MW01076322

TRACTS FOR THE TIMES

THE WORKS OF
CARDINAL JOHN HENRY NEWMAN
BIRMINGHAM ORATORY
MILLENNIUM EDITION
VOLUME X

SERIES EDITOR
JAMES TOLHURST DD

TRACTS FOR THE TIMES

BY

JOHN HENRY CARDINAL NEWMAN

with an Introduction and Notes by

JAMES TOLHURST DD

GRACEWING

NOTRE DAME

Individual Tracts originally published 1833–1841.

First published in the Birmingham Oratory Millennium Edition
in 2013 jointly by

Gracewing   University of Notre Dame Press
2 Southern Avenue   310 Flanner Hall
Leominster   Notre Dame
Herefordshire HR6 0QF   IN 46556 USA

Library of Congress Cataloging-in-Publication Data
Newman, John Henry, 1801-1890.
  Tracts for the times / by John Henry Cardinal Newman; with an
introduction and notes by James Tolhurst, DD Gracewing, Notre Dame.
      pages cm. - (The works of Cardinal Newman: Birmingham oratory
millennium edition, v.10)
  Includes bibliographical references.
  ISBN 978-0-85244-749-9 - ISBN 0-268-03612-8 (U.S. cloth: alk. paper)
1. Catholic Church - Doctrines. 2. Theology. 3. Catholic Church. I.
Tolhurst, James. II. Title.
  BX891.3.N495   2013
  230'.3'dc23
                                                        2013006722

                ISBN 978 0 85244 749 9 (Gracewing)
                ISBN 978 0 268 03612 6 (Notre Dame)

Typesetting by Action Publishing Technology Ltd,
Gloucester, GL1 5SR

Produced by Shore Books, Blackborough End, Norfolk.

Printed in England.

CONTENTS

Contents

ABBREVIATIONS

Apo	*Apologia pro Vita Sua*
Ari	*The Arians of the Fourth Century*
AW	Autobiographical Writings edited by Henry Tristram (London & New York, 1956)
BCP	*Book of Common Prayer*
BOA	Birmingham Oratory Archives
Cross	*The Oxford Dictionary of the Christian Church* (edited by F. L. Cross & E. A. Livingstone, 2nd edition, Oxford, 1974)
DA	*Discussions and Arguments on Various Subjects*
DEC	*Decrees of the Ecumenical Councils* (edited by Norman Tanner, SJ, 2 vols, London & Georgetown, 1990)
Dev	*An Essay on the Development of Christian Doctrine*
Diff	*Certain Difficulties felt by Anglicans in Catholic Teaching*, 2 vols
DS	Denzinger-Schönmetzer, *Enchiridion Symbolorum* (Herder, 1965)
Elu	Elucidations of Dr Hampden's Theological Statement (Oxford, 1836)
Ess	*Essays Critical and Historical*, 2 vols
GA	*An Essay in Aid of a Grammar of Assent*
Jfc	*Lectures on the Doctrine of Justification*

LD	*Letters and Diaries of John Henry Newman* edited by C. S. Dessain *et al* (Oxford and London, 1973–2006)
Mir	*Two Essays on Biblical and Ecclesiastical Miracles*
ML	Migne: *Patrologia Latina*
MS	Manuscript sermon in Birmingham Oratory Archives
OED	*Oxford English Dictionary*
Prepos	*Lectures on the Present Position of Catholics in England*
PPS	*Parochial and Plain Sermons*
S1	John Henry Newman Sermons, vol. 1 (ed. Placid Murray, Oxford, 1991)
SD	*Sermons Bearing on Subjects of the Day*
Tr	*Tracts for the Times*
US	Sermons preached before the University of Oxford
VM	*The Via Media of the Anglican Church,* 2 vols
VV	*Verses on Various Occasions*

INTRODUCTION

Newman's Tracts for the Times

The *Tracts for the Times* will always be connected with the Oxford Movement. The first Tract was published on 9 September 1833 and the ninetieth on 27 February 1841. Newman himself was either the author or the compiler of a third of the total number. They were published up until the Spring of 1834 by Turrill and King, and then by Gilbert and Rivington. Increasingly they expanded into treatises – especially after Tract 36 – often composed of quotations from patristic writers and the English Divines (Tract 81 runs to 424 pages). Newman did provide short introductions, but except in the case of the Tract on the Breviary (which is more extensive), these have been excluded.

Events leading up to the publication of the Tracts
By the end of Summer 1832, John Henry Newman was exhausted by his work on the volume for Hugh Rose and William Rowe Lyall's *Theological Library* which would eventually be published as *The Arians of the Fourth Century*. Archdeacon Froude proposed a sea voyage with his family to the Mediterranean, which Newman accepted. It was his first journey abroad. They left Falmouth on 8 December, and reached Rome on 2 March 1833.

Newman was alternately fascinated and appalled by

the city. After attending the papal ceremonies for the feast of the Annunciation, he wrote to his mother,

> As I looked on, and saw all Christian acts perform-
> ing the Holy Sacrament offered up, and the
> blessing given, and recollected I was in church, I
> could only say in very perplexity my own words,
> 'How shall I name thee, Light of the wide West,
> or heinous error-seat?' – and felt the force of the
> parable of the tares – who can separate the light
> from the darkness but the Creator Word who
> prophesied their union, and so I am forced to
> leave the matter, not at all seeing my way out of
> it. – How shall I name thee?[1]

There was also the problem of Church-State relations at home. The Whigs were now in power and the Church Temporalities Bill – which envisaged the elimination of ten (redundant) dioceses of the established Church in Ireland – was introduced into parliament. The same parliament was also passing the Coercion Act, which partially suspended *habeas corpus* and applied martial law in certain areas. At the same time, Dr Thomas Arnold put forward a liberal solution to inter-Church relations by proposing that all sects (except Quakers and Roman Catholics) should share Church premises.[2] Newman's reaction to all this can be gauged by his poem, *Sacrilege*:

---

[1] To Mrs. Newman, 25 March 1833, LD 3, p. 268. Cf. Matt. 13:24ff.
[2] *Principles of Church Reform,* 1833 and cf. To R. F. Wilson, 18 March 1833, LD 3, p. 258.

> Blest is a pilgrim Church! – yet shrink to share
> The curse of throwing down.
> So will we toil in our old place to stand,
> Watching, not dreading, the despoiler's hand.[3]

When the Froudes decided to return to England in April, Newman chose not to accompany them. He had heard that Keble "at length is roused, and (*if* once up) he will prove a second St Ambrose – and others too are moving."[4] The impact of the Reform Bill and Charles Grey's Whig government and the new foundation of the British Association (it was thought, in spite of being a scientific society, it could meddle in religion)[5] were very troubling to those who had the interests of the Church at heart. But it was all brought to a head by the government intervention in Ireland, which gave the impression that the civil authorities were preparing to encroach on the rights, and alter the constitution of the Church. It was accepted by most that England "was a nation which had for centuries acknowledged, as an essential part of its theory of government, that *as* a Christian nation, she is also a part of Christ's Church, and bound, in all her legislation and policy, by the fundamental laws of that Church."[6] This was now being called into question.

Newman decided to trek across Sicily with a guide and crossed the island from Catania to Syracuse, and then fell ill – called by the locals "gastric fever", but possibly typhoid. His guide, Gennaro, put him on a

---

[3] VV, p. 139.
[4] To Jemima, 20 March 1833, LD 3, p. 264.
[5] To David Brown, 4 April 1874, LD 27, p. 43.
[6] John Keble's Sermon on *National Apostasy*.

mule and brought him to the attention of a local good Samaritan who took him in and called the doctor. Newman lay at death's door for eleven days and recorded later that he did not think he would die, for "God has still work for me to do."[7] He reflected that he could almost think that the devil "saw I am to be a means of usefulness, and tried to destroy me."[8] Newman wrote to his mother at the beginning of June and included some verses:

> Christ will unloose His Church; yea, even now
> Begins the work; – and thou
> Shall spend in it thy strength but, ere He save,
> Thy lot shall be the grave.[9]

Newman returned to England on July 8, filled with renewed vigour for the fight ahead. Keble delivered on 14 July, his *Assize Sermon* in St Mary's on "National Apostasy": "There was once here a glorious Church, but it was betrayed into the hands of Libertines for the real or affected love of a little temporary peace and good order."[10] Newman considered the day as the start of the Oxford Movement.[11] But he regarded Hurrell Froude as, in many ways, the driving force.[12] At the end of July, a meeting was held at Hugh Rose's rectory in Hadleigh to discuss the implications of the Church Temporalities Bill, which resulted in a loose association

[7] AW, p. 124.

[8] Ibid., pp. 121-2.

[9] LD 3, p. 319 and VV, p. 136.

[10] *National Apostasy Sermon*.

[11] Apo, p. 35.

[12] In the case of Newman and Froude, "Each caught fire from each other", R. W. Church, *The Oxford Movement 1833–1845,* London, 1891, p. 40.

called *The Friends of the Church*. There was a difference
of opinion about whether the Church should remain
established, but no action was taken. In common with
Keble and Froude, Newman urged the formation of a
loose association "for the purpose of rousing the
clergy" to support the apostolical succession. "We shall
probably be printing tracts bearing on this subject"[13]
was the plan of action. William Palmer of Worcester
points out that pamphlets were already circulating
"recommending the abolition of the creeds (at least in
public worship) ... the removal of all mention of the
Blessed Trinity; of the doctrine of Baptismal
Regeneration; of the practice of absolution."[14]
Newman knew the topics which were required:
"canvassing support for 'Apostolical Succession',
defending the Prayer Book against alteration and
opposing heretical appointments in the Church."[15]

The Tracts
Newman was responsible for sixteen out of the forty-
six which made up the first volume of Tracts. They
were entitled *Tracts of the Times against Popery and
Dissent*. In all, he wrote twenty-nine: 1, 2, 3, 6, 7, 8,
10, 11, 15,[16] 19, 20, 21, 31, 33, 34, 38, 41, 45, 47, 71,
73, 74, 75, 76, 79, 82, 83, 85, 88 and 90. Of these, 38,
41, 71 and 82 have been published in *Via Media II* but
are also included; 73, which is in *Essays Critical &
Historical 1*, is printed here; 83 and 85 are in *Discussions*

---

[13] To C. P. Golightly, 11 August 1833, LD 4, p. 29.

[14] William Palmer, *Narrative of Events Connected with the Publication of the
Tracts for the Times* 1841, p. 3. Cf. Dr. Arnold's views *supra*.

[15] To C. P. Golightly, 11 August 1833, LD 4, pp. 28-9.

[16] By William Palmer, revised and completed by Newman.

and Arguments. These can be read in *The Millennium Edition*. The Treatise-Tracts of Numbers 74, 76 (*Catena Patrum 1 & 2*),[17] and 88 (*The Greek Devotions of Bishop Andrews*) have been omitted. In Tract 75, the introductory explanation of the breviary has been printed.

Newman never had much time for committees. He felt that they discussed matters but did not act: "If you correct according to the wishes of a board, you will have nothing but tame, dull compositions, which will take no one."[18] So Newman "out of my own head began the Tracts,[19] centering on the importance of apostolic succession and its ramifications for the parish: I am but one of yourselves, – a Presbyter; and therefore I conceal my name, lest I should take too much on myself by speaking in my own person. Yet speak I must; for the times are very evil, yet no one speaks against them."[20] He wrote to Hugh Rose of the distinctive style he envisaged for the future writers: "We do not want regular troops, but sharpshooters."[21] He likened the Tracts themselves to "a dose of volatile salts, pungent but restorative."

a) Apostolical Succession

So began the first tract, issued on 9 September 1833. It urged its readers, "Exalt our Holy Fathers, the Bishops as the Representatives of the Apostles, and the Angels of the Churches; and magnify your office, as being

---

[17] Not included in Newman's list to J. H. Parker (LD 29, p. 206).
[18] To John Keble, 24 September 1833, LD 4, p. 55.
[19] Apo, p. 40.
[20] Tract 1: *Thoughts on the Ministerial Commission.*
[21] To H. J. Rose, 15 December 1533, LD 4, p. 143.

ordained by them to take part in their Ministry."
Newman could not have overlooked the fact that of
the *Angels*, Bishop Blomfield of London was in favour
of the Irish Temporalities Bill; or that the Bill itself had
been described as a destruction of one of the seven
candelabra (Revelation 1:20).

He returned to the theme in Tract 4, "Why should
we talk of an *establishment*, and so little of an APOS-
TOLICAL SUCCESSION? Priests self-elected, or
appointed by the State ... not Priests commissioned,
successively from heaven." He concludes,

> Look on your pastor as acting by man's commission,
> and you may respect the authority by which he acts,
> you may venerate and love his personal character,
> but it can hardly be called a *religious* veneration;
> there is nothing, properly, *sacred* about him. But
> once learn to regard him as 'the Deputy of
> CHRIST, for reducing man to the obedience of
> God' and everything about him becomes changed,
> everything stands in a new light.

Newman backed his ideas up with a series of articles in
the *British Magazine* (edited by his friend Hugh Rose)
entitled *Letters on the Church of the Fathers* or "little
stories of the Apostles, Fathers etc., to familiarize the
imagination of the reader to an *Apostolical state* of the
Church" (later published as *The Church of the Fathers*).

If the bishops thought that Newman's comments
had merely a spiritual side to them, they had only to
read about St Ambrose and the Empress Justina in
Letters on the Church, in certain ecclesiastical proceedings in the city of Milan in A.D. 385. The Empress

required Ambrose to surrender the Portian basilica to the Arians. Ambrose refused and Newman comments,

> When a question arises now about the spoliation of the Church, we are obliged to betake ourselves to the rule of *national* law; we appeal to precedents, or we urge the civil consequences of the measure, or we use other arguments which, good as they may be, are too refined to be very popular. Ambrose rested his resistance on grounds which the people understood at once, and recognized as irrefragable ('The palace is the emperor's, the churches are the bishop's').[22]

Newman was obviously holding up to his episcopal contemporaries the example of Ambrose, as he had previously the figure of St Athanasius in *Arians*: "If we had one Athanasius, or Basil, we could bear with 20 Eusebiuses."[23] Newman would argue for a revival of the Convocations of York and Canterbury as "a really working court of heresy and false doctrine".[24] He would point out in Tract 15 that Convocation had signed the declaration that the bishop of Rome had no more jurisdiction in this country than the word of God, than any other foreign bishop and so "The Church by its proper rulers and officers reformed itself." He would speak of the Pope as tyrannically taking control of the Churches in Britain "which he

---

[22] *Church of the Fathers,* pp. 9, 8; cf. also Diff 1, pp. 55–6.

[23] To J. W. Bowden, 31 August 1833, LD 4, p. 33. Eusebius of Nicomedia (d. 341) was bishop of Berytus and disciple of Lucian of Antioch.

[24] To R. H. Froude, 10 January 1835, LD 5, p. 10. Cf. also Tract 41.

had no right at all to do ... because we were altogether independent of him."

The civil power, however, needed to be confronted by Episcopal authority. Newman, writing to Bowden says,

> These men in power ... will kick the Church for a while and exult over it, but the time will soon come when they will rouse its sleeping strength – the gift of excommunication will not for ever remain unused. If I were a Bishop, the first thing I should do would be to excommunicate Lord Grey and half a dozen more, whose names it is almost a shame and a pollution for a Christian to mention.[25]

He would however admit, in Tract 3, that the restoration of excommunication was *impracticable*. But there was clear evidence that confrontation worked. Newman had earlier reviewed the case of Praxeas, an exponent of Patripassianism, who meeting "determined resistance which honourably distinguishes the primitive Roman Church in its dealings with heresy, he (Praxeas) retired into Africa, and there, as founding no sect, he was soon forgotten."[26]

---

[25] To J. W. Bowden, 20 August 1833, LD 4, p. 32. Tract 37 contains Bishop Wilson's *Form of Excommunication:*
"In the name of JESUS CHRIST, and by the authority which we have received from Him,
We separate you from the communion of the Church ..."
[26] Ari, p. 117.

Oh, for the rod of ancient discipline
Unheeded and unheeding o'er the plain
They wandered shepherdless – are caught and slain,
With none to help ! Oh for a sacred sign
Of pastoral severity benign !
Spirit of Ambrose, wake again![27]

In Tract 7, Newman argues that the *form* of Church
government is not just a useful arrangement which we
take on trust, but rather a "permanent Body
Corporate" which we can trace "from St Peter to our
present Metropolitans." Newman later argues (in Tract
33) that the growth of the episcopate led to the
creation of subordinate sees and suffragan bishops. He
urges the furtherance of such practice in England
where many dioceses were top heavy but adds the
topical comment, "These statements are also made
with the view of keeping up in the minds of
churchmen a recollection of the injury which the Irish
branch of our Church has lately sustained in the
diminution of it." He would publish a more detailed
examination of the subject in 1835, which is in *Via
Media II*. Newman returns to the debate in Tract 45,
The Grounds of Our Faith. He argues that the tendency
to regard Scripture as the sole document for establishing the validity of episcopacy is flawed. We must
consider the practice of the early Church "which was
universally episcopal." We need to go to the Creeds to
find what is implicit in Scripture.

The problem which was thrown into prominence
by government interference in Church affairs did not
affect the Scriptural basis of the Church's authority but

[27] "Disciplina Externa", *British Magazine,* April 1835, p. 406.

rather urged greater insistence *on that very authority*. In Tract 31 Newman used the building of Israel's second temple as an analogy of the renewal which took place under the Elizabethan divines: "Ezra and Nehemiah are the forerunners of our Hookers and Lauds." A similar restoration was now called for. He would state later that it was a demand for a second reformation.[28]

Rowan Williams in his introduction to *Arians* (in the *Millennium Edition*) maintains that Newman "accepts in advance that the bishops will not be able to guarantee the privileges of the old Church of England. What is needed is a revival of the patristic Church."[29] It could also be argued that Newman put his faith in the contemporary episcopate, and hoped that they would be inspired by the courage and faith of their patristic ancestors. At the close of his life Pusey used to say that Newman had depended on the Bishops, while he himself had looked to God's Providence acting through the Church. To Newman it was a necessity that his Bishop should approve and support him. As late as 1841, Newman would lament to Pusey, "We have leant on the bishops, and they have broken under us."[30]

b) Defending the Prayer Book

Liturgy is always going to be a *casus belli* for some. The 1637 Laudian Prayer Book was the last straw for Jenny Geddes, the Edinburgh kailwife, who threw her stool at the Dean. Newman pointed out in Tract 3 that people "have long regarded the Prayer Book with

[28] Apo, p. 43. Cf. also S1 (MS Sermon 449), p. 161.

[29] *Introduction,* p. xliv.

[30] H. P. Liddon, *Life of E. B. Pusey,* Vol. 2, (London, 1893), pp. 57, 237.

reverence as the stay of their faith and devotion." He is mindful of the pamphlets urging change, and his answer is interesting. People are fickle: some do not want certain changes because they like the hallowed texts, some would regard change as concession to modern tastes, some would like shorter services, and some would prefer the service to be lengthened, "how few would be pleased by *any given* alterations; and how many pained!" Once we begin to tinker then where do you stop? "Have we any security, if we once begin, that we shall never end?" Among Roman Catholics, the liturgical changes of 1968 and the current process of re-translating the Missal into English, have thrown up the same arguments.

Newman pointed out that "the rage of the day is for concession. That is ever the way of the world; but it should not be the way of the Church." The bishops should be petitioned not to alter the prayer book, for how can they resist unless the clergy support them. "They consent to them (if they do) partly from the notion that they are thus pleasing you. Undeceive them." Whether such an approach would commend itself to Bishop Blomfield, Dr Maltby of Chichester, or even to Dr Lloyd, Newman's own bishop, remains a moot point.

Newman also reminds his readers that the structure of the Church as fellowship and communion was committed to the apostles and their successors, in Tract 8. The administration of the sacraments had ever continued in their hands as had the gathering together for public worship as recognized in the Acts of the Apostles. Newman takes issue with those "enlightened believers" who attack the ancient rules of the ecclesiastical system and he points out that the biblically based tithe has been incorporated into the law of the land "where reason and conscience have no means of determining."

Newman also argues from tradition in the case of various rites and customs. In Tract 34, *Rites and Customs of the Church*, he says, "Far from being unmeaning (they) are in their nature capable of impressing our memories and imagination with the great revealed verities." He argues from the Pauline letters, "that it would seem as if the very multiplicity of the details of the church ritual made it plainly impossible for St. Paul to write them all down, or to do more than *remind* the Corinthians of his way of conducting religious discipline when he was among them." So we see references to houses of prayer, the cup of blessing and the *Amen* at the conclusion of the *Synaxis*. Newman concludes, "This incidental information, vouchsafed to us in Scripture, should lead us to be very cautious how we put aside other usages of the early Church concerning this sacrament which do not happen to be *clearly* mentioned in Scripture." The English Church must value its *catholic* rites, while it declares its independence of Rome, and not be like men "who recover from some grievous illness with the loss or injury of their sight or hearing." Newman must have realized that such an appeal to antiquity would be fiercely resisted. Edward Hawkins (who would succeed Whately as Provost of Oriel) in his dissertation, had firmly rejected tradition as an independent authority and, as such, an error of the Roman Church. "The Church should teach, and the Scriptures prove, the doctrines of Christianity. Tradition is useful, and intended to be so, introducing us to those doctrines which Scripture, the only authority for such doctrines now, does not so reading, teach."[31] The Reverend Thomas Scott regretted that the reformers had "an undue regard" for the Fathers of the Church. Richard Whately had long referred to the Fathers as "certain old divines." Thomas Gaisford, Professor of Greek, indicating the volumes of the Fathers, referred to them as "sad rubbish."[32]

As far as catholic practices go, there is nothing as distinctive as the Roman breviary. From January 1836, Newman had been using it regularly, as well as his meditation and intercessory prayer in the chapel at Oriel and the practice of fasting. He had also published three volumes of his Sermons and the first volume of the Tracts, and had also begun daily service at St Mary's. Newman was already being suspected of Romish leanings, which subsequent tracts did nothing to negate.

Tract 90, of course, marks the end of the journey. Newman argues for a correct understanding of the Thirty-nine Articles of Religion. He considered that it was necessary to seek "the distinct Catholic sense, the sense of the Holy Fathers, of Athanasius, Ambrose, Augustine, and of all Doctors and Saints." The reaction was not long in coming. Bishop Sumner of Chester had already stated in 1839, "Under the specious pretence of deference to antiquity, and

---

[31] Dissertation *Upon the Use and Importance of Unauthoritative Tradition as an Introduction to Christian Doctrines,* Oxford, 1819, pp. 21–2, 30.

[32] *Works* II, p. 237, quoted in M. Ward, *Young Mr Newman,* Sheed & Ward, London, 1948, p. 95; Thomas Mozley, *Reminiscences, chiefly of Oriel College and the Oxford Movement* I, 1882, p. 356.

respect for primitive models, the *foundations* of our Protestant Church are *undermined* by men who dwell within her walls, and those who sit in the Reformers' seat are traducing the Reformation."[33]

c) The Spread of Heterodoxy

There was also the allied question which lay at the root of the crisis as Newman saw it: the spread of unorthodox teaching. As early as 1825 Newman had preached, "Are not the principles of unbelief certain to dissolve society?"[34] He would further develop this:

Now what do we see at this time? First a great variety of opinions and parties – an open licence to blaspheme, which men avail themselves of, and which is granted by the State, almost necessary to avoid what is considered worse, a contempt for the Church and an undervaluing of ancient notions on the ground that they *are* ancient, and a consequent avowed neglect and ignorance of the system of Christian truth – an opinion certainly increasing in quarters of most influence in civil matter, that one belief is as good as and no better than another, an incipient thrust after sacrilege, and lastly an indifference, an irreverent treatment of the subject of religion, a thoughtless jesting upon Scripture and heartless scoffing, which though it has partially obtained in other times and in all ages perhaps is the sin to which young persons are exposed yet seems to have become more a national sin now than ever it was before.[35]

[33] Ess 1, p. 265.
[34] PPS 8, p. 112.
[35] MS Sermon 273, pp. 22-3 (Birmingham Oratory Archives).

The problem, as Newman saw it, was widespread ignorance of theology, especially among the clergy. The Theological Society (which began to meet in November 1835), together with the Tracts, were specifically designed to answer this. Newman's aunt, Elizabeth, was informed,

> The most religiously-minded men are ready to give up important truths because they do not *understand their value.* A cry is raised that the creeds are unnecessarily minute, and even those who would defend, through ignorance cannot. What is most painful is that the clergy are so utterly ignorant on the subject. We have no *theological* education, and instead of profiting by the example of past times, we attempt to decide the most intricate questions whether of doctrine or conduct, by our blind and erring reason. In my present line of reading them, I am doing what I can to remedy this defect in myself, and (if so be) in some others.[36]

The beginning of the conflict could be said to have begun in August 1834, when Renn Dickson Hampden obtained the Chair of Moral Philosophy. Hampden then published a pamphlet in August 1834, *Observations on Religious Dissent.* In it he developed his previous Bampton lecture of 1832, arguing that "The Scripture intimates to us certain facts concerning the Divine Being; but conveying them to us by the medium of language, it only brings them before us darkly, under the signs appropriate to the thought of the human mind . . ." One should rather concentrate on the simple religion of

---

[36] To Elizabeth Newman, 9 August 1835, LD 5, p. 120.

Christ "as received into the heart and influencing conduct." Newman commented in a letter to him that "the principles contained in it, tending as they do in my opinion altogether to make a shipwreck of Christian faith."[37] When Hampden published a second edition Newman set himself the task of analyzing it.

His *Elucidations of Dr. Hampden's Theological Statements* was published on 13 February 1836. Newman states that

> [Dr Hampden] considers that no statement whatever, even though correctly deduced from the text of Scripture, is part of revelation; that no right conclusions about theological truth can be drawn from Scripture; that Scripture itself is a mere record of historical facts; that it contains no dogmatic statements, such as those about the Trinity, Incarnation, Atonement, Justification. The Articles of the Nicene and Athanasian Creeds are merely human opinions, scholastic, allowing of change.[38]

Nor was this an isolated example because Joseph Blanco White, a former colleague at Oriel had just published his *Observations on Heresy and Orthodoxy* in which he asserted, "You must frequently have observed the hopelessness of the attempts which are constantly being made to establish various points of Christian doctrine by logical arguments, founded on detached texts of Scripture . . . You cannot but have observed, moreover, how short all such attempts fall of the intended object."[39]

[37] From R. H. Froude, End of August 1833, LD 4, p. 37.
[38] *Elucidations of Dr. Hampden's Theological Statement,* Oxford, 1836, p. 5.
[39] Ibid., p. 12.

Tract 73, published in February 1836, was seen as
sufficiently important to be reprinted in *Via Media II*
(with an appendix, dealing with Schleiermacher's view
of the doctrine of the Trinity). Newman is careful not
to be accused of being anti-intellectual; he maintains
that *Rationalism* is

> a certain abuse of reason ... to rationalize in matters
> of Revelation is to make our reason the standard
> and measure of the doctrines revealed; to stipulate
> that those doctrines should be such as to carry with
> them their own justification; to reject them, if they
> come in collision with our existing opinions or
> habits of thought, or are with difficulty harmonized
> with our existing stock of knowledge ... It is
> Rationalism to accept the Revelation, and then to
> explain it away.

He gives the example of the captain of the King of
Samaria's army replying to Elisha's prophecy that the
siege would be ended by saying, "Though God shall
make windows in heaven, shall this thing be?" (2
Kings 7:2). This is rationalization, maintains Newman,
because the Captain said that he was unable to discover
how the prophecy would be fulfilled and was expressing himself in a way which would excuse his unbelief.

At the heart of Rationalism is the desire to make
oneself one's own centre instead of his Creator: "he
does not go to God, but he implies that God must
come to him." So we are talking in terms of religion
being subjective rather than objective truth. Faith
therefore "does not lie in the submission of the reason
to external realities partially disclosed, but in what he

calls that candid pursuit of truth which ensures the eventual adoption of that opinion on the subject, which is best for us individually, which is most natural according to the constitution of our minds, and, therefore, divinely intended for us."

Newman selects two exponents of Rationalism, Thomas Erskine from Angus and Jacob Abbott from Maine. Both regarded the Scriptures as merely giving us a *manifestation* of God's character to provide moral guidance, but not a basis for a definite Christian faith. Newman would preach about rationalists, "They say that the Object of the Gospel Revelation is merely practical, and therefore, that theological doctrines are altogether unnecessary, mere speculations, and hindrances to the extension of religion."[40] Schleiermacher would say that the object of Christianity was "to stir the affections and soothe the heart."[41] Newman consistently held this view about such rationalization and by 1841 traced it back to the origins of the Church of England: "The spirit of lawlessness came in at the Reformation – and Liberalism is its offspring."[42] Towards the end of his life he would declare, "Liberalism in religion is the doctrine that there is no positive truth in religion, but that one creed is as good as another ... It is inconsistent with any recognition of any religion as *true*. It teaches that all are to be tolerated, for all are matters of opinion. Revealed religion is not a truth, but a sentiment and a taste; not an objective fact, not mirac-

[40] PPS 2, p. 261.
[41] Ess 1, p. 97.
[42] To A. L. Phillipps, 12 September 1841, LD 8, pp. 269-70.

ulous; and it is the right of each individual to make it say just what strikes his fancy."[43]

d) The Influence of Hurrell Froude

Newman was the main contributor of *Tracts*, but looking back, he reflected that the original founders of the Oxford Movement "were the late Mr. Froude and Mr. Palmer."[44] As the brother of James Anthony, Hurrell was two years younger than Newman. His mother tells us, "he had (for his age) an unusually deep feeling of admiration for everything that was good and noble."[45] He became a fellow of Oriel in 1826, when he began his Journal.

Jeremy Taylor's *Holy Living and Holy Dying* and William Law's *Serious Call* set him on the road of living the Christian life with intensity and self-abnegation. A combination which found its way into the Tracts, either indirectly, modifying the attitude to Romanism, or directly, in the case of Tract 21.

In *Mortification of the Flesh. A Scriptural Duty,* Tract 21, in January 1834, Newman traces the argument for fasting. Pusey, in Tract 18 of the previous December, had already covered some of the ground (and had signed his contribution). Whether under Froude's influence or not, Newman began to fast every Friday, and sometimes on Wednesdays as well. In the Tract, he first considers the Old Testament, beginning with

---

[43] *Biglietto Speech*, Rome, 12 May 1879.

[44] To Messrs Griffin & Co., 19 January 1860, LD 19, p. 287. He would also say that Keble was "the true and primary author". R. W. Church *The Oxford Movement,* London, 1891, p. 27. Also H. P. Liddon, *Life of E. B. Pusey,* Vol. 1, p. 27.

[45] *Remains of the late Reverend Richard Hurrell Froude* I, p. 12.

Moses. He then answers the objection that this was not binding on Christians by saying that "Man is now what he was then; and if affliction of the flesh was good then, it is now." He asks people to consider "the *general austere character* of Christian obedience ... a circumstance much to be insisted on in an age like this, when what is really self-indulgence is thought to be a mere moderate and innocent use of this world's goods."

After Hurrell Froude's death in February 1836, Newman was asked to choose a keepsake from his library. He came away with his breviary, which he began to use from then onwards and which he kept by him until he died. He devoted some three to four hours each day to his prayers (including the breviary devotions) in the Oriel chapel. He noted, in a letter in 1837, "Another characteristic of the Breviary Services is the shortness of the prayers they contain. Dear Froude used to say that 'long prayers' were peculiar and came in at the Reformation ... Another excellence of the Breviary Services is their precise *method*."[46]

In his introduction to Tract 75, in June 1836, Newman is anxious to "wrest a weapon out of our adversaries' hands [i.e. Roman Catholics] who have in this, as in many other instances, appropriated to themselves a treasure which was ours as much as theirs." The tract deals with the history of the breviary, followed by an analysis of the separate seven daily offices and a translation of fifteen hymns. Altogether he translated some forty-seven of the Latin Office hymns.

---

[46] To H. Wilberforce, 25 March 1837, LD 6, p. 47; cf. D. L. Withey, *John Henry Newman and the Breviary,* London, 1992, pp. 114-23.

The 148 pages of the original tract were later expanded to 207 pages in its second edition in 1838. The fact that two young laymen, Samuel Wood and Robert Williams were translating the breviary at their own expense, explains the expansion. George Prevost, hearing of it, was greatly distressed and, writing in haste, with the agreement of Keble and Jeffreys, asked that the authors "could be persuaded on our earnest entreaty to suppress it", and said he would cover the expense.[47] Bowden wrote to Newman that he feared for the consequences of publishing the breviary because it will be asked "whether you are leading them to what Rome is or to what Rome was" and would seem "to mix ourselves up with the modern inventions, legends and the like of the Southern Church [i.e. Rome]."[48] Eventually the project was cancelled with Wood and Williams footing the bill.

Froude berated Newman on several occasions for his negative attitude to Rome. He insisted, for instance, on the term "Holy Eucharist" for "the Lord's Supper", "God's Priests" for "ministers of the word" and "Altar" instead of "the Lord's Table." When Newman asks Froude his opinion about *Home Thoughts Abroad* in 1833, he replies, "I think it not unlikely to do some pittance of good in the way of infusing sentiments. I only except from this general approbation your second and most superfluous hit at the poor Romanists – you have first set them down as demoniacally possest [sic] by the evil genius of pagan Rome, but notwithstanding are able to find some

[47] To George Prevost, 2 November 1838, LD 6, p. 336.
[48] LD 6, p. 338n.

thing to admire in their spirit."[49] At the same time, he was helping Newman in his correspondence with the Abbé Jean-Nicholas Jager who held the chair of Ecclesiastical History in the Faculty of Theology of the University of Paris.[50] Newman is perhaps influenced by Froude, together with his reading of Vincent of Lerins, who figures prominently in the Lectures on the Prophetical Office of the Church which Newman was delivering in St Mary's at the time and which he quotes in his letter to Abbé Jager.[51] In *Via Media II,* Laicus makes the point that "Fresh articles of faith are necessary to secure the Church's purity, according to the rise of successive heresies and errors. These articles are all hidden, as it were, in the Church's bosom, from the first, and brought out into form according to the occasion."

e) On Controversy with Romanists

It should not be forgotten that the Tracts were entitled *against Popery and Dissent.*[52] When Newman would give his *Lectures on the Prophetical Office of the Church*, they would be subtitled, *Viewed Relatively to Romanism and Popular Protestantism*. But the immediate concern was Romanism – the Dissenters would only come into the picture (with its implications for the Atonement) of Isaac Williams' Tract 80, *On Reserve*. The background was the repeal of the Test Act in 1828 and Catholic Emancipation in 1829. It should not be forgotten that

---

[49] From R. H. Froude, End of August 1833, LD 4, p. 37.
[50] Cf. L. Allen, *John Henry Newman and the Abbé Jager,* Oxford, 1975, pp. 116ff.
[51] VM 1, p. 321 and Allen *supra,* pp. 45, 77.
[52] Cf. Appendix 3: Advertisement to 1st Edition, concluding words.

Anti-Catholicism was rife at the time. One has only to read *Lectures on the Present Position of Catholics* to gauge the intensity of feeling. Newman argued at the outset,

> First we shall have inquirers turning Papists, if we do not draw lines between ourselves and Popery. Next it will do us good, if we show we do differ from the Papists. Thirdly, it is availing ourselves of a popular cry ... (viz. when there was a cry against Dissent) and we shall miss our opportunity if we do not do the like now as regards Popery. Fourthly, it [will] be anticipating other parties by giving our own views of Romanist – and fifthly, it is a very effectual though unsuspicious way of dealing a backhanded blow at ultra-protestantism.[53]

He had made his position quite clear in Tract 15, written in December 1833, which states, "True, Rome is heretical now – nay, grant she has thereby forfeited her orders; and, at least, she was not heretical in the primitive ages. If she has apostatized, it was at the time of the Council of Trent. Then indeed, it is to be feared the whole Roman Communion bound itself, by a perpetual bond and covenant, to the cause of Antichrist." He continues the theme in Tract 20, *The Visible Church*. Already doubts are circulating that the Tracts are papistical. Newman counters, "You have some misgivings, it seems, lest the doctrine I have been advocating 'should lead to Popery'. I will not, by way of answer, say that the question is not, whether it will *lead to Popery*, but whether it is *in the Bible*." The

---

[53] Quoted in I. Ker, *John Henry Newman*, p. 135.

Roman Church is unscriptural and the way to oppose it is to insist that the English Church is a "true branch of the Church Universal, yet withal preserved free from error ... It is Catholic and Apostolic, yet not Papistical." By 1836, when he came to write Tract 71, Newman itemizes the subjects for debate as: The denial of the cup to the laity, the necessity of the priest's intention for the validity of the sacraments, the necessity of confession, the power of Rome to anathematize, the doctrine of purgatory, the invocation of the saints and the worship of images; and again he uses the documents of Trent. But there is far less strident condemnation of Rome; in fact he quotes from *The Christian Year.*

> Speak gently of our sister's fall,
> Who knows but gentle love
> May win her, at our patient call,
> The surer way to prove.

Newman argues that the defects of the English Church "are but omissions", whereas Rome has positive errors. This is because she is "merely *Reformed*, not Protestant." He would say the same in a sermon preached in 1837, "We having reformed ourselves, and the Roman Catholics going on in the corruptions which had crept in."[54]

In a follow-up Tract, *On Purgatory* (Tract 79) in March 1837, Newman is even more dispassionate in his treatment of Roman Catholic doctrine, quoting from the Councils of Trent and Florence as well as

[54] Allen, *supra,* p. 148.

from Scripture, theologians and patristic authors in a tract that runs to 61 pages. At the same time, Newman had been secretly inserting a silent commemoration of the dead in the Communion Service. "It is so great a gift, if so be to *be able* to benefit the dead."[55] His introductory statement sets the tone: "Nor is it unprofitable to weigh accurate how much the Romanists have committed themselves in their formal determinations of doctrine, and how far, by God's merciful providence, they had been restrained and overruled; and again how far they must retract, in order to make amends to Catholic truth and unity." Newman would make the distinction in Tract 90 between the Romish doctrine and the *primitive* doctrine which lay behind the concept of pardons but already in 1837, the way ahead can be seen, and, with the publication of Froude's *Remains*, it is not surprising that there was increasing suspicion of crypto-Romanism in Newman himself and his colleagues. Newman writes to James Henin, "That my views on the Priesthood and Sacraments are such as the Romanists adopt is what *many* believe, that you consider my present views are effecting and [a] fearful deviation from the faith once delivered to the Saints and if not at present popery, will ere long lead to that awful apostasy."[56]

The Last Tract and its Immediate Aftermath
Tract 90, *Remarks on Certain Passages of the Thirty-Nine Articles*, published on 27 February 1841, proved

---

[55] To Hugh Rose, 23 May 1836, LD 5, p. 305 and cf. To Robert Wilberforce, 15 March 1837, LD 5, p. 260: "so great a gift … to *be able* to benefit the dead."
[56] To James Henin, 19 December 1836, LD 5, pp. 394–5.

to be the last. Newman thought that his tract attempted to see if the Articles "were patient, though not ambitious, of a Catholic interpretation."[57] His main argument was "Whether we shall give them feelings of awe, mystery, tenderness, reverence, devotedness, and other feeling which may be especially called Catholic or claim them for ourselves?"[58] The response was predictable. The Vice-Chancellor and the Heads of Houses resolved, "That modes of interpretation such as are suggested in the said Tract, evading rather than explaining the sense of the Thirty-Nine Articles, and reconciling subscription to them with the adoption of errors, which they were designed to counteract, defeat the object."[59] One modern reaction would be to say that Newman argued "with more ingenuity than was sensible"[60] but this does not fit well with one who said, "I am not pugnacious; I am only militant."[61] Newman's own bishop, Richard Bagot wrote in a letter to Pusey, which was forwarded to Newman,

> that there are opinions spoken of in the Tract, as not Catholic, yet not incompatible with the Articles, which Mr. Newman does not himself hold, and which he would not desire to see taught by the Clergy. If so, these he might disavow, and it might also be in his power to declare certain of the most

---

[57] VM 2, p. 265. "They but partially oppose Roman dogma" (Apo, p. 79).
[58] Ibid., p. 386.
[59] VM 2, p. 362.
[60] Diarmaid McCulloch, *A History of Christianity,* London, 2009, p. 841.
[61] Tract 82.

obnoxious opinions to be opposed to the *spirit* of the Articles, if not to the letter.[62]

Newman, who held that "a Bishop's lightest word *ex cathedra* is heavy. His judgment on a book cannot be light. It is a rare occurrence,"[63] suspended publication of the Tracts.

The question posing itself to Newman concerned the exact nature of the English Church. Newman did not *want* it to be papistical. But he also did not want it to be protestant. Where exactly did the Church stand? Newman wrote to S. L Pope, "How can that be practically a Church, how can it *teach*, which speaks half a dozen things in the same breath?"[64] Things would come to a head over the question of bishops, which started the Tracts in the first place.

In 1841, through the mediation of Chevalier Bunsen, Frederick William IV's agent in London, there was a proposal (which Newman had heard rumoured when he was with Bunsen in 1833) to erect a United Church, consisting of the National Churches of England and Prussia at Jerusalem. This received the backing of Palmerston and the Evangelicals as well as the Archbishop of Canterbury and Bishop Blomfield of London, together with Dr Arnold and the liberals. The Act became law in October. England and Prussia were to nominate in turn for the bishopric. Michael Solomon Alexander (1799–1845), Professor of

---

[62] 17 March 1841, LD 8, p. 94. He would later say on Visitation in 1842 that Tr. 90 was "objectionable and likely to disturb the peace of the Church", LD 9, p. xvii.

[63] To Archdeacon of Oxford, VM 2, p. 384; cf. Apo, p. 56.

[64] To S. L. Pope, 4 September 1842, LD 9, pp. 79–80.

Hebrew at King's College, London had converted from Judaism in 1825 and was consecrated bishop in 1842. Newman questioned the nature of a united Church which could combine acceptance of the Thirty-Nine Articles *and* the Confession of Augsburg. Newman comments in his *Apologia*,

> Now here, at the very time that the Anglican Bishops were directing their censure upon me for avowing an approach to the Catholic Church not closer than I believed the Anglican formularies would allow, they were on the other hand, fraternizing, by their act or by their sufferance, with Protestant bodies, and allowing them to put themselves under an Anglican Bishop, without any renunciation of their errors or regard to their due reception of baptism and confirmation.[65]

He concluded, despondently at the time, in a letter to his sister Jemima, "I begin to have serious apprehensions lest any religious body is strong enough to withstand the league of evil but the Roman Church. At the end of the first Millenary it withstood the fury of Satan – and now the end of the second is drawing on."[66]

So the Tracts would begin with the question of the Irish bishops and would end with the matter of the Jerusalem episcopate; thus apostolic succession and the authority it embodied would be the theme running the length of the Tracts themselves.

---

[65] Apo, pp. 142-3. The scheme failed in 1886, when subscription to the 39 Articles was insisted upon.

[66] H. Chadwick, *The Spirit of the Oxford Movement: Tractarian Essays,* Cambridge, 1990, p. 2.

The Tracts and the Movement

There is no doubt the Tracts owed their origin to political and ecclesiastical events, and by extension, the Oxford Movement, according to Chadwick.[67] But how influential were the Tracts *on* the Movement? R. W. Church maintained that they only made their *contribution*: "The Tracts were not the most powerful instrument in drawing sympathy to the Movement ... without those sermons [of Newman] the Movement might never have gone on."[68] The first volume on Newman's sermons and volume 1 (Tracts 1–46) of the Tracts were both published in 1834.

Jonathan Clark maintains that whereas this was not true of Newman's sermons, the Tractarians' point of view was "more political than sacramental."[69] There was the issue of Erastianism in the first Tracts, but always the underlying basis, if not overtly sacramental, was at least theological and moral. Faught would argue that the Tractarians sought to maintain "the Church of England's central role in social control."[70] Newman and Froude (and later Pusey) would put it higher than that. For the majority of contributors, the Church of England represented a cement which bound society together, but which needed to recover its holiness. Ironically Charles Grey's government in proposing the Ecclesiastical Commission in 1832, aimed to correct abuses, including the holding of multiple livings in the

---

[67] To Jemima (Mrs John Mozley), 25 February 1840, LD 7, p. 245.

[68] R. W. Church *The Oxford Movement 1833–1845,* London, 1891, pp. 129-30.

[69] J. C. D. Clark *English Society 1688–1832,* Cambridge, 1985, p. 415.

[70] C. B. Faught, *The Oxford Movement, A Thematic History of the Tractarians and Their Times* Pennsylvania University Press, 2003, p. 16.

Church. The Tractarians would go further by returning to the apostolic basis for episcopacy. Rune Imberg is the latest to emphasize the quest for authority in the Movement.[71] In retrospect it could be argued that too much was being demanded of the bishops, but this should not be exaggerated. There was an insistence on the nature of the Episcopal office as apostolical together with the awareness of the crucial importance of the word of Scripture and the transcendence of the Incarnate Word present in the Church's worship. There is no coincidence in the fact that Newman began weekly celebrations of the Eucharist in St Mary's in 1833.

Newman and the Tracts

The contribution of Pusey cannot be underestimated as regards the general acceptance of the Tracts. Not only was he Regius Professor of Hebrew and Canon of Christchurch, but he signed Tract 18, thus giving weight to the series. However the Tracts would have been bogged down in discussions with Palmer and Rose if it had not been for Newman's "first vehement feelings".[72] In Meriol Trevor's words, "Newman was the activating centre."[73] Although he did not take credit for their success, he could not hide his pleasure: "I am astonished to see how they take. A flame seems rising in many places to show no mortal incendiary is

---

[71] R. Imberg, *In Quest of Authority,* Lund University, 1987, and James Tolhurst, *The Church a Communion,* Leominster, 1987, pp. 170–1.

[72] Apo, p. 44.

[73] *The Pillar and the Cloud,* London, 1962, p. 150. Wilfrid Ward would call him "the life and soul". (*The Life of J. H. Cardinal Newman*, Vol. 1, London, 1921, p. 60.)

at work."[74] It is also noticeable that, unlike many pamphlets of the time, the *Tracts of the Times* were at times "severe" and hard-hitting, but without being personal. Newman would remind one editor,

> The writers nowhere attack your Magazine, or other similar publications, though they evidently as little approve of its theology, as your Magazine that of the Tracts. They have been content to go onward; to preach what is positive; to trust in what they did well, not in what others did ill; to leave truth to fight its own battle, in a case where they had no office or commission to assist it coercively. They have spoken against principles, ages, or historical characters, but not against persons living. They have not taken an eye for eye, or tooth for tooth. They have left their defence to time, or rather committed it to God.[75]

That this is not some sort of special pleading can be seen in the response of Jacob Abbot, the author of "Corner Stone", which Newman criticized in Tract 83. Mr Abbot subsequently visited Newman at Littlemore and "confessed that [Newman's words] had the greatest effect upon his mind, and that he would write very differently now ... [he] admitted the entire fairness of the review, and wished nothing to be withdrawn or altered."[76]

---

[74] To R. H. Froude, 16 July 1835, LD 5, p. 99.
[75] Tract 82. The Editor of the *Christian Observer* was Samuel Charles Wilks.
[76] From *The English Churchman,* Ess I, pp. 100-1 and cf. LD 9, pp. 435, 552.

It is hard to conceive how the Vicar of St. Mary's
and the Dean of Oriel, with all his college commit-
ments, could not only embark on the work of writing,
publishing and distributing what became best-sellers
(60,000 copies a year by 1834), but also continued as
Vicar of St Mary's, composing sermons and his *Lectures
on the Prophetical Office* (1834–1836). The Tracts played
a large part in the early years, but they were combined
with the sermons, as is clear from Newman's comment
to Froude, "That the said Tracts have been of essential
benefit, it is impossible to doubt. Pamphlets, sermons
etc., on the Apostolical Succession are appearing in
every part of the Kingdom – and every other Sunday
we have an University Sermon on the subject."[77] It is
significant that although six volumes of the Tracts
were published between 1834 and 1841, Newman
never considered re-issuing his Tracts when Copeland
was editing his *Parochial and Plain Sermons* in 1868.
Newman clearly considered that the Tracts were of a
past that had gone, and, in retrospect no longer seemed
relevant.

Yet the Tracts record the beginning of a movement
which had repercussions in the Church of England.
Newman recalled that undergraduates "went down to
the country, and became curates of parishes. Then they
had down from London parcels of Tracts, and other
publications. They placed them in the shops of local
booksellers, got them into newspapers, introduced
them to clerical meetings, and converted more or less
their Rectors and their brother curates."[78] Frances

---

[77] To R. H. Froude, 15 June 1834, LD 4, p. 271.
[78] Apo,. pp. 58-9.

Knight claims that there was an extremely limited impact in some dioceses and the overall importance of the Tracts has been exaggerated. But she is willing to admit that it is a thread in the tapestry of high church-manship.[79]

The controversies which occasioned their publication have not gone away. The debate about Erastianism may one day be solved by disestablishment but there still remains the key role of Episcopal authority and the conflict between rationalism and credal belief. The interest shown in the study of Patristics supported by *The Library of the Fathers* brought a new emphasis on doctrine, and over it all there loomed the cloud no bigger than a man's hand, as early as Tract 20, "True it is, were the Church to teach heretical doctrine, it might become incumbent on us (a miserable obligation!) to separate from it."

The Oxford Movement, as Clement Webb observed, "created a new ideal of the Church's ministry and a new type of clergyman."[80]. It also indirectly led to the formation of the Additional Curates Society in 1837 supporting poor parishes, and the restoration of religious communities in the Church of England – inaugurated by Pusey, and soon followed by the Wantage Community. It was also in embryo, in Newman's community of Littlemore.

It may be that there were only under a thousand clergy who would openly admit to Tractarian princi-

---

[79] F. Knight "The Influence of the Oxford Movement in the Parishes: A Reassessment" in *From Oxford to the People,* Leominster, 1996, pp. 133, 139.

[80] *Religious Thought in the Oxford Movement 1824–1843,* London, 1928, p. 71.

ples, if we follow Conybeare's somewhat partisan account.[81] But the issues raised by the Tracts saw fulfillment eventually in the parish ministries of Fr Jellicoe in Somerstown and Fr Lowder in St Peter's London Docks as well as Fr Wagner of Brighton and Canon Carter of Clewer. Harold Perkin maintained that both the Oxford Movement and the Evangelical revival "made the Church for the first time since the Reformation, to a limited extent at least, an independent force of moral and social reform."[82] As Newman said in 1833, "Then you will look at us, not as gentlemen, as now, not as your superiors in worldly station ... *we* must do our duty."[83] Such practical concern was shown by John Keble in his country parish of Hursley and would continue to be practised by John Henry Newman in the urban sprawl of the Midlands, for "Birmingham people had souls."[84]

I have preserved Newman's syntax and punctuation (with certain exceptions), including his use of capital letters in early Tracts. For Scriptural references in the text, I have used either the King James or the Revised Standard Versions, where appropriate. Newman's works are from the standard edition of 1910 by Longmans.

---

[81] W. J. Conybeare, "Church Parties", *Edinburgh Review,* October 1853, p. 338.
[82] *The Origins of Modern English Society* (2nd ed., London, 2002), p. 362.
[83] Tract 10 (4 November 1833).
[84] To Mgr Talbot, 25 July 1864, LD 21, p. 167.

TRACT 1

THOUGHTS ON THE MINISTERIAL COMMISSION

RESPECTFULLY ADDRESSED TO THE CLERGY

I AM but one of yourselves, – a Presbyter; and therefore I conceal my name, lest I should take too much on myself for speaking in my own person. Yet speak I must; for the times are very evil, yet no one speaks against them.

Is this not so? Do we not "look upon one another,"[1] yet perform nothing? Do we not all confess the peril into which the Church is come, yet sit still each in his own retirement, as if mountains and seas cut off brother from brother? Therefore suffer me, while I try to draw you forth from those pleasant retreats, which it has been our blessedness hitherto to enjoy, to contemplate the condition and prospects of our Holy Mother in a practical way; so that one and all may unlearn that idle habit, which has grown upon us, of owning the state of things to be bad, yet doing nothing to remedy it.

Consider a moment. Is it fair, is it dutiful, to suffer our Bishops to stand the brunt of the battle without doing our part to support them? Upon them comes "the care of the Churches."[2] This cannot be helped; indeed it is their glory. Not one of us would wish in the least to deprive them of the duties, the toils, the responsibilities of their high Office. And, black event as it would be, for the country, yet, (as far as they are concerned,) we could not wish them a more blessed termination of their course, than the spoiling of their goods, and martyrdom.

To them then we willingly and affectionately relinquish their high privileges and honours; we encroach not upon the rights of the SUCCESSORS OF THE APOSTLES; we touch not their sword and crosier. Yet surely we may be their shield-bearers in the battle without offence; and by our voice and deeds be to them what Luke and Timothy were to St. Paul.

Now then let me come at once to the subject which leads me to address you. Should the Government and country so far forget their GOD as to cast off the Church, to deprive it of its temporal honours and substance, *on what* will you rest the claim of respect and attention which you make upon your flocks? Hitherto you have been upheld by your birth, your education, your wealth, your connexions; should these secular advantages cease, on what must CHRIST'S Ministers depend? Is not this a serious practical question? We know how miserable is the state of religious bodies not supported by the State. Look at the Dissenters on all sides of you, and you will see at once that their Ministers, depending simply upon the people, become the *creatures* of the people. Are you content that this should be your case? Alas! can a greater evil befal Christians than for their teachers to be guided by them instead of guiding? How can we "hold fast the form of sound words," and "keep that which is committed to our trust,"[3] if our influence is to depend simply on our popularity? Is it not our very office to *oppose* the world? can we then allow ourselves to *court* it? to preach smooth things and prophesy deceits?[4] to make the way of life easy to the rich and indolent, and to bribe the humbler classes by excitements and strong intoxicating doctrine? Surely it must not be so; – and the question recurs, on *what* are we to rest our authority, when the State deserts us?

CHRIST has not left His Church without claim of its own upon the attention of men. Surely not. Hard Master He cannot be, to bid us oppose the world, yet give us no credentials for so doing. There are some who rest their divine mission on their own unsupported assertion; others, who rest it upon their popularity; others, on their success; and others, who rest it upon their temporal distinctions. This last case has, perhaps, been too much our own; I fear we have neglected the real ground on which our authority is built, – OUR APOSTOLICAL DESCENT.

We have been born, not of blood, nor of the will of the flesh, nor of the will of man, but of God.[5] The Lord JESUS CHRIST gave His Spirit to His Apostles; they in turn laid their hands on those who should succeed them; and these again on others; and so the sacred gift has been handed down to our present Bishops, who have appointed us as their assistants, and in some sense representatives.

Now every one of us believes this. I know that some will at first deny they do; still they do believe it. Only it is not sufficiently practically impressed on their minds. They *do* believe it; for it is the doctrine of the Ordination Service, which they have recognised as truth in the most solemn season of their lives. In order, then, not to prove, but to remind and impress, I entreat your attention to the words used when you were made Ministers of CHRIST'S Church.

The office of Deacon was thus committed to you: "Take thou authority to execute the office of a Deacon in the Church of GOD committed unto thee: In the name," &c.[6]

And the priesthood thus: "Receive the HOLY GHOST, for the office and work of a Priest in the Church of GOD, now committed unto thee by the imposition of our hands. Whose sins thou doest forgive, they are forgiven; and whose sins thou dost retain, they are retained. And be thou a faithful dispenser of the Word of GOD, and of His Holy Sacraments: In the name," &c.[7]

These, I say, were words spoken to us, and received by us, when we were brought nearer to GOD than at any other time of our lives. I know the grace of ordination is contained in the laying on of hands, not in any form of words; – yet in our own case, (as has ever been usual in the Church,) words of blessing have accompanied the act. Thus we have confessed before GOD our belief, that through the Bishop who ordained us, we received the HOLY GHOST, the power to bind and to loose, to administer the Sacraments, and to preach. Now *how* is he able to give these great gifts? *Whence* is his right? Are these words idle, (which would be taking GOD'S name in vain,) or do they express merely a wish, (which surely is very far below their meaning,) or do they not rather indicate that the Speaker is conveying a gift? Surely they can mean nothing short of this. But whence, I ask, his right to do so? Has he any right, except as having received the power from those who consecrated him to be a Bishop? He could not give what he had never received. It is plain then that he but *transmits*; and that the Christian ministry is a *succession*. And if we trace back the power of ordination from hand to hand, of course we shall come to the Apostles at last. We know we do, as a plain historical fact; and therefore all we, who have been ordained Clergy, in the very form of our ordination acknowledged the doctrine of the APOSTOLICAL SUCCESSION.

And for the same reason, we must necessarily consider none to be *really* ordained who have not *thus* been ordained. For if ordination is a divine ordinance, it must be necessary; and if it is not a divine ordinance, how dare we use it? Therefore all who use it, all of *us*, must consider it necessary. As well might we pretend the Sacraments are not necessary to Salvation, while we make use of the offices of the Liturgy; for when GOD appoints means of grace, they are *the* means.

I do not see how any one can escape from this plain view of the subject, except, (as I have already hinted,) by declaring, that the words do not mean all that they say. But only reflect what a most unseemly time for random words is that, in which Ministers are set apart for their office. Do we not adopt a Liturgy, *in order to* hinder inconsiderate idle language, and shall we, in the most sacred of all services, write down, subscribe, and use again and again forms of speech, which have not been weighed, and cannot be taken strictly?

Therefore, my dear Brethren, act up to your professions. Let it not be said that you have neglected a gift; for if you have the Spirit of the Apostles on you, surely this *is* a great gift. "Stir up the gift of GOD which is in you."[8] Make much of it. Show your value of it. Keep it before your minds as an honourable badge, far higher than that secular respectability, or cultivation, or polish, or learning, or rank, which gives you a hearing with the many. Tell *them* of your gift. The times will soon drive you to do this, if you mean to be still any thing. But wait not for the times. Do not be compelled, by the world's forsaking you, to recur as if unwillingly to the high source of your authority. Speak out now, before you are forced, both as glorifying in your privilege, and to ensure your rightful honour from your people. A notion has gone abroad, that they can take away your power. They think they have given and can take it away. They think it lies in the Church property, and they know that they have politically the power to confiscate that property. They have been deluded into a notion that present palpable usefulness, produceable results, acceptableness to your flocks, that these and such like are the tests of your Divine commission. Enlighten them in this manner. Exalt our Holy Fathers, the Bishops as the Representatives of the Apostles, and the Angels of the Churches; and magnify your office as being ordained by them to take part in their Ministry.

But, if you will not adopt my view of the subject, which I offer to you, not doubtingly, yet (I hope) respectfully, at all events, CHOOSE YOUR SIDE. To remain neuter much longer will be itself to take a part. *Choose* your side; since side you shortly must, with one or other party, even though you do nothing. Fear to be of those whose line is decided for them by chance circumstances, and who may perchance find themselves with the enemies of CHRIST, while they think but to remove themselves from worldly politics. Such abstinence is impossible in troublous times. HE THAT IS NOT WITH ME, IS AGAINST ME, AND HE THAT GATHERETH NOT WITH ME SCATTERETH ABROAD.[9]

TRACT 2

THE CATHOLIC CHURCH

*No weapon that is formed against thee shall prosper,
and every tongue that shall rise against thee in judgment*
THOU SHALT CONDEMN *(Isa 54:17)*

IT is sometimes said, that the Clergy should abstain from politics; and that if a Minister of Christ is political, he is not a follower of him who said, "My kingdom is not of this world."[1] Now there is a sense in which this is true, but, as it is commonly taken, it is very false.

It is true that the mere affairs of this world should not engage a Clergyman; but it is absurd to say that the affairs of this world should not at all engage his attention. If so, this world is not a preparation for another. Are we to speak when individuals sin, and not when a nation, which is but a collection of individuals? Must we speak to the poor, and not to the rich, and powerful? In vain does St. James warn us against having the faith of our LORD JESUS CHRIST with respect of persons.[2] In vain does the Prophet declare to us the word of the LORD, that if the watchmen of Israel "speak not to warn the wicked from his way," "his blood will be required at the watchman's hand." [3]

Complete our LORD'S declaration concerning the nature of His kingdom, and you will see it is not at all inconsistent with the duty of our active and zealous interference in matters of this world. "If my kingdom were of this world," He says, "*then would My servants fight.*"[4] – Here He has vouchsafed so to explain Himself, that there is no room for misunderstanding His meaning. No one contends that His ministers ought to use the weapons of a carnal warfare; but surely to protest, to warn, to threaten, to excommunicate, are not such weapons. Let us not be scared from a plain duty, by the mere force of a misapplied text. There is an unexceptionable sense in which a Clergyman may, nay must be *political*. And above all, when the Nation interferes with the rights and possessions of the Church, it can with even less grace complain of the Church interfering with the Nation.

With this introduction let me call your attention to what seems a most dangerous infringement of our rights, on the part of the State. The Legislature has lately taken upon itself to remodel the dioceses of Ireland;[5] a proceeding which involves the appointment of certain Bishops over certain Clergy, and of certain Clergy under certain Bishops without the Church being consulted in the matter. I do not say whether or not harm will follow from this particular act with reference to Ireland; but consider whether it be not in itself an interference with things spiritual.

Are we content to be accounted the mere creation of the State, as schoolmasters and teachers may be, or soldiers, or magistrates, or other public officers? Did the State make us? can it unmake us? can it send out missionaries? can it arrange dioceses? Surely all these are spiritual functions: and Laymen may as well set about preaching, and consecrating the LORD'S Supper, as assume these. I do not say the guilt is equal; but that, if the latter is guilt, the former is. Would St. Paul, with his good will, have suffered the Roman power to appoint Timothy, Bishop of Miletus, as well as of Ephesus? Would Timothy at such a bidding have undertaken the charge? Is not the notion of such an order, such an obedience, absurd? Yet has it not been realized in what has lately happened? For in what is the English state at present different from the Roman formerly? Neither can be accounted members of the Church of CHRIST. No one can say the British Legislature is in our communion, or that its members are necessarily even Christians. What pretence then has it for, not merely advising, but superseding the Ecclesiastical power?

Bear with me, while I express my fear, that we do not, as much as we ought, consider the force of that article of our Belief, "The One Catholic and Apostolic Church." This is a tenet so important as to have been in the Creed from the beginning. It is mentioned there as a *fact* and a fact *to be believed*, and therefore practical. Now what do we conceive is meant by it? As people vaguely take it in the present day, it seems only an assertion that there is a number of sincere Christians scattered through the world. But is not this a truism? who doubt it? who can deny that there are people in various places who are sincere believers? what comes of this? how is it important? why should it be placed as an article of faith, after the belief in the HOLY GHOST? Doubtless the only true and satisfactory meaning is that which our Divines have ever taken, that there is on earth an existing Society,[6] Apostolic as founded by the Apostles, Catholic because it spreads its branches in every place; i.e. the Church Visible with its Bishops, Priests, and Deacons. And this surely *is* a most important doctrine; for what can be better news to the bulk of mankind than to be told that CHRIST when He ascended, did not leave us orphans, but appointed representatives of Himself to the end of time?

"The necessity of believing the Holy Catholic Church," says Bishop Pearson in his Exposition of the Creed,[7] "appeareth first in this, that CHRIST has appointed it as the only way to eternal life. ... CHRIST never appointed two ways to heaven, nor did He build a Church to save some, and make another institution for other men's salvation. There is none other name under heaven given among men whereby we must be saved but the name of JESUS;[8] and that name is no otherwise given under heaven than in the

Church." "This is the congregation of those persons here on earth which shall hereafter meet in heaven. ... There is a necessity of believing the Catholic Church, because except a man be of that he can be of none. Whatsoever Church pretendeth to a new beginning, pretendeth at the same time to a new Churchdom, and whatsoever is so new is none." This indeed is the unanimous opinion of our divines, that, as the Sacraments, so Communion with the Church, is "generally necessary to salvation," in the case of those who can obtain it.

If then we express our belief in the existence of One Church on earth from CHRIST'S coming to the end of all things, if there is a promise it shall continue, and if it is our duty to do our part in our generation towards its continuance, how can we with a safe conscience countenance the interference of the Nation in its concerns? Does not such interference tend to destroy it? Would it not destroy it, if consistently followed up? Now, may we sit still and keep silence, when efforts are making to break up, or at least materially weaken that Ecclesiastical Body which we know is intended to last while the world endures, and the safety of which is committed to our keeping in our day? How shall we answer for it, if we transmit the Ordinance of GOD less entire than it came to us?

Now what am I calling on you to do? You cannot help what has been done in Ireland; but you may protest against it. You may as a duty protest against it in public and private; you may keep a jealous watch on the proceedings of the Nation, lest a second act of the same kind be attempted. You may keep it before you as a desirable object that the Irish Church should at some future day meet in Synod and protest herself against what has been done; and then proceed to establish or rescind the State injunction as may be thought expedient.

I know it is too much the fashion of the times to think any

earnestness for ecclesiastical rights unseasonable and absurd, as if it were the feeling of those who live among books and not in the world. But it is our *duty* to live among books, especially to live by ONE BOOK, and a very old one; and therein we are enjoined to "keep that good thing which is committed unto us," to "neglect not our gift."[9] And when men talk, as they sometimes do, as if in opposing them we were standing on technical difficulties instead of welcoming great and extensive benefits which would be the result of their measures, I would ask them, (letting alone the question of their beneficial nature, which *is* a question) whether this is not being wise above that is written, whether it is not doing evil that good may come. We cannot know the effects which will follow certain alterations; but we can decide that the means by which it is proposed to attain them are unprecedented and disrespectful to the Church. And when men say, "*the day is past*[10] for stickling about ecclesiastical rights," let them see to it lest they use substantially the same arguments to maintain their position as those who say, "The day is past for being a Christian."

Lastly, is it not plain that by showing a bold front and defending the rights of the Church, we are taking the only course which can make us respected? Yielding will not persuade our enemies to desist from their efforts to destroy us root and branch.[11] We cannot hope by giving something to keep the rest. Of this surely we have had of late years sufficient experience. But by resisting strenuously, and contemplating and providing against the worst, we may actually prevent the very evils we fear. To prepare for persecution may be the way to avert it.

TRACT 3

THOUGHTS ON ALTERATIONS IN THE LITURGY

RESPECTFULLY ADDRESSED TO THE CLERGY

ATTEMPTS are making to get the Liturgy altered. My dear Brethren, I beseech you, consider with me whether you ought not to resist the alteration of even one jot or tittle of it. Though you would in your own private judgments wish to have this or that phrase or arrangement amended, is this a time to concede one tittle?[1]

Why do I say this? because, though most of you would wish some immaterial points altered, yet not many of you agree in those points, and not many of you agree what is and what is not immaterial. If all your respective emendations are taken, the alterations in the Services will be extensive; and though each will gain something he wishes, he will lose more from those alterations which he did not wish. Tell me, are the present imperfections (as they seem to each) of such a nature, and so many, that their removal will compensate for the recasting of much which each thinks to be no imperfection, or rather an excellence?

There are persons who wish the Marriage Service emended; there are others who would be indignant at the changes proposed. There are some who wish the Consecration Prayer in the Holy Sacrament to be what it was in King Edward's first book;[2] there are others who think this would be an approach to Popery. There are some who wish the imprecatory Psalms omitted;[3] there are others who would lament this omission as savouring of the shallow and detestable liberalism of the day. There are some who wish the Services shortened, and more frequent attendance at public worship than we have.

How few would be pleased by *any given* alterations; and how many pained!

But once begin altering, and there will be no reason or justice in stopping, till the criticisms of all parties are satisfied. Thus will not the Liturgy be in the evil case described in the well-known story, of the picture subjected by the artist to the observations of passers-by?[4] And, even to speak at present of comparatively immaterial alterations, I mean such as do not infringe upon the doctrines of the Prayer Book, will not it even with these be a changed book, and will not that new book be for certain an inconsistent one, the alterations being made, not on principle, but upon chance objections urged from various quarters?

But this is not all. A taste for criticism grows upon the mind. When we begin to examine and take to pieces, our judgment becomes perplexed, and our feelings unsettled. I do not know whether others feel this to the same extent, but for myself, I confess there are few parts of the Service that I could not disturb myself about, and feel fastidious at, if I allowed my mind in this abuse of reason. First, e.g. I might object to the opening sentences; "they are not evangelical enough; CHRIST is not mentioned in them; they are principally from the Old Testament."[5] Then I should criticize the exhortation, as having too many words, and as antiquated in style.[6] I might find it hard to speak against the Confession; but "the Absolution," it might be said, "is not strong enough; it is a mere declaration, not an announcement of pardon to those who have confessed."[7] And so on.

Now I think this unsettling of the mind a frightful thing; both to ourselves, and more so to our flocks. They have long regarded the Prayer Book with reverence as the stay of their faith and devotion. The weaker sort it will make sceptical; the better it will offend and pain. Take, e.g. an alteration which some have offered in the Creed, to omit or otherwise word the clause, "He descended into *hell*." Is it no comfort for mourners to be told that CHRIST Himself has been in that unseen state, or Paradise, which is the allotted place of sojourn for the departed spirits? Is it not very easy to explain the ambiguous word,[8] is it any great harm if it is misunderstood, and is it not very difficult to find any substitute for it in harmony with the composition of the Creed? I suspect we should find the best men in the number of those who would retain it as it is. On the other hand, will not the unstable learn from us a habit of criticizing what they should never think of but as a divine voice supplied by the Church for their need?

But as regards ourselves, the Clergy, what will be the effect of this temper of innovation in us? We have the power to bring about changes in the Liturgy; shall we not exert it? Have we any security, if we once begin, that we shall never end? Shall not we pass from non-essentials to essentials? And then, on looking back after the mischief is done, what excuse shall we be able to make for ourselves for having encouraged such proceedings at first? Were there grievous errors in the Prayer Book, something might be said for beginning, but who can point out any? cannot we very well *bear* things as they are? does any part of it seriously disquiet us? no – we have before now freely given our testimony to its accordance with Scripture.

But it may be said that "we must conciliate an outcry which is made; that some alteration is demanded." By whom? no one can tell who cries, or who can be conciliated. Some of the laity, I suppose. Now consider this carefully. Who are these lay persons? Are they serious men, and are their consciences involuntarily hurt by the things they wish altered? Are they not rather the men you meet in company, worldly men, with little personal religion, of lax conversation and lax professed principles, who sometimes perhaps come to Church, and then are wearied and disgusted? Is it not so? You have been dining, perhaps, with a wealthy neighbor, or fall in with this great Statesman, or that noble Land-holder, who considers the Church two centuries behind the world, and expresses to you wonder that its enlightened members do nothing to improve it.[9] And then you get ashamed, and are betrayed into admissions which sober reason disapproves. You consider, too, that it is a great pity so estimable or so influential a man should be disaffected to the Church; and you go away with a vague notion that something must be done to conciliate such persons. Is this to bear about you the solemn office of a GUIDE and TEACHER in Israel, or to *follow a lead*?

But consider what are the concession which would conciliate such men. Would immaterial alterations? Do you really think they care one jot about the verbal or other changes which some recommend, and others are disposed to grant? whether "the unseen state" is substituted for "hell", "condemnation" for "damnation", or the order of Sunday Lessons is remodeled? No; – they dislike the *doctrine* of the Liturgy. These men of the world do not like the anathemas of the Athanasian creed[10] and other peculiarities of our Services. But even were the alterations, which would please them, small, are they the persons whom it is of use, whom it is becoming to conciliate by going out of our way?

I need not go on to speak against doctrinal alterations, because most thinking men are sufficiently averse to them. But, I earnestly beg you to consider whether we must not come to them if we once begin. For by altering immaterials, we merely *raise* without *gratifying* the desire of correcting; we excite the craving, but withhold the food. And it should be observed, that the changes called immaterial often contain in themselves the germ of some principle, of which they are thus the introduction. E. G. If we were to leave out the imprecatory Psalms, we certainly countenance the notion of the day, that love and love only is in the Gospel the character of ALMIGHTY GOD and the duty of regenerate man; whereas that Gospel, rightly understood, shows His Infinite Holiness and Justice as well as His Infinite Love; and it enjoins on men the duties of zeal towards Him, hatred of sin, and separation from sinners, as well as that of kindness and charity.

To the above observations it may be answered, that changes have formerly been made in the Services without leading to the issue I am predicting now; and therefore they may be safely made again. But, waving all other remarks in answer to this argument, is not this enough, viz. that there is *peril*? No one will deny that the rage of the day is for concession. Have we not already granted (political) points, without stopping the course of innovation? This is a fact. Now, is it worth while even to *risk* fearful changes merely to gain petty improvements, allowing those which are proposed to be such?

We know not what is to come upon us; but the writer for one will try so to acquit himself now, that if any irremediable calamity befalls the Church, he may not have to vex himself with the recollections of silence on his part and indifference, when he might have been up and alive. There was a time when he, as well as others, might feel the wish, or rather the temptation, of steering a middle course between parties; but if so, a more close attention to passing events has cured his infirmity.[11] In a day like this there are but two sides, zeal and persecution, the Church and the world; and those who attempt to occupy the ground between them, at best will lose their labour, but probably will be drawn back to the latter. Be practical, I respectfully urge you; do not attempt impossibilities; sail not as if in pleasure boats upon a troubled sea. Not a word falls to the ground,[12] in a time like this. Speculations about ecclesiastical improvements which might be innocent at other times, have a strength of mischief now. They are realized before he who utters them understands that he has committed himself.

Be prepared then for petitioning against any alterations in the Prayer Book which may be proposed. And, should you see that our Fathers the Bishops seem to countenance them, petition still. Petition *them*. They will thank you for such a proceeding. *They do not wish these alterations;* but how can they resist them without the support of their Clergy? They consent to them, (if they do,) partly from the notion that they are thus pleasing you. Undeceive them. They will be rejoiced to hear that you are as unwilling to receive them as they are. However, if after all there be persons determined to allow some alterations, then let them quickly make up their minds *how far* they will go. They think it easier to draw the line elsewhere, than as things now exist. Let them point out the limit of their concessions now; and let them keep to it then; and, (if they can do this,) I will say that, though they are not as wise as they might have been, they are at least firm, and have at last come right.

THE BURIAL SERVICE

We hear many complaints about the Burial Service, as unsuitable for the use for which it was intended. It expresses a hope, that the person departed, over whom it is read, will be saved; and this is said to be dangerous when expressed about all who are called Christians, as leading the laity to low views of the spiritual attainments necessary for salvation; and distressing the Clergy who have to read it.

Now I do not deny, I frankly own, it is sometimes distressing to use the Service; but this it must ever be in the nature of things; wherever you draw the line. Do you pretend you can discriminate the wheat from the tares?[13] of course not.

It is often distressing to use this Service, because it is often distressing to think of the dead at all; not that you are without hope, but because you have fear also.

How many are there whom you know well enough to dare to give any judgment about? Is a Clergyman only to express a hope where *he* has grounds for having it? Are not the feelings of relatives to be considered? And may there not be a difference of judgments? I may hope more, another less. If each is to use the precise words which suit his own judgment, then we can have no words at all.

But it may be said, "every thing of a *personal* nature may be left out from the Service." And do you really wish this? Is this the way in which your flock will wish their lost friends to be treated? a cold "edification," but no affectionate vale-diction to the departed? Why not pursue this course of (supposed) improvement, and advocate the omission of the Service altogether?

Are we to have no kind and religious thoughts over the good, lest we should include the bad?

But it will be said, that, at least we ought not to read the Service over the flagrantly wicked; over those who are a scandal to religion. But this is a very different position. I agree with it entirely. Of course we should not do so, and truly the Church never meant we should. She never wished we should profess our hope of the salvation of habitual drunkards and swearers, open sinners, blasphemers, and the like; not as daring to despair of their salvation, but thinking it unseemly to honour their memory. Though the Church is not endowed with a power of absolute judgment upon indi-viduals, yet she is directed to decide according to external indications, in order to hold up the *rules* of GOD'S gover-nance, and afford a type of it, and an assistance towards the realizing it. As she denies to the scandalously wicked the LORD's Supper, so does she deprive them of her other privileges.[14]

The Church, I say, does not bid us read the Service over open sinners. Hear her own words introducing the Service. "The office ensuing is not to be used for any that die unbaptized, or excommunicate, or have laid violent hands upon themselves." There is no room to doubt *whom* she meant to be excommunicated, open sinners. Those therefore who are pained at the general use of the Service, should rather strive to restore the practice of excommunication, than to alter the words used in the Service. Surely, if we do not do this, we are clearly defrauding the religious, for the sake of keeping close to the wicked.

Here we see the common course of things in the world. We omit a duty. In consequence our services become inconsistent. Instead of retracing our steps we alter the Service. What is this but, as it were, to sin upon principle? While we keep to our principles, our sins are inconsistencies; at length, sensitive of the absurdity which inconsistency involves, we accommodate our professions to our practice. This is ever the way of the world; but it should not be the way of the church.

I will join heart and hand with any who will struggle for a restoration of that "godly discipline," the restoration of which our Church publicly professes she considers desirable; but God forbid any one should so depart from her spirit, as to mould her formularies to fit the case of deliberate sinners! And is not this what we are plainly doing, if we alter the Burial Service as proposed? we are recognizing the right of men to receive Christian Burial, about whom we do not like to express a hope. Why should they have Christian burial at all?

It will be said that the restoration of the practice of Excommunication is impracticable; and that therefore the other alternative must be taken as the only one open to us. Of course it is impossible, if no one attempts to restore it; but if all willed it, how would it be impossible; and if no one stirs because he thinks no one else will, he is arguing in a circle.

But, after all, what have we to do with probabilities and prospects in matters of plain duty? Were a man the only member of the Church who felt it a duty to return to the Ancient Discipline, yet a duty is a duty, though he be alone. It is one of the great sins of our times to look to consequences in matters of plain duty. Is not this such a case? If not, prove that it is not; but do not argue from *consequences*.

In the mean while I offer the following texts in evidence of the duty:

> Matt. 18:15–17; Rom. 16:17; 1 Cor. 5:7–13; 2 Thess. 3:6, 14, 15;
> 2 Tim. 3:5; Tit. 3:10, 11; 2 John 10:11.

THE PRINCIPLE OF UNITY

Testimony of St. Clement, the associate of St. Paul (Phil 4:3) to the Apostolical Succession.

The Apostles knew, through our LORD JESUS CHRIST, that strife would arise for the Episcopate. Wherefore having received an accurate foreknowledge, they appointed the men I before mentioned, and have given an orderly succession, that on their death other approved men might receive in turn their office. Ep. 1.44.

Testimony of St. Ignatius, the friend of St. Peter, to Episcopacy.

Your celebrated Presbytery, worthy of GOD, is as closely knit to the Bishop, as the strings to a harp, and so by means of your unanimity and concordant love JESUS CHRIST is sung. Eph. 4.

There are who profess to acknowledge a Bishop, but do everything without him. Such men appear to lack a clear conscience. Magn. 4.

He for whom I am bound is my witness that I have not learned this doctrine from mortal man. The Spirit proclaimed to me these words: "Without the Bishop do nothing." Phil. 7.

With these and other such strong passages in the Apostolical Fathers, how can we permit ourselves in our present *practical* disregard of the Episcopal Authority? Are not we apt to obey only so far as the law obliges us? do we support the Bishop and strive to move all together with him as our bond of union and head; or is not our everyday conduct as if, except with respect to certain periodical forms and customs, we were each independent in his own parish?

TRACT 6

THE PRESENT OBLIGATION
OF PRIMITIVE PRACTICE

WHEN we look around upon the present state of the Christian Church, and then turning to ecclesiastical history acquaint ourselves with its primitive form and condition, the difference between them so strongly acts upon the imagination, that we are tempted to think, that to base our conduct now on the principles acknowledged then, is but theoretical and idle. We seem to perceive, as clear as day, that as a Primitive Church had its own particular discipline and political character, so have we ours; and that to attempt to revive what is past, is as absurd as to seek to raise what is literally dead. Perhaps we even go on to maintain, that the constitution of the Church, as well as its actual course of acting, is different from what it was; that Episcopacy now is in no sense what it used to be; that our Bishops are the same as the Primitive Bishops only in name; and that the notion of an Apostolical Succession is "a fond thing."[1] I do not wish to undervalue the temptation of sight to overcome faith, and of course not a slight one.

But the following reflection on the history of the Jewish Church may perhaps be considered to throw light upon our present duties.

1. Consider how exact are the injunctions of Moses to his people. He ends them thus: "These are the words of the covenant which the LORD commanded Moses to make with

the children of Israel in the land of Moab, beside the covenant which He made with them in Horeb. ... Keep therefore the words of this covenant, and do them, that ye may prosper in all that ye do. ... Neither with you only do I make this covenant and this oath; but with him that standeth here this day before the LORD our GOD, and also with him that is not here this day." (Deut. 29).

2. Next, survey the history of the chosen people for the several first centuries after taking possession of Canaan. The exactness of Moses was unavailing. Can a greater contrast be conceived than the commands and promises of the Pentateuch, and the history of the Judges? "Every man did that which was right in his own eyes." (Judges 17:6).

Samuel attempts a reformation on the basis of the Mosaic Law; but the effort ultimately fails, as being apparently against the stream of opinion and feeling then prevalent. The times do not allow of it. Again, contrast the opulent and luxurious age of Solomon, though the covenant was then openly acknowledged and outwardly accepted more fully than at any other time, with the vision of simple piety and plain straightforward obedience, which is the scope of the Mosaic Law. Lastly, contemplate the state of the Jews after their return from the captivity; when their external political relations were so new, the internal principle of their government so secular, GOD'S arm apparently so far removed. This state of things went on for centuries. Who would suppose that the Jewish Law was binding in all its primitive strictness at the age when CHRIST appeared? Who would not say that length of time had destroyed the obligation of a projected system, which had as yet never been realized?

Consider too the impossible nature (so to say) of some of its injunctions. An infidel historian somewhere asks scoffingly, whether "the ruinous law which required all the males of the chosen people to go up to Jerusalem three times a year, was ever observed in its strictness."[2] The same question may be asked concerning the observance of the Sabbatical year; – to which but a faint allusion, if that, is made in the books of Scripture subsequent to the Pentateuch.[3]

3. And now, with these thoughts before us, reflect upon our SAVIOUR'S conduct. He set about to fulfil the Law in its strictness, just as if He had lived in the generation next to Moses. The practice of others, the course of the world was nothing to Him; He received and He obeyed. It is not necessary to draw out the evidence of this in detail. Consider merely His emphatic words in the beginning of Matthew 23 concerning those, whom as individuals He was fearfully condemning. "The Scribes and Pharisees sit in Moses' seat; all therefore whatsoever they bid you observe, that observe and do." – Again reflect upon the praise bestowed upon Zacharias and his wife, that "they were both righteous before GOD, walking in all the commandments and ordinances of the LORD blameless."[4] – And upon the conduct of the Apostles.

Surely these remarkable facts impress upon us the necessity of going to the Apostles, and not to the teachers and oracles of the present world, for the knowledge of our duty, as individuals and as members of the Christian Church. It is no argument against a practice being right, that it is neglected; rather, we are warned against going the broad way of the multitude of men.

Nor is there any doubt in our minds, as to the feelings of the Primitive Church regarding the doctrine of the Apostolical Succession? Did not the Apostles observe, even in an age of miracles, the ceremony of the Imposition of Hands?[5] And are not we bound, not merely to acquiesce in, but zealously to maintain and inculcate the discipline which they established?

The only objection, which can be made to this view of our duty, is, that the injunction to obey strictly is *not* precisely given to us, as it was in the instance of the Mosaic

Law. But is not the real state of the case merely this; that the Gospel appeals rather to our love and faith, our divinely illuminated reason, and the free principle of obedience, than to the mere letter of its injunctions? And does not the conduct of the Jews just prove to us, that, *though* the commands of CHRIST were put before us ever so precisely, yet there would not be found in any extended course of history a more exact attention to them, than there is now; that the difficulty of resisting the influence, which the world's actual proceedings exert upon our imagination, would be just as great as we feel at present?

A SIN OF THE CHURCH

Remember from whence thou art fallen, and repent, and do thy first works; or else I will come unto thee quickly, and will remove thy candlestick out of his place, except thou repent.[6]

The following extract is from Bingham, Antiq. 15.9.[7]

In the primitive ages, it was both the rule and practice of all in general, both Clergy and Laity, to receive the Communion every Lord's day ... As often as they met together for Divine Service on the Lord's day, they were obliged to receive the Eucharist under pain of Excommunication ... And if we run over the whole history of the three first ages, we shall find this to have been the Church's constant practice ... We are assured farther, that in some places they received the Communion every day.

Is there anyone who will deny, that the Primitive Church is the best expounder in this matter of our SAVIOUR'S will as conveyed through His Apostles?

Can a learned Church, such as the English, plead ignorance of His will thus ascertained?

Do we fulfil it?

Is not the regret and concern of pious and learned writers among us, such as Bingham, at our neglect of it, upon record?

And is it not written, "THAT SERVANT WHICH KNEW HIS LORD'S WILL, AND PREPARED NOT HIMSELF, NEITHER DID ACCORDING TO HIS WILL, SHALL BE BEATEN WITH MANY STRIPES"?[8]

And putting aside this disobedience, can we wonder, that faith and love wax cold,[9] when we so seldom partake of the MEANS, mercifully vouchsafed us, of communion with our LORD and SAVIOUR?

THE EPISCOPAL CHURCH
APOSTOLICAL

———————————

THERE are many persons at the present day, who, from not having turned their minds to the subject, think they are Churchmen in the sense in which the early Christians were, merely because they are Episcopalians. The extent of their Churchmanship is, to consider that Episcopacy is the best form of Ecclesiastical Polity;[1] and, again, that it originated with the Apostles. I am far from implying, that to go thus far is nothing; or is not an evidence (for it is,) of a reverent and sober temper of mind; still the view is defective. It is defective, because the expediency of a system, though a very cogent, is not the highest line of argument that may be taken in its defence: and because an opponent may deny the fact of the Apostolicity of Episcopacy, and so involve its maintainer in an argument. Doubtless the more clear and simple principle for a Churchman to hold, is that of a *Ministerial Succession*; which is undeniable as a fact, while it is most reasonable as a doctrine, and sufficiently countenanced in Scripture for its practical reception. Of this, Episcopacy, i.e. *Superintendence*, is but an accident; though, for the sake of conciseness, it is often spoken of by us as synonymous with it. It shall be the object of the following Tract to insist upon this higher characteristic of our Church.

My position then, is this; – that the Apostles appointed

successors to their ministerial office, and the latter in turn appointed others, and so on to the present day; – and further, that the Apostles and their Successors have in every age committed portions of their power and authority to others, who thus become their delegates, and in a measure their representatives, and are called Priests and Deacons. The result is an Episcopal system, *because* of the practice of delegation; but we may conceive their keeping their powers altogether to themselves, and in the same proportion in which this was done would the Church polity cease to be Episcopalian. We may conceive the Order of Apostolic Vicars (so to call it,) increased, till one of them was placed in every village, and took the office of parish Priest. I do not say such a measure would be justifiable or pious; – doubtless it would be a departure from the rule of antiquity – but it is conceivable; and it is useful to conceive it, in order to form a clear notion of the Essence of the Church System, and the defective state of those Christian Societies which are separate from the Church Catholic. It is a common answer made to those who are called High Churchmen, to say, that "if GOD had intended the *form* of Church Government to be of great consequence, He would have worded His will in this matter more clearly in Scripture." Now enough has already been said to show the irrelevancy of such a remark. We need not deny to the Church the abstract right, (however we may question the propriety,) of altering its own constitution. It is not merely *because* Episcopacy is a *better or more scriptural form* than Presbyterianism, (true as this may be in itself,) that Episcopalians are right, and Presbyterians are wrong; but because the Presbyterian Ministers have assumed a power, which was never entrusted to them. They have presumed to exercise the power of ordination, and to perpetuate a succession of ministers, without having received a commission to do so. This is the plain fact that condemns them; and is a standing condemnation from which they cannot escape, except by artifices of argument, which will serve equally to protect the self-authorized teacher of religion. If *they* may ordain without being set to do so, *others* may teach and preach without being sent. They hold a middle position, which is untenable as destroying itself; for if Christians can do without Bishops (i.e. Commissioned Ordainers), they may do without Commissioned Ministers (i.e. the Priests and Deacons). If an imposition of hands is necessary to convey one gift, why should it not be to convey another?

1. As to the *fact* of the Apostolical Succession, i.e. that our present Bishops are the heirs and representatives of the Apostles by successive transmission of the prerogative of being so, this is too notorious to require proof. Every link in the chain is known from St. Peter to our present Metropolitans. Here then I only ask, looking at this plain fact by itself, is there not something of a divine providence in it? can we conceive that this Succession has been preserved, all over the world, amid many revolutions, through many centuries, *for nothing*? Is it wise or pious to despise or neglect a gift thus transmitted to us in matter of fact, even if Scripture did not touch upon the subject?

2. Next, consider how *natural* is the doctrine of a Succession. When an individual comes to me, claiming to speak in the name of the Most High, it is natural to ask him for his authority. If he replies, that we are all bound to instruct each other, this reply is intelligible, but in the very form of it excludes the notion of a ministerial order, i.e. a class of persons set apart *from* others for religious offices. If he appeals to some miraculous gift, this too is intelligible, and only unsatisfactory when the alleged gift is proved to be a fiction. No other answer can be given except a reference to some person, who has given him license to exercise ministerial functions; then follows the question, *how* that individual gained his authority to do so. In the case of the Catholic Church, the person referred to, i.e. the Bishop, has received

it from a predecessor, and he from another, and so on, till we arrive at the Apostles themselves, and thence our LORD and SAVIOUR. It is superfluous to dwell on so plain a principle, which in matters of this world we act upon daily.

3. Lastly, the *argument from Scripture* is surely quite clear to those, who honestly wish direction for *practice*. CHRIST promised He would be with His Apostles always, as ministers of His religion even unto the end of the world.[2] In one sense the Apostles were to be alive till He came again; but they all died at the natural time. Does it not follow, that there are those now alive who represent them? Now who were the most probable representatives of them in the generation next their death? They surely, whom they have ordained to succeed them in the ministerial work. If any persons could be said to have CHRIST'S power and presence, and the gifts of ruling and ordaining, of teaching, of binding and loosing, (and comparing together the various Scriptures on the subject, all these seem included in His promise to be with the Church always,) surely those, on whom the Apostles laid their hands, were they. And so in the next age, if any were representatives of the first representatives, they must be the next generation of Bishops, and so on. Nor does it materially alter the argument, though we suppose the blessing upon Ministerial Offices made, not to the Apostles, but to the whole body of Disciples; i.e. the Church. For, even if it be the Church that has the power of ordination committed to it, still it exercises it through the Bishops as its organs; and the question recurs, *how* has the Presbytery in this or that country obtained the power? The Church certainly has from the first committed it to the Bishops, and has never resumed it; and the Bishops have no where committed it to the Presbytery, who therefore cannot be in possession of it.

However, it is merely for argument sake that I make this allowance, as to the meaning of the text in Matt. 28; for our LORD'S promise of his presence "unto the end of the world," was made to the Apostles *by themselves*. At the same time, let it be observed what force is added to the argument for the Apostolical Succession, by the acknowledged existence in Scripture of a standing Church or permanent Body Corporate for spiritual purposes. For, if Scripture has formed all Christians into one continuous community through all ages (which I do not here prove,) it is but according to the same analogy, that the Ministerial Office should be vested in an order, propagated from age to age, on a principle of Succession. And, if we proceed to considerations of utility and expedience, it is plain that, according to our notions, it is more necessary that a Minister should be perpetuated by a fixed law, than that the community of Christians should be, which can scarcely be considered to be vested with any powers such as to require the visible authority which a Succession supplies.

TRACT 8

THE GOSPEL A LAW OF LIBERTY

IT is a matter of surprise to some persons, that the ecclesiastical system under which we find ourselves, is so faintly
enjoined on us in Scripture. One very sufficient explanation
of the fact will be found in considering that the Bible is not
intended to teach us matters of *discipline* so much as matters
of *faith*; i.e. those doctrines, the reception of which are
necessary to salvation. But another reason may be suggested,
which is well worth our attentive consideration.

The Gospel is a Law of *Liberty*. We are treated as sons, not
as servants; not subjected to a code of formal commands, but
addressed as those who *love* God, and *wish* to please Him.
When a man gives orders to those whom he thinks will
mistake him, or are perverse, he speaks pointedly and explicitly; but when he gives directions to friends, he will trust
much to their knowledge of his feelings and wishes, he leaves
much to their discretion, and tells them not so much what he
would have done in detail, as what are the objects he would
have accomplished. Now this is the way CHRIST has spoken
to us under the New Covenant; and apparently with this
reason, to *try* us, whether or not we really love Him as our
LORD and SAVIOUR.

Accordingly, there is no part, perhaps of the ecclesiastical
system, which is not faintly traced in Scripture, and no part
which is much more than faintly traced. The question which
a reverend and affectionate faith will ask, is, "what is *most*

likely to please CHRIST?" And this is just the question that obtains an answer in Scripture; which contains just so much as *intimations* of what is most likely to please Him. Of course different minds will differ as to the degree of clearness with which this or that practice is enjoined, yet I think no one will consider the state of the case, as I have put it, exaggerated on the whole.

Many duties are intimated to us by example, not by precept – many are implied merely – others can only be inferred from a comparison of passages – and others perhaps are contained only in the Jewish Law. I will mention some specimens to assist the reflection of the reader.

The early Christians were remarkable for keeping to the Apostles' *fellowship*.[1] Who are *more likely* to stand in the Apostles' place since their death, than that line of Bishops which they themselves began? for that the Apostles *were* in some sense or other to remain on earth to the end of all things, is plain from the text, "Lo, I am with you always," &c. (Matt 28:20).

St. Paul set Timothy over the Church at Ephesus, and Titus over the Churches of Crete; i.e. as Bishops; therefore it is *safer* to have Bishops now, it is more likely to be pleasing to Him with the heart, not with formal service.

Our LORD committed the Administration of the LORD'S SUPPER *to His Apostles*; "Do this in remembrance of Me;"[2] – therefore the Church has ever continued it in the hands of their Successors, and the delegates of these.

From CHRIST'S words, "Suffer the little children," &c.[3] and from His blessing them, we infer His desire that children should be brought near to Him in baptism; as we do also from St. Paul's conduct on several occasions. Acts 16:15, 33; 1 Cor 1:16.

So also we continue the practice of Confirmation, from a desire to keep as near the Apostles' rule as possible.

Again, what little is there of express command in the New

Testament for our meeting together in *public worship*, in large congregations! Yet we see what the custom of the Apostolic Church was from the book of Acts, 1 Cor. &c. and we follow it.

In like manner, the words of Genesis 2 and the practice of the Apostles in the Acts, are quite warrant enough for the sanctification of the LORD'S Day, even though the fourth Commandment be not binding on us.[4]

For the same reason we continue the Patriarchal and Jewish rule of paying tithe to the Church. Some portion of our goods is evidently due to GOD; – and the ancient Divine Command is a *direction* to us, which the law of the land has made obligatory, in a case where reason and conscience have no means of determining.[5]

These may be taken as illustrations of a general principle. And at this day it is most needful to keep it in view, since a cold spirit has crept into the Church of demanding rigid demonstration of every religious practice and observance. It is the fashion now to speak of those who maintain the ancient rules of the ecclesiastical system, not as zealous servants of CHRIST, not as wise and practical expounders of His will, but as *inconclusive reasoners*, and *fanciful theorists*, merely because, instead of standing still and arguing, they have a heart to obey. Are there not numbers in this day, who think themselves enlightened believers, yet who are but acting the part of the husbandman's son in the Gospel, who said, "I go, sir," – AND WENT NOT.[6]

TRACT 10

HEADS OF A WEEK-DAY LECTURE

BEFORE we meet again, we shall have celebrated the feast of St. Simon and St Jude, the Apostles. You will be at your daily work, and will not have the opportunity to attend the Service in Church.[1] For that reason, it may be as well, you should lay up some good thoughts against that day; and such, by God's blessing, I will now attempt to give you.

As you well know, there were twelve Apostles; St. Simon and St. Jude were two of them. They preached the Gospel of CHRIST; and were like CHRIST, as far as sinful man may be accounted like the Blessed SON of GOD. They were like CHRIST in their deeds and in their sufferings. The Gospel for the festival[2] shows us this. They were like CHRIST in their *works*, because CHRIST was a witness of the FATHER, and they were witnesses of CHRIST. CHRIST came in the name of GOD the FATHER ALMIGHTY; He "came and spoke" and "did works which none other man did."[3] In like manner, the Apostles were sent to bear witness of CHRIST, to declare His power, His great mercy, His sufferings on the cross for the sins of all men, His willingness to save all who come to Him.

But again, they were like CHRIST in their *sufferings*. "If the world hate you," He says to them, "you know that it hated Me, before it hated you. If ye were of the world, the world would love his own; but because ye are not of the world, but

I have chosen you out of the world, therefore the world hateth you. Remember the word that I said unto you, The servant is not greater than his lord. If they have persecuted Me, they will also persecute you; if they have kept My saying, they will keep yours also."[4]

Thus, they were like CHRIST in *office*. I do not speak of their holiness, their faith, and all their other high excellencies, which GOD the HOLY GHOST gave them. I speak now, not of their personal graces, but of their *office*, of preaching, of witnessing CHRIST, of suffering for being His servants. Men ought to have listened to them, and honoured them; some did: but the many, the world did not, – they *hated* them; they hated them, for their office-sake; not because they were Paul, and Peter, and Simon, and Jude, but because they bore witness to the SON of GOD, and were chosen to be His Ministers.

Here is a useful lesson for us at this day. The Apostles indeed are dead; yet it is quite as possible for men still to hate their preaching and to persecute them, as when they were alive. For in one sense they are still alive; I mean, they did not leave the world without appointing persons to take their place; and these persons represent them, and may be considered with reference to us, as if they were the Apostles. When a man dies, his son takes his property, and represents him; that is, in a manner he still lives in the person of his son. Well, this explains how the Apostles may be said to be still among us; they did not indeed leave their sons to succeed them as Apostles, but they left *spiritual* sons; they did not leave this life, without first solemnly laying their hands on the heads of certain of their brethren, and these took their place, and represented them after their death.

But it may be asked, are these spiritual sons of the Apostles still alive? no; – all this took place many hundred years ago. These sons and heirs of the Apostles died long since. But then they in turn did not leave the world without committing their sacred office to a fresh set of Ministers, and they in turn to another, and so on even to this day. Thus the Apostles had, first, spiritual sons; then spiritual grandsons; then great grandsons; and so on, from one age to another, down to the present time.

Again, it may be asked, *who* are at this time the successors and spiritual descendants of the Apostles? I shall surprise some people by the answer I shall give, though it is very clear, and there is no doubt about it; THE BISHOPS. They stand in the place of the Apostles, as far as the office of ruling is concerned;[1] and whatever we ought to do, had we lived when the Apostles were alive, the same ought we to do for the Bishops. He that despiseth them, despiseth the Apostles.[5] It is our duty to reverence them for their office-sake; they are the shepherds of CHRIST'S flock. If we knew them well, we should love them for the many excellent graces they possess, for their piety, loving-kindness, and other virtues. But we do not know them; yet still, for all this, we may honour them as the Ministers of CHRIST, without going so far as to consider their *private* worth; and we may keep to their "fellowship",[2] as we should to that of the Apostles. I say, we may all thus honour them even without knowing them in private, because of their high office; for they have the marks of CHRIST'S presence upon them, in that they *witness* for CHRIST, and *suffer* for Him, as the Apostles did. I will explain to you how this is.

There is a temptation which comes on many men to honour no one, except such as they themselves know, such as have done a favour or kindness to them personally. Thus

---

[1] As far as the office of *ruling*, not as far as the office of *teaching* is concerned. The Apostles were both *inspired teachers* (Acts ii. 3, 4) and *Bishops* (John xx. 21–23). Their successors are Bishops only, not inspired teachers; and rule *according* to the Apostles' teaching, – not absolutely, as the Apostles may be said to have done.

[2] Acts ii. 42.

sometimes people speak against those who are put over them in this world's matters, as the King. They say, "What is the King to me? he never did me any good." Now, I answer, whether he did or not, is nothing to the purpose. We are bound *for* CHRIST'S sake, to honour him, *because* he is King, though he lives far from us; and this all well-disposed, right-minded people do. And so, in just the same way, though for much higher reasons, we must honour the Bishop because he *is* the Bishop; – for his *office*-sake;–– because he is CHRIST'S Minister, stands in the place of the Apostles, is the Shepherd of our souls on earth, while CHRIST is away. This is FAITH, to look at things not seen, but as unseen;[6] to be as sure that the Bishops is CHRIST'S appointed Representative, as if we actually saw him work miracles as St. Peter and St. Paul did, as you have read in the book of the Acts of the Apostles.

But you will say, how do we know this, since we do not see it? I repeat, the Bishops are Apostles to us, from their *witnessing* CHRIST, and *suffering* for Him.

1. They witness our LORD in their very *name*, for He is the true Bishop of our souls, as St. Peter says,[7] and they are Bishops. They witness CHRIST in their *station*; – there is but One LORD to save us, and there is but one Bishop in each place. The meetingers[8] have no head, they are all of them mixed together in one confused way; but we of CHRIST'S Holy Church (blessed be God!) have one Bishop over us, and our Bishop is the Bishop of –––––––––. Many of you have seen him lately, when he confirmed in our Church.[9] That very *confirmation* is another ordinance, in which the Bishop witnesses CHRIST. Our LORD and SAVIOUR confirms us with the SPIRIT in all goodness; the Bishop is His figure and likeness when he lays his hands on the heads of children. Then CHRIST (as we trust,) comes to them, to confirm in them the grace of Baptism. Moreover, the Bishop *rules* the whole Church here below, as CHRIST, the true and eternal Sovereign, rules it above; and here again the Bishop is a

figure or witness to our LORD. And further it is the Bishop who is commissioned to make us Clergymen GOD'S Ministers. He is CHRIST'S instrument; and he visibly chooses those whom CHRIST vouchsafes to choose invisibly, to serve in the Word and Sacraments of the Church. And thus, in one sense, it is from the Bishop that the *news of redemption and the means of grace*[10] have come to all men; this again is a witnessing CHRIST. I, who speak to you concerning CHRIST, was ordained to do so by the Bishop; he speaks in me, – as CHRIST wrought in him, and as GOD sent CHRIST. Thus the whole plan of salvation hangs together. – CHRIST the True Mediator above; His servant, the Bishop, His earthly likeness; mankind the subjects of His teaching; GOD the Author of Salvation.

2. But I must now mention the more painful part of the subject, i.e. the *sufferings* of the Bishops, which is the second mark of their being our living Apostles. I may say, Bishops have undergone this trial in every age. As the first Apostles were hated and opposed by the world, so have they ever been. I do not say they have been always opposed in the same way. In these latter times, they have experienced the lesser sufferings of bearing slander, reproach, threats, vexations, and thwartings in their efforts to do good. Time was, when they were even persecuted, cruelly slain by fire and sword. That time, (though GOD avert it!) may come again. But, whether or not Satan is permitted so openly to rage, certainly some kinds of persecution are to be expected in our day; nay, such have begun. It is not so very long since the great men of the earth told them to *prepare for persecution*; it is not so very long since the mad people answered the summons, and furiously attacked them, and seemed bent on destroying them, in all parts of the country.[11]

Yes! the day may come, even in this generation, when the Representatives of CHRIST are spoiled of their sacred possessions, and degraded from their civil dignities. The day may come, when each of us inferior Ministers – when I myself, whom you know – may have to give up our Churches, and be among you, in no better temporal circumstances than yourselves; with no larger dwelling, no finer clothing, no other fare, with nothing different beyond those gifts, which I trust we received from the All-gracious GOD when we were made Ministers; and those again, which have been vouchsafed to us before and after that time, for the due fulfillment of our Ministry. Then you will look at us, not as gentlemen, as now; not as your superiors in worldly station; but still, nay, more strikingly so than now, still as messengers from Him, who seeth and worketh in secret, and who judgeth not by outward appearance. Then you will honour us, with a purer honour than many men do now, namely, as those (if I may say so) who are entrusted with the keys of heaven and hell, as the heralds of mercy, as the denouncers of woe to wicked men, as entrusted with the awful and mysterious privilege of dispensing CHRIST'S Body and Blood, as far greater than the most powerful and the wealthiest of men in our unseen strength and our heavenly riches. This may all come in our day; *we* must do our duty; go straight forward, looking neither to the right hand or the left, "in patience possessing our souls,"[12] watching and praying, and so preparing for the evil day. And after all, if GOD'S loving kindness spares both us and you the trial, still it will have been useful to have steadily thought about it beforehand, and to have prepared our hearts to meet it.

TRACT 11

THE VISIBLE CHURCH
(In Letters to a Friend)

———————

LETTER I

YOU wish to have my opinion on the doctrine of "the Holy Catholic Church," as contained in Scripture, and taught in the Creed. So I send you the following lines, which perhaps may serve, through GOD'S blessing, to assist you in your search after the truth in this matter, even though they do no more; indeed no remarks, however just, can be much more than an assistance to you. You must search for yourself, and GOD must teach you.

I think I partly enter into your present perplexity. You argue, that true *doctrine* is the important matter for which we must contend, and a *right state of the affections* is the test of vital religion in the heart: and you ask, "Why may I not be satisfied if my Creed is correct, and my affections spiritual?[1] Have I not in that case enough to evidence a renewed mind, and to constitute a basis of union with others like minded? The love of CHRIST is surely the one and only requisite for Christian communion here, and the joys of heaven hereafter." Again you say, that —— and —— are constant in their prayers for the teaching of the HOLY SPIRIT; so that if it be true, that every one who asketh receiveth, surely they must receive, and are in a safe state.[2]

Believe me, I do not think lightly of these arguments. They are very subtle ones; powerfully influencing the imagination, and difficult to answer. Still I believe them to be

mere fallacies. Let me try them in a parallel case. You know
the preacher at −, you have heard of his flagrantly immoral
life;[3] yet it is notorious that he can and does speak in a
moving way of the love of CHRIST, &c. It is very shocking to
witness such a case, which (we will hope) is rare; but it has its
use. Do you not think him in peril, in spite of his impressive
and persuasive language? Why? − you will say, his life is bad.
True; it seems then that more is requisite for salvation than
an orthodox creed, and keen sensibility; viz. consistent
conduct. − Very well then, we have come to an additional
test of true faith, obedience to God's word, and plainly a
scriptural test, according to St John's canon, "He who *doeth*
righteousness is righteous."[4] Do not you see then your
argument is already proved to be unsound? It seems that true
doctrine and warm feelings are not enough. How am I to
know what *is* enough? you ask. I reply, *by searching Scripture.*
It was your original fault that, instead of inquiring what GOD
has told you is necessary for being a true Christian, you chose
out of your own head to *argue* on the subject; − e.g. "I can
never believe that to be such and such is not enough for
salvation," &c. Now this is *worldly wisdom.*

Let us join issue then on this plain ground, whether or not
the doctrine of "the Church" and the duty of obeying it, be
laid down *in Scripture.* If so, it is no matter as regards our
practice, whether the doctrine is primary or secondary,
whether the duty is much or little insisted on. A Christian
mind will aim at obeying the *whole* counsel and will of God;
on the other hand, to those who are tempted arbitrarily to
classify and select their duties, it is written, "Whosoever shall
break one of these least commandments, and shall teach men
so, he shall be called the least in the kingdom of heaven."[5]

And here first, that you may clearly understand the ground
I am taking, pray observe that I am not attempting to contro-
vert any one of those high evangelical points, on which
perhaps we do not altogether agree with each other. Perhaps

you attribute less efficacy to the Sacrament of Baptism than I do; bring out into greater system and prominence the history of an individual's warfare with his spiritual enemies; fix more precisely and abruptly the date of his actual conversion from darkness to light; and consider that Divine Grace acts more arbitrarily against the corrupt human will, than I think is revealed in Scripture.[6] Still, in spite of this difference of opinion, I see no reason why you should not accept heartily the Scripture doctrine of "the Church." And this is the point I wish to press, not asking you at present to abandon your own opinions, but to *add to them* a practical belief in a tenet which the Creed teaches and Scripture has consecrated. And this surely is quite possible. The excellent Mr. —— of —, who has lately left ——, was both a Calvinist, and a strenuous High-Churchman.

You are in the practice of distinguishing between the Visible and Invisible Church.[7] Of course I have no wish to maintain, that those who shall be saved hereafter are exactly the same company that are under the means of grace here; still I must insist on it, that Scripture makes the existence of a Visible Church a condition of the existence of the Invisible. I mean the *Sacraments* are evidently in the hands of the Church Visible; and these, we know, are generally necessary to salvation, as the Catechism says.[8] Thus it is an undeniable fact, as true as that souls will be saved that a Visible Church must exist as a means towards that end. The Sacraments are in the hands of the Clergy; this few will deny, or that their efficacy is independent of the personal character of the administrator. What then shall be thought of any attempts to weaken or exterminate that Community, or that Ministry, which is an appointed condition of the salvation of the elect? But everyone, who makes or encourages a schism, *must* weaken it. Thus it is plain, schism must be wrong in itself, even if Scripture did not in express terms forbid it, as it does.[9]

But further than this; it is plain this Visible Church is a *standing* body. Everyone who is baptized, is baptized *into* an existing community. Our Service expresses this when it speaks of baptized infants being *incorporated* into GOD'S holy Church.[10] Thus the Visible Church is not a voluntary association of the day, but a continuation of one which existed in the age before us, and then again in the age before that; and so back till we come to the age of the Apostles. In the same sense, in which Corporations[11] of the State's creating, are perpetual, is this which CHRIST has founded. This is a matter of fact hitherto; and it necessarily will be so always, for is not the notion absurd of an unbaptized person baptizing others? which is the only way in which the Christian community can have a new beginning.

Moreover Scripture directly *insists* upon the doctrine of the Visible Church as being of importance. E.g. St. Paul says; – "There is *one body,* and one Spirit, even as ye are called in one hope of your calling; one LORD, one faith, one baptism, one GOD and Father of all." (Eph. 4:5, 6). Thus, as far as the Apostle's words go, it is as false and unchristian, (I do not mean in degree of guilt, but in its intrinsic sinfulness,) to make more bodies than one, as to have many Lords, many Gods, many Creeds. Now, I wish to know, how it is possible for anyone to fall into this sin, if Dissenters are clear of it? What *is* the sin, if separation from the Existing Church is not it?

I have shown that there is a divinely instituted Visible Church, and that it has been one and the same by successive incorporation of members from the beginning. Now I observe further, that the word Church, as used in Scripture, ordinarily means this actually existing visible body. The possible exception to this rule, out of about 100 places in the New Testament, where the word occurs, are four passages in the Epistle to the Ephesians; two in the Colossians; and one in the Hebrews. (Eph. 1:22; 3:10, 21; 5:23–32; Col. 1:18, 24; Heb.

12:23) – And in some of these exceptions the sense is at most but doubtful. Further, our SAVIOUR uses the word twice, and in both times of the Visible Church. They are remarkable passages, and may here be introduced, in continuation of my argument.

Matt. 16:18. "Upon this rock I will build My Church, and the gates of hell shall not prevail against it." Now I am certain, any unprejudiced mind, who knew nothing of controversy, considering the Greek word ἐκκλησία means simply an *assembly*, would have no doubt at all that it means in this passage a visible body. What right have we to disturb the plain sense? why do we impose a meaning, arising from some system of our own? And this view is altogether confirmed by the other occasion of our LORD'S using it, where it can *only* denote the Visible Church. Matt. 18:17. "If he (thy brother) shall neglect to hear the Church, let him be unto thee as a heathen man and a publican."

Observe then what we gain by these two passages; – the grant of *power* to the Church; and the promise of *permanence*. Now look at the fact. The body then begun has continued; and has always claimed and exercised the power of a corporation or society. Consider merely the article in the Creed, "The Holy Catholic Church;" which embodies this notion. Do not Scripture and History illustrate each other?

I end this first draught of my argument with the text in 1 Tim 3:15, in which St. Paul calls the Church "the pillar and ground of the truth," – which can refer to nothing but a Visible Body; else martyrs may be invisible, and preachers, and teachers, and the whole order of the Ministry.

My paper is exhausted. If you allow me, I will send you soon a second Letter; meanwhile I sum up what I have been proving from Scripture thus; that ALMIGHTY GOD might have left Christianity as a sort of sacred literature, as contained in the Bible, which each person was to take and use by himself; just as we read the works of any human

philosopher or historian, from which we gain practical
instruction, but the knowledge of which does not bind us to
be Newtonians, or Aristotelians, &c., or to go out of our line
of life in consequence of it. This, I say, He might have done;
but in matter of fact, He has ordained otherwise. He has
actually set up a Society, which exists even this day all over
the world, and which (as a general rule) Christians are bound
to join; so that to believe in CHRIST is not a mere opinion or
a secret conviction, but a social or even a political principle,
and quite inconsistent with the supercilious mood of those
professed Christians of the day, who stand aloof, and
designate their indifference as philosophy.

LETTER II

I AM sometimes struck with the inconsistency of those, who
do not allow us to express the gratitude due to the Church,
while they do not hesitate to declare their obligation to individuals who have benefited them. To avow that they owe
their views of religion and their present hopes of salvation to
this or that distinguished preacher, appears to them as
harmless, as it may be in itself true and becoming; but if a
person ascribed his faith and knowledge to the Church, he is
thought to forget his peculiar and unspeakable debt to that
SAVIOUR who died for him. Surely, if our LORD makes man
His instrument of good to man, and if it is possible to be
grateful to man without forgetting the Source of all grace and
power, there is nothing wonderful in His having appointed a
company of men as the especial medium of His instruction
and spiritual gifts, and in consequence, of His having laid
upon us the duty of gratitude to it. Now this is all I wish to
maintain, what is most clearly (as I think) revealed in
Scripture, that the blessings of redemption come to us

through a Visible Church; so that, as we betake ourselves to a Dispensary for medicine, without attributing praise or intrinsic worth to the building or the immediate managers of its stores, in something of the like manner we are to come to that One Society, to which CHRIST has entrusted the office of stewardship in the distribution of gifts, of which He alone is the Author and real Dispenser.

In the letter I sent you the other day, I made some general remarks on this doctrine; now let me continue the subject.

First, the Sacraments which are the ordinary means of grace, are clearly in possession of the Church. Baptism is an incorporation into a body; and invests with spiritual blessings, because it is the introduction into a body so invested. In 1 Cor. 12. We are taught first, the SPIRIT'S indwelling in the Visible Church or body; I do not say, *in every member of it*, but generally *in* it; – next, we are told that the SPIRIT baptizes individuals *into* that body. Again, the LORD'S Supper carries evidence of its social nature even in its name; it is not a solitary individual act, it is a joint communion. Surely nothing is more alien to Christianity than the spirit of Independence; the peculiar Christian blessing, i.e. the presence of CHRIST, is upon *two or three* gathered together, not on mere individuals.[12]

But this is not all. The Sacraments are committed, not into the hands of the Church Visible assembled together, (though even this would be no unimportant doctrine practically,) but into certain definite persons, who are selected from their brethren for that trust.[13] I will not here determine who these are in each successive age, but will only point out how far this principle itself will carry us. The doctrine is implied in the original institution of the LORD'S Supper, where CHRIST says to His Apostles, "Do this." Further, take that remarkable passage in Matt. 24:45–51. Luke 12:42–46, "Who then is that faithful and wise Steward, whom his Lord shall make ruler over His household, to give them their portion of meat in due season? Blessed is that servant, whom his Lord, when he cometh, *shall* find so doing!" &c. Now I do not inquire *who* in every age are the stewards spoken of, (though in my own mind I cannot doubt the line of Bishops is that Ministry, and consider the concluding verses fearfully prophetic of the Papal misuse of the gift; – by the bye, at least it shows this, that bad men may nevertheless be the channels of grace to GOD'S "household",) I do not ask who are the stewards, but surely the words, *when He cometh*, imply that they are to continue till the end of the world. This reference is abundantly confirmed by our LORD'S parting words to the eleven; in which after giving them the baptismal commission, He adds, "Lo! I am with you *always*, even unto the end of the world." If then He was with the Apostles in a way in which He was not present with teachers who were strangers to their "fellowship," (Acts 2:42) which all will admit, so, in like manner, it cannot be a matter of indifference in *any* age, what teachers and fellowship a Christian selects; there must be those with whom CHRIST is present, who are His "Stewards" and whom it is our duty to obey.

As I have mentioned the question of faithfulness and unfaithfulness in Ministers, I may refer to the passage in 1 Cor. 4 where St. Paul, after speaking of himself and others as "*Stewards* of the mysteries of God," and noticing that "it is required of Stewards, that a man be found faithful," adds, "With me it is a very small thing that I should be judged of you or of man's judgment ... therefore *judge nothing before the time*."

To proceed, consider the following passage: "Obey them that have rule over you, and submit yourselves." Heb. 13:17. Again, I do not ask *who* these are; but whether this is not a duty, however it is to be fulfilled, which multitudes *in no sense* fulfil. Consider the number of people, professing and doubtless in a manner really actuated by Christian principle, who yet wander about from church to church, or from church to meeting, as sheep without a shepherd, or who choose a preacher merely because he pleases their taste, and whose first movement towards any clergyman they meet, is to examine and criticize his doctrine: what conceivable meaning do they put upon these words of the Apostle? Does any one *rule over* them? do they in any way *submit themselves*? Can these persons excuse their conduct, except on the deplorably profane plea, (which yet I believe is in their hearts at the bottom of their disobedience,) that it matters little to keep CHRIST'S "least commandments,"[14] so that we embrace the peculiar doctrines of His gospel?

Some time ago I drew up a sketch of the Scripture proof of the doctrine of the Visible Church; which with your leave I will here transcribe. You will observe, I am not arguing for this or that form of Polity, or for the Apostolical Succession, but simply the duties of order, union, ecclesiastical gifts, and ecclesiastical obedience; I limit myself to these points, as being persuaded that, when they are granted, the others will eventually follow.

I. That there was a Visible Church in the Apostles' day.

  1. General texts. Matt. 16:18; 18:17; 1 Tim. 3:15; Acts passim, &c.

  2. Organization of the Church.

    (1.) Diversity of ranks. 1 Cor. 12; Eph. 4:4–12; Rom. 12 4–8; 1 Pet. 4:10, 11.

    (2.) Governors. Matt. 28:19; Mark 16:15, 16; John 20:22, 23; Luke 22:19, 20; Gal. 2:9, &c.

    (3.) Gifts. Luke 12: 42,43; John 20:22,23; Matt. 18:18.

    (4.) Order. Acts 8:5, 6, 12, 14, 15, 17; 11:22, 23; 11:2, 4; 9:27; 15:2, 4, 6, 25; 16:4; 18:22; 21:17–19. conf. Gal. 1:1, 12; 1 Cor. 14:40; 1 Thess. 5:14.

    (5.) Ordination. Acts 6:6; 1 Tim. 4:14; 5:22; 2 Tim. 1:6; Tit. 1:5; Acts 13:3. conf. Gal. 1:1,12.

    (6.)   Ecclesiastical obedience. 1 Thess. 5:12, 13; Heb. 13:17; 1 Tim. 5:17.

    (7.)   Rules and discipline. Matt. 28:19; Matt. 18:17; 1 Cor. .5:4–7; Gal. 5:12, &c.
           1 Cor. 16:1, 2; 1 Cor. 11:2, 16 &c.

    (8.)   Unity. Rom. 16:17; 1 Cor. 1:10; 3:3; 14:26; Col. 2:5; 1 Thess. 5:14; 2 Thess. 3:6.

II. That the Visible Church, thus instituted by the Apostles, was intended to continue.

1. Why should it not? The *onus probandi*[15] lies with those who deny this position. If the doctrines and precepts already cited are obsolete at this day, why should not the following texts? e.g. 1 Pet. 2:13, or e.g. Matt. 7:14; John 3:3.

2. Is it likely so elaborate a system should be framed, yet with no purpose of its continuing?

3. The objects to be obtained by it are as necessary now as then. (1.) Preservation of the faith. (2.) Purity of doctrine. (3.) Edification of Christians. (4.) Unity of operation. Vid. Epists. to Tim. and Tit. passim.

4. If system were necessary in a time of miracles, much more is it now.

5. 2 Tim. 2:2; Matt. 28:20, &c.

Take these remarks, as they are meant, as mere suggestions for your private consideration.

TRACT 15

ON THE APOSTOLICAL SUCCESSION
IN THE ENGLISH CHURCH

WHEN Churchmen in England maintain the Apostolical Commission of their Ministers,[1] they are sometimes met with the objection, that they cannot prove it without tracing their orders back to the Church of Rome; a position, indeed, which in a certain sense is true. And hence it is argued, that they are reduced to the dilemma, either of acknowledging they had no right to separate from the Pope, or, on the other hand, of giving up the Ministerial Succession altogether, and resting the claims of their pastors on some other ground; in other words, that they are *inconsistent* in reprobating Popery, while they draw the line between their Ministers and those of Dissenting Communions.

It is intended in the pages that follow, to reply to this supposed difficulty; but first, a few words shall be said, by way of preface, on the doctrine itself, which we Churchmen advocate.

The Christian Church is a body consisting of Clergy and Laity; that is generally agreed upon, and may here be assumed. Now what we say is, that these two classes are distinguished from each other, and united to each other, by the commandment of GOD Himself; that the Clergy have a commission from GOD ALMIGHTY through regular succession from the Apostles, to preach the Gospel, administer the Sacraments, and guide the Church; and, again, that in conse-

quence the people are bound to hear them with attention,
receive the Sacraments from their hands, and pay them all
dutiful obedience. I shall not prove this at length, for it has
been done by others, and indeed the common sense and
understanding of men, if left to themselves, would be quite
sufficient in this case. I do but lay before the reader the
following considerations.

1. We hold, with the Church in all ages, that, when our
LORD, after His Resurrection, breathed on His Apostles, and
said, "Receive ye the HOLY GHOST, – as My FATHER hath
sent Me, so send I you;"[2] He gave them the power of
sending *others* with a divine commission, who in like manner
should have the power of sending others, and so on even
unto the end; and that our LORD promised His continual
assistance to these successors of the Apostles in this and all
other respects, when He said, "Lo I am with you" (that is,
with you, and those who shall represent and succeed you,)
"alway, even unto the end of the world."[3]

And, if it is plain that the Apostles left successors after
them, it is equally plain that the Bishops are these Successors.
For it is only the Bishops who have ever been called by the
title of Successors; and there has been actually a perpetual
succession of these Bishops in the Church, who alone were
always esteemed to have the power of sending other
Ministers to preach and administer the Sacraments. So that
the proof of the doctrine seems to lie in a very small space.

2. But, perhaps, it may be as well to look at it in another
point of view. I suppose no man of common sense thinks
himself entitled to set about teaching religion, administering
Baptism, and the LORD'S Supper, and taking care of the souls
of other people, unless he has *in some way* been called to
undertake the office. Now, as religion is a business between
every man's own conscience and GOD ALMIGHTY, no one
can have any right to interfere in the religious concerns of
another with the authority of a teacher, unless he is able to

show, that it is GOD that has in some way called and sent him to do so. It is true, that men may as *friends* encourage and instruct each other with consent of both parties; but this is something very different from the office of a Minister of religion, who is entitled and called to "exhort, rebuke," and "rule, with all authority"[4] as well as love and humility.

You may observe that our LORD Himself did not teach the Gospel, without proving most plainly that His FATHER had sent Him. He and His Apostles proved their divine commission by miracles. As miracles, however, have long ago come to an end,[5] there must be some *other* way for a man to prove his right to be a Minister of religion. And what other way can there possibly be, except a regular call and ordination by those who have succeeded to the Apostles?

3. Further, you will observe, that all sects think it necessary that their Ministers should be ordained by other Ministers. Now, if this be the case, then the validity or ordination, even with *them*, rests on a *succession*; and is it not plain that they ought to trace that succession to the Apostles? Else, why are they ordained at all? And, how, if *their* Ministers have a commission, who derive it from private men, much more do the Ministers of our Church, who actually do derive it from the Apostles. Surely those who dissent from the Church have *invented* an ordinance, as they themselves much allow; whereas Churchmen, wither rightly or wrongly, still maintain *their* succession not to be an invention, but to be GOD'S ordinance. If Dissenters say, that *order* requires there should be some such *succession*, this is true, indeed, but still it is only a testimony to the mercy of CHRIST, in having, as Churchmen maintain, *given us* such a succession. And this is *all* it shows: it does nothing for *them;* for their succession, not professing to come from GOD, has no power to restrain any fanatic from setting up to preach of his own will, and a people with itching ears choosing for themselves a teacher.[6] It does but witness to a need, without supplying it.

4. I have now given some slight suggestions by way of evidence for the doctrine of the Apostolical Succession, from Scripture, the nature of the case, and the conduct of Dissenters. Let me add a word on the usage of the Primitive Church. We know that the succession of Bishops, and ordination from them, was the invariable doctrine and rule of the early Christians. Is it not utterly inconceivable, that this rule should have prevailed from the first age, everywhere, and without exception, had it not been given them by the Apostles?

But here we are met by the objection, on which I propose to make a few remarks, that, though it is true there was a continual Succession of pastors and teachers in the early Church who had a divine commission, yet that no Protestants can have it; that we gave it up, when our communion ceased with Rome, in which Church it still remains; or, at least, that no Protestant can plead it without condemning the Reformation itself, for that our own predecessors then revolted and separated from those spiritual pastors, who, according to our principles, then had the commission of JESUS CHRIST.

Our reply to this is a flat denial of the alleged facts on which it rests. The English Church did *not* revolt from those who in that day had authority from the Apostles. On the contrary, it is certain that the Bishops and Clergy in England and Ireland remained the same as before the separation, and that it was these, with the aid of the civil power, who delivered the Church of those kingdoms from the yoke of Papal tyranny and usurpation, while at the same time they gradually removed from the minds of the people various superstitious opinions and practices which had grown up during the middle ages, and which, though never formally received by the judgment of the whole Church, were yet very prevalent. I do not say the case might never arise, when it might become the duty of private individuals to take upon themselves the office of protesting against and abjuring the heresies of a corrupt Church. But such an extreme case it is unpleasant and unhealthy to contemplate. All I say here is, that this was not the state of things at the time of the Reformation. The Church then by its proper rulers and officers reformed itself. There was no new Church founded among us, but the rights and the true doctrines of the Ancient existing Church were asserted and established.

In proof of this we need only look to the history of the times. In the year 1534, the Bishops and Clergy of England assembled in their respective convocations of Canterbury and York,[7] and signed a declaration that the Pope or Bishop of Rome had no more jurisdiction in this country by the word of GOD, than any other foreign Bishop; and they also agreed to those acts of the civil government, which put an end to it among us.[1] [8]

The people of England, then, in casting off the Pope, but obeyed and concurred in the acts of their own spiritual Superiors, and committed no schism. Queen Mary, it is true, drove out after many years the orthodox Bishops, and reduced our Church again under the Bishop of Rome, but this submission was only exacted by force, and in itself null and void; and, moreover, in matter of fact it lasted but a little while, for on the succession of Queen Elizabeth, the true Successors of the Apostles in the English Church were reinstated in their ancient rights. So, I repeat, there was no revolt, in any part of these transactions, against those who had a commission from God; for it was the Bishops and Clergy themselves, who maintained the just rights of their Church.

But, it seems, the Pope has ever said, that our Bishops were bound by the laws of GOD and the Church to obey

---

[1] Vide Collier, Eccl. Hist. v. ii, p. 94.

him; that they were subject to him; and that they had not right to separate from him, and were guilty of doing so, and that accordingly they have involved the people of England in their guilt; and, at all events, that *they* cannot complain of their flock disobeying and deserting them, when they have revolted from the Pope. Let us consider this point.

Now that there is not a word in *Scripture* about our duty to obey the Pope, is quite clear. The Papists indeed say, that he is the Successor of St. Peter; and that therefore he is Head of all Bishops, because St. Peter bore rule over the other Apostles. But though the Bishops of Rome were often called the Successors of St. Peter in the early Church, yet every other Bishop had the *same* title. And though it be true, that St. Peter was the *foremost* of the apostles, that does not prove he had any *dominion* over them. The eldest brother in a family has certain privileges and a precedence, but he has no power, over the younger branches of it. And so Rome has ever had what is called the *primacy* of the Christian Churches; but it has not therefore any right to interfere in their internal administration; not more of a right, than an elder brother has to meddle with his younger brother's household.

And this is plainly the state of matters between us and Rome, *in the judgment of the Ancient Church* also, to which the Papists are fond of appealing, and by which we are quite ready to stand or fall. In early times, as is well known, all Christians thought substantially alike, and formed one great body all over the world, called the Church Catholic, or Universal. This great body, consisting of a vast number of separate Churches, with each of them its own Bishop at its head, was divided into a number of portions called Patriarchates; these again into others called Provinces, and these were made up of the separate Dioceses or Bishopricks. We have among ourselves an instance of this last division in the Provinces of Canterbury and York, which constitute the English Church each of them consisting of a number of distinct Bishopricks or Churches. The head of a Province was called Archbishop, as in the case of Canterbury and York; the Bishops of those two sees being, we know, not only Bishops with Dioceses of their own, but having, over and above this, the place of precedence among the Bishops in the same Province. In like manner, the Bishop at the head of a Patriarchate was called the Patriarch, and had the place of honour and certain privileges over all other Bishops within his own Patriarchate. Now, in the early Christian Church, there were four or five Patriarchates; e.g. one in the East, the Head of which was the Bishop of Antioch; one in Egypt, the Head of which was the Bishop of Alexandria; and again, one in the West, the Head of which was the Bishop of Rome. These Patriarchates, I say, were the primates or Head Bishops of their respective Patriarchates; and they had an order of precedence among themselves, Rome being the first of them all. Thus the Bishop of Rome, being the first of the Patriarchs in dignity, might be called the honorary Primate of all Christendom.

However, as time went on, the Bishop of Rome, not satisfied with the honours which were readily conceded to him, attempted to gain *power* over the whole Church. He seems to have been allowed the privilege of *arbitrating* in case of appeal from other Patriarchates.[9] If, e.g. Alexandria and Antioch had a dispute, he was a proper referee; or if the Bishops in those Churches were at any time unjustly deprived of their sees, he was a fit person to interfere and defend them. But, I say, he became ambitious, and attempted to *lord it* over GOD'S heritage. He interfered in the internal management of other Patriarchates; he appointed Bishops to sees, and Clergy to parishes which were contained within them, and imposed on them various religious and ecclesiastical usages illegally. And in doing so, surely he became a remarkable contrast to the Holy Apostle, who, though inspired, and an universal Bishop, yet suffered not himself to control the proceedings even of the Churches he founded; saying to the Corinthians, "not for that we have dominion over your faith, but are helpers of your joy; for by faith ye stand." 2 Cor. 1:24. This impressive declaration, which seems to be intended almost as a prophetic warning against the times of which we speak, was neglected by the Pope, who among other tyrannical proceedings, took upon him the control of the Churches in Britain, and forbade us to reform our doctrine and usages, which he had no right at all to do. He had no pretence for so doing, because we were altogether independent of him; the English and Irish Churches, though in the West, being exterior to his Patriarchate. Here, again, however some explanation is necessary.

You must know, then, that from the first there were portions of the Christian world, which were not included in any Patriachate, but were governed by themselves. Such were the Churches of Cyprus, and such were the British Churches. This need not here be proved; even Papists have before now confessed it. Now, it so happened, in the beginning of the 5th century, the Patriarch of Antioch, who was in the neighbourhood of Cyprus, attempted against the Cyprian Churches what the Pope has since attempted against us; viz. took measures to reduce them under his dominion. And, as a sign of his authority over them, he claimed to consecrate their Bishops. Upon which the Great Council of the whole Christian world assembled at Ephesus, A.D. 341, made the following decree, which you will find is a defence of England and Ireland against the Papacy, as well as of Cyprus against Antioch.

"An innovation upon the Rule of the church and the Canons of the Holy Fathers, such as to affect the general liberties of Christendom, has been reported to us by our venerable brother Rheginus, and his fellow Bishops of Cyprus, Zeno, and Evagrius. Wherefore, since public disorders call for extraordinary remedies, as being more perilous, and whereas it is against ancient usage, that the Bishop of Antioch should ordain in Cyprus, as has been proved to us in this Council both in words and in writing, by most orthodox men, We therefore decree, that the Prelates of the Cyprian Churches shall be suffered without let or hindrance to consecrate Bishops by themselves; and moreover, that the *same rule shall be observed also in other dioceses and provinces everywhere, so that no Bishop shall interfere in another province, which has not from the very first been under himself and his predecessors;* and further, that, if any one has so encroached and tyrannized, he must relinquish his claim, that the Canons of the Fathers be not infringed, nor the Priesthood be made an occasion and pretence for the pride of worldly power, nor the least portion of that freedom unawares be lost to us, which our LORD JESUS CHRIST, who bought the world's freedom, vouchsafed to us, when He shed His own blood. Wherefore it has seemed good to this Holy Ecumenical Council, that *the rights of every province should be preserved pure and inviolate, which have always belonged to it, according to the usage which has ever obtained,* each Metropolitan having full liberty to take a copy of the acts for his own security. And, should any rule be adduced repugnant to this decree, it is hereby repealed."[10]

Here we have a remarkable parallel to the dispute between Rome and us; and we see what was the decision of the General Church upon it. It will be observed, the decree is past *for all provinces in all future times,* as well as for the immediate exigency. Now this is a plain refutation of the Romanists on their own principles. *They* profess to hold the Canons of the Primitive Church: the very line they take, is to declare the Church to be one and the same in all ages. Here then they witness against themselves. The Pope *has* encroached on the rights of other Churches, and violated the Canon above cited. Herein is the difference between his relation to us, and that of any civil Ruler, whose power was in its origin illegally acquired. Doubtless we are bound to obey the Monarch under whom we are born, even though his ancestor were an usurper. Time legitimizes a conquest. But this is not the case in spiritual matters. The Church goes by *fixed laws*; and this usurpation has all along been counter to one of her acknowledged standing ordinances, founded on reasons of universal application.

After the Canon above cited, it is almost superfluous to refer to the celebrated rule of the First Nicene Council, A.D. 325, which, in defending the rights of the Patriarchates, expresses the same principle in all its simple force and majesty.

"*Let the ancient usages prevail,* which are received in Egypt, Libya, and Pentapolis, relative to the authority of the Bishop of Alexandria; as they are observed in the case of the Bishop of Rome. And so in Antioch too, and other provinces, let the prerogatives of the Churches be preserved."[11]

On this head of the subject, I will but notice, that, as the Council of Ephesus controlled the ambition of Antioch, so in like manner did St. Austin rebuke Rome itself for an encroachment of another kind on the liberties of the African Church.

Bingham says,

"When Pope Zosimus and Celestine took upon them to receive Appellants from the African Churches, and absolve those whom they had condemned, St. Austin and all the African Churches sharply remonstrated against this, as an irregular practice, *violating the laws of unity,* and the settled rules of ecclesiastical commerce; which required, that no delinquent excommunicated in one Church should be absolved in another, without giving satisfaction to his own church that censured him. And therefore, to put a stop to this practice and check the exorbitant power which Roman Bishops assumed to themselves, they first made a Law in the Council of Milevis,[12] That no African Clerk should appeal to any Church beyond sea, under pain of being excluded from communion in all the African Churches. And then, afterwards, meeting in a general Synod, they dispatched letters to the Bishop of Rome, to remind him how contrary this practice was to the Canons of Nice, which ordered, That all controversies should be ended in the places where they arose, before a Council and the Metropolitan."[2]

Thus I have shown, that our Bishops, at the time of the Reformation, did but vindicate their ancient rights; were but acting as grateful, and therefore jealous champions of the honour of the old Fathers, and the sanctity of their institutions. Our duty surely in such matters lies in neither encroaching nor conceding to encroachment; in taking our rights as we find them, and using them; or rather in regarding them altogether as trusts, the responsibility of which we cannot avoid. As the same Apostle says, "Let every man abide in the same calling, wherein he is called."[13] And, if England and Ireland had a plea for asserting their freedom under any circumstances, much more so, when the corruptions imposed on them by Rome even made it a duty to do so.

I shall answer briefly one or two objections, and so bring these remarks to an end.

1. First, it may be said, that Rome has withdrawn our orders, and excommunicated us; therefore we cannot plead any longer our Apostolical descent. Now I will not altogether deny, that a Ministerial Body might become so plainly apostate, as to lose its privilege of ordination. But, however this may be, it is a little too hard to *assume*, as such an objection does, the very point in dispute. *When* we are proved to be heretical in doctrine, then will be the time to begin to consider, whether our heresy is of so grievous a character as to invalidate our orders; but, *till then*, we may fairly and fearlessly maintain, that our Bishops are still invested with the power of ordination.

2. But it may be said on the other hand that if we do

---

[2] Bingham, *Antiquities of the Christian Church,* vol. 1 §14.

not admit ourselves to be heretic, we necessarily must accuse the Romanists of being such; and that therefore, on our own ground, we have really no valid orders, as having received them from an heretical Church. True, Rome may be so considered now; but she was not heretical in the primitive ages. If she has apostatized, it was at the time of the Council of Trent. Then, if at any time, surely not before, did the Roman Communion bind itself in covenant to the cause of Antichrist.[3] But before that time, grievous as might be the corruptions in the Church, no individual Bishop, Priest, or Deacon, was bound by oath to maintenance of them.[14] Extensively as they were spread, no Clergyman was shackled with obligations which prevented his resisting them; he could but suffer persecution for so doing. He did not commit himself in one breath to two vows, to serve faithfully in the Ministry, and yet to receive the superstitions and profanities which man had, in course of ages, introduced into the most gracious and holiest of God's gifts. On the contrary, we may say with the learned Dr. Field, "that none of these points of false doctrine and error which Romanists now maintain, and we condemn, were the doctrines of the Church before the Reformation constantly delivered or generally received by all them that were of it, but doubtfully broached, and devised without all certain resolution, or factiously defended by some certain only, who as a dangerous faction adulterated the sincerity of the Christian

---

[3] The following is from the Life of Bernard Gilpin, vid. Wordsworth's Ecclesiastical Biography, vol. 4, p. 94. "Mr. Gilpin would often say that the Churches of the Protestants were not able to give any firme and solid reason of their separation besides this, to wit, that the Pope is Antichrist ... The Church of Rome kept the rule of faith intire, until that rule was changed and altered *by the Council of Trent, and from that time it seemed to him a matter of necessitie to come out of the Church of Rome,* that so that Church which is true and called out from thence might follow the word of God ... But he did not these things violently, but by degrees."

verity, and brought the Church into miserable bondage."[4] Accordingly, acknowledging and deploring all the errors of the middle ages, yet we need not fear to maintain, that after all they were but the errors of individuals, though of large numbers of Christians; and we may safely maintain, that they no more interfere with the validity of the ordination received by our Bishops from those who lived before the Reformation, than errors of faith and conduct in a priest interfere with the grace of the Sacraments at his hands.

3. It may be said, that we throw the blame on Luther, and others of the foreign Reformers, who *did* act without the authority of their Bishops. But we reply, that it has been always agreeable to the principles of the Church, that if a bishop taught and upheld what was contrary to the orthodox faith, the Clergy and people were not bound to submit, but were obliged to maintain the true religion; and if excommunicated by such Bishops, they were never accounted to be cut off from the Church. Luther and his associates upheld in the main the true doctrine; and though it is not necessary to defend *every* acts of fallible men like them, yet we are fully justified in maintaining, that the conduct of those who defended the truth against the Romish party, even in opposition to their spiritual rulers, was worthy of great praise. At the same time it is impossible not to lament, that they did not take the first opportunity to place themselves under orthodox Bishops of the Apostolical Succession.[15] Nothing, as far as we can judge, was more likely to have preserved them from that great decline of religion, which has taken place on the Continent.[16]

---

[4] See Field on the Church, Appendix to Book iii, where he proves all this. See also Birkbeck's Protestant's Evidence.

TRACT 19

ON ARGUING CONCERNING THE APOSTOLICAL SUCCESSION

MEN are sometimes disappointed with the proofs offered in behalf of some important doctrines of our religion; such especially as the necessity of Episcopal Ordination, in order to constitute a Minister of CHRIST. They consider these proofs to be not so strong as they expected, or as they think desirable. Now such persons should be asked, whether these arguments they speak of are in their estimation weak as a guide to their own practice, or weak in controversy with hardheaded and subtle disputants. Surely, as Bishop Butler has convincingly shown, the faintest probabilities are strong enough to determine our *conduct* in a matter of duty.[1] If there be but a reasonable likelihood of our pleasing CHRIST more by keeping than by not keeping to the fellowship of Apostolic Ministry, this of course ought to be enough to lead those, who think themselves moved to undertake the Sacred Office, to seek for a licence to do so from it.

It is necessary to keep this truth distinctly in view, because of the great temptation, that exists among us, to put it out of sight. I do not mean the temptation, which results from pride, – hardness of heart, – a profane disregard of the details and lesser commandments of the Divine Law, – and other such like bad principles of our nature, which are in the way of our honestly confessing it. Besides these, there is a still more subtle temptation to slight it, which will bear insisting on here, arising from an over-desire to convince others, or, in other words, a desire to out-argue others, a fear of seeming inconclusive and confused in our notions and arguments. Nothing, certainly, is more natural, when we hold a truth strongly, than to wish to persuade others to embrace it also. Nay, without reference to persuasion, nothing is more natural than to be dissatisfied in all cases with our own convictions of a principle or opinion, nay suspicious of it, till we are able to set it down clearly in words. We know, that, in all matters of thought, to write down our meaning is one important means of clearing our minds. Till we do so, we often do not know what we really hold and what we do not hold. And a cautious and accurate reasoner, when he has succeeded in bringing the truth of any subject home to his mind, next begins to look round about the view he has adopted, to consider what others will say to it, and to try to make it unexceptionable. At least we are led thus to fortify our opinion, when it is actually attacked; and if we find we cannot recommend it to the judgment of the assailant, at any rate we endeavour to make him feel that it is to be respected. It is painful to be thought a weak reasoner, even though we are sure in our minds that we are not such.

Now, observe how these feelings will affect us, as regards such arguments as were alluded to above; *viz.* such as are open to exception, though they are sufficiently strong to determine our conduct. We state them, and he sifts them. He observes, that our conclusions do not necessarily follow from our premises. E.g. to take the argument for the Apostolical Succession derived from the ordination of St. Paul and St. Barnabas (Acts 13:2, 3), he will argue, that their ordination *might* have been an accidental rite, intended merely to commission them for their Missionary journey, which followed it, in Asia Minor; again, that St. Paul's direction to Timothy (1 Tim 5:22), to "lay hands suddenly on no man," may refer to confirmation, not ordination.

We should reply (and most reasonably too), that, *considering the undeniable fact* that ordination has ever been thought necessary in the Church for the Ministerial Commission, our interpretation is the most probable one, and therefore the safest to act upon; on which our friend will think awhile, then shake his head, and say, that "at all events this is an *unsatisfactory* mode of reasoning, that it does not convince *him*, that he is desirous of clearer light," &c.

Now what is the consequence of such a discussion as this on ourselves? not to make us *give up* the doctrine, but to make us afraid of *urging* it. We grow lukewarm about it; and, with an appearance of judgment and caution (as the world will call it), confess that "to rest the claims of our Clergy on an Apostolical Descent is an unsafe and inexpedient line of argument; that it will not convince men, the evidence not being sufficient; that it is not a practical way of acting to insist upon it." – whereas the utmost that need be admitted, is, that it is out of place to make it the subject of a speculative dispute, and to argue about it on that abstract logical platform which virtually excludes a reference to conduct and duty. And indeed, it would be no unwise caution to bear about us, wherever we go, that our first business, as Christians, is to address men as responsible servants of CHRIST, not as antagonists; and that it is but a secondary duty (though a duty) to "refute the gainsayers."

And, as on the one hand it continually happens, that those who are most skilled in debate are deficient in sound practical piety, so on the other it may be profitable to us to reflect, that doctrines, which we believe to be most true, and which are received as such by the most profound and enlarged intellects, and which rest upon the most irrefragable proofs, yet may be above *our* disputative powers, and can be treated by us only with reference to our conduct. And in this way, as in others, is fulfilled the saying of the Apostle, that "the preaching of the Cross is to them that perish foolishness; but unto us, who are saved, it is the power of GOD ... Where is the wise? where is the scribe? where is the disputer of this world? ... The foolishness of GOD is wiser than men; and the weakness of GOD is stronger than men."[2]

ON RELUCTANCE TO CONFESS
THE APOSTOLICAL SUCCESSION

If a Clergyman is quite convinced that the Apostolical Succession is lost, then of course he is at liberty to turn his mind from the subject. But if he is not quite sure of this, it surely is his duty seriously to examine the question, and to make up his mind carefully and deliberately. For if there be a chance of its being preserved to us, there is a chance of his having had a momentous talent committed to him, which he is burying in the earth.[3]

It cannot be supposed that any serious man would treat the subject scoffingly. If anyone is tempted to do so, let him remember the fearful words of the Apostle. "Esau, *a profane person*, who for one morsel of meat, sold his birthright."[4]

If any are afraid, that to insist on their commission will bring upon them ridicule, and diminish their usefulness, let them ask themselves whether it be not cowardice to refuse to leave the event to GOD. It was the reproach of the men of Ephraim, that, though they were "harnessed and carried bows," they "turned themselves back in the day of battle."[5]

And if any there be, to take upon them to contrast one doctrine of the Gospel with another, and preach only those which they consider the more essential, let them consider our SAVIOUR'S words, "These things ought ye to have done, and not to leave the other undone."[6]

TRACT 20

THE VISIBLE CHURCH

LETTERS TO A FRIEND
No. III

You have some misgivings, it seems, lest the doctrine I have been advocating "should lead to Popery." I will not, by way of answer, say that the question is not, whether it will *lead to Popery*, but whether it is *in the Bible*; because it would bring the Bible and Popery into one sentence, and seem to imply the possibility of a "communion" between "light and darkness."[1] No; it is the very enmity I feel against the Papistical corruptions of the Gospel, which leads me to press upon you a doctrine of Scripture, which we are sinfully surrendering, and the Church of Rome has faithfully retained.

How comes it that a system, so unscriptural as the Popish, makes converts? because it has in it an element of truth and comfort amid its falsehoods. And the true way of opposing it, is, not to give up to them that element, which GOD's providence has preserved to us also, thus basely surrendering "the inheritance of our Fathers," but to claim it as our own, and to make use of it for the purposes for which GOD has given it to us. I will explain what I mean.

Before CHRIST came, Divine Truth was, as it were, a pilgrim in the world. The Jews excepted, men who had portions of the SPIRIT of GOD, knew not their privilege. The whole force and current of the external world was against them, acting powerfully on their imagination, and tempting them to set sight against faith, to trust the many witnesses who prophesied falsehood (as if) in the name of the LORD, rather than the still small voice which spoke within them. Who can undervalue the power of this fascination, who has had experience of the world ever so little? Who can go at this day into mixed society, who can engage in politics or other active business, and not find himself gradually drifting off from the true Rock on which his faith is built, till he begins in despair to fancy, that solitude is the only safe place for the Christian, or, (with a baser judgment) that strict obedience will not be required at the last day of those who have been engaged in active life? If such is now the power of the world's enchantments, surely much greater was it before our SAVIOUR came.

Now what did He do for us, in order to meet this evil? His merciful Providence chose means which might act as a counter influence on the imagination. The visible power of the world enthralled men to a lie; He set up a Visible Church, to witness the other way, to witness for Him, to be a matter of fact, as undeniable as the shining of the sun, that there *was* such a principle as conscience in the world,[2] as faith, as fear of GOD; that there *were* men who considered themselves bound to live as his servants. The common answer which we hear made every day to persons who engage in any novel undertaking, is, "You will get no one to join you; nothing can come of it; you are singular in your opinion; you do not take practical views, but are smit with a fancy, with a dream of former times," &c. How cheering it is to a person so circumstanced, to be able to point to others elsewhere, who actually hold the same opinions as himself, and exert themselves for the same objects! Why, because it is an appeal to a *fact*, which no one can deny; it is an evidence that the view which influences him is something external to his own mind, and not a dream. What two persons see, cannot be an ideal apparition. Men are governed by such facts much more than by argumentative proof. These act upon the imagination. Let a person be told ten times over that an opinion is true, the *fact* of its being said becomes an argument for the truth of it; *i.e.* it is so with most men. We see from time to time the operation of this principle of our nature in political matters. Our American colonies revolt; France feels the sympathy of the event, and is revolutionized. Again, in the same colonies, the Episcopal Church flourishes;[3] we Churchmen at home hail it as an omen of the Church's permanence among ourselves. On the other hand, what can be more dispiriting than to find a cause, which we advocate, sinking in some other country or neighbourhood, though there be no reason for concluding, that, *because* it has failed elsewhere, therefore it will among ourselves. In order then to supply this need of our minds, to satisfy the imagination, and so to help our faith, for this among other reasons CHRIST set up a visible Society, His Church, to be as a light upon a hill, to all the ends of the earth, while time endures. It is a witness of the unseen world; a pledge of it; and a prefiguration of what hereafter will take place.[4] It prefigures the ultimate separation of good and bad, holds up the great laws of GOD's Moral Governance, and preaches the blessed truths of the Gospel. It pledges to us the promises of the next world, for it is something (so to say) in hand; CHRIST has done one work as the earnest of another. And it witnesses the truth to the whole world; awing sinners, while it enspirits the fainting believer, And in all these ways it helps forward the world to come; and further, as the keeper of the Sacraments, it is an essential means of the realizing it at present in our fallen race. Nor is it much to the purpose, as regards our duty towards it, what are the feelings and spiritual state of the individuals who are its officers. True it is, were the Church to teach heretical doctrine, it might become incumbent on us (a miserable obligation!) to separate from it. But, while it teaches substantially the Truth, we ought to look upon it as one whole, one ordinance of GOD, not as composed of individuals, but as a house of GOD's building; – as an instrument in His hand, to be used and reverenced for the sake of its Maker.

Now the Papists have retained it; and so they have the advantage of possessing an instrument, which is, in the first place suited to the needs of human nature; and next, is a special gift of CHRIST, and so has a blessing with it. Accordingly we see that in its measure success follows their zealous use of it. They act with great force upon the imaginations of men. The vaunted antiquity, the universality, the unanimity of their Church puts them above the varying fashions of the world, and the religious novelties of the day.[5] And truly when one surveys the grandeur of their system, a sigh arises in the thoughtful mind, to think that we should be separate from them; *Cum talis esses, utinam noster esses*![6] – But, alas, AN UNION IS IMPOSSIBLE. Their communion is infected with heterodoxy; we are bound to flee it, as a pestilence. They have established a lie in the place of GOD's truth; and, by their claim of immutability in doctrine, cannot undo the sin they have committed. They cannot repent. Popery must be destroyed; it cannot be reformed.

Now then what is the Christian to do? Is he forced back upon that cheerless atheism (for so it practically must be considered which prevailed in the world before CHRIST's coming, poorly alleviated, as it was, by the received polytheisms of the heathen? Can we conceive a greater calamity to have occurred at the time of our Reformation, one which the Enemy of man would have been more set on effecting, than to have entangled the whole of the Church Catholic in the guilt of heterodoxy, and so have forced everyone who worshipped in spirit and in truth, to flee out of doors into the bleak world, in order to save his soul? I do not think that Satan could have desired any event more eagerly, than such

an alternative; viz. to have forced Christians, either to remain
in communion with error, or to join themselves in some
such spontaneous union among themselves, as is dissolved as
easily as it is formed. Blessed be GOD! His malice has been
thwarted. I do believe it to be one most conspicuous mark of
GOD'S adorable Providence over us, as great as if we saw a
miracle, that Christians in England escaped in the evil day
from either extreme, neither corrupted doctrinally, or secularized ecclesiastically. Thus in every quarter of the world,
from North America to New South Wales, a Zoar has been
provide for those who would escape Sodom, yet dread to be
without shelter.[7] I hail it as an omen amid our present perils,
that our Church will not be destroyed. He hath been mindful
of us; He will bless us. He has wonderfully preserved our
Church as a true branch of the Church Universal, yet withal
preserved it free from doctrinal error. It is Catholic and
Apostolic, yet not Papistical.

With this reflection before us, does it not seem to be utter
ingratitude to an astonishing Providence of GOD'S mercy, to
be neglectful, as many Churchmen now are, of the gift; to
attempt unions with those who have separated from the
Church, to break down the partition walls, and to argue as if
religion were altogether and only a matter of each man's
private concern, and that the State and Nation were not
bound to prefer the Apostolical Church to all self-originated
forms of Christianity? But this is a point beside my purpose.
Take the matter merely in the light of human expedience.
Shall we be so far less wise in our generation than the
children of this world,[8] as to relinquish the support which
the Truth receives from the influence of a Visible Church
upon the imagination, from the energy of operation which a
well disciplined Body ensures? Shall we not foil the Papists,
not with their own weapons but with weapons which are
ours as well as theirs? or, on the other hand, shall we with a
melancholy infatuation give them up to them? Depend upon

it, to insist on the doctrine of the Visible Church is not to favour the Papists, it is to do them the most serious injury. It is to deprive them of their only strength. But if we neglect to do so, what will be the consequence? Break down the Divine Authority of our Apostolical Church, and you are plainly preparing the way for Popery in our land. Human nature cannot remain without visible guides; it chooses them for itself, if it is not provided for them. If the Aristocracy and the Church fall, Popery steps in. Political events are beyond our power, and perhaps out of our sphere; but ecclesiastical matters are in the hands of all Churchmen.

OXFORD,
Dec. 24, 1833.

MORTIFICATION OF THE FLESH A SCRIPTURAL DUTY

IF we take the example of the Holy men of Scripture as our guide, certainly bodily privation and chastisement are a very essential duty of all who wish to serve GOD, and prepare themselves for His presence.

1. First we have the example of Moses. His recorded Fasts were miraculous; still they were Fasts, and the ordinance was recommended to the notice of all believers afterwards, by the honour put upon it. "I abode in the mount forty days and forty nights; I neither did eat bread nor drink water." Again; "I fell down before the LORD, as at the first, forty days and forty nights; I did neither eat bread nor drink water, because of all your sins." (Deut. 9:9, 18). Fasting is in the former instance subservient to divine contemplation, in the latter to humiliation and intercession for sinners.

Elijah. "He said unto him, What manner of man was he which came up to meet you, and told you these words? And they answered him, He was an hairy man, and girt with a girdle of leather about his loins. And he said, It is Elijah the Tishbite." (2 Kings 1:7, 8). It is indeed needless to show the ascetic character of him who was in fact the chief and type of those who "wandered about in sheepskins and goatskins," "in deserts and in mountains, and in dens and caves of the earth."[1] He too fasted by the power of GOD for forty days and nights; "He arose and did eat and drink, and went in the strength of that meat forty days and forty nights, unto Horeb the mount of GOD." (1 Kings 19:8).

Daniel. "I set my face unto the LORD GOD, to seek by prayer and supplications, with fasting, and sackcloth, and ashes; and I prayed unto the LORD my GOD, and made my confession." (Dan 9:3, 4). It must be observed, that Daniel was not bound by any vow, as Samson and Samuel. Moreover it would appear the gift of prophecy was given him in reward for his self-chastisements, as the following passage shows. "In those days I Daniel was mourning three full weeks; I ate no pleasant bread, neither came flesh nor wine in my mouth; neither did I anoint myself at all, till three whole weeks were fulfilled ... And he said unto me, O Daniel, a man greatly beloved, understand the words that I speak unto thee, and stand upright; for unto thee am I now sent ... Fear not, Daniel; for *from the first day* that thou didst set thine heart to understand, and *to chasten thyself* before thy GOD, thy words were heard, and I am come for thy words." (Dan. 10:2, 3, 11, 12. Vide also Luke 2:37; Acts 10:30).

2. Now here it will be objected, perhaps, that these instances are taken from the Old Testament, and belong to the Law of Moses, which is not binding on Christians.

I answer :

(1.) That in the above passages Fasting is connected with moral acts, humiliation, prayer, meditation, which are equally binding on us as on the Jews. Man is now what he was then; and if affliction of the flesh was good then, it is now.

(2.) In matter of fact, *private* Fasting , such as instanced in the passages above quoted, was no special duty of the Mosaic Law. Public fasting, indeed, was on one occasion enjoined by Moses himself, and on others by subsequent Rulers; but this was in part a ceremonial act, not a moral discipline, and was doubtless abolished with the other rites of the Law.

"Of Fasts," says Lewis, "there was not more than one appointed by the Law of Moses, called the Fast of Expiation ... [2] was a most severe Fast, kept every year upon the tenth day of the month of Tizri, which answers to our September ... This solemnity was observed with fasting and abstinence, not only from all meat and drink, but from all other pleasure whatsoever; insomuch that they did not wash their faces, much less anoint their heads, nor wear their shoes ... nor, (if their Doctors say true,) read any portion of the law which would give them delight. They refrained likewise not only from pleasure, but from labour, nothing being to be done upon this day, but confessing of sins and repentance." [1]

Nay, it may rather be said, that the Jewish Law, as such, was rather opposed than otherwise to austerities. The Nazarites and Rechabites, being exceptions to the rule, are evidence of it. Vide, on the other hand, Deut. 12; Eccles. 5:18.[2] [3]

Such then being the character of the Law in its formal letter, it tells just the contrary way to that which superficial reasoners might expect. For it is most remarkable, first, that the greatest prophets under it, such as Elijah and Daniel, were without express command singularly austere and self-afflicting men, in the midst of a people, who from the first went lusting after "the fish which they eat in Egypt freely; the cucumbers, and the melons, and the leeks, and the onions, and the garlick, and said, Who shall give us flesh to eat?"[4] Next there is something of a very startling and admonitory nature in the *miraculous* fasts of Moses and Elijah, under this same imperfect dispensation. The miracle evidently was for some purpose; yet it did not sanction, in any direct way, any injunction of the Law. Was it not an admonition to the Israelites, that there was a more excellent

---

[1] Lewis, *Hebrew Republic* IV, 15.
[2] Vide Spencer *de Regg. Hebraeor.* Lib 3 diss. 1. ii; 3. Diss. 4. i. 5, &c.

way of obedience than that which ALMIGHTY GOD as yet thought fit to promulgate by solemn enactment? Is it not an intimation serviceable for Christian practice, as much as Moses' announcement of the destined "Prophet like unto him"[5] is intended for the comfort of Christian faith?

Surely the duty of bodily discipline might be rested on the answer to this plain question, *Why* did Daniel use austerities not enjoined by the Law?

3. Now turn to the New Testament, and observe what clear light is therein thrown upon the duty already recommended to us by the Old Testament Saints.

First, there is the instance of St. John the Baptist. "John came neither eating nor drinking." (Matt 11:18): and his disciples fasted (Matt 9:14).

Our SAVIOUR did *not* statedly fast; but here also the exception proves the rule. He who did not fast statedly was the only one born of woman who was untainted by sinful flesh; which seems to imply, that all who are natural descendants of guilty Adam ought to fast.

He bade His disciples to fast. Consider his implied precept, which is an express command to those who obey the Law of Liberty. "When thou fastest, anoint thy head, and wash thy face, that thou appear not unto men to fast." (Matt 6:17, 18).

Consider, moreover, the *general austere character* of Christian obedience, as enjoined by our LORD; – a circumstance much to be insisted on in an age like this, when what is really self-indulgence is thought to be a mere moderate and innocent use of the world's goods. I will but refer to a few, out of the many texts, which I am persuaded are now forgotten by numbers of educated and amiable men who are fond of extolling what they call the mild, tolerant, enlightened spirit of the Gospel. Matt 5:29, 30; 7:13, 14; 10:37–39; Mark 9:43–50; 10:25; Luke 14:12, 26–33.[6]

And reflect, too, whether the spirit of texts such as the following will not move every true member of the Church

Militant. "The ark, and Israel, and Judah abide in tents; and my lord Joab, and the servants of my lord, are encamped in the open fields; shall I then go into mine house, to eat and to drink? . . . as thou liveth, and as thy soul liveth, I will not do this thing." (2 Sam. 11:11).

Now take the example of the Apostles. St. Peter was fasting, when he had the vision which sent him to Cornelius (Acts 10:10). The prophets and teachers at Antioch were fasting, when the HOLY GHOST revealed to them His purpose about Saul and Barnabas: Acts 3:2, 3. Vide also Acts 14: 23; 2 Cor. 6:5; 11:27.

Weigh well the following text, which I am persuaded many men would deny to be St. Paul's writing, had not a gracious Providence preserved to us the epistle containing it. "I keep under my body, and bring it into subjection; lest by any means, when I have preached to others, I myself should be a cast-away." (1 Cor. 9:27).

4. Lastly, consider the practice of the Primitive Christians.

The following account of the early Christian Fasts, is from Bingham, [*Antiquities of the Christian Church,* vol. 21].

THE QUADRAGESIMAL OR LENT FAST – "The Quadragesimal Fast before Easter," says Sozomen, "some observe six weeks, as the Illyrian and Western Churches, and all Libya, Egypt, and Palestine; others make it seven weeks, as the Constantinopolitans and neighbouring nations as far as Phoenicia; others fast three only of those six or seven weeks, by intervals; others the three weeks next immediately before Easter."

The manner of observing Lent among those that were piously disposed to observe it, was to abstain from all food till evening. For anciently a change of diet was not reckoned a fast; but it consisted in perfect abstinence from all sustenance for the whole day till evening.

THE FASTS OF THE FOUR SEASONS – The next anniversary fasting days were those which were called *Jejunia quattuor temporum,* the Fasts of the Four Seasons of the Year . . . These were at first designed . . . to beg a blessing of God upon the several seasons of the year, or to return thanks for the benefits received in each of them, or to exercise and purify both body and soul in a more particular manner, at the return of these certain terms of stricter discipline and more extraordinary devotion. [These afterwards became the Ember Fasts.]

MONTHLY FASTS – In some places they had also Monthly Fasts throughout the year excepting in the two months of July and August . . . because of the sickness of the season.

WEEKLY FASTS – Besides these they had their weekly Fasts on Wednesday and Friday, called the Stationary Days, and Half-Fasts, or Fasts of the Fourth and Sixth Days of the Week . . . These Fasts being of continual use every week throughout the Year, except in the Fifty Days between Easter and Pentecost, were not kept with that rigour and strictness which was observed in the time of Lent . . . [but] ordinarily held no longer than 9 o'clock, i.e. 3 in the afternoon.

OXFORD,
The Feast of the Circumcision.

TRACT 31

THE REFORMED CHURCH

> All the people shouted with a great shout, when they praised the Lord, because the foundation of the House of the Lord was laid. But many of the Priests and Levites, the chief of the fathers, who were ancient men that had seen the first House, when the foundation of this House was laid before their eyes, wept with a loud voice. – Ezra 3:11, 12

SOME remarks may, perhaps, be profitably made on the following well known lines of Herbert's[1] *Church Militant*, in which the text above quoted is applied to our own period:

> The second Temple could not reach the first,
> And the late Reformation never durst
> Compare with ancient times and purer years,
> But in the Jews and us, deserveth tears.
> Nay, it shall every year decrease and fade,
> Till such a darkness shall the world invade
> At CHRIST'S last coming, as His first did find;
> Yet must their proportions be assigned
> To these diminishing, as is between
> The spacious world and Jewry to be seen.

Surely there is a close analogy between the state of the Jews after the captivity, and our own; and, if so, a clear understanding and acknowledgement of it will tend to teach us our own place and suggest to us our prospects.

1. It is scarcely necessary to notice the general correspondence between the fortunes of the two Churches. Both Jews and Christians "left their first love,"[2] mixed with the world, were brought under the power of their enemies, went into captivity, and at length, through GOD'S mercy, were brought back again from Babylon. Ezra and Nehemiah are the forerunners of our Hookers and Lauds; Sanballat and Geshem of the disturbers of our Israel. Samaria has set up its rival temple among us.[3]

2. The second Temple lacked the peculiar treasures of the Temple of Solomon, The Prince of Peace; such as the Ark, the visible glory of GOD, the tables of the Covenant, Aaron's rod, the manna, the oracle. In like manner the Christian Church was, in the beginning, set up in unity; unity of doctrine, or *truth,* unity of discipline, or *Catholicism*, unity of heart, or *charity*. In spite of the heresies which then disturbed the repose of Christians, consider the evidences which present themselves in ecclesiastical history of their firm endurance of persecution, their tender regard for the members of CHRIST, however widely removed by place and language, their self-denying liberality in supplying their wants, the close correspondence of all parts of the body Catholic, as though it were but one family, their profound reverential spirit towards sacred things, the majesty of their religious services, and the noble strictness of their life and conversation. Here we see the "Rod" of the Priesthood, budding forth with fresh life; the "Manna" of the Christian ordinances uncorrupted; the "Oracle" of Tradition fresh from the breast of the Apostles; the "Law" written in its purity on "the fleshly tables of the heart;"[4] the "Shechinah," which a multitude of Martyrs, Saints, Confessors, and gifted Teachers, poured throughout the Temple. But where is our unity now? our ministrations of self-denying love " our prodigality of pious and charitable works? our resolute resistance of evil? We are reformed; we have come out of

Babylon, and have rebuilt our Church; but it is Ichabod; "the glory is departed from Israel."[5]

3. The Jewish polity was, on its restoration, so secularized, that the vestiges of a Theocracy scarcely remained in the eyes of any but attentive believers. That it really existed as before, is plain from the prophetic gift possessed by Caiaphas, wicked man as he was.[6] Consider the anomaly of the political relation of the Jews toward the Ptolemies[7] and Seleucidae,[8] their alliance with Rome, their dispersion over the Roman Empire, their disuse of certain of the Mosaic ordinances, the cruelties and blasphemies of Antiochus, the reign of Herod, and his virtual rebuilding of the Temple, a remarkable omen as regards ourselves. Turn to the restored Christian Church, and reflect upon the perplexed questions concerning the union of Church and State, to which the politics of the last three centuries have given rise; the tyrannical encroachments of the civil power at various eras; the profanations at the time of the Great Rebellion;[9] the deliberate impiety of the French Revolution; and the present breaking up of Ecclesiastical Polity everywhere, the innumerable schisms, the mixture of men of different creeds and sects, and the contempt poured upon any show of Apostolical zeal.

4. Consider the following passages from the Prophets, after the Captivity, and see if they do not apply to present times.

Hagg. i. 4–10. "Is it time for you, O ye, to dwell in your veiled houses, and this house to lie waste? Now, therefore, thus saith the LORD of Hosts, Consider your ways. Ye have *sown much* and *bring in little*; ye eat, but ye have not enough; ye drink, but ye are not filled with drink; ye clothe you, but there is none warm; and he that earneth wages, *earneth wages to put it into a bag with holes.*"&c.

Mal. i. 6–13. "A son honoureth his father, and a servant his master; if then I be a Father, where is Mine honour? and if I be a Master, where is My fear? ... Ye say, The *table of the Lord is polluted*, and *the fruit thereof even His meat, contemptible.* Ye say also, Behold what a *weariness* is it ... and *ye brought that which was torn and the lame, and the sick;* thus ye brought an offering; should I accept this of your hands, saith the LORD?"

Mal. ii. 1–9. "And now, O ye Priests, this commandment is for you ... And ye shall know that I have sent this commandment unto you, that My covenant might be with Levi, saith the LORD of Hosts. My covenant was with him of life and peace, and I gave them to him, for the fear wherewith he feared Me, and was afraid before My Name. The Law of Truth was in his mouth, and iniquity was not found in his lips; he walked with Me in peace and equity, and did turn many away from iniquity. For the Priest's lips should keep knowledge, and they shall seek the Law at his mouth; for he is the messenger of the LORD of Hosts. *But ye are departed out of the way*; ye have caused many to stumble at the Law; *ye have corrupted the covenant of Levi,* saith the LORD of Hosts. *Therefore have I also made you contemptible and base before all the people*." Does not the history of the times of Hoadley[10] and such as he, and our present trials throw light upon the parallel?

Mal. iii. 8–9. "Will a man rob God? yet ye have robbed Me; but ye say, Wherein have we robbed Thee? *in tithes and offerings. Ye are cursed with a curse;* for ye have robbed Me, even this whole nation."

5. It is remarkable that, while the reinstated Jewish Church was so deficient in zeal, piety, and consistent obedience, and was punished by failure and disorganization; yet it never fell into those gross and flagrant offences, which were the opprobrium of its earlier period. *It was clear of the sin of idolatry*.

6. Moreover consider the *parties*, unknown to the era of the Theocracy, which divided the Church after the captivity; the Pharisees, Sadducees, and the rest; the necessary conse-

quence of a relaxation of the original principle of national union. The case is the same in this day; as if the Church were already dead, new forms of organization, multiplied varieties of life and action, show themselves within her.

7. Lastly. The following texts suggest hope to all true Christians. "*According to the word that I covenanted with you, when ye came out of Egypt,* so MY SPIRIT REMAINETH AMONG YOU: fear ye not." (Hagg. ii. 5–9). He will be with us even in this base and groveling age, as with St. Paul, St. Cyprian, and St. Athanasius.

> "Thou wilt; for Thou art Israel's God;
> And thine unwearied arm
> *Is ready yet* with Moses' rod," &c[11]

"The glory of this latter house SHALL BE GREATER THAN OF THE FORMER, saith the LORD of HOSTS."

Strange it now seems before the event, how the Church should close both with glory and yet in unbelief; yet surely, as in the history of Jerusalem, so now both predictions will be at once fulfilled : "The day cometh that shall burn as an oven and *all the proud,* yea and *all who do wickedly shall be stubble: but unto you that fear My name shall the Sun of Righteousness arise with healing in His wings.* "(Mal. iv. 1, 2).

And let it be remembered, that when our Lord seems at greatest distance from His Church, then He is even at the doors. Doubtless when the Angel appeared in the Temple to Zacharias,[12] the news of a miraculous interposition was as great a marvel to the world at large as if it were now noised abroad of one of our own Ministers in the course of his Christian Service.

OXFORD,
The Feast of St. Mark.

TRACT 33

PRIMITIVE EPISCOPACY

IN primitive times the first step towards evangelizing a heathen country seems to have been to seize upon some principal city in it, commonly the civil metropolis, as a centre of operation; to place a Pastor, *i.e.* (generally) a Bishop there; to surround him with a sufficient number of associates and assistants; and then to wait, till, under the blessing of Providence, this Missionary College was able to gather around it the scattered children of grace from the evil world, and invest itself with the shape and influence of an organized Church. The converts would, in the first instance, be those in the immediate vicinity of the Missionary or Bishop, whose diocese nevertheless would extend over the heathen country on every side, either indefinitely, or to the utmost extent of the civil province; his mission being without restriction to all to whom Christian faith had never been preached. As he prospered in the increase of his flock, and sent out his clergy to greater and greater distances from the city, so would the homestead (so to call it) of his Church enlarge. Other towns would be brought under his government, openings would occur for stations in isolated places; till at length "the burden becoming too heavy for him," he would appoint others to supply his place in this or that part of the province. To these he would commit a greater or lesser share of his spiritual power, as might be necessary; sometimes he would make them fully his representatives, or ordain them Bishops; at other times he would employ presbyters for his purpose.

These assistants, or (as they were called) Chorepiscopi,[1] would naturally be confined to their respective districts; and if Bishops, an approximation would evidently be made to a division of the large diocese into a number of smaller ones connected with and subordinate to the Bishop of the metropolitan city. Thus, from the very Missionary character of the Primitive Church, there was a tendency in its polity to what was afterwards called the Provincial and Patriarchal system.

It is not indeed, to be supposed that this was the only way in which the graduated order of sees (so to call it) originated; but, at least, it is one way. And there is this advantage in remarking it: we learn from it, that large dioceses are the characteristics of a church in its infancy or weakness; whereas, the more firmly Christianity was rooted in a country, and the more vigorous its rulers, the more diligently were its sees multiplied throughout the ecclesiastical territory. Thus, St. Basil, in the fourth century, finding his exarchate defenceless in the neighbourhood of Mount Taurus, created a number of dioceses to meet the emergency.[2] These subordinate sees may be called suffragan[3] to the Metropolitan Church, whether their respective rulers were mere representatives of the Bishop who created them, *i.e,* Chorepiscopi; or, on the other hand, substantive authorities, sovereign within their own limits, though bound by external ties to each other and to their Metropolitan. The most perfect state of a Christian country would be, where there was a sufficient number of separate dioceses; the next to it, where there were Chorepiscopi, or Suffragan Bishops in the modern sense of the word.

Few persons, who have not expressly examined the subject, are aware of the minuteness of the dioceses into which many parts of Christendom were divided in the first ages. Some Churches in Italy were more like our rural deaneries than what we now consider dioceses; being not above ten or twelve miles in extent, and their Sees not above five or six miles from each other. Even now (or, at least, in Bingham's time[4]) the kingdom of Naples contains 147 sees, of which twenty are Archbishopricks.[5] Asia Minor is 630 miles long, 210 broad; yet in this country there were almost 400 dioceses. Palestine is in length 160 miles, in breadth 120; yet the number of dioceses amounted to 48. Again, in the province of Syria Secunda, the see of Larissa (*e.g.*) was about 14 miles from Apamea, Arethusa 16 from Epiphania. And so again, turning to the West, though the dioceses were generally larger, as partaking more of a Missionary character, yet we shall find in Ireland at one time from 50 to 60 sees.

Such was the character of the Primitive Regimen, where Christianity especially flourished in the zeal and number of its professors. But, where the country was mountainous or desert, the inhabitants scanty, or but partially Christian, it was considered advisable to leave all to the management of one chief Pastor, who appointed assistants to himself according to his discretion, as the circumstances of the times required. The office of these Chorepiscopi, or country Bishops, was to preside over the country clergy, inquire into their behavior, and report to their principal; also to provide fit persons for the inferior ministrations of the Church. They had the power of ordaining the lower ranks of the clergy, such as the readers, subdeacons, and exorcists; they might ordain priests and deacons with the leave of the city Bishop, and administer the rite of confirmation; and were permitted to sit and vote in councils. Thus their office bore a considerable resemblance to that of our Archdeacons; except of course, that they had the power of ordination; whereas the latter are only presbyters.[6] And, in matter of fact, by such presbyters (*visitors*, as they were called)there were superseded in the course of the fourth and following centuries, till at length the Pope caused the order to be set aside almost altogether in the ninth.

Little use was made of Suffragans during the middle ages;

but, at the time of the Reformation, Archbishop Cranmer[7] felt the deficiency of the English Church in respect of Bishopricks, and projected several measures to supply it. The most complete was that of increasing the number of dioceses; availing himself of existing circumstances, he advised the King to apply the Abbey lands to the founding of twenty additional sees. Bishop Burnet[8] gives some the particulars in the following passage:

"On the 23rd of May, in the session of Parliament, a bill was brought in by Cromwell[9] for giving the King the power to erect new bishopricks by his letters-patent.[1] It was read that day for the first, second, and third time, and sent down to the Commons. The preamble of it was, 'that it was known what slothful and ungodly life had been led by those who were called religious. But that these houses might be converted to better uses; that GOD'S word might be better set forth; children brought up in learning; clerks nourished in the universities; and that old decayed servants might have livings; poor people might have almshouses to maintain them; readers of Greek, Hebrew, and Latin, might have good stipends; daily alms might be administered, and allowance might be made for mending of the highways, and exhibitions for ministers of the Church; for these ends, if the King thought fit to have more bishopricks or cathedral churches erected out of the rents of these houses, full power was given him to erect and found them, and to make rules and statutes for them, and such translations of sees, or divisions of them, as he thought fit.' In the same paper, there is a list of the sees which he intended to found; of which what was done afterwards came so far short, that I know nothing to which it can be so reasonably imputed, as the declining of Cranmer's interest at court, who had proposed the erecting the new cathedrals and sees, with

---

[1] It is scarcely necessary to observe that parliament was then the lay synod of the Church of England.

other things mentioned in the preamble of the statute, as a great mean of reforming the Church.[2] Some of the proposed additional dioceses are then enumerated; Essex. Hertford, Bedfordshire and Buckinghamshire, Oxford and Berkshire, Northampton and Huntingdon, Middlesex, Leicester and Rutland, Gloucestershire, Lancashire, Suffolk, Stafford and Salop, Nottingham and Derby, Cornwall. As to the means by which they were to be endowed, no opinion is here expressed on its lawfulness, as the present sketch is confined to the consideration of the spiritual part of the ecclesiastical system. It is scarcely necessary to add, that Cranmer's view were partly realized in the subsequent creation of the dioceses of Chester, Bristol, Gloucester, Oxford, and Peterborough.

The same prelate, whose episcopate has had so important an influence upon the constitution of our Church ever since, also projected with great wisdom, a system of suffragan bishops or Chorepiscopi, which he was able to bring into effect, and which lasted till the reign of King James. Twenty-six such bishops were appointed; the bishop of the diocese having the power of presenting two persons to the king, who might choose either of them, and present them to the archbishop of the province for consecration. These suffragans exercised such jurisdiction as their principal gave them, or as had formerly been committed to suffragans; their authority lasting no longer than he continued their commission to them. "These were believed," says Burnet,[3] "to be the same with the Chorepiscopi in the primitive church; which, as they were begun before the first council of Nice,[10] so they continued in the Western Church till the 9th century, and then a decretal of Damascus being forged, that condemned them, they were put down everywhere by degrees, and now revived in England. The suffragan sees were as follows:

[2] Burnet, *History of the Reformation,* 3.
[3] *History of the Reformation,* 2.

Thetford, Ipswich, Colchester, Dover, Guildford, Southampton, Taunton, Shaftesbury, Molton, Marlborough, Bedford, Leicester, Gloucester, Shrewsbury, Bristol, Penrith, Bridgwater, Nottingham, Grantham, Hull, Huntingdon, Cambridge, Perth, Berwick, St. Germain's, and the Isle of Wight.

After the disuse of suffragans in the reign of James I there was a fresh project for establishing them on the Restoration. Charles, in one of his declarations, promises to increase the number of bishops, in accordance with Archbishop Ussher's plan for episcopal government.[11] However, his intention was not put into execution, doubtless owing to existing circumstances, which reasonably interfered with it.

The following extract is made from Bingham, Antiqu. ix.8,[12] "One great objection against the present diocesan episcopacy, and that which to many may look the most plausible, is drawn from the vast extent and greatness of most of the northern diocese of the world, which makes it so extremely difficult for one man to discharged all the offices of the episcopal function ... The Church of England has usually followed the larger model, and had very great and extensive dioceses; for at first she had but seven bishopricks in the whole nation, and those commensurate in a manner to the seven Saxon kingdoms. Since that time she has thought it a point of wisdom to contract her dioceses, and multiply them into above 20; and if she should think fit, to add 40 or 100 more, she would not be without precedent in the practice of the Primitive Church ... In Ireland there are not now above half the number of dioceses that there were before, and consequently they must needs be larger by uniting them together. In England, there are more in number than formerly, some new ones being created out of the old ones, and at present the whole number augmented to three times as many as they were for some ages after the first conversion. Besides that, we have another way of contracting dioceses in effect here in England appointed by law, which law was never yet repealed; which is by devolving part of the bishop's care upon the Chorepiscopi, or suffragan bishops, as the law calls them: – a method commonly practiced in the ancient Church in such large dioceses as those of St. Basil and Theodoret, one of which had not less than fifty chorepiscopi under him, if Nazianzen[13] rightly informs us. And it is a practice which was continued here all the reign of Queen Elizabeth, and even to the end of King James; and is what may be revived again, whenever any bishop thinks his diocese too large, or his burden too great to be sustained by himself alone."

To the above statements, may be subjoined the present number of souls, and the area of square miles, in certain of our dioceses, as given in a pamphlet lately published, which has come into the writer's hands since the foregoing was put on paper. (Vide Plan for a New Arrangement, &c. by Lord Henley.)[14]

	Souls	Square Miles
Chester	1,806,722	4140
London	1,676,725	1942
York	1,526,288	5300
Lincoln	920,011	5775
Lichfield	978,655	3344

By this table, it is not here intended to insinuate the necessity of any immediate measure of multiplying the English sees or appointing suffragans, (the expediency of which is to be determined by a variety of considerations, which it were unprofitable here to detail,) but to show that the *genius* of our ecclesiastical system tends towards such an increase, and that the only question to be determined is one of time. These statements are also made with the view of keeping up in the minds of churchmen a recollection of the injury which the

Irish branch of our Church has lately sustained in the diminution of its sees.

OXFORD,
The Feast of St. Philip and St. James.

————————

P.S. – Since this was written, a new arrangement of Dioceses and Sees has been made by authority of a Royal Commission, composed of members the greater part of whom were laymen, and without confirmation of their acts on the part of the Church.

TRACT 34

THE RITES AND CUSTOMS OF THE CHURCH

Ὁ μὲν οὖν πιστός, ὡς χρή, καὶ ἐρρωμένος οὐδὲ δεῖται λογου καὶ αἴτας, ὑπέρ ὧν ἄν ἐπιταχθῇ, ἀλλ ἀρκεῖται τῇ παραδόσει μονῇ.

He who is duly strengthened in faith, does not go so far as to require argument and reason for what is enjoined, but is satisfied with the *tradition* alone.

Chrysost. In 1 Cor. Hom. 26.

———————

THE reader of ecclesiastical history is sometimes surprised at finding observances and customs generally received in the Church at an early date, which have not express warrant in the Apostolic writings; *e.g.* the use of the cross in baptism. The following pages will be directed to the consideration of this circumstance; with a view of suggesting from those writings themselves, that a minute ritual was contemporaneous with them, that the Apostles recognized it as existing and binding, that it was founded on religious *principles*, and tended to the inculcation of religious truth. Not that any formal proof is attainable or conceivable, considering the brevity and subjects of the inspired documents; but such fair evidence of the fact, as may recommend it to the belief of the earnest and single-minded Christian. It is abundantly evident that the Epistles were not written to prescribe and enforce the Ritual of Religion; all then we can expect, if it existed in the days of the Apostles, is an occasional allusion to it in their Epistles as existing, and a plain acquiescence in it: and thus much we find.

Let us consider that remarkable passage, (1 Cor. 11:2–16) which, I am persuaded, most readers pass over as if they could get little instruction from it. St. Paul is therein blaming the Corinthians for not adhering to the *custom* of the Church, which prescribed that men should wear their hair short, and that women should have their head covering during divine service; a custom apparently most unimportant, if any one ever was, but in his view strictly binding on Christians. He begins by implying that it is one out of many rule or traditions (πάράδοσείς) which he had given them, and they were bound to keep. He ends by refusing to argue with any one who obstinately cavils at it and rejects it : "If any man seems to be contentious, we have no such custom, neither the Churches of GOD."[1] Here then at once a view is opened to us which is quite sufficient to remove the surprise we might otherwise feel at the multitude of rites, which were in use in the Primitive Church, but about which the New Testament is silent; and further, to command our obedience to such as come down to us from the first ages, and are agreeable to Scripture.

In accordance with this conclusion, is the clear and forcible command given by the Apostle, (2Thess. 2:15) "Brethren, stand fast, and hold the traditions which ye have been taught, whether *by word*, or our epistle."

To return. St. Paul goes on to give the reason of the usage, for the satisfaction of the weak brethren at Corinth. It was, he implies, a symbol or development (so to say) of the principle of the subordination of the woman to the man, and a memorial of the history of our creation; nay it was founded in *"nature,"* *i.e.* natural reason. And lastly, it had a practical object: the women ought to have her head covered *"because* of the angels."* We need not stop to inquire *what* this reason was; but it was a reason of a practical nature which the

Corinthians understood, though we may not. If it mean, as is probable "because she is in the sight of the heavenly angels." (1 Tim 5:21) it gives a still greater importance to the ceremonies of worship, as connecting them with the unseen world.

It would seem as if the very multiplicity of the details of the Church ritual made it plainly impossible for St. Paul to write them all down, or to do more than *remind* the Corinthians of his way of conducting religious discipline when he was among them. "Be ye *followers* of me;" he says, "I praise you that *ye remember me in all things*."[2] It is evident there are ten thousand little points in the working of any large system, which a present instructor alone can settle. Hence it is customary at present, when a school is set up, or when any novel manufacture in trade or extraordinary machinery, is to be brought into use, to set it going by sending a person fully skilled in its practical details. Such was St. Paul as regards the system of Christian discipline and worship; and when he could not go himself, he sent Timothy in his place. He says in the 4th chapter; "I beseech you, be ye followers of me. *For this cause* have I sent unto you Timotheus, who shall bring you into remembrance *of my ways which be in* CHRIST*, as I teach everywhere in every Church*." Here there is a like reference to an uniform system of discipline, – whether as to Christian conduct, worship, or Church government.

Another important allusion appears to be contained in the 22nd verse of the chapter above commented on. "What, have ye not houses to eat and drink it? or despise ye the *Church of* GOD?"[3] This is remarkable as being a solitary allusion in Scripture to *houses* of prayer under the Christian system, which nevertheless we know from *ecclesiastical history* were used from the very first. Here then is a most solemn ordinance of primitive Christianity, which barely escapes, if it escapes, omission in Scripture.

A passing allusion is made in another passage of the same Epistle, to the use of the word Amen at the conclusion of the Eucharistical prayer, as it is preserved after it and all other prayers to this day.[4] Thus the ritual of the Apostles descended to minutiae, and these so invariable in their use, as to allow of an appeal to them.

In the original institution of the Eucharist, as recorded in the Gospels, there is no mention of *consecrating* the cup; but in 1 Cor. 10:16, St. Paul calls it "the cup *of blessing, which we bless*." This incidental information, vouchsafed to us in Scripture, should lead us to very cautious how we put aside other usages of the early Church concerning this sacrament, which do not happen to be *clearly* mentioned in Scripture; as *e.g.* the solemn offering of the elements to GOD by way of pleading His mercy through CHRIST, which seems to have been universal in the Church, till Popery corrupted it.[5]

As regards the same Sacrament, let us consider the use of the word *ministering* λείτουργουντων (Acts 13:2); a word which, dropt (so to say) by accident, and interpreted, as is reasonable, by its use in the services of the Jewish Law, (Luke 1:23; Heb 10:11) remarkably coincides with the λείτουργία of the Primitive Church, according to which the offering of the Altar was intercessory, as pleading CHRIST'S merits before the throne of grace.[6]

Again, in 1 Cor. 15:29, we incidentally discover the existence of persons who are styled "the baptized for the dead." Perhaps it is impossible to determine what is meant by this phrase, on which little light is thrown by early writers. However, any how it seems to refer to a *custom* of the Church, which was so usual as to admit of an appeal to it, which St. Paul approved, yet which he did not in the Epistle directly enforce, and but casually mentions.

In 1 Cor. 1:16, St. Paul happens to inform us that he baptized the *household* of Stephanus. It has pleased the HOLY SPIRIT to preserve to us this fact; by which is detected the existence of a rule of discipline for which the express doctrinal parts of Scripture afford but indirect warrant, viz. the custom of household baptism. (Vid. also Acts 16:15, 33) This accidental disclosure accurately anticipates the after practice of the early Church, according to which families, infants included, were baptized, and that on a weighty doctrinal *reason*; viz. that all men were born in sin and in the wrath of God,[7] and needed to be individually translated into that kingdom of grace, in which baptism is the initiation.

These instances, then, not to notice others of the like or a different kind, are surely sufficient to reconcile us to the complete ritual system which breaks upon us in the writings of the Fathers. If any parts of its indeed are contrary to Scripture, that is of course a decisive reason at once for believing them to be additions and corruptions of the original ceremonial; but till this is shown, we are bound to venerate what is certainly primitive, and probably is apostolic.

It will be remarked, moreover, that many of the religious observances of the early Church are expressly built upon words of Scripture, and intended to be a visible memorial of them, after the manner of St. Paul's directions about the respective habits of men and women, which was just now noticed. Metaphorical or mystical descriptions were represented by a corresponding literal action. Our LORD Himself authorized this procedure when He took up the metaphor of the prophets concerning the fountain opened for our cleansing (Zech. 13:1) and represented it in the visible rite of baptism.[8] Accordingly, from the frequent mention of *oil* in Scripture as the emblem of spiritual gifts, (Isa. 41:1–3, &c.) it was actually used in the Primitive Church in the ceremony of admitting catechumens, and in baptizing. And here again they had the precedent of the Apostles, who applied it in effecting their miraculous cures. (Mark 6:13; James 5:14) And so from the figurative mention in Scripture of *salt*, as the necessary preparation of every religious sacrifice, it was in use in the Western Church in the ceremony of admitting converts into the rank of catechumens. So again from Phil. 2:10, it was customary to bow the head at the name of JESUS. It were endless to multiply instances of a similar pious attention to the very words of Scripture, as their custom of continual public prayer from such passages as Luke 18:7; or of burying the bodies of martyrs under the altar, from Rev. 6:9; or of the white vestments of the officiating ministers, from Rev. 4:4.

Two passages on the subject from the Fathers shall now be laid before the reader, by way of further illustration, and first from Tertullian:

"Though this observance has not been determined by any text of Scripture, yet it is established by custom, which doubtless is derived from Apostolic tradition. For how can an usage ever obtain, which has not first been given by tradition? But you say, even though tradition can be produced, still a written (Scripture) authority must be demanded. Let us examine, then, how far it is true, that an Apostolic tradition itself, unless written in Scripture, is inadmissible. Now I will give up the point at once, if it is not already determined by instances of other observances, which are maintained without any Scripture proof, on the mere plea of tradition, and the sanction of consequent custom. To begin with baptism. Before we enter the Water, we solemnly renounce the devil, his pomp, and his angels, in church in the presence of the Bishop. Then we are plunged into the water thrice, and answer certain questions over and above what the LORD has determined in the written gospel. After coming out of it, we taste a mixture of milk and honey; and for a whole week from that day we abstain from our daily bath. The sacrament of the Eucharist, though given by the LORD to all and at supper time, yet is celebrated in our meetings before day break, and only at the hand of our presiding ministers ... We sign our foreheads with the cross whenever we set out and walk, go in or out, dress, gird on our sandals, bathe, eat, light our lamps, sit or lie down to rest, whatever we do. If you demand a scripture rule for these and such like observances, we can give you none; all we say to you is, that tradition directs, usage sanctions, faith obeys. That reason justifies this tradition, usage, and faith, you will soon yourself see, or will easily learn from others; meanwhile you will do well to believe that there is a law to which obedience is due. I add one instance from the old dispensation. It is so usual among the Jewish females to veil their head, that they are even known by it. I ask where the law is to be found; the Apostle's decision of course is not to the point. Now if I nowhere find a law, it follows that tradition introduced the custom, which afterwards was confirmed by the Apostle when he explained the reason of it. These instances are enough to show that a tradition, even though not in Scripture, still binds our conduct, if a continuous usage be preserved as the witness of it." – (Tertullian, de Corona. § 3).[9]

Upon this passage, it may be observed, that Tertullian, flourishing A.D. 200, is on the one hand a very early witness for the existence of the general doctrine which it contains, while on the other he gives not sanction to those later customs, which the Church of Rome upholds, but which cannot be clearly traced to primitive times.

St. Basil, whose work on the HOLY SPIRIT, § 66, shall next be cited, flourished in the middle of the fourth century, 150 years after Tertullian, and was of a very different school; yet he will be found to be in exact agreement with him on the subject before us, viz. that the ritual of the Church was derived from the Apostles, and was based on religious principles and doctrines. He adds a reason for its not being given us in Scripture, which we may receive or reject as our judgment leads us, viz. that the rites were memorials of doctrines not intended for publication except among baptized Christians, whereas the Scriptures were open to all men.[10] This at least is clear, that the ritual could scarcely have been given in detail in Scripture without imparting to the Gospel the character of a burdensome ceremonial, and withdrawing our attention from its doctrines and precepts.

"Of those articles of doctrine and preaching, which are in the custody of the Church, some come to us in Scripture itself, some are conveyed to us by a continuous tradition in mystical depositories. Both have equal claims on our devotion, and are received by all who are in any respect Churchmen. For, should we attempt to supersede the usages which are not enjoined in Scripture as if unimportant, we should do most serious injury to Evangelical truth; nay, reduce it to a bare name. To take an obvious instance; which Apostle has taught us in Scripture to sign believers with the cross? Where does Scripture teach us to turn to the east in prayer? Which of the saints has left us recorded in Scripture the words of invocation at the consecration of the bread of the Eucharist, and of the cup of blessing? Thus we are not content with what Apostle or Evangelist has left on record, but we add other rites before and after it, as important for the celebration of the mystery, receiving them from a teaching distinct from Scripture. Moreover, we bless the water of baptism, and the oil for anointing, and also the candidate for baptism himself ... After the example of Moses, the Apostles and Fathers who modeled the Churches, were accustomed to lodge their sacred doctrine in mystic forms, as being secretly and silently conveyed ... This is the reason why there is a tradition of observances independent of Scripture, lest doctrines, being exposed to the world, should be so familiar as to be despised ... We stand instead of kneeling at prayer on the Sunday; but all of us do not know the reason of this ... Again, every time we kneel down and rise up, we show by our outward action, that sin has leveled us with the ground, and the loving mercy of our Creator has recalled us to heaven."[11]

The conclusion to be drawn from all that has been said in these pages is this: – That rites and ordinances, far from being unmeaning, are in their nature capable of impressing our memories and imaginations with the great revealed verities; far from being superstitious, are expressly sanctioned in Scripture as to their principle, and delivered to the Church in their form by tradition. Further, that they varied in different countries, according to the respective founder of the Church in each. Thus e.g., St John and St. Philip[12] are known to have adopted the Jewish rule for observing Easter-day; while the other Apostles celebrated it always on a Sunday. Lastly, that, although the details of the early ritual varied in importance, and corrupt additions were made in the middle ages, yet, that, as a whole, the Catholic ritual was a precious possession; and if we, who have escaped from Popery, have lost not only the possession, but the sense of its value, it is a serious question whether we are not like men who recover from some grievous illness with the loss or injury of their sight or hearing; – whether we are not like the Jews returned from captivity, who could never find the rod of Aaron or the Ark of the Covenant, which, indeed, had ever been hid from the world, but then was removed from the Temple itself.

OXFORD,
The Feast of St. Philip and St. James

TRACT 38

VIA MEDIA
No. I[1]

LAICUS.[2] – Will you listen to a few free quotations from one who has not known you long enough to be familiar with you without apology? I am struck by many things I have heard you say, which show me that, somehow or other, my religious system is incomplete; yet at the same time the world accuses you of Popery, and there are seasons when I have misgivings whither you are carrying me.

Clericus. – I trust I am prepared, most willing I certainly am, to meet any objections you have to bring against doctrines which you have heard me maintain. Say more definitely what the charge against me is.

L. That your religious system, which I have heard some persons style Apostolical, and which I so name by way of designation, is like that against which our forefathers protested at the Reformation.

C. I will admit it, *i.e.*. if I may reverse your statement, and say, that the Popish system resembles the Apostolical. Indeed, how could it be otherwise, seeing that all corruptions of the truth must be like the truth which they corrupt, else they would not persuade mankind to take them instead of it?

L. A bold thing to say, surely; to make the earlier system an imitation of the later?

C. A bolder, surely, to assume that mine is the later, and the Popish the earlier. When think you that my system (so to call it) arose? – not with myself?

L Of course not; but whatever individuals have held it in our Church since the Reformation, it must be acknowledged that they have been but few, though some of them doubtless eminent men.

C. Perhaps you would say (*i.e.* the persons whose views your are representing), that at the Reformation, the stain of the old theology was left among us, and has shown itself in its measure ever since, as in the poor, so again in the educated classes; – that the peasantry still use and transmit their Popish rhymes, and the minds of students still linger among the early Fathers; but that the genius and principles of our Church have ever been what is commonly called Protestant.

L. This is a fair general account of what would be maintained.

C. You would consider that the Protestant principles and doctrines of this day were those of our Reformers in the sixteenth century; and that what is called Popery now, is what was called Popery then.

L. On the whole: there are indeed extravagances now, as is obvious. I would not defend extremes; but I suppose our Reformers would agree with moderate Protestants of this day, in what they meant by Protestantism and by Popery.

C. This is an important question, of course; much depends on the correctness of the answer you have made to it. Do you make it as a matter of history, from knowing the opinions of our Reformers, or from what you consider probable?

L. I am no divine. I judge from a general knowledge of history, and from the obvious probabilities[3] of the case, which no one can gainsay.

C. Let us then go by *probabilities*, since you lead the way. Is it not according to probabilities that opinions and principles should *not* be the same now as they were three hundred years since? that though our professions are the same, yet we should not mean by them what our Reformers meant? Can you point to any period of Church history, during which doctrine remained for any time uncorrupted? Three hundred years is a long time. Are you quite sure we do not need A SECOND REFORMATION?

L. Are your really serious? Have we not Articles and a Liturgy, which keep us from deviating from the standard of truth set up in the sixteenth century?

C. Nay, I am maintaining no paradox. Surely there is a large religious party all around us who say the great body of the Clergy *has* departed from the doctrines of our Martyrs at the Reformation. I do not say I agree with the particular charges they prefer; but the very circumstance that they make them is a proof there is nothing extravagant in the notion of our Church having departed from the doctrine of the sixteenth century.

L. It is true; but the persons you refer to, bring forward, at least, an intelligible charge; they appeal to the Articles, and maintain that the Clergy have departed from the doctrine therein contained. They may be right or wrong; but at least they give us the means of judging for ourselves.

C. This surely is beside the point. We are speaking of *probabilities*. *What* change actually *has* been made, if any, is a further question, a question of *fact*. But before going on to examine the particular case, I observe that change of some sort was *probable*; probable in itself you can hardly deny, considering the history of the universal Church; not extravagantly improbable, moreover, in spite of Articles, as is sufficiently proved by the extensively prevailing opinion to which I referred, that the clergy *have* departed from them. Now consider the course of religion and politics, domestic and foreign, during the last three centuries, and tell me whether events have not occurred to increase this probability almost to a certainty; the probability, I mean, that the

members of the English Church of the present day differ
from the principles of the Church of Rome more than our
forefathers differed. First, consider the history of the Puritans
from first to last. Without pronouncing any opinion on the
truth or unsoundness of their principles, were they not
evidently further removed from Rome than were our
Reformers?[4] Was not their influence all on the side of
leading the English Church farther from Rome than our
Reformers placed it? Think of the fall of the Scottish
Episcopal Church.[5] Reflect upon the separation and extinction of the Nonjurors,[6] upon the rise of Methodism, upon
our political alliances with foreign Protestant communities.
Consider especially the history and the school of Hoadley.
That man, whom a high authority of the present day does
not hesitate to call a Socinian,[1] was for near fifty years a
bishop in our Church.

L. You tell me to think on these facts. I wish I were versed
enough in our ecclesiastical history to do so.

C. But you are as well versed in it as the generality of
educated men; as those whose opinions you are now maintaining. And they surely ought to be well acquainted with
our history and the doctrines taught in our different schools
and eras, considering they scruple not to charge such as me
with a declension from the true Anti-popish doctrine of our
Church. For what the doctrine of the Church is, what it has
been for three centuries, is a matter of fact which without
reading cannot be known.

L. Let us leave, if you please, this ground of *probability*,
which, whatever you may say, cannot convince me while I
am able to urge that strong objection to it which you would
not let me mention just now. I repeat, we have Articles; we
have a Liturgy; the dispute lies in a little compass, without

---

[1] "It is true he was a Bishop, though a Socinian." – Bishop Blomfield's Letter
  to C. Butler, Esq. 1825.[7]

need of historical reading: – do you mean to say we have departed from *them*?

C. I am not willing to follow you a second time, and will be explicit. I reply, we *have* departed from them. Did you ever study the Rubrics of the Prayer Book?

L. But surely they have long been obsolete; – they are impracticable!

C. It is enough; you have answered your own question without trouble of mine. Not only do we not obey them, but it seems we style them impracticable. I take your admission. Now, I ask you, are not these Rubrics (I might mention parts of the Services themselves which have fallen into disuse), such as in the present day incur the odium of being called Popish? and, if so, is not this a proof that the spirit of the present day has departed (whether for good or evil) from the spirit of the Reformation? – and is it wonderful that such as I should be called Popish, if the Church Services themselves are considered so?

L. Will you give me some instances?

C. Is it quite in accordance with our present Protestant notions, that unbaptized persons should not be buried with the rites of the Church? – that every Clergyman should read the Daily Service morning and evening at home, if he cannot get a congregation?[8] – that in college chapels the Holy Communion should be administered every week?[9] – that Saints' Days should be observed?[10] – that stated days of fasting should be set apart by the Church?[11] Ask even a sober-minded really serious man about the observance of these rules; will he not look grave, and say that he is afraid of formality and superstition if these rules were attended to?

L. And is there not the danger?

C. The simple question is, whether there is more danger now than three centuries since? was there not far more superstition in the sixteenth century than in the nineteenth century? and does the spirit of the nineteenth move with the spirit of the sixteenth, if the sixteenth commands and the nineteenth draws back?

L. But you spoke of parts of the Services themselves laid aside?

C. Alas! . . .

What is the prevailing opinion or usage respecting the form of absolution in the office for Visiting the Sick?[12] What is thought by a great body of men of the words in which the Priesthood is conveyed?[13] Are there no objections to the Athanasian Creed?[14] No murmurs against the Commination Service?[15] Does no one stumble at the word "oblations," in the Prayer for the Church Militant?[16] Is there no clamour against parts of the Burial Service? No secret or scarcely secret complaints against the word "regeneration" in the Baptismal?[17] No bold protestations against reading the Apocrypha?[18] Now do not all these objections rest upon one general ground: viz. That these parts of our Services savour of Popery? And again, are not these the popular objections of the day?

L. I cannot deny it.

C. I consider then that already I have said enough to show that the Churchman of this day has deviated from the opinions of our Reformers, and has become more opposed than they were to the system they protested against. And therefore, I would observe, it is not fair to judge of men, or of such as me, in the off-hand way which many men take the liberty to adopt. Men seem to think that we are plainly and indisputably proved to be Popish, if we are proved to differ from the generality of Churchmen nowadays. But what if it turn out that they are silently floating down the stream and we are upon the shore?

L. All, however, will allow, I suppose, that our Reformation was never completed in its details. The final judgment was not passed upon parts of the Prayer Book. There was, you know, alterations in the second edition of it published in King Edward's time; and these tended to a more Protestant doctrine than that which had first been adopted. For instance, in King Edward's first book the dead in CHRIST were prayed for; in the second this commemoration was omitted. Again, in the first book the elements of the LORD'S Supper were more distinctly offered up to GOD, and more formally consecrated than in the second edition, or at present.[19] Had Queen Mary not succeeded, perhaps the men who effected this would have gone further.

C. I believe they would; nay indeed they did at a subsequent period. They took away the Liturgy altogether, and substituted a Directory.

L. They? the same men?

C. Yes, the foreign party: who afterwards went by the name of Puritans. Bucer, who altered in King Edward's time,[20] and the Puritans, who destroyed in King Charles's, both came from the same religious quarter.

L. Ought you so to speak of the foreign Reformers? to them we owe the Protestant doctrine altogether.

C. I like foreign interference, as little from Geneva, as from Rome. Geneva at least never converted a part of England from heathenism, nor could lay claim to patriarchal authority over it. Why could we not be let alone and suffered to reform ourselves?

L. You separate then your creed and cause from that of the Reformed Churches of the Continent?

C. Not altogether; but I protest against being brought into that close alliance with them which the world nowadays would force upon us. The glory of the English Church is, that it has taken the VIA MEDIA, as it has been called.[21] It lies *between* the (so called) Reformers and the Romanists; whereas there are religious circles, and influential too, where it is thought enough to prove an English Clergyman unfaithful to his Church, if he preaches anything at variance with the opinions of the Diet of Augsburg[22] or the Confessions of the Waldenses.[23] However, I will, if you will still listen to me, strengthen my argument by an appeal to them.

L. That argument being, that what is now cried up as Protestant doctrine, is not what was considered such by the Reformers.

C. Yes; and I am going to offer reasons for thinking that the present age has lapsed, not only from the opinions of the English Reformers, but from those of the foreign also. This is too extensive a subject to do justice to in a conversation, even had I the learning for it; but I may draw your attention to one or two obvious proofs of the fact.

L. You must mean from Calvin; for Luther is, in some points, reckoned nearer the Romish Church that ourselves.

C. I mean Calvin,[24] about whose extreme distance from Rome there can be no doubt. What is the popular opinion now concerning the necessity of an Episcopal Regimen?

L. A late incident has shown what it is; that it is uncharitable to define the Catholic Church, as the body of Christians in every country governed by Bishops, Priests, and deacons; such a definition excluding pious Dissenters and others.

C. But what thought Calvin? "Calvin held those men worthy of anathema who would not submit themselves to truly Christian bishops, if such could be had."[2] What would he have said then to the Wesleyan Methodists,[25] and that portion of the (so called) Orthodox Dissenters, which is friendly at present to the Church? These allow that we, or that numbers among us, are truly Christian, yet make no attempts to obtain Bishops from us. Thus the age is more Protestant now than Calvin himself.

L. Certainly in this respect; unless Calvin spoke rhetorically under circumstances.

C. Now for a second instance. The following is his statement concerning the LORD'S Supper: "I understand

---

[2] Vide Mr Perceval's *Churchman's Manual*, p. 13.

what is to be understood by the words of CHRIST; that He doth not only offer us the benefits of His death and Resurrection, but His very body, wherein He died and rose again. I assert that the body of CHRIST is really (as the usual expression is), that it is truly given to us in the Sacrament, to be the saving food of our souls."[26] ... "The SON of GOD offers daily to us in the Holy Sacrament, the same body which He once offered in sacrifice to His Father, that it may be our spiritual food." ... "If anyone ask me concerning the manner, I will not be ashamed to confess that it is a secret too high for my reason to comprehend, or my tongue to express."[3] Now, if I were of myself to use these words, (in spite of the qualification at the end, concerning the *manner* of His presence in the Sacrament,) would they not be sufficient to convict me of Popery in the judgment of this minute and unlearned generation?

L. You speak plausibly, I will grant; yet surely, after all, it is not unnatural that the Reformers of the sixteenth century should have fallen short of a full Reformation in matters of doctrine and discipline. Light breaks but gradually on the mind: one age begins a work, another finishes.

C. I am arguing about a matter of fact, not defending the opinions of the Reformers. As to this notion of their being but partially illuminated, I am not concerned to oppose such a view, being quite content if the persons whom you are undertaking to represent are willing to admit it. And then, in consistency, I shall beg them to reproach me not with *Popery* but with *Protestantism*, and to be impartial enough to assail not only me, but "the Blessed Reformation," as they often call it, using words they do not understand. It is hard, indeed, that when I share in the opinions of the Reformers, I should have no share in their praises of them.

L. You speak as if you really agreed with the Reformers.

---

[3] Vide Tract 27, *The History of Popish Transubstantiation.*

You may say so in an argument, but in sober earnest you cannot mean to say you really agree with the great body of them. Neither you nor I should hesitate to confess they were often inconsistent, saying, at one time, what they disowned at another.

C. That they should have said different things at different times, is not wonderful, considering they were searching into Scripture and Antiquity, and feeling their way to the Truth. Since, however, they did vary in their opinions, for this very reason it is obvious I should be saying nothing at all, in saying that I agreed with them, unless I stated explicitly at what period of their lives, or in which of their writings. This I do state clearly: I say I agree with them as they speak in the formularies of the Church; more cannot be required of me, nor indeed is it possible to say more.

L. What persons complain of is, that you are not satisfied with the formularies of the Church, but add to them doctrines not contained in them. You must allow there is little stress laid in the Articles on some points, which are quite cardinal in your system, to judge by your way of enforcing them.

C. This is not the first time you have spoken of this supposed system of ours. I will not stop to quarrel with you for calling it ours as if it were not rather the Church's; but explain to me what you consider it to consist in.

L. The following are some of its doctrines: that the Church has an existence independent of the State; that the State may not religiously interfere with its internal concerns; that none may engage in ministerial works except such as are episcopally ordained; that the consecration of the Eucharist is especially entrusted to Bishops and Priests. Where do you find these doctrines in the formularies of the Church; that is, so prominently set forth, as to sanction you in urging them at all, or at least so strongly as you are used to urge them?

C. As to urging them at all, we might be free to urge them even though not sanctioned in the Articles; unless indeed the Articles are our rule of faith. Were the Church first set up at the Reformation, then indeed it might be right so to exalt its Articles as to forbid to teach "whatsoever is not read therein, nor may be proved thereby."[27] I cannot consent, I am sure the Reformers did not wish me, to deprive myself of the Church's dowry, the doctrines which the Apostles spoke in Scripture and impressed upon the early Church. I receive the Church as a messenger from CHRIST, rich in treasures old and new, rich with the accumulated wealth of ages.

L. Accumulated?

C. As you will yourself allow. Our Articles are one portion of that accumulation. Age after age, fresh battles have been fought with heresy, fresh monuments of truth set up. As I will not consent to be deprived of the records of the Reformation, so neither will I part with those of former times. I look upon our Articles as in one sense an addition to the Creeds; and at the same time the Romanists added their Tridentine articles.[28] Theirs I consider unsound; ours as true.

L. The Articles have surely an especial claim upon you; you have subscribed them, and are therefore more bound to them, than to other truths, whatever or wherever they be.

C. There is a popular confusion on this subject. Our Articles are not a *body of divinity,* but in great measure only protests against certain errors of a certain period of the Church. Now I will preach the whole counsel of GOD,[29] whether set down in the Articles or not. I am bound to the Articles by subscription; but I am bound, more solemnly even than by subscription, by my baptism and by my ordination, to believe and maintain the *whole* Gospel of CHRIST. The grace given at those seasons comes through the Apostles, not through Luther or Calvin, Bucer or Cartwright.[30] You will presently agree with me in this statement. Let me ask, do you not hold the inspiration of Holy Scripture?

L. Undoubtedly.

C. Is it not a clergyman's duty to maintain and confess it?

L. Certainly.

C. But this doctrine is nowhere found in the Articles; and for this plain reason, that both Romanists and Reformers admitted it; and the difference between the two parties was, not whether the Old and New Testament were inspired, but whether the Apocrypha was of canonical authority.

L. I must grant it.

C. And in the same way, I would say, there are many other doctrines unmentioned in the Articles, only because they were not then disputed by either party; and others again, for other reasons, short of disbelief in them. I cannot indeed make my neighbor preach them, for he will tell me he will believe only just so much as he has been obliged to subscribe; but it is hard if I am therefore to be defrauded of the full inheritance of faith myself. Look at the subject from another point of view, and see if we do not arrive at the same conclusion. A statesman of the last century is said to have remarked that we have Calvinistic Articles, and a Popish Liturgy.[31] This of course is an idle calumny. But is there not certainly a distinction of doctrine and manner between the Liturgy and the Articles? And does not what I have just stated account for it, viz. that the Liturgy, as coming down from the Apostles, is the depository of their complete teaching; while the Articles are polemical, and except as they embody the creeds, are mainly protests against certain definite errors? Such are my views about the Articles; and if in my teaching, I lay especially stress upon doctrines only indirectly contained in them, and say less about those which are therein put forth most prominently, it is because times are changed. We are in danger of unbelief more than of superstition. The Christian minister should be a witness against the errors of his day.

L. I cannot tell whether on consideration I shall agree with you or not. However, after all, you have said not a word to explain what your real differences from Popery are; what those false doctrines were, which you conceive our Reformers withstood. You began by confessing that your opinions and the Popish opinions had a resemblance, and only disputed whether yours should be called like the Popish, or the Popish like yours. But in what are yours different from Rome?

C. Be assured of this – no party will be more opposed to our doctrine, if it ever prospers and makes noise, than the Roman party. This has been proved before now. In the seventeenth century the theology of the divines of the English Church was substantially the same as ours is; and it experienced the full hostility of the Papacy. It was the true Via Media; Rome sought to block up that way as fiercely as the Puritans did. History tells us this. In a few words then, before we separate, I will state some of my irreconcilable differences with Rome as she is;[32] and in stating here errors, I will closely follow that order observed by Bishop Hall in his treatise on "The Old Religion",[33] whose Protestantism is unquestionable.

I consider that it is unscriptural to say with the Church of Rome that "we are justified by inherent righteousness."

That it is unscriptural that "the good works of a man justified do *truly* merit eternal life."[34]

That the doctrine of transubstantiation, as not being revealed, but a theory of man's devising, is profane and impious.

That the denial of the cup to the laity, is a bold and unwarranted encroachment on their privileges as CHRIST'S people.

That the sacrifice of masses, as it has been practiced in the Roman Church, is without foundation in Scripture or antiquity, and therefore blasphemous and dangerous.

That the honour paid to images is very full of peril, in the case of the uneducated, that is, of the great part of Christians.

That indulgences, as in use, are a gross and monstrous invention of later times.

That the received doctrine of purgatory is at variance with Scripture, cruel to the better sort of Christians, and administering deceitful comfort to the irreligious.

That the practice of celebrating divine service in an unknown tongue is a great corruption.

That forced confession is an unauthorized and dangerous practice.

That the direct invocation of Saints is a dangerous practice, as tending to give, often actually giving, to creatures the honour and reliance due to the Creator alone.

That there are not seven sacraments.

That the Roman Doctrine of Tradition is unscriptural.

That the claim of the Pope to be Universal Bishop is against Scripture and antiquity.

I might add other points in which also I protest against the Church of Rome, but I think it enough to make my confession in Hall's order, and so leave it. And having done so, I will ask you but one question. Which says more against Popery, the Articles or I? The only severe words in the Articles being, that "the Sacrifice of Masses" "were blasphemous fables and dangerous deceits;"[35] whereas the "doctrines concerning Purgatory, Pardons, Worshipping, and Adoration, as well of Images as of relics, and also Invocation of saints," are only called "a fond thing", vainly invented, and grounded upon no warranty of Scripture, but rather repugnant to the Word of GOD."[36]

L. Thank you for this conversation; from which I hope to draw matter for reflection, though the subject seems to involve such deep historical research, I hardly know how to find my way through it.

OXFORD,
The Feast of St. James

TRACT 41

VIA MEDIA
No. II[1]

LAICUS. I am come for some further conversation with you; or rather, for another exposition of your views on Church matters. I am not well read enough to argue with you; nor, on the other hand, do I profess to admit all you say: but I want, if you will let me, to get at your opinions. So will you lecture if I give the subjects?

Clericus. To lecture, as you call it, is quite beyond me, since at best I have but a smattering of reading in Church history. The more's the pity; though I have as much as a great many others: for ignorance of our historical position as Churchmen is one of the especial evils of the day. Yet even with a little knowledge, I am able to see certain facts which seem quite inconsistent with notions at present received. For my *practice*, I should be ashamed of myself if I guided it by any theories. Here the letter and spirit of the Liturgy is my direction, as it is of all classes of Churchmen, high and low. Yet, though I do not lay a great stress on such views as I gather from history, it is to my mind a strong confirmation of them, that they just account for and illustrate the conclusions to which I am led by plain obedience to my ordination vows.

L. If you only wish to keep to the Liturgy, not to change, what did you mean the other day by those ominous words, in which you suggested the need of a *second Reformation*?

C. Because I think the Church has in a measure *forgotten* its own principles, as declared in the 16th century; nay under stranger circumstances, as far as I know, than have attended any of the errors and corruptions of the Papists. Grievous as are their declensions from primitive usage, I never heard in any case of their practice directly contradicting their Services; – whereas we go on lamenting once a year the absence of discipline in our Church, yet do not even dream of taking any one step towards its restoration. Again, we confess in the Articles the excommunication is a solemn duty of the Church under certain circumstances, and that the excommunicated person must be openly reconciled by penance, before he is acknowledged by the faithful as a brother;[2] yet excommunication, I am told, is now a civil process, which takes place as a matter of course at a certain stage of certain law proceedings. Here a *reformation* is needed.

L. Only of discipline, not of doctrine.

C. Again, when the Church, with an unprecedented confidence, bound herself hand and foot, and made herself over to the civil power, in order to escape the Pope, she did not expect that infidels (as it has lately been hinted) would be suffered to have the absolute disposal of the crown patronage.[3]

L. This, again, might be considered matter of discipline. Our Reformation in the 16th century was one in matters of *faith*; and therefore we do not need a second Reformation *in the same sense* in which we needed it first.

C. In what points would you say the Church's *faith* was reformed in the 16th century?

L. Take the then received belief in purgatory and pardons, which alone was a sufficient corruption to call for a reformation.

C. I conceive the presumption of the Popish doctrine on these points to lie in adding to the means of salvation set forth in Scripture. ALMIGHTY GOD has said that His Son's merits shall wash away all sin, and that they shall be conveyed to believers through the two Sacraments;[4] whereas, the Church of Rome has added other ways of gaining heaven.

L. Granted. The belief in purgatory and pardons disparages the sufficiency, first of CHRIST'S merits, next of His appointed sacraments.

C. And by "received" belief, I suppose you mean that it was the popular belief, which clergy and laity acted on, not that it was necessarily contained in any particular doctrinal formulary.

L. Proceed.

C. Do you not suppose that there are multitudes both among clergy and laity at the present day, who disparage, not indeed CHRIST'S merits, but the Sacraments He has appointed? and if so, is not their error so far the same in kind as that of the Romish Church – the preferring Abana and Pharpar to the waters of Jordan?[5] Take the Sacrament of Baptism. Have not some denominations of schismatics *invented* a rite of dedication instead of Baptism?[6] and do not Churchmen find themselves under the temptation of countenancing this Papist-like presumption? – Again, there is a well-known sect, which denies both Baptism and the LORD'S Supper.[7] A Churchman must believe its members to be altogether *external* to the fold of CHRIST. Whatever benevolent works they may be able to show, still, if we receive the Church's doctrine concerning the means "generally necessary to salvation,"[8] we must consider such persons to be mere heathens, except in knowledge. Nor would there not be an outcry raised, as if I were uncharitable, did I refuse the rites of burial to such an one?

L. This censure would not proceed from the better informed or the rulers of our Church.

C. Happily, we are not yet so corrupted as at the era of the Reformation. Our Prelates are still sound, and know the difference between what is modern and what ancient. Yet is not the mode of viewing the subject I refer to, a *growing* one?

and how does it differ from the presumption of the Papists? In both cases, the power of CHRIST'S Sacraments is denied; in the one case by the unbelief of restlessness and fear, in the other by the unbelief of profaneness.

L. Well, supposing I grant that the Church of this day is in a measure faulty in faith and discipline; more or less, of course, according to the diocese and neighbourhood. Now in the next place, what do you mean by your *Reformation*?

C. I would do what our reformers in the 16th century did: they did not touch the existing documents of doctrine – there was no occasion – they kept the creeds as they were; but they *added* protests against the corruptions of faith, worship, and discipline, which had grown up round them. I would have the Church do the same thing now, if I could: she should not *change* the Articles, she should *add* to them: add protests against the erastianism and latitudinarianism[9] which have incrusted them. I would have her append to the Catechism a section on the power of the Church.

L. You have not mentioned any corruptions at present in *worship*; do you consider that there are such, as well as errors of faith and discipline?

C. Our Liturgy keeps us right in the main, yet there are what may be considered such, though for the most part occasional. To board over the altar of a Church, place an orchestra there of playhouse singers, and take money at the doors, seems to me as great an outrage as to sprinkle the forehead with holy water and to carry lighted tapers in a procession.

L. Do not speak so harshly of what has often been done piously. George the third was a patron of concerts in our Cathedrals.[10]

C. Far be it from my mind to dare to arraign the actions of that religious king! The same deed is of a different nature at different times and under different circumstances. Music in a Church may as reverentially subserve the feelings of devotion as pictures or architecture; but *it may not*.

L. You could not prevent such a desecration by adding a fortieth article to the thirty-nine.

C. Not directly: yet though there is no article directly condemning religious processions, they have nevertheless been discontinued. In like manner, were an article framed (to speak by way of illustration) declaratory of the sanctity of places set apart to the worship of GOD and the reception of the saints that sleep, doubtless Churchmen would be saved from many profane feelings and practices of the day, which they give into unawares, such as the holding vestries in Churches,[11] the flocking to preachers rather than to sacraments, (as if the servant were above the Master, who is LORD over His own house), the luxurious and fashionable fitting up of town Churches, the proposal to allow schismatics to hold their meetings in them,[12] the off-hand project of pulling them down for the convenience of streets and roads, and the wanton preference (for it frequently is wanton) of unconsecrated places, whether for preaching to the poor, or for administering sacred rites to the rich.

L. It is visionary to talk of such a reformation: the people would not endure it.

C. It is; but I am not *advocating* it, I am but raising a *protest*. I say this ought to be, "because of the angels,"[1] but I do not hope to persuade others to think as I do.

L. I think I quite understand the ground you take. You consider that, as time goes on, fresh and fresh articles of faith are necessary to secure the Church's purity, according to the rise of successive heresies and errors. These articles are all hidden, as it were, in the Church's bosom, from the first, and brought out into form according to the occasion.[13] Such was the Nicene explanation against Arius; the English Articles against Popery: and such are those now called for in this Age of schism, to meet the new heresy, which denies the

[1] 1 Cor. 11:10.

holy Catholic Church – the heresy of Hoadley, and others like him.

C. Yes – and let it never be forgotten that, whatever were the errors of the Convocation of our Church in the beginning of the 18th century, it expired in an attempt to brand the doctrines of Hoadley.[14] May the day be merely delayed!

L. I understand you further to say, that you hold to the Reformers as far as they have spoken out in our formularies, which at the same time you consider as incomplete; that the doctrines which may appear wanting in the Articles such as the Apostolical Commission, are the doctrines of the Church Catholic; doctrines, which a member of the Church holds *as such,* prior to subscription; that, moreover they are quite consistent with our Articles, sometimes are even implied in them, and sometimes are clearly contained in the Liturgy, though not in the Articles, as the Apostolical Commission in the Ordination Service; lastly, that we are clearly bound to believe, and all of us do believe, as essential, doctrines which nevertheless are not contained in the Articles, as *e.g.* the inspiration of Holy Scripture.

C. Yes – and further I maintain, that, while I fully concur in the Articles, as far as they go, those who call one Papist, do not acquiesce in the doctrine of the Liturgy.

L. This is a subject I especially wish drawn out. You threw out some hints about it the other day, though I cannot say you convinced me. I have misgivings, after all, that our Reformers only *began* their work. I do not say they saw the tendency and issue of their opinions; but surely, had they lived, and had the opportunity of doing more, they would have given into much more liberal notions (as they are called) than you are disposed to concede. It is not by producing a rubric, or an insulated passage from the services, that you can destroy this impression. Such instances only show they were inconsistent, which I will grant. Still, is not the genius of our formularies towards a more latitudinarian system than they reach?

C. I will cheerfully meet you on the grounds you propose. Let us carefully examine the Liturgy in its separate parts. I think it will decide the point which I contended for the other day, viz. that we are more Protestant than our Reformers.

L. What do you mean by Protestant in your present use of the word?

C. A number of distinct doctrines are included in the notion of Protestantism: and as to all these, our Church has taken the VIA MEDIA between it and Popery. At present I will use it in the sense most apposite to the topics we have been discussing; viz. as the religion of so-called freedom and independence, as hating superstition, suspicious of forms, jealous of priestcraft,[15] advocating heart-worship;[16] characteristics, which admit of a good or a bad interpretation, but which, understood as they are instanced in the majority of persons who are zealous for what is called Protestant doctrine, are (I maintain) very inconsistent with the Liturgy of our Church. Now let us begin with the Confirmation Service.

L. Will not the Baptismal be more to your purpose? In it regeneration is connected with the *formal* act of sprinkling a little water on the head of an infant.

C. It is true; but I would rather shew the general spirit of the Services, than take those obvious instances which, it seems, you can find out for yourself. Is it not certain that a modern Protestant, even though he granted that children were regenerated in Baptism, would, in the Confirmation Service, have inserted some address to them about the necessity of spiritual renovation, of becoming new creatures, &c.? I do not say such warning has not its appropriateness; nor do I propose to account for our Church's not giving it; but is it not quite certain that the present *prevailing* temper in the Church would have given it, judging from the prayers and sermons of the day, and that the Liturgy does not? Were that day like this, would it not have been deemed formal and cold, and to argue a want of spiritual-mindedness, to have proposed a declaration, such as has been actually adopted, that "to the end that Confirmation may be ministered to the more edifying of such as shall receive it . . . none hereafter shall be confirmed, but such as can *say* the Creed, the LORD'S Prayer, and the Ten Commandments," &c.; nothing being said of a change of heart, or spiritual affections? And yet, upon this mere external profession, the children receive the imposition of the Bishop's hands, "to *certify* them by this sign, of GOD'S favour and gracious goodness towards them."

L. From the line you are adopting, I see you will find Services more Anti-Protestant (in the *modern* sense of Protestant) than that for Confirmation.

C. Take again, the Catechism. What can be more technical and formal (as the persons I speak of would say), than the division of our duties into our duty towards GOD and our duty towards our neighbor? Indeed, would not the very word *duty* be objected to by them, as obscuring the evangelical character of Christianity? Why is there no mention of newness of heart, of appropriating the mercies of redemption, and such like phrases, which are now common among so-called Protestants? Why no mention of justifying faith?

L. Faith is mentioned in an earlier part of the Catechism.

C. Yes, and it affords a remarkable contrast to the modern use of the word. Nowadays the *prominent* notion conveyed by it regards its properties, whether spiritual or not, warm, heartfelt, vital. But in the Catechism, the *prominent* notion is that of its *object*, the believing "*all* the *Articles* of the Christian faith," according to the Apostle's declaration that it is "the substance of things hoped for, the evidence of things not seen."[17]

L. I understand; and the Creed is also introduced into the service for Baptism.

C. And still more remarkably into the Order for Visiting the Sick: more remarkably, both because of the season when it is introduced, when a Christian is drawing near his end, and also as being a preparation for the Absolution. Most comfortable, truly, in his last hour, is such a distinct rehearsal of the great truths on which the Christian has fed by faith, with thanksgiving, all his life long; yet it surely would not have suggested itself to a modern Protestant. He would rather have instituted some more searching examination (as he would call it,) of the state of the sick man's heart; whereas the whole of the minister's exhortation is what the modern school calls cold and formal. It ends thus: – "I require you to examine yourself and your estate, both towards GOD and man; so that, accusing and condemning yourself for your own faults, you may find mercy at our heavenly FATHER's hand for CHRIST's sake, and not be accused and condemned in that fearful judgment. Therefore, I shall rehearse to you the *Articles* of our Faith, *that you may know whether you believe as a Christian man should or no.*"

L. You observe the Rubric which follows: it speaks of a further examination.

C. True; still it is what would now be called formal and external.

L. Yet it mentions a great number of topics for examination: – "Whether he repent him truly of his sins, and be in charity with all the world; exhorting him to forgive, from the bottom of his heart, all persons that have offended him; and, if he hath offended any other, to ask them forgiveness; and where he hath done injury or wrong to any man, that he make amends to the uttermost of his power. And, if he hath not before disposed of his goods, let him then be admonished to make his will, and to declare his debts, what he oweth, and what is owing to him; for the better discharging of his conscience, and the quietness of his executors. Here is an exhortation to repentance, charity, forgiveness of injuries, humbleness of mind, honesty, and justice. What could be added?

C. You will be told that worldly and spiritual matters are mixed together; and, besides, not a word said of looking to CHRIST, resting on Him, and renovation of heart. Such are the expressions which modern Protestantism would have considered necessary, and would have inserted as such. They are good words; still they are not those which our Church considers *the words* for a sick-bed *examination*. She does not give them the prominence which is now given them. She adopts a manner of address which savours of what is now called formality. That our Church was no stranger to the more solemn kind of language, which persons now use on every occasion, is evident from the prayer "for a sick person, when there appeareth small hope of recovery," and "the commendatory prayer;" still she adopts the other as her ordinary manner.

L. I can corroborate what you just now observed about the Creed, by what I lately read in some book or books, advocating a revision of the Liturgy. It was vehemently objected to the Apostles' Creed, that it contained no confession of the doctrine of the atonement, nor (I think) of original sin!

C. It is well to see persons consistent. When they go full lengths, they startle others, and, perhaps (please GOD) themselves. Indeed, I wish men would stop a while, and seriously reflect whether the mere verbal opposition which exists between their own language and the language of the Services (to say nothing of the difference of spirit) is not a sort of warning to them, if they would take it, against inconsiderately proceeding in their present course. But nothing is more rare at this day than *quiet* thought. Every one is in a bustle, being bent to do a great deal. We preach, and run from house to house;[18] we do not pray or meditate. But to return. Next, consider the first exhortation to the Communion: would it not be called, if I said it in discourse of my own, dark, cold, and formal? "The way and means thereto [to receive worthily] is, – First, to examine your lives and conversations by the rule of GOD'S *Commandments, &c. ...* Therefore, if any of you be a *blasphemer* of GOD, an *hinderer* or *slanderer* of His word, an *adulterer,* or be in *malice,* or *envy,* or any other grievous crime, repent you of your sins," &c. Now this is what is called, in some quarters, by a great abuse of terms, "mere morality."

L. If I understand you, the Liturgy, all along, speaks of the Gospel dispensation, under which it is our blessedness to live, as being, at the same time, a moral *law*; that this is its *prominent* view; and that external observances and definite acts of duty are made the means and the tests of faith.

C. Yes; and that, in thus speaking, it runs quite counter to the innovating spirit of this day, which proceeds rashly forward on large and general views, – sweeps alone, with one or two prominent doctrines, to the comparative neglect of the details of duty, and drops articles of faith and positive and ceremonial observances, as beneath the attention of a spiritual Christian, as monastic and superstitious, as forms, as minor points, as technical, lip-worship, narrow-minded, and bigoted. – Next, consider the wording of one part of the Commination Service: – "He was wounded for our offences, and smitten for our wickedness.[19] Let us, therefore, return unto Him, who is the merciful receiver of all true penitent sinners; assuring ourselves that He is ready to receive us, and most willing to pardon us, if we come unto Him with faithful repentance; if we will submit ourselves unto Him, and *from henceforth walk* in His ways; if we will take *His easy yoke and light burden*[20] upon us, to follow Him in *lowliness, patience, and charity,* and be *ordered* by the governance of His Holy Spirit; seeking *always His glory*, and *serving* Him duly in our vocation with thanksgiving: *This if we do,* CHRIST *will deliver us from the curse of the law,*"[21] &c. Did another say this, he would be accused by the Protestant of this day of interfering with the doctrine of justification by faith.

L. You have not spoken of the daily service of the Church or of the Litany.

C. I should have more remarks to make than I like to trouble you with. First, I should observe on the absence of what are now called, *exclusively*, the great Protestant doctrines, or, at least, of the modes of expression in which it is at present the fashion to convey them. For instance, the Collects are *summaries* of doctrine, yet I believe they do not once mention what has sometimes been called the articulus stantis vel cadentis Ecclesiae.[22] This proves to me that, true and important as this doctrine is in a controversial statement, its direct mention is not so apposite in devotional and practical subjects as modern Protestants of our Church would consider it. Next, consider the general Confession, which prays simply that GOD would grant us "hereafter to live a godly, righteous, and sober life." *Righteous and sober!* alas! this is the very sort of words which Protestants consider superficial; good, *as far as they go,* but nothing more. In like manner, the priest, in the Absolution, bids us pray GOD "that the rest of our life hereafter may be *pure and holy.*" But I have given instances enough to explain my meaning about the Services generally: you can continue the examination for yourself. I will direct your notice to but one instance more, – the Introduction of the Psalms into the Daily Service. Do you think a modern Protestant would have introduced them into it?

L. They are inspired.

C. Yes, but they are also what is called *Jewish.* I do certainly think, I cannot doubt, that had the Liturgy been compiled in a day like this, but a *selection* of them, at most, would have been inserted in it, though they were all used in the primitive worship from the very first. Do we not hear objections to using them in singing, and a wish to substitute hymns? Is not this a proof what judgment would have been passed on their introduction into the Service, by reformers of the nineteenth century? First, the imprecatory Psalms, as they are called, would have been set aside, of course.[23]

L. Yes, I cannot doubt it; though some of them, at least, are prophetic, and expressly ascribed in the New Testament to the inspiration of the Holy Ghost.

C. And surely numerous other passages would have been pronounced unsuitable to the spiritual faith of a Christian. I mean all such as speak of our being rewarded according to the cleanness of our hands, and of our walking innocently,[24] and of the LORD's doing well to those that are good and true of heart.[25] Indeed, this doctrine is so much the characteristic of that heavenly book, that I hardly see any part of it could have been retained but what is clearly predictive of the Messiah.

L. I shall now take my leave, with many thanks, and will think over what you have said. However, have you not been labouring superfluously? We know all along that the *Puritans* of Hooker's[26] time *did* object to the Prayer Book: there was no need of proving that.

C. I am not speaking of those who would admit they were Puritans; but of that arrogant Protestant spirit (so called) of the day, in and out of the Church (if it is possible to say what is in and what is out), which thinks it takes bold and large views, and would fain ride over the superstitions and formalities which it thinks it sees in those who (I maintain) hold to the old Catholic faith; and, as seeing that this spirit is coming on apace, I cry out betimes whatever comes of it, that corruptions are pouring in, which sooner or later will need a SECOND REFORMATION.

OXFORD,
The Feast of St. Bartholomew

TRACT 45

THE GROUNDS OF OUR FAITH

EVERY system of theology has its dangers, its tendencies toward evil. Systems short of the truth have this tendency inherent in themselves, and in process of time discover it, and work out the anticipated evil, which is but the legitimate though latent consequence of their principles. Thus, we may consider the present state of Geneva the fair result on the long run of the system of self-will which was established there in the sixteenth century.[1] But even the one true system of religion has its dangers on all sides, from the weakness of its recipients, who pervert it. Thus the Holy Catholic doctrines, in which the Church was set up, were corrupted into Popery, not legitimately, or necessarily, but by various external causes acting on human corruption, in the lapse of many ages. St. Paul's command of obedience to rulers, was changed into the tyrannical rule of *one* Bishop over *all* countries; his recommendation of an unmarried life, for certain religious objects, was made a rule of celibacy in the case of the clergy. Now let us ask, what are the bad *tendencies* of Protestantism? for this is a question which nearly concerns ourselves. We are nearly 300 years from its rise in this country; have any evils yet shown themselves from it? It is not here proposed to examine the question at large; but a hint on one part of the subject, may be made in answer to it.

At the Reformation, the authority of the Church was discarded by the spirit then predominant among Protestants, and Scripture was considered as the sole document for ascertaining and proving our faith. The question immediately arose, "Is this or that doctrine in Scripture?" – and in consequence, various intellectual Gifts, such as argumentative subtlety, critical acumen, knowledge of the languages, rose in importance, and became the interpreters of Christian truth. Exposition lay through controversy. Now the natural effect of disputation is to make us shun all but the strongest proofs, those which an adversary will find substantial impediments in his line of reasoning; and, therefore, to generate a cautious discriminative turn of thought, to fix in the mind a *standard* of proof simulating demonstration, and to make light of mere probabilities. This intellectual habit, resulting from controversy, would also arise from the peculiar exercises of thought necessary for the accurate scholar or antiquarian. It followed, that in course of time, all the delicate shades of truth and falsehood, the unobtrusive indications of GOD'S will, the low tones of the "still small voice"[2] in which Scripture abounds, were rudely rejected; the crumbs from the rich man's table,[3] which Faith eagerly looks about for, were despised by the proud-hearted intellectualist, who (as if it were a favour in him to accept the Gospel,) would be content with nothing short of certainty, and ridiculed as superstitious and illogical whatever did not approve itself to his own cold, hard, and unimpassioned temper. For instance, if the case of Lydia, of the jailer, of Stephanas,[4] were brought to show our LORD'S wish as to the baptism of households, the actions of his apostles to *interpret* his own commands, it was answered; "This is no satisfactory *proof*; it is not certain that everyone of those households was not himself a believer; it is not *certain* there were any children among them:" – though surely, in as many as *three* households, the probability is on the side which the Church has taken, especially viewing the texts in connexion with our Saviour's words, "Suffer the little children,"[5] &c. Again, while the observance of the Lord's day was grounded upon the *practice* of the apostles, it was somehow felt, that this proof was not *strong enough* to bind the mass of Protestants: and so the chief argument now in use is one drawn from the Jewish law, viz. the direct Scripture *command*, contained in the fourth commandment.

Our Saviour has noticed the frame of mind here alluded to, in Mark 8:11, 12, where his feelings and judgment upon it are also told us: – "And the Pharisees came forth, and began to question Him, seeking of Him *a sign from heaven,* tempting Him. And *He sighed deeply in His spirit,* and saith, Why doth this generation seek after a sign? Verily I say unto you, *There shall no sign be given unto his generation.*[6] And he left them."

We are warned against the same hard, intractable temper in the book of Psalms: "I will inform thee, and teach thee in the way wherein thou shalt go; *and I will guide thee with Mine eye.* Be ye not like to horse or mule, *which have no understanding;* whose mouths must be held *with bit and bridle,* lest they fall upon thee." (Ps. 32:9, 10). This stubborn spirit, which yields to nothing but violence, is determined to *feel* Christ's yoke ere it submits to it, will not see except in broad daylight, and like the servant who hid his talent, is ever making excuses, murmuring, doubting, grudging obedience, and stifling docile and open-hearted faith, is the spirit of ultra-Protestantism, *i.e.* that spirit, to which the principles of Protestantism *tend*, and which they have in a great measure *realized*. On this subject the reader may consult Nos. 4, 8 and 19 of this series of Tracts.

Now to apply this to the doctrines, at present so much undervalued, which it is the especial object of these Tracts to enforce.

When a clergyman has spoken strongly in defence of Episcopacy, a hearer will go away saying, that there is much very able and forcible, much very eloquent and excellent, in what he has just heard; but after all, *there is very little about Episcopacy in Scripture.* This is the point to which a shrewd, clear-headed reasoner will resort, – *"after all;"* we come round and round to it; the doctrine advocated is plausible, useful, generally received hitherto; – granted, – *but* Scripture says very little about it.

Now it cannot be for a moment allowed, that Scripture *contains* little on the subject of Church government; though it may readily be granted that it *obtrudes* on the reader little about it. The doctrine is in it, not on it; not on the surface. This need not be proved here, since the subject has been variously considered in former Numbers of this series.[7] But it may be useful in a few words to show how the state of the argument and controversy concerning Episcopacy, illustrates the above remarks, and how parallel it is to the state in which other religious truths are found, which no Churchman ventures to dispute.

1. Now in the first place, let us suppose, *for the sake of argument,* that Episcopacy is in fact not at all mentioned in Scripture: even then it would be our duty to receive it. Why? because the first Christians received it. If we wish to get at the truth, no matter how we get at it, *if* we get at it. If it be a fact, that the earliest Christian communities were universally Episcopal, it is a reason for our maintaining Episcopacy; and *in proportion* to our conviction, is it incumbent on us to maintain it.

Nor can it be fairly dismissed as a non-essential, or ordinance indifferent and mutable, though formerly existing over Christendom; for, *who* made us judges of essentials and non-essentials? *how* do we determine them? In the Jewish law, the slightest transgression of the commandment was followed by the penalty of death; vide Lev. 8:35; 10:6. Does not its universality imply a necessary connexion with how the business of the world depends on punctuality in minutes;

how "great a matter" a mere spark dropped on gunpowder "kindleth."[8]

But, it may be urged, that we Protestants believe the *Scriptures* to contain the whole rule of duty. – Certainly not; they constitute a rule of *faith*, not a rule of *practice;* a rule of *doctrine*, not a rule of *conduct* or *discipline*. Where (*e.g.*) are we told in Scripture, that gambling is wrong? or again, suicide? Our article is precise: "Holy Scripture containeth all things necessary to salvation, so that whatsoever is not read therein, &c. is not to be required of any man, that it should be *believed* as an article of *faith*." Again it says, that the Apocrypha is *not* to be applied "to establish any *doctrine*," implying that *this* is the use of the canonical books.

2. However, let us pass from this argument, which is but founded on a *supposition*, that the Episcopacy is not enjoined in Scripture. Suppose we maintain, as we may well maintain, that it *is* enjoined in Scripture. An objector will say, that, at all events it is but obscurely contained therein, and cannot be drawn out from it without a great deal of delicate care and skill. Here comes in the cooperation of that principle of *faith* in opposition to *criticism*, which was above explained; the principle of being content with a little light, where we cannot obtain sunshine. If it is *probably* pleasing to CHRIST, let us maintain it. Now take a parallel case: *e.g.* the practice of infant baptism; where is this *enjoined* in Scripture? Nowhere. Why do we observe it? Because the primitive Church observed it, and because the Apostles in Scripture *appear* to have sanctioned it, though this is not altogether clear *from* Scripture. In a difficult case we do as well as we can, and carefully *study* what is most agreeable to our LORD and SAVIOUR. This is how our Church expresses it in the 27th Article: "The baptism of young children is in any wise to be retained in the Church, as *most agreeable* with the institution of CHRIST." This is true wariness and Christian caution; very different from that spurious caution which ultra-

Protestantism exercises. Let a man only be consistent, and apply the same judgment in the case of Episcopacy: let him consider whether the duty of keeping to Bishops, be not "*most agreeable* with the institution of CHRIST." If, indeed, he denies this altogether, these remarks do not apply, but they are addressed to waverers, and falsely moderate men, who cannot deny, that the evidence of Scripture is in favour of Churchmen, but say it is not strong enough. They say, if Almighty GOD had intended an uniformity in Church Government among Christians, he would have spoken more clearly.

Now if they carried on this line of argument consistently, they would not baptize their children: happily they are inconsistent. It would be more happy still, were they consistent on the other side; and as they baptized their children, because it is safer to observe than to omit the sacrament, did they also keep to the Church , as the safer side. The received practice, then, of infant baptism seems a final answer to all who quarrel with the Scripture evidence for Episcopacy.

3. But further still, infant baptism, like Episcopacy, is but a case of *discipline*. What shall we say, when we consider that a case of *doctrine*, necessary doctrine, doctrine the very highest and most sacred, may be produced, where the argument lies as little on the surface of Scripture, − where the proof, though *most conclusive* is as indirect and circuitous as that for Episcopacy; viz. the doctrine of the Trinity? Where is this solemn and comfortable mystery formally stated in Scripture, as we find it in the creeds? Why is it not? Let a man consider whether all the *objections* which he urges against the Scripture argument for Episcopacy may not be turned against his own belief in the Trinity. It is a happy thing for themselves that men are inconsistent; yet it is miserable to advocate and establish a *principle*, which, not in their own case indeed, but in the case of others who learnt of them, leads to Socinianism. This being considered, can we any longer

wonder at the awful fact, that the descendants of Calvin, the first Presbyterian, are at the present day in the number of those who have denied the LORD who bought them?

OXFORD,
The Feast of St. Luke.

TRACT 47

THE VISIBLE CHURCH

LETTER IV

My Dear ——

I am sorry my delay has been so considerable in answering your remarks on my Letters on the Church. Indeed it has been ungrateful in me, for you have given me an attention unusual with the multitude of religious persons; who, instead of receiving the arguments of others in simplicity and candour, seem to have a certain number of types, or measures of professing Christians, set up in their minds, to one or other of which they consider every one they meet with belongs, and who, accordingly, directly they hear an opinion advanced, begin to consider whether the speaker be a No. 1, 2, or 3, and having rapidly determined this, treat his views with consideration or disregard, as it may be. I am far from saying our knowledge of a person's character and principles should not influence our judgment of his arguments; certainly it should have great weight. I consider the cry "measures not men," to be one of the many mistakes of the day.[1] At the same time there is surely a contrary extreme, the fault of fancying we can easily look through men, and *understand* what each individual is; and arbitrary classing of the whole Christian family under but two or three *counte-nances*, and mistaking one man's doctrine for another's. You at least have not called me an Arminian,[2] or a high Churchman, or a Borderer,[3] or one of this or that school, and so dismissed me.

To pass from this subject. You tell me that in my zeal in advocating the doctrine of the Church Catholic and Apostolic, I "use expressions and make assumptions which imply that the Dissenters are without the pale of salvation."[4] So let me explain myself on these points.

You say that my doctrine of the one Catholic Church in effect excludes Dissenters, nay, Presbyterians, from salvation. Far from it. Do not think of me as of one who makes theories for himself in his closet, who governs himself by book-maxims, and who, as being secluded from the world, has not temptation to let his sympathies for individuals rise against his abstract positions, and can afford to be hard-hearted, and to condemn by wholesale the multitudes in various sects and parties whom he never saw. I have known those among Presbyterians whose piety, resignation, cheerfulness, and affection, under trying circumstances, have been such, as to make me say to myself, on the thoughts of my own higher privileges, "Woe unto thee Chorazin, woe unto thee Bethsaida !"[5] Where little is given, little will be required;[6] and that return, though little, has its own peculiar loveliness, as an acceptable sacrifice to Him who singled out for praise the widow's two mites.[7] Was not Israel apostate from the days of Jeroboam; yet were there not even in the reign of Ahab, seven thousand souls who were "reserved," an elect remnant?[8] Does any Churchman wish to place the Presbyterians, where, as in Scotland, their form of Christianity is in occupation, in a worse condition under the Gospel, than Ephraim held under the Law? Had not the ten tribes the schools of the Prophets, and has not Scotland at least the word of God? Yet what would be thought of the Jew who had maintained that Jeroboam and his kingdom were in no guilt? and shall we from a false charity, from a fear of condemning the elect seven thousand, scruple to say that Presbyterianism has severed itself from our temple privileges, and undervalue the line of Levi and the house of Aaron?

Consider our Saviour's discourse with the woman of Samaria. While by conversing with her he tacitly condemned the Jews' conduct in refusing to hold intercourse with the Samaritans, yet He plainly declared that "salvation was of the Jews." "Ye worship ye know not what;" He says, "we know what we worship."[9] Can we conceive of His making light of the difference between Jew and Samaritan?

Further, if to whom much is given, of him much will be required, how is it safe for us to make light of our privileges, if we have them? is not this to reject the birth-right? to hide our talent under a napkin?[10] When we say that God has done more for us than for the Presbyterians, this indeed *may* lie hid (to our great shame) among those who have not themselves the certainty of our especial approaches to His glorious majesty. Was not Elijah sent to a widow of Sarepta? did not Elisha cure Naaman?[11] are not these instances set forward by our Lord Himself as warnings to us "not to be high-minded but to fear;"[12] and, again, as a gracious consolation when we think of our less favoured brethren? Where is the narrowness of view and feeling which you impute to me? Why may I not speak out, in order at once to admonish myself, and to attempt to reclaim to a more excellent way those who are at present severed from the true Church?

And what has here been said of an established Presbyterianism, is true (in its degree) of dissent, when it has become hereditary, and embodied in institutions.

Further, it is surely parallel with the order of Divine Providence that there should be a variety, a sort of graduated scale, in His method of dispensing His favour of Christ. So far from its being a strange thing that Protestant sects are not "in Christ," in the same fullness that we are, it is more accordant to the scheme of the world that they should lie between us and heathenism. It would be strange if there were but two states, one absolutely of favour, one of disfavour. Take the world at large, one form of paganism is better than another. The North American Indians are theists, and as such more privileged than polytheists. Mahometanism is a better religion than Hinduism. One may believe that long established dissent affords to such as are born and bred in it a sort of pretext, and is attended with a portion of blessing, (where there is no means of knowing better,) which does not attach to those who *cause* divisions, found sects, or wantonly wander from the Church to the Meeting House; – that what is called an orthodox sect has a share of Divine favour, which is utterly withheld from heresy. I am not speaking of the next world, where we shall all find ourselves as individuals, and where there will be but two states, but of existing bodies or societies. On the other hand, why should the corruptions of Rome led us to deny her Divine privileges, when even the idolatry of Judah did not forfeit hers, annul her temple-sacrifice, or level her to Israel?

I say all this, merely for the purpose of suggesting to those who are "weak"[13] some idea of possible modes in which Eternal Wisdom may reconcile the exuberance of His mercy in Christ to the whole race of man, with the placing of it in its fullness in a certain ordained society and ministry. For myself I prefer to rely upon the simple word of truth, of which Scripture is the depository, and since Christ has told me to preach the *whole* counsel of God, to do so fearlessly and without doubting; not being careful to find ways of smoothing strange appearances in His counsels, and of obviating difficulties, being aware on the one hand that His thoughts are not our thoughts, nor our ways His ways,[14] and on the other, that He is ever justified in His sayings, and overcomes when He is judged.[15]

Ever yours, &c.

Oxford,
The Feast of All Saints.

TRACT 71

ON THE CONTROVERSY WITH THE ROMANISTS[1]

(Against Romanism – No. 1)

THE controversy with the Romanists has overtaken us "like a summer's cloud."[2] FWe find ourselves in various parts of the country preparing for it, yet, when we look back, we cannot trace the steps by which we arrived at our present position. We do not recollect what our feelings were this time last year on the subject, – what was the state of our apprehensions and anticipations. All we know is, that here we are, from long security ignorant why we are not Roman Catholics, and they on the other hand are said to be spreading and strengthening on all sides of us,[3] vaunting of their success, real or apparent, and taunting us with our inability to argue with them.

The Gospel of CHRIST is not a matter of mere argument; it does not follow that we are wrong, and they are right, because we cannot defend ourselves. But we cannot claim to direct the faith of others, we cannot check the progress of what we account error, we cannot be secure (humanly speaking) against the weakness of our own hearts some future day, unless we have learned to analyze and to state formally our own reasons for believing what we do believe, and thus have fixed our creed in our memories and our judgments. This is the especial duty of Christian Ministers, who as St. Paul in the Acts of the Apostles, must be ready to dispute, whether Jews or Greeks. That we are at present very ill practised in this branch of our duty (a point it is scarcely necessary to prove) is owing in a very great measure to the protection and favour which have long been extended to the English clergy by the state. Statesmen have felt that it was their interest to maintain a Church, which, absorbing into itself a great portion of the religious feeling of the country, sobers and chastens what it has so attracted, and suppresses by its weight the intractable elements which it cannot persuade; and, while preventing the political mischief resulting whether from fanaticism or pride, is altogether free from those formidable qualities which distinguish the ecclesiastical genius of Rome. Thus the clergy have been in that peaceful condition in which the civil magistrate supersedes the necessity of struggling for life and ascendency; and amid their privileges it is not wonderful that they should have grown secure, and have neglected to inform themselves on subjects on which they were not called to dispute. It must be added, too, that a feeling of the untenable nature of the Romanistic doctrines, a contempt for their arguments, and a notion that they could never prevail in an educated country,[4] have not a little contributed to expose us to our present surprise.

In saying all this, it is not forgotten that there is still scattered about the Church much learning upon the subject of Romanism, and much intelligent opposition to it: nor on the other hand does the present series of Tracts pretend to be more than an attempt towards a suitable consideration of it on the part of persons who feel themselves, and see in others a deficiency of information.

It will be the object, then, of these Tracts, should it be allowed the editor to fulfil his present intention, to consider variously, the *one* question, with which we are likely to be attacked, why, in matters of fact, we remain separate from Rome. Some general remarks on the line of argument hence resulting, will be the subject of this paper.

Our position is this. We are seated at our own posts, engaged in our own work, secular or religious, interfering with no one, and anticipating no harm, when we hear of the encroachments of Romanism around us.[5] We can but honour all good Romanists for such aggression; it marks their earnestness, their confidence in their own cause, and their charity towards those whom they consider in error. We need not be bitter against them; moderation and candour, are virtues under all circumstances. Yet for all that, we may resist them manfully, when they assail us. This then, I say, is our position, a defensive one; we are assailed, and we defend ourselves and our flocks. There is no plea for calling on us in England to do more than this, – to defend ourselves. We are under no constraint to go out of our way spontaneously to prove charges against the Romanists, but when asked about our faith, we give a reason why we are this way of thinking, and not that. This makes our task in the controversy incomparably easier, than if we were forced to exhibit an offensive front, or volunteered articles of impeachment against the rival communion. "Let every man abide in the same calling wherein he was called,"[6] is St. Paul's direction. We find ourselves under the Anglican regimen; let every one of us, cleric and layman, remain in it, till our opponents have shown cause why we should change, till we have reason to suspect we are wrong. The *onus probandi* plainly lies with them. This, I say, simplifies our argument, as allowing us to content ourselves with less of controversy than otherwise would be incumbent on us. We have the strength of possession and prescription. We are not *obliged* to prove them incurably corrupt and heretical; no, nor our own system unexceptionable. It is in our power, if we will, to take very low ground; it is quite enough to ascertain that reasons cannot be brought why we should go over from our side to theirs.

But besides this, there are the Apostle's injunctions against disorder. Did we go over to the Roman Catholics, we should be fomenting divisions among ourselves, which

would be a *prima facie* case against us. Of course, there are
cases where division is justifiable. Did we believe, for
instance, the English Church to be absolutely heretical, and
Romanism to be pure and Catholic, it would be a duty, as
the lesser evil, to take part in a division which truth
demanded. Else it would be a sin. Those dissenters, who
consider union with the state to be apostasy, or the doctrine
of baptismal regeneration a heresy, are wrong, not in that
they separate from us, but in that they so think.[7]

And further, a debt of gratitude to that particular branch of
the Church Catholic through which GOD made us
Christians, by which we were new born, instructed, and (if
so be) ordained to the ministerial office; a debt of reverence
and affection towards the saints of that Church; the tie of that
invisible communion with the dead as well as the living, into
which the sacraments introduce us; the memory of our great
teachers, champions, and confessors, now in Paradise, especially those of the seventeenth century, – Hammond's name
alone, were there no other, or Hooker's,[8] or Ken's,[9] – bind
us to the Anglican Church, by cords of love,[10] except
something very serious can be proved against it. But this
surely is impossible. The only conceivable causes for leaving
its communion are, I suppose, the two following; first, that it
is involved in some damnable heresy, or secondly, that it is
not in possession of the sacraments: and so far we join issue
with the Romanist, for these are among the chief points
which he attempts to prove against us.

However, plain and satisfactory as is this account of our
position, it is not sufficient, for various reasons, to meet the
need of the multitude of men. The really pious and sober
among our flocks will be contented with it. They will
naturally express their suspicion and dislike of any doctrine
new to them, and it will require some considerable body of
proof to convince them that they ought even to open their
ears to it. But it must be recollected that there is a mass of

persons, easily caught by novelty, who will be too impetuous to be restrained by such advice as has been suggested. Curiosity and feverishness of mind do not wait to decide of which side of a dispute the *onus probandi* lies. The same feelings which carry men now to dissent will carry them to Romanism, novelty being an essential stimulant of popular devotion, and the Roman system, to say nothing of the intrinsic majesty and truth which remain in it amid its corruptions, abounding in this and other stimulants of a most potent and effective character. And further, there will ever be a number of refined and affectionate minds, who, disappointed in finding full matter for their devotional feelings in the English system, as at present conducted, betake themselves, through human frailty, to Rome. Besides *ex parte* statements may easily suggest scruples even to the more sensible and sober portion of the community; and though they will not at all be moved ultimately from the principle above laid down, viz. not the change unless clear reason for change is assigned, yet they may fairly demand of their teachers and guides what they have to say in answer to these statements, which do seem to justify a change, not indeed at once, but in the event of their not being refuted.

Thus then we stand as regards Romanism. Strictly speaking, and in the eyes of soberly religious men, it ought not to be embraced, even could it be made appear in some points superior to (what is now practically) the Anglican system; St. Paul even advising a slave to remain a slave,[11] though he had the option of liberty. If all men were rational, little indeed would be necessary in the way of argument, only so much as would be enough to set right the misconceptions which might arise on the subject in dispute. But the state of things being otherwise, we must consult for men as they are; and in order to meet their necessities, we are obliged to take a more energetic and striking line in the controversy than can in strict logic be required of us, to defend ourselves by an offensive warfare, and to expose our opponents' argument with a view of recommending our own.

This being the state of the case, the arguments to be urged against Romanism, ought to be taken from such parts of the general controversy as bear most upon *practice*, and at the same time keep clear of what is more especially sacred and painful to dispute about. Its adherents' assault on us will turn (it is to be presumed) on strictly practical considerations. They will admit that the English Church approaches in many points very near to themselves, and for that very reason was wrong in separating from them:- that it is in danger far more as being schismatical than as heretical: – that our Lord commanded and predicted that His Church should be one; therefore, that the Roman and the Anglican communions cannot both be His Church, but that one must be external to it: – that the question to be considered by us is, what our *chance* is of being the true Church; and in consequence, of possessing the sacraments: – that we confess Rome to be a branch of CHRIST'S Church, and admit her orders, but that Rome does not acknowledge us; hence that it is safer for us to unite to Rome: – that we are, in matter of fact, cut off from the great body of the Church Catholic, and stand by ourselves: that we suffer all manner of schism and heresy to exist, and to propagate itself among us, which is inconceivable that the true Church, guided by the HOLY SPIRIT should ever do: – that this circumstance, if there were no other, being an inconsistency, involves a *prima facie* case against us, for the consideration of those who are not competent to decide in the matter of doctrine: – that, if our creed were *true*, GOD would prosper us in *maintaining* it, according to the promise:[12] – moreover, were there no other reason, that our forms of administering the sacraments are not such as to make us sure that we receive GOD'S grace in them. These, and the like arguments, we may suppose, will be urged upon the attention of our members, being not of a technical and scholastic, but of a powerfully practical character; and such must be ours to oppose them. Much might be said on this part of the subject. There are a number of arguments which are scarcely more than ingenious exhibitions, such as would be admired in any game where skill is everything, but which as arguments tell only with those on our own side, while an adversary thinks them unfair. Their use is not here denied in matter of fact, viz. in confirming those in an opinion, who already hold it, and wish reasons for it. When a man is (rightly or wrongly) of one particular way of thinking, he needs, and (it may be added) allowably needs very little argument to support him in it to himself. Still it is right that that argument should be substantially sound; substantially, because for many reasons, certain accidental peculiarities in the form of it may be necessary from the peculiarities of his mind, which has been accustomed to move in some one line and not in another. If the argument is radically unreal, or (what may be called) rhetorical or sophistical, it may serve the purpose of encouraging those who are really convinced, though scarcely without doing mischief to them, but certainly it will offend and alienate the more acute and sensible; while those who are in doubt, and who desire some real and substantial ground for their faith, will not bear to be put off with such shadows. Thus, for instance, to meet the Romanists' charge against us of scepticism, because we do not believe this or that portion of their doctrine, an argument has been sustained by Protestants, in proof of the scepticism of the Roman system. Who does not see that Romanism erring on the whole in superstition not in unbelief, this is an unreal argument, which will but offend doubting and distressed minds, as if they were played with; however plausibly and successfully it might be sustained in a trial of strength, and whatever justice there really may be in it? Nor is it becoming, over and above its inexpediency, to dispute for victory not for truth, and to be careless of the manner in which we urge conclusions, however sound and important. Again, when it is said that the saints cannot hear our prayers, unless GOD reveal them to them; so that Almighty GOD, on the Romanist theory, conveys from us to them those requests which they are to ask back again of Him for us, we are certainly using an unreal, because an unscriptural argument; Moses on the Mount having the sin of his people revealed to him by GOD, that he in turn might intercede with GOD for them.[13] Indeed, it is through him "in whom we live, and move, and have our being,"[14] that we are able in *this* life to hear the requests of each other, and to present them to him in prayer. Such an argument then, while shocking and profane to the feelings of a Romanist, is shallow even in the judgment of a philosopher. Here may be mentioned the unwarrantable application of texts, such as that of John 5:39: "Search the Scriptures" in disproof of the Roman doctrine that the Apostles have handed down some necessary truths by Catholic Tradition;[15] or again, Eccles. 11:3: "If the tree falls towards the south, or towards the north, in the place where the tree falleth, there it shall be," in disproof of Purgatory.

The arguments, then, which we use, must be such as are likely to convince serious and earnest minds, which are really seeking for the truth, not amusing themselves with intellectual combats, or desiring to support an existing opinion anyhow. However popular these latter methods may be, of however long standing, however easy both to find and to use, they are a scandal; and, while they lower our religious standard from the first, they are sure of hurting our cause in the end.[16] But again, our arguments must not only be true and practical, they must avoid being abstract arguments and on abstract points. For instance, it will do us little good with the common run of men, in the question of the Pope's power, to draw the distinction, true though it is, between his primacy in honour and authority, and his sovereignty or his universal jurisdiction. The force of the distinction is not here questioned, but it will be unintelligible to minds unpractised in ecclesiastical history. Either the Bishop of Rome has really a claim upon our deference, or he has not; so it will be urged; and our safe argument at the present day will lie in waiving the question altogether, and saying that, even if he has, according to the primitive rule, ever so much authority, (and that he has some, e.g. a precedence over other bishops, need not be denied,) that it is in matter of fact altogether suspended, and under abeyance, while he holds a corrupt system against which it is our duty to protest. At present all will see he ought to have "no jurisdiction, power, superiority, preeminence, our authority, within this realm."[17] It will be enough to settle his legitimate claims, and make distinctions, when he removes all existing impediments to our acknowledging him; it will be time enough to argue on this subject, after first deciding the other points of the controversy. Again the question of the Rule of Faith is an abstract one to men in general, till the progress of the controversy opens its bearings upon them. True, the intelligible argument of ultra-Protestantism may be taken, and we may say, "The Bible, and nothing but the Bible." But this is an unthankful rejection of another great gift, equally from GOD, such as no true Anglican can tolerate. If, on the other hand, we proceed to take the sounder view, that the Bible is the *record* of necessary truth, or of matters of faith, and the Church Catholic's tradition is the *interpreter* of it, then we are involved in refined and intricate questions, which are uninteresting and uninfluential with the many. It is not till they are made to see that certain notable tenets of Romanism depend solely on the Apocrypha, or on tradition, not on Scripture, that they will understand why the question of the Rule of Faith is an important one.

It has been already said that our arguments must also keep clear, as much as possible, of the subjects more especially

sacred. This is our privilege in these latter days, if we understand it, that with all that is painful in our controversies, we
are spared that distressing necessity which lay upon the early
Church, of discussing questions relative to the divine nature.
The doctrines of the Trinity and Incarnation, form a most
distressing subject of discussion, for two reasons; first, as
involving the direct contemplation of heavenly things, when
one should wish to bow the head and be silent; next as
leading to arguments about things possible and impossible
with GOD, that is (practically) to a rationalistic line of
thought. How He is Three and yet One, how He could
become man, what were the peculiarities of that union, how
He could be everywhere as GOD, yet locally present as man,
in what sense GOD could be said to suffer, die, and rise again,
– all these questions were endured as a burden by the early
Christians for our sakes, who come after; and with the
benefit of their victories over error, as if we had borne the
burden and heat of the day,[18] it were perverse indeed in us,
to plunge into needless discussions of the same character.
This consideration will lead us to put into the background
the controversy about the Holy Eucharist, which is almost
certain to lead to profane and rationalistic thoughts in the
minds of many, and cannot well be discussed in words at all,
without the sacrifice of "godly fear,"[19] while it is well nigh
anticipated by the ancient statements, and the determinations
of the Church concerning the Incarnation.[1] It is true that
learned men, such as Stillingfleet, have drawn lines of distinction between the doctrine of transubstantiation and that high
mystery;[20] but the question is, whether they are so level to
the intelligence of the many, as to secure the Anglican
disputant from fostering irreverence, whether in himself or
his hearers, if he ventures on such an argument. If transub-

---

[1] e.g, Chrysost. ep. ad Caesar. Vid. Hooker's remarks on the subject, Eccl.
Pol. v.

stantiation must be opposed, it is in another way; by showing, as may well be done, and as Stillingfleet himself has done, that, in matter of fact, it was not the doctrine of the early Church, but an innovation at such or such a time; a line of discussion which requires learning both to receive and to appreciate.

In order to illustrate the above view, the following are selected by way of specimen of those *practical grievances*, to which Christians are subjected in the Roman Communion, and which should be put in the foreground in the controversy.

1. The denial of the cup to the laity.[21] Considering the great importance of the holy eucharist to our salvation, this seems a very serious consideration for those who seek to be saved. Our Lord says, "Except ye eat the flesh of the Son of Man and drink His blood, ye have no life in you."[22] If it be recriminated, as it sometimes is, that we think it no risk to sprinkle instead of immersing in baptism,[23] it is obvious to answer that we not only do not forbid, we enjoin immersion; we only do not forbid sprinkling in the case of infants, and that the laity are defrauded, if defrauded, by their own fault, or the fault of the age, not the fault of the Church.

2. The necessity of the priest's intention to the validity of the Sacraments. The Church of Rome has determined, that a Sacrament does not confer grace unless the priest means to do so; so that if he be an unbeliever, nay, if he, from malice or other cause, withholds his intention, it is not a means of salvation.[24] Now, considering what the Romanists themselves will admit, the great practical corruption of the Church at various times, – considering that infidels and profligates have been in the Papal Chair, and in other high stations, – who can answer, on the Church of Rome's own ground, that there is still preserved to it the Apostolical succession as conveyed in its sacrament of Orders ? what individual can answer that he himself really receives in the

consecrated wafer, even that moiety of the great Christian blessing which alone remain to him in the Roman Communion? *We* indeed, believe, (and with comfort) that the administration of the Sacrament is effectual in those Churches, in spite of their undermining their own claim to the gift. Still let it be recollected no one can become a Romanist without believing that the communion he has joined has no truer certainty of possessing it than that which, probably on the very account of its uncertainty in this matter, he has deemed it right to abandon.

3. The necessity of confession. By the council of Trent, every member of the Church must confess himself to a priest once a year at least. This confession extends to all mortal sins, that is to all sins which either are done willingly or are of any magnitude.[25] Without this confession, which must be accompanied by hearty sorrow for the things confessed, no one can be partaker of the Holy Communion. Here is a third obstacle in the way of our receiving the grace of the Sacraments in the Roman Church, which surely requires our diligent examination, before it be passed over. That there is no such impediment sanctioned in Scripture is plain, yet to believe in it is a point of faith with the Romanist. The practice is grievous enough; but it is not enough to submit to it; you must believe that it is part of the gospel doctrine, or you are committing one of those mortal sins which are to be confessed; and you must believe, moreover, that everyone who does not believe it, is excluded from the hope of salvation. But, not to dwell on the belief in the necessity of confession itself, consider the number of points of faith which the Church of Rome has set up. You must believe every one of them; if you have allowed yourself to doubt anyone of them you must repent of it, and confess it to the priest. If you knowingly omit any one such doubt you have entertained, and much more if you still cherish it, your confession is worse than useless; nay such conduct is consid-

ered sacrilege, or the sin against the Holy Ghost. Further, if, under such circumstances, you partake of the Communion, it is a partaking of it unworthily to your condemnation.[26]

4. The unwarranted anathemas of the Roman Church is a subject to which the last head has led us. Here let us put aside, at present, the prejudice which has been excited in the minds of Protestants, against the principle itself of anathematizing by the variety and comparative unimportance of the subject upon which the Roman Church has applied it in practice. Let us consider merely the state of the case in that Church. Every Romanist is, by the creed of his Church, in mortal sin, unless he believes everyone else excluded from Christian salvation, who, with means of knowing, yet declines any one of those points which have been ruled to be points of faith. If a man for instance, who has had the means of instruction, doubts the Church's power of granting indulgences, he is exposed, according to the Romanists, to eternal ruin.[27] Now this consideration, one would think, ought to weigh with those of our own Church who may be half converts to the Roman; not that our own salvation is not our first concern, but that such cruelty as this is, such narrowing the Scripture terms of salvation, (for no one can say this doctrine is found in Scripture,) is a presumption against the purity of that Church's teaching. But a further reflection may be added to the above. Such as we have not had an opportunity of knowing the truth, are, it must be observed, *not* exposed to this condemnation. This at first sight would seem a comfort to those whose relations and friends have died in Protestantism. But observe, the Church of Rome, we know, retains the practice of praying for the dead. It will be natural for a convert from Protestantism, first of all to turn his thoughts towards those dearest relations, say his parents, who have lived and died in involuntary ignorance of Catholicism. He is not allowed to do so, he can only pray for the souls in *Purgatory*; none have the privilege of being in Purgatory but

such as have died in the communion of the Roman Church, and his parents died in Protestantism.[28]

5. Purgatory may be mentioned as another grievous doctrine of Romanism. Here again, if Scripture, as interpreted by tradition, taught it, we should be bound to receive it; but knowing as we do that even St. Austin questioned the doctrine in the fifth century, we may well suspect the evidence for it.[29] The doctrine is this; that a certain definite punishment is exacted by Almighty GOD for all sins committed after baptism; and that they who have not by sufferings in this life, whether trouble, penance, and the like, run through it, must complete it during the intermediate state in a place called Purgatory. Again, all who die in venial sin, that is in sins of infirmity, such as are short of mortal, go to Purgatory also. Now what a light does this throw upon the death of beloved and revered friends! Instead of their "resting from their labours,"[30] as Scripture says, there are (ordinarily speaking,) none who have not to pass a time of trial and purification, and, as Romanists commonly believe, in fire, or a torment analogous to fire. There is no one who can for himself look forward to death with hope and humble thankfulness. Tell the sufferer upon a sick bed that his earthly pangs are to terminate in Purgatory, what comfort can he draw from religion? If it be said that it is a comfort in the case of bad men who have begun to repent on their death bed; this is true, I do not deny it; still the doctrine, in accordance, be it observed, with the ultra- Protestantism of this age, evidently sacrifices the better part of the community to the less deserving. Should the foregoing reasoning seem to dwell too much on the question of comfortableness and uncomfortableness, not of truth, I reply, first, that I have already stated that Scripture, as interpreted by tradition, does not teach the doctrine; next that I am arguing against the Romanists, who are accustomed to recommend their communion on the very ground of its being safer, more satisfactory, and more comfortable.

6. The Invocation of Saints. Here again the *practice* should be considered, not the *theory*. Scripture speaks clearly and solemnly about CHRIST as the sole mediator.[31] When prayer to the Saints is recommended *at all times and places,* as ever present guardians, and their good works pleaded in God's sight, is not this such an infringement upon the plain word of God, such a violation of our allegiance to our only Saviour, as must needs be an insult to Him? His honour He will not give to another.[32] Can we with a safe conscience do it? Should we act thus in a parallel case even with an early friend? Does not St. John's example warn us against falling down before angels?[33] Does not St. Paul warn us against a voluntary humility and worshipping of angels?[34] And are not these texts *indications* of GOD's will, which ought to guide our conduct? Is it not *safest* not to pay them this extra-ordinary honour? As an illustration of what I mean, I will quote the blessing pronounced by the Pope[35] on the assembled people at Easter.

"The holy Apostles Peter and Paul, from whom has been derived our power and authority, themselves intercede for us to the LORD. Amen.

For the prayers and righteous deeds of the blessed Mary, ever Virgin, of the blessed Michael the Archangel, of the blessed John the Baptist, of the holy Apostles Peter and Paul and of all the saints, Almighty GOD have mercy upon you, and JESUS CHRIST absolve you from all your sins, and bring you to life everlasting. Amen.

The Almighty and merciful LORD, grant to you pardon, absolu-tion, and remission of all your sins, time for true and fruitful penitence, an ever penitent heart, and amendment of life, the grace and comfort of the HOLY GHOST, and final perseverance in good works. Amen.

And the blessing of GOD Almighty, the FATHER, the SON, and the HOLY GHOST, come down upon you and remain with you always. Amen."

7. The Worship of Images might here be added to these instances of grievances which Christians endure in the Communion of Rome, were it not that in England, its rulers seem, at present, to have suspended the practice out of policy, though it is expressly recommended by the Council of Trent, as if an edifying usage.[36] In consequence of this decree of the Church, no one can become a Romanist, without implying his belief that the usage is edifying and right, and this itself is a grievance, even though the usage be in this or that place dispensed with.

Such are the *subjects* which, it is conceived, may be profitably brought into question remains to be discussed; viz. What the *sources* are, whence we are to gather our opinions of Popery. Here the Romanists complain of their opponents, that, instead of referring to the authoritative documents of their Church, Protestants avail themselves of any errors or excesses of individuals in it, as if the Church were responsible for acts or opinions which it does not enjoin. Thus the legends of relics, superstitions about images, the cruelty of particular prelates or kings, or the accidental fury of a populace, are unfairly imputed to the Church itself. Again the profligacy of Popes, at various periods, is made an argument against their religious pretensions as successors to St. Peter; whereas Caiaphas himself had the gift of prophecy,[37] and it is, as they consider, a memorable and instructive circumstance, that in matter of fact, among their worst popes are found the instruments, in God's hand of some of the most salutary acts of the Church. Accordingly they claim to be judged of their formal documents, especially by the decrees of the Council of Trent.

Now here we shall find the truth to lie between the two contending parties. Candour will oblige us to grant that the mere acts of individuals should not be imputed to the body; certainly no member of the English Church can in common prudence as well as propriety do otherwise, since he is exposed

to an immediate retort, in consequence of the errors and irreg-
ularities which have in Protestant times occurred among
ourselves. King Henry VIII, the first promoter of the
Reformation, is surely no representative of our faith or feelings; nor Hoadley,[38] in a later age, who was suffered to enjoy
his episcopate for 46 years; to say nothing of the various parties
and schools which have existed, and do exist, among us.

So much then must be granted to the Romanists; yet not
so much as they themselves desire. For though the acts of
individuals are not the acts of the Church, yet they may be
the results, and therefore illustrations of its principles. We
cannot consent then to confine ourselves to a mere reference
to the text of the Tridentine decrees, as Romanists would
have us, apart from the teaching of their doctors, and the
practice of the Church, which are surely the legitimate
comment upon them. The case stands as follows. A certain
system of teaching and practice has existed in the churches of
the Roman communion for many centuries; this system was
discriminated and fixed in all its outlines at the Council of
Trent. It is therefore not unnatural, or rather it is the
procedure we adopt in any historical research, to take the
general opinions and conduct of the Church in elucidation of
their Synodal decrees; just as we take the tradition of the
Church Catholic and Apostolic as the legitimate interpreter
of Scripture, or of the Apostles' Creed. On the other hand, it
is as natural that these decrees, being necessarily concise and
guarded, should be much less objectionable than the actual
system they represent. It is not wonderful then, yet it is
unreasonable, that Romanists should protest against our
going beyond these decrees in adducing evidence of their
Church's doctrine, on the ground that nothing more than an
assent to them is requisite for communion with her: *e.g.* the
Creed of Pope Pius, which is framed upon the Tridentine
decrees, and is the Roman Creed of Communion, only says
"I firmly hold there is a Purgatory, and that souls therein

detained are aided by the prayers of the faithful,"[39] nothing being said of its being a place of punishment, nothing, or all of nothing, which doses not admit of being explained of merely an intermediate state.

Now supposing we found ourselves in the Roman Communion, of course it would be a great relief to find that we were not bound to believe more than this vague statement, nor should we (I conceive) on account of the received interpretation about Purgatory superadded to it, be obliged to leave our Church. But it is another matter entirely, whether we who are external to that Church, are not bound to consider it as one whole system, written and unwritten, defined indeed and adjusted by general state-ments, but not limited to them or coincident with them.

The conduct of the Catholics during the troubles of Arianism affords us a parallel case, and a direction in this question. The Arian Creeds were often quite unexception-able, differing from the orthodox only in this, that they omitted the celebrated word ´ομοουσιον[40] and in conse-quence did not obviate the possibility of that perverse explanation of them, which in fact their framers adopted. Why then did the Catholics refuse to subscribe to them? Why did they rather submit to banishment from one end of the Roman world to the other? Why did they become confessors and martyrs? The answer is ready. They inter-preted the language of the creeds by the professed opinions of their framers. They would not allow error to be intro-duced into the Church by an artifice. On the other hand, when at Ariminum they were seduced into a subscription of one of these creeds, though unobjectionable in its wording, their opponents triumphed, and circulated the news that the Catholic world had come over to their opinion.[41] It may be added that, in consequence, ever since that era, phrases have been banished from the language of theology which hereto-fore had been innocently used by orthodox teachers.

Apply this to the case of Romanism. We are not indeed
allowed to take at random the accidental doctrine or practice
of this or that age, as an explanation of the decrees of the
Latin Church; but when we see clearly that certain of these
decrees have a natural tendency to produce certain evils,
when we see those evils actually existing far and wide in that
Church, in different nations and ages, existing especially
where the system is allowed to act most freely, and only
absent where external checks are present, sanctioned
moreover by its celebrated teachers and expositors, and
advocated by its controversialists with the tacit consent of the
whole body, under such circumstances surely it is not unfair
to consider our case parallel to that of the Catholics during
the ascendancy of Arianism. Surely it is not unfair in such a
case to interpret the formal document of belief by the
realized form of it in the Church, and to apprehend that, did
we express our assent to the creed of Pope Pius, we should
find ourselves bound hand and foot,[42] as the fathers at
Ariminum, to the corruptions of those who profess it.

To take the instances of the Adoration of Images and the
Invocation of Saints. The Tridentine decrees declares that it
is good and useful suppliantly to invoke the Saints, and that
the Images of CHRIST, and the Blessed Virgin, and the other
Saints should "receive due honour and veneration;"[43]
words, which themselves go to the very verge of what could
be received by the cautious Christian, though possibly
admitting of a honest interpretation. Now we known in
matters of fact that in various parts of the Roman Church, a
worship approaching to idolatrous is actually paid to Saints
and Images, in countries very different from each other, as
for instance, Italy and the Netherlands, and has been countenanced by eminent men and doctors, and that, without any
serious or successful protest from any quarter: further that,
though there may be countries where no scandal of the kind
exists, yet these are such as have, in their neighbourhood to

Protestantism, a practical restraint upon the natural tendency of their system.

Moreover, the silence which has been observed, age after age by the Roman Church, as regards these excesses, is a point deserving of serious attention; – for two reasons: first, because of the very solemn warnings pronounced by our LORD and His Apostle, against those who introduce scandals into the Church,[44] warnings which seem almost prophetic of such as exist in the Latin branches of it. Next it must be considered that the Roman Church has had the power to denounce and extirpate them. Not to mention its use of the its Apostolical powers in other matters, it has had the civil power at its command, as it has shown in the case of errors which less called for its interference; all of which shows it has not felt sensitively on the subject of this particular evil.

This may be suitably illustrated by an example. Wake,[45] in his controversy on the subject of Bossuet's[46] Exposition, observed that a Jesuit named Crasset, had published an account of the worship due to the Virgin Mary, quite opposed to that which Bossuet had expounded as the doctrine of the Roman Church. Bossuet replies, "I have not read the book, but neither did I ever hear it mentioned there was anything in it contrary to mine, and that Father would be much troubled I should think there was." Wake, in answer, expresses his great surprise that Bossuet should not have heard any mention of a fact so notorious.

Bossuet replies, "I still continue to say that I have never read Father Crasset's[47] book which they bring against me." "I will only add here," he continues, "that Father Crasset himself, troubled and offended that anyone should report his doctrine to be different from mine, has made complaints to me; and in a preface to the second edition of his book, has declared, that he varied in nothing from me, unless perhaps in the manner of expression; which, whether it be so or no, I leave them to examine, who will please to give themselves the trouble." Bossuet is known as the special champion of a more moderate exposition of the Romanistic doctrine than that which has generally been put upon them. Now he either did agree with the Jesuit or he did not. If he did, not a word more need be said against the Roman doctrine, as will appear when I proceed to quote his words; if he did not, let the reader judge of the peculiar sensitiveness of a faith, (as illustrated in a prelate, who for his high qualities is a very fair representative of his Church,) which can anathematize a denial of Purgatory, or a disapproval of the Invocation of Saints, yet can pass *sub silentio*[48] a class of blasphemies, of which the following extracts are an instance.

It must be first observed that Father Crasset's book is an answer to a Cologne tract entitled, "Salutary Advertisements of the Blessed Virgin to her indiscreet Adorers;" which is said, by Wake, truly or not, (for this is nothing to the purpose,) to agree with Bossuet in its exposition of doctrine. This tract was sent into the world with the approbation of the Suffragan Bishop of Cologne, of the Vicar-general, the Censure of Ghent, the Canons and Divines of Mechlin, the Universithy of Louvain, and the Bishop of Tournay. Father Crasset's answer was printed at Paris, licensed by the Provincial, approved by three fathers of the Jesuit's body appointed to examine it, and authorized by the King. I mention these circumstances to show that this controversy was not conducted in a corner; to which I may add that, according to Crasset, learned men of various nations had also written against the Tract, that the Holy See had condemned the author, and that Spain had prohibited him and his word from its dominions. We have nothing to do with the doctrine of this Tract, good or bad, but let us see what this Crasset's doctrine is on the other hand, thus put forth by the Jesuits in a notorious controversy, and accepted on hearsay by Bossuet, with a studious abstinence from the sight of it after the matter of it had been brought before him.

"Whether a Christian that is devout towards the Blessed Virgin can be damned.

Answer. The servants of the Blessed Virgin have an assurance, morally infallible, that they shall be saved.

"Whether GOD ever refuses anything to the Blessed Virgin?

Answer. 1. The Prayers of a Mother so humble and respectful are esteemed a command by the Son so sweet and so obedient. 2. Being truly our Saviour's mother, as well in heaven as she was on earth, she still retains a kind of natural authority over His person, over His goods, and over His omnipotence; so that, as Albertus Magnus[49] says, she can not only entreat Him for the salvation of her servants, but by her motherly authority can command him; and as another expresses it, the power of the Mother and the Son is all one, she being by her omnipotent Son made herself omnipotent.

"Whether the blessed Virgin has ever fetched any out of hell?

Answer. 1. As to purgatory, it is certain that the Virgin has brought several souls from thence, as well as refreshed them whilst they were there. 2. It is certain she has fetched many out of hell: *i.e.* from a state of damnation before they were dead. 3. The Virgin can, and has fetched men that were dead in mortal sin out of hell, by restoring them to life again, that they might repent . . .

"The practice of devotion towards her. 1. To wear her scapulary;[50] which whoso does shall not be damned, but this habit shall be for them a mark of salvation, a safeguard in danger, and a sign of peace and eternal alliance. They that wear this habit, shall be moreover delivered out of Purgatory the Saturday after their death. 2. To enter her congregation.[51] And if any man be minded to save himself, if it is impossible for him to find out any more advantageous means than to enroll himself into these companies. 3. To devote oneself more immediately to her service, &c.

"Woe unto the world because of offences! for it must needs be that offences come, but woe to that man by whom the offence cometh. Wherefore if thy hand or thy foot offend thee, cut them off and cast them from thee: it is better for thee to to enter into life with one eye, rather than having two eyes, to be cast into hell fire."[52]

Bossuet's name has been mentioned in evidence of the

really existing connection between the decrees of Trent and the popular opinions and practices in the Roman Church, as regards the matters they treat of. But the labours of that celebrated divine in the cause of his Church introduce us to very varied and extensive illustrations of another remark which has been incidentally made in the course of our discussion.

It was observed that the legitimate meaning of the Tridentine decrees might be fairly ascertained by comparing together those of the Latin Churches, where the system was allowed to operate freely, and those in which the presence of Protestantism acted as a check upon it. This has been remarkably exemplified in the history of the controversy during the last one hundred and fifty years, that is since the time of Bossuet, who seems to have been nearly[2] the first who put on the Tridentine decrees a meaning more consonant with Primitive Christianity, distinguishing between the doctrines of the Church, and of the Schools. This new interpretation has been widely accepted by the Romanists, and, as far as our own islands are concerned, may be considered to be the received version of their creed; and one should rejoice in any appearance of amelioration in their system, were not the present state of Italy and Spain, where no check exists, an evidence what that system still is, and what, in course of time, it would, in all probability, be among ourselves, did an universal reception of it put an end to restraint which controversy at present imposes on them.

Bossuet's Exposition,[54] which contains the modified doctrine above spoken of, was looked at with great suspicion at Rome, on its first appearance, and was with difficulty acknowledged by the Pope. It is said to have been written originally with the purpose of satisfying Marshall

---

[2] Véron[53] had preceded him in France, and an exposition on the same basis is said to have been published in England in Queen Mary's time.

Turenne,[55] who became, in consequence, a convert to
Romanism. It was circulated in manuscript several years, and
was considered to be of so liberal a complexion, according to
the doctrine of the day,[56] as to scandalize persons of his own
communion, and to lead Protestants to doubt whether the
author dare ever own it. In the year 1671, it was, with
considerable alterations, committed to the Press with the
formal approbation of the Archbishop of Rheims and nine
other Bishops, but on objections being urged against it by the
Sorbonne the press was stopped, and not till after various
alterations was it resumed, with the suppression of the copies
which had already been struck off. It is affirmed by Wake
without contradiction (I believe) from his opponents, that
even with these corrections it was of so novel an appearance
to the Romanists of that day, that an answer from one of
Bossuet's own communion was written to it, before the
Protestants began to move, though the publication was
suppressed. The Roman See at last accorded its approbation,
but not before the conversions which it effected had recommended it to its favour.[3]

It may be instructive to specify some instances of this
change of doctrine, or of interpretation of doctrine, (if it
must so be called,) which Bossuet is accused of introducing.

In the private impression of his Exposition, as the
suppressed portion of the edition may be called, Bossuet says,

"Furthermore, there is nothing so unjust as to accuse the Church of
placing all her piety in these devotions to the Saints; *since on the
contrary she lays no obligation at all on particular persons to join in this
practice* . . . By which it appears clearly that the Church condemns

---

[3] Nine years intervened between its publication and the Pope's approval of
   it. Clement X (1670–1676) refused it absolutely. Several priests were
   rigourously treated for preaching the doctrine contained in it; the
   University of Louvain formally condemned it in 1685. Vid. Mosheim,
   Hist., vol. 5, p. 126, note.

only those who refuse it *out of contempt, or by a spirit of dissension and revolt."*

In the second or published edition, the words printed in italics were omitted, the first clause altogether, and the second with the substitution of *"out of disrespect or error."*

2. Again in the private impression he had said,

"So that it (the Mass) *may very reasonably be called a sacrifice."*

He raised his doctrine in the second as follows:

"So that *there is nothing wanting to it, to make it a true sacrifice."*

In giving these instances, I am far from insinuating that there is any unfairness in such alterations. Earnestly desiring the conversion of Protestants, Bossuet did but attempt to place the doctrines of his Church in the light most acceptable to them. But they seem to show thus much: first that he was engaged in a novel experiment, which circumstances rendered necessary, and was trying how far he might safely go; secondly that he did not carry with him the body of the Gallican[57] divines. In other words, we have no security that this new form of Romanism is more stable than one of the many forms of Protestantism which rise and fall around us in our own country, which are matters of opinion, and depend upon individuals.[4] [58]

3. But again, after all the care bestowed on his work, Bossuet says in his exposition as ultimately published:

"When the Church pays an honour to the Image of an Apostle or Martyr, the intention is not so much to honour the image, as to honour the apostle or martyr in the presence of the image ... Nor do we attribute to them *any other virtue* but that of *exciting in us the remembrance* of those they represent," p. 8.

---

[4] Mosheim observes [ut supra] that none of the attempts to reconcile Protestants to the Church, from Richelieu downwards, were avowed by the Church itself, or much more than the acts of individuals.

To this his Vindicator adds,

"The use we make of images or pictures is purely as *representatives*, or commemorative signs, which call the originals to our remembrance," p. 35.

Now with these passages contrast the words of Bellarmine,[59] who, if any one, might be supposed a trustworthy interpreter of the Roman doctrine.

"The images of Christ and of the saints are to be venerated *not only by accident and improperly, but properly and by themselves,* so that *they themselves are the end of the veneration* [ut ipsae terminent venerationem] as considered in themselves, and *not only as they are copies.*" De Imagin. lib. 2, ch. 21.

Again, in the Pontifical we are instructed that to the wood of the Cross "divine worship *(latria)* is due;"[60] and that saving virtues for soul and body proceed form it; which surely agrees with the doctrine of Bellarmine as contained in the above extract, not with that of Bossuet.

4. The Vindicator of Bossuet speaks of the Mass to the following effect:

"The Council tells us that it was instituted *only to represent* that which was accomplished on the Cross, to perpetuate the memory of it to the end of the world, and apply to us the saving virtue of it, for those sins which we commit every day … When we say that CHRIST is offered in the Mass, we do not understand the word *offer* in the strictest sense, but *as we are said to offer to God what we present before him.* And thus the Church does not doubt to say, that she offers up our Blessed JESUS to His Father in the Eucharist, in which He vouchsafes to render Himself present before Him."

But the Tridentine Fathers say in their Canons that,

"the Mass is a true and proper sacrifice; a sacrifice *not only commemoratory of that of the Cross,* but also truly and properly propitiatory for the dead and the living."[61]

And Bellarmine says,

"A true and real sacrifice requires a true and real death or destruction of the thing sacrificed." De Missa, lib. i, ch. 27.

And then he proceeds to show how this condition of the notion of sacrifice is variously fulfilled in the Mass.

Leaving Bossuet, let us now turn to the history of the controversy in our own country, whether in former or recent times; and here I avail myself of an article of a late lamented Prelate of our Church, in a periodical work ten years since.[5] As to the particular instances adduced, it must be recollected that they are not dwelt on as a sufficient evidence by themselves of that difference of vie between members of the Roman Church at various times and places, which is under consideration, but as mere illustrations of what is presumed to be an historical fact.

The following extract is from Dr. Doyle's[62] Evidence before the Committee of the House of Commons on the subject of Roman Catholic doctrines:

"The Committee find, in a treatise called 'A Vindication of the Roman Catholics', the following curse: 'Cursed is every goddess worshipper, that believes the Virgin Mary to be any more than a creature, that honours her, worships here, or puts his trust in her more than in GOD; that honours her above her Son, or believes that she can in any way command Him.' Is that acknowledged? *Ans.* That is acknowledged; and every Roman Catholic in the world would say with Gother,[63] Accursed be such person."

Such is the received Romanism of the English Papists at this day; and accordingly Dr. Challoner[64] has translated the famous words in the office of the Blessed Virgin:

---

[5] In the *British Critic*, October 1825. [By Charles Lloyd, Bishop of Oxford (1784–1829)].

> "Monstra te esse Matrem
> Sumat per te preces,"

by

> "Exert the *Mother's care*,
>   And us *thy children own*,
> To Him convey our prayer," &c.

On the other hand consider the following passage in the controversy between Jewell and Harding.[65] Jewell accused the Roman Church with teaching that the blessed Virgin could command her Son. Harding replies as follows,

"If now any spiritual man, such as St. Bernard[66] was, deeply considering the great honour and dignity of Christ's mother, do in excess of mind, spiritually sport with her, bidding her to remember that she is a Mother, and that *thereby she has a certain right to command* her Son, and require, in the most sweet manner, that she use her right; is this either impiously or imprudently spoken? Is not he, rather, most impious and imprudent that findeth fault therewith?"

Again, we find in Peter Damiani,[67] a celebrated divine of the eleventh century,

"She approaches to that golden tribunal of divine Majesty, not asking, but commanding, not a handmaid but a Mistress."[6]

Albertus Magnus in like manner,

"Mary prays as a daughter, requests as a sister, commands as a mother."

Another writer says,

---

[6] Prosa, quam Dallaeus allegat, ut invidiam faciat Catholicis, quasi B. Virginem Filio imperare putemus ad Patris dexteram sedenti, non est ab Ecclesia probata, et quibusdam tantum Missalibus olim inserta fuit; quamvis innoxius esset iste loquendi modus, "Jure Matris impera Redemptori," quemadmodum ... Scriptura ait, "Deum obedisse voci hominis," quando orante Josue sol stet. ... Hoc sensu B. Patrus Damiani, &c. Natal. Alex. Hist. Saec. v. Diss. 25. Art. 2. Prop. 2.

"The blessed Virgin, for the salvation of her supplicants, can not only supplicate her Son, as other saints do, but also by her maternal authority command her Son. Therefore the Church prays, 'Monstra te esse Matrem;' as if saying to the Virgin, Supplicate for us after the manner of a command, and with a mother's authority."

After these instances the article from which I cite asks, not unreasonably, "Upon whom does the anathema of Gother fall?"

Another instance of this unsteady, and (if it may so be called) untrustworthy conduct of the Roman Church, occurs in respect to their doctrine of Repentance;[68] which is well pointed out by a recent writer in the British Magazine. His account is as follows.

"The Romish tenet most pregnant with moral mischief is, probably, that which promises salvation to mere Attrition [i.e. sorrow for sin arising from a view of its turpitude, or fear of punishment[69]] ... Now it should be generally known that a Romish divine pressed into argument is very likely to pronounce salvability from Attrition only, as nothing more than a *Scholastic* doctrine, to which his Church does not stand committed. He might be reminded of the Tridentine Catechism, which declares real Contrition, [i.e. hearty sorrow for sin proceeding immediately from the love of GOD above all things, and joined with a firm purpose of amendment,] to be found in very few; and hence deduces the necessity of an *easier way* for the salvation of men in general. His answer would be, that the Catechism is *not a decree of the Council,* and, therefore, *not like one binding as an article of faith.* It is indeed true, that the Council here has spoken more vaguely and guardedly than the Catechism. Pallavincino[70] represents the Trentine Fathers accordingly as intending merely to condemn an opinion of their adversaries, which branded the fear of punishment with baseness ... However a nice scrutiny may dispose of this doctrine, it is in fact broadly asserted in the manual drawn up for instructing ordinary clergymen, under authority of the Trentine Council, though not completed till that body was dissolved.[71] This manual too was promulged under papal sanction, expressly conferred upon the Roman See for that very purpose by the Council. The *Catechismus ad Parochos* has been accordingly ever since, what it was intended to be, a text book for the Romish clergy ... Nor is it doubtful that it speaks the feeling and intention of this council upon the question of Attrition; only the Trentine fathers here knew themselves to be upon treacherous ground, and therefore they discreetly left a vague outline which might be filled up by better, because less responsible hands."[7]

The following are further illustrations of the distinction observed in the Roman Church between Catholic verities and the opinions of the schools. In presenting them to the reader, I have no purpose of denying that there is a distinction really, and that it may properly be insisted on, but I deny it exists in the particular cases; in which what is professed to be but an *opinion*, is more or less the genuine practical meaning of the Tridentine decrees.

"It is *de fide*[72] to believe that there is a purgatory; it is not *de fide* to believe that the fire of purgatory is true and proper, or of the same species as the material element, – or that it is in this or that place, or that it lasts for this or that period. It is *de fide* that the saints may well and profitably be invoked; it is not *de fide* that they hear our prayers, though it be certain and true. It is *de fide* that the relics of the saints should be venerated; it is not *de fide* that these or those relics are genuine. It is *de fide* that man is justified by inherent righteousness; it is not *de fide* that justifying righteousness is a habit or quality."[8]

Enough, perhaps, has now been said on the mode in which it is expedient at the present day to carry on the controversy with Romanism, – which of its doctrines are to be selected for attack, what authorities are to be used in ascertaining them, and what arguments are to be employed against them. Some remarks shall be added before concluding, as to the best mode of conducting the defence of our own Church.

Let it be observed that, in our argument with the

---

[7] *British Magazine,* February 1836.
[8] Annati's *Apparatus ad Theologiam* ... 1,4. (Pietro Annati, 1636–1710).

Romanists, we might, if needful, be very liberal in our confessions about ourselves, without at all embarrassing our position in consequence. While we are able to maintain the claim of our clergy to the ministration of the Sacraments, and our freedom from any deadly heresy, we have nothing to fear from any historical disclosures which the envy of adversaries might contrive against our Church, or from any external appearances which it may present at this day to the superficial observer. Whatever may be the past mistakes of individual members of it, or the tyranny of aliens over it, or its accidental connexion with Protestant persuasions, still these hinder not its having "the ministration of the Word and Sacraments;"[73] and having them, it has sufficient claims on our filial devotion and love. This being understood then, the following remarks are made with a view of showing *how far*, if necessary, we may safely go in our admissions.

1. We may grant in the argument that the English Church has committed mistakes in the practical working of its system; nay is *incomplete* even in its formal doctrine and discipline. We require no enemy to show us the probability of this, seeing that her own Article expressly states that the primitive Churches of Antioch and Alexandria, as well as that of Rome, have erred, "not only in their living and manner of ceremonies, but also in matters of faith."[74] Much more is a Church exposed to imperfection, which embraces but a narrow portion of the Catholic territory, has been at the distance of 1500 to 1800 years from the pure fountains of tradition, and is surrounded by political influences of a highly malignant character.

2. Again, the remark may seem paradoxical at first sight, yet surely it is just that the English Church is for certain deficient in particulars, because it does not profess itself infallible. I mean as follows. Every thoughtful mind must at times have been beset by the following doubt: "*How is it* that the particular Christian body to which I belong *happens* to be the

right one? I hear everyone about me saying *his own* society is alone right, and others wrong: is not everyone as much justified as I am? In other words, the truth is surely nowhere to be found pure, unadulterated and entire, but is shared through the world, each Christian body having a portion of it, none the whole of it." A certain liberalism is commonly the fruit of this perplexity. Men are led on to gratify the pride of human nature, by standing aloof from all systems, forming a truth for themselves, and countenancing this or that denomination of Christians according as each maintains portions of that which they have already assumed to be the truth. Now the primitive Church answered this question, by appealing to the simple fact that all the Apostolic Churches all over the world did agree together. True there were sects in every country, but they bore their own refutation on their forehead, in that they were of recent origin; but all those societies in every country, where the Apostles had founded, did agree together in one, and no time short of the Apostles' could be assigned, with any show of argument, for the rise of their existing doctrine. This doctrine in which they agreed was accordingly called *Catholic* truth, and there was plainly no room at all for asking, "Why should my own Church be more true than another's?" – But at this day, it need not be said, such an evidence is lost, except as regards the articles of the Creeds. It is a very great mercy that the Church Catholic over the world, as descended from the Apostles, does at this day speak one and the same doctrine about the Trinity and Incarnation, as it has always spoken it, excepting in one single point, which rather *probat regulam*[75] than interferes with it, viz. as to the procession of the HOLY GHOST from the SON.[76] With this solitary exception, we have the certainty of possessing the entire truth as regards the high theological doctrines, by an argument which supersedes the necessity of arguing from Scripture against those who oppose them. It is quite impossible that all countries should have

agreed to that which was not Apostolic. They are a number
of concordant witnesses to certain definite truths, and while
their testimony is one and the same from the very first
moment they publicly utter it, so, on the other hand, if there
be bodies which speak otherwise, we can show historically
that they rose later than the Apostles. This majestic evidence,
however, does not extend to any but to the articles of the
Creed, especially those relating to the Trinity and
Incarnation.[9] The primitive Church was never called upon,
whether in Council or by its divines, to pronounce upon
other points of faith, and the later Church has differed about
them; especially about those on which the contest turns
between Romanism and ourselves. Here neither Rome nor
England can in the same sense appeal to *Catholic* testimony;
and, this being the case, a member of the one or the other
Church *might* fairly have the antecedent scruple rise in his
mind, why his own communion should have the *whole* truth,
why on the contrary the rival communion should not have a
share of it, and the truth lie midway between them. This is
the question of a philosophical mind, and the Church of
Rome meets it with a theory, perfectly satisfactory, *provided
only* it be established as a fact, viz. the theory of infallibility.
The actual promise made, as they contend, to St. Peter's
chair as the centre of unity, would undoubtedly *account* for
truth being wholly in the Roman Communion, not in the
English, and solve the antecedent perplexity in question. But
the English Church, taking no such high ground as this,
certainly is open to the force, such as it is, of the objection,
or (as it was just now expressed) on the *prima facie* view of the
case is unlikely to have embraced the *whole counsel* of GOD,[77]

---

[9] By a great misapprehension, the word "Incarnation" here used has been
understood by some readers as if it *excluded* the Atonement; whereas, in its
more Catholic sense, it includes the whole dispensation or οἰκονομία of
Christ's taking flesh.

because she does not assume infallibility; and consequently no surprise or distress should be felt by her dutiful sons, should that turn out to be the fact, which her own principles, rightly understood, would lead them to anticipate. At the same time it must carefully be remembered, that this admission involves no doubt or scepticism as regards the more sacred subjects of theology, of which the Creed is the summary; these having been witnessed from the first by the whole Church, – being witnessed too at this moment, in spite of later corruptions, both by the Latin and Greek Communions.

A consideration has been suggested in the last paragraph on which much might be said on a fitting occasion; it is (what may be called) a great Canon of the Gospel, that Purity of faith depends on the *Sacramentum Unitatis*.[78] Unity is the whole body of the Church, as it is the divinely blessed symbol and pledge of the true faith, so also it is the obvious means (even humanly speaking) of securing it. The *Sacramentum* was first infringed during the quarrels of the Greeks and Latins; it was shattered in that great schism of the sixteenth century which issued in some parts of Europe in the Reformation, in others in the Tridentine Decrees, our own Church keeping the nearest of any to the complete truth. Since that era at least, Truth has not dwelt simply and securely in any visible Tabernacle. This view of the subject will illustrate for us the last words of Bishop Ken[79] as contained in his will: – "As for my religion, I die in the Holy Catholic and Apostolic faith, *professed by the whole Church before the disunion of East and West*; more particularly I die in the communion of the Church of England, *as it stands distinguished from* all Papal and Puritan innovations, and *as it adheres* to the doctrine of the Cross."

3. Another antecedent ground for anticipating wants and imperfections in the English Church lies in the circumstances under which the reformation of its doctrine and worship was

effected. It is now universally admitted as an axiom in ecclesiastical and political matters that sudden and violent changes must be injurious; and though our own revolution of opinion and practice was happily slower and more carefully considered than those of our neighbours, yet it was too much influenced by secular interests, sudden external events, and the will of individuals, to carry with it any vouchers for the perfection and entireness of the religious system thence emerging. The proceedings for instance of 1536,[80] remind us at once of the dangers to which the Church was exposed, and of its providential deliverance from the worst part of them: the articles then framed being, according to Burnett,[81] "in several places corrected and tempered by the King's (Henry's) own hand." Again the precise *structure* of our present liturgy, so primitive and edifying in its *matter*, is confessedly owing to the successive and counteracting influences exerted on it, among others, by Bucer[82] and Queen Elizabeth. The Church did not make the circumstances under which it found itself, and therefore is free from the responsibility of imperfections to which these gave rise. These imperfections followed in two ways. First, the hurry and confusion of the times led, as has been said, to a settlement of religion incomplete and defective: secondly, the people, not duly apprehending even what was soundly propounded as being new to them, and unable to digest healthy food after long desuetude, gave a false meaning to it, went into opposite extremes, and fashioned into unseemly habits and practices those principles which in themselves conveyed a wholesome and edifying doctrine. These considerations cannot fairly be taken in disparagement of the celebrated men who were the instruments of providence in the work, and who doubtless felt far more keenly than is here expressed the perplexities of their situation; but they will serve perhaps to reconcile our minds to our circumstances in these latter ages of the Church, and will cherish in us a sobriety of mind, salutary in itself, and calculated more than anything else to arm us against the arguments of Rome, and to turn us in affection and sympathy towards the afflicted Church, which has been the "Mother of our new-birth."[83] They will but lead us to confess that she is in a measure in that position which we fully ascribe to her Latin sister,[10] *in captivity*; and they will make us understand and duly use the prayers of our wisest doctors and rulers, such as Bishop Andrewes,[84] that GOD would please to "look down upon His holy Catholic and Apostolic Church, *in her captivity*;to visit here once more with His salvation, and to bring her out to serve Him in the beauty of holiness."[11]

4. A further antecedent reason for anticipating practical imperfections in the Anglican system, (and to those mainly allusion is here made), arises from the circumstance that our Articles, so far as distinct from the ancient creeds, are scarcely more than protests against specific existing errors of the 16th century,[85] and neither are nor profess to be a system of doctrine. It is not unnatural however that they should have practically superseded that previous Catholic teaching altogether, which they were but modifying in parts, and, though but corrections, should be mistaken for the system corrected.

These reasonings *prepare* us to acquiesce in much of plausible objection being admissible against our Church, even in the judgment of those who love and defend it.

---

[10] At Rome she wears it, as of old,
   Upon the accursed hill,
By Monarchs clad in gems and gold
   She goes a mourner still, &c. &c.

Speak gently of our sister's fall,
   Who knows but gentle love
May win her, at our patient call,
   The surer way to prove.
                    Keble, *The Christian Year* (1827)
                    [Omitted from VM 2]

[11] Devotions. Liturgy of Jerusalem.

When, however, we proceed to examine what its defects really are, we shall find them to differ from those of Rome in this all-important respect, which indeed has already been in part hinted, that they are but *omissions*. Rome maintains positive errors, and that under the sanction of an anathema; but nothing can be pointed out in the English Church which is not true, as far as it goes, and even when it opposes Rome, with a truly Apostolical toleration, it utters no ban or condemnation against its adherents. On the other hand the omissions, such as they are, or rather obscurities of Anglican doctrine, may be supplied for the most part by each of us for himself, and thus do not interfere with the perfect development of the Christian temper in the hearts of individuals, which is the charge fairly adducible against Romanism. Such for instance is the phraseology used in speaking of the Holy Eucharist, which though on the whole protected safe through a dangerous time by the cautious Ridley,[86] yet in one or two places was clouded by the interpolations of Bucer,[87] through an anxiety to unite all the reformed Churches under episcopal government against Rome. And such is the omission of any direct safeguard in the Articles, against disbelief of the doctrine of Apostolical Succession.

And again, for specimens of the perverse reception by the nation, as above alluded to, of what was innocently intended, I would refer to the popular sense put upon the eleventh article,[88] which though clearly and soundly explained in the Homily on Justification or Salvation, has been taken to countenance the wildest Antinomian doctrine,[89] and is now so associated in the minds of many with this wrong interpretation, as to render almost hopeless the recovery of the true meaning.

And such again is the mischievous error, in which the Church in her formal documents certainly has no share, that we are but one among many *Protestant* bodies, and that the differences between Protestants are of little consequence;

whereas the English Church, as such, is *not* Protestant, only politically, that is, externally, or so far as it has been made an establishment, and subjected to national and foreign influences. It claims to be merely *Reformed*, not Protestant, and it repudiates any fellowship with the mixed multitude which crowd together, whether at home or abroad, under a mere political banner. That this is no novel doctrine, is plain from the emphatic omission of the word Protestant in all our Services, even in that for the fifth of November, as remodeled in the reign of King William;[90] and again from the protest of the Lower House of Convocation at that date, on this very subject, which would have had no force, except as proceeding upon recognized usages. The circumstance here alluded to was as follows. In 1689 the Upper House of Convocation agreed on an address to King William, to thank him "for the grace and goodness expressed in his message, and the zeal shown in it for the *Protestant Religion in general,* and the Church of England in particular." To this phrase the Lower House objected, as importing, as Birch in his Life of Tillotson[91] says, "*their owning common union with the foreign Protestants.*" A conference between the two houses ensued, when the Bishops supported their wording of the address, on the ground that the Protestant Religion was the known denomination of the *common doctrine* of such parts of the West as had separated from Rome. The Lower House proposed, with other alterations of the passage, the words "Protestant Churches" for "Protestant Religion," being unwilling to acknowledge religion as separate from the Church. The Upper House in turn amended thus, – "the interests of the Protestant Religion in *this* and *all other* Protestant Churches;" but the Lower House, still jealous of any diminution of the English Church by this comparison with foreign Protestants, persisted in their opposition, and gained at length that the address, after thanking the King for his zeal for the Church of England, should proceed to anticipate, that thereby "the interests of the Protestant Religion in" [not "this and" but] "all other Protestant Churches would be better secured." Birch adds, "the King well understood why this address omitted the thanks which the Bishops had recommended, for . . . the zeal which he had shown for the Protestant Religion; and *why there was not expression of tenderness to the Dissenters, and but a cool regard to the Protestant Churches.*"

Another great *practical error* of members of our Church, has been their mode of defending its doctrines; and this has arisen, not from any direction of the Church itself, but, as it would appear, from the mistake, already mentioned, of the specific protests contained in its Articles for that Catholic system, which is the rightful inheritance of it as well as other branches of the Church. We have indeed too often fought the Romanists on wrong grounds, and given up to them the high principles maintained by the early Church. We have tacitly yielded the major premise of our opponents' argument, when we should have denied the fact expressed in the minor. For instance; they have maintained that Transubstantiation was an Apostolical doctrine, as having been ever taught everywhere in the Church. We instead of denying this fact as regards Transubstantiation, have acted as if it mattered very little whether it were true or not, (whereas the principle is most true and valuable,) and have proceeded to oppose Transubstantiation on supposed grounds of *reason*. Again, we have argued for the sole Canonicity of the Bible to the exclusion of tradition, not on the ground that the Fathers so held it (which would be an irrefragable argument,) but on some supposed internal witness of Scripture to the fact, or some abstract and antecedent reasons against the Canonicity of unwritten teaching. Once more, we have urged the *unscripturalness* of image worship as its only condemnation; a mode of argument, which I am very far indeed from pronouncing untenable, but which opens the door to a multitude of refined distinctions and pleas; whereas the way lay clear before us to appeal to *history*, to appeal to the usage of the early Church Catholic, to review the circumstance of the introduction of image worship, the Iconoclast controversy, the Council of Frankfort,[92] and the late reception of the corruption of the West.

So much then, on the objections which may be urged against the English Church, which relate either to mere *omissions* not positive errors, or again to faults in the *practical working* of the system, and are in these respects dissimilar from those which lie against the Church of Rome, and which relate to clear and direct perversions and corruptions of divine truth. Should it, however, be asked, *whence* our knowledge of the truth should be derived, since there is so much of meagerness and mistake in our more popular expounders of it, it may be replied, first, that the writings of the Fathers contain abundant directions how to ascertain it; next, that their directions are distinctly propounded and supported by our Divines of the seventeenth century, though little comparatively at present is known concerning these great authors. Nor could a more acceptable or important service be done to our Church at the present moment, than the publication of some systematic introduction to theology, embodying an illustrating the great and concordant principles and doctrines set forth by Hammond,[93] Taylor,[94] and their brethren before and after them.

Lastly, should it be inquired whether this admission of incompleteness in our own system does not lead to projects of change and reform, it must be answered plainly in the negative. The admission has but reference to the question of *abstract* perfection; as a practical matter, it will bed our wisdom to enjoy what GOD'S good providence has left us, lest, striving to obtain more, we lose what we still possess.

OXFORD,
The Feast of the Circumcision

TRACT 73

ON THE INTRODUCTION OF RATIONALISTIC PRINCIPLES INTO RELIGION[1]

It is not intended in the following pages to enter into any general view of so large a subject as Rationalism, nor to attempt any philosophical account of it; but, after defining it sufficiently for the purpose in hand, to direct attention to a very peculiar and subtle form of it existing covertly in the popular religion of this day. With this view two writers, not of our own Church, though of British origin, shall pass under review, Mr. Erskine[2] and Mr. Jacob Abbott.[3]

This is the first time that a discussion of (what may be called) a *personal* nature has appeared in these Tracts, which have been confined to the delineation and enforcement of *principles* and *doctrines*. However, in this case, while it was important to protest against certain views of the day, it was found that this could not be intelligibly done, without referring to the individuals who have inculcated them. Of these the two authors above mentioned seemed at once the most influential and the most original; and Mr. Abbott being a foreigner, and Mr. Erskine having written sixteen years since, there seemed a possibility of introducing their names without seriously encroaching on the province of a Review.

It will be my business first to explain what I mean by Rationalism, and then to illustrate the description given of it from the writings of the two authors in question.

§1. *The Rationalistic and the Catholic Spirit compared together.*

To Rationalize[4] is to ask for *reasons* out of place; to ask improperly how we are to *account* for certain things, to be unwilling to believe them unless they can be accounted for, i.e. referred to something else as a cause, to some existing system as harmonizing with them or taking them up into itself. Again, since whatever is assigned as the reason for the original fact canvassed, admits in turn of a like question being raised about itself, unless it be ascertainable by the senses, and be the subject of personal experience, Rationalism is bound properly to pursue onward its course of investigation on this principle, and not to stop till it can directly or ultimately refer to self as a witness, whatever is offered to its acceptance. Thus it is characterized by two peculiarities; its loves of systematizing, and its basing its system upon personal experience, on the evidence of sense. In both respects it stands opposed to what is commonly understood by the word Faith, or belief in Testimony; for which it deliberately substitutes System (or what is popularly called Reason) and Sight.

I have said that to act the Rationalist is to be unduly set upon *accounting* for what is offered for our acceptance; *unduly*, for to seek reasons for what is told us, is natural and innocent in itself. When we are informed that this or that event has happened, we are not satisfied to take it as an isolated fact; we are inquisitive about it; we are prompted to refer it, if possible, to something we already know, to incorporate it into the connected family of truths or facts which we have already received. We like to ascertain its position relatively to other things, to view it in connection with them, to reduce it to a place in the series of what is called cause and effect. There is no harm in all this, until we insist upon receiving this *satisfaction* as a necessary condition of believing what is presented for our acceptance, until we set up our existing system of knowledge as a legitimate test of the credibility of testimony, until we claim to be told the mode of reconciling alleged truths to other truths already known, the *how* they are, and *why* they are; and then we Rationalize.

When the rich lord in Samaria said, "Though God shall make windows in heaven, shall this thing be?"[5] he rationalized, as professing his inability to discover *how* Elisha's prophecy was to be fulfilled, and thinking in this way to excuse his unbelief. When Naaman objected to bathe in Jordan, it was on the ground of his not seeing the *means* by which Jordan was to cure his leprosy above the rivers of Damascus.[6] "*How* can these things be?" was the objection of Nicodemus to the doctrine of regeneration;[7] and when the doctrine of the Holy Communion was first announced, "the Jews strove among themselves," in answer to their Divine Informant, "saying *How* can this man give us His flesh to eat?"[8] When St. Thomas doubted of our LORD's resurrection, though his reason for so doing is not given, it plainly lay in the astonishing, unaccountable nature of such an event. A like desire of judging for oneself is discernible in the original fall of man. Eve did not believe the Tempter, any more than GOD's word, till she perceived that "the fruit was good for food."[9]

So again, when infidels ask, *how* prayer can really influence the course of GOD's providence, or *how* everlasting punishment consist with GOD's infinite mercy, they rationalize.

The same spirit shows itself in the restlessness of others to decide *how* the sun stopped at Joshua's word,[10] *how* the manna was provided, and the like; forgetting what our Saviour suggests to the Sadducees, – "*the power of* GOD."[11]

Rationalism[12] then in fact is a forgetfulness of GOD's power, disbelief of the existence of a First Cause sufficient to account for any events or facts, however marvelous or extraordinary, and a consequent measuring of the credibility of things, not by the power and other attributes of GOD, but by our own knowledge; a limiting the possible to the actual, and denying the indefinite range of GOD's operations beyond our means of apprehending them. Mr. Hume[13] openly avows this principle, declaring it to be unphilosophical to suppose that Almighty GOD can do anything, but what we see He does. And, though we may not profess it, we too often, it is to be feared, act upon it at the present day. Instead of looking out of ourselves, and trying to catch glimpses of GOD's workings, from any quarter, – throwing ourselves forward upon Him and waiting on Him, we sit at home bringing everything to ourselves, enthroning ourselves as the centre of all things, and refusing to believe anything that does not force itself upon our minds as true. Our private judgment is made everything to us, – is contemplated, recognized, and referred to as the arbiter of all questions, and as independent of every-thing external to us. Nothing is considered to have an existence except so far forth as our minds discern it. The notion of half views and partial knowledge, of guesses, surmises, hopes and fears, of truths faintly apprehended and not understood, of isolated facts in the great scheme of prov-idence, in a word, of Mystery, is discarded. Hence a distinction is drawn between what is called Objective and Subjective Truth, and religion is said to consist in a reception of the latter. By Objective Truth is meant the Religious System considered as existing in itself, external to this or that particular mind: by Subjective, is meant that which each mind receives in particular, and considers to be such. To believe in Objective Truth is to throw ourselves forward upon that which we have but partially mastered or made Subjective, to embrace, maintain, and use general proposi-tions which are greater than our own capacity, as if we were contemplating what is real and independent of human judgment. Such a belief seems to the Rationalist superstitious and unmeaning, and he consequently confines faith to the province of Subjective Truth, or to the reception of doctrine, as, and so far as it is met and apprehended by the mind, which will be differently in different persons, in the shape of orthodoxy in one, heterodoxy in another; that is, he professes to *believe* in that which he *opines*, and he avoids the apparent extravagance of such an avowal by maintaining that the moral trial involved in faith does not lie in the submission of the reason to external truths partially disclosed, but in that candid pursuit of truth which ensures the eventual adoption of that opinion on the subject which is best for us, most natural according to the constitution of our minds and so divinely intended. In short he owns that faith, viewed with reference to its objects, is never more than an opinion, and is pleasing to GOD, not as an active principle apprehending definite doctrines, but as a result and fruit, and therefore an evidence, of past diligence, independent inquiry, dispassion-ateness, and the like. Rationalism takes the words of Scripture as signs of Ideas; Faith, of Things or Realities.

For an illustration of Faith, considered as the reaching forth after and embracing what is beyond the mind or Objective, we may refer to St. Paul's description of it in the Ancient Saints; "These all died in faith, *not having received* the promises, but *having seen them afar off,* and were persuaded of them, and embraced them, and confessed that they were strangers and pilgrims on the earth;"[14] or to St. Peter's; "Of which salvation the Prophets have inquired and searched diligently, who *prophesied* of the grace that should come *unto your, searching what, or what manner of time* the Spirit of CHRIST, which was in them, did signify, when it testified beforehand the sufferings of CHRIST, the glory that should follow; unto whom it was revealed, that *not unto themselves,* but unto us they did minister the things *which are now reported unto you* by them that have evangelized you."[15] Here the faith of the ancient Saints is described and employed, not on truths so far mastered by the mind, but truths beyond it, and even to the end withheld from its clear apprehension.

On the other hand, if we would know to what a temper

of mind the Rationalist Theory of Subjective Truth really tends, we may study the following passage from a popular review.[16] It will be found to make use of the wonders of nature, not as "declaring the glory of GOD, and showing His handywork,"[17] but in order to exalt and deify the wisdom of man. Of the almost avowed infidelity contained in it, I do not speak.

"For the civil and political historian the past alone has existence, the present he rarely apprehends, the future never. To the historian of science it is permitted however, to penetrate the depths of past and future with equal clearness and certainty; facts to come on to him as present, and not unfrequently more assured than facts which are past. Although this clear perception of causes and consequences characterizes the whole domain of physical science, and clothe the natural philosopher with powers denied to the political and moral inquirer, yet *foreknowledge is eminently the privilege of the astronomer.* Nature has raised the curtain of futurity, and displayed before him the succession of her decrees, so far as they affect the physical universe, for countless ages to come; and the *revelations* of which she has made him the instrument, are supported and verified by a never-ceasing train of predictions fulfilled. He [the astronomer] "shows us the things which will be hereafter;"[18] not obscurely shadowed out in figures and in parables, as must necessarily be the case with other revelations, but attended with the most minute precision of time, place, and circumstance. He converts the hours as they roll into an ever-present miracle, *in attestation of those laws which his Creator through him has unfolded;* the sun cannot rise, the moon cannot wane, a star cannot twinkle in the firmament without bearing testimony to *the truth of his* [the astronomer's] *prophetic records.* It has pleased the "Lord and Governor" of the world, in his inscrutable wisdom, to baffle our inquiries into the nature and proximate cause of that wonderful faculty of intellect, – that image of his own essence which he has conferred upon us, &c. &c ... . But how nobly is the darkness which envelopes metaphysical inquiries compensated by the flood of light which is shed upon the physical creation! *There* is all harmony, and order, and majesty, and beauty. From the chaos of social and political phenomena exhibited

in human records, phenomena unconnected to our imperfect vision
by any discoverable law, a war of passions and prejudices governed
by no apparent purpose, tending to no apparent end, and setting all
intelligible order at defiance, – *how soothing and yet how elevating* it is
to turn to the splendid spectacle which offers itself to the habitual
contemplation of the astronomer! How favourable to the development of all the *best and highest feelings* of the soul are such objects!
The only passion they inspire being *the love of truth,* and the chiefest
pleasure of their votaries arising from excursions through the
imposing scenery of the universe, scenery on a scale of grandeur
and magnificence compared with which whatever we are accustomed to call sublimity on our planet, dwindles into ridiculous
insignificancy. Most justly has it been said, that nature has
implanted in our bosoms *a craving after the discovery of truth*, and
assuredly that glorious instinct is never more irresistibly awakened
than when our notice is directed to what is going on in the
heavens, &c."[19]

Here desire after Truth is considered as irreconcilable with
acquiescence in doubt. Now if we do not believe in a First
Cause, then indeed we know nothing except so far as we
know it clearly, consistency and harmony being the necessary
evidence of reality; and so we may reasonably regard doubt
as an obstacle in the pursuit of Truth. But, on the other hand,
if we *assume the existence of* an unseen Object of Faith, then
we already possess the main truth, and may well be content
even with half views as to His operations, for whatever we
have is so much gain, and what we do not know does not in
that case tend at all to invalidate what we do know.

A few words may be necessary to bring together what has
been said. Rationalism then, viewed in its essential character,
is a refusal to take for granted the existence of a First Cause,
in religious inquiries, which it prosecutes as if commencing
in utter ignorance of the subject. Hence it receives only so
much as may be strictly drawn out to the satisfaction of the
reason, advancing onwards in belief according to the range of
the proof; it limits Truth to our comprehension of it, or

subjects it to the mind, and admits it only so far as it is subjected. Hence again it considers faith to have reference to a *thing* or *system*, far more than to an *agent,* for an agent may be supposed as acting in unknown ways, whereas a system cannot be supposed to have existence beyond what is ascertained of it. Hence moreover it makes the credibility of any alleged truth to lie solely in its capability of coalescing and combining with what is already known.

Mr. Hume, as has been observed, avowed the principle of Rationalism in its extent of Atheism. The writers, I shall have to notice, have religious sensibilities, and are far less clearsighted. Yet even Mr. Erskine maintains or assumes that the main *object* of Christian faith is, not Almighty GOD, but a certain work or course of things which He has accomplished; as will be manifest to any reader either of His *Essay on Internal Evidence,* or *on Faith.* He says, for instance, in the latter of these works,

"I may understand many things which I do not believe: but I cannot believe anything which I do not understand, unless it be something addressed to my senses, and not to my thinking faculty. A man may with great propriety say, I understand the Cartesian System of Vortices,[20] though I do not believe in it. But it is absolutely impossible for him to believe in that system without knowing what it is. *A man may believe in the ability of the maker of a system without understanding it*; but he cannot believe in the *system itself* without understanding it. Now there is a meaning, and this system, must be understood, before we can believe the Gospel. We are not called on to believe the Bible merely that we may give a proof of our willingness to submit in all things to God's authority, but that we may be influenced by the objects of our belief, &c."

Every word of this extract tells in illustration of what has been drawn out above. And it is cited here merely in illustration; what judgment is to be formed of it shall be determined in its place. To resume the thread of our discussion.

We shall now perhaps be prepared to understand a very characteristic word, familiarly used by Mr. Erskine among others to designate his view of the Gospel dispensation. It is said to be a *Manifestation*, as if the system presented to us were such as we could trace and connect into one whole, complete and definite. Let me use this word "Manifestation," as a token of the philosophy under review; and let me contrast it with the word "Mystery" which on the other hand may be regarded as the badge or emblem of orthodoxy. Revelation considered as a Manifestation, is a doctrine variously received by various minds, but nothing more to each than that which it appears to be. Considered as a Mystery,[21] it is a doctrine enunciated by inspiration, in human language, as the only possible medium of it, and suitably according to the capacity of language from the first by every mind, whatever be its separate power of under-standing, entered into more or less by this or that mind, as it may be; and admitting of being apprehended more and more perfectly according to the diligence of the person receiving it. It is one and the same, independent and real, of depth unfathomable, and illimitable in its extent.

This is a fit place to make some remarks on the Scripture sense of the word Mystery. It may seem a contradiction in terms to call Revelation a Mystery; but is not the book of the Revelation of St. John as great a mystery from beginning to end as the most abstruse doctrine the mind ever imagined? yet it is even called a *revelation*. How is this? The answer is simple. No revelation can be complete and systematic, from the weakness of the human intellect; *so far* as it is not such, it is mysterious. When nothing is revealed, nothing is known, and there is nothing to contemplate or marvel at; but when something is revealed and only something, for all cannot be, there are forthwith difficulties and perplexities. A Revelation is religious doctrine viewed on its illuminated side; a Mystery is the self-same doctrine viewed on the side unilluminated.

Thus Religious Truth is neither light nor darkness, but both together; it is like the dim view of a country seen in twilight, with forms half extricated from the darkness, with broken lines, and isolated masses. Revelation, in this way of considering it, is not a revealed *system,* but consists of a number of detached and incomplete truths belonging to a vast system unrevealed, of doctrines and injunctions mysteriously connected together, that is, connected by unknown media, and bearing upon unknown portions of the system. And in this sense we see the propriety of calling St. John's prophecies, though highly mysterious, yet a revelation.

And such seems to be the meaning of the word Mystery in Scripture, a point which is sometimes disputed.[22] Campbell,[23] in his work on the Gospels, maintains that the word means a *secret*, and that, whatever be the subject of it in the New Testament, it is always, when mentioned, associated with the notion of its being revealed. Thus it is, in his view, a word belonging solely to the Law, which was a system of types and shadows, and is utterly foreign to the Gospel which has brought light instead of darkness. This sense might seem to be supported by our Lord's announcement, for instance, to His disciples that to them was given to know the mysteries of His kingdom;[24] by His command to them at another time to speak abroad what they had heard from Him in secret.[25] And St. Paul in like manner glories in the revelation of mysteries hid from the foundation of the world.[26]

But the sense of Scripture will more truly be represented as follows. What was hidden altogether before CHRIST came could not be a Mystery; it became a Mystery then, for the first time by being disclosed at all, at His coming. What had never been dreamed of by "righteous men",[27] before Him, when revealed *as being* unexpected, if for no other reason, would be strange and startling. And such unquestionably is the meaning of St. Paul, when he uses the word; for he applies it, not to what was passed and over, but what was the then state of the doctrine revealed. Thus in the 1 Cor. 15:51–52, "Behold I show you a Mystery; we shall not all sleep, but we shall all be changed in a moment, in the twinkling of an eye, at the last trump." The resurrection and consequent spiritualizing of the human body, was not dreamed of by the philosophy of the world till CHRIST came, and, when revealed, was "mocked,[28] as then first becoming a Mystery. Reason was just where it was; and, as it could not discover it beforehand, so now it cannot account for it, or reconcile it to experience, or explain the manner of it: the utmost it does is by some faint analogies to show it is not inconceivable. Again, St. Paul, speaking of marriage, says, "This is a great Mystery, I mean, in its reference to CHRIST and to the Church;"[29] that is, the ordinance of marriage has an inward and spiritual meaning, contained in it and revealed through it, a certain bearing, undefined and therefore mysterious, towards the heavenly communion existing between CHRIST and the Church: – as if for persons to place themselves in that human relation, interested themselves in some secret way in the divine relation of which it is a figure. Again: "Great is the Mystery of piety, GOD was manifested in the flesh, justified in the Spirit, seen of Angels, preached unto the Gentiles, believed on in the world, received up into glory." 1 Tim. 3:16. Now is the revelation of these truths a Manifestation (as above explained) or a Mystery? Surely the great secret has, by being revealed, only got so far as to be a Mystery, nothing more; nor could become a Manifestation (i.e. a system connected in its parts by the human mind,) without ceasing to be anything great at all. It must ever be small and superficial, viewed only as received by man; and is vast only when considered as that external truth into which each Christian may grow continually, and ever find fresh food for his soul. As to the unknown and marvelous system of things spoken of in the text just quoted, it is described again, in an almost parallel passage, as regards the subject, though differently worded, in the epistle to the Hebrews, "Ye are come unto Mount Zion, and unto the city of the Living GOD, the heavenly Jerusalem, and to an innumerable company of Angels, to the full concourse and assembly of the first-born enrolled in heaven, and to GOD the judge of all, and to the spirits of the perfected just, and to Jesus the Mediator of the New Covenant, and to the blood of sprinkling, that speaketh better things than that of Abel." Heb. 12:22–24. In like manner when St. Paul speaks of the election of the Gentiles as a Mystery,[30] revealed, the facts of the case show that it was still a Mystery, not a secret explained. We know that the Jews did stumble at it:[31] why if it was clear and obvious to reason? Certainly it was still a Mystery to them. Will it be objected that it had been plainly predicted? Surely not. The calling indeed of the Gentiles had been predicted, but not their equal participation with the Jews in all the treasures of the covenant of grace, not the destruction of the Mosaic system. The prophets everywhere speak of the Jews as the head of the Gentiles; it was a new doctrine altogether (at least to the existing generation) that the election henceforth was to have no reference whatever to the Jews as a distinct people. It had hitherto been utterly hidden and unexpected; it emerged into a stumbling block, or Mystery, when the Gospel was preached, as on the other hand it became to all humble minds a marvel or mystery of mercy. Hence St. Paul speaks of the Mystery "which in other ages was not made known to the sons of men ... that the Gentiles should be *fellow heirs*, and of the *same body,* and *partakers of His promise in* CHRIST by the Gospel."[32]

In these remarks on the meaning of the word Mystery, some of the chief doctrines of the Gospel revelation have been enumerated; before entering, however, into the particular subjects to be discussed, it may be right briefly to enumerate the revealed doctrines according to the Catholic, that is the anti-rationalistic notion of them. They are these;

the Holy Trinity; the Incarnation of the Eternal SON; His atonement and merits; the Church as the medium and instrument through which He operates on the world in the communication of them; the Sacraments, and Sacramentals (as Bishop Taylor[33] calls them) as the principal channels through which His merits are applied to individuals; Regeneration, the Communion of Saints, the Resurrection of the body, consequent upon their administration; and lastly, our faith and works, as a condition of the availableness and success of these divine appointments. Each of these doctrines is a Mystery; that is, each stands in a certain degree isolated from the rest, unsystematic, connected with the rest by unknown intermediate truths, and bearing upon subject unknown. Thus the Atonement, *why* it was necessary, *how* it operates, is a Mystery; that is, the heavenly truth which is revealed, extends on each side of it into an unknown world. We see but the skirts of GOD's glory in it.[34] The virtue of the Holy Communion; how it conveys to us the body and blood of the Incarnate Son crucified, and how by partaking it body and soul are made spiritual. The Communion of Saints; in what sense they are knit together into one body of which CHRIST is the head. Good works, how they, and how prayers again, influence our eternal destiny. In like manner what our relation is to the innumerable company of Angels, some of whom, as we are told, minister to us; what to the dead in CHRIST, the spirits of the just perfected,[35] who are ever joined to us in a heavenly communion; what bearing the Church has upon the fortunes of the world, or, it may be, the universe.

That there are some such mysterious bearings, not only the incomplete character of the Revelation, but even its documents assure us. For instance. The Christian dispensation was ordained, "to the intent that now unto the *principalities* and powers in heavenly places, might be known by *the Church*, the manifold wisdom of GOD." (Eph. 3:10).

Such is its relation to the Angels. Again to lost spirits; "We wrestle not against flesh and blood, but against principalities, against powers, against the rulers of darkness in this world, against spiritual wickedness in heavenly places." (Eph. 6:12). In like manner our Lord says, "the gates of hell shall not prevail against" the Church (Matt. 16:18) implying thereby a contest. Again, in writing the following text, had not St. Paul thoughts in his mind, suggested by the unutterable sights of the third heaven,[36] but to us unrevealed and unintelligible? "I am persuaded that neither death, nor life, nor angels, nor principalities, nor powers, nor things present, nor things to come, nor height, nor depth, nor any other creature, shall be able to separate us" (that is, the Church,) "from the love of GOD, which is in CHRIST JESUS our LORD." (Rom. 8:38–39).

The practical inference to be drawn from this view, is first, that we should be very reverent in dealing with revealed truth; next, that we should avoid all theorizing and systematizing as relates to it, which is pretty much what looking into the ark was under the Law;[37] further, that we should be solicitous to hold it safely and entirely; moreover, that we should be zealous and pertinacious in guarding it; and lastly, which is implied in all these, that we should religiously adhere to the form of words and the ordinances under which it comes to us, through which it is revealed to us, and apart from which the revelation does not exist, there being nothing else given us by which to ascertain or enter into it.

Striking indeed is the contrast presented to this view of the Gospel by the popular theology of the day! That theology is as follows; – that the Atonement is the chief doctrine of the Gospel; – again that it is chiefly to be regarded, not as a wonder in heaven, and in its relation to the attributes of GOD and the unseen world, but in its experienced effects on our minds, in the change it effects where it is believed.[38] On this, as on the horizontal line of a picture, all the portions of the Gospel system are placed and made to converge; as if it might fearlessly be used to regulate, adjust, correct, complete, everything else. Thus the doctrine of the Incarnation is viewed as necessary and important to the Gospel *because* it gives sacredness to the Atonement; of the Trinity, *because* it includes the revelation, not only of the Redeemer, but also of the Sanctifier, by whose aid and influence the Gospel message is to be blessed to us. It follows that faith is nearly the whole of religion, for through it the message or Manifestation is *received*; on the other hand, the scientific language of Catholicism is disparaged, as having no tendency to enforce the operation of the revelation of the Atonement on our minds, and the Sacraments are limited to the office of representing, and promising, and impressing on us the promise of divine influences, in no measure of conveying them. Thus the Dispensation is practically identified with its Revelation or rather Manifestation. Not that the reality of the Atonement is formally denied, but it is cast into the background, except so far as it can be discovered to be influential, viz. to show GOD's hatred of sin, the love of CHRIST and the like; and there is an evident *tendency* to consider it as a *mere* Manifestation of the love of CHRIST, to the denial of all real virtue in it as an expiation of sin; as a sign of GOD's infinite mercy, to calm and assure us, without any *real* connexion existing between it and GOD's forgiveness of our sins. And the dispensation thus being hewn and chiseled into an intelligible human system, is represented, when thus mutilated, as affording a remarkable evidence of the truth of the Bible, an evidence level to the *reason*, and superseding the *testimony* of the Apostles. That is, according to the above observations, that Rationalism, or want of faith, which has first invented a spurious gospel, next looks complacently on its own offspring, and pronounces it to be the very image of that notion of the Divine

Providence according to which it was originally modeled; a procedure, which, besides more serious objections, incurs the logical absurdity of arguing in a circle.

§2. *Remarks on Mr. Erskine's "Internal Evidence."*

This is in fact pretty nearly Mr. Erskine's argument in his *Internal Evidence*, an author, concerning whom personally I have not wish to use one harsh word, not doubting that he is better than his own doctrine, and is only the organ, eloquent and ingenious, of unfolding a theory, which it has been his unhappiness to mistake for the Catholic faith revealed in the Gospel. Let us now turn to the Essay in question.

Mr. Erskine begins in the following words.

There is a principle in our nature, which makes us dissatisfied with unexplained and unconnected facts; which leads us to theorize all the particulars of our knowledge, or to form in our minds some system of causes sufficient to explain or produce the effects which we see; and which teaches us to believe or disbelieve in the truth of any system which may be presented to us, just as it appears adequate or inadequate to afford that explanation of which we are in pursuit. We have an intuitive perception, that the appearances of nature are connected by the relation of cause and effect; and we have also an instinctive desire to classify and arrange the seemingly confused mass of facts with which we are surrounded, according to this distinguishing relationship." pp. 1, 2.

He then speaks of two processes of reasoning which the mind uses in searching after truth.[39]

"When we are convinced of the real existence of a cause in nature, and when we find that a class of physical facts is explained by the supposition of this cause, and tallies exactly with its ordinary operation, we resist both reason and instinct when we resist the conviction that this class of facts does result from this cause." p. 2.

Again:

"There is another process of reasoning ... by which, instead of ascending from effects to a cause, we descend from a cause to effects When we are once convinced of the existence of a cause, and are acquainted with its ordinary mode of operation, we are prepared to give a certain degree of credit to a history of other effects attributed to it, provided we can trace the connexion between them." p. 3.

Presently he says,

"In [all] these processes of reasoning we have examples of conviction, upon an evidence which is, most *strictly speaking*, internal, - an evidence altogether independent of our *confidence in the veracity* of the narrator of the facts." p. 8.

Now, before explaining the precise argument he draws from the contents of Scripture, be it observed, that in these passages he countenances the principle of "believing or disbelieving in the truth of any system which may be presented to us," according as it contains in it or not, a satisfactory adjustment of causes to effects, the question of testimony being altogether superseded. Accordingly he says a little further on of the Apostles; "Their system is true in the nature of things, even were they proved to be impostors." p. 17. And it will appear from other passages of his work, that he does not hesitate to receive the other alternative contained in the original proposition with which he opens it, viz. that that professed revelation is to be rejected, which implies a system of causes and effects incongruous in man's judgment with each other. To proceed.

His argument is as follows: —

"*The first faint outline of Christianity,*" he says, "presents to us a view of GOD operating on the characters of men through a manifestation of His own character, in order that, by leading them to participate in some measure of His moral likeness, they may also in some measure participate of His happiness. p. 12.

Again,

"If the actions attributed to GOD, by any system of religion, be really such objects as, when present to the mind, do not stir the affections at all, that religion cannot influence the character, and is *therefore* utterly useless." p. 23.

"The *object* of Christianity is to bring the character of man into harmony with that of GOD." p. 49.

"The *reasonableness* of a religion seems to me to consist in there being a direct and natural *connexion between* a believing the doctrines which it inculcates, *and* a being formed by these to the character which it recommends. If the belief of the doctrines has *no* tendency to train the disciple in a more exact and more willing discharge of its moral obligations, *there is evidently a very strong probability against the truth of that religion* ... What is the history of another world to me, unless it have some *intelligible relation* to my duties or happiness?" p. 59.

Now in these passages there is, first, this great assumption, that the object of the Christian revelation is ascertainable by us. It is asserted that its object is "to bring the character of men into harmony with that of GOD." That this is *an* object is plain from Scripture, but that it is *the* object in such sense, that we may take it as a key or rule, whereby to arrange and harmonize the various parts of the revelation, – which is the use to which the author puts it. GOD's works look many ways; they have objects (to use that mere human word) innumerable; they are full of eyes before and behind, and, like the cherubim in the Prophet's vision, advance forward to diverse points at once.[40] But it is plainly unlawful and presumptuous to make one of those points which happen to be revealed to us, the τελος τελειοτατου[41] of His providence, and to subject everything else to it. It plainly savours of the Rationalism already condemned; for what is it but to resolve, that what is revealed to us, is and shall be a complete system; to reject everything but what is so complete; and to disallow the notion of revelation as a collection of fragments of a great scheme, the notion under which the most profound human philosophy is accustomed to regard it?

"Christianity," says Bishop Butler, "is a scheme quite beyond our comprehension. The moral government of GOD is exercised by gradually conducting things so in the course of His providence, that every one at length and upon the whole shall receive according to his deserts; and neither fraud nor violence, but truth and right, shall finally prevail. Christianity is a particular scheme under this general plan of providence, and a part of it, conducive to its completion, with regard to mankind; consisting itself also of various parts and a mysterious economy, which has been carrying on from the time the world came into its present wretched state, and is still carrying on for its recovery by a divine person, the Messiah, who is to 'gather together in one the children of GOD, that are scattered abroad,'[42] and establish 'an everlasting kingdom wherein dwelleth righteousness.'[43] ... Parts likewise of this economy, are the miraculous system of the HOLY GHOST, and His ordinary assistance as given to good men; the invisible government which CHRIST exercises over His Church ... and His future return to judge the world in righteousness, and completely re-establish the kingdom of GOD ... Now little, surely need be said to show, that *this system or scheme of things is but imperfectly comprehended by us.* The Scripture expressly asserts it to be so. And indeed, *one cannot read a passage relating to this great mystery of godliness, but what immediately run up into something which shows us our ignorance in it,* as everything in nature shows our ignorance in the constitution of nature."[1] [44]

In this passage, the great philosopher, though led by his line of argument to speak of the Dispensation entirely in its reference to mean, still declares that even then its object is not identical with man's happiness, but that it is justice and truth; while, viewed in itself, every part of it runs up into mystery. Right reason, then, and faith combine to lead us, instead of measuring a divine revelation by human standards, or systematizing, except so far as it does so itself, to take what is given as we find it, to use it and be content. *E.g.* Scripture says that CHRIST died for sinners, – *so far* we may systematize;

[1]Anal. ii. 4.

that He rose for our justification, that He went that the Spirit may come. Such and such like portions of a scheme are revealed, and we may use them, but no farther. On the other hand the Catholic doctrine of the Trinity is a mere juxtaposition of separate truths, which to our minds involve inconsistency, when viewed together; nothing more being attempted, for nothing more is told us. Arrange and contrast them we may and do; systematize (*i.e.* reduce them into an intelligible dependence on each other, or harmony with each other) we may not; unless indeed any such oversight of revealed truth, such right of subjecting it to our understandings, is committed to us by itself. What then must be thought of the confident assumption, without proof attempted, contained in the following sentence, already quoted?

"The first faint outline of Christianity presents to us a view of GOD operating on the characters of men through a Manifestation of his own character, in order that, by leading them to participate in some measure in His moral likeness, they may also in some measure participate in His happiness."

That GOD intends us to partake in His moral likeness, that He has revealed to us His own moral character, that He has done the latter in order to accomplish the former (to speak as a man) I will grant, for it is in Scripture; but that it is the *leading idea* of Christianity, the chief and sovereign principle of it, this I altogether deny. I ask for proof of what seems to us an assumption, and (if an assumption) surely an unwarranted and presumptuous one.[45]

Notice was above taken of the selfishness of that philosophy, which resolves to sit at home and make everything subordinate to the individual. Is not this painfully instanced in one of the foregoing passages? "What is the history of another world *to me*, unless it have some intelligible relation to my duties and happiness?" Was this Moses' temper, when he turned aside to see the great sight of the fiery bush![46]

Further, be it observed, the above theory has undeniably a tendency to disparage, if not supersede the mysteries of religion, such as the doctrine of the Trinity. It lays exclusive stress upon the *character* of GOD, as the substance of the Revelation. It considers Scripture as a *Manifestation* of GOD's character, an intentional subjecting it in an intelligible shape to our minds, and nothing more. The author says: —

"The *reasonableness* of a religion seems to me to consist in there being a direct and natural connexion between a believing [its] doctrines, and being formed by the character which it recommends."[47]

Again,

"These terms ['manifestation' and 'exhibition'] suit best with the *leading idea* which I wish to explain, viz. that the facts [*i.e.* doctrines, as is just before explained] of revelation are developments of the moral principle of the Deity, and carry an influential address to the feelings of man." p. 26.

Now, is the theological doctrine of the Trinity such a development? Is it influentially addressed to our feelings? Is it "an act of the divine government," as the author expresses himself? Further, does he not also tell us the "reasonableness" of a religion seems to consist in there being a *direct and natural* connexion between a believing the doctrines which it inculcates, and a being formed by these to the character which it recommends? We need not dwell on the assumption hazarded in this passage; for surely it is conceivable that reasons may exist in the vast scheme of the Dispensation, (of the bearings of which we know nothing perfectly,) for doctrines being revealed which do not directly and naturally tend to influence the formation of our characters, or at least which we cannot see to do so. We have at least the authority of Bishop Butler to support us in considering that "we are *wholly ignorant what degree of new knowledge* it were to be expected GOD would give mankind by Revelation, upon supposition of His affording one; or how far, or in what way, he would interpose miraculously to qualify them to whom He should originally make the Revelation, for *communicating the knowledge given to it*; and to secure their doing it to the age in which they should live, and to secure its being transmitted to posterity."[2]

But even though Butler, and other deep thinkers, had not said a word on the subject, the immediate and inevitable result, or rather operation of Mr. Erskine's principle, when applied to the matter of the Scripture Revelation, is a sufficient refutation of it. It will be found to mean nothing, or to lead pretty nearly to Socinianism.[48] Let us take an instance: he says that the reasonableness of a religion, and therefore its claim on our acceptance, consists in there being a direct and natural tendency in belief in its doctrines to form that moral character which it recommends. Now, I would ask it ourselves, – "What is the *harm* of being, *e.g.,* a Sabellian?[49] And is not the habit of thought, from which such questionings proceed, owing to the silent influence of such books as this of Mr. E's? Further, do we not hear persons say, "As to the Athanasian doctrine, I do not deny there is a Mystery about the Manifestations of the Divine Nature in Scripture, but this Mystery, whatever it is, as it does not interfere with the practical view of the doctrine, so, on the other, it cannot subserve it. It is among the secret things of GOD and must be left among them;" – as if we might unthankfully throw back again into the infinite abyss, any of the jewels which GOD has vouchsafed to bring us thence.

The reader may at first sight be tempted to say, "This is an overstrained handling of Mr. Erskine's words. What he does mean, is, not that the *want* of connexion between doctrine and precept is an objection, (though his word strictly taken

[2] Anal. ii. 3.

may say this,) but that where such a connexion does exist, as
we see it does in Christianity, *there* is a strong argument in
behalf of the divinity of a professed Revelation." Probably
this was his original meaning, and it would have been well
had he kept to it. But it is the way with men, particularly in
this day, to generalize freely, to be impatient of such concrete
truth as existing appointments contain, to attempt to
disengage it, to hazard sweeping assertions, to lay down principles, to mount up above GOD's visible doings, and to
subject them to tests derived from our own speculations.
Doubtless He, in some cases, vouchsafes to us the knowledge
of truths more general than those works of His which He has
set before us; and when He does so, let us thankfully use the
gift. This is not the case before us. Mr. E. seems to have been
led on, from the plain fact, that in Christianity there is
evidently a certain general bearing of faith in doctrine upon
character, and so far a proof of its *consistency*, which is a token
of divine working, – led on, to the general proposition, that
"in a genuine Revelation all doctrines revealed must have a
direct bearing upon the moral character enjoined by it;" and
next to the use of it as a test for rejecting such alleged
doctrines of the gospel, *e.g.* the Catholic doctrine of the
Trinity, as do not perceptibly come up to it.

That I am not unfair upon Mr. Erskine will appear from
the following passages.

"*The abstract fact* that there is a plurality in the unity of the Godhead,
really makes *no address either to our understandings, or our feelings, or our
consciences*. But the *obscurity* of the doctrine, as far as *moral* purposes
are concerned, is dispelled, when it comes in such a form as this
'But the comforter, which is, &c.'[50] – Our *metaphysical* ignorance
of the Divine Esssence is not indeed in the slightest degree removed
by this mode of stating the subject; but our moral ignorance of the
Divine character is enlightened, and *that is the thing with which we
have to do*." p. 96.

Now I do not say that such a passage as this is a denial of the doctrine of the Athanasian Creed; but I ask, should a man be disposed to deny it, *how* would the writer refute him? Has he not, if a Trinitarian, cut away the ground from under him? Might not a Socinian or Sabellian convince him of the truth of their doctrine by his own arguments? Unquestionably. He has laid down the principle, that a Revelation is *only so far* reasonable as it exhibits a direct and natural connexion between belief in its doctrines and conformity to its precepts. He then says, that in matter of fact the doctrine of the Trinity is only influential as it exhibits the moral character of GOD; that is, that so far as it does not, so far as it is abstract (as he calls it) and in scientific form *i.e.* viewed as the Catholic Doctrine, it is not influential, or reasonable, or by consequence important, or even credible. He has cut off the *Doctrine* from its roots, and has preserved only that superficial part of it which he denominates a "*Manifestation*," – only so much as bears visibly upon another part of the system, the character of man, – so much as is perceptibly connected with it, so far as may be comprehended.

But he speaks so clearly on this subject that comment is perhaps needless.

"In the Bible the Christian doctrines ... stand as indications of the character of GOD, and as the exciting motives of a corresponding character in man."

This assumption must not pass without notice; often they so stand, not always, as he would imply. When St. Paul bids Timothy hold fast the form of sound words,[51] or St. Jude exhorts us to contend earnestly for the faith,[52] these Apostles seem so to direct for the sake of the faith itself, not for any ulterior reason. When St. John requires us to reject anyone who brings not the true doctrine,[53] nothing is said of it as an "exciting motive" of a certain character of mind, though viewed on one side of it, that doctrine certainly is so. St. Paul glories in the doctrine of CHRIST crucified, as being

a strange doctrine and a *stumbling block*.[54] St. John states the
doctrine of the Incarnation in the first chapter of his gospel as
a heavenly truth, which was too glorious for men, and
believed on only by a few, by which, indeed the Father was
declared, but which *shone in darkness*.[55] But to return:

"In the Bible, the Christian doctrines are always stated in this
connexion, they stand as indications of the character of GOD, and as
the exciting motives of a corresponding character in man. Forming
thus the connecting link between the character of the Creator and
the creature, they possess a majesty which it is impossible to despise,
and exhibit a form of consistency and truth which it is difficult to
disbelieve. Such is Christianity in the Bible; *but in creeds and Church
articles it is far otherwise*. These tests and summaries originated from
the introduction of doctrinal errors and metaphysical speculations
into religion; and in consequence of this, they are not so much
intended to be the repositories of the truth, as barriers against the
encroachment of erroneous opinions. The doctrines contained in
them, therefore, are not stated with any reference to their *great object*
in the Bible. – the regeneration of the human heart by the
knowledge of the divine character. *They appear as detached propositions,* indicating no *moral* cause, and pointing to no *moral* effect.
They do not look to GOD on the one hand as their source; nor to
man on the other as the object of their moral urgency. *They appear
like links severed from the chain to which they belonged*; and *thus* they lose
all that evidence which arises from their consistency, and all that
dignity which is connected with their high design. I do not talk of
the propriety or impropriety of having Church Articles, but the
evils which spring from receiving impressions of religion exclusively or chiefly from this source." pp. 93, 94.

It is always a point gained to be able to come to issue in a
controversy, as I am able to do here with the writer under
consideration. He finds fault with that disjoined and isolated
character of the doctrines of the old Catholic creed, that
want of system, which to the more philosophical mind of
Bishop Butler would seem an especial recommendation from
its analogy to the course of nature. He continues,

"I may instance the ordinary statements of the doctrine of the Trinity, as an illustration of what I mean. It seems difficult to conceive that any man should read through the New Testament candidly and attentively, without being convinced that this doctrine is essential to, and implied in every part of the system: but it is not so difficult to conceive, that although his mind is perfectly satisfied on this point, he may yet, if his religious knowledge is exclusively derived from the Bible, feel a little surprised and staggered, when he for the first time reads the terms in which it is announced in the articles and confessions of all Protestant Churches. In these summaries, the doctrine in question is stated by itself, divested of all its Scriptural accompaniments, and is made to bear simply on *the nature of the* Divine essence, and the *Mysterious fact* of the existence of Three in One. *It is evident that this fact, taken by itself, cannot in the smallest degree tend to develop the Divine character,* and therefore cannot make any moral impression on our minds." pp. 94, 95.

Now here, if it were to the purpose, this author might be encountered on his own ground. Surely, if it were religious to do so, it might be asserted, in contradiction to his last remark, that the Catholic doctrine of the Trinity, *does* "tend to develop the Divine character," *does* "make a moral impression on our minds;" for does not the notion of a Mystery lead to reverence, awe, wonder, and fear? and are these not moral impressions? He proceeds:

"In the Bible it assumes quite a different shape; it is there *subservient to the manifestation* of the moral character of GOD. The Doctrine of GOD's combined justice and mercy, in the redemption of sinners, and of his continued spiritual watchfulness over the progress of truth through the world, and in each particular heart, could not have been communicated without it, so as to have been distinctly and vividly apprehended; but it is never mentioned, except in connection with these objects; nor is it ever taught as a separate subject of belief. There is a great and important difference between these two modes of statement. In the first, *the doctrine stands* as an isolated fact of a strange and unintelligible nature, and is apt even to suggest the idea that *Christianity holds out a premium for believing improbabilities*. In the other, it stands indissolubly united with an act of Divine holiness and compassion, which radiates to the heart an appeal of tenderness most intelligible in its nature and object, and most constraining in its influence." pp. 95, 96.

Here, at length, Rationalism stands confessed, and we hear openly the "mouth speaking great things," described in prophecy.[56] Again;

"The hallowed purpose of restoring men to the lost image of their Creator is in fact the very soul and spirit of the Bible; and *whenever this object does not distinctly appear, the whole system becomes dead and useless*."

If so, what judgment are we to pass upon such texts as the following? "We are unto GOD a *sweet savour of Christ,* in them that are saved, *and in them that perish; to the one we are savour of death unto death;* and to the other, the savour of life unto life." "What if GOD *willing to show His wrath and to make his power known,* endured with much long suffering the vessels of wrath fitted to destruction, and that He might make known the riches of His glory on the vessels of mercy, which He had afore prepared unto glory?" "He hath appointed a day in which *He will judge the world in righteousness,* by that Man whom he hath ordained." "*Behold, I come quickly,* and my reward is with Me, *to give every man according as his work shall be.*"[3] The glory of God, according to Mr. Erskine, and the maintenance of truth and righteousness are *not* objects sufficient, were there no other, to prevent "the whole system" of revealed truth from "becoming dead and useless." Does not this philosophy tend to Universalism?[57] Can its upholders maintain for any long while the eternity of future punishment? Surely its upholders speak at random, and have no notion what they are saying. He proceeds:

---

[3] 2 Cor. ii. 15, 16; Rom. ix. 22, 23; Acts xvii. 31; Rev. xxii. 12.

"In creeds and Confessions this great purpose is not made to stand forth with its real prominency; its intimate connexion with the different articles of faith is not adverted to; the *point* of the whole argument is thus lost, *and Christianity is misapprehended to be a mere list of mysterious facts.* One who understands the Bible may read them with profit, *because hi own mind may fill up the deficiencies,* and when their statements are correct, they may assist inquirers in certain stages, by bringing under their eyes a concentrated view of all the points of Christian doctrine; and they may serve, according to their contents, either as public invitations to their communion, or as public warnings against it; ... but they are not calculated to impress on the mind of a learner a vivid and *useful* apprehension of Christianity ... [58] Any person who draws his knowledge of the Christian doctrines, exclusively or principally from such sources, must run considerable risk of losing the benefit of them, by over-looking their moral object; and, in so doing, he may be tempted to reject them altogether, because he will be blind to their *strongest evidence, which consists in their perfect adaptation to these objects.* The bible is the only perfectly pure source of Divine knowledge, and the man who is unacquainted with it, is, in fact, ignorant of the doctrines of Christianity, however well read he may be in the schemes, and systems, and controversies, which have been written on the subject ... The habit of viewing the Christian doctrine and the Christian character as two separate things has a most pernicious tendency. A man who in his scheme of Christianity, says, 'here are so many things to be believed, and here are so many things to be done,' has already made a fundamental mistake. The doctrines are the principles which must excite and animate the performance &c." pp. 139–141.

It is not the design of this Paper to refute Mr. Erskine's principles, so much as to delineate and contrast them with those of the Church Catholic. Since, however, he has already, in several of these extracts, *assumed* that Scripture ever speaks of revealed doctrines in a directly practical way, – not as objects of faith merely, but as motives to conduct, – I would call attention to the following passage, in addition to those which have been above pointed out. "JESUS answered and said unto him, Verily, verily I say unto thee, *Except a man be born again, he cannot see the kingdom of* GOD. Nicodemus saith unto Him, *How* can a man be born when he is old? can he enter the second time into his mother's womb and be born? JESUS answered, Verily, verily, I say unto thee, *Except a man be born of water and the Spirit, he cannot enter the kingdom of* GOD. That which is born of the flesh is flesh, and that which is born of the Spirit is Spirit, *Marvel not* that I said to thee, Ye must be born again. The wind bloweth where it listeth, and thou hearest the sound thereof, but *canst not tell* whence it cometh and whither it goeth: so is everyone that is born of the Spirit. Nicodemus answered and said unto Him, How can these things be? JESUS answered and said unto him, Art thou a master in Israel, and knowest not these things? Verily, verily, I say unto thee, We speak that We do know, and testify that We have seen; and *ye receive not Our witness.* If I have told you earthly things, and ye *believe not, how shall ye believe* if I tell you of heavenly things? And *no man ascended up to heaven, but He that came down from heaven, even the Son of man which is in heaven.*"[4]

Some persons, doubtless, are so imbued with modern glosses and the traditions of men, that they will discern in all this but a practical exhortation to conversion, change of heart, and the like; but anyone who gets himself fairly to look at the passage in itself, will, I am persuaded, see nothing more or less than this, – that CHRIST enunciates a solemn *Mystery* for Nicodemus to receive in *faith*, that Nicodemus understands His words, and hesitates at it; that our LORD reproves him for hesitating, tells him that there are even higher Mysteries than that he had set forth, and proceeds to instance that of the Incarnation. In what conceivable way would a supporter of Mr. E's views make the last awful verse "subservient to the manifestation of the moral character of

---

[4] John iii. 3–13.

God," or directly influential upon practice? unless, indeed, he explained its clauses away altogether, as if they meant nothing more than is contained in the next verses, "As Moses, &c." and "God so loved the world, &c." All this is too painful to dwell upon. The latter part, particularly the conclusion, of the sixth chapter of the same Gospel, would afford another instance in point.

Now let us hear what Mr. Erskine says in like manner on the doctrine of the Atonement, which he would exalt, indeed, into the substance of the Gospel, but in his account of which, as well as of the other Mysteries of revelation, he will, I fear, be found wanting.

"The doctrine of the Atonement through Jesus Christ, which is the corner-stone of Christianity, and to which *all the other doctrines of Revelation are subservient.*"

Here is the same, (what I must call,) presumptuous assumption, —

"— has had to encounter the misapprehension of the understanding as well as the pride of the heart."

Now let us observe, he is going to show *how* the understanding of the Church Catholic has *misapprehended* the doctrine.

"This pride is natural to man, and can only be overcome by the power of truth; but the misapprehension might be removed by the simple process of reading the Bible with attention; because it has arisen from neglecting the record itself, and taking our information from the discourses or the *systems of men,* who have engrafted the metaphysical subtleties of the schools upon the perplexed statement of the word of God. In order to understand the fact of Revelation, we *must* (sic) form a system to ourselves; but if any subtlety, *of which the application is unintelligible to common sense, or uninfluential on conduct,* enters into our system, *we may be sure that it is a wrong one.*"

The author here alludes to the Catholic teaching in the words "systems of man;" indeed it has been fashionable of late so to speak of it; but let me ask, which teaching has the more of system in it, that which regards the doctrines of revelation as isolated truths, so far as they are not connected in Scripture itself, or that which pares away part, and forcibly deals with the rest till they are all brought down to an end cognizable by the human mind? It must be observed that the author expressly sanctions the formation *of a system,* which Catholic believers do not. He proceeds,

"The common sense system of a religion consists in two connexions, – first the connexion between the doctrines and the character of GOD which they exhibit; and secondly, the connexion between these same doctrines and the character which they are intended to impress on the mind of man. When, therefore, we are considering a religious doctrine, our questions ought to be, first, what view does this doctrine give of the character of GOD in relation to sinners? And secondly, what influence is the belief of it calculated to exercise on the character of man? ... The first of these questions leads us to consider the Atonement as an act necessarily resulting from, and simply developing principles in the Divine mind, altogether independent of its effects on the hearts of those who are interested in it. The second leads us to consider the adaptation of the history of the Atonement, when believed, to the moral wants and capacities of the human mind ... There is something very striking and wonderful in this adaptation; and the deeper we search into it, the stronger reasons shall we discover for admiration and gratitude, and the more thoroughly shall we be convinced that it is not a lucky coincidence, not an adjustment contrived by the precarious and temporizing wisdom of this world, but that it is stamped with the uncounterfeited seal of the universal Ruler, and carries on it the traces of that same mighty will, which has connected the sun with his planetary train, and fixed the great relations in nature, appointing to each atom its bound that it cannot pass." pp. 97–100.

These last remarks are true of course in their place: so far as we think we see an adaptation, even though Scripture does not expressly mention it, let us praise GOD and be thankful; – but it is one thing to trace humbly and thankfully what we surmise to be GOD's handiwork, and so far as we think we see it, and quite another thing to propound our surmises dogmatically, not only as true, but as the substance of the revelation, the test of what is important in it, and what not; nay, of what is really part of it, and what not. Presently he says as follows; —

"The doctrine of the Atonement is the great subject of Revelation. GOD is represented as delighting in it, as being glorified by it, and as being most fully manifested by it. *All the other doctrines radiate from this as their centre.* In *subservience to it.,* the distinction in the unity of the Godhead has been revealed. It is described as the everlasting theme of praise and song amongst the blessed who surround the throne of GOD." pp. 101, 102.

Now that the doctrine of the Atonement is so essential a doctrine that none other is more so, (true as it is,) does not at all hinder other doctrines in their own place being so essential that they may not be moved one inch from it, or made to converge towards that doctrine ever so little, beyond the sanction of Scripture. There is surely a difference between being prominent and being paramount. To take an illustration of the human body: the brain is the noblest organ, but have not the heart, and the lungs their own essential rights, (so to express myself,) their own independent claims upon the regard of the physician? Will not he be justly called a theorist who resolves all diseases into one, and refers general healthiness to one organ as its seat and cause?

One additional observation is to be made on Mr. Erskine's view of the Atonement. He consider, in common with many other writers of his general way of thinking, that in that most solemn and wonderful event, we have a Manifestation, not only of GOD's love, but of His justice. *E.*g.

"The distinction of persons in the Divine nature we cannot comprehend, but we can easily comprehend the high and engaging morality of that character of GOD, which is developed in the history of the New Testament. GOD gave His equal and well-beloved SON, to suffer in the stead of an apostate world: *and through this exhibition of awful justice,* He publishes the fullest and freest pardon. He thus teaches us, that it forms no part of His scheme of mercy to dissolve the eternal connexion between sin and misery. No; this connexion stands sure; and one of the chief objects of Divine Revelation, is to convince men of this Truth; and *Justice* does the work of mercy, when it alarms us to a sense of danger, &c." p. 74.

Again:

"The design of the Atonement was *to make mercy towards this offcast race consistent with the honour and the holiness of the Divine Government.* To accomplish this gracious purpose, the Eternal Word, who was GOD, took on himself the nature of man, and as the elder brother and representative and champion of the guilty family, he solemnly acknowledged the justice of the sentence pronounced against sin, and submitted Himself to its full weight of woe, in the stead of His adopted kindred. GOD's *justice found rest here;* His law was magnified and made honourable, &c." pp. 102, 103.

The view maintained in these and other extracts, and by others besides Mr. Erskine, is remarkable for several reasons. First for the *determination* it evinces not to leave us anything in the gospel system unaccounted for. One might have thought that here at least somewhat of awful Mystery would have been allowed to hang over it; here at least some "depth" of GOD's counsels would have been acknowledged and accepted on *faith.* For though the death of CHRIST manifests GOD's *hatred of sin,* as well as His love for man, (inasmuch as it was sin that made His death necessary, and the greater the sacrifice the greater must have been the evil that caused it,) yet *how* His death expiated our sins, and what satisfaction it was to GOD's *justice,* are surely subjects quite above us. It is in no sense a great and glorious *Manifestation* of His *justice,* as men speak nowadays; it is an event ever *mysterious* on account of its necessity, while it is *fearful* from the hatred of sin implied in it, and most *transporting and elevating* from its display of GOD's love to man. But Rationalism would account for everything.

Next it must be observed, as to Mr. Erskine himself, that he is of necessity forced by his hypothesis thus to speak of it, however extravagant it may be to do so. For unless GOD's justice *were* manifested to our comprehension in the Atonement, the dispensation would not be a "Manifestation," the revealed scheme would be imperfect, doctrines would be severed from ascertainable moral effects on the character, – which the Catholic Church has ever considered, but which Mr. E pronounces in the outset to be contrary to reason, and fatal to the claims of a professed revelation.

An additional remark is in place.[59] The difficulty here pointed out has been felt by writers who agree with Mr. Erskine, and they have contrived to get rid of the remaining Mystery of the Dispensation, resulting from the question of justice, as follows. They refer GOD's justice to the well-being of His creation, as a *final end,* as if it might in fact be considered a modification of benevolence. Accordingly, they say GOD's justice was satisfied by the Atonement, inasmuch as He could then pardon man consistently with the good of His creation; consistently with the due order of His government. This should be carefully noted, as showing us the tendency of the Rationalistic principle under review towards Utilitarianism.[60] The following passage is given in illustration, from the Essays of Mr. Scott of Aston Sandford.[61]

"The story of Zaleucus, prince of the Locrians, is well-known:[62] to show his abhorrence of adultery, and his determination to execute the law he had enacted, condemning the adulterer to the loss of both his eyes, and at the same time to evince his love to his son who had committed that crime, he willingly submitted to lose one of his own eyes, and ordered at the same time one of his son's to be put out! Now what adulterer could *hope to escape,* when *power was vested in a* man whom neither *self love* nor *natural affection* in its greatest force, could induce to dispense with the law, or relax the rigour of its sentence?"

True, this act would show intense energy of determination to uphold the existing laws, clearly enough; and so did Mucius Scaevola in burning off his hand;[63] but what is this to the question of *justice*?

One more subject of examination, and that not the least important, is suggested by the foregoing passages. Mention has been made in them once or twice of the *facts* of revelation; the doctrines are said to be facts, and such facts to be all in all. Now according to Catholic teaching, doctrines are divine truths, which are the objects of faith, not of sight; we may call them facts, if we will, so that we recollect that they are sometimes facts of the unseen world, not of this, and that they are not synonymous with actions or works. But Mr. E., by a remarkable assumption, rules it that doctrines are facts of the revealed divine *governance*, so that a doctrine is made the same as a divine action or work. As Providence has given us a series of moral facts by nature, as in the history of nations or of the individual, from which we deduce the doctrines of a natural religion, so Scripture is supposed to reveal a second series of facts, or works, in the course of the three dispensations,[64] especially the Christian, which are the *doctrines* of religion, or at least, which together with the principle involved in them, are the doctrines. Thus CHRIST's death upon the cross is an historical fact; the meaning of it is what illustrates and quickens it, and adapts it for influencing the soul. Now if we ask, how on this theory the doctrine of the Trinity is a fact in the divine governance, we are answered that it must be thrown into another shape, if I may so express myself; it must be made subordinate, and separated into parts. The series of Christian facts passes from the birth to the death of CHRIST, and thence to the mission of the HOLY GHOST.

We must view the divinity of CHRIST in His death, the divinity of the SPIRIT in His mission. That they are therein exhibited, I grant; but the theory requires us to consider this *the* scriptural mode of their exhibition. This theory is supposed by some of its upholders to be sanctioned by Butler; for they seem to argue, that *as* the course of nature is a collection of manifested facts, so is the course of grace.[65] But that great divine knew better than to infer, from what he saw, what was to be expected in a Revelation, were it to be granted. He asserts plainly the contrary; his whole argument is merely negative, defending Christianity as far as nature enable him to do so, – not limiting the course of the revelation to the analogy of nature. Accordingly the Church Catholic has ever taught, (as in her Creeds,) that there are facts revealed to us, not of this world, not of time, but of eternity, and that absolutely and independently; not merely embodied and indirectly conveyed in a certain historical course, not subordinate to the display of the Divine character, not revealed merely relatively to us, but primary objects of our faith, and essential in themselves, whatever dependence or influence they may have upon other doctrines, or upon the course of the Dispensation. In a word, it has taught the existence of *Mysteries* in religion, for such emphatically must truths ever be which are external to this world, and existing in eternity; whereas this narrow-minded, jejune, officious, and presumptuous human system teaches nothing but a *Manifestation, i.e.* a series of historical works conveying a representation of the moral character of GOD; and it dishonours our holy faith by the unmeaning reproach, unmeaning and irreverent, just as much so as it *would* be on the other hand to call the historical facts earthly or carnal.

I will quote some passages from Mr. E's work, to justify my account of his view, and then shall be able, at length to take leave of him.

"It may be proper to remark, that the acts attributed to the Divine Government are usually termed 'doctrines,' to distinguish them from the moral precepts of a religion." p. 25.

Thus the doctrine of the Trinity, *as such,* is not a doctrine of the Gospel. Again":

"It is not enough to show, in proof of its authenticity, that the facts which it affirms concerning the dealings of GOD with His creatures, do exhibit His moral perfections in the highest degree, it must also be shown that these facts, when present to the mind of men, do naturally, according to the constitution of his being, tend to excite and suggest that combination of feelings which constitutes his moral perfection. But when we read a *history* which authoritatively claims, to be an *exhibition* of the character of GOD in His dealings with men; if we find in it that which fills and overflows our most dilated conception of moral worth, &c.; ... and if our reason farther discovers a system of powerful moral stimulants, embodied *in the facts* of this *history*; ... if we discern that the spirit of this history gives peace to the conscience, &c; ... to clothe the eternal laws which regulate His spiritual government, in such a form as may be palpable to our conceptions, and adapted to the urgency of our necessities." pp.18, 19.

"I mean to show that there is an intelligible and necessary connection between the *doctrinal facts* of revelation and the character of GOD ... and farther, that the belief of these *doctrinal facts*, has an intelligible and necessary tendency to produce the Christian character, &c." p. 20, 21.

"The object of this dissertation, is to analyse the component parts of the Christian scheme of doctrine, with reference to its bearings both on the character of GOD and on the character of man; and to demonstrate that *its facts*, not only present an expressive *exhibition* of all the moral qualities which can be conceive to reside in the divine mind, but also contain all those objects which have a natural tendency to excite and suggest in the human mind, that combination of moral feelings which has been termed moral perfection." p. 16.

"GOD has been pleased to present to us a most interesting *series of actions,* in which His moral character, *as far as we are concerned*, is fully and perspicaciously embodied. In this *narration*, &c. p. 55.

"It [the Gospel] addresses the learned and unlearned, the savage and the civilized, the decent and the profligate; and to all it speaks precisely the same language? What then is this universal language? It cannot be the language of metaphysical discussion, or what is called abstract moral reasoning . . . Its argument consists in a relation of *facts*." p. 55.

Now that in these passages,[66] the doctrines of the Gospel are resolved into facts which took place in GOD's governance, and that its mysteries are admitted, only so far as they are qualities or illustrations of these historical facts, seems to me, not only true, but the only interpretation to be put upon his words. If they do not mean this, let this at least be proposed, as an approximation to the real meaning; in the meanwhile, let it be observed that nothing which has been said in the former portions of this discussion is at all affected by any failing, if so, in having fully elicited it.

§3. *Remarks on Mr. Abbotts, "Corner Stone."*

Here then we have arrived at a point where we part company with Mr. Erskine, and join Mr. Abbott, who advances further in a most perilous career. The principle with which Mr. E. began has been above discovered to issue in a view of the Gospel which may be contemplated apart from that principle. That the human mind may criticize and systematize the divine revelation, that it may identify it with the Dispensation, that it may limit the uses of the latter to its workings through our own reason and affections, and such workings as we can ascertain and comprehend, in a word, that the Gospel is a *Manifestation*, this is the fundamental principle of Mr. Erskine's Essay. Mr. Jacob Abbott seems so fully to take this principle for granted, that it would be idle to do more than notice his doing so; it will be more to the purpose to direct attention to this treatment of the theory, in which Mr. Erskine's principle seems to issue, viz. that the Gospel is a *Collection of facts.* I am now referring to Mr. Abbott's works called 'the Corner Stone," which I do not hesitate to say approaches within a hairs' breath of Socinianism; a charge which I would by no means urge against Mr. E, whatever be the *tendency* of his speculations.

In the work in question, Mr. Abbott disclaims entering into *theological* questions, properly so called (Preface, p. vi.); nor is there any necessity for his entering into them, so that the line of discussion which he does take, does not intrude upon them or provoke them.

"I have made this *exhibition* of the Gospel," he says, "with reference to its *moral* effect on human hearts, and not for the purpose of taking sides in a controversy between different parties of Christians."

Again,

"A system of theology is a map or plan, in which every feature of the country must be laid down in its proper place and proportion; this work is on the other hand a series of views, as the traveler sees them in passing over a certain road. In this case the road which I have taken, leads indeed through the heart of the country, but it does not by any means bring to view all which is interesting or important. The reader will perceive, that the history of JESUS CHRIST is the clue which I have endeavoured to follow; that is, the work is intended to exhibit religious truth, as it is connected with the various events in the life of our SAVIOUR. In first introducing Him to the scene, I consider His exalted nature as the *great Moral Manifestation of the Divinity to us.* Then follows a view *of His personal character, and of His views of religious duty, &c.*" pp. vi, vii.

Let us observe here the similarity of language between the two writers I am speaking of. They are evidently of the same school. They both direct their view to the Gospel *history* as a Manifestation of the Divine Character; and though, in the above extract, Mr. Abbott speaks more guardedly than Mr. Erskine, there will be found to be little or no practical difference between them. But there seems this most important distinction in their respective applications of their theory, though not very distinct or observable at first sight, that Mr. E. admits into the range of divine facts such as are not of this world, as the voluntary descent of CHRIST from heaven to earth, and his Incarnation, whereas Mr. A. virtually limits it to the witnessed history of CHRIST upon earth. This, so far as it exists, is all the difference between orthodoxy and Socinianism.

For this encroachment Mr. E. indeed had prepared the way; for he certainly throws the high doctrines of religion into the background; and the word "Manifestation" far more naturally fits on to a history witnessed by human beings, than to dispositions belonging to the unseen world. But Mr. E. certainly has not *taught* this explicitly.

If we wish to express the sacred Mystery of the Incarnation accurately, we should rather say that GOD is man, than that man is GOD. Not that the latter proposition is not altogether Catholic in its wording, but the former expresses the *history* of the Economy, (if I may so call it,) and confines our LORD's personality to His divine nature, making His manhood an adjunct; whereas to say that man is GOD does the contrary of both of these, – leads us to consider Him a man personally, with some vast and unknown dignity superadded, and that acquired of course after His coming into existence as man. The difference between these two modes of speaking is well illustrated in the recent work of a Socinian writer, whom on account of the truth and importance of his remarks, it is right, with whatever pain, to quote.

"A quick child, though not acquainted with logic, ... will perceive the absurdity of saying that Edward is John ... As the young pupil must be prepared to infer from the New Testament, that a perfect man is perfect GOD, he ... must be imperceptibly led to consider the word GOD as expressing a quality, or an aggregate of qualities, which may be predicated of more than one, as the name of a species; just as when we say John is man, Peter is man, Andrew is man ... And so it is, with the exception of a few who, in this country, are still acquainted with that ingeniously perverse system of word, by means of which the truly scholastic Trinitarians (such as Bishop Bull and Waterland, who had accurately studied the fathers and the schoolmen,[67]) appear to evade the logical contradictions with which the doctrine of the Trinity abounds; all, as I have observed for many years, take the word of GOD, in regard to Christ, as the name of a species, and more frequently of a dignity." *Heresy and Orthodoxy,* p. 91.[68]

It will be observed at this passage, that the writer implies that the orthodox mode of speaking of the Incarnation is not exposed to a certain consequence, to which the mode at present popular is exposed, viz. the tendency to explain away CHRIST's divinity. Man is GOD is the popular mode of speech, GOD is man is the Catholic. To return. It seems that Mr. Erskine proceeds in the orthodox way, illustrating the doctrine that GOD became man; Mr. A. starting with the earthly existence of our LORD, does but enlarge upon the doctrine that a man is GOD. Mr. Erskine enforces the Atonement, as a Manifestation of GOD's moral character; Mr. A. the life of CHRIST with the same purpose, – with but slight reference to the doctrine of the Expiation, for of course he whose life began with his birth from Mary, had given up nothing, and died merely because other men die. Here then is something very like Socinianism at first sight.

But again, let us see how he conducts his argument. Here again he differs from Mr. E. The latter considers the incarnation of the SON of GOD to be a manifestation of GOD's mercy. Here then in his view, which so far is correct, there is a double Manifestation, – of the SON of GOD personally in human nature, and of GOD morally in the history and circumstances of His incarnation; though Mr. E's argument leads him to insist on the latter. Mr. A. assumes the latter as the sole Manifestation, thus bringing out the tendency of Mr. E's argument. In other words, he considers our LORD JESUS CHRIST as a man primarily, not indeed a mere man, any more than the conversion of the world was a mere human work aided and blessed by GOD; a man in intimate union with GOD, as Moses might be on the Mount, but not more than Moses except in degree. He considers that certain attributes of the Godhead were manifested in JESUS CHRIST, in the sense that the solar system manifests His power, or animal economy His wisdom; which is a poorly concealed Socinianism. – So this, it appears, is what really comes of declaiming against "metaphysical" notions of the revelation, and enlarging on its moral character!

That I may not be unfair to Mr. A., I proceed to cite his words:

"In the first place, let us take a survey of the *visible universe*, that we may see what *manifestations* of GOD appear in *it*. Let us imagine that we can see with the naked eye all that the telescope would show us; and then, in order that we may obtain an uninterrupted view, let us leave this earth, and, ascending from its surface, take a station where we can look, without obstruction, upon all around. As we rise above the summits of the loftiest mountains, the bright and verdant regions of the earth begin to grow dim. City after city, &c. As the last breath of its atmosphere draws off from us, it leaves us in the midst of universal night, with a sky extending without interruption all around us, and bringing out to our view, in every possible direction, innumerable and interminable vistas of stars. . . . Our globe itself cuts off one half of the visible universe at all times, and the air spreads over us a deep canopy of blue, which during the day, shuts out entirely the other half. But were the field open, we should see in every direction the endless perspective of suns and stars, as I have described them. . . . The conception of childhood, and it is one which clings to us in maturer years, that above the blue sky there is a *heaven* concealed, where the Deity sits enthroned, is a delusive one. GOD is everywhere. ... The Deity is the *All-pervading Power*, which lives and acts throughout the whole, He is not a separate existence, having a special habitation in a part of it. ... The striking and beautiful metaphors of the Bible never were intended to give us this idea. GOD is a Spirit, it says, in its most emphatic tone. A Spirit; that is, he has no form, no place, no throne. Where he acts, there only can we see Him. He is the widespread omnipresent power, which is everywhere employed, but which we can never see, and never know, except so far as He shall manifest Himself by His doings.

"If we thus succeed in obtaining just conceptions of the Deity, as the invisible and universal *power*, pervading all space, and existing in all time, we shall at once perceive that the only way by which He can make Himself known to His creatures is by *acting Himself* out, as it were, in His works; *and of course the nature of the Manifestation which is made will depend upon the nature of the works*. In the structure of the solar system, with its blazing centre and revolving worlds, the Deity, invisible itself, acts out its mighty power, and the unerring perfection of its intellectual *skill*. At the same time, while it is carrying on these mighty movements, it is exercising, in a very different scene, its untiring *industry*, and unrivalled *taste*, in clothing a mighty forest with verdure, &c. &c. ... And so everywhere this unseen and universal essence *acts out its various attributes, by its different works*. We can learn its nature only by the character of the effects which spring from it ...

"This universal essence, then, must display to us its nature, by acting itself out in a thousand places, *by such manifestations* of itself as it wishes us to understand. Does GOD desire to impress us with the idea of His *power*? He darts the lightning, &c. &c. Does he wish to beam upon us in *love*? What can be more expressive than the sweet summer sunset, &c. ... How can He make us acquainted with His *benevolence* and *skill*? Why, by acting them out in some mechanism which exhibits them. He may construct an eye or a hand for man, &c. How can he give us some conception of His *intellectual powers*? He can plan the motions of the planets, &c. &c. ... But the great question, after all, is to come. It is the one to which we have meant that all we have been saying should ultimately tend. *How can such a Being exhibit the moral principle by which His mighty energies are all controlled*? pp. 6–14.

It is impossible to do justice to one's feelings of distress and dismay on studying this passage, – to explain what one thinks of it, and why, – to convince a careless reader that one's language about it is not extravagant. Nor is it necessary perhaps, as it does not directly bear upon the subject before us, – to which I will hasten on. I interrupt the course of this exposition merely to put in a protest against the doctrine of it, which, to speak shortly and plainly, is pantheistic, and against the spirit of it, which breathes an irreverence approaching on blasphemy. Should the reader think the tone of this paragraph is out of keeping with the remarks as yet made, he will see in a little time that Mr. Abbott does not allow one to preserve that didactic or critical air, which is commonly appropriate to a discussion such as the present. To proceed, however, with our immediate subject, the author's views, not of natural, but revealed religion: —

"He is an unseen, universal power, utterly invisible to us, and imperceptible, except so far as He shall act out His attributes in what He does. *How shall He act out moral principle?* It is easy, by his material creation to make any impression upon us, which material objects can make; but how shall He exhibit to us the moral beauty of justice and benevolence and mercy between man and man? ... He might *declare* His moral attributes as He might have declared His power; but if He would bring home to us the one as vividly and distinctly as the other, He must act out His moral principles by a moral *manifestation*, in a moral scene; *and the great beauty of Christianity* is, that it represents Him as doing so. He brings out the purity, and spotlessness, and moral glory of the Divinity, through the workings of a human mind, called into existence for this purpose, and stationed in a most conspicuous attitude among men. ... Thus the moral perfections of divinity show themselves to us in the only way by which, so far as we can see, it is possible directly to show them, by coming out in action, in the very field of human duty, by a mysterious union with a human intellect and human powers. It is GOD manifest in the flesh; *the visible moral image of an all-pervading moral Deity,* Himself for ever invisible." pp. 14, 15.

On this explanation of the Incarnation, now alas, not unpopular even in our own Church, viz. that "GOD manifest in the flesh" is "the *visible moral image*" of GOD, let us hear the judgment of one who was a Trinitarian, and has lately avowed Socinianism.[69] He thus relates the change in his own religious profession:

"In my anxiety to avoid a separation from the Church by the deliberate surrender of my mind to my old Unitarian convictions, I took refuges in a modification of the Sabellian theory, and availed myself of the moral unity which I believe to exist between GOD the FATHER and CHRIST, joined to the consideration that CHRIST is called in the New Testament the *Image* of GOD, and addressed my prayers to GOD *as appearing in that Image.* I left nothing untried to cultivate and encourage this feeling by devotional means. But such efforts of mere feeling (and I confess with shame their frequency on my part for the sake of what seemed most religious) were always vain and fruitless. *Sooner or later my reason has not only frustrated, but punished them.* In the last mentioned instance, the devout contrivance would not bear examination. *Sabellianism is only Unitarianism disguised in words;* and as for the worship of an image in its absence, the idea is most unsatisfactory. In this state, however, I passed five or six years; but the return to the clear and definite Unitarianism in which I had formerly been, was as easy as it was natural." *Heresy and Orthodoxy*, p. viii.

This passage proves thus much, not that the philosophizing in question *leads* to Socinianism, but that it is one under which Socinianism may *lie* hid, even from a man's own consciousness; and this is just the use I wish to make of it against Mr. Abbott. He ends as follows:

"The substance of the view, which I have been wishing to impress upon your minds, is, that we are to expect to see Him solely through *the manifestations He makes of Himself in His works.* We have seen in what way some of the traits of His character are displayed in the visible creation, and how at last He determined to *manifest His moral character,* by bringing into action *through the medium of a human soul.* The plan was carried into effect, and the mysterious person thus formed appears for the first time to our view in the extraordinary boy, &c." pp. 15, 16.

In these passages it seems to be clearly maintained that our LORD is a Manifestation of GOD in precisely that way in which His creatures are, though in a different respect, viz. as regards His moral attributes, – a Manifestation not having anything in it essentially peculiar and incommunicable, and therefore "*a* Manifestation" as he in one passage expresses himself, not *the* Manifestation of the FATHER.

Further he expressly disclaims any opinion concerning the essential and superhuman relation, or (as he calls it) the "metaphysical" relation of the SON to the FATHER, in a passage which involves a slight upon other doctrines of a most important, though not such a sacred character.

"Another source of endless and fruitless discussions, is disputing about questions *which can be of no practical consequence,* however they may be decided; such as the origin of sin,"

does this mean original sin?

"the state of the soul between death and the resurrection, the salvation of infants,"

is it possible he should thus talk?

"The *precise metaphysical relationship* of the SON to the FATHER." p. 323.[5]

Why called metaphysical, I do not understand, but we have been already introduced to this word by Mr. Erskine, whose original fallacy also, be in observed, is faithfully preserved in this passage; – "questions which can be of no practical consequence," as if we have any warrant thus to limit, or to decide upon the gracious revelations of GOD. He continues,

[5] Vide also p. 197.

"We have said they are of no practical consequences; *of course* an ingenious reason *can contrive* to connect practical consequences with *any subject whatever,* and in his zeal he will exaggerate the importance of the connexion;"

I interrupt the reader, to remind him that the subjects spoken of in this careless self-satisfied way, are those which from the first have been preserved in Creeds and Confessions as the most necessary, most solemn truths; —

"in fact, *every subject in the moral world is more or less connected with every other one;* nothing stands out entirely detached and isolated, and *consequently* a question which its arguers will admit to be merely a theoretical one, will never be found." p. 24.

But if so, who shall draw the line between truths practical and theoretical? Shall we trust the work to such as Mr. A? Surely this passage refutes his own doctrine. *We* also say that there are no two subjects in religion but may be connected by our minds, and therefore, for what we know, perchance are connected in fact. All we maintain in addition, is, that evidence of the fact of that connexion is not necessary for the proof of their importance to us, and further, that we have no right to pronounce that they are revealed, merely with a view to their importance to us.

He disposes of the Catholic doctrine of CHRIST's eternal Sonship by calling it metaphysical; how he escapes from the Catholic doctrine of the Incarnation we have already seen, - he resolves it into a moral Manifestation of GOD in the person of CHRIST. But his view requires a few more words of explanation. First he speaks of GOD in pantheistic language, as an Anima Mundi,[70] or universal essence, who has no known existence except in His works, as an all-pervading power or principle not external to the created world, but in it, and developed through it. He goes on to say that ALMIGHTY GOD, who is thus illimitable and incomprehensible, is exhibited in *personal* attributes in CHRIST, as if all the

laws and provisions in which He energizes in nature imper-
sonally, were condensed and exemplified in a real personal
being. Hence he calls our LORD by a strange term, the *personification* of GOD, i.e. (I suppose) the personal image, or the
Manifestation in a person. In other words GOD, whose
person is unknown in nature, in spite of His works, is
revealed in CHRIST, who is the express image of His person;
and just in this, and (as I conceive) nothing more, would he
conceive there was a difference between the Manifestation of
GOD in CHRIST and the Manifestation of Him in a planet or
a flower. CHRIST is a *personal* Manifestation. Whether there
be any elements of truth in this theory, I do not concern
myself to decide, thus much is evident, that he so *applies* it as
utterly to explain away the real divinity of our LORD. The
passages are as follows: –

"It is by JESUS CHRIST that we have access to the Father. This vital
exhibition of His character, this *personification of His moral attributes,*
opens to us the way., Here we see a manifestation of divinity, an
image of the Invisible GOD, which comes as it were down to us; it
meets our feeble faculties with a personification," &c. p. 40.

"We accordingly commenced with His childhood, and were led
at once into a train of reflection on the nature and the character of
that eternal and invisible essence, *whose attributes were personified in
Him."* p. 192.

"The human mind ... reaches forward for some vision of the
Divinity, the great unseen and inconceivable essence. JESUS CHRIST
is the *personification of the divinity for us,* the brightness of His glory
and the express image of His person." p. 200.

Next, as to his opinions concerning the doctrine of the
Atonement. I will not deny that some of his general expressions are correct, and taken by themselves, would be
satisfactory; but they are invalidated altogether by what he
has at other times advanced. It may be recollected that Mr.
E., in his treatise on Internal Evidence, lays such a stress upon
the use of the Atonement *as a Manifestation*, as to throw the

real doctrine itself into the shade. Viewed in itself, CHRIST's death is, we believe, a sacrifice acting in some unknown way for the expiation of human sin; but Mr. E. views it, (as indeed it may well be viewed, but exclusively as it should not be viewed,) as a mark and pledge of GOD's love to us, which it would be, though it were not an Expiation. Even though CHRIST's incarnation issued in nothing more than His preaching to the world and sealing His doctrine with His blood, it would be a great sign of His love, and a *pledge* now of our receiving blessings through Him; for why should He die except He meant to be merciful to us? but this would not involve the necessity of an Expiation. St. Paul died for the Church, and showed his love for it in this sense. When then the view of the Christian is limited, as Mr. E. would almost wish it to be, to the *Manifestation* of the Atonement, or the effect of the Atonement on our minds, no higher doctrine is *of necessity* elicited than that of its being a sign of GOD's mercy, as the rainbow might be, and a way is laid, by obscuring to obliterate the true doctrine concerning it. So far Mr. E. proceeds, not denying it (far from it) but putting it aside in his philosophical evidence: Mr. A., upon the very same basis, is bolder in his language, and almost, if not alto-gether gets rid of it.

In the following pages he applies Mr. Erskine's doctrine of the moral lesson, taught in CHRIST's death, of the justice and mercy of GOD; and he will be found distinctly to assert that the virtue of it *lay in this,* viz. that it was a *declaration* of GOD's hatred of sin, the same in kind as the punishment of the sinner would have been, only more perfect, a means of impressing *on us* His hatred of sin; not as if it really reconciled us to an offended Creator.

"The balm for your wounded spirit is this, that the moral impres-sion in respect to the nature and tendencies of sin, which *is the only possible reason* GOD can have in leaving you to suffer its penalties," one would think the reason might be that "the wages of sin is death,"[71]

"is accomplished far better by the life and death of His Son;—"

surely it is a greater balm to know that CHRIST has put away the wrath of GOD, as Scripture says,[72] than to theorize about "moral impressions" beyond the word of Scripture. Observe too, he says "the *life* and death," excluding the proper idea of Atonement, which lies in the death of CHRIST,[73] and so tending to resolve it into a Manifestation.

"GOD never could have wished to punish you for the sake of doing evil;"

how unspeakably bold;[74] when GOD says He does punish the sinner, not indeed for the sake of evil, but as a just and holy GOD!

"and all the good which He could have accomplished by it, is already effected in another and a better way." p. 179.[6]

Here is the same assumption which was just now instanced from the writings of Mr. Scott, of Aston Sandford, that GOD cannot afflict punishment except for the sake of a greater good, or, (as Mr. A. himself has expressed it just before) "because the welfare of His government requires" it, which is an altogether gratuitous statement.

Again:

"A knowledge of the death of CHRIST, with the explanation of it given in the Scriptures, touches men's hearts, it shows the nature and tendencies of sin, it produces fear of GOD's displeasure, and resolution to return to duty; and thus *produces effects by which* justice is satisfied,"—

---

[6] Vide also p. 173.

observe, not by an expiation, but by the repentance of the offender in consequence of the "moral impression" attendant on the "manifestation" of CHRIST's death, —

"and the authority of the law sustained for better in fact, than it would be by the severest punishment of the guilty sinner." p. 174.

"Look at the *moral effect* of this great sacrifice, and feel that it takes off all the necessity of punishment, and all the burden of your guilt." p. 190.

The necessity of punishment is (according to Mr. A.) the well being of the Universe: and the virtue of the great sacrifice is, not expiation, atonement in GOD's sight, but the *moral effect* of CHRIST's death on those who believe in it. So again, in a passage lately quoted for another purpose:

"It is by JESUS CHRIST that we have access to the Father. *This vivid exhibition of His character,* this personification of His moral attributes, *opens to us the way.*" p. 40.

Lastly, we have the same stress laid upon the facts of the Gospel as in Mr. Erskine's work, with this difference, that Mr. Erskine supposes the orthodox doctrine, or what he considers such, to be conveyed in the facts; Mr. Abbott with the liberalism to which his predecessor leads, but which is more characteristic of this day than of fifteen years ago, seems to think that various theories may be raised about the facts, whether orthodox or otherwise, but that the facts alone are of consequence to us.

"Such are the three great *Manifestations* of Himself to man, which the one Unseen All-pervading Essence has made, and exhibited to us in the Bible, and in our own experience and observation," —

—This sentence, be it observed in passing, savours strongly of Sabellianism; he has spoken of what he calls three Manifestations of ALMIGHTY GOD, as our natural Governor, as influencing the heart, and as in JESUS CHRIST, without there being anything in his way of speaking to show that he attributed these Manifestations respectively to THREE PERSONS. He proceeds:

"Though there have been interminable disputes in the Christian Church about the language which has been employed to describe these *facts,* there has been comparatively little dispute among even nominal[75] Christians about the *facts* themselves." p. 39.

Such is the theology to which Mr. E's principle is found to lead in the hands of Mr. Abbott; a theology (so to name it,) which violently robs the Christian Creed of all it contains, except those outward historical facts through which its divine truths were fulfilled and revealed to men.

This brief explanation of Mr. Abbott's theological system may be fitly followed up by some specimens of the temper and tone of his religious sentiments. In this way we shall be able to ascertain the state of mind which such speculations presuppose and foster.

"JESUS CHRIST had a taste for beauty, both of nature and art; He admired the magnificent architecture of the Temple, and deeply lamented the necessity of its overthrow, and his dress was at least of such a character, that the disposal of it was a subject of importance to the well paid soldiers who crucified him." pp. 50, 51.

I put aside the utter unreasonableness of this last remark; but let us think seriously, is CHRIST GOD, or is He not? If so, can we dare talk of Him as having "a taste for nature?" It is true Mr. A. does speak in this way of the ALMIGHTY FATHER also; so that it may be said rather to prove that He has a grovelling conception of GOD than of CHRIST. Perhaps it will be more truly said that his irreverence towards the SAVIOUR, has led on to the other more direct profaneness. Yet a "taste for beauty of *art*!" This of the Eternal SON of GOD, the Creator; will it be said that He is man also? true; – but His personality is in his Godhead, if I may express myself in theological language. He did not undo what He was, He did not cease to be the Infinite GOD, but He added to Him the substance of a man, and thus participated in human thoughts and feelings, yet with no impairing (GOD forbid) of His divine perfection. The Incarnation was not "a conversion of the Godhead into the flesh, but a taking of the manhood into GOD." It seems there is *need* of the Athanasian Creed in these dangerous times.[76] A Mystery, indeed, results from this view, for certain attributes of Divinity and of manhood seem incompatible; and there may be some revealed instances in our Lord's history on earth of less than divine thought and operation; but *because* of all this, we never must speak, of the Person of the ETERNAL WORD as thinking and feeling like a mere man, like a child, or a boy, as simply ignorant, imperfect, and dependent on the creature, which is Mr. A's way. In saying this, I am quite aware that the sensitiveness of a Christian mind will at once, without argument, shrink from a passage such as that commented on, but I say it by way of accounting for its aversion, which, perhaps, it may not be able to justify to others. To proceed: —

"JESUS CHRIST was in some respects the *most* bold, energetic, decided, and courageous man *that ever lived*; but in others he was the most flexible, submissive and yielding." p. 51.

The SON of GOD made flesh, though a man, is beyond comparison with other men; His person is not human; but to say "most of all men" is to compare.

"There never was a mission, or an enterprise of any kind, conducted with a more bold, energetic, fearless spirit, than the SAVIOUR's mission." p. 62.

This sentence may not seem objectionable to many people, and as it is similar to many others in the work, it may be right to remark upon it. The truth is, we have got into a way of, what may be called, panegyrizing our LORD's conduct, from our familiarity with treatises on external evidence. It has been the fashion of the day to speak as to unbelievers and, therefore, to level the sacred history to the rank of a human record, by way of argument. Hence we have learned to view the truth merely externally, i.e. as an unbeliever would view it; and so to view and treat it even when we are not arguing, which involves, of course, an habitual disrespect towards what we hold to be divine, and ought to treat as such. This will in part account for the tone in which the history of the Jews is sometimes set forth. And it is remarkably illustrated in the work before us, which though pointedly addressed only to those who "have confessed their sins and asked forgiveness," who "strive against temptation, and seek help from above," (vide p. 1.) yet is continually wandering into the external view of CHRIST's conduct, and assumes in a didactic treatise, what is only accidentally allowable in controversy.

"There is something very bold and energetic in the measures He adopted in accomplishing His work ... In fact, there perhaps, never was so great a moral effect produced in three years, on any community so extensive, if we consider at all the disadvantages incident to the customs of those days. There was no press, no modes of extensive written communication, no regularly organized channels of intercourse whatever between the different portions of the community. He acted under every disadvantage." pp. 53, 54.

Under no disadvantage, if He were GOD. But this is only part of one great error under which this writer lies. "There was no press!" What notions he has concerning the nature, the strength, and the propagation of moral truth!

"He sought solitude, he shrunk from observation; in fact, almost the only *enjoyment* which he seemed really to love, was His *lonely ramble* at midnight, for rest and prayer ... It is not surprising that *after the heated crowds and exhausting labours of the day,* He should love to retire to silence and seclusion, to enjoy the cool and balmy air, the refreshing stillness, and all the beauties and glories of midnight among the solitudes of the Galilean hills, to find there happy communion with his Father, &c." p. 55.

The more ordinary and commonplace, the more like vulgar life, the more carnal the history of the Eternal SON of GOD is made, the more does this writer exult in it. He exults in sinking the higher notion of CHRIST, and in making the flesh the '*ηγεμονίκον*[77] of a Divine Essence. Even a prophet or apostle *might* be conceived to subdue the innocent enjoyments of His lower nature to the sovereignty of faith, and enjoy this world as an emblem and instrument of the unseen. But it is the triumph of Rationalism to level everything to the lowest and most tangible form into which it can be cast, and to view the SAVIOUR Himself, not in His mysterious greatness, acting by means of human nature, and ministered unto by Angels in it,[78] but as what I dare not draw out, lest profane words be necessary, as akin to those lower natures which have but an animal existence.

"Another thing which exhibits the *boldness and enterprise,* that characterized his plans for making an impression on the community, was the *peculiarly new and original style of public speaking* He adopted." p. 55.

"This then is the key to the character of JESUS CHRIST in respect to *spirit and decision.*" p. 57.

"For the real sublimity of courage, the spectacle of this deserted and defenceless sufferer coming at midnight to meet the betrayer and his band, far exceeds that of Napoleon urging on his columns over the bridge of Lodi, or even that of Regulus returning to his chains."[79] pp. 59, 60.

One seems to incur some ceremonial pollution by repeating such miserable words.

"He *evidently observed, and enjoyed* nature. There are many allusions to His solitary walks in the fields, and on the mountains, and by the sea side; but the greatest evidence of His *love for nature* is to be seen in the manner in which He speaks of its beauties. *A man's metaphors* are drawn from the sources with which he is most familiar, or which interest him most." p. 60.

"We learn in the same manner how distinct were the *impressions of beauty or sublimity,* which the works of nature made upon the SAVIOUR, by the manner in which He alluded to them. ... Look at the lilies of the field says He.[80] ... *A cold heartless man,* without *taste or sensibility,* would not have said such a thing as that. He could not; and we may be as sure, that JESUS CHRIST *had stopped to examine and admire* the grace and beauty of the plant, &c." pp. 61, 62.

"Now JESUS CHRIST noticed these things. He *perceived* their beauty and enjoyed it." p. 62.

Surely such passages as these are direct evidence of Socinianism. Does any one feel curiosity, or wonder, does anyone search and examine, in the case of things fully known to Him? Could the Creator of nature "stop to *examine*" and "enjoy the grace and beauty" of His own work? Were indeed this said of Him, we should say, "Here is one of the Mysteries which attend on the Incarnation," but since we cannot suspect such writers as Mr. A. inventing a Mystery for the sake of it, we must take it as evidence of a carnal and Socinian view of the SAVIOUR of mankind.

"He observed everything, and His *imagination was stored* with an inexhaustible supply of images, drawn from every source, and with these He illustrated and enforced His principles in a manner altogether unparalleled by any writings, sacred or profane." p. 63.

So this is the ashes to be given as children's meat to those who "confess" and repent, and try to know GOD's will in the Gospel!

"Even His disciples, till they came to see Him die, had no conception of His love. They learned it at last, however. They saw Him suffer and die; and inspiration from above explained to them something about the influence of His death. *They enjoyed its benefits long before.*" –

All this is presumptuous and unsatisfactory, but let it pass.

"It is hard to tell which touches our gratitude most sensibly; the ardent love which led Him to do what He did, or *the delicacy with which He refrained from speaking of it* to those who were to reap its fruits." p. 94.

—that is, the delicacy towards sinners of an injured Creator, coming to atone in some mysterious way by His own sufferings for their sins in the sight of GOD His FATHER.

"There is in fact no moral or spiritual safety without these feelings, and *our* SAVIOUR *knew this full well.*" p. 204.

"JESUS CHRIST *understood human nature better.* ... He was *wiser* than the builders of the pyramids. ... The SAVIOUR did the work and *did it better,* by a few parting words." p. 217.

Such are the feelings which this writer ventures to express concerning Him, who is His LORD and His GOD. In condemning, however, his most unclean and miserable imaginings, I have neither wish nor occasion to speak against him as an individual. We have no concern with *him*. We know nothing of his opportunities of knowing better, nor how far what appears in his writings is an index of his mind. We need only consider him as the organ, involuntary (if you will) or unwittingly, but still the organ of the spirit of the Age, the voice of that scornful, arrogant, and self-trusting spirit, which has been unchained during these latter ages, and waxes stronger in power day by day, till it is fain to stamp under foot all the host of heaven.[81] This spirit we may steadily contemplate to our great edification; but to do more than denounce it *as such,* to judge or revile its instruments, would involve another sin besides uncharitableness. For surely, this is a spirit which has tempted others besides those who have yielded to its influences; and like an infection in the air,[82] it has perchance ere now, in some degree, not perhaps the high doctrines of the gospel, but in some way or other, breathed upon those who, at the present crisis of things, feel themselves called upon solemnly to resist it. The books of the day are so full of its evil doctrine in a modified shape, if not in its grosser forms, the principles (I may say,) of the nation are so instinct with it or based in it, that the best perhaps that can be said of any of us, or at most of all but a few, is that they have escaped from it "so as by fire,"[83] and that the loudness of their warning is but a consequence of past danger, terror and flight.

I view the works, then, of this writer, whether in their publication, or in their general reception, as signs of the religious temper of this Age. What shall be said of the *praise* that has been lavished on them? the *popularity* they have acquired? Granting that there are many things in them, from which a religious mind may gain something (for no one accuses Mr. A. of being deficient in quickness and intelligence,[84] and he evidently has had opportunities of studying human nature, whatever success has attended him in it, – and it must be confessed that his first work[85] published here was of a less objectionable character, and might well interest at first sight those who "thought no evil") but, allowing all this, yet it may be fairly asked, is the book from which I have cited, one which Christian minds can come very near without revolting from? How is it then that so many men professing strict religion, have embraced and dwelt on its statements without smelling the taint of death which is in them? And is there not something of a self-convicted mischief in that View of religion, the upholder of which, independent of each other, and disagreeing with each other materially in other points of doctrine and discipline, attempt to support by editing a book, as conducive to it, which turns out to be all but Socinian? The reason (I believe), why many pious persons tolerate a writer such as this, is, that they have so fully identified spirituality of mind with the use of certain phrases and professions, that they cannot *believe* that a person who uses them freely and naturally can be but taught of the Holy Spirit: to believe it otherwise, would be unsettling their minds from the very foundation, – which indeed must take place sooner or later whether they will or not.

With some quotations from the preface of one of Mr. A's editors,[86] one of the most learned, orthodox, and moderate of the Dissenters of the day, I will bring this discussion to an end.

"Mr Abbott has so much of originality in his manner of thinking, and of *unguarded simplicity* in his style of expression," [as render a friendly editor useful,] "There might be peril that, without such a precaution, some readers would take a premature alarm, when they found some essential doctrines of Christianity conveyed in *terms of simplicity*, and elucidated by very familiar analogues, which appear considerably removed from our accredited phraseology. ... *Whatever use we make of the language of the theological schools, we should never go beyond our ability to translate it into the plain speech of common life.*"

As far as the *words* go, this means, when duly explained, though the writer could not of course intend it. that Mr. A's merit consists in having translated Trinitarianism into Socinianism. And that this is no unfair interpretation of the *words*, is plain from what presently follows, in which he speaks of the *prejudice* which the orthodox language and doctrine of divinity create against orthodoxy in the minds of those who are orthodox, *all but* receiving these orthodox statements. In other words, expressly specifying the Socinians, he requires us to adopt Mr. A's language in order to reconcile them to us. I quote his words.

"But there is one department in the inseparable domain of theology and religion, upon Mr. Abbott's treatment of which, I should be very blameable, were I to withhold my convictions. Among us, as well as in the New England States, there is a body, large and respectable if considered absolutely, but far from large when viewed in comparison with the numbers of other professed Christians. It consists of those who believe the doctrines held, as to their essential principles, by all other Christian denominations, with respect to the way in which sinful, guilty, degraded mankind may regain the favour of GOD and the pure felicity of the world to come; – the doctrines of a divine SAVIOUR, His assumption of our nature, His propitiation and righteousness, and the restoration of holiness and happiness by His all-gracious SPIRIT. This class of persons is treated, by some public men, and in some influential writings, chiefly periodical, with scorn and contumely, and are held up to hatred, not to say persecution; they are continually represented as blasphemers and infidels, alike dangerous to the state, and inimical to all vital religion. Hence, thousands of excellent persons, deriving their only knowledge from the source to which I have alluded, regard this portion of their neighbours with horror, never think of treating them with tenderness, never attempt to obtain a lodgment for truth and holy affections in their hearts. Ah, little think these well meaning persons, &c. ... The circumstances of my life have put me into a condition of more correctly knowing this class of our fellow professors of Christianity; I know that there are among them serious, thoughtful, amiable persons, whose minds are prepossessed with prejudices against us and our system, much to the same extent as we are against them and theirs. I know, not merely how they reason, but how they feel. They in general have extremely erroneous conceptions of the orthodox system of faith. They have imbibed those misconceptions in early years; and subsequent circumstances, of no trivial power to confirm prejudice, we have to blame ourselves. This is a state of things full of mischief and danger. Surely it is a pressing duty, to do all that we can for clearing away the clouds of ignorance and misrepresentation which, with so dire effect, discolour and distort the objects seen through them. For this purpose, it is to me an heartfelt pleasure to say that Mr. Abbott's 'Corner Stone' is admirably adapted. Notions producing feelings, and those feelings so deep and wide activity in the formation of religious sentiments, have been derived from Pelagius, Socinus, and Episcopius, from Clarke, Law, and Watson, from Lardner, Priestley, and Channing;[87] and it is the thoroughly pervading influence on the mind of those mutually acting feelings and sentiments, which produces all that is formidable in the theoretical objections, and much of that which is effective in the practical repugnance, which are entertained by many against the doctrines of grace and holiness through the Atonement and the Spirit of Christ. How desirable to meet those feelings in their germinating principle; to anticipate those sentiments, by the dissolution of the causes which would from them. This is what our author has done. His *reasonings and official attributes* of our Lord and Saviour, are such as may be compared to the *correctness of anatomical knowledge, the delicacy of touch, and the astonishing preciseness of applying the probe and the knife, which we admire in the first surgeons of the age.*"

A correct and memorable witness indeed, to the kind of treatment offered by these religionists to Him, whom, after His exposure on the cross, His true disciples reverently "took down," and "wrapped in fine linen," and "laid in a sepulchre wherein never man before was laid."[88]

I will conclude by summing up in one sentence, which must be pardoned me, if in appearance harsh, what the foregoing discussion is intended to show. There is a widely spread, though variously received School of doctrine among us, within and without the Church, which intends and professes peculiar piety, as directing its attention to the *heart itself*, not to anything external to us, whether creed, actions, or ritual. I do not hesitate to assert that this doctrine is based upon error, that it is really a specious form of trusting man rather than God, that it is in its nature Rationalistic, and that it tends to Socinianism. How the individual supporters of it will act as time goes on is another matter, – the good will be separated from the bad; but the School, as such, will pass through Sabellianism, to that "God-denying Apostasy,"[89] to use the ancient phrase, to which in the beginning of its career it professed to be especially opposed.

Oxford,
The Feast of the Purification

N.B. For reasons, not necessary here to explain, it may be proper to observe, that this Tract was written before the commencement of 1836.

Postscript

Since the above Essay was in type, an account of Dr. Schleiermacher's[90] view of the doctrine of the Trinity, as contained in an American Periodical[7] has been put into the writer's hands, and raises very painful feelings.

It seems, indeed, impossible to doubt that a serious doctrinal error is coming as a snare over the whole of the Protestant part of Christendom, (every part, at least, which is not fallen into worse and more avowed heterodoxy,) being the result of an attempt of the intellect to delineate, philosophise, and justify that religion, (so called) of the heart and feelings, which has long prevailed. All over the Protestant world, – among ourselves, in Ireland, in Scotland, in Germany, in British America,[91] – the revival of religious feeling during the last century has taken a peculiar form, difficult to describe or denote by any distinct appellation, but familiarly known to all who ever so little attend to what is going on in the general Church. It has spread, not by talents or learning in its upholders, but by their piety, zeal, and sincerity, and its own incidental and partial truth. At length, as was natural, its professors have been led to a direct contemplation of it, to a reflection upon their own feelings and belief, and the genius of their system; and thence has issued that philosophy of which Mr. Erskine and Mr. Abbott have in the foregoing pages afforded specimens.

The American publication above alluded to, is a melancholy evidence that the learning and genius of Germany are to be made to bear in favour of this same (as the writer must call it) spurious Christianity, by the theologians of the United States. Some passages from it shall be here extracted, which

---

[7] *The Biblical Repository*, Nos 18 and 19, in which is translated and reviewed[92] Schliermacher's Comparison of the Athanasian and Sabellian views of the Trinity."

will be found to tend to one or other of these three objects, all of them also professed in the two works above analysed.

1. That the one object of the Christian Revelation, or Dispensation, is to stir the affections, and soothe the heart.

2. That it really contains nothing which is unintelligible to the intellect.

3. That misbelievers, such as Socinians, &c., are made so, for the most part, by the Creeds, which are to be considered as the great impediments of the Gospel, both as being stumbling-blocks to the reason, and shackles and weights on the affections.

"With regard to Schleiermacher's views as a Trinitarian, I can truly say that I have met with scarcely any writer, ancient or modern, who appears to have a deeper conviction of, or more hearty belief in, the doctrine of the real Godhead of the FATHER, SON and HOLY SPIRIT . . . 'God manifest in the flesh,' seems to be inscribed, in his view, on every great truth of the Gospel, and to enter as a necessary ingredient into the composition of its essential nature. Yet Schleiermacher was not made a Trinitarian by creeds and confessions. Neither the Nicene or Athanasian symbol, nor any succeeding formula of Trinitarian doctrine, built on this, appears to have had any influence in the formation of his views. From the Scriptures, and from arguments flowing, as he believed, out of Scriptural premises, he became, and lived, and died, a hearty and constant believer in the One Living and True GOD, *revealed to us as* FATHER, SON, and HOLY GHOST . . . He ventured to inquire whether, in the vehemence of dispute, and in the *midst of philosophical mists,* the former survey had been in all respects made with thorough and exact skill and care, and whether a report of it *in all respects intelligible and consistent* had been made out." – Translator, No. 18, pp. 268–9.

"After defending in various places, in the most explicit manner, and with great ability, the doctrine of the Godhead of the SON and the SPIRIT, and *showing that such a development of the Deity is demanded by our moral wants as sinners, in order that we may obtain peace and sanctification;* he concludes," &c. *ibid.*

"Of his view of the Trinity, we may at least say that *it is intelligible.*

But who will venture to say, that any of the definitions heretofore given of personality in the Godhead in itself considered, I mean such definitions as have their basis in the Nicene or Athanasian Creeds, are *intelligible and satisfactory* to the mind?" p. 277.

"The sum of Schleiermacher's opinions ... is that ... the Unity ... is GOD *in se ipso*;[93] but as to the Trinity, the FATHER is GOD as revealed in the works of creation, providence, and legislation: the SON is GOD in human flesh, the divine Logos incarnate; the HOLY GHOST is GOD the sanctifier, who renovates the hearts of sinners, and dwells in the hearts of believers. The personality of the Godhead consists in these developments, made in time, and made to intelligent and rational beings. Strictly speaking, personality is not in his view eternal; and from the nature of the case as thus viewed, it could not be, because it consists in developments of the Godhead to intelligent beings, &c." p. 317.

"That GOD has developed himself in these three different ways, is what they [Sabellius and Schleiermacher,] believe to be taught in the Scriptures, and to be commended to our spiritual consciousness by the nature of our wants, woes and sins." No. 19, p. 81.

"Dr. Schleiermacher asks, with deep emotion, what more is *demanded*? what more is *necessary*? what more can *further the interests of practical piety*?" p. 82.

"I can see no *contradiction*, no *absurdity*, nothing even *incongruous* in the supposition that the Divine Nature has *manifested* itself as FATHER, &c." p. 88.

"Why should it ever have any more been overlooked that the names FATHER, &c. are names that have a *relative* sense ... than that such names as Creator, &c." p. 110.

"It may be proper for me to say, that the results of this re-examination of the doctrine of the Trinity are, in their essential parts, the same which I some years since advocated in my letters addressed to the Rev. Dr. Channing, &c." p. 115.

These extracts are perhaps sufficient to justify the apprehensions above expressed, as far as the more religious part of Protestant Germany is concerned. It is believed that Protestant France could be made to afford similar evidence of the Sabellian tendencies of the day.

TRACT 75

ON THE ROMAN BREVIARY AS EMBODYING THE SUBSTANCE OF THE DEVOTIONAL SERVICES OF THE CHURCH CATHOLIC

———————————

> Teach her to know and love her hour of prayer,
>> And evermore,
>> As faith grows rare,
> Unlock her heart, and offer all its store,
>> In holier love and humbler vows,
>> As suits a lost returning spouse.
>> (The Christian Year)

THERE is so much of excellence and beauty in the Services of the Breviary, that, were it skillfully set before the Protestant by Romanistic controversialists as the book of devotions received in their communion, it would undoubtedly raise a prejudice in their favour, if he were ignorant of the circumstances of the case, and but ordinarily candid and unprejudiced. To meet this danger is one principal object of the following pages; in which, whatever is good and true in those Devotions will be claimed, and on reasonable grounds, for the Church Catholic in opposition to the Roman Church, whose only real claim above other Churches is that of having adopted into the Service certain additions and novelties, ascertainable to be such in history, as well as being corruptions doctrinally. In a word, it will be attempted to wrest a weapon out of our adversaries' hands; who have in this, as in many other instances, appropriated to themselves a treasure which was ours as much as theirs; and then, on our attempting to recover it, accuse us of borrowing what we have but lost through inadvertence. The publication then of the selections, which it is proposed presently to give from these Services, is, as it were, an act of re-appropriation.[1] Were however the Breviary even so much the property of the Romanists, by retaining it in its ancient Latin form, they have defrauded the Church of the benefit which, in the vernacular tongue, it might have afforded to the people at large.

Another reason for the selections which are to follow, lies in the circumstance, that our own daily Service is confessedly formed upon the Breviary; so that an inspection of the latter will be found materially to illustrate and explain our own Prayer-Book.

It may suggest, moreover, character and matter for our *private* devotions, over and above what our Reformers have thought fit to adopt into our public Services; a use of it which will be but carrying out and completing what they have begun.

And there is a further benefit which, it is hoped, will result from an acquaintance with the Breviary Services, viz. that the adaptation and arrangement of the Psalms therein made, will impress many persons with a truer sense of the excellence and profitableness of those inspired compositions than it is the fashion of this age to entertain.

Lastly, if it can be shown, as was above intimated, that the corruptions, whatever they be, are of a late date, another fact will have been ascertained, in addition to those which are ordinarily insisted on, discriminating and separating off the Roman from the primitive Church.

With these views a sketch shall first be given of the history of the Breviary; then the selections from it shall follow.

INTRODUCTION

On the history of the Breviary[1]

The word *Breviarium*[2] first occurs in the work of an author of the eleventh century, and is used to denote a compendium or systematic arrangement of the devotional offices of the Church. Till that time they were contained in several independent volumes, according to the nature of each. Such, for instance, were the *Psalteria, Homilaria, Hymnaria* and the like, to be used in the service in due course. But at this memorable era, and under the auspices of the Pontiff who makes it memorable, Gregory VII,[3] an Order was drawn up, for the use of the Roman Church, containing in one all these different collections, introducing the separate members of each in its proper place, and harmonizing them together by the use of rubrics. Indeed, some have been led to conclude that in its first origin the word *Breviary* was appropriated to a mere collection of rubrics, not to the offices connected by them. But even taking it in its present sense, it will be obvious to anyone who inspects the Breviary how well it answers to its name Yet even thus digested, it occupies four thick volumes of duodecimo size.[4]

Gregory VII did but restore and harmonize these offices; which seem to have existed more or less the same in constituent parts though not in order and system from Apostolic times. In their present shape they are appointed for seven distinct seasons in the twenty-four hours,[5] and consist of prayers, praises, and thanksgivings of various forms; and as regards both contents and hours, are the continuation of a system of worship observed by the Apostles and their converts. As to *contents*, the Breviary Services consist of the

---

[1] The authorities used in this account are Gavanti's *Thesaurus Rituum,* cum notis Merari; Zaccaria's *Bibliotheca Ritualis*; and Mr. Palmer's *Origines Liturgicae.*

Psalms; of Hymns, and Canticles; of Lessons and Texts from inspired and ecclesiastical authors; of Antiphons, Verses and Responses, and Sentences; and of Collects. And analogous to this seems to have been the usage of the Corinthian Christians, whom St. Paul blames for refusing to agree in some common order of worship; when they came together, *everyone of them* having a Psalm, a doctrine, a tongue, a revelation, an interpretation.[2] On the other hand, the Catholic *seasons* of devotion are certainly derived from Apostolic usage. The Jewish observance of the third, sixth, and ninth hours for prayer, was continued by the inspired founders of the Christian Church. What Daniel had practiced, even when the decree was signed forbidding it, "kneeling on his knees three times a day, and praying, and giving thanks unto his GOD."[6] St Peter and the other Apostles were solicitous in preserving. It was when "they were all with one accord in one place," at "the *third* hour of the day,"[7] that the HOLY GHOST came down on them at Pentecost. It was at the *sixth* hour, that St. Peter "went up upon the housetop to pray,"[8] and saw the vision revealing to him the admission of the Gentiles into the Church. And it was at the *ninth* hour that "Peter and John went up together into the temple," "the hour of prayer."[9] But though these were the more remarkable seasons of devotion, there certainly were others besides them, in the first age of the Church. After our SAVIOUR's departure, the Apostles, we are informed, "all *continued* with one accord in prayer and supplication with the women, and Mary the mother of Jesus, and with His brethren;"[10] and with this accords the repeated exhortation to pray together without ceasing, which occurs in St. Paul's Epistles. It will be observed that he insists in one passage on prayer to the abridgement of sleep;[3] and one recorded passage of his life

[2] 1 Cor. 14:26.
[3] Eph. 6:18.

exemplifies his precept. "And at midnight Paul and Silas prayed, and sang praises unto GOD, and the prisoners heard them.[11] Surely it is more natural to suppose that this act of worship came in course, according to their wont, and was only not omitted because of their imprisonment, somewhat after Daniel's pattern, than that they should have gone aside to bear this sort of indirect testimony to the Gospel.

Such was the Apostolic worship as far as Scripture happens to have preserved it; that it was as systematic, and as apportioned to particular times of the day, as in the aftertimes of peace and prosperity, is not to be supposed; yet it seems to have been as ample and extended, as then, under ordinary circumstances. If St. Paul thought a prison and a prison's inmates no impediment to vocal prayer, we may believe it was no common difficulty which ever kept him from it.

In subsequent times the Hours of prayer were gradually developed from the three, or (with midnight) the four seasons, above enumerated, to seven, viz. by the addition of Prime (the first hour), Vespers (the evening), and Compline (bedtime); according to the words of the Psalm, "Seven times a day do I praise Thee, because of Thy righteous judgments."[12] Other pious and instructive reasons existed, or have since been perceived, for this number. It was a memorial of the seven days of creation; it was an honour done to the seven petitions given us by our LORD in His prayer; it was a mode of pleading for the influence of that Spirit who is revealed to us as sevenfold;[13] on the other hand, it was a preservative against those seven evil spirits, which are apt to return to the exorcised soul more wicked than he who has been driven out of it;[14] and it was a fit remedy of those seven successive falls, which Scripture says happen to "the just man" daily.[15]

And, as the particular number of their Services admitted of various meanings, so did each in its turn suggest separate events in our SAVIOUR's history. He was born, and He rose again at midnight. At Prime, (or 7 a.m. according to our reckoning,) He was brought before Pilate. At the third (or 9 a.m.,) He was devoted to crucifixion by the Jews, and scourged. At the sixth (or noon,) He was crucified. At the ninth (or 3 p.m.,) He expired. At Vespers He was taken down from the cross; at which hour He had the day before eat the Passover, washed His Apostles' feet, and consecrated the Eucharist. At Completorium, or Compline, He endured the agony in the garden.

These separate Hours, however, require a more distinct notice. The night Service was intended for the end of the night, when it was still dark, but drawing towards day; and, considering that the hour for rest was placed soon after sunset, it did not infringe upon the time necessary for repose. Supposing the time of sleep to extend from 8 or 9 p.m. to 3 or 4 in the morning, the worshipper might then rise without inconvenience to perform the service which was called variously Nocturns,[16] or Matins, as we still indifferently describe the hours in which it took place, as night or morning. It consist, when full, of three parts, or Nocturns, each made up of Psalms and Lessons; and it ended in a Service, supposed to be used shortly before sunrise, and called Lauds, or Praises. This termination of the Nocturn Service is sometimes considered distinct from it, so as to make eight instead of seven Hours in the day; as if in accordance with the text, "Give a portion to seven, and also to eight."[17] Accordingly it is sometimes called by the name of Matins, instead of the Nocturns; and sometimes both together are so called.

This subdivision of the night-service has the effect of dividing the course of worship into two distinct parts, of similar structure with each other; the three Nocturns, Lauds, and Prime, corresponding respectively to the three day hours (of the 3rd, 6th, and 9th) Vespers and Compline. Of these the three day hours are made up of Psalms, Hymns, and

Sentences.[18] These are the simplest of the Services, and differ very little from each other through the year. Lauds answers to Vespers, the sun being about to rise or about to set in the one and the other respectively. Each contains five Psalms, a Text, Hymn, Evangelical Canticle, Collect, and Commemoration of Saints. These hours are considered to answer to the morning and evening sacrifice of the Jews.[19]

Prime and Compline were introduced at the same time (the fifth century), and are placed respectively at the beginning of the day and the beginning of night. In each there is a Confession, four Psalms, a Hymn, Text, and Sentences.

The ecclesiastical day is considered to begin with the evening or Vesper service; according to the Jewish reckoning, as alluded to in the text, "In the evening, and morning, and at noon-day will I pray, and that instantly."[20] The ancient Verspers are regarded by some to be the most solemn hour of the day. They were sometimes called the *Officium Lucernarum.*[4] Prayers were in some places offered while the lamps were lighting; and this rite was called *lumen offerre.*[5] [21] The Mozarabic service supplies an instance of this, in which the Office ran as follows:

"Kyrie eleyson, Christe eleyson, Kyrie eleyson. Pater noster, &c. In nomine Domini Jesu Christi, lumen cum pace. R. Amen. Hoc est lumen oblatum. R. Deo gratias."[22]

On Festivals, the appropriate Services, beginning on the evening of the preceding day, are continued over the evening of the day itself; so that there are in such cases two Vespers, called the First and the Second, of which the First are the more solemn.

---

[4] Vid. Socrates, *History* 5.22. Vide also ' Lyra Apostolica', xv [in *British Magazine,* March 1834].

[5] This ceremony must not be confused with the *Lucernarium,* or prayers at lighting the lamps, which took place before the evening.

This is the stated succession of the sacred offices through the day, but the observance of the precise hours has not been generally insisted on at any time, but has varied with local usages or individual convenience. Thus the Matin and Laud Services may be celebrated on the preceding evening, as is done for instance in the Sestine Chapel at Rome during Passion week, the celebrated *Miserere* being the first Psalm of Lauds.[23] Prime may be used just before or after sunrise; the Third soon after the Sixth; the Ninth[24] near dinner; Vespers and Compline after dinner. Or Prime, the Third, Sixth and Ninth may come together two or three hours after sunrise. The hour of dinner, which, in most ages, as now abroad, has been the meal of the day, is made to divide the Services; there is a rule, for instance, against Compline coming before dinner.[25]

Such is the present order and use of the Breviary Service, as derived more or less directly from Apostolic practice. Impressed with their antiquity, our Reformers did not venture to write a Prayer-Book of their own, but availed themselves of what was ready to their hands; in consequence our Daily Service is a compound of portions of this primitive ritual, Matins being made up of the Catholic Matins, Lauds, and Prime, and Evensong of Vespers and Compline. The reason why these changes were brought about will be seen in the following sketch of the history of the breviary from the time of Gregory VII.

The word has been already explained to mean something between a directory and an harmony of offices; but it is to be feared there was another, and not so satisfactory reason for the use of it. It implied an abridgement or curtailment of Services, and so in particular of the Scripture readings, whether Psalms of Lessons, at least in practice.[26] Of course there is no reason why the Church might not, in the use of her discretion, limit as well as select the portions of the inspired volume, which were to be introduced into her devotions; but there were serious reasons why she should not defraud her children of "their portion of meat in due season,"[27] and it would seem, as if the eleventh or at least the twelfth century, a time fertile in other false steps in religion,[28] must be charged also, as far as concerns Rome and its most intimate dependencies, with a partial removal of the light of the written Word from the Sanctuary. Whatever benefit attended the adjustment of the offices in other respects, so far as the reading of Scripture was omitted, it was productive of evil, at least in prospect. An impulse was given, however slight in itself, which was followed up in the centuries which succeeded, and in all those churches which either then, or in the course of time, adopted the usages or Rome.

Even now that usage is not in universal use in the Latin Communion, and it was in no sense enjoined on the whole communion till after the Council of Trent;[29] but from the influence of the papal see and of the monastic orders, it seems to have affected other countries from a much earlier date. This influence would naturally be increased by the circumstance that the old Roman Breviary had long before Gregory's time been received in various parts of Europe: in England, since the time of Gregory the Great, who, after the pattern of Leo, and Gelasius before him, had been a Reformer of it;[30] in Basle, since the ninth century; in France and Germany by means of Pepin and Charlemagne;[31] while Gregory VII himself effected its reception in Spain. Other breviaries however still were in use, as they are at this day. The Ambrosian Breviary used in the Church in Milan, derives its name from the great St. Ambrose;[32] and in the ninth century Charles the Bald,[33] while sanctioning the use of the Roman, speaks also of the usage of Jerusalem, of Constantinople, of Gaul, of Italy, and of Toledo.

In Gregory's Breviary there are no symptoms of a neglect

of Scripture. It contains the offices for festival–days, Sundays, and weekdays; Matins on festivals having nine Psalms and nine Lessons, and on Sundays, eighteen Psalms and nine Lessons, as at present. The course of the Scripture Lessons was the same as it had been before his time; as it is preserved in a manuscript of the thirteenth century. It will be found to agree in great measure both with the order of the present Breviary and with our own. From Advent to Christmas were read portions of the prophet Isaiah; from the Octave of Epiphany to Septuagesima,[34] St Paul's Epistle to the Romans; from Septuagesima to the third Sunday in Lent, the book of Genesis, chapters 1, 12 and 27 on the Sundays to which they are allotted in our own offices; on the fourth in Lent to Wednesday in Passion Week, Jeremiah; from Easter to the third Sunday after, the Apocalypse; from the third to the fifth, St. James; from the Octave of the Ascension to Pentecost, the Acts; after the Octave of Trinity to the last Sunday in July, the books of Kings; in August, Proverbs; in September, Job, Tobit, Judith, and Esther; in October, Maccabees; and in November, Ezekiel, Daniel and other prophets.

Well would it have been if this laudable usage, received from the first ages, and confirmed by Pope Gregory VII had been observed, according to his design,[35] in the Roman Church; but his own successors were the first to depart from it. The example was set in the Pope's chapel of curtailing the sacred Services, and by the end of the twelfth century it had been followed in all the churches of Rome, except that of St. John Lateran. The Fratres Minores, (Minorists or Franciscans) adopted the new usage, and their Breviaries were in consequence remarkable for the title "secundum consuetudinem Romanae Curiae,"[36] contrary to the usage of such countries as conformed to the Roman Ritual, which were guided by the custom of the churches in the city. Haymo,[37] the chief of this order, had the sanction of

Gregory X in the middle of the thirteenth century, to correct
and complete a change, which as having begun in irregularity, was little likely to have fallen of itself into an orderly
system; and his arrangements, which were conducted on the
pattern of the Franciscan Devotions, nearly correspond to the
Breviary, as it at present stands.

Haymo's edition, which was introduced into the Roman
Church by Nicholas III[38] in AD 1278, is memorable for
another and still more serious fault. Graver and sounder
matter being excluded, apocryphal legends of Saints were
used to stimulate and occupy the popular mind; and a way
was made for the use of the Invocations to the Virgin and
other Saints, which heretofore were unknown in public
worship. The Addresses to the blessed Mary in the Breviary,
as it is at present constituted, are such as the following: – the
Ave Mary, before commencing every office through the day
and at the end of Compline; at the end of Lauds and Vespers,
and Antiphon invocatory of the Virgin; the Officium B.
Mariae, on the Sabbath or Saturday, and sundry other offices,
containing Hymns and Antiphons in her honour.[39] These
portions of the Breviary carry with them their own plain
condemnation in the judgment of an English Christian; no
commendation of the general structure and matter of the
Breviary itself will have any tendency to reconcile him to
them; and it has been the strong feeling that this is really the
case, that has led the writer of these pages fearlessly and
securely to admit the real excellences, and to dwell upon the
antiquity, of the Roman Ritual. He has felt that, since the
Romanist required an unqualified assent to the *whole* of the
Breviary, and that there were passages which no Anglican
ever could admit, praise the true Catholic portion of it as
much as he might, he did not in the slightest degree approximate to a recommendation of Romanism. But to return; –
these Invocations and Services to the Blessed Virgin have
been above enumerated, with a view of observing that, on

the face of them, they do not enter into the *structure* of the Breviary; they are really, as they are placed, additions,[40] and might easily have been added at some later period, as (e.g.) was the case of our own Thanksgiving, or the Prayer for the Parliament.[41] This remark seems to apply to all the intrinsically exceptionable Addresses in the Breviary; for as to the Confession at Prime and Compline, in which is introduced the name of the Blessed Virgin and the other Saints, this practice stands of a different ground. It is not a simple gratuitous Invocation made to them, but an address to Almighty GOD *in his heavenly court*, as surrounded by His Saints and Angels, answering to St. Paul's charge to Timothy, "before GOD and the LORD JESUS CHRIST and the elect Angels,"[42] and to Daniel and St. John's address to the Angels who were sent to them. The same may even by said of the Invocation "Holy Mary and all Saints,"[6] &c. in the Prime Service, which Gavanti[43] describes as being of great antiquity. These usages certainly *now* do but sanction and encourage that direct worship of the Blessed Virgin and the Saints, which is the great practical offence of the Latin Church, and so are a serious evil;[44] but it is worth pointing out, that, as on the one hand they have more claim to be considered an integral part of the service, so on the other more can be said towards their justification than for those whose addresses which are now especially under our consideration.

This is what occurs to observe on the first sight of these Invocations; but we are left to draw a conjectural judgment about them. Their history is actually known, and their recent introduction into the Church Services is distinctly confessed by Roman ritualists.

The Ave Mary, for instance, is made up of the Angel's salutation, "Hail, thou," &c., Elizabeth's "Blessed art thou

---

[6] The words 'Holy Mary' do not occur in ancient monastic breviaries. The Confession at Prime and Compline does not occur in the Paris breviary of 1735.

among women," &c., and the words "Holy Mary, Mother of GOD, pray for us sinners, now and in the hour of our death." The last clause "now and," was confessedly added by the Franciscans in the beginning of the sixteenth century; and the words preceding it, "Holy Mary," &c., which Gavanti, after Baronius,[45] wishes to attribute to the Council of Ephesus (AD 431) are acknowledged by the later critics, Grancolas and Merari[46] to have had no place in any form of prayer till the year 1508. Even the Scripture portion of the Ave Mary, which, as Merari observes, is an Antiphon rather than a Prayer and which occurs as such in the lesser Office of the Blessed Virgin, and in St. Gregory's Sacramentary, in the Mass Service for the fourth Sunday of Advent, is not mentioned by any devotional writer, nor by Councils nor Fathers up to the eleventh century, though they do enjoin the universal and daily use of the Creed and LORD's Prayer, which are in the present Breviary used with it. It first occurs among forms of prayer prescribed for the people in the statutes of Otho,[47] Bishop of Paris, AD 1195,[48] who was followed after the interval of a hundred years by the Council of Oxford[49] and elsewhere. Another space of at least fifty years intervenes before the introduction of rosaries and crowns in honour of the Virgin. As to the Roman breviary, it did not contain any part of the Ave Mary, till the promulgation of it by Pope Pius V,[50] after the Tridentine Council, AD 1550.

The four antiphons to the Blessed Virgin, used at the termination of the offices, are known respectively by their first words; the *Alma Redemptoris*, the *Ave Regina*, the *Regina Caeli*, and the *Salve Regina*. Gavanti and Merari plainly tell us that are not to be found in ancient authors. The *Alma Redemptoris* is the composition of Hermannus Contractus,[51] who died AD 1054. The author of the *Ave Regina* is unknown, as is that of the *Regina Caeli*. The *Salve Regina* is to be attributed either to Hermannus, or to Peter of

Compostella.[52] Gavanti would ascribe the last words "O Clemens, O pia, O dulcis," &c. to St. Bernard, but Merari corrects him, the work in which they are contained being suppositions. These Antiphons seem to have been used by the Franciscans after Compline from the thirteenth century; but are found in no breviary before AD 1520.

The Saturday or Sabbath office of the Blessed Virgin was introduced, according to Baronius, by the monks of the Western Church, about AD 1056.

The Officium Parvum B.V.M. was instituted by the celebrated Peter Damiani at the same date.[53] It is said indeed to have been the restoration of a practice three hundred years old, and observed by John Damascene;[54] which it may well have been; but there is nothing to show the identity of the Service itself with the ancient one, and that is the only point on which evidence would be important. Thirty years after its introduction by Damiani, it was made part of the daily worship by decree of Urban II.[55]

The Breviary then, as it is now received, is pretty nearly what the Services became *in practice* in Rome, and among the Franciscans, by the middle of the thirteenth century; the two chief points of difference between it and the ancient Catholic Devotions, being on the one hand its diminished allowance of Scripture reading, on the other its adoption of certain legends, and of Hymns and Prayers to the Virgin. However, the more grievous of these changes were not formally made in the Breviary itself; till the Pontificate of Pius V after the Tridentine Council; at which time also it was imposed in its new form upon all the Churches in union with Rome, except such as had used some other Ritual for above two hundred years. Not even at the present day, however, is this Roman novelty, as it may be called, in universal reception; the Paris Breviary, as corrected by the Archbishop of that city AD 1735, differs from it considerably in detail, though still disfigured by the Invocations.[56]

Before concluding this account of the Roman Breviary, it is necessary to notice one attempt which was made in the first part of the sixteenth century to restore it to a more primitive form. In the year 1536, Quignonius, Cardinal of Sancta Crux,[57] compiled a Breviary under the sanction of Clement VII, and published it under his successor, Paul III. This Ritual, the use of which was permitted but not formally enjoined by the Holy See, was extensively adopted for forty years, when it was superseded by the Franciscan Breviary, as the now authorized one may be called, in consequence of a Bull of Pius V.[58] The Cardinal's Breviary was drawn up on principles far more agreeable to those on which the Reformation was conducted, and apparently with the same mixture of right and wrong in the execution. With a desire of promoting the knowledge of Scripture, it showed somewhat of rude dealing with received usages, and but a deficient sense of what is improperly called the *imaginative* part of religion. His object was to adapt the Devotions of the Church for private reading, rather than chanting in choir, and so to encourage something higher than that almost theatrical style of worship, when, when reverence is away, will prevail, alternatively with a slovenly and hurried performance, in the performance of Church Music. Accordingly he left out the Versicles, Responses, and Texts, which, however suitable in Church, yet in private took more time, as he says, to find out in the existing formularies than to read when found. He speaks in his preface expressly of the "perplexus ordo,"[59] on which the offices were framed. But his great reform was as regards the reading of Scripture. He complains that, whereas it was the ancient rule that the Psalms should be read through weekly and the Bible yearly, both practices had been omitted. The ferial or weekday service, had been superseded by the Service for feast days, as being shorter; and for that reason every day, even through Lent, was turned into a festival. To obviate the temptation which led to this irregularity, he made the Ferial Service about the length of that of the old feast day; and he found space in these contracted limits for the reading of the Psalms and the whole Bible, except parts of the Apocalypse, in the week and the year respectively, by omitting the popular legends of the Saints which had been substituted for them.[60] He observes, that these compositions had been sometimes introduced without any public authority, or sanction of the Popes, merely at the whim of individuals. Those which he retained, he selected from authors of weight, whether of the Greek or Latin Church. Besides, he omitted the Officium Parvum B.V.M. on the ground that there were sufficient services in her honour independently of it. In all his reforms he professes to be returning to the practice of antiquity; and he made use of the assistance of men versed "in Latin and Greek, in divinity and ius pontificium."[61]

This Breviary was published at Rome, AD 1536, under the sanction, as has been said, of Paul III.[62] However, it was not of a nature to please the divines of an age which had been brought up in the practice of the depraved Catholicism then prevalent; and its real faults, as they would appear to be, even enabled them to oppose it with justice. The Doctors of the Sorbonne proceeded to censure it as running counter in its structure to antiquity and the Fathers; and though they seem at length to have got over their objections to it, and various editions at Venice, Antwerp, Lyons, and Paris, showed that it was not displeasing to numbers in the Roman Communion, it was at length superseded by the Bull of Pius V establishing the Franciscan Breviary, which had more or less grown into use in the course of the preceding three hundred years.

This account of Cardinal Quignonius's Breviary, and the circumstances under which it was compiled, will remind the English reader of the introductory remarks concerning the Service of the Church, prefixed to our own Ritual; which he may read more profitably than heretofore, after the above illustrations of their meaning. For this reason they shall be here cited:

"There was never anything by the will of man so well devised, or so sure established, which in continuance of time hath not been corrupted; as, among other things, it may plainly appear by the Common Prayers in the Church, commonly called Divine Service. The first original and ground whereof, if a man would search out by the Ancient Fathers, he shall find, that the same was not ordained but of a good purpose, and for a great advancement of godliness. For they so ordered the matter, that all the whole Bible, (or the greatest part thereof,) should be read over once every year; intending thereby, that the Clergy, and especially such as were Ministers in the Congregation, should (by often reading and meditation in GOD's Word) be stirred up to godliness themselves, and be more able to exhort others by wholesome doctrine, and to confute them that were adversaries to the truth; and further, that the people (by daily hearing of Holy Scripture read in the Church,) might continually profit more and more in the knowledge of GOD, and be the more inflamed with the love of His true religion.

"But these many years past, this godly and decent order of the ancient Fathers hath been so altered, broken, and neglected, by planting in uncertain Stories and Legends, with multitude of Responds, Verses, vain Repetitions, Commemorations, and Synodals; that commonly when any book of the Bible was begun, after three or four chapters were read out all the rest were unread.[63] And in this sort the book of Isaiah was begun in Advent, and the book of Genesis in Septuagesima; but they were only begun, and never read through. After like sort were other books of Holy Scripture used. And furthermore, notwithstanding that the ancient Fathers have divided the Psalms into seven portions, whereof everyone was called a Nocturn, now of late time a few of them have been daily said, and the rest utterly omitted.

Moreover, the number and hardness of the rules called the Pie,[64] and the manifold changings of the service, was the cause, that, to turn the book only was so hard and intricate a matter, that many times there was more business to find out what should be read, than to read it when it was found out.

"These inconveniences therefore considered, here is set forth such an Order, whereby the same shall be redressed. And for a readiness in this matter, here is drawn out a Calendar for that purpose, which is plain and easy to be understood; wherein (so much as may be) the reading of Holy Scripture is to set forth, that all other things shall be done in order, without breaking one piece from another. For this cause be cut off Anthems, Responds, Invitatories, and such like things as did break the continual course of the reading of the Scripture."

It remains but to enumerate the selections from the Breviary which follow. First has been drawn out, an Analysis of the Weekly Service, as well for Sundays as other days. This is followed by an ordinary Sunday Service at length, as it runs when unaffected by the occurrence of special feast or season, in order to ground the reader, who chooses to pursue the subject, in the course of worship as a system. With the same object a Week-day Service has also been drawn out. Two portions of extraordinary Services are added, one from the Service for the Transfiguration, the other for the Festival of St. Lawrence, with a view of supplying specimens of a more elevated and impressive character. Next follows a design for a Service for March 21st, the day on which Bishop Ken was taken from the Church below, and another for a Service of thanksgiving and commemoration for the anniversaries of the days of death of friends or relations. These have been added, to suggest to individual Christians a means of carrying out in private the principle and spirit of those inestimable forms of devotion which are contained in our authorized Prayer Book.[65] The series is closed with an abstract of the

Services for every day in Advent, fitting on to sections 2 and 3, which contain respectively the types of the Sunday and Week-day Service. Except by means of some such extended portion, it is impossible for the reader to understand the general structure, and appreciate the harmony of the Breviary.

Lastly, the writer of these pages feels he shall have to ask indulgence for such chance mistakes, in the detail of the following Services, as are sure to occur when an intricate system is drawn out and set in order, with no other knowledge of it than is supplied by the necessarily insufficient directions of a Rubric.

There follows:
An Analysis of the Seven Daily Services of the Church.
Service for Sunday, June 21, 1801.
Part of the Service for August 6th – (The Transfiguration).
Part of the Service for August 10th (St. Lawrence).
Matin Service for March 21 (Bishop Ken's Day).
Service in Commemoration of the Dead in Christ.

OXFORD,
The Feast of St. John the Baptist

TRACT 79

ON PURGATORY[1]

(*Against Romanism – No 3*)

THE extract from Archbishop Ussher's Answer to a Jesuit,[2] contained in Tract 72, on the subject of the ancient Commemorations for the Dead in Christ, may fitly be succeeded by an inquiry as to what degree and sort of proof remains for the Roman tenet of Purgatory, after deducting from the evidence those usages or statements of the early Church, which are commonly supposed, but, as Ussher shows, improperly, to countenance it. Ussher's explanations have had the effect, it is presumed, of cutting away the *prima facie* evidence, on which the doctrine is usually rested; and it now remains to see what is left when it is withdrawn. With this view it is proposed in the following pages to draw out in detail the evidence alleged by the Romanists in behalf of their belief, with such remarks as may be necessary, in order to form a fair estimate of it. A plain statement of the doctrine itself, and of its rise, shall be also attempted, as not unseasonable at a time when the strength of Romanism rests in no small degree in its opponents mistaking the points in debate, and making or refuting propositions which but indirectly or partially bear upon the errors which they desire to combat.

Before commencing, it is necessary to warn the reader against estimating the magnitude or quality of any of those errors by its apparent dimensions in the theory. What seems to be a small deviation from correctness in the abstract system, becomes considerable and serious when it assumes a substantive form. This is especially the case with all doctrinal discussions, in which the undeveloped germs of many diversities, of practice and moral character lie thick together and in small compass, and as if promiscuously and without essential differences. The highest truths differ from the most miserable delusions by what appears to be a few words or letters. The discriminating mark of orthodoxy, the Homoousion, has before now been ridiculed, however irrationally, as being identical, all but the letter '*i*', with the heretical symbol of the Homoiousion.[3] What is acknowledged in the Arian controversy, must be endured without surprise in the Roman, in whatever degree it occurs. We may be taunted as differing from the Romanists only in phrases and modes of expression; and we may be taunted, or despised, according to the fate of our Divines for three centuries past, as taking a middle, timid, unsatisfactory ground, neither quite agreeing nor quite disagreeing with our opponents.[4] We may be charged with dwelling on trifles and niceties, in a way inconsistent with plain, manly good sense; but in truth it is not we who are the speculatists, and unpractical controversialists, but they who forget that *hae nugae seria ducunt in mala*.[5]

But again there is another reason, peculiar to the Roman controversy, which occasions a want of correspondence between the appearance presented by the Roman theology in theory, and its appearance in practice. The separate doctrines of Romanism are very different, in position, importance, and mutual relation, in the abstract, and when developed, applied, and practiced. Anatomists tell us that the skeletons of the most various animals are formed on the same type; yet the animals are dissimilar and distinct, in consequence of the respective differences of their developed proportions. No one would confuse between a lion and a bear; yet many of us at first sight would be unable to discriminate between their respective skeletons. Romanism in the theory may differ little from our own creed; nay, in the abstract type, it might even by identical, and yet in the actual framework, and still further in the living and breathing form, it might differ essentially. For instance, the doctrine of Indulgences[6] is, in the theory, entirely connected with the doctrine of Penance; that is, it has relation solely to *this world* so much so that Roman apologists sometimes speak of it without even an allusion to its bearings elsewhere: but we know that in practice it is mainly, if not altogether, concerned with the next world, – with the alleviation of sufferings in Purgatory.

And further still, as regards the doctrine of Purgatorial suffering, there have been for many ages in the Roman Church gross corruptions of its own doctrine, untenable as that doctrine is even by itself.[7] The decree of the Council of Trent, which will presently be introduced, acknowledges the fact. Now we believe that those corruptions still continue; that Rome has never really set herself in earnest to eradicate them. The pictures of Purgatory so commonly seen in countries in communion with Rome, the existence of Purgatorian societies,[8] the means of subsistence accruing to the clergy from belief in it,[9] afford a strange contrast to the simple wording and apparent innocence of the decree by which it is made an article of faith. It is the contrast between poison in its lifeless seed, and the same developed, thriving, and rankly luxuriant in the actual plant.

And lastly, since we are in no danger of becoming Romanists, and may bear to be dispassionate and (I may say) philosophical in our treatment of their errors, some passages in the following account of Purgatory are more calmly written than would satisfy those who were engaged with a victorious enemy at their doors. Yet whoever be our opponent, Papist or Latitudinarian, it does not seem to be wrong to be as candid and conceding as justice and charity allow us. Nor is it unprofitable to weigh accurately how much the Romanists have committed themselves in their formal determinations of doctrine, and how far, by GOD's merciful providence, they had been restrained and overruled; and again how far they must retract, in order to make amends to Catholic truth and unity.

§1. Statement of the Roman Doctrine Concerning Purgatory.

§2. Proof of the Roman Doctrine Concerning Purgatory.

§3. History of the Rise of the Doctrine of Purgatory, and Opinions
in the Early Church Concerning It.

§4. The Council of Florence.

---

§1. STATEMENT OF THE ROMAN DOCTRINE CONCERNING PURGATORY.

The Roman doctrine is expressed in the Creed of Pope Pius IV.

"Constanter teneo Purgatorium esse, animasque ibi detentas fidelium suffragiis juvari."

"I hold without wavering that there is a Purgatory, and that souls there detained are aided by the suffrages of the faithful."

The words of this article are taken from the decree of the Council of Trent on the subject, (Sess. 25)[1] which runs as follows:

"Whereas the Church Catholic, fully instructed by the Holy Ghost, hath from the Sacred Scriptures and ancient tradition of the Fathers, in sacred Councils, and last of all in this present Oecumenical

---

[1] Session 25 took place on 3–4 December 1563. Pius IV reigned from 1559–1565 and reconvened Trent in 1562.

Synod, taught that there is a Purgatory, and that souls there detained are aided by the suffrages of the living, and above all by the acceptable sacrifice of the Altar, this holy Synod enjoins on Bishops, to make diligent efforts that the sound doctrine concerning Purgatory, handed down from the holy Fathers and sacred Councils, be believed, maintained, taught, and everywhere proclaimed by the disciples of Christ. At the same time, as regards the uneducated multitude, let the more difficult and subtle questions, such as tend not to edification nor commonly increase piety, be excluded from popular discourses. Moreover, let them disallow the publication and discussion of whatever is uncertain or suspicious; and prohibit whatever is of a curious or superstitious nature, or savours of filthy lucre as the scandals and stumbling blocks of believers. And let them provide, that the suffrages of believers living, that is, the sacrifices of masses, prayers, alms, and other works of piety, which believers living are wont to perform for other believers dead, be performed according to the rules of the Church, piously and religiously; and whatever are due for them from the endowments of testators, or in other way, be fulfilled, not in a perfunctory way, but diligently and accurately by the Priests and Ministers of the Church, and others who are bound to do this service."

Such is the Roman doctrine; and taken in the *mere letter* there is little in it against which we shall be able to sustain formal objections. Purgatory is not spoken of at all as a place of pain; it need only mean, what its name implies, a place of purification. There is indeed much presumption in asserting definitively that there is such a place; and assuredly there is not only presumption, but very great daring and uncharitableness in including belief in it, as Pope Pius' Creed goes on to do, among the conditions of salvation; but if we could consider it as confined to the mere opinion that that good which is begun on earth is perfected in the next world, the tenet would be tolerable. The word "*detentas*" indeed expresses a somewhat stronger idea; yet after all hardly more than that the souls in

Purgatory would be happier out of it than in it, and that they cannot of their own will leave it: which is not much to grant. Further, that the prayers of the living benefit the dead in Christ, is, to say the least, not inconsistent, as Ussher shows us, with the primitive belief. So much as to the *letter* of the decree; but it is not safe to go by the letter: on the contrary, we are bound to take the universal and uniform doctrine taught and received *in* the Roman Communion, as the real and true interpreter of words which are in themselves comparatively innocent. What that doctrine is, may be gathered from the words of the Catechism of Trent, in which the spirit of Romanism, not being bound by the rules which shackle it in the Council,[10] speaks out. The account of Purgatory which the formulary supplies, shall here be taken as our text, and Cardinal Bellarmine's Defence[11] shall be used as a comment upon it.

The Catechism then speaks as follows :

"Est Purgatorius ignis, quo piorum animae ad definitum tempus cruciatae expiantur, ut eis in aeternam patriam ingressus patere posit, inquam nihil coinquinatum ingreditur."

"There is a Purgatorial fire, in which the souls of the pious are tormented for a certain time and cleansed, in order that an entrance may lie open to them into their eternal home, into which nothing defiled enters."[12]

In like manner Bellarmine says,

"Purgatory is a certain place in which, as if in a prison, souls are purged after this life, which have not been fully purged in it, in order, (that is,) that thus purged they may be enabled to enter heaven, which nothing defiled shall enter."

A painful light is at once cast by these comments on the Synodal Decree. "There is a Purgatory" in the Decree, is interpreted by Bellarmine "there is a sort of *prison*;" and by the Catechism, "there is a Purgatorial *fire*." And whereas the Decree merely declares that souls are "*detained* there," the Catechism says they are "tormented and cleansed." Moreover, both the Catechism and Bellarmine imply that this is the ordinary mode of attaining heaven, inasmuch as no one scarcely can be considered, and no one can be surely known, to leave this world, "fully purged"; whereas the Decree speaks vaguely of "the souls there." So much at first sight; now to consider the persons with which Purgatory is concerned, the sins, condition of souls, place, time, punishment, and remedies; Bellarmine likening it to a *carcer*, the Catechism saying that the "*animae piorum* ad *definitum tempus cruciatae* expiantur purgatorio *igne*."[13]

1. *The Persons who are reserved for Purgatory.*

The Roman Church holds that Christians or believers only are tenants of Purgatory, as for Christians only are offered their prayers, alms, and masses. The question follows, whether all Christians? not all Christians, but such as die in GOD's favour, yet with certain sins unforgiven. Some Christians die simply in GOD's favour with all their sins forgiven; others die out of His favour, as the impenitent, whether Christians or not; but others, and that the great majority, die according to the Romanists, in GOD's favour, yet more or less under the bond of their sins. And so far we may unhesitatingly allow to them, or rather we ourselves hold the same, if we hold that after Baptism there is no plenary pardon for sins in this life to the sinner, however penitent, *such* as in Baptism was once vouchsafed to him. If for sins committed after Baptism we have not yet received a simple and unconditional absolution, surely penitents from this time up to the day of judgment may be considered in that double state of which the Romanists speak, their *persons* accepted, but certain sins uncancelled. Such a state is plainly revealed to us in Scripture as a real one, in various passages, to which we appeal as well as the Romanists. Let the case of David suffice. On his repentance Nathan said to him, "The Lord also *hath put away thy sin; thou shalt not die; howbeit,* because by this deed thou hast given great occasion to the enemies of the LORD to blaspheme, the child also that is born unto thee shall surely die." (2 Sam. 12:13–14) Here is a perspicacious instance of a penitent restored to GOD's favour at once, yet his sins afterwards visited; and it needs very little experience in life to be aware that such punishments occur continually, though no one takes them to be an evidence that the sufferer himself is under GOD's displeasure, but rather accounts them punishments even when we have abundant proofs of his faith, love, holiness, and fruitfulness in good works. So far then we cannot be said materially to oppose the Romanists. They on the other hand agree with us in maintaining that CHRIST's death *might,* if GOD so willed, be applied for the removal even of these specific punishments of sins, which they call *temporal* punishments, as fully as it really is for the acceptance of the *soul* of the person punished, or the removal of eternal punishment. Further, both parties agree, that in matter of fact it is not so applied; the experience of life shows it; else every judgment might be taken as evidence of the person suffering it being under GOD's wrath. The death of the disobedient prophet from Judah would, in that case, prove that he perished eternally, which surely would be utterly presumptuous and uncharitable. As far as this then we have no violent difference of *principle* with the Romanists; but at this point we separate from them; *they* say these temporal punishments on sin are inflicted on the faults incurring them, in a certain fixed proportion; that every sin of a certain kind has a definite penalty or price; in consequence, that if it not fully discharged in this life, it must be hereafter; and that Purgatory is the place of discharging it.

2. *The sins for which persons are confined in Purgatory.*

The next question is, *what* are the sins which are thus punished? not all sins of Christians, for some incur an eternal punishment. There are sins, it is maintained, which in themselves merit eternal damnation, are directly opposed to love or charity, quench grace, and throw the doer of them out of God's favour. These in consequence are called mortal; such as murder, adultery, or blasphemy. Such sins do not lead to Purgatory; hell is their portion if unrepented of. But all these, all but *unrepented mortal* sins are in the case of Christians punished in Purgatory. Of these it follows there are two kinds, sins though *repented of*, and sins though not *mortal*; concerning which a few words shall be said.

1. Mortal sins, though repented of, and though the offender cease to be under God's displeasure, yet have visibly their own punishment in many cases as in the instance of David. But the Romanists consider that these sins have their penalty assigned to them as if by weight and measure; moreover, that we can ourselves take part in discharging it, and by our own act anticipate and supersede God's judgment, according to the text: "If we would judge ourselves, we should not be judged."[14] This voluntary act on our part is called Penance, and is said to expiate the sin, that is, to wash away its temporal effects. Should we die before the full temporal punishment, or satisfaction, has been paid for all our mortal sins, we must pay the rest hereafter, *i.e.* in Purgatory.

2. Sins which are not mortal, are called *venial*, and are such as do not quench grace, or run counter to love. Bellarmine thus contrasts them:

"Mortal sins are they which absolutely turn from GOD, and merit eternal punishment; Venial are those which somewhat impede our course to Him, but do not turn it and are with little pains blotted out. The former are crimes, the latter sins … Mortal sin is like a deadly wound, which suddenly kills: Venial is a slight stroke, which does not endanger life, and is easily healed. The former fights with love, which is the soul's life; the latter is rather beside than against love."[15]

Venial sins differ from Mortal in two ways, in *kind* and *degree*. An idle word, excessive laughter, and the like are sins in kind distinct from perjury and adultery. Again, anger is a venial sin when slight and undesigned, but when indulged interferes with love and is mortal; a theft of a large sum may be mortal, of a small venial.

Venial sins, being such, are considered by Romanists not to deserve so much as eternal punishment, – to be pardonable not merely by an express and immediate act of GOD's mercy, or again through the virtue of our state of regeneration, but to be intrinsically venial, to offend GOD, but not so as to alienate Him. They rest this doctrine upon such passages as the following: "Sin, when it is *finished*, bringeth forth *death* (James 1:15); therefore, before it is finished and perfected, it has no such fearful power. Still they say it requires *some* punishment; which it receives in the next world, should it not receive it in this, that is, in Purgatory.

Such then are the sins of GOD's true servants, penitent believers, for which, according to the Romanists, they suffer in Purgatory; mortal sins repented of, and those sins of infirmity which befall them so continually and so secretly, that they cannot repent of them specifically if they would, and which do not deserve eternal punishment, though they do not. They consider the Purgatorial punishment of *venial* sins to be meant by the Apostle, when he speaks of those who, building on the true foundation "wood, hay, and stubble," are "saved so *as by fire,*"[16] and the punishment for *mortal* sins, in our SAVIOUR's declaration that certain prisoners shall not go out till they have "paid the very last mite." (Luke 12:59) It may be added, that Martyrdom is supposed to be a full expiation of whatever guilt of sin still rests on the Christian undergoing it; and therefore to stand instead of Purgatory. Martyrs then are at once admitted to the Beatific vision,[17] which is the privilege in which Purgatory terminates.

From this account of the inmates of Purgatory, and the causes why they are there detained, we gather that what has already been hinted, that the one main or rather sole reason of the appointment is *a satisfaction to* GOD's *justice.* The persons concerned are believers destined for bliss eternal; but before they pass on from earth to heaven, the course of their existence is, as it were, suspended, and they are turned aside to discharge a debt; *how* they effect it, or in what *length* of time, or with what *effect* on themselves, being questions as beside the mark, as if they were used with reference to the payment of a charge in worldly matters. It is an appointment altogether with bearing upon their moral character in eternal prospects; and after it is over, is wiped out as though it had never been.

3. *The moral condition of the souls in Purgatory.*

Bellarmine well illustrates the supposed mental state of believers while in Purgatory by comparing them to travelers who come up to a fortified town after nightfall, and have to wait at the gates till the morning. Such persons have come to the end of their journey; they are not on the way, they have attained; they are sure of admittance, which is a matter of time only. Accordingly the Romanists hold that souls in Purgatory become neither better or worse, neither sin or add to their good works; they are one and all perfect in love, and ready for heaven, were it not for this debt, which hangs about them as so much rust or dross, and cannot be purged away except for certain appointed external remedies. They support this view of the stationary condition of the soul in Purgatory by such texts as the following: "The night cometh when no man can work." "Where the tree falls, there it shall be." "We must all appear before the judgment seat of Christ, that every one may receive the things *done in his body*."(John 9:4; Eccles. 11:3; 2 Cor. 5:10)

Next, with the exception of some few theologians, they consider that souls in Purgatory are comforted with the assurance that their eternal happiness is secured to them. Their state in consequence is thus described by Bellarmine.

"You will object that they may be in doubt whether they are in hell or in Purgatory. Not so; for in hell God is blasphemed, in Purgatory He is praised; in hell there is neither habit of faith, nor hope, nor love of GOD, in Purgatory all of these. A soul then which shall understand that it hopes in GOD, praises and loves GOD, will clearly know it is not in hell. But perhaps it will fear it is to be sent to hell, though not there yet; neither can this be, for the same faith remains in it, which it had here. Here it believed according to the plain word of Scripture, that after death none can become of good bad, or of bad good, and none but the bad are to be sent into hell. When then it perceives that it loves GOD, and is therefore good, it will not fear damnation."[18]

4. *The place and time of Purgatory.*

On this subject the Church has not formally determined anything: but the common opinion of Schoolmen is, that it is one of four prisons or receptacles, which are situated at the heart of the earth,[19] Hell for the damned, the *Limbus Puerorum*[20] for children dying without baptism, the *Limbus Patrum* for the just who died before the passion of CHRIST, and who since that time have all been transferred from it to heaven, and Purgatory for believers under punishment. In other words, whereas all punishment is either for a time or eternal, either positive (*poena sensus)* or negative (*poena damni*),[21] that of good men before CHRIST's coming is the *poena damni*, or absence of GOD's light and joy for a time, that of unbaptized infants is the *poena damni* for ever, that of Purgatory the *poena sensus* for a time, that of Hell the *poena sensus* for ever. To these some Romanists have added a fifth, that is, of faithful souls, who without being yet admitted into heaven are yet secured against all pain; but these according to Bellarmine, as at least enduring the *poena damni*, are to be considered in Purgatory, though in the most tolerable place in it, as being but in the condition of the old Fathers before CHRIST came.

The time of Purgatory depends of course upon the state of the debt which is to be liquidated in each case, and varies consequently with the individual. Martyrs, as has been above stated, are supposed to satisfy it in the very act of Martyrdom; others will not be released until the day of judgment. Again, the period of suffering depends upon the exertions of survivors, by prayers, alms, and masses, which have power not only to relieve but to shorten the pain.

5. *The nature of the Punishment.*

Here the Roman Church has defined nothing; its catechism, as we have seen, and its theologians in accordance, consider it to be material fire, but in the Council of Florence,[22] the Greeks would not do more than subscribe to the existence of Purgatory; they denied that the punishment was fire; the question accordingly remains open, that is, it is not determined either way *de fide*. The difficulty, how elementary fire, or anything of a similar nature can affect the disembodied soul, is paralleled by St. Austin by the mystery of the union of soul and body.

The pains of Purgatory are considered to be horrible and far exceeding any in this life; "*Poenas Purgatorii est atrocissimas; et cum illis nullas poenas hujus vitae comparandas, docent constanter Patres,*" says Bellarmine,[23] and proceeds to refer to Austin, Pope, Gregory, Bede, Anselm, and Bernard. Yet on this point theologians differ. Some consider the chief misery to consist in the *poena damni*, or absence of GOD's presence, which to holy souls, understanding and desiring it, would be as intolerable as extreme thirst or hunger to the body; and in this way seem to put all purgatorial pain on a level, or rather assign the greater pain to the more spiritually-minded. Others consider the *poena damni* to be alleviated by the certainty of heaven and of the continually lessening term of their punishment. With them then the *poena sensus*, or the fire, is the chief source of torment, which admits of degrees according to the will of GOD.

6. *The efficacy of the suffrages of the Church.*

By suffrages are meant, co-operations of the living with the dead; prayers, masses, and works, such as alms, pilgrimages, fastings, &c. These aids which individuals can supply, alms, prayers, &c., only avail when offered by good persons; for he who is not accepted himself, cannot do acceptable service for another. Moreover these aids may be directed either to the benefit of all souls in Purgatory indiscriminately, or specially to the benefit of a certain soul in particular.

There is one other means of escaping the penalties due to sin in Purgatory, which may be briefly explained, viz. by the grant of indulgences; these are dispensed on the following theory. Granting that a certain fixed temporary penalty attached to every act of sin, in such case, it would be conceivable that, as the multitude of Christians did not discharge their total debt in this life, so some extraordinary holy men might more than discharge it. Such are the

Prophets, Apostles, Martyrs, Ascetics, and the like, who have committed few sins, and have undergone extreme labours and sufferings, voluntary or involuntary. This being supposed, the question rises, what becomes of the overplus; and then there seems a fitness that what is not needed for themselves, should avail for their brethren who are still debtors. It is accordingly stored, together with CHRIST's merits, in a kind of treasure-house,[24] to be dispensed according to the occasion, and that at the discretion of the Church. The application of this treasure is called an Indulgence, which stands instead of a certain time of penance in this life, or for the period, whatever it be, to which that time is commuted in Purgatory. In this way, the supereroga-tory works of the Saints are supposed to go in payment of the debts of ordinary Christians.

---

§2. PROOF OF THE ROMAN DOCTRINE CONCERNING PURGATORY.

1. *Proofs from supernatural appearances.*

The argumentative ground, on which the belief in Purgatory was actually introduced, would seem to lie in the popular stories of apparitions witnessing to it. Not that it rose in consequence of them historically, or that morally it was founded in them; only that when persons came to ask them-selves why they received it, this was the ultimate ground of evidence on which the mind fell back; viz. the evidence of miracles, not of Scripture, or of the Fathers.

Bellarmine enumerates it as one of the confirmatory arguments. With this view he refers in particular to some relations of Gregory of Tours, AD 573; of Pope Gregory, AD 600; of Bede, AD 700; of Peter Damiani, AD 1100; of St.

Bernard, AD 1100; and of St Anselm, AD 1100. The dates are worth noticing, if it be true, as is here assumed, that such supernatural accounts as then were put forth, are really the argument on which the doctrine was and is received; for it would thence appear, first, that the doctrine was not taught as divine before the end of the sixth century, next, that when it was propagated, it was so on an (alleged) new revelation. The following miraculous narratives are found in a Protestant Selection from Roman writers, published in 1688, and entitled "Purgatory proved by Miracles".

"St. Gregory the Great writes that the soul of Paschasius appeared to St. Germanus, and testified to him, that he was freed from the pains of Purgatory for his prayers.

"When the same St. Gregory was abbot of his monastery, a monk of his called Justus, now dead, appeared to another monk, called Copiosus, and advertized him, that he had been freed from the torments of Purgatory, by thirty masses, which Pretiosus, Prefect of the monastery by the order of St. Gregory, had said for his soul, as is recounted in his life.

"St. Gregory of Tours writes of a holy damsel, called Vitaliana, that she appeared to St. Martin, and told him she had been in Purgatory for a venial sin which she had committed, and that she had been delivered by the prayers of the Saint.

"Peter Damiani writes, that St. Severin appeared to a clergyman, and told him that he had been in Purgatory, for not having said the Divine Service at due hours, and that afterwards GOD had delivered him and carried him to the company of the blessed.

"St. Bernard writes that St. Malachy freed his sister from the pains of Purgatory by his prayers; and that the same sister had appeared unto him, begging of him that relief and favour.

"And St. Bernard himself by his intercession freed another, who had suffered a whole year the pains of Purgatory, as William Abbot writes in his life." *Flowers of the Lives of the Saints,* p. 830.

These instances among others are adduced by Bellarmine; and he adds, "plura similia legi possunt apud, &c . . . .*sed quae attulimus sunt magis authentica.*" I. 11.[25]

2. *Proofs from the Old and New Testaments.*

Bellarmine adduces the following texts from the Old and New Testaments; in doing which he must not be supposed to mean, that each of them contains in itself the evidence of its relevancy and availableness, or could be understood without some authoritative interpretation; only, if it is asked, "*is* Purgatory the doctrine of Holy Scripture, and *where*?" he would answer, that in matter of fact it *is* taught in the following passages, according to the explanations of them found in various writers of consideration.

1. 2 Macc. 12:42–45. "Besides that noble Judas exhorted the people to keep themselves from sin, forsomuch as they saw before their eyes the things that come to pass for the sins of those that were slain. And when he had made a gathering throughout the company to the sum of two thousand drachms of silver, he sent it to Jerusalem, *to offer a sin offering*, doing therein very well and honestly, in that he was mindful of the Resurrection; for if he had not hoped that they that were slain should have risen again, it had been superfluous and vain to pray for the dead. And also, in that he perceived that there was great favour laid up for those that died godly, *it was an holy and good thought.* Whereupon he made *a reconciliation for the dead, that they might be delivered from sin.*"

2. Tob. 4:17. "Pour out thy bread on the burial of the just, but give nothing to the wicked;" that is, at the burial of the just, give alms; which were given to gain for them the prayers of the poor.

3. 1 Sam. 31:13. "And they took their bones," [of Samuel and his sons,] and *buried* them under a tree at Jabesh, and *fasted seven* days." Vid. also 2 Sam.1:12; 3:35. This fasting was an offering for their souls.

4. Ps 38: 1 "O Lord, rebuke me not in Thy *wrath*; neither chasten me in *Thy hot displeasure."* By *wrath* is meant Hell; by *hot displeasure,* Purgatory.

5. Ps. 46:12. We went through *fire* and through *water,* but Thou broughtest us out into a wealthy place" (*refrigerium*). Water is Baptism; fire is Purgatory.

6. Isa. 4:4. "When the Lord shall have washed away the filth of the daughters of Zion, and shall have *purged* the blood of Jerusalem from the midst thereof, by the spirit of judgment and by the spirit of *burning.*"

7. Isa 9:18. "Wickedness burneth as the fire; it shall devour the briers and the thorns."

8. Mic. 7:8.9. "Rejoice not against me, O mine enemy; when I fall, I shall arise; when I *sit in darkness*, the Lord shall be a light unto me. I will bear the *indignation* of the Lord, because I have sinned against Him, *until He plead my cause*, and execute judgment for me: *He will bring me forth to the light,* and I shall behold His righteousness.

9. Zech. 9:11. "As for Thee also, by the blood of Thy covenant, I have *sent forth Thy prisoners out of the pit,* wherein is not water." This text is otherwise taken to refer to the *Limbus Patrum*.

10. Mal 3:3. "He shall sit as a refiner and purifier of silver; and He shall *purify* the sons of Levi, and *purge* them as gold and silver," &c.

From the New Testament he adduces the following texts:

1. Matt. 12:32. "Whosoever speaketh against the Holy Ghost, it shall not be forgiven him, neither in this world, *neither in the world to come;*" that means, "neither in

Purgatory," for in hell the very supposition of forgiveness is excluded.

2. 1 Cor. 3:15. "He himself shall be saved; *yet so as by fire.*"

3. 1 Cor. 15:29. "Else what shall they do, which are *baptized.*" i.e.. who undergo the baptism of tears and humiliation, who pray, fast, give alms, &c. "for the dead, if the dead rise not at all?"

4. Matt. 5: 25–26; Luke 12:58–59. "Agree with thine adversary quickly, whilst thou art in the way with him; lest at any time the adversary deliver thee to the judge, and the judge deliver thee to the officer, and thou be cast into *prison.* Verily, I say unto thee, *thou shalt by no means come out thence, till* thou hast paid the uttermost farthing." By the *way,* is means this present life; by the *adversary,* the Law; by the *Judge,* our Saviour; by the *officer,* or executioner, the Angels; by the *prison,* Purgatory.

5. Matt 5:22. "Whosoever is angry with his brother without a cause, shall be in danger of the *judgment*; and whosoever shall say to his brother, Raca, shall be in danger of the *Council*: but whosoever shall say, Thou fool, shall be in danger of hell fire." Here are three kinds of punishment spoken of. Hell belongs to the next world; therefore also do the other two. Hence there are in the next world, besides eternal punishment, punishments short of eternal.

6. Luke 16:9. "Make to yourselves friends of the mammon of unrighteousness, that, when ye fail, they may receive you into everlasting habitations." To *fail,* is to die; the *friends* are the Saints in glory, and they *receive* us, *i.e.* from Purgatory, in consequence of their prayers.

7. Luke 23:42. "Lord, *remember* me, *when* Thou comest into Thy kingdom." That is, there is a remembrance and a remission of sin, not only in this life, but after it, in Christ's future kingdom.

8. Acts 2:24. "Whom God raised up, having loosed the *pains* of death (*inferi*); because it was not possible that He

should be holden of it." Christ Himself was released from no *pains* on being raised, nor were the ancient Fathers in the *Limbus:* nor were lost souls released at all. Therefore the pains which God loosed, were those of souls in Purgatory.

9. Phil 2:10. "That at the name of Jesus every knee should bow, of things in heaven, and things in earth, *and things under the earth.*" Vid. also Rev. 5:3. "And no *man* in heaven, nor in earth, *neither under the earth,* was able to open the book, neither to look thereon."

Now as to many of these texts, we who have not been educated in the belief of Purgatory, may well wonder how they come to be enlisted in support of Purgatory at all. This may be explained in some way as the following – which may be of use in helping us to understand the state of mind under which the Romanists view them. It is obvious, as indeed has been already remarked, that they do not of themselves *prove* the doctrine, nor are they chosen by Bellarmine himself, but given on the authority of writers of various times. Could indeed competent evidence be brought from other quarters, that the doctrine really was true and Apostolical, we should not unreasonably have believed that some of them did allude to it; especially if writers of name, who might speak from tradition, so considered. We could not have taken upon ourselves to say at first sight that it certainly was not contained in them, only we should have waited for evidence that it was. Some of the texts in question are obscure, and seem to desiderate a meaning; and so far it is a sort of gain when they have any meaning assigned them, as though they were unappropriated territory which the first comer might seize. Again, the coincidence of several of them in one and the same mode of expression, implies that they have a common drift, whatever that drift is, – that there is something about them which seems to have reference to secrets untold to man. Amid these dim and broken lights, the text in the Apocrypha first quoted, comes as if to combine and steady them.[26] All this is said *by way of analyzing how* it is that such a class of texts, though of so little cogency critically, has that influence with individuals, which it certainly sometimes has. The reason seems to be that the doctrine of Purgatory professes to interpret texts which God's word has left in obscurity. Yet, whatever be the joint force of such arguments from Scripture, in favour of the doctrine, it vanishes surely, at once and altogether, before one single clear text, such as the following: "Blessed are the dead *which die in the Lord,* from henceforth; yea saith the Spirit, *that they may rest from their labours*." Or again, if anyone is destined to endure Purgatory for the temporal punishment of sins, one should think it would be persons circumstanced as the thief on the cross, – a dying penitent; yet to him it is expressly said, "Verily I say unto thee, *today* shalt thou be with me in Paradise."

3. *Proofs from Antiquity*

After Scripture, Bellarmine brings the testimony of early Church in Council, as follows :

1. The African Church : "Let the Altar Sacrament be celebrated fasting; if however, there be any Commendation of the Dead made in the afternoon, let prayers only be used." Conc. Carth. 4. c. 79.[27]

2. The Spanish enjoins that suicides should not be prayed for, &c. Conc. Bracar. I c. 39.[28]

3. The Gallic : "It has seemed fit, that in all celebrations of the Eucharist, the Lord shall be interceded with in a suitable place in Church, for the spirits of the dead." Conc. Cabilon.[29]

4. The German defines, (Conc. Wormat. c.10[30] that prayers and offerings should be made even for those who are executed.

5. The Italic declares (Conc. 6 under Symmachus[31] that it is sacrilege to defraud the souls of the dead of prayer, &c.

6. The Greek in like manner.

Moreover, the Liturgies of St. James, St Basil, &c. all contain prayers for the dead.[32]

Now these professed instances are here enumerated in order to show how plainly and entirely they fall short of the point to be prove. Not one of them implies the doctrine of Purgatory; or goes beyond the doctrine which Archbishop Ussher (vide Tract 72,) has shown to have existed in the early Church, that the Saints departed were not at once in their full happiness, and that prayers benefited them. One of these instanced indeed is somewhat remarkable, the allowing prayers for malefactors executed;[33] but all were the subject of prayer who were not excluded from hope, and malefactors are, even by us, admitted to Holy Communion, and are allowed the Burial Service. To pray for them was merely the expression of hope.

Next, Bellarmine appeals to the Fathers, of whom I shall only cite those within the first hundred years; viz. Tertullian, Cyprian, Eusebius, Cyril of Jerusalem, Gregory Nazianzen, Ambrose, Jerome, Chrysostom, Paulinus, Augustine, Theodoret, and one or two others. Now in order to keep the point in controversy clearly in view, let it be recollected that we are not disputing the existence in the Ritual of the Church, of the custom of praying for the dead in Christ;[34] but *why* prayer was offered was a question in dispute, a point unsettled by any Catholic tradition, but variously treated by various Doctors at various times. There is nothing contrary to the genius of religion, natural and revealed, that duties should be prescribed, yet the reasons for them not told us, as Bishop Butler[35] has abundantly showed; and the circumstances that the ancients do agree in the usage, but differ as to the reasons, shows that the reasons were built upon the usage, not the usage on the reasons. And while this variety of opinions in the early Church, as to the meaning of the usage, forfeits for anyone of these any claim to be considered apostolical, of course it deprives the doctrine of Purgatory of authority inclusively, even supposing for argument's sake it was received by some early writers as true. Purgatory is but a violent hypothesis to give meaning to a usage, for which other hypotheses short of it and very different from it, and equally conjectural with it, may be assigned, nay, and were assigned before it, and far more extensively. Let it be remembered then, when the following list of passages, professedly in behalf of Purgatory, is read, that, what we have to look for, is, not evidence of a certain usage, which we grant did exist, but of an opinion, of a particular opinion explaining it, not of Prayer for the dead simply, nor of the opinion that Prayer for the dead profits, but that such Prayer is intended and tends to rescue them from a state of suffering. Further what we look for is not the testimony of one or two writers to the truth of this opinion, even if one or two could be brought, but an agreement of all in its favour.[36] If however it be said that the usage of Prayer in itself tends to the doctrine of Purgatory, I answer, that so far from it, in its primitive form it included prayers for the Virgin Mary and Apostles, which while retained were an indirect but forcible standing witness against the doctrine.

Tertullian, in his *de Corona*, §3,[37] speaks of "oblationes pro defunctis' offerings for the dead.

Again, "Let her" [the widow] "pray for the soul of" [her deceased husband] "and ask for him a place of refreshment in the interval before the judgment, and a fellowship in the first resurrection, and let her offer on the anniversary of his falling asleep." *De Monogam.* §10. *Vid. also de Pudicit.*[38]

Cyprian. "The Bishops or predecessors ... decreed that no one dying should nominate clerics as guardians or executors, and if anyone had done this, no offering should be made for him, or sacrifice celebrated for his sleeping well." *Epist.* I.9. *et infra.*[39]

Eusebius (vid. Constant. 4)[40] says that Constantine had wished to be buried in a frequented Church, in order to have the benefit of many prayers. On his death they offered the Holy Eucharist over his remains."[41]

Cyril of Jerusalem. "We pray for all our community who are dead, believing that this is the greatest benefit to those souls for whom the offering is made." *Mystagog,* 5.[42]

Gregory Nazianzen. "Let us commend to God our own souls, and the souls of those who, as men more advanced on the same road, have arrived before us at their resting place." *Orat. In Caesar. fin.*[43]

Ambrose. "Therefore she is, I think, not so much to be lamented as to be followed with your prayers; she is not to be mourned over with your tears, but rather her soul is to be commended to GOD by your oblations." *Ep* 2.8 *ad Faustinum.* Vid also *de ob. Theod. &c. &c.*[44]

Jerome. "Other husbands scatter on their wives' graves violets, roses, lilies, and purple flowers; but our Pammachius waters her holy ashes and reverend relics with the balsams of almsgiving; with such embellishments and perfumes he honours the sleeping remains, knowing what is written, 'As water quenches fire, so doth alms sin' " *Ad Pammach.*[45]

Chrysostom. "The dead is aided not by tears, but by prayers, by supplications, by alms … Let us not weary in giving aid to the dead, offering prayers for them." *Hom.* 41 *in 1 ad Cor.*[46]

Again. "Not without purpose has it been ordained by the Apostles, that in the awful Mysteries a commemoration should be made of the dead; for they know that thence much gain accrues to them, much advantage." *Hom.* 69 *ad pop.* Vid also *Hom.* 32. *in Matt. In Joan. Hom* 84. *In Philipp.* 3. *In Act. Apost.* 21.

Paulinus, writing to Delphinus, Bishop of Bordeaux: "Do thy diligence that he may be granted to thee, and that from the least of thy sacred fingers the dews of refreshment may sprinkle his soul."[47]

Augustine. "We read in the book of Maccabees that sacrifice was offered for the dead; but though it were not even found in the Old Scriptures, the authority of the universal Church is not slight, which is explicit as to this custom, viz. that in the Priests' prayers which are offered to the LORD GOD at His altar, the commendation of the dead is included." *De cur. Pro mortuis*, c. 2. *et alibi*.[48]

Theodoret (Hist. 5.26) mentions that Theodosius the younger fell down at the tomb of St. John Chrysostom, and prayed for the souls of his parents, then dead, Arcadius and Eudoxia.[49]

Isidore. "Unless the Church Catholic believed that sins are remitted to the dead in Christ, she would not do alms, or offer sacrifice to GOD for their spirits." *De off. Div.* 1.18.[50]

Gregory the Great. "Much profiteth souls even after death the sacred oblation of the lifegiving Sacrifice, so that the souls of the dead themselves sometimes seem to ask for it." *Dial.* 4.55.[51]

Again: "They who are not weighed down by grievous sins, are profited after death by burial in the Church, because that their relatives, whenever they come to the same sacred places, remember their own kin whose tombs they behold, and pray to the LORD for them."

It is evident that the above passages go no way to prove the point in debate, being nothing more in fact than Ussher allows to be found in the early Fathers. They contain the musings of serious minds finding a mystery, and attempting to solve it, at least by conjecture. They state that prayers benefit the dead in Christ, but *how* is either not mentioned, or vaguely, or hesitatingly, or discordantly. Accordingly, Bellarmine begins anew, and draws out a series of authorities for the doctrine of *Purgatory* expressly; and this certainly demands our attention more than the former. It contains such as the following:

For instance, Origen says that "he who is saved, is saved by fire, that if he has any alloy of lead, the fire may melt and separate it, that all may become pure gold." *Hom. 6. in Exod.*[52]

Tertullian speaks of our being "committed into the prison beneath, which will detain us till every small offence is expiated, during the delay of the resurrection." *De Anim.* 17.[53]

Cyprian contrasts the being purged by torment in fire, and by martyrdom. *Epist.* 4.2.

Gregory Nazianzen speaks of the last Baptism being "one of fire, not only more bitter, but longer than the first Baptism." *In Sancta lum. circ. Fin.*[54]

Ambrose speaks of our being "saved through faith, as if through fire," which will be a trial under which grievous sinners will fall, while others will pass safe through it." *In Ps. 36.*[55]

Basil speaks of the "Purgatorial fire," in cap. 10, *Isa.*[56]

Gregory Nyssen, of "our recovering our lost happiness by prayer and religiousness in this life, or after death by the *purgatorial fire.*" *Orat pro Mort.*[57] Elsewhere too he speaks of the Purgatorial fire.

Eusebius Emissenus uses such determined words, as to require quoting. "This punishment under the earth will await those, who, having lost instead of preserving their Baptism, will perish for ever; whereas those who have done deeds calling for temporal punishments, shall pass over the fiery river and that fearful water the drops of which are fire."[58]

Hilary declares that we have to undergo "that ever-living fire, which is a punishment of the soul in cleansing of sin." In *Ps.* 118.[59] Lactantius speaks to the same effect. *Div. Inst.* 7.21.[60]

Jerome contrasts the eternal torments of the devil, and of atheists and infidels, with "the judgment tempered with mercy, of sinners and ungodly men, yet Christian, whose works are to be tried purified in the fire." *In fin. comment. In Isa.* In another place in a like contrast he speaks of Christians, if overtaken in a fault, being saved after punishment. Lib. 1 *in Pelag.*[61]

Augustine has various passages in point, such as *Civ Dei*, 21.24, where, speaking of believers who die with lighter sins, he says, "It is certain that these being purified before the day of judgment by means of temporal punishment, which their souls suffer, are not to be given over to eternal fire." Pope Gregory the first expresses the same doctrine,[62] as do some others.

These instances are at first sight to the point, and demand serious consideration. Yet there is nothing in them really to alarm the inquirer whither he is being carried. I say this, that no one may be surprised at the deliberateness and over-patience with which I may seem to loiter over the explanation of them. First, then, let it be observed, were they ever so strong in favour of something more than we believe, it does not therefore follow that they take that very view which the Romanists take, nay, it does not necessarily follow that they take any one view at all, or agree with each other. Now it so happens neither the one or the other of these suppositions is true, as regards those passages, though they ought both to hold, if the Roman doctrine is to be satisfactorily maintained. These Fathers, whatever they teach, do not teach any one view at all on the subject. Romanists consider Purgatory to be an article of faith, necessary to be believed in order to salvation; or in Bellarmine's words, "Purgatory is an article of faith, so that he who disbelieves its existence, will never have experience of it, but will be tormented in hell with everlasting fire."[63] Now it can only be an article of faith, supposing it is held by Antiquity, and that unanimously. For such things only are we allowed to maintain, as come to us from the Apostles; and that only (ordinarily speaking) has evidence of so originating, which is witnessed by a number of independent witnesses in the early Church. We must have the unanimous "consent of Doctors,"[64] as an assurance that the Apostles have spoken; and much less can we tolerate their actual disagreement, in a case where unanimity was promised us. Now as regards Purgatory, not only are early writers silent as to the modern view of Rome, but they do not agree with each other; which proves they knew little more about the matter than ourselves, whatever they might conjecture; that they possessed no Apostolic Tradition, only at most entertained floating opinions on the subject. Nay it is obvious, if we wished to believe them, we could not; for *what* is it we are to believe? If, as I shall show, various writers speak various things, which of their statements is to be taken? If this or that, it is but the language of an individual: if all of them at once, a doctrine results, discordant in its details, and in general outline, if it have any, vague and imperfect at the best.

Now as to the passages quoted by Bellarmine, it will be observed that in the number are extracts from the works of Origen, St. Ambrose, St. Jerome, and Lactantius. He introduces the list with these words, "*Sunt apertissima loca in Patribus, ubi asserunt Purgatorium, quorum pauca quaedam afferam,*" 1.10. "There are most perspicuous passages in the Fathers, in which they assert Purgatory, of which I will adduce some few." Will it be believed that in his second book on these Fathers, nay, for the most part in the very extracts, which he has before adduced in proof of the doctrine, are enumerated as at variance with it, and mistaken in their notion of it? He quotes a passage of Origen, (not the same) the very same two passages from

St. Ambrose, the very same passage from St. Hilary, the very same from Lactantius, and a passage (not the same) from St. Jerome. Then he says, "*Haec sententiae, accepta ut sonat, manifestum errorem continent*; for" (he proceeds) "it is defined in the Council of Florence," &c. 2.1. Next he observes, "*Adde, quod Patres adducti, Origene except . . . videntur sano modo intelligi posse.*"[65] At length after he has given the two most favourable explanations assignable to their words, he adds of one one the two, "*Sane hanc sententiam [quae docet omnes transituros per ignem, licet non omnes laedendi sint ab igne] nec auderem pro vera asserere, nec ut errorem improbare.*"[66] "The only alleviation of this strange inconsistency," says a work which has recently appeared, "if that he quotes not the very same sentences both for and against his Church, but adjoining ones." The work referred to, thus comments on Bellarmine's conduct, as throwing light upon the state of feeling under which Romanists engage in controversy. "A Romanist," the writer says, "cannot really argue in defence of the Roman doctrines. He has too firm a confidence in their truth, if he is sincere in his profession, to enable him critically to adjust the due weight to be given to this or that evidence. He assumes his Church's conclusion is true; and the facts or witnesses he adduces, are rather brought to receive an interpretation than to furnish a proof. His highest aim is to show the mere consistency of his theory, its possible adjustment, with the records of antiquity. I am not here inquiring how much of high but misdirected moral feeling is implied in this state of mind; certainly as we advance in perception of the truth, we all of us become less fitted to be controversialists. If this, however, be the true explanation of Bellarmine's strange error, the more it tends to exculpate him, the more deeply it criminates[67] his system. He ceases to be chargeable with unfairness, only in proportion as the notion of the infallibility of Rome is admitted

to be the sovereign and engrossing tenet of his communion, the foundation stone, or (as it may be called) the
fulcrum of its theology. I consider then, that when he first
adduces the aforementioned Fathers in proof of Purgatory,
he was really but interpreting them; he was teaching what
they ought to mean, what in *charity* they must be supposed
to mean, what they *might* mean as far as the very words
went, *probably* meant *considering* the Church so meant, and
might be taken to mean, even if their authors did not so
mean from the notion that they spoke vaguely, and, as
children, really meant something besides what they
formerly said, and that after all, they were but the spokes-
men of the then existing Church, which, though in silence,
held, as being the Church, the same doctrine which Rome
has since defined and published. This is to treat Bellarmine
with the same charity with which he has on this supposition treated the Fathers, and it is to be hoped, with a
nearer approach to the matter of fact. So much as to his
first use of them: but afterwards, in noticing what he
consider erroneous opinions on this subject, he treats them,
not as organs of the Church infallible, but as individuals,
and interprets their language by its literal sense or by the
context, and in consequence condemns it ... How hopeless then is it to contend with Romanists, as if they
practically agreed to the foundation of faith, however much
they pretend to it! Ours is antiquity: theirs the existing
Church. Its infallibility is their first principles; belief in it
is a deep prejudice, quite beyond the reach of anything
external. It is quite clear that the combined testimonies of
all the Fathers, supposing such a case, would not have a
feather's weight against a decision of the Pope in Council,
nor would matter at all, except for the Fathers' sake who
had by anticipation opposed it. They consider that the
Fathers ought to mean what Rome has since decreed, and
that Rome knows their meaning better than they them-

selves did. That venturesome Church has usurped their place, and thinks it merciful, only not to banish outright the rivals she has dethroned. By an act, as it were, of grace she has determined, that when they contradict her, though not available as witnesses against her, yet, as living in times of ignorance, they are only heterodox, and not heretical; and she keeps them around her, to ask their advice when it happens to agree with her own.

"Let us then understand the position of the Romanists towards us; they do not really argue from the Fathers, though they seem to do so. They may affect to do so on our behalf, happy if by an innocent stratagem they are able to convert us; but all the while in their own feelings, they are taking a far higher position. They are teaching, not disputing or proving. They are interpreting what is obscure in antiquity, purifying what is alloyed, correcting what is amiss, perfecting what is incomplete, harmonizing what is various. They claim and use all its documents as ministers and organs of that one infallible Church, which once forsooth kept silence, but since has spoken, which by a divine gift must ever be consistent with itself, and which bears with her own evidence of divinity."

Leaving Bellarmine then, let us proceed to inquire what the opinion of the Fathers in the foregoing passages really is.

———————

§3. HISTORY OF THE RISE OF THE DOCTRINE OF PURGATORY AND OPINIONS IN THE EARLY CHURCH CONCERNING IT.

The argumentative ground of the doctrine of Purgatory, as far as the Infallibility of the Church has not superseded any, has ever been, I conceive, the report of miracles and visions attesting it; but the historical origin is to be sought elsewhere, viz. in the anxious conjectures of the human mind about its future destinies, and the apparent coincidences of these with certain obscure texts of Scripture.

These may be supposed to have operated as follows; as described in the work already cited. "HOW ALMIGHTY GOD will deal with the mass of Christians, who are neither very good nor very bad, is a problem with which we are not concerned, and which it is our wisdom , and may be our duty, to put from our thoughts. But when it has once forced itself upon the mind, we are led in self-defence, with a view of keeping ourselves from dwelling unhealthily on particular cases, which come under our experience and perplex us, to imagine modes, not by which GOD *does*, (for that would be presumptuous to conjecture,) but by which He may solve the difficulty. Most men, to our apprehensions, are too unformed in religious habits either for heaven or for hell, yet there is no middle state when CHRIST comes in judgment. In consequence it is obvious to have recourse to the interval before His coming, as a time during which this incomplete-ness might be remedied; a season, not of changing the spiritual bent and character of the soul departed, whatever that be, for probation ends with mortal life, but of develop-ing it into a more determinate form, whether of good or of evil. Again, when the mind once allows itself to speculate, it will discern in such a provision a means, whereby those, who not without true faith at bottom yet have committed great crimes, or those who have been carried off in youth while still undecided, or who die after a barren, though not an immoral or scandalous life, may receive such chastisement as may prepare them for heaven, and render it consistent with GOD's justice to admit them thither. Again, the inequality of the sufferings of Christians in this life, compared one with another, would lead the unguarded mind to the same specu-lations, the intense suffering, *e.g.* which some men undergo on their death bed, seeming as if but an anticipation in their case of what comes after death upon others, who without greater claims on GOD's forbearance, have lived without chastisement and die easily. I say, the mind will inevitably dwell upon such thoughts, unless it has been taught to subdue them by education or by the experience of their dangerousness.

"Various suppositions have, accordingly, been made, as pure supposition, as mere specimens of the capabilities, (if one may so speak,) of the Divine Dispensation, as efforts of the mind reaching forward and venturing beyond its depth into the abyss of the divine counsels. If one supposition could be produced to solve the problem, ten thousand others were conceivable, unless indeed the resources of GOD's Providence are exactly commensurate with man's discernment of them. Religious men, amid these searching of heart, have naturally gone to Scripture for relief, to see if the inspired word anywhere gave them any clue for their inquiries. And for what was there found, and from the speculations of reason upon it, various notions have been hazarded at different times; for instance, that there is a certain momentary ordeal to be undergone by all men after this life, more or less severe according to their spiritual state; or that certain gross sins in good men will be thus visited, or their lighter failings and habitual imperfections; or that the very sight of divine perfection in the invisible world will be in itself a pain, while it constitutes the purification of the imperfect but believing soul; or that, happiness admitting of various degrees of intensity, penitents late in life may sink for ever into a state, blissful as far as it goes, but more or less approaching unconsciousness; infants dying after baptism may be as gems paving the courts of heaven, or as the living wheels in the Prophet's vision;[68] while matured Saints may excel in capacity of bliss, as well as in dignity, the highest Archangels. Such speculations are dangerous when indulged; the event proves it; from some of these in fact seems to have resulted the doctrine of Purgatory.

"Now the texts to which the minds of the early Christians seem to have been principally drawn, and from which they ventured to argue in behalf of these vague notions, were these two: 'The fire shall try every man's work,' &c. and 'He shall baptize you with the Holy Ghost and with fire.'[69] These texts, with which many more were found to accord, directed their thoughts one way, as making mention of '*fire*' whatever was meant by the word, as the instrument of trial and purification; and that, at some time between the present time and the judgment, or at the judgment. And accordingly without perhaps having any definite or consistent meaning in what they said, or being able to say whether they spoke literally or figuratively and with an indefinite reference to this life, as well as to the intermediate state,[70] they sometimes named fire as the instrument of recovering those who had sinned after their baptism. That this is the origin of the notion of a Purgatorial fire, I gather from these circumstances, first that they do frequently insist on the texts in question, next, that they do not agree in the particular sense they put upon them. That they quote them shows they rest upon them; that they vary in explaining them, that they had no Catholic sense to guide them. Nothing can be clearer, if these facts be so, than that the doctrine of the Purgatorial fire in all its senses, as far as it was more than a surmise, and was rested on argument, was the result of private judgment exerted in defect of Tradition, upon the text of Scripture ...

"As the doctrine, thus suggested by certain striking texts, grew in popularity and definiteness, and verged towards its present Roman form, it seemed a key to many others. Great portions of the books of Psalms, Job, and the Lamentations, which express the feelings of religious men under suffering, would powerfully recommend it by the forcible and most affecting and awful meaning which they received from it. When this was once suggested, all other meanings would seem tame and inadequate.

"To these must be added various passages from the Prophets, as that in the beginning of the 3rd chapter of

Malachi,[71] which speaks of fire as the instrument of judgment and purification when CHRIST comes to visit His Church.

"Moreover there were other texts of obscure and indeterminate bearing which seemed on this hypothesis to receive a profitable meaning, such as our LORD's words in the Sermon on the Mount, 'Verily, I say unto thee, thou shalt by no means come out thence till thou hast paid the uttermost farthing;"[72] and St. John's expression in the Apocalypse, that 'no man in heaven, nor in earth, *neither under the earth*, was able to open the book.'"[73]

"Further, the very circumstance that no second instrument of a plenary and entire cleansing from sin was given after Baptism, such as Baptism, led Christians to expect that that unknown means, when accorded, would be of a more painful nature than that which they had received so freely and instantaneously in infancy, and confirmed, not only the text already cited, 'He shall baptize you with the Holy Ghost and with fire,' but also St. Paul's announcement of the 'judgment and fiery indignation'[74] which awaits those who sin after having been once 'enlightened,' and by CHRIST's warning to the impotent man to sin no more lest a worse thing come unto him.[75]

"Lastly, the universal and apparently apostolical custom of praying for the dead in CHRIST, called for some explanation, the reason for it not having come down to posterity with it. Various reasons may be supposed quite clear of this distressing doctrine, but it supplied an adequate and a most constraining motive for its observance to those who were not content to practice it in ignorance."

Should anyone for a moment be startled by anything that is here said, as if investing the doctrine with some approach to plausibility, I would have him give GOD thanks for the safeguard of Catholic Tradition, which keeps us from immoderate speculation upon Scripture or a vain indulgence

of the imagination, by authoritatively declaring the contents
and the limits of the Creed necessary to salvation and profitable to ourselves.

There seem, on the whole, to be two chief opinions on
the subject embraced in the early Church. One of these is
Origen's, which I shall first exhibit in the language of St.
Ambrose, being the very passage referred to by Bellarmine.
The notion is this, that the fire at the day of judgment will
burn or scorch everyone in proportion to his remaining
imperfections. St. Ambrose then thus comments on Ps.
37(38):14.

"'Thou hast proved us by fire,' says David; therefore we shall all be
proved by fire, and Ezekiel (Malachi) says, 'Behold the LORD
ALMIGHTY cometh, and who may abide the day of his coming? ...
for He is like a refiner's fire and like fuller's soap; and He shall sit as
a refiner and purifier of silver; and He shall purify the Sons of Levi,
and purge them as gold and silver ... Therefore the Sons of Levi
will be purged by fire; *by fire Ezekiel, by fire Daniel.* But these,
though proved by fire, yet shall say, 'We *passed* through fire and
water.' (Ps. 46:12) Others shall remain in the fire: and the fire shall
be as dew to them, (Song of the Three Children)[76] as to the
Hebrew children who were exposed to the fire of the burning
furnace. But the ministers of impiety shall be consumed in the
avenging flame. Woe is me should my work be burned, and I suffer
this worsting of my labour! Although the Lord will save His
servants, we shall be saved by faith, but so saved as by fire. Although
we shall not be consumed, yet we shall be burned. But how some
remain in the fire, others escape through it, learn from another
Scripture. The Egyptians were drowned in the Red Sea, the
Israelites passed over; Moses escaped to land, Pharaoh sank, for his
heavy sins drowned him. In like manner the irreligious will sink in
the lake of burning fire."[77]

It is plain that St. Ambrose, so far from imagining a Roman
Purgatory, definite in period, place and subjects, speaks of an
ordeal by fire which *all* Christians must undergo at the last

day, and grounds it on the solemn text already referred to, 1
Cor. 3:12–15. Which whether rightly so interpreted or not,
a point we cannot determine, since it is an *ἅπαξ λεγόμενον*[78]
in Scripture, yet at least may be so understood without
violence to the wording. "If any man build upon this foundation, gold, silver, precious stones, wood, hay, stubble,
every man's work shall be made manifest; for the Day shall
declare it, because it, (the Day) shall be revealed in fire; and
the fire shall try every man's work of what sort it is. If any
man's work abide which he hath built thereupon, he shall
receive a reward. If any man's work shall be burned, he shall
suffer loss; but he himself shall be saved, yet so as by fire."
Now it would seem plain that in this passage the *searching
process* of final Judgment, essaying our works of righteousness,
is described by the word *fire*. Not that we may presume to
limit the word fire to that meaning, or on the other hand to
say it is a merely *figurative* expression denoting judgment;
which seems a stretching somewhat beyond our measure.
Doubtless there is a mystery in the word *fire*, as there is a
mystery in the words *day of judgment*. Yet it anyhow has
reference to the *instrument* or *process* of judgment. And in this
way the Fathers seem to have understood the passage;
referring it to the last Judgment, as Scripture does, but at the
same time religiously retaining the use of the word *fire*, as not
affecting to interpret and dispense with what seems some
mysterious economy, lest they should be wiser than what is
written.

Next let us turn to the same Father's 20th Sermon on Ps.
119, which is also referred to by Bellarmine.

"As long as the Israelites were in Egypt, they were in the *iron*
furnace, that is, in the furnace of temptation, in the furnace of
affliction, when they were afflicted by cruel tyranny. Whence also
it is written, 'I brought them forth out of the land of Egypt, from
the iron furnace.'[79] The furnace was iron, because, while the
people was yet in Egypt, no one's works were illuminated by

holiness, no one's gold had been there assayed, no one's lead of iniquity burned away. It was a cruel furnace, a furnace of perpetual death, which none could escape, which consumed everyone, in which pain and sorrow dwell only. But the furnace, in which Ananias, Azarias, and Misael sang their hymn to the Lord was a golden furnace, not an iron; by means of which wisdom hath shown forth in the faith of true obedience all over the world. It was indeed in Babylon, where spiritual gold was not, unless perchance in captivity, for 'the Lord led captivity captive.'[80] This is the gold in God's saints who were captives among the Babylonians in body, but in spirit were freemen with God, delivered from the chains of human captivity, and bearing the yoke of spiritual grace. And perchance the same furnace would be iron to the unstable, and gold to those who persevere.

"*All must be proved through fire*, as many as desire to return to Paradise; for it is not said for nothing, that, when Adam and Eve were expelled from Paradise, God placed at the outlet a fiery sword which turned every way. *All must pass through the flames, whether he be John the Evangelist*, whom the Lord so loved as to say to Peter of him, 'If I wish him to tarry, what is that to thee? Follow thou me.'[81] Some have doubted of his death; of his passage through the fire we cannot doubt, for he is in Paradise, not separated from Christ. Or *whether he be Peter*; he who received the keys of the kingdom of Heaven, who walked upon the sea, must still say, 'We passed through fire and water, and Thou broughtest us out into a place of refreshment.'[82] But the fiery sword will soon be turned by St. John, for iniquity is not found in him, whom righteousness itself loved. Whatever human defect was in him, Divine Love melted it away; for her wings are as the wings of fire. (Cant. 8:6)

"He who possesses this fire of love, will have no cause to fear there the fiery sword. To Peter, who so often exposed his life for Christ, He will say, 'Go and sit down to meat.'[83] But he shall say, 'Thou hast tried us with fire, as silver is tried; for when many waters do not drown love,[84] how can fire consume then?' But he shall be tried as silver, I as lead; *I shall burn till the lead melts away*. If no silver is found in me, ah me! I shall be plunged down into the lowest pit, or consume entire as the stubble. Should ought of gold or silver be found in me, not for my works, but through the mercy and grace of Christ, by the ministry of the priesthood, I shall peradventure say, 'They that hope in Thee, shall not be ashamed.'[85]

"The fiery sword then shall consume iniquity, which is placed on the leaden scale. One only could not feel that fire, Christ the Righteousness of God, who did no sin; for the fire found nought in Him which it might consume."

It is now sufficiently clear what St. Ambrose's belief was. The only point of approximation between it and the doctrine of Purgatory is this; that he conceived that for all but the highest saints, in whom love dissolved all remaining dross whatever, some transient suffering, more or less in duration, was in store in the day of judgment. And hence the force of the ordinary prayers of the early Church, as based on Scripture, (and described at length by Archbishop Ussher, in Tract 72,) that departed believers might have "a merciful trial at the last day."

St. Hilary is another witness, whom Bellarmine, in his former book quotes, in his latter surrenders. He, too, will be found to hold this same view of the purgatorial nature of the fire of the last judgment.

"The prophet [the Psalmist] observes, that it is difficult and most perilous to human nature, to desire God's judgments: for, since no one is clean in His sight how can His judgment be desirable? Considering we shall have to give an account for every idle word, shall we long for the day of judgment, in which we must undergo that ever-living fire, and those heavy penalties for cleansing the souls from its sins? Then will a sword pierce through the soul of Mary, that the thoughts of many hearts may be revealed.[86] If that Virgin which could compass God is to come into the severity of the judgment, who shall dare desire to be judged by God? Job, when he had finished his warfare with all calamities of man and had triumphed, who, when tempted, said, 'The Lord gave,'[87] and confessed himself but [dust and] ashes when the heard God's voice from the cloud, and determined that he ought not to speak another word.[88] And who shall venture to desire God's judgments, whose voice from heaven neither so great a Prophet endured, nor the Apostles again, when they were with the Lord on the Mount ?"[89] – Tract. in Ps. 118(119) lit. 3 §12. Vid also §5.

Again,

He [John the Baptist] marks the season of our salvation and judgment in the Lord, saying, 'He shall baptize you with Holy Ghost and with fire;' for to those who are baptized in the Holy Ghost, it remains to be perfected in the fire of judgment." – Comm. in Matt. 2 §4.

Let us now proceed to Origen, who is historically the first who has put forward the theory under review. Even Origen, be it remembered, is at first alleged by Bellarmine, though afterwards absolutely relinquished. His words, as quoted by that author himself, are as follows:

"I consider that even after the resurrection from the dead, we need a sacrament to wash us thoroughly and cleanse us; for no one will rise without dross upon him, nor can the soul be found which at once is free from all defects." Hom. 14 in Luc.

Again,

"We must all come to that fire, be we Paul or Peter." In Ps. 37.

Lactantius expresses the same, or almost the same doctrine in the following passage, as referred to by Bellarmine.

"Moreover, when He shall have judged the just. He will also try them in the fire. Then they whose sins prevail in weight or number, will be tortured in the fire and partially burned; but they, who are mature in righteousness and ripeness of virtue, shall not feel that flame; for they have somewhat of God within them, to repel and throw off the force of the flame. Such is the force of innocence, that from it that fire recoils without mischief, as having received this property from God to burn the irreligious, to recede from righteousness." Div. Inst.7. 21.[90]

Two more writers may be mentioned, as holding the same view, both of whom are quoted by Bellarmine in his favour. St. Jerome, as referred to by him, speaks as follows:

"The fire," he says, commenting on Amos 7:4, "being called for judgment, devours first the deep; that is all kinds of sins, wood, hay, stubble, and afterwards consumes also a part, that is, reaches to his saints, who are accounted the Lord's portion."

St. Paulinus of Nola is the other, who thus writes to Severus:[91]

"If we attain by these works to be citizens with the saints, our works shall not be burned; and that sagacious fire will, on our passing its ordeal, surround us with no severe heat of punishment; but as if we were commended to its care it will play around us with a kind caress, so that we may say, 'We have passed through fire and water,' &c." Ep. 28, 9.

To these passages, others similar might be added from St. Basil and St. Gregory Nazianzen.

So much on this speculation or foreboding concerning the fire of the last judgment. Before proceeding to consider the second notion of a Purgatory, which existed in the early Church, I stop to make a remark. What has been said will illustrate what is meant by Catholic Tradition, and how it may be received without binding us to accept everything which the Fathers say. It must be *Catholic* to be of authority; that is, all the writers who mention the subject, must agree together in their view of it, or the exceptions, if there by any, must be such as *probare regulam*.[92] And again, they must profess it *is* Traditionary teaching. For instance, supposing all the Fathers agreed together in their interpretation of a certain text, I consider that agreement would invest that interpretation with such a degree of authority, as to make it at first sight most rash (to say the very least) to differ from them; yet it is conceivable that on some points, as the interpretation of

unfulfilled prophecy, they might be mistaken. It is abstract-
edly conceivable, that a modern commentator *might* on
certain occasions plausibly justify his dissent from them: –
this is conceivable, I say, *unless* they were explaining a
doctrine of the creed, which is otherwise known to come
from the Apostles, – or professed, (which would be equivalent) that such an interpretation had ever been received in
their respective Churches as coming from the Apostles.
Catholic Tradition is something more than Catholic
teaching. Great as is the authority of the latter, (and we
cannot well put it too high,) Tradition is something beyond
it. This remark is in point here, for it might be objected that
so many Fathers agree together in the notion of a last-day
Purgatory, that, were it not for the accident of others
speaking differently, we should certainly have received it as
Catholic Tradition. I answer, no; whatever the worth of so
many witnesses could have been, – and it is certainly for
safety's sake ought to have been taken for very much, – still,
Origen, Hilary, Ambrose, and the rest, do not approximate
in their remarks to the authoritative language in which they
would speak of the Trinity or the benefits of Baptism. They
do not profess to be delivering an article of the Faith once
delivered to the saints. – Now, to consider the second theory
in the early Church on the subject of Purgatory.

While the Greek Churches, and thence the Italian held
the doctrine of a judgment Purgatory, a doctrine far more
like the Roman is found from an early age in the African
Church; at the same time, it was so far from being considered
as a necessary article of faith, that even St. Austin, who brings
it out most fully, expresses his doubt about its truth.[93] It was
in fact only an opinion or conjecture.

Tertullian speaks thus, when discussing the question,
whether souls suffer in the intermediate state, or wait till the
resurrection of the body:

"In short, considering we understand that prison, which the gospel discloses, to be the places under the earth (inferos), and explain the very last farthing to mean, that every slightest fault is then to be washed away in the interval before the resurrection, no one will doubt that the soul pays something in those nether places without intrenching on the fullness of the resurrection also through the flesh." De Anim. fin.

Next comes St. Cyprian. Cyprian is arguing in favour of readmitting the lapsed, when penitent, and his argument seems to be, that it does not follow we absolve them simply, by restoring them to the Church; we do not admit them to present privileges, the judgment being reserved in God's hands. He thus writes to Antonianus.

"Neither suppose, dearest brother, that the virtue of the brethren will be impaired, or martyrdoms fail, though penitence be indulged to the lapsed, and hope of reconciliation set before the penitent. Strength unmoveable abides with those who have true faith; and to those who fear and love God with their whole heart, integrity endures in firmness and courage. Even to adulterers a period of penitence is granted by us, and reconciliation allowed; yet not on that account does virginity decline in the Church, or the glorious resolve of continence languish through the sins of others. The Church is still embellished by the crown of so many virgins, and chastity and purity are as glorious as before; nor though the adulterer is indulged with penitence and pardon, is the vigour of continence relaxed. It is one thing to stand for pardon, another to arrive safe at glory; one to be sent to prison, there to remain till the last farthing be paid; another to receive at once the reward of faith and virtue; one thing to be tormented for sin in long pain and so to be cleansed, and to be purged a long while in the fire, another to have washed away all sin in martyrdom; one thing in short, to wait for the Lord's sentence in the day of judgment, another at once to be crowned by Him." Ep. 55 ad Antonian[94]

Rigaltius, Faber,[95] and some others understand this passage to refer to the penitential discipline of the Church which was imposed on the penitent; and, as far as the context goes, certainly no sense could be more apposite. Yet, if I may venture on an opinion apart from such high authorities, the words in themselves seem to go beyond any mere ecclesiastical, though virtually divine censure, especially "missum in carcerem" and "purgari diu igne."[96]

Further, the passage in Tertullian, weak in itself, for its was perhaps written after he was a Montanist,[97] fixes a sense, though it rest for authority on Cyprian's language. Tertullian explains Cyprian, Cyprian sanctions Tertullian. It should be recollected, moreover, that Cyprian used to call Tertullian his Master; and the inference deducible from all this is greatly strengthened, when we come to consider the views of St. Austin, another African. At the same time it is worth noticing, the *occasion* and *manner* of St. Cyprian's statement, whatever it means. He will be found to speak conjecturally, and as if in disputation. He is *accounting* for a difficulty; as if he said, – "You suppose that, should the lapsed be received, this makes it all one as if they had never fallen. Far from it; they do not receive an *absolute* pardon; they are reserved to the judgment of the great day. Had they endured and suffered martyrdom, they would have had their pardon sealed at once; as it is, it is uncertain, and *who knows but* in God's judgment such a recompense is in store for them as will allow the Church to be merciful to them without God ceasing to be just?"

St. Austin is lastly to be mentioned; who speaks neither in one uniform way, nor with one and the same degree of certainty. Sometimes he seems to hold the Greek opinion of the final purgatorial conflagration.[98] In the following passage, after alluding to Abraham's sacrifice, (Gen. 15) in which the beasts were divided, but not the birds, and "when the sun went down," "a smoking furnace and a burning lamp passed between the pieces," and interpreting the birds of the spiritual members of the Church, and the beasts of carnal men, some of whom are within, some outside the Church, he says,

"The smoking furnace will come; for Abraham sat there till the evening, and then comes the great terror of the day of judgment. For the evening is the end of the world, and the furnace is the coming day of judgment. It went between those things which were already divided, separating them to the right and the left. Thus there are certain carnal men who are yet in the Church's bosom, living according to their own way, who are in danger of seduction from heretics. While they remain carnal, they are divisible; he did not divide the birds, but the carnal are divided. 'I could not speak unto you as unto spiritual, but as unto carnal ... .'[99] Whoso shall remain such, and in a way of life suitable to the carnal, and yet has not receded from the bosom of the Church, not been seduced by heretics, so as to be divided off the other way, the furnace will come, nor will he be able to stand on the right without undergoing it. If then he would escape that furnace, let him be changed now into the turtle-dove and pigeon. Let him receive it, who can. But if not, but he shall have built on the foundation, wood, hay, stubble; that is, if he has heaped over the foundation of his faith worldly likings, – yet if Christ be there, so as to have the first place in his heart, above all other objects, such are endured, are suffered. The furnace shall come, and shall burn the wood, hay, and stubble; and 'he shall be saved, yet so as by fire.' This will the furnace do; separating off some to the left, - others it will in a manner strain off unto the right: but it did not divide the birds." In Ps. 104 Serm. 3 and De Civ. Dei 16.24. Vid. also, in Ps. 6, De Civ. Dei 20.25; 21.16 and in Gen. contra Man. 2.20 fin.[100]

This is one notion St. Austin had of Purgatory; another was, that it would be of a certain duration, in proportion to the sins of each individual. Without asserting that this view is plainly inconsistent with the former, it may be called a distinct one. The following passage will be found to contain it:

"Some suppose that those who do not renounce the name of Christ, and are baptized in his font in the Church, nor are cut off therefrom by any schism or heresy, whatever be their crimes, though neither washed away by penitence nor ransomed by alms, but preserved in obstinately to the last day of life, will yet be saved by fire, punished indeed according to the greatest of their excesses and wickednesses, but not with eternal fire ... but since those clear and positive apostolical testimonies to the contrary (James 2:14, 17; 1 Cor. 6:9, &c.) cannot be false, the former obscure text concerning those who build on this foundation, which is Christ, not gold, silver, precious stones, but wood, hay, stubble ... must be so explained as not to contradict passages which are clear. Wood, then, hay, stubble, may naturally mean such desires of lawful things of this world as cannot be foregone without some pain of mind. But when that pain burns, if Christ abides in the heart as a foundation, so that nothing is preferred to him, and the man who feels the fire of that pain, has rather lose the things which he so loves than Christ, he is saved through fire ... The trial of tribulation is a certain fire, of which Scripture speaks plainly in another place. 'Earthen vessels are proved by the furnace, and righteous men by the trial of tribulation.'[101] That fire fulfils the Apostle's words in this life; for instance, should it befall two Christians, one caring for the things of God, how he may please God; that is, building upon the foundation of Christ, gold, silver, precious stones; the other caring for the things of the world, how he may please his wife, that is building on the same foundation wood, hay, stubble; the work of the former is not burned away, for he has not loved things, the loss of which would distress him; but the other's work is burned away, since those things are not lost without suffering which are possessed with enjoyment. But since, when an alternative comes, he had rather lose them than Christ, nor from apprehension of losing such things renounces Christ, though he may feel a pain during the loss, yet he is 'saved so as by fire;' for though the loss of what he loved is a burning pain, yet it does not subvert or consume one who is secured by the firmness and indestructibility of his foundation. *Such a suffering too, it is not impossible may happen after this life;* and it is a fair question, whether it can be settled or not; viz. that some Christians, according to their love of the perishing goods of this world, attain salvation *more slowly or speedily* through a certain purgatorial fire; not such, however, of whom it is said 'that they shall not inherit the kingdom of God,'[102] unless they repent suitably, and gain remission of their crimes." Enchirid. 68. 69. vid. also ad Dulcitium, §6–13. De Fide et Operib. §16.[103]

In his *de Civitate Dei*, after speaking (as above noticed) of the fire at the judgment, he goes on to change its position in the course of the Divine Economy, and places it between death and the resurrection; yet still he observes his hesitating and conjectural tone.

"After the death of the body, until the arrival of that last day of condemnation and reward after the resurrection [of the body], should it be said that in this interval the spirits of the dead suffer a fire, such as they do not feel who had not habits and likings in the life of this body, which requires their wood, hay, and stubble to be burned up, but they feel who have not carried with them the like worldly tabernacles, whether these only, or how and then, or not then because here, though they experience the fire of transitory tribulation rescuing venial offences from damnation by consuming them, I *do not oppose, for perchance it is true.*"

He then proceeds to speak, as before, of the other senses of the word *fire*, as used in the text, which affords matter for his inquiry.

And now the reader has before him the whole extent of Augustine's much-talked-of admissions in behalf of Purgatory; and he may see how hesitating and incomplete they are. It is remarkable that the passages on which Bellarmine chiefly relies, are rejected by the Benedictines[104] as not Augustine's; so that Romanists, if they would use this celebrated Father in the controversy, must betake themselves to such as the two extracts last quoted, in which Augustine speaks but doubtfully, and which (it is remarkable) Bellarmine introduces, not in his own favour, but on an opponent's challenge, to explain, as if from their conjectural tone rather making against him. It really would appear, as if in the African Church, there had been no advance in definiteness of doctrine in this matter since the days of Cyprian; but that what was a speculation then, remained as little insisted on or settled when St. Austin wrote.

If it were necessary to add any other evidence, how little the Fathers knew on this mysterious subject, I might mention, that in one place St. Austin implies that the impenitent are in Purgatory; and that St. Jerome seems to say, all baptized persons, however they suffer in Purgatory, are eventually saved.[105]

I have now finished my account of what the early Fathers said about Purgatory; but very imperfect justice is done to the subject, till the reader is put into possession of those decisive testimonies of the Fathers the other way, (that is, in favour of the peace and rest of the intermediate state to true believers,) which will reduce the opinions already described to a mere conjecture, pious indeed and solemnly made, yet received one moment, and abandoned the next. Without determining whether the strict wording of the following passages be such as necessarily to exclude the doctrine of Purgatory, which is a poor way of seeking after what the fact really was, simply consider whether persons who *practically hold* that doctrine, who kept it simply before them as the whole truth and acted upon it, could possibly have written them.

Cyprian, on occasion of the famous plague of AD 252,

"Let him fear death, who has never been born anew of water and the Spirit, and is sold over to the flames of hell; him, who has not been given an interest in the cross and passion of Christ; who is to pass from temporal to the second death;[106] whose departure from the world will be followed by the torments of eternal flame of punishment; who by a longer delay gains but a longer respite from pangs and groans. Many of our people are dying in this pestilence, that is, are delivered from the world; and what is truly a plague to Jews, heathen and enemies of Christ, is to God's servants an end bringing salvation. That you witness righteous and wicked dying together without any distinction of man from man, is no reason for your supposing that destruction is common to good and evil; *the righteous are called to a place of refreshment, the wicked are hurried to punishment,* shelter is promptly afforded to the believing, punishment to infidels. We are undiscerning and ungrateful, well-beloved brethren, in return for God's benefits, nor do we recognize the mercy vouchsafed to us. Lo the virgins depart in peace safe, and with their glory secured, without the dread of the threats, the seductions, and the impurities of approaching Antichrist; youths escape the perils of their anxious age, and happily receive the prize of continence and chastity; the delicate matron no more fears the tortures, the fury of persecution, the violent hands and the cruelties of the executioner, receiving the gain of a speedy death. By fear of the pestilence the lukewarm are kindled, the languid are braced, the slothful are roused, deserters are driven back, the heathen are constrained to believe; *the multitude of those who are already believers is called to peace;* recruits are collected in abundance and with increased strength, prepared to fight without fear of death, when the action comes on, as having joined in a season when death was busy." De Mortal. 9.[107]

"Our brethren should not cause us sorrow, whom the Lord's call has delivered from the world, knowing as we do that they are not lost to us but sent before us, they do not recede, but precede: we should behave as towards men going a journey or a voyage, regret but not deplore them, nor go into mourning *for those who have already put on white raiment,*"[108] &c. Ibid., 14.

"It is not an exit, but a passage, a travelling to things eternal, when time has been journey through. *Who would not hasten to what is better?*" Ibid., 15.

That in this last passage St. Cyprian is speaking of heavenly felicity after the resurrection is certain from the context; but it is as plain that he looks upon the intermediate state as the beginning of it, or the outpost, which he could not do, unless she thought that at least, on the whole, and to the generality, it was a state of rest and peace.

St. Ambrose:

"Death is in every way a good; because it puts away those principles in us which war against each other, and because it is *a sort of
harbor for those* who after tossing on the wide sea of this life, *seek an
anchorage of secure peace;* and because it puts an end to the chance of
deterioration, but, as it finds a man in that condition it consigns him
to the future judgment, and comforts him with the rest itself, and
withdraws him from such present goods as raise envy, and quiets
him with the expectation of the future." De Bono Mortis, 4.

"Unwise persons fear death as the greatest of ills; but the wise
desire it, *as if a rest after toil, and the end of ills."* Ibid., 8.

"Relying on these considerations, let us betake ourselves courageously to our Redeemer Jesus; courageously to the council of
Patriarchs, to our father Abraham, when our day shall arrive; courageously to that holy assembly and congregation of the just. We shall
go to our fathers, to our preceptors in the faith, so that, though our
works fail us, our faith may succor us, our birthright plead for us. We
shall go where holy Abraham opens his arms to receive the heavy and
sharp afflictions ... We shall go to those, who sit down in the
kingdom of God with Abraham, Isaac and Jacob,[109] because when
asked to supper they did not excuse themselves.[110] We shall go
thither, where there is a paradise of delight, where Adam, who fell
among thieves, has forgotten to lament his wounds, where too the
thief himself rejoices in the fellowship of the kingdom of heaven,
where are no clouds, where no thunder, no lightning, no storm of wind,
no darkness, no evening, no summer, nor the presence of this sun,
moon, or stars; but the brightness of Light will shine forth." Ibid.,
12[111]

St. Hilary:

"The vengeance of hell overtakes us at once; and immediately we
depart from the body, if we have so lived, we 'perish from the right
way.' The rich and poor man in the gospel show us this: the one
placed by angels in the abode of the blessed and in Abraham's
bosom, the other at once received into the place of punishment. So
quickly did punishment come upon the dead, that even his brothers
were still alive.[112] There is no deferring or delaying there. For, as

the day of judgment is the eternal reward either of bliss or punishment, so the time of death orders the interval for every man by its own laws, committing every one to Abraham or to punishment till the judgment." In Psalm 2 § 48.

Nazianzen thus speaks of the death of his father:

"There is but one life, to look forward towards life; and one death, even sin, which is the destruction of the soul. Whatever else men exult in, is but a vision in sleep in mockery of realities, and a phantom seducing the soul. If these be our feelings, O my Mother, we shall neither exult in life, nor be much distressed at death. What heavy misfortune has befallen us, if we have passed hence to the true life, released from meat and drink, from dizziness, from surfeiting, from base money-getting, and placed amid stable not transitory possessions, as lesser lights circling in festive dance round the Great Luminary?" Orat. 19 fin.

Macarius,[113] in answer to the question what shall become of those who have two principles, of sin and grace, within them, answers that they will go to that place on which their heart is stayed: for

"The Lord, beholding thy mind, that thou fightest and lovest Him with thy whole soul, separateth death from thy soul in one hour, (for it is not for him to do so,) and receiveth thee unto his bosom and to light. For He snatcheth thee in an hour's turn from the mouth of darkness, and forthwith translates thee into His kingdom. For to God all things are easy to do in an hour's turn, so that thou hast the love of Him." Hom. 26.

The hour's space spoken of seems to imply that the hour of death would supply the necessary purification of the soul from sin;[114] but, whatever it means, the passage is quite irreconcilable with the Roman tenet, for the *state* of the dead is made one of bliss, and that "forthwith" upon death. The following passage is to the same effect; after saying that the guilty soul is upon death carried away by the devil, he proceeds,

"When they" (the righteous) "depart from the body, the choirs of angels receive their souls to their own place, to the pure world, and so bring them to the Lord." Hom. 22.

St. Jerome:

"Let the dead be bewailed, but it must be he whom hell receives, whom the pit swallows up, for whose punishment the everlasting fire is in motion. We, whose departure a crowd of angels accompanies, whom Christ goes out to meet, let us rather feel distress, if we have longer to dwell in this tabernacle of death, for as long as we delay here, we are pilgrims from the Lord." Ep. 25.

So much on the theology of the first five hundred years. But it may be shown that not even Pope Gregory at the end of that period, held the doctrine of Purgatory in the modern Roman form of it. He seems to have gone little further than maintain the Greek notion of the fire of judgment, as above explained, but, from the circumstance of his considering the end of the world close at hand, he so expressed himself as to give it a different character. Nothing has been more common in every age than to think the day of judgment approaching;[115] and perhaps it was intended that the Church should ever so supposed. Perhaps so to suppose is even a mark of a Christian mind; which at least will ever be on its watchtower to see whether it be coming or no, from desire of its Saviour's return. But anyhow, as at other times, so in St. Gregory's case, this expectation prevailed; and, as thinking that the end was all but arrived, he seems to have fancied that "fire upon earth" was almost "kindled," that last judicial and purgatorial trial, which the Greeks and some of the Latins had made attendant upon it. If then he speaks of Purgatory in language since adopted by Romanism, it was not as intending thereby to sanction the idea to which it is appropriated in that theology, viz. that of a regular and ordinary *system* of fiery cleansing in the intermediate state; but, because he imagined the world was on the eve and under the incipient symptoms of an extraordinary crisis, when the sun was to be darkened, and the earth dissolved, and the graves opened, and all souls to be judged which were in earth and under the earth. He says,

"As, when night is ending and day beginning, before the sun rises there is a sort of twilight, while the remains of the departing darkness are changing perfectly into the radiance of the day which succeeds, so the end of this world is already mingling with the commencement of the next, and the very gloom of what remains has begun to be illuminated with the incoming of things spiritual." Dial. 4. 41.[116]

To the same effect he says:

"Why is it, I ask, that in these last times so many things *begin to be clear* about souls which before were hidden; so that by open revelations and disclosures the age to come seems forcing itself on us and to be dawning?" Ibid., 40.

Conformably with this view, he considered the pains of Purgatory to be diverse and various in their modes and circumstances, in this earth as well as under the earth, and consisting in other torments as well as those of fire, being but the pangs and shuddering of intellectual natures, when their judge was approaching and disclosing themselves in a supernatural agony parallel to that trembling of the earth or the failing of the sun, which will precede the dissolution of the physical world.[117] Occasion has already been taken to speak of the belief in visions and miracles, as occurring in attestation of the doctrine, and of the predisposition of the popular mind to receive it. The state of the evidence, of the popular feeling, and of the doctrine itself, is strikingly set before the reader in the following passage of Bishop Jeremy Taylor, though perhaps with somewhat less of considerateness in the wording of it, than such a subject might bear.

"The people of the Roman Communion have been principally led into belief of Purgatory by their fear, and by their credulity; they have been softened and enticed into this belief, by perpetual tales and legends, by which they love to be abused. To this purpose, their priests and friars have made great use of the apparition of St. Jerome, after death, to Eusebius, commanding him to lay his sack upon the corpse of three dead men, that they, arising from death, might confess Purgatory, which formerly they had denied. The story is written in an epistle imputed to St. Cyril; but the ill luck of it was, that St. Jerome outlived St. Cyril, and wrote his life, and so confuted the story; but all is one for that, they believe it nevertheless; but these are enough to help it out; and if they be not firmly true, yet, if they be firmly believed, all is well enough. In the *Speculum Exemplorum*[118] it is said, that a certain priest, in an ecstasy, saw the soul of Constantinus Turritanus in the eaves of his house, tormented with frosts and cold rains, and afterwards climbing up to heaven upon a shining pillar.[119] And a certain monk saw some souls roasted upon spits, like pigs, and some devils basting them with scalding lard; but a while after, they were carried to a cool place, and so proved Purgatory. But Bishop Theobald[120] standing upon a piece of ice to cool his feet, was nearer Purgatory than he was aware, and was convinced of it, when he heard a poor soul telling him, that under that ice he was tormented; and that he should be delivered if for thirty days continual he would say for him thirty masses. And some such thing was seen by Conrade and Udelric [121] in a pool of water: for the place of Purgatory was not yet resolved on, till St. Patrick had the key of it delivered to him; which, when one Nicholas borrowed of him, he saw as strange and true things there, as ever Virgin dreamed of in his Purgatory, or Cicero in his dream of Scipio, or Plato in his Gorgias, or Phaedo,[122] who indeed are the surest authors to prove Purgatory. But, because to preach false stories was forbidden by the Council of Trent,[123] there are yet remaining more certain arguments, even revelations made by angels, and the testimony of St. Odilio[124] himself, who heard the devil complain ... that the souls of dead men were daily snatched out of his hands, by the alms and prayers of the living; and the sister of St. Damianus[125] being too much pleased with hearing of a piper, told her brother, that she was to be tormented for fifteen days in Purgatory.

"We do not think that the wise men in the Church of Rome believe these narratives; for if they did, they were not wise; but this we know, that by such stories the people were brought into a belief of it, and having served their turn of them, the master builders used them as false arches and centries, taking them away when the parts of the building were made firm and stable by authority. But even the better sort of them do believe them; or else they do worse, for they urge and cite the Dialogues of St. Gregory, &c." *Dissuasive from Popery*, Part 1, ch. 1 §4.[126]

Yet not even after Pope Gregory's times was the doctrine unhesitatingly received. Ussher (*Answer* Ch. 6.) quotes the words of the Council of Aix la Chapelle in Charlemagne's time,[127] near 250 years after Gregory, to the effect that there are "three way in which sins are punished; two in this life, and the third in the life to come; that of the former one is the punishment with which the sinner, GOD inspiring, by penitence, takes vengeance on himself, the other the punishment which ALMIGHTY GOD inflicts; and that the third is that of everlasting fire. He also quotes the author of the tracts *de Vanitate Saeculi,* and *de Rectitudine Catholicae Conversationis,*[128] wrongly ascribed to St. Austin; the former of which says, "Know that when the soul is separated from the body, presently it is either placed in paradise for its good works, or plunged into the bottom of hell for its sins;" and the latter, "The departing soul, which is invisible to eyes of flesh is received by the angels, and placed either in Abraham's bosom, if it be faithful, or, if a sinner, in the keeping of the prison beneath, till the appointed day arrive for it to receive its own

body again and give account of its works before the judgment
seat of CHRIST, the true Judge." Even in the days of Otto
Frisingensis, AD 1146,[129] the doctrine of Purgatory was
considered but a private opinion, not an article of faith universally received; for he writes, "Some affirm there is in the
unseen state a place of Purgatory, in which those who are to be
saved are either troubled with darkness only, or are refined by
the fire of expiation."

However, without entering further into the history of the
gradual reception of the doctrine, which, if the circumstances
of its rise be clear, is unnecessary, even could it be given, I
conclude this head of the subject with one or two avowals on
the part of Romanists confirmatory of what has been said. As
to the text of Scripture, we have the candid admission of the
celebrated M. Trevern, present bishop of Strasbourg,[130] that
it is silent as regards this doctrine, at least so Mr. Faber understands him.

"Instead of vainly laboring to establish the doctrine on
some one or two misinterpreted texts of the New Testament,
he fairly and honestly confesses, that we have received no
revelation concerning it from JESUS CHRIST. Hence he judi-
ciously wastes not his time in adducing passages of Holy
Writ, which are altogether irrelevant. 'Had it been necessary
for us,' says he, 'to be instructed in such questions, JESUS
would doubtless have revealed the knowledge of them.
He has not done so. We can therefore, only form conjectures
on the subject more or less probable.' "[2]

It seems then the doctrine is not taught in *Scripture*. The
silence of *Antiquity* concerning it is avowed by Fisher, Bishop
of Rochester,[131] Alphonsus de Castro,[132] and Polydore
Virgil.[133]

Of these the celebrated Cardinal Fisher speaks as follows:

---

[2] Faber's *Difficulties of Romanism* 1.12. This reference is made on the
authority of Mr. Faber.

"It weighs perhaps with many, that we lay such stress upon indulgences, which are apparently of but recent usage in the Church, not being found among Christians till a very late date. I answer, that it is not clear from whom the tradition of them originated. They are said not to be without precedent among the Romans from the most ancient times; as may be understood from the numerous stations in that city.[134] Moreover Gregory the First is said to have granted some in his own time. We all indeed are aware, that by means of the acumen of later times many things both from the Gospels and the other Scriptures are now more clearly developed and more exactly understood than they once were; whether it was that the ice was not yet broken by the ancients, and their times were unequal to the task of accurately sounding the open sea of Scripture, or that it will ever be possible in so extensive a field, let the reapers be ever so skilful, to glean somewhat after them. For there are even now a great number of obscure passages in the Gospel, which I doubt not posterity will understand much better. Why should we despair of it when the Gospel is given for this very purpose, to be understood thoroughly and exactly? Seeing then that the love of CHRIST towards His Church continues not less strong now than before, nor His power less, and that the Holy Ghost is her perpetual guardian and restorer, whose gifts flow into her as unceasingly and abundantly as from the beginning, who can question that the minds of posterity will be enlightened unto the clear knowledge of those things which remain still unknown in the Gospel?"

After a sentence or two, he adds:

"Whoever reads the commentaries of the ancient Greeks, will find no mention, as far as I can see, or the slightest possible concerning Purgatory. Nay, even the Latins did not all at once, but only gradually enter into the truth of this matter ... For a while it was unknown, at a later date it was known, to the Church Universal. Then it was believed by some, by little and little, partly from Scripture, partly from revelations." Assert. Luther. Confutat. 18.[135]

It will be observed how accurately Bishop Fisher's words bear out, as far as they go, our foregoing account. First, he candidly gives up the Greek Church, and almost gives up the

Latin. He says it was gradually introduced, that at length it became universal. What can we desire more in disproof of the Roman doctrine? He implies too, that the doctrine, though not suggested by the plain text of Scripture, was recommended by it, when once suggested in whatever way; as if what it did was just what has been above supposed, viz. bring out in a touching way a certain possible deep sense which the sacred text could not be said to teach but might contain; else why should it be understood only after a long delay? Further, he illustrates and confirms what has above been observed, that the Church of Rome, relying on its supposed gift of enunciating the truth, cares not to *prove* its doctrines ancient, and rather interprets the Fathers by its present teaching than thinks it necessary to depend upon them. And lastly, he is a witness that, as far as Rome has cared to argue in this matter, she has rested the doctrine on *revelations;* – a true and honest account of the matter of fact, but decidedly opposed to the more accurate, though inapplicable, theory established after his death at Trent, which is this, that the revelation was concluded once for all in the Apostles, that all that the Church does is to discriminate and define their doctrine, and that he is Anathema, though an angel from heaven, who adds to it.[136] "That alone is matter of faith," says Bellarmine, "which is revealed by GOD either mediately or immediately; but divine revelations are *partly written, partly unwritten.* The decrees of Councils, and Popes, and the consent of Doctors, ... *then only* make an article of faith, when they *explain the Word of God or deduce* any thing from it."[3]

Polydore Virgil appeals to Fisher's statement as above given and adds, "Moreover by the Greeks, even to this day, the doctrine is not believed." Alphonsus de Castro says, "Concerning Purgatory there is scarcely any mention, espe-

---

[3] Bellarmine *de Purgatorio* 1.15.

cially among the Greek writers; for which reason, even to this day, it is not believed by the Greeks."[4]

Lastly, the following is the avowal of the Benedictine Editor of St. Ambrose's Works in his preface to the *de Bono Mortis*, on certain passages concerning the state of the dead, some of which have been extracted in the course of these remarks.

"If we interpret the words of our author strictly and literally, we must plainly confess that in his judgment souls are kept shut up in certain dwellings till the general resurrection, and there wait the award due to their deeds, which will not however be paid them before the last day; meanwhile that they are visited with some good or punishment, according as each of them has deserved. Lastly, the joy of the righteous is dispensed according to certain ranks.

"It is not surprising that Ambrose should have written in this way concerning the state of souls; but what might seem almost incredible, is the uncertainty and inconsistency of the Holy Fathers on the subject from the very times of the Apostles down to the Pontificate of Gregory XI,[137] and the Council of Florence,[138] that is for nearly the whole of fourteen centuries. For, not only do they differ one from the other, as commonly happens in such questions not yet defined by the Church, but they are not even consistent with themselves, sometimes appearing to grant that those souls enjoy the clear sight of the divine nature, of which at other times they deprive them.

---

§4. THE COUNCIL OF FLORENCE.

It remains to give a brief notice of the Council of Florence, by which the doctrine of Purgatory was first made an article of faith. With it I shall bring this paper to an end.

The Council of Constance, which had been summoned

---

[4] These passages are from Taylor's *Dissuasive* Part 2, 2.2.

principally with a view to the reformation of the clergy, terminated in April 1418, without having taken any effectual measures for their object. Five years afterwards the remonstrance which the existing state of things occasioned, obliged the then Pope Martin V to summon another, which in consequence of his sudden death, eventually opened at Basle, 23rd of July, 1431, in the pontificate of Eugenius,[139] under the presidency of Cardinal Julian Caesarini.[140] Basle, as being across the Alps, was removed from the influence of the Roman see; and the Fathers assembled at once applied themselves to determine a question, which already been agitated at Constance, the superiority, viz. of a General Council to the Pope. They passed a decree that the jurisdiction of the representatives of the Church Catholic in Council Assembled was supreme and universal, and that they could not be dissolved, prorogued, or transferred without their own consent. They proceeded to summon, threaten, and censure Eugenius; and at length when he resisted their proceedings, they suspended him from all his powers unless he submitted to them within 60 days. In these acts they were supported by the Emperor and other chief powers of Europe, as well as by the clergy; and the Pope was forced to submit.

They next attempted to reconcile the Greeks to the Latin Church. At this time Constantinople was much pressed by the Turkish arms; and the Emperor John Palaeologus, the second of that name,[141] after the example of his father, hoped by holding out the prospect of a union of the Churches to gain succours from the West. The Fathers of Basle invited him to attend their meeting with the Patriarch and other chief ecclesiastics of his division of Christendom; but, on his objecting to a journey across the Alps, an opening was afforded to Eugenius, who was not slow to avail himself of it, to propose to the Greeks to transfer the seat of the Council from the Rhine to Italy. In spite of the opposition of the Fathers at Basle, Eugenius was successful in his overtures. The Greek Emperor and ecclesiastics accepted the place of meeting which he proposed, which was Ferrara, and proceeded thither, that is, besides Palaeologus himself, the Patriarch, and twenty chief bishops, amon whom were the metropolitans of Heraclea, Cyzicus, Nice, Nicomedia, Ephesus, and Trebizond; representatives also attended from Alexandria, Antioch, and Jerusalem; and the Primate of Russia. Such were the members of the Greek Church present at this Council, who, however, high in station as they were, evidently were too few to express the voice of the East. It is well known that on the ancient principle of Councils, decisions were made not by authority, but by the independent and concordant testimony of all the Bishops of Christendom, or what was virtually all, to the doctrines declared. On the side of the Latins there were but five archbishops, eighteen abbots, the greater part of whom were subjects or countrymen of the Pope. This scanty representation however of the Latin Church received, as it happened, a considerable reinforcement from Basle; for a reaction taking place there in the Pope's favour, some chief members of the rival Council coming over to him, the whole number of subscribers which he at last obtained to the synodical decree, amounted to eight cardinals, two patriarchs, eight archbishops, fifty-two bishops, and forty-five abbots. After all, however, these are at first sight scarcely to be considered representatives of the whole of Christendom; yet such was the composition of the assembly, known in history as the Council of Florence, (whither a plague had driven it from Ferrara) which established the doctrine of Purgatory.

This is a sketch of its external history: but the point to be considered is the part taken by the Greeks in its proceedings. At the first glance here is this circumstance, almost in itself decisive against its authority, that the Greeks were actuated by motives of interest, and at least by the influence and the presence of a Sovereign. Were they in number fifty times as many, they would not have appeared in Italy at all, had not the Ottomans been at the gates of Constantinople.[142] Next they were unprotected in a strange country, depending even for their daily food on the bounty of those who were bent upon the reconciliation of the Churches; and they were detained by delays which, whether necessary or not, were sufficient to alarm them, and to make them impatient to bring their dispute to a termination. After the first session of the Council at Ferrara, the public proceedings were adjourned about six months. The Greek ecclesiastics were allowed each three or four gold florins a month; at one time there was an arrear of four months in the payment, at another of three, and at the time of their agreeing to unite with the Latins, of five and a half. Besides, even had they the means, their withdrawal from the Council was absolutely forbidden: passports were required at the gates of Ferrara, the Venetian Government had engaged to intercept all fugitives, and civil punishment awaited them at Constantinople. Their condition is vividly described by Syropulus or Sguropulus,[143] the ecclesiarch or preacher, who was present at the Council as one of the Patriarch's five attendants, and whose history of the proceedings is extant. Some extracts shall be introduced from his work; which, besides proving what I have said about the position of the Greeks, will introduce us in particular to the course taken in their discussions on the subject of Purgatory. There were four points of difference between the Churches: the use of leaven in the Eucharistic bread, the supremacy of the Pope, the nature of Purgatory, and the double procession of the Holy Ghost. Concerning the subject which concerns us, Syropulus says,

"At our fourth meeting the Bishop of Ephesus[144] said, 'In our last meeting, venerable Fathers, you laid before us four heads for discussion, out of which we might take our choice … Julian (the legate of Eugenius at Basle) said … it seems to us best, to treat first of the purgatorial fire, that our own minds may be cleared by the discussion. Let us then now dispute upon this subject. The Bishop of Ephesus answered, Be it so as you have decided; but tell us first whence has your Church her traditions about it, and when did she receive and profess it, and what is her exact doctrine on the subject. These inquiries will help us forward. This was agreed to, and we separated.

"*Meanwhile our allowance of provisions was demanded, but not given us. Though we made frequent demands on account of our need, it was not given until we came into the proposed conditions. When we had come round, we received the second monthly allowance on the 12th of May.*

"While we were so circumstanced, serious news kept coming that Amurath[145] was preparing an attack on Constantinople. The Venetians sent the despatches to our Emperor and the Patriarch; afterwards came letters from the city itself, intimating the same, and begging them to do their utmost to gain succours. On hearing this, we were sadly afflicted, were sick of life, prayed to God for help, took it to heart, and with groans and tears begged for some escape from so great a calamity … The Emperor had much talk with the Cardinals on this subject, and made representations through them to the Pope. We, indignant at their unbecoming conduct, betook ourselves to such private friends as we might have among them. When some of us had intreated in this way brother Ambrose, he said to them, 'Be not out of heart, *but do your utmost to bring about a union,* and then we shall make great preparations, and will send a formidable force to Constantinople.'

"Meanwhile some of our company said, that if a subscription for raising forces was proposed to our Archbishops, they would be ready according to their power. The Emperor catching at this, immediately went to the Patriarch, and called us all together, and made us a speech concerning contribution, saying that he himself had set the pattern by borrowing money to fit out a vessel of his own, that he felt confident the Pope would send some also, and that it was a duty in the case of those who had the means to be liberal in the service of their country. To this the principal Archbishop made answer, that were they in Constantinople, they would contribute even more than they could well afford; but being at present in a foreign land, and not knowing what was coming upon them, they felt it necessary to keep what they had, even supposing some among them had anything left ... however, under the necessity, they would each give something. Accordingly four of them promised 50 aspers apiece.

"The Bishop of Nicea (the celebrated Bessarion[146]) said, 'I have no ducats, but I have three urns, of which I will contribute two.' The Bishop also who came next said, 'I have no ducats, but I have two woolen cloaks, and I give one of them.' The Emperor on hearing as far as this, gave up the attempt as vain, for he had reckoned that the Archbishops together might have almost fitted out one vessel ... ' "In the fifth meeting, Julian began to discuss the subject of Purgatory, and said that the Roman Church, even from the very first had received and held this doctrine, from the time of the Holy Apostles, receiving it from St. Peter and St. Paul ... and then from the Doctors of the Church who succeeded them."

To complete the imbecility of the Greek party, they were at variance with each other, Bessarion of Nicea inclining to the Latins, Gregory the Penitentiary taking either said as it happened, and both opposing Mark of Ephesus, the resolute defender of the Greek doctrines. The Latins having put their argument on paper, the Greeks had to do the same, and the Emperor commanded Mark to draw it up, who declined the office, unless it was understood that what he should present would be accepted. The following childish scene ensued which is here introduced merely to show that the Greek cause was not fairly represented in that Council, since it was in the hands, as will be seen, of two rival Bishops and an Emperor as umpire, and not as it to imply that a Council must be composed of none but superior men in order to come to a right conclusion.

"It appeared proper that some among ourselves should stay with the Bishop of Ephesus, and that the paper should be drawn in our presence and hearing, and with our assistance, if it happened to be needed. Accordingly the Bishop of Nicaea, the great Ecclesiarch" (the writer) "Gregory the Penitentiary, the Secretary of the Holy Consistory, met him. The Bishop of Nicea began to converse carelessly and to digress into a variety of subjects. The Penitentiary followed, and rivaled him in the irrelevancy of his discourse. They took up each other, and emulated each other in wasting time on trifles and impertinences. I at intervals begged them to spare words and attend to the writing, but they persisted; when good part of the day was thus wasted, the Bishop of Ephesus said, 'At this rate I shall not be able to write a word: leave me with the Secretary of the Consistory and I will draw up something. Afterwards you shall look over it, and correct anything that is amiss?' On this we left the room. Then the Bishop of Ephesus began to write; but the Bishop of Nicea did the same at the suggestion of the Penitentiary, who praised what he drew up to the Emperor, and wished him to send it to the Latins, as more striking in style, and more eloquent. At his command both compositions were brought to him an read in the presence of select judges. Then the Emperor said to the Bishop of Ephesus, 'Your composition is good: it has many strong points. But it has some things too which will give advantage to the Latins, such as the story of St. Macarius asking the skull (of an idolater) and receiving an answer; for you can bring no unexceptionable testimony to this and they will at once put it aside, and some other arguments also. Better let alone what can be easily met, and urge a little and strong than a parade of arguments, come of which may be easily overset for your opponent will fix on your weak points, and if he masters you on one or two, he will appear to the many, or rather he will be heralded forth as having defeated you altogether. Therefore put out these passages.' ... Then turning to the Bishop of Nicea, he remarked, 'You too have your own faults, you begin by saying, 'O men of Latium;' this is unsuitable. It is more becoming to say, 'Venerable Fathers,' or something of the same respectful and acceptable nature; you have other mistakes too.' He ended by saying that the proem and previous statements of the Bishop of Nicea were the better, but the course of the argument, the proofs, and collateral remarks stronger in the paper of the Bishop of Ephesus; and that it seemed advisable to take the commencement of the former, and any other serviceable passages, and the body of the latter."

The reply thus compounded by two men of discordant sentiments was submitted to the Latins, and an answer drawn up to it in due form. A reply followed, and the discussion became animated.

"Meanwhile in private conversations the Latins begged the Bishop of Ephesus to propound plainly the doctrine which our Church holds concerning souls departed hence. *But he did not state it, being hindered by the Emperor.* And in proportion as they perceived him resisting, and not wishing to set forth our Church doctrine on the matter, so much the more did they press him, and intreat him, and remonstrate with him, and asked what he meant by his reserve, saying that every regular member of any Church was bound, when asked what was the Church's view on any question, at once to give it without hesitation or ambiguity. But the Bishop had his mouth stopped by the royal command."

John, a Spanish Bishop, then entered into a discussion with the Bishop of Ephesus with great dialectic skill, and Bessarion deserted to the Latins; at length, however, the Emperor consented to Mark's speaking out, and he put the Latins into full possession of the Greek notions on the subject of Purgatory. The next sentences run as follows:

"Our allowance was expended, and nothing more was given us in spite of our frequent demands: but when we yielded to their demand, and told them our Church's opinion on the question in discussion, then they gave us three month's allowance on the 30th of June, 689 florins." 5 §18.

This was all that passed on the subject of Purgatory, before the final decree, which, as in other points, so in this, was overruled by the determination of the Latins and the need of the Emperor. But here let me instance another hardship inflicted on the Greeks, for which I have already prepared the reader.

"We sat down in sorrow, not only because of existing and expected perils, but for the loss of our liberty, for we were shut up as slaves. And when months and more were passed, and all were indignant at our dependence upon strangers, the straits we were in, and our want of provision, ... three clerics under the spur of necessity, found an escape ... But the Patriarch learning it, and being indignant at it, wrote at once to the Doge of Venice, who found out the men and sent them to him."

After many months' discomfort from the causes that have been enumerated, the Greeks came to an understanding with the Latins: indeed, from the first, they had very little trust or attachment to their view. There doctrine is said to have been, that the souls of imperfect Christians went to a place of darkness and sadness, where they were for some time in affliction and deprived of the light of GOD's countenance, in which state they were benefited by Eucharistic offerings and by alms; to this the Latins wished to add, that souls without stain enter at once into heavenly glory, while those who have repented of sin, but have not had time to complete the necessary penance, are consigned for a longer or shorter time to purgatorial fire. This was the difference between the Churches, and they compromised the matter thus: the Latins did not press the doctrine of *fire*, and the Greeks gave up – not a word, but a truth, – they allowed, contrary to the belief with which they had come to the Council, that those who are not in Purgatory are immediately beatified, and enjoy the sight of GOD.

It may be objected, and readily admitted, that the narrative of which the above are extracts, is drawn up by a writer unfriendly and unfair to the Latins. But it would seem to prove as much as this, viz. what was the popular view in Greece on the subject of these discussions and their termination, immediately upon it.

A high ecclesiastic, as Syropulus was, would hardly have ventured to have set himself against a recent and solemn act of his own Church, sanctioned by the Court, unless he had had a strong feeling with him. The very fact of his opposition proves that the conduct of the Greeks at Florence was but the act of a party at most in the Church; while the line of history, their sufferings and compelled decision, is too clearly guaranteed to us as true by the known circumstances of the case. But we need not thus painfully deduce the real dissatisfaction of the Greek Church with the articles imposed upon its delegates at Florence. On their return home, they had to encounter so general an indignation and resentment at their conduct, that they were obliged at once to recant and confess their weakness, and throw themselves on the mercy of their brethren. Mark of Ephesus had not signed the decree, and became a rallying point for all who held by the popular religion; while the successor of the Patriarch was deserted even by his cross-bearers, and presided in an empty Cathedral. The feeling spread north and south; the patriarchs of Alexandria, Antioch, and Jerusalem assembled a numerous Council, and disowned the acts of their representatives in Italy; and Isidore, the Primate of Russia,[147] on returning to his country, was synodically condemned and imprisoned in a monastery.

Again, it may be objected that the great article of difference between Greeks and Latins was the question of the procession, not that of Purgatory, and after all, that the real point of repulsion between them lay in national jealousies; whereas they agreed together, as the Council shows, or at least with the slightest difference, on the question in which we are concerned, while the subsequent resentment of the Greeks at home had little or no reference to it; and that their agreement under such circumstances was the more remarkable. It may be replied, that the object of the foregoing account has been to show that the Greeks at

Florence were not trustworthy, that they had neither the ease of circumstances, the learning, or the composure of mind to be witnesses of the traditionary and universal doctrine of the Churches. If this is proved by after circumstances, by the popular indignation as regards one doctrine, it takes all credit from their testimony as regards another. Moreover as regards the doctrine of Purgatory, they did not agree with the Latins in an important point, yet that point they gave up to them; most unfaithfully, considering them as stewards of Gospel truth; and, had they discerned the bearings of the Latin doctrine, which doubtless they did not, most treacherously. They admitted, against the national belief, the beatification of soul under specific circumstances, before the judgment, and in so doing they admitted practically almost as much, as if they had subscribed to the doctrine of purgatorial fire. For, as the mention of fire on the one hand is definite, and ascertains Purgatory to be strictly a place of punishment, which the general expressions of the Greeks did not strictly imply, so in like manner to separate off from it all the perfected saints, and transfer them to a better and heavenly state, does in effect sink it, by the contrast, to a place of privation and suffering. The presence of the souls of all saints, (to speak in general terms, that is, not to include the Martyrs whom the early Church has excepted) in Hades, Paradise, or Abraham's bosom, or by whatever other name we designate the Intermediate State, is our guarantee for the substantial blessedness of that State. We cannot spare the higher Saints from Paradise, in that they are our pledges for its heavenly character in the case of all believers. Thus as regards their own doctrine, the Greeks made most important admissions to the Latins, for making which they had no warrant, and therefore cannot be considered of authority in witnessing a Purgatory at all, any more than in the account they gave of it.

And with these remarks shall terminate a discussion, which has extended far beyond the limits which were originally proposed by the writer.

OXFORD,
The Feast of the Annunciation

TRACT 82

LETTER TO A MAGAZINE
ON THE SUBJECT OF DR. PUSEY'S[1]
TRACT ON BAPTISM

In answer to a Correspondent who had asked, "on what authority," certain "statements" in Dr. Pusey's Tract on Baptism,[2] pp. 133–135, rested, the Editor of the Magazine[3] in question made the following remarks: —

We are not sure that we perfectly understand all H. C.'s[4] remarks; and we differ from his opinion that Bishop Burnet[5] "ought to be allowed to have great weight in controversies respecting the doctrine of our Church." But, in reply to the question which he puts to us, as to "what authority" the doctrine which he quotes from the Oxford Tracts rests upon, we can only say, Upon the authority of the darkest ages of Popery, when men had debased Christianity from a spiritual system, a "reasonable service," to a system of forms, and ceremonial rites, and *opera operata*[6] influences; in which, what Bishop Horsley[7] emphatically calls "the mysterious intercourse of the soul with its Creator," was nearly super-seded by an intervention of "the Church" – not as a congregation of faithful men, in which the pure word of God is preached and the sacraments are "duly administered according to Christ's ordinance,"[8] as the Church of England defines it – but as a sort of "mediator between God and man," through whom all things relating to spiritual life were to be conveyed. Those who could not understand that "God is a Spirit, and they that worship him must worship him in spirit and in truth,"[9] and those who had neither the reality nor "the appearance of spiritual life," readily allied themselves to a religion of ceremonials, in which the Church stood in the place of God. And as the Popish priesthood found their gain in encouraging these ritual and non-spiritual views of Christianity, they eventually prevailed throughout Christendom, till the Reformation restored the pure light of Scripture, and taught men to look less to the priest and more to God; less to "outward and visible signs," and more to "inward and spiritual graces;" and not to infer, that, because their names stood upon the register of baptism, that it was therefore enrolled in the Lamb's book of life,[10] when there was no "appearance" of spiritual vitality in their heart or conduct.

This fatal reliance upon signs, to the forgetfulness of the things signified, was rendered more proclivious,[11] from the circumstance that in the early Church persecution so purified its ranks, that there was little temptation for men to call themselves Christian who were not such in heart; and as adult converts were the first candidates for baptism, the outward and visible sign of regeneration was not resorted to till the inward and spiritual grace was already actually possessed; for there had been spiritually "a death unto sin and a new birth unto righteousness,"[12] before the party applied to make a public confession of his faith in Christ, at the risk of subjecting himself to all the secular perils which it involved.

We have devoted so many scores, nay, hundreds, of pages to the questions propounded in the extract from the Oxford Tracts (especially at the time of the Baptismal Controversy, upon occasion of Bishop Mant's[13] tract, when not a few of our readers were thoroughly wearied with the discussion), that we are not anxious to obtrude a new litigation; but we have readily inserted the extract furnished by our correspondent, because, nothing that we could say would so clearly show the unscriptural character of the whole system of the Oxford Tracts, as to let them speak for themselves. When the Christian reader learns that Noah, and Abraham, and Moses, and Job, and David, and Isaiah, and Daniel, are not regenerate persons, were not sons of God, were not born again, but that Voltaire was all this, because he had been baptized by a Popish priest, we may surely leave such an hypothesis to be crushed by its own weight. It is the very bathos of theology, an absurdity not worthy to be gravely replied to, that men were "sanctified," "greatly sanctified;" were the friends of God, that "the Spirit of God dwelt in their hearts, and wrought incorruption, self-denial, patience, and unhesitating, unwearied faith;" who yet, having been "by nature born in sin, and the children of wrath,"[14] and never having been baptized, so as to be made "the children of grace," were still "unregenerate," and therefore, in Scripture language, "children of the devil." Sanctified, unregenerate friends of God! The Spirit of God dwelling in men, who, not being "born again," were of necessity, being still in their natural condition, "children of the devil!" What next?

We defy a score of Dr. Hampden's,[15] even were they to give lectures in favour of pure Socinianism, to do so much mischief to the cause of religion, in a high academical station, as is done by setting forth such doctrine as that contained in the following passage from one of the Oxford Tracts; – for Socinianism makes no pretensions to be the doctrine of the Church of England, nor do any members of that Church profess to find it in Scripture; whereas the absurdity, the irrational fanaticism, the intellectual drivelling under the abused name of faith, which dictates such sentiments as the following, must disgust every intelligent man and make him an infidel, if he is really led to believe that Christianity is a system so utterly opposed to common sense. The writer complains, that "We have almost embraced the doctrine, that

God conveys grace only through the instrumentality of the mental energies, that is, through faith, prayer, active spiritual contemplations, or (what is called) communion with God, in contradiction to the primitive view, according to which the Church and her Sacraments are the ordained and direct visible means of conveying to the soul what is in itself supernatural and unseen. For example, would not most men maintain, on the first view of the subject, that to administer the Lord's Supper to infants, or to the dying and insensible, however consistently pious and believing in their past lives, was a superstition? and yet both practices account for the prevailing indisposition, to admit that Baptism conveys regeneration? Indeed, this may even be set down as the essence of Sectarian doctrine (however its mischief may be restrained or compensated, in the case of individuals), to consider faith and not the Sacraments, as the *instrument of justification* and other Gospel gifts."

Did ever any man, but the most ignorant Popish fanatic, till these our modern days, write thus? Administering the Lord's Supper (by which we feed upon Christ "*by faith with thanksgiving*"[16] – that is, in a purely spiritual banquet) to infants, or to the dying or insensible, is not superstition if it can be proved that there were in some former age some persons weak and ignorant enough to act or advocate such folly and impiety! Why not equally vindicate the Pope's sprinkling holy water upon the horses, or St. Anthony's preaching to the fishes?[17] We will only say, Let those who adopt a portion of this scheme, and not the whole, mark well whither they are tending. Upon the showing of the Oxford Tracts themselves, the whole system hangs together. You are to adopt some irrational mystical system, by which grace is conveyed – not through "faith, prayer, active spiritual contemplations, or (what is called) communion with God," but – in the same manner that the Lord's Supper conveys grace when administered to an infant, or an insensible person. We have never been extreme in our views respecting the language used in our Liturgy concerning Baptism. We have thought that the words might be consistently used, either with reference to the undoubted privileges of Christian baptism; or in faith and charity, upon the principle stated in the Catechism, where is its said, "Why, then are infants baptized, when, by reason of their tender age, they cannot perform them? (faith and repentance.) Because they promise them both by their sureties;[18] which promise, when they come of age, themselves are bound to perform." Upon either of these principles we can cheerfully use our Baptismal Service. But if the use of it is to sanction the doctrine stated in this tract; if we are to believe that baptism "conveys to the soul what is in itself supernatural and unseen," in the selfsame way that the Popish wafer is alleged to convey grace to infants and insensible persons – (why not to idiots?) – and if our Church Service is to be tortured to bear this meaning; then we confess, that the sooner such a stumbling-block is removed the better. The Oxford Tract writers will not allow us to connect the outward and visible sign of Baptism, or the Lord's Supper, with the inward and spiritual grace, through the medium of "faith, prayer, active spiritual contemplations, or (what is called) communion with God,"[19] but only through the selfsame channel by which "primitive usage" supposed grace to flow to an infant or insensible person, when operated upon with the holy Eucharist. Nay, they sneer at and ridicule "what is called" communion with God (poor Bishop Horsley's "mysterious intercourse of the soul with its Creator"), as being something "so called," but without warrant; whereas true communion with God is through the intervention of "the Church:" by which intervention there is this communion when the priest puts a consecrated wafer upon the lips of an infant or insensible person. The Church of England teaches, after Holy Scripture, that we are "justified by faith;" Professor Pusey[20] teaches that the Sacraments are the appointed instruments of justification. The learned Professor ought to lecture at Maynooth,[21] or the Vatican, and not in the chair at Oxford, when he puts forth this Popish doctrine. It is afflicting beyond expression to see our Protestant Church – and in times like these – agitated by the revival of these figments of the darkest ages of Papal superstition. Well may Popery flourish! well may Dissent triumph! well may Unitarianism sneer! well may all Protestantism mourn, to see the spot where Cranmer and Latimer shed their blood for the pure Gospel of Christ,[22] overrun (yet not overrun, for, blessed by God, the infection is not – at least so we trust – widely spread) with some of the most baneful absurdities of Popery. We ask Professor Pusey how, as a conscientious man, he retains any office in a church which requires him to subscribe to all the Thirty-Nine Articles, and to acknowledge as Scriptural the doctrines set forth in the Homilies? Will any one of the writers, or approvers of the Oxford Tracts, venture to say that he does really believe all the doctrines of the Articles and Homilies of our Church? He may construe some of *the offices* of the Church after his own manner; but what does he do with the Articles and Homilies? We have often asked this question in private, but could never get an answer. Will any approver of the Oxford Tracts answer it in print?

The demand here made had been met; and the following number of the Magazine had contained the following notice on the subject.

In reply to the communication of the Rev. ————, of ———— College, requesting to know whether we will insert a letter in which he says his is prepared "both as regards Dr. Pusey and the Oxford Tracts" to furnish an answer to our inquiry, how the writers reconcile some of the statements in them respecting the Sacraments, with some of those in the Articles and Homilies; we can only say, that we are surprised that he should think it necessary to ask that question; for what honesty or love of truth would there be in our putting a query, and refusing to insert a responsible and properly written reply?

The following letter was the consequence of this permission.

Letter to the Editor of the —————————[23]

Part I

————————— College, Jan. 11, 1837

Sir, – Through that courtesy, which is on the whole characteristic of your Magazine, in dealing with opponents, I am permitted to answer in its pages the challenge, made in a late number, to Dr. Pusey and the writers of the Tracts for the Times, on certain points of their theology. The tone of that challenge, I must own, or rather the general conduct of your Magazine towards the Tracts, since their first appearance, has been an exception to its usual mildness and urbanity. However, I seize, as an ample amends, this opportunity of a reply, which, if satisfactory, will, as appearing in its pages, be rather a retractation on your part than an explanation on mine.

One would think that the Tracts had introduced some new articles of faith into English theology, such surprise have they excited in some quarters; yet, much as they have been censured, no attempt, that I know of, has been made to prove against them – I will not say, article of faith, but – even any theological opinion, which is not consonant to that religious system which has been received among us since the date of the Ecclesiastical Polity.[24] Indeed, nothing is more striking than the contrast exhibited in the controversy between the great definiteness and precision of the feelings, and the vagueness of the outcry, raised against these Tracts. From the excitement on the subject for the last three years, one would think nothing was more obvious and tangible than the offence they contained; yet nothing, not only to refute, but even to describe their errors definitely, has yet been attempted. Extracts have been made; abuse has been lavished;[25] invidious associations excited; irony and sarcasm have lent their aid: their writers have been called Papist, and Non-Jurors, and Lauds, and Sacheverells,[26] and that not least of all by your own Magazine: yet I much doubt whether, as far as you have thrown light on the subject, its readers have, up to this hour, any more definite idea of the matter than they have of Sacheverell himself, or of the Non-jurors, or any other vague name which is circulated in the world, meaning the less the oftener it is used. If they were examined, perhaps they would not get beyond this round of titles and epithets: or, at the utmost, we should but hear that the Tracts were corruptions of the Gospel, human inventions, systems of fallible men, and so forth. These are the fine words which you give them to feed upon, for bread.

Even now, Mr. Editor, when you make your formal challenge concerning Dr. Pusey, you do not distinctly and pointedly say, as a man who was accusing, not declaiming, *what* you want answered. You ask "will any of the writers or approvers of the Oxford Tracts venture to say that he [Dr. Pusey][1] does really believe *all* the doctrines of the Articles and Homilies of our church?" How unsuitable is this! Why do you not tell us *which* doctrine of the Articles you have in your mind, and then prove your point, instead of leaving us to guess it? One used to think it was the business of the accuser to bring proof, and not to throw upon the accused the *onus* of proving a negative. What! am I, as an approver of

---

[1] The Editor meant by 'he,' not Dr. Pusey, but 'any of the writers,' &c.

the Tracts, to go through the round of doctrines in Articles and Homilies, measuring Dr. Pusey first by one, then by the other, while the ———— sits still, as judge rather than accuser? What! are we not even to have the *charge* told us, let alone the proof? No; we are to find out both the dream and the interpretation.[27]

So much for the formal challenge which your Magazine puts forth; and I can find nothing, either in the remarks which precede it, nor in its acceptance of my offer, precisely coming to the point, and informing me *what* the charge against Dr. Pusey is. It is connected with the Sacraments: you wish him and his friends, according to your subsequent notice, "to reconcile *some* of the statements in them [the Tracts] respecting the Sacraments, with *some* of those in the Articles and Homilies!" In your remarks which precede the challenge, you do mention two opinions which you suppose him to hold, which I shall presently notice; but you are still silent as to the Article or Homily transgressed. This is not an English mode of proceeding; and I dwell on it, as one of the significant tokens in the controversy, what is the real state of the case and its probable issue? Here are two parties: one clamours loudly and profusely against the other, and does no more; that other is absorbed in its *subject*, appeals to Scripture, to the Fathers, to custom, to reason, in *its* defence, but answers not. Put the case before any sharp-sighted witness of human affairs, and he will give a good guess which is in the right. If, indeed, there is one thing more than another that brings home to me that the Tracts are mainly on the side of Truth – more than their reasonings, their matter, and their testimonies; more than proof from Scripture, or appeal to antiquity, or sanction from our own divines; more than the beauty and grandeur, the thrilling and transporting influence, the fullness and sufficiency of the doctrines they desire to maintain – it is this: the evidence which their writers bear about them, that they are the reviled party, not the revilers. I challenge the production of anything in the Tracts of an unkind, satirical, or abusive character; anything personal. One Tract only concerns individuals at all, No. 73; and that treats of them in a way which no one, I think, will find to be any exception to this remark. The writers nowhere attack your Magazine, or other similar publication, though they evidently as little approve of its theology, as your Magazine that of the Tracts.[28] They have been content to go onward; to preach what is positive; to trust in what they did well, not in what others did ill; to leave truth to fight its own battle, in a case where they had no office or commission to assist it coercively. They have spoken against *principles, ages, or historical characters*, but not against persons living. They have taken no eye for eye, or tooth for tooth. They have left their defence to time, or rather committed it to God. Once only have they accepted of defence, even from a friend,[29] a partner he indeed also, but not in those Tracts which he defended. This, then, is the part they have chosen; what your Magazine's choice has been, is plain even from the article which leads me to write this letter. We are told of Oxford writers, "relying on the authority of the darkest ages of Popery;" of their advocating "bathos in theology, an absurdity not worthy to be gravely replied to," of their "absurdity," "irrational fanaticism," "intellectual driveling," of their writing like "the most ignorant Popish fanatic," of their "sneering and ridiculing," of their reviving the "figments of the darkest ages of Papal superstition," "some of the most vain and baneful absurdities of Popery;" and all this with an avowal you do not wish to discuss the matter. Brave words surely! Well and good, take your fill of these, Mr. Editor, since you choose them for your portion. It does but make *our* spirits rise cheerily and hopefully thus to be encountered. Never were such words on one side, but *deeds* were on the other. We know our place, and our fortunes; to give a witness and to be contemned, to be ill used and to *succeed.* Such is the law which God has annexed to the promulgation of the truth; its preachers suffer, but its cause prevails. Be it so. Joyfully will we all consent to this compact; and the more you attack us personally, the more, for the very omen's sake, will we exult in it.

With these feelings, then, I have accepted your challenge, not for the sake of Dr. Pusey, much as I love and revere him; not for the sake of the writers of the Tracts; but for the sake of the secret ones of Christ, lest they be impeded in their progress towards Catholic truth by personal charges against those who are upholding it against the pressure of the age. As for Dr. Pusey himself, and the other writers, they are happy each in his own sphere, wherever God's providence has called them, in earth or in heaven; and they literally do not know, and do not care, what the world says of them.

Now, as I have already said, I cannot distinctly make out the precise charge brought against Dr. Pusey; that is, I cannot determine *what* tenet of his is supposed to be contrary to *which* of the Thirty-nine Articles. However, you condemn two, the notion that the Sacraments may, for what we know, in certain cases be of benefit to persons unconscious during their administration; and next that Regeneration is a gift of the new covenant exclusively. I will take them in the order you place them.

1. And first of Regeneration, as a gift peculiar to the Gospel. – You remain upon a passage from Dr. Pusey's work on Baptism (in which he contrasts regeneration and sanctification, and says, that the former is a gift of the Gospel exclusively, the latter of all good men), thus: "We have devoted so many scores, nay hundreds of pages to the questions propounded in the extract from the Oxford Tracts (especially at the time of the Baptismal controversy, upon occasion of Bishop Mant's Tract, when not a few of our readers were wearied with the discussion), that we are not anxious to obtrude a new litigation; but we have readily

inserted the extract furnished by our correspondent, because nothing that we could say would so clearly show the unscriptural character of the whole system of the Oxford Tracts, as to let them speak for themselves." Now, it might seem at first sight as if there were an inconsistency in persisting for some years in speaking *instead of us*, then suddenly saying, it is best to let the Tracts "*speak for themselves*," and then in the very next sentences, relapsing *in eandem cantilenam*, [30] into the same declamatory tone of attack as before; which, as you candidly confess, and very likely with good reason, you are tired of. I doubt not you are discouraged at finding that you have still to argue what you have already done your utmost to settle. Or rather, if you will let me speak plainly, and tell you my mind, perhaps there has been that in the religious aspect of the hour, which has flattered many who agree with you, and perhaps yourself, that the day of mere struggle was past, and that of triumph was come; that your principles were professed by all the serious, all the active men in the Church, the old defenders of opposite view drooping or dying off; and that now, by the force of character, or by influence in high places, they would be secured a permanent impression upon our religious system. And if so, you are not unnaturally surprised to find "uno avulso, non deficit alter;" [31] to find a sudden obstacle in your path, and that from a quarter when you looked not for it; and, in consequence you feel stimulated to remove it hastily rather than courteously. And hence partly from weariness, partly from vexation, you prefer to act as if you were judge rather than —————, and to pronounce sentence by acclamation, not after discussion. If all this be so, you are quite consistent, whether you quote our words without comment, or substitute your own comment for them. In one point alone you are irretrievably inconsistent, to have inserted your challenge at the end of the article.

But what is the very doctrine that has created this confusion? Dr. Pusey's asserting after the primitive teachers that the Old Fathers, though sanctified, were not regenerated. Is *this*, after all, the doctrine which is against the Articles, and such that he who holds it should quit his Professorship? In which of them is a syllable to be found referring to the subject, one way or the other – except so far as they tend our way as implying, from their doctrine of regeneration *in* baptism, that those who are not baptized, and therefore the Old Fathers, are not regenerate? If then, the plain truth must be spoken, what your Magazine wishes is to *add* to the Articles. Let this be clearly understood. This Magazine, which has ever, as many think, been over-liberal in its interpretations of our Services, and in concessions to Dissenters, desires to forge for us a yoke of commandments, and, as I should hold, of commandments of men. Years ago, indeed, we heard of much from it in censure of Bishop Marsh's Eighty-seven Questions; [32] but it would seem that your Magazine may do what a Bishop may not. In reviewing those Questions in 1821, it pointedly spoke of the wisdom of the framers of the Royal Declaration prefixed to the Articles, which prescribes that they shall be taken in no new or peculiar sense; contrasting, to use its own words, "the spirit of peace, of moderation, of manly candour, and comprehensive liberality, which breathes throughout this Declaration, with the subtle, contentious, dogmatical, sectarian, and narrow-minded spirit which," it proceeded, "we grieve to say, pervades the Bishop of Peterborough's Eighty-seven Questions." (— March 1821). But why is liberality to develop on one side only? Why must Baptismal Regeneration be an open point, but the Regeneration of the Patriarchs a close one? Why must Zuinglius[33] be admitted, and the school of Gregory and Augustine excluded? Or do persons by a sort of superstition so cleave to the word Protestant, that a Saint who had the misfortune to be born before 1517[34] is less of kin to them than heretics since? But such is your Magazine's rule: it is as zealous against Bishop

Marsh for coercing one way, as against us for refusing to be coerced the other.

Will it be said that Dr. Pusey and others would do the same, if they could; that is, would limit the Articles to their own sense. No; the Articles are confessedly wide in their wording, though still their width is within bounds; they seem to include a number of shades of opinion. Your Magazine may rest satisfied that Dr. Pusey's friends will never assert that the Articles have any *particular* meaning at all. They aspire, and (by God's blessing) intend, to have a successful fight; but not by narrowing the Articles to Lutheranism, Calvinism, or Zuinglianism, but as feeling that they are contending for the Truth, and that Providence seems wonderfully to be raising up witnesses and champions of the Truth, not in one place only, but at once in many, as armed men from the ground.

But to return. It is hard to be put on our defence, as it appears we are, for opinions not against the Articles; but be it so. Let us hear the form of the accusation. Your Magazine speaks thus: "When the Christian reader learns that Noah, and Abraham, and Moses, and Job, and David, and Isaiah, and Daniel, were not regenerate persons, were not sons of God, were not born again; but that Voltaire was all this, because he had been baptized by a Popish Priest; we may surely leave such an hypothesis to be crushed by its own weight." To be sure the hypothesis *is* absurd, if your Magazine's own sense is to be put upon the word "regenerate;" but it will be observed, that it all depends upon this; and it is not evident that it will be absurd when Dr. Pusey's own sense is put upon his own words. If all who are sanctified are regenerate, then I say, it *is* absurd to say that Abraham was *not* regenerate, being not a Christian. What trifling upon words is this! what is the use of oscillating to and fro upon their different meanings? Your business, Mr. Editor, was to *prove his sense wrong*, not to assume your sense and interpret his words by it; else, when *you* assert, "no one shall enter heaven unless regenerated, on earth," *he*, in turn, might accuse you, quite as fairly, of denying the salvation of Abraham, because in his view, Abraham was not regenerated on earth.

I will now state briefly the view of Dr. Pusey, derived from the goodly fellowship of the Fathers, proved from Scripture, and called by your Magazine "the very bathos of theology." All of us, I suppose, grant that the Spirit in some sense is given under the Gospel, in which it was not given under the Law. The Homily (2nd on Faith) says so expressly: "Although they," the Old Testament saints mentioned in Heb. 11, "were not named Christian men, yet was it a Christian faith that they had: God gave them then grace to be His children, as He doth us now. But now, by the coming of our Saviour Christ, we have received *more abundantly* the Spirit of God in our hearts, whereby we may conceive a greater faith, and a surer trust, than many of them had. But in effect, they and we be all one: we have the same faith," &c. Though man's duties were the same, his gifts were greater after Christ came. Whatever spiritual aid was vouchsafed before, yet afterwards it was a Divine presence in the soul, abiding, abundant, and efficacious. In a word, it was the Holy Ghost Himself; who influenced indeed the heart before, but is not revealed as residing in it. Now, when we consider the Scripture proof of this in the full, I think we shall see that his special gift, which Christians have, is really something extraordinary and distinguishing. And, whether it should be called Regeneration or no, so far is clear, that all persons who hold that there *is* a great gift since Christ came, which was not given before, do, in their degree, incur your Magazine's censure, as holding a "very bathos of theology." You might say of them just as of Dr. Pusey, "when the Christian reader learns that Abraham was sanctified, yet 'had not the Spirit, because that Jesus was not yet glorified,' [35] we may leave the hypothesis to be crushed by its own weight."

Now, according to Scripture, I contend, first, that there is a spiritual difference between Christians and Jews; and, next, that the accession of spiritual power, which Christians have, is called Regeneration. Let it be understood, however, that I am not desirous here to bring *proofs* of the doctrine, for which you have no claim on me; but to show your readers that, even at first sight, it is not so utterly irrational and implausible a notion as to account for your saying, "What next?" in short, to show that the "absurdity" does not lie with Dr. Pusey.

The prophets had announced the *promise*. Ezek. 36:25–27: "I will sprinkle clean water upon you, and ye shall be clean ... *a new heart* also will I give you, and *a new spirit* will I put *within* you ... and I will put *My spirit within you*." Again, 37:27: "My *tabernacle* also shall be with them." Vid. also Heb. 8:10. In Isa. 44:3, the gift is expressly connected with the person of the Messiah: "I will pour water upon him that is thirsty, and floods upon the dry ground: I will pour *my Spirit* upon Thy seed, and My blessing upon Thine offspring."

Our Saviour refers to this gift as the *promise* of his Father, Luke 24:49; Acts 1:4. He enlarges much upon it, John 14–16. It flows to us from Him, "Of his fullness have all we received." (John 1:16).

St. John expressly tells us that it was *not* given *before* Christ was glorified (John 7:39). In like manner St. Paul says, that though the old fathers lived by faith, yet they received not the *promise*." (Heb. 11:39) And St. Peter, that even the prophets, though they *had* the prophetic Spirit – "the Spirit of Christ which was in them" – yet, after all, had not "the glory which should follow;" which was "the Gospel *with the Holy Ghost sent down from heaven*;" the Spirit, in the special Christian sense. [36] Consider also St. Paul's use of the term "spirit," e.g. Rom. 8, as the characteristic of the Gospel. [37]

It is described in the New Testament under the same images as it is promised in the Old, – a tabernacle, and a fount of living water (1 Cor. 3:17; 2 Cor. 6:16–18; John 4:14; 7:38).

Nothing, I think, but the inveterate addiction to systematizing so prevalent, can explain away texts which so expressly say that we have a Divine presence which the Jews had not.

Now, secondly, is this gift to be called Regeneration? I grant that in one sense all the terms applicable to Christian privileges are also applicable to Jewish. The Jews were "sons of God," were "begotten" of God, had "the Spirit," saw "the glory of God," and the like; but, in like manner, the Saints in heaven, as their peculiar gift, will see "the glory of God," and Angels are "sons of God;" [38] yet we know that Angels and Saints are in a state different from the Jews. The question, then, still remains open, whether, in spite of the absence of discriminating terms, Christians also have not a gift which the Jews had not, and whether the word regeneration in its *proper* sense, does not denote it.

Our proof, then, is simple. The word regeneration occurs twice only in Scripture: in neither can it be interpreted to include Judaism; in one, most probably in both, it is limited to the Gospel; in Titus 3:4, 5, certainly; and in Matt. 19:28, according as it is stopped, it will mean the coming of Gospel grace, or the resurrection.

Such is some small portion of the Scripture notices on the general subject, which I bring to show that Scripture does not so speak as to make the view maintained by Dr. Pusey, with all Saints, guilty of absolute "absurdity" on the face of the matter, and a "bathos in theology." And the following consideration will increase this impression. In truth, the view in question is simply *beyond* not *against*, the opinion of your Magazine. It is a view which the present age cannot be said to deny, because it does not see it. The Catholic Church has ever given to Noah, Abraham, and Moses, all that the present age gives to Christians. You cannot mention the grace, in kind or degree, which you ascribe to the Christian, which Dr. Pusey will not ascribe to Abraham; except, perhaps, the intimate knowledge of Christian doctrine. But he considers that Christians have a something beyond this, even a portion of that heaven brought down to earth, which will be for ever in heaven the portion of Abraham and all saints in its fullness. It is not, then, that Dr. Pusey defrauds Abraham, but your Magazine defrauds Christians. That special gift of grace, called "the glory of God," is as unknown to the so-called religious world as to the "natural man." The Catholic religion teaches, that, when grace takes up its abode in us, we have so superabounding and awful a grace tabernacled in us, that no other words describe it more nearly than to call it an Angel's nature. Now mark the meaning of this. Angels are holy; yet Angels before now have become devils. Keeping this analogy in view, you will perceive that it is as little an absurdity to say that Abraham was not regenerate, as to say that he was not an Angel; as little unmeaning to say that Voltaire was unregenerate, as to say he became a devil, as Judas is expressly called. [39] Let me suit one or two of your sentences to this view of the subject, and then I will release you from the trouble of hearing more upon it. You will then speak thus: "When the Christian reader learns that Noah, Abraham, and Moses, were not Angels, yet that Voltaire was a devil, we may surely leave such an hypothesis to be crushed by its own weight. It is the very bathos of theology – an absurdity not worthy to be gravely replied to – that men are sanctified, the friends of God, had the grace of God in their hearts, and yet were not Angels. Sanctified, non-angelic friends of God! grace dwelling in any but Michael, Gabriel, the Cherubims and the Seraphims? What next?"

Alas! Sir, that you should so speak of your own privileges! Perhaps it is my turn now to ask you, "What next?" and this I mean to do. Before proceeding to the other opinion attributed to Dr. Pusey, I wish to see what you will say to what is now offered you. Only I would remark, that the subjects which I have not yet touched upon *are* to come, when due attention shall be shown to your remarks about Justification, the Homilies, and kindred points.

PART II

March 3, 1837

2. I now proceed to the second of the charges which you made against Dr. Pusey. After saying what is necessary, I shall, as I promised, notice the subject of Justification,[40] the Homilies, and the Articles; and shall intersperse the discussion with some remarks, as brief as is practicable, on the various matter "ramblingly and cursory set before you readers," as you happily express it, in your animadversions on the portion of my letter already published.

That portion occupies not so much as seven pages of your larger type, and that in the course of two numbers. It has elicited from you in answer about sixty pages of your closest. I think then I have a claim in courtesy, nay in justice, that you should put in the *whole* of this reply without a word of your own. I will not embrace the entire subject in it, but leave one portion for an after Number of your Magazine, that you may not say I burden you with too much at once. But what I send, I hope to see inserted without mutilation. Do grant me this act of fairness – you will have months upon months, nay, the whole prospective duration of your Magazine, for your reply: I, on the other hand, limit myself to *one* letter. All I ask is the right of an Englishmen, a fair and uninterrupted hearing.

The second charge you bring against Dr. Pusey is this: – that he holds that the sacraments may, for what we know, in certain cases, be of benefit to persons unconscious during their administration. You quarrel, however, with this mode

of stating his supposed opinion; you say, Mr ————
misstates what we said. We were denying the utility of
administering the Lord's Supper to infants or insensible
persons, as the Papists employ extreme unction; which Mr.
———— skilfully turns into a charge of our denying that
there is any benefit in Infant Baptism" (p. 124). Now, I must
think you leave the matter as you found it. You have said,
the notion of the Holy Eucharist benefitting infants was "an
absurdity," intellectual driveling," irrational fanaticism," &c.
I ask, then, *why* is not the doctrine that Holy Baptism
benefits them, all these bad things also? Surely you are
speaking of the very *notion* of infants being benefitted by
means of external rites, when you say it implies "a system
utterly opposed to common sense." You must mean there is
an *antecedent* absurdity; antecedent to a consideration of the
particular case. You speak, just as I have worded it, against
the very notion that "the sacraments," one as well as the
other,[41] "may, for what we know, in certain cases, be of
benefit to persons unconscious during their administration."
What is an absurdity when supposed in one case, is an
absurdity surely in the other. I cannot alter my wording of
your objection.

Next let us consider the very passage which has led you to
use these free epithets. It stands thus: "We have almost
embraced the doctrine that God conveys grace only through
the instrumentality of the mental energies, that is through
faith, prayer, active spiritual contemplation, or (what is
called) communion with God, in contradiction to the
primitive view, according to which the church and her sacraments are the ordained and direct invisible means of
conveying to the soul what is in itself supernatural and
unseen. For example: would not most men maintain, on the
first view of the subject, that to administer the Lord's Supper
to infants, or to the dying and insensible, however consistently pious and believing in their past lives, was a

superstition? and yet both practices have the sanction of primitive usage. And does not this account for the prevailing indisposition to admit at baptism conveys regeneration? Indeed, this may even by set down as the essence of sectarian doctrine (however its mischief may be restrained or compensated in the case of individuals), to consider faith, and not the sacraments, as the instrument of justification and other Gospel gifts." – These words you attribute to Dr. Pusey. You say, "Professor Pusey teaches that the sacraments are the appointed instruments of justification; the learned Professor ought to lecture at Maynooth, or the Vatican, and not in the chair of Oxford, when he puts forth this Popish doctrine." Again, in pp. 118, 119, you speak of Dr. Pusey's saying that the grace of the sacrament is unconnected "with the mental energies, that is, through faith, prayer, active spiritual contemplations, or what is called communion with God;" (here you interpose of your own "for shame, Dr. Pusey to speak thus lightly of 'communion with God!' "[42]); that "to administer the Lord's Supper to infants, or to the dying and insensible," is not "superstition," but "a practice having the sanction of primitive usage," and "primitive usage," you add, "the Oxford Tracts" [Tracts for the Times] "teach is of Apostolical authority." It is quite clear you attribute the above sentences to Dr. Pusey.

Now, Mr. Editor, let me ask you a question. Should any one accuse *you* of having written them, should you not be startled? Supposing I boldly attributed them to you, and retorted your interjection of indignation upon yourself, would you not consider it somewhat outrageous? Should I have any reason to complain if you accused me of exceeding assurance, of being under a delusion, or at least of unpardonable carelessness? Be judge then in your own case. Those sentences no more belong to Dr. Pusey than to you. They are not in his Tract. They are not his writing. No one man is chargeable with the work of another man. Not even were

Dr. Pusey to profess he approved the general sentiment of the passage, would you have any right to charge him with the very wording of it. Every man has his own way of expressing himself; I have mine, and you have yours. Dr. Pusey might approve the sentiment, yet criticize the wording. All these strong sayings then against Dr. Pusey, are misdirected. Learn, Mr. Editor, to be sure of your man, before you attack him.

To proceed. The words in the Advertisement to the second volume of the Tracts.[43] Let us examine them, whosesoever they are. Now, in what they say about administering the Holy Eucharist to children or the insensible, they do not enforce it, as you suppose, on "Apostolical authority." A usage may be primitive, yet not universal; may belong to the first *ages*, but only to some *parts* of the Church. Such a usage is either not apostolical, else it would be everywhere observed; or at least not binding, as not being delivered by the Apostles *as* binding. For instance, the Church of Ephesus, on St. John's authority, celebrated the Easter-feast after the Jewish manner, on the fourteenth day of Nisan; yet such a custom is not binding on us. Now, supposing I said, "the great reverence in which the Jewish dispensation was held in the best and purest ages, is shown in this, that the quartodec-imam[44] usage has primitive, nay Apostolic sanction;" must I necessarily mean that all Christendom, all the Apostles, observed Easter on the fourteenth day? must I mean that we are bound to keep it on that day? must I mean to extol such a usage, and to advocate it? Apply this instance to the sentence of this writer who is not Dr. Pusey, this Pseudo-Pusey, as I may call him; and see whether it will not help your conception of his meaning. He does not say, he does not imply, that to administer the Second Sacrament to infants is Apostolic, he does not consider it a duty binding to us. He does but say, that, since it has a sanction in early times, it is not that "absurdity," "irrational fanaticism," and so forth, which your Magazine says it is: and his meaning may be thus worded: "Here is a usage existing up and down the early Church, which *right or wrong*, argues quite a different *temper* and *feeling* from those of the present day. This day, *on the first view of the subject*, calls it an absurdity; that day did not." Surely it is fair to estimate inward states of mind by such spontaneous indications. To warn men against the religious complexions of certain persons at present, I should point to the Pastoral Aid-Society,[45] though some who agree with them in general sentiments may not approve it. To describe that of our Bishops 130 years since, I should refer to the then attempt, nearly successful, of formally recognizing the baptism of Dissenters.[46] Again, the character of Laud's religion may be *gathered* even from the exaggerated account of his consecrating St. Catherine Cree's church, without *sanctioning* that account.[47]

When such indications occur in primitive times, though they are not of authority more than in modern times, yet they are tokens of what *is* of authority, – a certain religious temper, which *is* found everywhere, always, and in all,[48] though the particular exhibitions of it be not. In like manner the spiritual interpretations of Scripture, which abound in the Fathers, may be considered as proving the Apostolicity of the *principle* of spiritualizing Scripture; though I may not, if it so happen, acquiesce in this or that particular application of it, in this or that Father. And so the administration of the Lord's Supper to infants in the Church of Cyprian, Saint and Martyr, is a sanction of a *principle*, which your Magazine, on the other hand, calls "an absurdity," "intellectual drivelling," and "irrational fanaticism." For my part, I am not ashamed to confess that I should consider Cyprian a better interpreter of the Scripture doctrine of the Sacraments, of "the minding of the Spirit" about them, than even the best divines of this day, did they take, which I am far from accusing them of doing, an opposite view. You, however, almost class him among and at least make him the associate and abettor of, "ignorant fanatics," p. 119.

Now, if this interpretation of the passage in question be correct, as I conscientiously and from my heart believe it to be, it will follow that you have not yet made good even the shadow of a shade of a charge of opposition to the Articles – not only against Dr. Pusey, but against the Tracts generally; for no one can say that any one of the Articles formally *forbids* us to consider that grace is conveyed *through* the outward symbols; while, on the other hand, one of them expressly *speaks* of "the body of Christ" as "given," as well as "taken, in the Supper;"[49] words, moreover, which are known to have meant, in the language of that day, "given by the administrator;" and therefore, *through* the consecrated bread. At the same time, let it be observed I do not consider the writer of the Advertisement to say *for certain* that the outward elements benefit true Christians when insensible; only as much as this, that we cannot be sure they do not.

Before closing this head of my subject, I shall remark on the words upon which you exclaim, "For shame, Dr. Pusey!" though he has no reason to be ashamed of what he did not write. They are these: "or what is called, communion with God." You often mistake, Mr. Editor, by not laying the emphasis on the right word in the sentence on which you happen to be commenting. This is a case in point. The stress is to be placed on the word "*called*" – "what is *called* communion with God." The author meant, had he supplied his full meaning, "what is *improperly* called." There is nothing to show that he denies "the communion of saints" with God and with each other, and, in subordination to the mystical union, the conscious union of mind and affections. He only condemns that indulgence of mere excited feeling which has nowadays engrossed that sacred title.

To show that this is no evasion or disingenuousness on my part (for you sometimes indulge in hints about me to this effect), I will give your readers one or two more instances of the same failing in your mode of arguing, and one a very painful instance.

For example: I said, in the former part of my letter, that Dr. Pusey's friends insist on *no particular* or *peculiar* sense of the Articles, – a fault which I had just charged upon you. I had said you were virtually imposing additions: then I supposed the objection made, that *we* should do so, had we the power, – as is often alleged. To this I answer, "Your Magazine may rest satisfied that Dr. Pusey's friends will never assert that the Articles have any *particular* meaning at all." You have missed the point of this sentence: accordingly, you detach it from the context, and prefix it to the opening of the discussion, before it appears in its proper place in print; and when it does, you print it in italics. This is taking a liberty with my text. However, to this subject I shall have occasion to recur.

Another instance occurs in your treatment of the Homilies and Mr. Keble.[50] The Homily speaks of "the stinking puddles of *men's* traditions." You apply this as an answer to Mr. Keble's sermon, who speaks of *God's* traditions, even those which St. Paul bids us "hold;"[51] and who considers, moreover, that no true traditions of doctrine exist but such as may be proved from Scripture; whereas the Homily clearly means by men's traditions, such as *cannot* be proved from Scripture. You would have escaped this mistake, Mr. Editor, had you borne in mind that traditions, "devised by men's imagination," are not Divine traditions, and that it as little follows that Catholic Traditions are to be rejected because Jewish and Roman are, as that the Christian Sabbath is abolished because the Jewish is abolished. But you saw that Mr. Keble said something or other about tradition, and you were carried away with the word.

The last mistake of this kind is a distressing one. I hardly like to mention it; so serious is it. I must call it an "idle word."

It is a charge brought against Dr. Pusey. He has said; "To those who have fallen, God holds out only a light in a dark place, sufficient for them to see their path, but not bright or cheering, as they would have it; and so, in different ways, man would forestall the sentence of his Judge; the Romanist by the *sacrament* of penance, a modern class of divines by the *appropriation* of the merits and righteousness of our blessed Redeemer." You add three notes of admiration, and say, "We tremble as we transcribe these awful words," p. 123. I dare not trust myself to speak about such heedless language as it deserves. I will but say, in explanation of your misconception, that Dr. Pusey compares to Roman restlessness, not the *desiring* and *praying* to be clothed, or the doctrine that every-one who is saved must be clothed in "the merits and righteousness of our blessed Redeemer," but the *appropriation* of them without warrant on the part of individuals.[52] He denies that individuals who have fallen into sin have any right to *claim* them as their own already; he denies that they may "*forestall* the sentence of the Judge" at the last day; he main-tains they can but flee to Christ, and adjure Him by His *general* promises, by His past mercies to themselves, by His present distinct mercies to them in the Church; but they had no personal assurance, no right to appropriate again what was given them *plenarily* in baptism. This is his meaning; whereas you imply that he denies the duty of looking in faith to be saved *by* Christ's merits and righteousness; that he denies backsliders the *hope* of it. If you do not imply this, if you really and simply mean that the *act of claiming* Christ's merits by this or that individual (for of this Dr. P. speaks) is, as you express it, "a most Scriptural and consoling truth," and that it is "blas-phemous," but for "the absence of wicked intentions in the writer," to compare to the Roman penance the *confidence* which sinners are taught to feel that their past offences are *already* forgiven them, – if this be your meaning, I am wrong, but I am charitable, in saying you have mistaken Dr. Pusey.

Now I come to the consideration of (1) the Homilies, (2) the Articles, and (3) Justification. And first concerning the Homilies.

1. You ask, "How do these clergymen ... *reconcile their* consciences to such declarations as those which abound in the Homilies, affirming that the Church of Rome is 'Antichrist,' &c.? And you say that you are considered "persecutors" or a persecutor, because you ask how I and others "reconcile such things in the Homilies with the Oxford Tracts." Who considers you a persecutor? Not I; nor should I ever so consider you for asking a simple question in argument. What I have censured you for, has been the use of vague epithets, calling names, and the like, which I really believe you in your sober reason disapprove as heartily as I do. For instance: I am sure you would think it wrong to proclaim to the world that such a one is an ultra-Protestant. It is classing him with a party. There are ultra-Protestants in the world, we know; but we can know so little of individuals that we have seldom right to call them so, unless they take the name. A person may hold certain ultra-Protestant *notions*, and we may say so; this is deciding about him just as far as we know, and no farther. The case is the same in the more solemn matters of heaven and hell. We say, for instance, that they who hold anti-Trinitarian doctrines will perish everlastingly; but we dare not apply this anathema to this or that person; the utmost we say is that he holds damnable errors, leaving his person to God. To say nothing of the religiousness of such a proceeding, you see how much of real kindness and consideration it throws over controversy. Of course I do not wish to destroy what are facts; men *are* of different opinions, and they do act in sets. There is no harm in denoting this; many confess they so act. In conversation we never should get on, if we were ever using circumlocutions. But in controversy it does seem both Christian and gentle-manlike to subject oneself to rules; and as one of these, to

make a distinction between opinions and persons; to condemn opinions, to condemn them *in* persons, but not to give bad names to the persons, till public authority sanctions it. If I think you have aught of the spirit of persecution in you – (and to be frank with you, and in observance of my own distinction, though you are not "a persecutor," you speak in somewhat of a persecuting *tone*,) it is not for perplexing me with questions, or overwhelming me with refutations, but because your style is "rough, rambling, and cursory." I think it *like* a persecutor to prefer *general* charges, to use unmeasured terms, to be oratorical and theatrical, and when challenged to speak definitely, to accuse the party challenging of complaining, being angry, and the like.

Now to return to the Homilies.[53] You ask how I reconcile my conscience to the Homilies calling Rome Antichrist, I holding the doctrines of the Tracts. To this I answer by asking, if I may do so without offence, how *you* reconcile to your conscience the Homilies saying that "the Holy Ghost doth teach" in the book of Tobit? how you reconcile to your "subscription" that they five times call the books of the Apocrypha "Scripture;" that Baruch is quoted as a "prophet" and as "holy Baruch," Tobit as "holy Father Tobit," the author of Wisdom and the Son of Sirach as "the Wise Man," and the latter is said "certainly to assure us" of a heavenly truth; in a word, that the Apocrypha is referred to as many as fifty-three times? Here you see I have the advantage of you, Mr. Editor. Though I believe the Old and New Testaments alone to be *plenarily* inspired, yet I do believe, according to the Homily, what you do not believe, that the Holy Ghost spoke by the mouth of Tobit. Here you see is the advantage of what you call my "scholastic distinctions," p. 193. When I said that the great gift of the Holy Ghost, called regeneration, was reserved for Christians, and yet that the Jews might be under his blessed guidance, you said that I was drawing a scholastic distinction. This is one instance of your part of *calling names*. What do you mean by *scholastic*? Beware, lest, when you come to define it, you include unwittingly the most sacred truths under it. There are persons who think the Catholic doctrines of the Trinity and Atonement "scholastic;" and so they are, but they are something more, they are Apostolic also. The Church went down into Egypt before it came out of it; nor is it any proof that the distinction in question is not Scriptural, that it is, if it is, scholastic. However, and how, it serves me in good stead in this instance from the Homilies; it enables me to *understand* and to assent to their doctrine concerning the Apocrypha. I consider the gifts and operations of the Blessed Spirit are manifold. What He is towards Angels, towards glorified Saints and Moses and Elias, towards the faithful departed, towards Adam in Paradise, towards the Jews, towards the Heathen, towards Christians militant; what he is in the Church, in the individual, in the Evangelist, in the Apostle, in the Prophet, in the Apocryphal writer, in the Doctor and Teacher, is one and the same so far as this, that it is *holy*; but it may differ in kind in each case. Life is the same in all living things; yet there is one flesh of men, another of fishes, another of birds: and so the spiritual gift in like manner may be the same, yet diverse; it may be applied to the heart or to the head, as an inward habit or an external impression, plenarily or partially; for one purpose, not for another; for a time, or for ever. This view of God's gracious influences you call scholastic. I, on the other hand, call the common division, into miraculous and moral or spiritual, jejune and unauthorized. However, whether I be right or you, I am at least able to do with mine, what you cannot, – agree with the Homily. If you will not take my explanation, which I sincerely believe to be the right one, you must "reconcile your conscience" to a better; till you find one, you must reconcile it to a disagreement with the Homily.

Now I will put another difficulty to you, which will be found in the event to put you into a greater strait as regards the Homilies, than you suppose me to be in. The last Homily in the volume is "Against Disobedience and Wilful Rebellion."[54] It is one of the most elaborate of them, consisting of no less than six parts. *I* hold this doctrine, you do not.[2] Let me put before you some of the statements of this Homily, – the direct, explicit, developments of its title. "If servants," it says, "ought to obey their masters, not only being gentle, but such as be froward, as well, as much more, ought subjects to be obedient, *not only to their good and courteous, but also to their sharp and rigorous princes*," Part I. "A rebel is worse than the worst prince," ibid. "But what if the prince be indiscreet and evil indeed, and it is also evident to all men's eyes that he so is? I ask again, what if it belong to the wickedness of the subjects, that the prince is indiscreet and evil? shall the subjects both by their wickedness provoke God, for their deserving punishment, to give them an indiscreet and evil prince, and also rebel against him, and withal against God, *who for the punishment of their sins did give them such a prince*?" (ibid.) Now considering the high Tory doctrine, as it is called, contained in extracts such as these, I call upon you, Mr. Editor, as you would earn the meed[55] of consistency and impartiality, to designate the writers and abettors of them, and all "subscribers" to them, "Lauds and Sacheverells."

I think I have shown that *you* are not the person to take my conscience to task for not receiving every sentence of the Homilies as a formal enunciation of doctrine. I might, indeed, were it worth while, enlarge upon the venturesomeness of a writer, who seems according to my apprehension,

---

[2] The charge against the Magazine was not of disloyalty, but of holding the *doctrine* that subjects may, under circumstances, rebel against their civil governors, *e.g.* as in the instance of the Revolution of 1688 in England, in Greece in 1821, in Spain in 1823, in France in 1830.

to hold that baptism is not a *means* of grace, but only "a sign, seal and pledge," p. 167, and yet uses the Liturgy, being the man to make appeals to the conscience of others. But let this pass. Here, in the very instance you bring, you do not come into court with clean hands. You shrink from certain portions of the Homilies; and yet you use strong language about my supposed difference from other portions. Under these circumstances, were I merely writing for you I should leave you to marvel at my conscience, or to turn to your own; but I write to your readers; and in what I say in explanation of my own behavior towards the Homilies, I may perchance do something towards excusing yours.

I say plainly, then, I have not *subscribed* the Homilies, though you say I have, pp. 151, 153; though you *add* to my subscription to the Articles this further subscription also; nor was it ever intended that any member of the English Church should be subjected to what, if considered as an extended *confession*, would indeed be a yoke of bondage. Romanism surely is innocent, compared with that system which should impose upon the "conscience" a thick octavo volume, written flowingly and freely by fallible men, to be received exactly sentence by sentence. I cannot conceive any grosser instance of a Pharisaical tradition than this would be. No: the Reformers would have shrunk from the thought of so unchristian a proceeding – a proceeding which would render it impossible (I will say) for any one member, lay or clerical, of the Church to remain in it, who was subjected to such an ordeal. For instance: I do not suppose any reader would be satisfied with the political reasons for fasting, though indirectly introduced, yet fully admitted and dwelt upon in the Homily on that subject. He would not like to subscribe the declaration that eating fish was a duty, not only as being a kind of fasting, but as making provisions cheap, and encouraging the fisheries.[56] He would not like the association of religion with earthly politics.

How, then, are we bound to the Homilies? By the Thirty-fifth Article, which speaks as follows: "The Second Book of Homilies ... doth *contain* a godly and wholesome *doctrine*, and necessary for these times, as doth the former Book of Homilies."[57] Now observe, this Article does not speak of every statement made in them, but of the "doctrine." It speaks of the view or cast or body of doctrine contained in them. In spite of ten thousand prepositions, as in any large book, there is, it is obvious, a certain line of doctrine, which may be contemplated continuously in its shape and direction. For instance: if you say you disapprove the doctrine contained in the Tracts for the Times, no one supposes you to mean that every sentence is a lie. If this were so, then you are most inconsistent, after denouncing them, to imply, p. 167, that they "contain much that is godly and edifying, much that you are grateful for, and much that, if separated from its adjuncts, would be highly valuable in these days of liberalism and laxity." You even give logical reasons to show that there is no inconsistency, and protest against the notion. Now, sir, I am going to turn your "medium not distributed"[58] against yourself. I say then, that, in like manner, when the Article speaks of the *doctrine* of the Homilies, it does not measure the letter of them by the inch, it does not imply they contain no propositions which admit of two opinions; but it speaks of a certain determinate line of doctrine, and moreover adds, it is "*necessary* for *these times*." If a man said, The Tracts of the Times are *seasonable* at this moment, as their title signifies, would he not speak of them as taking a certain line and bearing a certain way? Would he not be speaking, not of phrases or sentences, but of a "doctrine" in them tending one way, viewed as a whole? Would he be inconsistent, if after praising them, as seasonable, he continued, "Yet I do not pledge myself to every view or sentiment; there are some things in them hard of digestion, or overstated, or doubtful, or subtle?"

Let us, then, have no more such superfluous appeals to our consciences in such a matter. Reserve them for graver cases, if you think you see such. If anything could add to the irrelevancy of the charge in question, it is the particular point in which I dissent from the Homilies, even if I do, which will not be so easy to prove; − a question concerning the fulfillment of prophecy: viz. whether Papal Rome is Antichrist! An iron yoke indeed you would forge for the conscience, when you oblige us to assent, not only to all matters of *doctrine* which the Homilies contain, but even to their opinion concerning the fulfillment of *prophecy*. Why, *we* do not ascribe authority in such matters even to the unanimous consent of all the Fathers. But *you* allow us no private judgment whatever; your private judgment is all particular and peculiar.

I will put what I have been saying in a second point of view. The Homilies are subsidiary to the Articles; therefore they are of authority as far as they *bring out* the sense of the Articles; and are not of authority when they do not. For instance, they say that David, though unbaptized, was regenerated, as you have quoted. This statement cannot be of authority, because it not only does not agree, but it even disagrees, with the Ninth Article, which translated the Latin word "renatis" by the English "baptized." But, observe, if this mode of viewing the Homilies be taken, as it fairly may, *you* suffer; for, the Apocrypha *being the subject of an Article,* the comment furnished in the Homily is binding on you, whereas you reject it.

A further remark will bring us to the same point. Another test of acquiescence in the doctrine of the Homilies is this: Take their table of contents; examine the headings; these surely, taken together, will give the substance of their teaching. Now I maintain that I hold fully and heartily the doctrine of the Homilies under every one of these headings: nor, (excepting the question of justification, on which I am myself thoroughly convinced I hold it, and which I intend to discuss; and of Repentance, in which the Homily says not a sentence which I do not hold); will you yourself be inclined to doubt it. The only point to which I should not accede, nor think myself called upon to accede, would be certain matters, subordinate to the doctrines to which the headings refer – matters not of doctrine, but of opinion, as that Rome is the Antichrist; or of historical fact, as that there was a Pope Joan, which, by the bye, I doubt whether you hold any more than I do.[59] But now, on the other hand, can *you* subscribe the doctrine of the Homilies under every one of its formal headings? I believe you *cannot.* The Homily against Disobedience and Wilful Rebellion is in many of its elementary principles decidedly opposed to your sentiments.[60] And yet *you* are the writer to tax another with not holding by the Homilies! Unless I had some experience that to be represented as "troublers of Israel"[61] and "pestilent fellows"[62] is the portion of those who fight against the Age, I should feel astonished at this.

I verily and in my conscience believe, that whether we take the text or the spirit of the Homilies, I do hold both the one and the other more exactly than those who question me. Do not, then in future appeal to me, as if I for an instant granted that the Homilies were on your side; – but I propose to say more on this subject when I come to speak on Justification.

2. It follows to speak of the Articles. You imply that I put no sense at all upon them, but take them to mean anything; and subscription to be no test or engagement of my opinions. Now is not this somewhat a strong charge to bring against a Clergyman? and particularly a member of a University which has, within the last two years shown extraordinary, and almost unanimous, earnestness in maintaining the necessity of subscription, even in the case of undergraduates, against the external pressure?[63] Why did not Dr. Pusey's friends

quietly sit by, and leave others to set them free? Surely the facts of the case are strong enough to excuse a little charity, had persons any to give. Persons really do astonish me, after all – prepared as I am for such exhibitions – by the ease and vigour with which they fling about accusations; showing themselves perfect masters of their weapon. In one place you say that we hold that there is "not one baptized person, not one regenerated person, not one communicant, among all the Protestant Churches, Lutheran or Reformed, except the Church of England, and its daughter churches," p. 122. Now, what would you say if we affirmed that you held that men could be saved by faith without works? You would think us very unscrupulous, and might use some strong words. Well, then, there is not a word, which you would apply to such a statement, that I might not with perfect sincerity and truth apply to yours. You have touched on a large subject, on which we have nowhere ventured any opinion whatever, and in which we do not hold what you have expressed – the subject of lay baptism – but on which an opinion is forthcoming when needed. Another remarkable exhibition of the same science is your asserting that one of the Tracts called the Dissenters "a mob of Tiptops, Gapes, and Yawns," pp. 172, 174, 177, 185, 186. Five times you say or imply it. Now it so happens that the Tract in question has nothing to do with Dissenters; but with persons who wish alterations in the Liturgy on insufficient grounds,[64] a circumstance which in itself excludes Dissenters. To those of your readers who do not know this Tract (it is one of the parts of Richard Nelson), the following explanation will be acceptable. The subject of the Tract is the shortening of the Church Service. Tiptop is a "travelling man from Hull or Preston," who "quarters at" a public house at Nelson's village, "sometimes for a fortnight at a time," and "dabbles in religion *as well* as in politics;" a man who is praised by his admirers as "talking beautifully, and expounding on *any* subject a person might choose to mention, politics, trade, agriculture, learning, religion, and what not." He "lectures about the Church Prayers" among other things; and I suppose that this word "lecture" which has caught your eye, and led you into error; if so, it is a sort of indication what attention you give to the matter of the Tracts. But to continue. Yawn is a farmer whose sons go to the Church school; and he himself "scarcely ever," as he boasts, "misses a Sunday," coming into the service "about the end of the First Lesson." Ned Gape too is a churchgoer, though a late one. In what sense of the words, then, Mr. Editor, do you assert that when Richard Nelson, in the end of the story, says, that he "cannot stand by and see the noble old Prayer-book pulled to pieces, just to humour a mob of Tiptops, Gapes and Yawns," that the writer calls Dissenters by those titles?

I shall give one more instance of this freedom, and then return to the consideration of the Articles. I said in the former part of my letter, that you called Dr. Pusey's belief that the old Fathers were not regenerated on earth, "the very bathos of theology." On this you observe, "Mr. ————— still finds it necessary to misapply our statement. The remark respecting 'the bathos of theology' referred to the doctrine quoted from some old writers, of the conveyance of Divine grace to an insensible person, by placing in his lips the bread and wine by which believers partake mystically of Christ's body – not however in a state of insensibility, but, 'by faith, with thanksgiving.'[65] This obsolete superstition we did and do consider the bathos of theology; but Mr. —————, not venturing to defend it, *turns aside our remark,* as if we had said that it is the bathos of theology that 'by the coming of our Saviour Christ,' quoting the Homily, 'we have received more abundantly the Spirit of God.' " p. 192. Now, without dwelling on the unreasonableness of saying, "Mr. ————— not *venturing to defend it,*" when the doctrine I did not defend was to be the subject of the *second* head of my letter, and I was not engaged in *proving* my belief on these points, but *demanding* proof that they were against the Articles; waving all this, let the reader reflect upon your Magazine's original words, which you now accuse me of misstating. "It is the very bathos of theology, an absurdity not worthy to be gravely replied to, that *men were* '*sanctified*,' 'greatly sanctified,' 'were the friends of God,' &c. &c. &c. yet ... were still 'unregenerate.' " (p. 790.) Thus you *do* call the non-regeneration of the Patriarchs "the bathos of theology;" and when I *say* so in my letter, "No" you retort, "it is a misstatement; I said the doctrine of insensible persons benefiting from the Sacrament is the bathos." It is kindest to account for this strange mistake of yours by attributing it to what you yourself are partly conscious of, your "rough and rambling" ways.

And with a like heedlessness you imply that I hold the Articles as a *nasus cereus*,[66] to use the controversial term. And you wish me to caution "indiscreet 'approvers' " of the Tracts against saying that "the Articles are the *weak point* in our Church; we may indeed sign them, for 'is there any tasted in the white of an egg?' " All this being as pertinent, when addressed to me, as if I were to accuse you of teaching salvation by faith without works.[67] However, such unfounded charges are, I repeat, our omen of ultimate success; I cheerfully bear them; and now proceed to disabuse at least some of your readers, and perhaps to silence yourself.

You seem to me to confuse between two things very distinct; the holding a certain sense of a statement to be *true*, and imposing that sense upon others. Sometimes the two go together; at other times they do not. For instance, the meaning of the Creed (and again, of the Liturgy) is *known;* there is no opportunity for doubt here; it means but one thing, and he who does not hold that meaning, does not hold it at all. But the case is different (to take an illustration), in the drawing up of a Political Declaration, or a Petition to Parliament. It is composed by persons, differing in matters of detail, agreeing together to a certain point and for a certain end. Each narrowly watches that nothing is inserted to prejudice his own particular opinion, or stipulates for the insertion of what may rescue it. Hence general words are used, or particular words inserted, which by superficial inquirers afterwards are criticized as vague and indeterminate on the one hand, or inconsistent on the other; but, in fact, they all have a meaning and a history, could we ascertain it.[3] And, if the parties concerned in such a document are legislating and determining for posterity, they are respective representatives of corresponding parties in the generations after them. Now the Thirty-nine Articles lie between these two, between a Creed and a mere joint Declaration; to a certain point they have one meaning, beyond that they have no one meaning. They have one meaning, so far as they embody the doctrine of the Creed; they have different meaning, so far as they are drawn up by men influenced by the discordant opinions of the day. This is what I have expressed in the former part of my letter: "the Articles," I say, "are confessedly wide in their meaning, but still their width is within bounds: they seem to include a number of shades of opinion."[68]

Next, as to those points (whatever they are) in which they cannot be said to have one meaning. Each subscriber indeed attaches that meaning which he at once holds and thinks the meaning; but this is his "particular" meaning and he has no right to impose it on another. In saying, then, I shall put no "particular meaning" on portions of the Articles, I spoke, not of *my own belief*, but of my enforcing that belief upon others. I do sincerely and heartily consider my sense of the Articles, on certain points to be presently mentioned, to be the true sense: but I do not feel sure that there were not present, at the drawing up of the Articles, persons or feelings which led

---

[3] Hence *faith, justification, infection*, &c. are used, not defined in the Articles.

the framers (not as doing so on a principle, but spontaneously, from the existing hindrances to perfect unanimity)
to abstain from perfect precision and uniformity of statement.
What can be more truly liberal and forbearing than this view?
yet for thus holding that Calvinists and others, whom I think
mistaken, may sign the Articles as well as myself, I am said
myself to sign them with "no meaning whatever." And you
actually take my own sentiment out of my mouth, clothe it
in the words of the Royal Declaration, and then gravely
make a present of it to me back again, as if it were something
wise and high of your own. "The Royal Declaration," you
say, "prefixed to the Articles, congratulates the Church that
all the clergy had 'most willingly subscribed' to them, 'all
sorts taking them to be for them:'[69] which shows that each
conscientious individual had carefully examined into their
meaning, and not that he signed them without attaching any
'particular meaning at all.' " p. 191. Of course, these are just
my sentiments.

Accordingly I go on to say, that I look forward to success,
not by *compelling* others to take one view of the Articles, but
by *convincing* them that mine is the right one. And this will
explain what you call my "pugnacious terms." Were I
fighting against individuals or a party in the Church, *this*
would be party spirit: but then I should wish to coerce them
or cast them out; whereas I am opposing principles and
doctrines – so, I would fain persuade and convert, not
triumph over those who hold them. I am not pugnacious; I
am only "militant."

It will explain, too, what you consider my overweening
and provoking language. For I consider I am but speaking
what the Catholic Fathers witness to be Christ's Gospel. I am
exercising no private judgment on Scripture; and while I will
not enforce it coercively, having no authority to do so I will
never put it forward hesitatingly, as if I did not think all other
doctrines plainly wrong.

So much about myself. On the other hand, my charge against you is, and I repeat it, that you do wish to *add* to the Articles; that is, in the same sense in which you accused Bishop Marsh of wishing to do so. You wish to impose upon me your particular notion that the Patriarchs were regenerated; which is an invasion of private judgment, as permitted in our Church, as gross as if I strove to enforce on you my particular notion, in accordance with the Homily, that the Holy Ghost spoke "by the mouth of Tobit." Till you name the particular points of opinion for which you call on Dr. Pusey to resign his Professorship, and state the Article or determination of the Church which he transgresses, I will never cease to say that you do unwittingly – not of course with bad intention – that you do wish and aim to add to the Articles of subscription.

To sum up what I have said, and be at the same time more specific. I consider that the first five Articles have one definite, positive, dogmatic view, even that which has been from the beginning, the Catholic and Apostolic Truth on which the Church is built.[70]

From the Sixth to the Eighteenth, I conceive to have one certain view also, brought out in that particular form at the Reformation; but, as in the Seventeenth, not clearly demonstrated to be such to the satisfaction of the world.

In the remaining Articles, taken *as a body,* I think there is less strictness, perspicuity, and completeness of meaning. Some, though clear and definite in their meaning, are but negative, or protestant, as being directed against the Romanists; others, which are positive, are derived from various schools; in others the view is left open, or inchoate.

The first division I humbly receive as Divine, provable from Scripture, but descending to us by Catholic tradition also. The next I admit and hold as deducible from Scripture by private judgment, tradition only witnessing here and there. The last division I receive only in the plain letter, according to the injunction of the Declaration, because I do believe in my conscience that they were not written upon any one view, and cannot be taken *except* in the letter; because I think they *never* had any one simple meaning; because I think I see in them the terms of various schools mixed together – terms known by their historical associations to be theologically discordant, though in the mere letter easy and intelligible.

And now, lastly, I will mention *why* I take these last Articles in that one particular meaning in which I do take them, and not in another. This again is from no mere private liking or opinion; it is because I verily think the Church wishes me so to take them. We at this day receive the Articles, not on the authority of their framers, whoever they were, English or foreign, but on the authority, *i.e.* in the sense, of the Convocation imposing them, that is, the Convocation of 1571.[71] That Convocation, which imposed them, also passed the following Canon about Preachers: – "In the first place, let them be careful never to teach anything in their sermons, as if to be religiously held and believed by the people, but what is agreeable to the doctrine of the Old and New Testament, *and collected from that very doctrine by the catholic Fathers and ancient Bishops.*" This is but one out of the hundred appeals to Antiquity, which, in one way or other, our Church has put forth; but it is rendered unique by its originating in the Convocation from which we receive the Articles. It is quite possible that that Convocation wished us to receive and explain the doctrines contained in them in any other sense than that which "the catholic Fathers and ancient Bishops" drew from Scripture. Far from explaining away, I am faithfully maintaining them, when I catholicize them. It were well for themselves, had others as good a reason for Calvinizing or Zuinglizing them.

And all this shows how right I am in saying that the Articles must not be viewed as in themselves *a perfect system* of doctrine, p. 189. They are, on the face of them, but protests against existing errors, Socinianism and Romanism. For instance, how else do you account for the absence of any statement concerning the *Inspiration* of Scripture? On the other hand, the Canon of 1571, just cited, is a proof that the whole range of catholic doctrines is professed by our Church; not only so much as is contained in the Articles. Its reception of the primitive Creeds is another proof; for they reach to many points not contained in the Articles without them. To these documentary evidences may be added the 30th Canon of 1603. Speaking of the use of the Sign of the Cross, it says, "The abuse of a thing doth not take away the lawful use of it.[72] Nay, *so far was it from the purpose* of the Church of England to *forsake and reject* the churches of Italy, France, Spain, Germany, or any such like churches, in *all* things which they held and practiced, that, as the Apology of the Church of England[73] confesseth, it doth with reverence retain those ceremonies which do neither endamage the church of God nor offend the minds of sober men; and *only* departed from them in those *particular* points wherein they were fallen, both from themselves *in their ancient integrity,* and from the Apostolical churches, which were their *first founders.*"

It is clear, then, that the English Church holds all that the primitive church held, even in ceremonies, *except* there be some particular reason assignable for not doing so in this or that instance; and only does not hold the modern corruptions maintained by Romanism. In these corruptions it departs from Rome; *therefore* these are the points in which it thinks it especially necessary to declare its opinion. To these were added the most sacred points of faith, in order to protest against those miserable heresies to which Protestantism had already given birth. Thus the Church stands in a *via media*; the first five Articles being directed against extreme Protestantism, the remaining ones against Rome. And hence, when the Royal Declaration says that they "contain the true doctrine of the Church of England, agreeable to God's word," which you quote, p. 169, as if it made against me, it speaks of the doctrine of the English Church *so far* as distinguished from other churches: it does not say the doctrine of the Gospel, the doctrine of the church catholic, or the whole faith; but it speaks of it in contrast with existing systems. This is evident from its wording; for the clause "agreeable to God's word" evidently glances at Rome; and the history of its promulgation throws abundant light on the fact that it was aimed against Calvinism and Arminianism. There is nothing, then, in these words to show that the Articles are a system of doctrine, or more than the English doctrine in those points in which it differs from Romanism and Socinianism and embraces Arminianism and Calvinism.

No: our Apostolical communion inherits, as the promises, so the faith, enjoyed by the Saints in every age; the faith which Ignatius, Cyprian, and Gregory[74] received from the Apostles. We did not begin on a new foundation in King Edward's[75] time; we only reformed, or repaired, the superstructure. You must not defraud us, Mr. Editor, of our birthright, by turning what is a salutary protest into a system of divinity.

Before proceeding to the subject of Justification, I will conclude what I have otherwise to say on your sixty pages, by adducing some further instances of what I consider misconceptions in them.

(1) You say (p. 120) that Mr. ———— in his Parochial Sermons "most unscripturally" expresses himself to this effect – even "the most hardened sinner" may "recollect those times of his youth when he was free [pure] from sin." You say this doctrine involves a "confidence of boasting," and is "fearful." Now he uses the word "sin" in the same sense in which our Church prays that Christ may "vouchsafe to keep

us this day without *sin*;" and "that this day we fall into no *sin*." It seems, then, all we of the English Church pray every day in a state which involves "a confidence of boasting." Your misconception has arisen from not observing there are different kinds of sin. You may call me indeed, and the Church in consequence, "scholastic" in this distinction; I call you "technical," and my epithet is as availing as yours.

(2) You speak, p. 146, of Mr. Hook's[76] University Sermons as embodying some of the leading principles of the Oxford Tracts. But you do not, I suppose, mean thereby to imply that he has taken his opinions from the Tracts. No, Mr. Hook is an independent witness, who has boldly put forth the Catholic doctrines in less promising times than these, and before some of the writers of the Tracts had any formed views upon the subjects he treats of. His sermons were listened to with extraordinary interest, and have made a deep impression on the minds of his hearers. In this instance, indeed, two distinct lines of usefulness are united, which have been granted together to no other clergyman of the day; viz. the successful preaching of Catholic truth both to a manufacturing population, and to the young. I say this, lest you should seem to be paying the Tracts an honour which they cannot claim, that of having influenced Mr. Hook's opinions.

(3) You say of the Fathers, p. 147, "they were discrepant in their opinions, so that, beyond their general testimony to a few striking particulars, above all, the Divinity of our Lord, they cannot be referred to with any certainty or confidence, for the opinion of one might not be that of another, much less of the Catholic Church." Now, Mr. Editor, observe what I am going to say, and never again accuse me of wishing to enslave the Protestant mind to the Fathers. I as well as you, hold the Fathers not to demand our assent, except on those points in which they agree together, in the same sense in which they agree in witnessing "the Divinity of our Lord."

You will find nothing in the Tracts for the Times stronger than this doctrine, which is appears is your own also. You and I, then, agree in *principle* in the matter; we differ in the *matter of fact,* what doctrines are unanimously attested, and what not.

This mistake is the more remarkable, because the exposition of our view on the subject occurs in the very Tract which you analyze and discuss at length, No. 71. It is there said, "It is quite impossible that *all countries* should have agreed in that which was not Apostolic. They are a number of concordant witnesses to certain definite truths; and while their testimony is one and the same from the very first moment they publicly utter it, so, on the other hand, if there be bodies which speak otherwise, we can show historically that they rose later than the Apostles. This majestic evidence, however, *does not extend to any but to the articles of the Creed, especially those relating to the Trinity and the Incarnation,*"[4] p.28. For the future, then, do not accuse us of what we do not hold, that one Father is of authority in a point in which others are against him. This instance will be sufficient to show your readers, that at least you cannot guide them into our views concerning tradition. They had better have recourse to Mr. Hook and Mr. Keble, if not to be converted, art least to ascertain how things stand.

(4) Here let me observe, you attribute most gratuitously, and (I must even say) officiously, this same Tract, No. 71, to Dr. Pusey;[77] and, as assuming it to be his, you accuse him of saying that it is "safest not," p. 149, to pray to the saints; and that "what the Fathers held" would be an "irrefragable argument" against transubstantiation. Again you say, "Professor Pusey considers the Eleventh Article as having been the cause of infinite mischief, by leading to 'the wildest

---

[4] A misconception in unexpected quarters makes it just necessary to observe, that in the language of the Primitive Church here used, "the Incarnation" was taken to include under it the doctrine of the Atonement.

Antinonmian doctrine;'[78] yet that, upon the whole –
bountiful concession for an Oxford Professor to the glorious
Eleventh Article of the Anglican Church – it was 'innocently
intended!!' " p. 135; see also p. 189. I do really think this is a
very great liberty to take with Dr. Pusey's name. It is the
second instance of the kind into which you have been
betrayed. This is very heedless. This Tract is not Dr. Pusey's
writing. Dr. Pusey has written nothing to which he has not
put either his name or his initials.[79] One should have
thought even the internal evidence of style would have saved
you from such an awkwardness. The writer of it is as
unwilling to surrender his claim to it, as to let others bear the
imputation; nor is he in danger of losing, or Dr. Pusey of
being laden with, a property which all careful readers will see
to want the exuberance of thought and language which is Dr.
Pusey's characteristic.

As to the principal charge brought against this Tract, that
it attacks the Eleventh Article, it will be best answered by
quoting the passage referred to. It is as follows. "For
specimens of the *perverse reception by the nation,* as above
alluded to, of what was innocently intended, I would refer to
the *popular sense* put upon the Eleventh Article, which, *though
clearly and soundly explained in the Homily on Justification or
Salvation,* has been *taken* to countenance the wildest
Antinomian doctrine; and is now so associated *in the minds of
many,* with this *wrong* interpretation, as to render almost
hopeless the recovery of the *true meaning.*"

(5) You quote Dr. Comber[80] against us as an "*argumentum
ad hominem.*"[81] But a single divine is no authority with us; it
is as one of a *catena,*[82] it is as coinciding with the consensus
Patrum,[83] in matters of doctrine, that he is valuable. There
are things in Jeremy Taylor, Hooker, Ussher, Laud, and
Field, which one may well scruple to admit.

(6) You say, "As Dr. Pusey considers this anointing" in
baptism "as Apostolical (and if so, it is a Divinely appointed,

and therefore an essential portion of baptism), we do not see how he can use the Church of England office, which omits it; thus violating a sacred precept of transmissive religion," &c. &c. – By "ordinance of the Lord" Dr. Pusey meant baptism. But, again, he holds with the Thirty-fourth Article: that "traditions and ceremonies may be changed according to the diversity of countries, times, and men's manners, so that nothing be ordained against God's word." He only questions the *advisableness* of the alteration in the particular instance, not the legality of the act.

(7) You say that "Mr Palmer[84] must surely have learned" certain "languages" in his learned work on the Prayer-book, "at Trent," p. 163. Mr. Palmer does not need defence from me. I notice him merely as additional instance how certain a writer of our Church is to be called Popish by you, if he has any learning. Depend upon it, Mr. Editor, your only chance of maintaining your ultraism, is by keeping men in ignorance of theology. If even your staunchest advocate were to study theology, he would become either a professed Rationalist, or what *you* would call a Papist.

(8) You say, speaking of Sacraments, "the Church of England, you believe, has gone *as far* as Scripture, and not beyond it, in the threefold expression of a sign, a seal, and a pledge," p.167. *vid. also* pp. 169, 180. Now it has gone further; it considers them "*means* of grace." Since, then our Church would, according to you, have gone *as far* as Scripture in making them "signs, seals, and pledges," it follows that, in making them *means,* it has gone beyond Scripture. This again is heedless.

(9) You find fault with Ussher's argument against Purgatory (viz. that it is distinct from the objects contemplated in the primitive prayers for the dead in Christ), as "injudicious." It is as I said, Mr. Editor, you cannot endure a learned man. Ussher even, in spite of his alleged Calvinism,[85] is not enough of a Protestant for you.

However, I shall now close for the present. One subject and a most important one, remains; that of Justification. Before I commence it, I invite you to do, what you cannot decline. You have accused me frequently of "evasions," though not intentional ones, of course. I on the other hand accuse you, instead of coming to the point, of vague and illogical declamation, though not intentional either. Now, then, state definitely *what* Dr. Pusey's opinions are, for which he ought to give up his Professorship; and state also *why,* that is, *what statements* of our Church his own opposed. *Till you do this,* I shall persist in saying you wish to add to the Articles of subscription. I challenge you to do this, and call your readers to attend to your answer; and then, in my next I will do my best to meet it.

———————

This letter was not continued further, partly on account of the mode in which the above was printed in the pages of our Magazine, and partly because the challenge, repeated in its closing words, had not been met.

TRACT 83

This comprises four sermons (MS 394–397) originally preached from 29 November to 20 December 1835. They were re-published in 1838 in *Discussions and Arguments* with minor corrections.

TRACT 85

TWELVE lectures were given in Adam de Brome's chapel in St. Mary's between 8 May and 7 August 1835 on the scriptural basis for the System of Christian Doctrine which relies too much on Tradition and against the Latitudinarian stance which denies there is a sound basis for Christian doctrine. Eight were included in the Tracts.

The text is reproduced in *Discussions & Arguments* with Newman's slight corrections but with the exception of the following passage in Lecture 7, between the end of section 5 and the beginning of section 6 (DA, pp. 230ff.):

"I conceive that under the same circumstances men will begin to be offended at the passage in the Revelation, which speaks of the "*number* of the beast." Indeed, it is probable that they will reject the Book of Revelation altogether, not sympathizing in the severe tone of doctrine which runs through it. Again: there is something very surprising in the importance attached to the Name of GOD and CHRIST in Scripture. The Name of Jesus is said to work cures and frighten away devils. I anticipate that this doctrine will become a stone of stumbling to those who set themselves to inquire into the trustworthiness of the separate parts of Scripture. For instance, the narrative of St. Peter's cure of the impotent man, in the early chapters of the Acts: – first, "Silver and gold," he says, "have I none; but such as I have, give I thee, In the *Name* of JESUS CHRIST of Nazareth, rise up and walk." Then, "And His *Name*, through faith in his *Name*, hath made this man strong." Then the question, "By what power, or by what *name*, have ye done this?" then the answer, "By the *Name* of JESUS CHRIST of Nazareth ... even *by It* does this man now stand before you whole ... there is none other *Name* under heaven given among men whereby we must be saved." Then the threat, that the apostles should not "speak at all, nor teach in the *Name* of JESUS." Lastly, their prayer that GOD would grant "that signs and wonders might be done by the *Name* of His Holy Child JESUS." In connexion with which must be considered St. Paul's declaration, "that at the *Name* of JESUS every knee should bow." Again: I conceive that the circumstances of the visitation of the Blessed Virgin to Elizabeth would startle us considerably if we lost our faith in Scripture. Again: can we doubt but that the account of CHRIST's *ascending* into heaven will not be received by the science of this age, when it is carefully considered what is implied in it? Where is heaven? Beyond all the stars? If so, it would take years for any natural body to get there. We say, that with GOD all things are possible. But this age, wise in its own eyes, has already decided the contrary, in maintaining, as it does, that He who virtually annihilated the distance between earth and heaven on His SON's ascension, cannot annihilate it in the celebration of Holy Communion, so as to make us present with Him, though He be on GOD's right hand in heaven.[1]

---

[1] Rev. 13:18; Acts 3:6, 16; 4:7, 10, 12, 17, 30; Phil. 2:10.

TRACT 90

REMARKS ON CERTAIN PASSAGES IN THE THIRTY-NINE ARTICLES[1]

INTRODUCTION

IT is often urged, and sometimes felt and granted, that there are in the Articles propositions or terms inconsistent with the Catholic faith; or, at least, when persons do not go so far as to feel the objection as of force, they are perplexed how best to reply to it, or how most simply to explain the passages on which it is made to rest. The following Tract is drawn up with the view of showing how groundless the objection is, and further of approximating towards an argumentative answer to it, of which most men have an implicit apprehension, though they may have nothing more. That there are real difficulties to a Catholic Christian in the Ecclesiastical position of our Church at this day, no one can deny; but the statements of the Articles are not in the number; and it may be right at the present moment to insist upon this. If in any quarter it is supposed that persons who profess to be disciples of the early Church will silently concur with those of very opposite sentiments in furthering a relaxation of subscriptions,[2] which, it is imagined, are galling to both parties, though for different reasons, and that they will do this against the wish of the great body of the Church, the writer of the following pages would raise one voice, at least, in protest against any such anticipation. Even in such points as he may think the English Church deficient, never can he, without a great alteration of sentiment, be party to forcing the opinion or project of one school upon another. Religious changes, to be beneficial, should be the act of the whole body; they are worth Little if they are the mere act of a majority. No good can come of any change which is not heartfelt,[1] a development of feelings springing up freely and calmly within the bosom of the whole body itself. Moreover, a change in theological teaching involves either the commission or the confession of sin; it is either the profession or renunciation of erroneous doctrine, and if it does not succeed in proving the fact of past guilt, it, *ipso facto*, implies present. In other words, every change in religion carries with it its own condemnation, which is not attended by deep repentance. Even supposing then that any changes in contemplation, whatever they were, were good in themselves, they would cease to be good to a Church, in which they were the fruits not of the quiet conviction of all, but of the agitation, or tyranny, or intrigue of a few; nurtured not in mutual love, but in strife and envying; perfected not in humiliation and grief, but in pride, elation and triumph. Moreover it is a very serious truth, that persons and bodies who put themselves into a disadvantageous state, cannot at their pleasure extricate themselves from it. They are unworthy of it; they are in prison, and CHRIST is the keeper. There is but one way towards a real reformation,[3] – a return to Him in heart and spirit, whose sacred truth they have betrayed; all other methods, however fair they may promise, will prove to be but shadows and failures.

On these grounds, were there no others, the present writer for one, will be no party to the ordinary political

---

[1] This is not meant to hinder acts of Catholic consent, such as occurred anciently, when the Catholic body aids one portion of a particular Church against another portion.

methods by which professed reforms are carried or compassed in this day. We can do nothing well till we act "with one accord;" we can have no accord in action till we agree together in heart; we cannot agree without a supernatural influence; we cannot have a supernatural influence unless we pray for it; we cannot pray acceptably without repentance and confession. Our Church's strength would be irresistible, humanly speaking, were it but at unity with itself: if it remains divided, part against part, we shall see the energy which was meant to subdue the world preying upon itself, according to our SAVIOUR's express assurance, that such a house "cannot stand."[4] Till we feel this, till we seek one another as brethren, not lightly throwing aside our private opinions which we seem to feel we have received from above, from an ill-regulated, untrue desire of unity, but returning to each other in heart, and coming together to GOD to do what we cannot do for ourselves, no change can be for the better. Till [we her children] are stirred up to this religious course, let the Church[5] [our Mother] sit still; let [us] be content to be in bondage: let [us] work in chains; let [us] submit to [our] imperfections as a punishment; let [us] go on teaching [through the medium of indeterminate statements][6] and inconsistent precedents, and principles but partially developed. We are not better than our fathers, let us bear to be what Hammond was, or Andrews, or Hooker; let us not faint under the body of death, which they bore about in patience: nor shrink from the penalty of sins, which they inherited from the age before them.[2]

But these remarks are beyond our present scope, which is merely to show that, while our Prayer Book is acknowledged on all hands to be of Catholic origin, our Articles also, the

---

[2] "We, thy sinful creatures," says the Service for King Charles the Martyr, "here assembled before Thee, do, in behalf of all the people of this land, humbly confess, that they were the *crying sins* of this nation, which brought down this judgment upon us," i.e. King Charles's murder.

offspring of an uncatholic age, are, through GOD's good providence, to say the least, not uncatholic, and may be subscribed by those who aim at being catholic in heart and doctrine. In entering upon the proposed examination, it is only necessary to add, that in several places the writer has found it convenient to express himself in language recently used, which he is willing altogether to make his own.[3] He has distinguished the passages introduced by quotation marks.

§1. *Holy Scripture and the Authority of the Church.*

Articles 6 and 20 – "Holy Scripture containeth all things necessary to salvation; so that whatsoever is not read therein, nor may be proved thereby, is not required of any man, that it should be believed as an article of the Faith, or be thought requisite or necessary to salvation … The Church hath [power to decree (*statuendi*) rites and ceremonies, and][4] authority in controversies of faith; and yet it is not lawful for the Church to [ordain (*instituere*) anything that is contrary to God's word written, neither may it] so expound one place of Scripture, that it be repugnant to another. Wherefore, although the Church be a witness and a keeper of Holy Writ, yet [as it ought not to decree (*decernere*) anything against the same, so] besides the same, ought it not to enforce (*obtrudere*) anything to be believed for necessity of salvation."

Two instruments of Christian teaching are spoken of in these Articles, Holy Scripture and the Church.

Here then we have to inquire, first, what is meant by Holy Scripture; next, what is meant by the Church; and then, what their respective offices are in teaching revealed truth,

---

[3] The passages quoted are the author's own writing on other occasions.

[4] The passages in brackets relate to rites and ceremonies, which are not here in question.

and how these are adjusted with one another in their actual exercise.

1. Now, what the Church is, will be considered below in Section 4.

2. And the Books of Holy Scripture are enumerated in the latter part of the Article, so as to preclude question. Still two points deserve notice here.

    First, the Scriptures or Canonical Books are said to be those "of whose authority was never any doubt in the Church." Here it is not meant that there never was any doubt in *portions* of the Church or *particular* Churches concerning certain books, which the Article includes in the Canon; for some of them, – as, for instance, the Epistle to the Hebrews, and the Apocalypse – have been the subject of much doubt in the West or East, as the case may be. But the Article asserts that there has been no doubt about them in the Church Catholic; that is, at the very first time that the Catholic or whole Church had the opportunity of forming a judgment on the subject, it pronounced in favour of the Canonical Books. The Epistle to the Hebrews was doubted by the West, and the Apocalypse by the East, only while those portions of the Church investigated separately from each other, only till they compared notes, interchanged sentiments and formed a united judgment. The phrase must mean this, because, from the nature of the case, it can mean nothing else.

    And next, be it observed, that the books which are commonly called Apocrypha,[7] are not asserted in this Article to be destitute of inspiration, or to be simply human, but to be not canonical; in other words, to differ from Canonical Scripture, specially in this respect, *viz.* that they are not adducible in proof of doctrine. "The other books (as Hierome[8] saith) the Church doth read for example of life and instruction of manners, but yet doth not apply them to *establish any doctrine.*" That this is the limit to which our disparagement of them extends, is plain, not only because the Article mentions nothing beyond it, but also from the reverential manner in which the Homilies speak of them, as shall be incidentally shown in Section 11. [The compatibility of such reverence with such disparagement is also shown from the feeling towards them of St. Jerome, who is quoted in the Article, who implies more or less their inferiority to Canonical Scripture, yet uses them freely and continually, as if Scripture. He distinctly names many of the books which he considers not canonical, and virtually names them all by naming what *are* canonical. For instance, he says, speaking of Wisdom and Ecclesiasticus, "As the Church reads Judith, Tobit, and the Maccabees without receiving them among the Canonical Scriptures, so she reads these two books for the edification of the people, not for the confirmation of the authority of ecclesiastical doctrines." (*Praef. In Libr. Salom*[9].) Again, "The Wisdom, as it is commonly styled, of Solomon, and the book of Jesus, son of Sirach, and Judith, and Tobias, and the Shepherd, are not in the Canon." (*Praef ad Reges*) Such is the language of a writer who nevertheless is, to say the least, not wanting in reverence to towards the books he thus disparages.

A further question may be asked, concerning our received version of the Scripture, whether it is in any sense imposed on us as a true comment on the original text; as the Vulgate[10] is upon the Roman Catholics. It would appear not. It was made and authorized by royal command, which cannot be supposed to have any claim upon our interior assent. At the same time everyone who reads it in the Services of our Church, does, of course thereby imply that he considers that it contains no deadly heresy or dangerous mistake. And about it simplicity, majesty, gravity, harmony, and venerableness, there can be but one opinion.

3. Next we come to the main point, the adjustment which this Article effects between the respective offices of the Scripture and the Church: which seems to be as follows.

It is laid down that, 1. Scripture contains all necessary articles of the faith; 2. either in its text, or by inference; 3. The Church is the keeper of Scripture; 4. and a witness of it; 5. and has authority in controversies of faith; 6. but may not expound one passage of Scripture to contradict another; 7. nor enforce as an article of faith any point not contained in Scripture.

From this it appears, first, that the Church *expounds and enforces the faith;* for it is forbidden to expound in a particular way, or so to enforce as to obtrude; next, that it derives the faith *wholly from Scripture;* thirdly, that its office is to educe an *harmonious interpretation* of Scripture. Thus much the Article settles.

Two important questions, however, it does not settle, viz. whether the Church judges, first, at her *sole discretion*, next, on her *sole responsibility;* i.e. first, what the *media*[11] are by which the Church interprets Scripture, whether by a direct divine gift, or catholic tradition, or critical exegesis of the text, or in any other way; and next, who is to decide whether it interprets Scripture rightly or not; – what is her method, if any; and who is her judge, if any. In other words, not a word is said, on the one hand, in *favour* of Scripture having no rule or method to fix interpretation by, or, as it is commonly expressed, *being the sole rule of faith;* nor on the other, of the *private judgment of the individual* being the ultimate standard of interpretation. So much has been said lately on both these points, and indeed on the whole subject of these two Articles, that it is necessary to enlarge upon them; but since it is often supposed to be almost a first principle of our Church, that Scripture is "the rule of faith," it may be well before passing on, to make an extract from a paper,[12] published some years since, which shows, by instances from our divines, that the application of the phrase to Scripture is but of recent adoption. The other question about the ultimate judge of the interpretation of Scripture, shall not be entered upon.

"We may dispense with the phrase 'Rule of Faith,' as applied to Scripture, on the ground of its being ambiguous; and, again, because it is then used in a novel sense; for the ancient Church made the Apostolic Tradition, as summed up in the Creed, and not the Bible, the *Regula Fidei*, or Rule. Moreover, its use as a technical phrase, seems to be of late introduction in the Church, that is, since the days of King William the Third.[13] Our great divines use it without any fixed sense sometimes for Scripture, sometimes for the whole and perfectly-adjusted Christian doctrine, sometimes for the Creed; and, at the risk of being tedious, we will prove this, by quotations, that the point may be put beyond dispute.

"Ussher, after St. Austin, identifies it with the Creed; – when speaking of the Article of our LORD's Descent to Hell,[14] he says,

"'It having here likewise been further manifested, what different opinions have been entertained by the ancient Doctors of the Church, concerning the determinate place wherein our Saviour's soul did remain during the time of the separation of it from the body, I leave it to be considered by the learned, whether any such controverted matter may fitly be brought in to *expound the Rule of Faith*, which, being common both to the great and small ones of the Church, must contain such varieties only as are generally agreed upon by the common consent of all true Christians.' *Answer to a Jesuit*, p. 362.[15]

"Taylor speaks to the same purpose: 'Let us see with what constancy that and the following ages of the Church did adhere to the Apostles' Creed, as the sufficient and perfect

Rule of Faith.' Dissuasive, part 2, 1.4, p. 270.[16] Elsewhere he calls Scripture the Rule: 'That the Scripture is a full and sufficient *Rule* to Christians in faith and manners, a full and perfect declaration of the Will of GOD, is therefore certain, because we have no other.' (*Ibid.,* part 2, 1.2, p. 384) Elsewhere, Scripture and the Creed: 'He hath, by His wise Providence, preserved the plain places of Scripture and the Apostles' Creed, in all Churches, to be the *Rule* and Measure of Faith, by which all Churches are saved.' *Ibid.* part 2. 1.1.1, p. 346. Elsewhere he identifies it with Scripture, the Creeds, and the first four Councils:[17] 'We also [after Scripture] do believe the Apostles' Creed, the Nicene, with the additions of Constantinople, and that which is commonly called the symbol of St. Athanasius; and the four first General Councils are so entirely admitted by us, that they, together with the plain words of Scripture, are made the *Rule* and Measure of judging heresies among us.' – *Ibid.* part 1,1, p. 131.

"Laud calls the Creed, or rather the Creed with Scripture, the Rule : 'Since the Fathers make the Creed the *Rule of Faith*; since the agreeing sense of Scripture with those Articles are the *Two Regular Precepts*, by which a divine is governed about his faith,' &c. – *Conference with Fisher,* p. 42.[18]

"Bramhall[19] also: 'The Scripture and the Creed and not two different Rules of Faith, but *one and the same Rule, dilated in Scripture, contracted in the Creed*.' – *Works,* p. 402. Stillingfleet[20] says the same (*Grounds,* 1.4,3.); as does Thorndike[21] (*De Rat. Fin. Controv.,*p. 144, &c). Elsewhere, Stillingfleet calls Scripture the Rule (Ibid., p. 1.6.2); as does Jackson[22] (vol. 2, p. 226). But the most complete and decisive statement on the subject is contained in Field's work on the Church,[23] from which shall follow a long extract.

"'It remained to show,' he says, 'what is the rule of that judgment whereby the Church discerneth between truth and falsehood, the faith and heresy, and to whom it properly pertaineth to interpret those things which, touching this Rule, are doubtful. The Rule of our Faith in general, whereby we know it to be true, is the infinite excellency of GOD ... It being presupposed in the generality that the doctrine of the Christian faith is of GOD, and containeth nothing but heavenly truth, in the next place, we are to inquire by what Rule we are to judge of particular things contained within the compass of it.

" 'This *Rule*, is, 1. The summary comprehension of such principal articles of this divine knowledge, as are the principles whence all other things are concluded and inferred. These are contained in the *Creed of the Apostles*.

" '2. All such things as every Christian is bound expressly to believe, by the light and direction whereof he judgeth of other things, which are not absolutely necessary so particularly to be known. These are rightly said to be the Rule of our Faith, because the principles of every science are the Rule whereby we judge of the truth of all things, as being better and more generally known than any other thing, and the cause of knowing them.

" '3. The analogy, due proportion, and correspondence, that one thing in this divine knowledge hath with another, so that men cannot err in one of them without erring in another; nor rightly understand one, but they must likewise conceive the rest.

" '4. Whatsoever *Books* were delivered unto us, as written by them, to whom the first and immediate revelation of the divine truth was made.

" '5. Whatsoever hath been delivered by all the saints with one consent, which have left their judgment and opinion in writing.

" '6. Whatsoever the most famous have constantly and uniformly delivered as a matter of faith, no one contradicting, though many other ecclesiastical writers be silent, and say nothing of it.

" '7. That which the most, and most famous in every age, constantly delivered as a matter of faith, and as received of them that went before them, in such sort that the contradictors and gain-sayers were in their beginnings noted for singularity, novelty, and division, and afterwards, in process of time, if they persisted in such contradiction, charged with heresy.

" 'These three latter Rules of our Faith we admit, not because they are equal with the former, and originally in themselves contain the direction of our Faith, but because nothing can be delivered, with such and so full consent of the people of GOD, as in them is expressed; but it must need be from those first authors and founders of our Christian profession. The Romanists add unto these the decrees of Councils and determination of Popes, making these also to be the Rules of Faith; but because we have no proof of *their* infallibility, we number them not with the rest.

" 'Thus we see how many things, in several degrees and sorts, are said to be Rules of our Faith. The infinite excellence of GOD, as that whereby the truth of the heavenly doctrine is proved. The Articles of Faith, and other verities ever expressly known in the Church as the first principles, are the Canon by which we judge of conclusions from thence inferred. The Scripture, as containing in it all that doctrine of Faith which CHRIST the SON of GOD delivered. The uniform practice and consenting judgment of them that went before us, as a certain and undoubted explication of the things contained in Scripture. . . . So, then *we do not make Scripture the Rule of our Faith, but that other things in their kind are Rules likewise;* in such sort that it is *not safe, without respect had unto them, to judge things by the Scripture alone.*' &c. – 4.14, pp. 364, 365.

"These extracts show not only what the Anglican doctrine is, but, in particular, that the phrase 'Rule of Faith' is no symbolical expression with us, appropriated to some one sense; certainly not as a definition or attribute of Holy Scripture. And it is important to insist upon this, from the very great misconceptions to which the phrase gives rise. Perhaps its use had better be avoided altogether. In the sense in which it is commonly understood at this day, Scripture, it is plain, is *not* on Anglican principles, the Rule of Faith."

§2. *Justification by Faith Only*.

Article 11 – "That we are justified by Faith only, is a most wholesome doctrine."

The Homilies add that Faith is the sole *means*, the sole

instrument of justification. Now to show briefly what such statements imply, and what they do not.

1. They do *not* imply a denial of *Baptism* as a means and an instrument of justification; which the Homilies elsewhere affirm, as will be shown incidentally in a later section.

"The instrumental power of Faith cannot interfere with the instrumental power of Baptism; because Faith is the sole justifier, not in contrast to *all* means and agencies whatever, (for it is not surely in contrast to our LORD's merits, or GOD's mercy,) but to all other *graces*. When, then, Faith is called the sole instrument, this means the sole *internal* instrument, not the sole instrument of any kind.

"There is nothing inconsistent, then, in Faith being the sole instrument of justification, and yet Baptism also the sole instrument, and that at the same time, because in distinct senses; and inward instrument in no way interfering with an outward instrument, Baptism may be the hand of the giver, and Faith the hand of the receiver."

Nor does the sole instrumentality of Faith interfere with the doctrine of *Works* being a mean also. And that it is a mean, the Homily of Alms-deeds declares in the strongest language, as will also be quoted in Section 11.

"An assent to the doctrine that Faith alone justifies, does not at all preclude the doctrine of Works justifying also. If, indeed, it were said that Works justify in *the same sense* as Faith only justifies, this would be a contradiction in terms; but Faith only may justify in one sense – Good Works in another: – and this is all that is here maintained. After all, does not CHRIST only justify? How is it that the doctrine of Faith justifying does not interfere with our LORD's being the sole Justifier? It will, of course, be replied, that our LORD is the *meritorious* cause,[24] and Faith the *means*; that Faith justifies in a different and subordinate sense. As, then, CHRIST justifies *in the sense* in which He justifies alone, yet Faith also justifies in its own sense; so Works, whether moral or ritual, may justify us in their own respective senses, though in the sense in which Faith justifies, it only justifies. The only question is, *What* is that sense in which Works justify, so as not to interfere with faith only justifying? It may, indeed, turn out on inquiry, that the sense alleged will not hold, either as being unscriptural, or for any other reason; but whether so or not, at any rate the apparent inconsistency of language should not startle persons; nor should they so promptly condemn those who, though they do not use *their* language, use St James's.[25] Indeed, is not this argument the very weapon of the Arians, in their warfare against the Son of God? They said, Christ is not God, because the Father is called the '*Only* God.' "[26]

2. Next we have to inquire *in what sense* Faith only does justify. In a number of ways, of which here two only shall be mentioned.

First, it is the pleading or impetrating[27] principle, or constitutes our *title* to justification; being analogous among the graces to Moses lifting up his hands on the Mount,[28] or the Israelites eyeing the Brazen Serpent, – actions which did not merit God's mercy, but *asked* for it. A number of means go to effect our justification. We are justified by Christ alone, in that He has purchased the gift; by Faith alone, in that Faith asks for it; by Baptism alone, for Baptism conveys it; and by newness of heart alone, for newness of heart is the life of it.

And secondly, Faith as the beginning of perfect or justifying righteousness, is taken from what it tends towards, or ultimately will be.[29] It is said by anticipation to be that which it promises; just as one might pay a labourer his hire before he began his work. Faith working by love is the seed of divine graces, which in due time will be brought forth and flourish – partly in this world, fully in the next.

§3. *Works before and after Justification.*

Articles 12 and 13 – "Works done before the grace of
CHRIST, and the inspiration of His SPIRIT, ['before justification,' *title of the Article*] are not pleasant to GOD (*minime Deo
grata sunt*); forasmuch as they spring not of Faith in JESUS
CHRIST, neither do they make man meet to receive grace, or
(as the school authors say) deserve grace of congruity[30]
(*merentur gratiam de congruo*); yea, rather for that they are not
done as GOD hath willed and commanded them to be done,
we doubt not but they have the nature of sin. Albeit good
works, which are the fruits of faith, and follow after justification (*justificatos sequuntur*), cannot put away (*expiare*) our sins,
and endure the severity of GOD's judgment, yet are they
pleasing and acceptable (*grata et accepta*) to GOD in CHRIST,
and do spring out necessarily of a true and lively Faith."

Two sorts of works are here mentioned – works before
justification, and works after; and they are most strongly
contrasted with each other.

1. Works before justification, are done "before the grace
of CHRIST, and the inspiration of HIS SPIRIT."

2. Works before, "do not spring of Faith in JESUS
CHRIST;" works after are "the fruits of Faith."

3. Works before "have the nature of sin;" works after are
"good works."

4. Works before "are not pleasant (*grata*) to GOD;" works
after "are pleasing and acceptable (*grata et accepta*) to GOD."

Two propositions, mentioned in these Articles, remain,
and deserve consideration. First, that works *before* justification
do not make or dispose men to receive grace, or, as the
school writers say, deserve grace of congruity; secondly, that
works *after* "cannot put away our sins, and endure the
severity of GOD's judgment."

1. As to the former statement, - to deserve *de congruo,* or of
congruity, is to move the divine regard, not from any claim

upon it, but from a certain fitness or suitableness; as for instance, it might be said that dry wood had a certain disposition or fitness toward heat which green wood had not. Now the Article denies that works done before the grace of CHRIST, or in a mere state of nature, in this way dispose towards grace, or move GOD to grant grace. And it asserts, with or without reason, (for it is a question of *historical fact*, which need not specially concern us,) that certain schoolmen maintained the affirmative.

Now, that this is what it means, is plain from the following passages of the Homilies, which in no respect have greater claims upon us than as comments upon the Articles:—

"Therefore they that teach repentance *without a lively faith*, in our SAVIOUR JESUS CHRIST, do teach none other but Judas's repentance, as all the schoolmen do, which do *only* allow these three parts of repentance, – the contrition of the heart, the confession of the mouth, and the satisfaction of the work. But all these things we find in Judas's repentance, which, in outward appearance, did far exceed and pass the repentance of Peter … This was commonly the penance which CHRIST enjoined sinners, 'Go thy way, and sin no more;' which penance we shall never be able to fulfil, *without the special grace* of Him that doth say, 'Without Me, ye can do nothing.' "[31]

To take a passage which is still more clear:

"As these examples are not brought in to the end that we should thereby take a boldness to sin, presuming on the mercy and goodness of GOD, but to the end that, if, through the frailness of our own flesh, and the temptation of the devil, we fall into like sins, we should in no wise despair of the mercy and goodness of GOD: even so must we beware and take heed, that we do in no wise think in our hearts, imagine, or believe *that we are able to repent aright or to turn effectually unto the LORD by our own might and strength*." Ibid., part I. fin.

The Article contemplates these two states, – one of justifying grace, and one of the utter destitution of grace; and it says, that those who are in utter destitution cannot do anything to gain justification; and, indeed, to assert the contrary would be Pelagianism.[32] However, there is an intermediate state, of which the Article says nothing, but which must not be forgotten, as being an actually existing one. Men are not always either in light or in darkness, but are sometimes between the two; they are sometimes not in a state of Christian justification, yet not utterly deserted by God, but in a state something like that of the Jews or of Heathen, turning to the thought of religion. They are not gifted with *habitual* grace, but they still are visited by divine influences, or by *actual* grace,[33] or rather *aid;* and these influences are the first fruits of the grace of justification going before it, and are intended to lead on to it, and to be perfected in it, as twilight leads to day. And since it is a Scripture maxim, that "he that is faithful in that which is least, is faithful also in much;" and "to whomsoever hath, to him shall be given;"[34] therefore it is quite true that works done *with* divine aid, and in faith, *before* justification, *do* dispose men to receive the grace of justification; – such were Cornelius's alms, fastings, and prayers, which led to his baptism.[35] At the same time it must be borne in mind that, even in such cases, it is not the works themselves which make them meet, as some schoolmen seem to have said, but the secret aid of GOD, vouchsafed, equally with the "grace and Spirit," which is the portion of the baptized, for the merits of CHRIST's sacrifice.

[But it may be objected, that the silence observed in the Article about a state between that of justification and grace, and that of neither, is a proof that there is none such. This argument, however, would prove too much; for in like manner there is a silence in the Sixth Article about a *judge* of the scripturalness of doctrine, yet a judge there must be. And, again, few, it is supposed, would deny that Cornelius, before the angel came to him, was in a more hopeful state than

Simon Magus or Felix.[36] The difficulty then, if there was one, is common to persons of whatever school of opinion.]

2. If works *before* justification, when done by the influence of divine aid, gain grace, much more do works *after* justification. They are, according to the Article, "grata," "pleasing to GOD;" and they are accepted, "accepta;" which means that GOD rewards them, and that of course according to their degree of excellence. At the same time, as works before justification may nevertheless be done under a divine influence, so works after justification are still liable to the infection of original sin; and, as not being perfect, "cannot expiate our sins," or "endure the severity of GOD's judgment."

§4. *The Visible Church*.

Article 19 – "The Visible Church of CHRIST is a congregation of faithful men (coetus fidelium), in which the pure Word of GOD is preached, and the Sacraments duly ministered according to CHRIST's ordinance, in all those things that of necessity are requisite to the same."

This is not an abstract definition of *a* Church, but a description of *the* actually existing One Holy Catholic Church diffused throughout the world; as if it were read, "The Church is a certain society of the faithful," &c. This is evident from the mode of describing the Catholic Church, familiar to all writers from the first ages down to the age of this Article. For instance, St. Clement of Alexandria says, "I mean by the Church, not a place, but the *congregation of the elect*." Origen: "The Church, the *assembly of all the faithful*." St. Ambrose: "*One congregation*, one Church." St. Isidore: "The Church is a *congregation of saints*, collected on a certain faith, and the best conduct of life." St. Augustine: "The Church is *the people of God* through all ages." Again: "The Church is *the multitude of the pious*." Theodoret: "The Apostle calls the Church the *assembly of the faithful.*" Pope Gregory: "The Church, *a multi-tude of the faithful* collected, of both sexes." Bede: "The Church is the *congregation of all saints.*" Alcuin: "The Holy Catholic Church, – in Latin the *congregation of the faithful.*" Amalarius: "The Church is *the people* called together by the Church's ministers." Pope Nicholas I: "The Church, that is, the *congregation of Catholics.*" St. Bernard: "What is the Spouse but *the congregation of the just?*" Peter the Venerable: "The Church is called *a congregation,* but not all things, not of cattle, but *of men, faithful,* good, just. Though bad among these good, and just among the unjust, are revealed or concealed, yet it is called a Church." Hugo Victorinus: "The Holy Church, that is *the university of the faithful.*" Arnulphus: "The Church is called *the congregation of the faithful.*" Albertus Magnus: "The Greek word church means in Latin convocation; and whereas works and callings belong to rational animals, and reason in man is inward faith, therefore it is called *the congregation of the faithful.*" Durandus: "The Church is in one sense material, in which divers offices are celebrated; in another spiritual, which is the *collection of the faithful.*" Alvarus: "The Church is the *multitude of the faithful,* or the university of Christians." Pope Pius II: "The Church is the *multitude of the faithful* dispersed through all nations."[5] [And so the Reformers, in their own way; for instance, the Confession of Augsburg. "The one Holy Church will remain for ever. Now the Church of Christ properly is the congregation of the members of Christ, that is, of saints who truly believe and obey Christ; though with this congregation many bad and hypocrites are mixed in this life, till the last judgment." vii. – And the Saxon: "We say then that the visible Church in this life is an assembly of those who embrace the Gospel of Christ and rightly use the Sacraments," &c. xii.]

These illustrations of the phraseology of the Article may

---

[5] These instances are from Launoy.[37]

be multiplied in any number. And they plainly show that it is not laying down any logical definition *what* a Church is, but is describing, and as it were, pointing to the Catholic Church diffused throughout the world; which being but one, cannot possibly be mistaken, and requires no other account of it beyond this single and majestic one. The ministration of the Word and Sacraments is mentioned as a further note of it. As to the question of its limits, whether Episcopal Succession or whether intercommunion with the whole be necessary to each part of it, – these are questions, most important indeed, but of detail, and are not expressly treated of in the Articles.

This view is further illustrated by the following passage from the Homily for Whitsunday:

"Our Saviour CHRIST, departing out of this world unto His FATHER, promised His Disciples to send down another COMFORTER, that should continue with them for ever, and direct them into all truth. Which thing to be faithfully and truly performed, the Scriptures do sufficiently bear witness. Neither must we think that this COMFORTER was either promised, or else given, only to the Apostles, but also to *the universal Church of* CHRIST, *dispersed through the whole world*.[38] For, unless the HOLY GHOST had always been present, governing and preserving the Church from the beginning, it could never have suffered so many and great brunts[39] of affliction and persecution, with so little damage and harm as it hath. And the words of CHRIST are most plain in this behalf, saying that 'the SPIRIT of Truth should abide with them for ever;' that 'He would be with them always (he meaneth by grace, virtue, and power) even to the world's end.'[40]

"Also in the prayer that He made to his FATHER a little before His death, He maketh intercession, not only for Himself and His Apostles, but indifferently for all them that should *believe* in Him through their words, that is, to wit, for His whole Church.[41] Again, St. Paul saith, "If any man have not the SPIRIT of CHRIST, the same is not His.' Also, in the words following: 'We have received the Spirit of adoption, whereby we cry, Abba, Father.' Hereby, then, it is evident and plain to all men, that the HOLY

GHOST was given, not only to the Apostles, but also to the *whole body of* CHRIST's *congregation,* although not in like form and majesty as He came down at the feast of Pentecost. But now herein standeth the controversy, – whether all men do justly arrogate to themselves the HOLY GHOST, or no. The Bishops of Rome have for a long time made a sore challenge thereto, reasoning with themselves after this sort: 'The HOLY GHOST,' say they, 'was promised to the Church, and never forsaketh the Church. But we are the chief heads and the principal part of the Church, therefore we have the HOLY GHOST for ever: and whatsoever things we decree are undoubted verities and oracles of the HOLY GHOST.' That ye may perceive the weakness of this argument, it is needful to teach you, first, what the true Church of CHRIST is, and then to confer the Church of Rome therewith, to discern how well they agree together. The true Church is *an universal congregation or fellowship of* GOD's *faithful and elect people,* built upon the foundation of the Apostles and Prophets, JESUS CHRIST Himself being the head cornerstone. And it hath always three notes or marks, whereby it is known; pure and sound doctrine, the Sacraments ministered according to CHRIST's holy institution, and the right use of ecclesi-astical discipline. This description of the Church is agreeable both to the Scriptures of GOD, and also to the doctrine of the ancient Fathers, so that none may justly find fault therewith. Now, if you will compare this with the Church of Rome, not as it was in the beginning, but as it is at present, and hath been for the space of nine hundred years and odd;[42] you shall well perceive the state thereof to be so far wide from the nature of the Church, that nothing can be more."

This passage is quoted, not for all it contains, but in that respect in which it claims attention, viz. as far as it is an illus-tration of the Article. It is speaking of the one Catholic Church, not of an abstract idea of a Church, which may be multiplied indefinitely in fact; and it uses the same terms of it which the Article does of "the visible Church." It says that "the true Church is an *universal* congregation or fellowship of GOD's faithful and elect people," &c. which as closely corresponds to the *coetus fidelium*, or "congregation of faithful men" of the Article, as the above descriptions from Fathers or Divines do. Therefore, the *coetus fidelium* spoken of in the Article is not a definition, which kirk, or connexion,[43] or other communion, may be made to fall under, but the enunciation of a fact.

§5. *General Councils*.

Article 21 – "General councils may not be gathered together without the commandment and will of princes. And when they be gathered together, forasmuch as they be an assembly of men, whereof all be not governed with the SPIRIT and Word of GOD, they may err, and sometimes have erred, in things pertaining to GOD.

That great bodies of men, of different countries, may not meet together without the sanction of their rulers, is plain from the principles of civil obedience and from primitive practice. That, when met together, though Christians, they will not be all ruled by the SPIRIT or Word of GOD, is plain from our Lord's parable of the net,[44] and from melancholy experience. That bodies of men, deficient in this respect, may err, is a self-evident truth, – *unless,* indeed, they be favoured with some divine superintendence, which has to be proved, before it can be admitted.

General councils then may err, [as *such;* may err] *unless* in any case it is promised, as a matter of express supernatural privilege, that they shall *not* err; a case which [as consisting in the fulfillment of additional or subsequent conditions,] lies beyond the scope of this Article, or at any rate beside its determination.

Such a promise, however, *does* exist, in cases when general councils are not only gathered together according to "the commandment and will of princes," but *in the Name of* CHRIST, according to our Lord's promise.[45] The Article merely contemplates the human prince, not the King of Saints. While councils are a thing of earth, their infallibility of course is not guaranteed; when they are a thing of heaven, their deliberations are overruled,[46] and their decrees author-itative. In such cases they are *Catholic* councils; and it would seem, from passages which will be quoted in Section 11, that the Homilies recognize four, or even six, as bearing this character. Thus Catholic or Oecumenical Councils are general councils, and something more. Some general councils are Catholic, and others are not. Nay, as even Romanists grant, the same councils may be partly Catholic, partly not.[6]

If Catholicity be thus a *quality*, found at times in general councils, rather than the *differentia*[47] belonging to a certain class of them, it is still less surprising that the Article should be silent about it.

What those *conditions* are, which fulfil the notion of a gathering "in the Name of CHRIST," in the case of a partic-ular council, it is not necessary here to determine. Some have included among these conditions, the subsequent reception of its decrees by the universal Church; others a ratification by the pope.

Another of these conditions, however, the Article goes on to mention, *viz.* that in points necessary to salvation, a council should prove its decrees by Scripture.

St.Gregory Nazianzen[48] well illustrates the consistency of this Article with a belief in the infallibility of Oecumenical Councils, by his own language on the subject on different occasions.

In the following passage he anticipates the Article:

"My mind is, if I must write the truth, to keep clear of every

---

[6] Bellarmine speaks of 'Concilia *generalia* approbata . . . and Concilia generalia *reprobata*' being a contemporary of the Articles. *De Conc.* 1.5,6. [Newman's note in VM 2, p. 292.]

conference of bishops, for of conference never saw I good come, or a remedy so much as an increase of evils. For there is strife and ambition, and these have the upper hand of reason." Ep. 55.

Yet, on the other hand, he speaks elsewhere of "the holy Council of Nicea, and that band of chosen men whom the HOLY GHOST brought together." Orat. 21.

§6. *Purgatory, Pardons, Images, Relics, Invocation of Saints.*[49]

Article 22 – "The Romish doctrine concerning purgatory, pardons (de indulgentiis), worshipping (de veneratione) and adoration, as well of images as of relics, and also invocation of saints, is a fond thing (res est futilis) vainly (inaniter) invented and grounded upon no warranty of Scripture, but rather repugnant (contradicit) to the Word of GOD."

Now the first remark that occurs on perusing this Article is, that the doctrine objected to is "the Romish doctrine." For instance, no one would suppose that the *Calvinistic* doctrine concerning purgatory, pardons, and image-worship is spoken against. Not every doctrine on these matters is a fond thing, but the *Romish* doctrine. Accordingly, the *Primitive* doctrine is not condemned in it, unless, indeed, the Primitive doctrine be the Romish, which must not be supposed. Now there *was* a primitive doctrine on all these points, – how far Catholic or universal is a further question, – but still so widely received and so respectably supported, that it may well be entertained as a matter of opinion by a theologian now; this, then, whatever be its merits, is not condemned by this Article.

This is clear without proof on the face of the matter, at least as regards pardons. Of course, the Article never meant to make light of *every* doctrine about pardons, but a certain doctrine, the Romish doctrine, [as indeed the plural form itself shows].

And [such an understanding of the Article is supported by] some sentences in the Homily on Peril of Idolatry, in which, as far as regards relics, a *certain* "veneration" is sanctioned by its tone in speaking of them, though not of course the Romish veneration.

The sentences referred to run as follows:

"In the Tripartite Ecclesiastical History,[50] the Ninth Book, and Forty-eighth Chapter, is testified, that Epiphanius,[51] being yet alive, did work miracles; and that after his death, devils *being expelled at his grave or tomb,* did roar.' Thus you see what authority St. Jerome (who has just been mentioned) and that most ancient history, give unto the holy and learned Bishop Epiphanius."

Again:

"St. Ambrose, in his Treatise on the Death of Theodosius the Emperor, saith, 'Helena found the Cross, and the Title on it. She worshipped the King, and not the wood, surely (for that is an heathenish error and the vanity of the wicked), but she worshipped Him that hanged on the Cross, and whose Name was written on the title,' and so forth. See both the godly empress' fact and St. Ambrose's judgment at once; they thought it had been an heathenish error and vanity of the wicked *to have worshipped the Cross itself, which was imbued with our* SAVIOUR CHRIST's *own precious blood.*" Peril of Idolatry, part 2, circ. Init.

In these passages the writer does not positively commit himself to the miracles at Ephiphanius' tomb, or the discovery of the true Cross, but he evidently wishes the hearer to think he believes in both. This he would not do, if he thought all honour paid to relics wrong.

If, then, in the judgment of the Homilies, not all doctrine concerning the veneration of relics is condemned in the Article before us, but a certain toleration of them is compatible with its wording; neither is all doctrine concerning purgatory, pardons, images, and saints, condemned by the Article, but only "the Romish."

And further, by "the Romish doctrine," is meant the Tridentine [statement], because this Article was drawn up before the decree of the Council of Trent.[52] What is opposed is the *received doctrine* of the day, and unhappily of this day too, or the doctrine of the *Roman schools;* a conclusion which is still more clear, by considering that there are portions in the Tridentine [statements] on these subjects, which the Article, far from condemning, by anticipation approves, as far as they go. For instance, the Decree of Trent enjoins concerning purgatory thus; – "Among the uneducated vulgar let *difficult and subtle questions*, which make not for edification, and seldom contribute aught toward piety, be kept back from popular discourses. Neither let them suffer the public mention and treatment of *uncertain points,* or such as *look like falsehood*." Session 25. Again, about images: "*Due* honour and veneration is to be paid unto them, *not that we believe that any divinity or virtue is in them,* for which they should be worshipped (colendae), or that *we should ask anything* of them, or that trust should be reposed in images, as formerly was done by the Gentiles, which used to place their hope on idols." *Ibid*.

If then, the doctrine condemned in this Article concerning purgatory, pardons, images, relics, and saints, be not the Primitive doctrine, nor the Catholic doctrine, nor the Tridentine [statement], but the Romish *doctrina Romanensium,* let us next consider *what* in matter of fact it is. And,

1. As to the doctrine of the Romanists concerning Purgatory. Now here there *was* a primitive doctrine, whatever its merits, concerning the fire of judgment, which is a possible or a probable opinion, and is *not* condemned. That doctrine is this; that the conflagration of the world, or the flames which attend the Judge, will be an ordeal through which all men will pass; that great saints such as St. Mary will pass it unharmed; that others will suffer loss; but no one will

fail under it who are built upon the right foundation. Here is one [purgatorian doctrine] not "Romish."

Another doctrine, purgatorian, but not Romish, is that said to be maintained by the Greeks at Florence, in which the cleansing, though a punishment, was but a *poena damni*, not a *poena sensus*;[53] not a positive sensible infliction, much less the torment of fire, but the absence of GOD's presence. And another purgatory is that in which the cleansing is but a progressive sanctification and has no pain at all.

None of these doctrines does the Article condemn; any of them may be held by the Anglo Catholic as a matter of private belief; not that they are here advocated, one or other, but they are adduced as an *illustration* of what the Article does *not* mean, and to vindicate our Christian liberty in a matter where the Church has not confined it.

[For what the doctrine which is reprobated is, we might refer, in the first place, to the Council of Florence, where a decree was passed on the subject, were not that decree almost as vague[54] as the Tridentine; viz., that deficiency of penance is made up by *poenae purgatoriae*.][55]

"Now doth St. Augustine say, that those men which are cast into prison after this life, on that condition, may in no wise be holpen,[56] though we would help them never so much. And why? Because the *sentence* of GOD is *unchangeable,* and cannot be *revoked again.* Therefore, let us not deceive ourselves, thinking that either we may help others, or others may help us, by their good and charitable prayers in time to come. For, as the preacher saith, 'Where the tree falleth, whether it be toward the south, or toward the north, what place soever the tree falleth, there it lieth;'[57] meaning thereby, that every mortal man *dieth either in the state of salvation or damnation,* according as the words of the Evangelist John do plainly import, saying, 'He that believeth on the SON of GOD hath eternal life; but he that believeth not on the SON, shall never see life, but the wrath of GOD abideth upon him,'[58] where is then the third place which they call purgatory? or where shall our prayers help and profit the dead? St. Augustine doth only acknowledge two places after this life, heaven and hell. As for the third place, he doth plainly deny that there is any such to be found in all Scripture. Chrysostom likewise is of this mind, that unless we wash away our sins in this present world, we shall find no comfort afterward. And St Cyprian saith that, after death, repentance and sorrow of pain shall be without fruit, weeping also shall be in vain, and prayer shall be to no purpose.[59] Therefore he counselleth all men to make provision for themselves while they may, because, when they are once departed out of this life, there is no place for *repentance,* nor yet for satisfaction." *Homily concerning Prayer*, pp. 282, 283.

Now it [would seem] from this passage, that the Purgatory contemplated by the Homily was one for which no one will for an instant pretend to adduce even those Fathers who most favour Rome, *viz.* one *in which our state would be changed* in which GOD's sentence could be reversed. "The sentence of GOD," says the writer, "is *unchangeable,* and cannot be revoked again; there is no place for *repentance.*" On the other hand, the Council of Trent, and Augustine and Cyprian, so far as they express or imply any opinion approximating to that of the Council, held Purgatory to the a place for *believers*, not unbelievers, not where men who have lived and *died* in GOD's *wrath,* may gain pardon, but where those who have *already* been pardoned in this life, may be cleansed and purified for beholding the face of GOD. The Homily, then, and therefore the Article, [as far as the Homily may be taken to explain it,] does not speak of the Tridentine purgatory.

The mention of Prayers for the dead in the above passage, affords an additional illustration of the limited and [relative] sense of the terms of the Article now under consideration. For such prayers are obviously not condemned in it in the abstract, or in every shape, but, *as offered to rescue the lost from eternal fire.*

[Hooker, in his Sermon on Pride,[60] give us a second view of the "Romish doctrine of Purgatory," from the schoolmen. After speaking of the *poena damni*, he says –

"The other punishment, which hath in it not only loss of joy, but also sense of grief, vexation, and woe, is that whereunto they give the name of purgatory pains, *in nothing different form those very infernal torments which the souls of the castaways, together with the damned spirits, do endure,* save only in this, there is an appointed term to the one, to the other none; but for the time they last they are *equal.*" Vol. 3, p. 798.]

Such doctrine, too, as the following may well be included in that which the Article condemns under the name of "Romish." The passage to be quoted has already appeared in these Tracts.[61]

"In the 'Speculum Exemplorum' it is said, that a certain priest, in an ecstasy, saw the soul of Constantius Turritanum in the eaves of his house, tormented with frosts and cold rains, and afterwards climbing up to heaven upon a shining pillar. And a certain monk saw some souls roasted upon spit like pigs, and some devils basting them with scalding lard; but a while after, they were carried to a cool place, and so proved purgatory. But Bishop Theobald, standing upon a piece of ice to cool his feet, was nearer purgatory than he was aware, and was convinced of it, when he heard a poor soul telling him, that under that ice he was tormented: and that he should be delivered, if for thirty days continual, he would say for him thirty masses. And some such thing was seen by Conrade and Udalric in a pool of water; for the place of purgatory was not yet resolved on, till St. Patrick had the key of it delivered to him, which when one Nicholas borrowed of him, he saw as strange and true things there, as ever Virgin dreamed of in his purgatory, or Cicero in his dream of Scipio, or Plato in his Gorgias or Phaedo, who indeed are the surest authors to prove purgatory. But because to preach false stories was forbidden by the Council of Trent, there are yet remaining more certain arguments, even revelations made by angels, and the testimony of St. Odilio himself, who heard the devil complain (and he had great reason surely), that the souls of dead men were daily snatched out of his hands, by the alms and prayers of the living; and the sister of St. Damianus, being too much pleased with hearing of a piper, told her brother, that she was to be tormented for fifteen days in purgatory.

"We do not think that the wise men in the Church of Rome believe these narratives; for if they did, they were not wise; but this we know, that by such stories the people were brought into a belief of it, and having served their turn of them, the master builders used them as false arches and centres, taking them away, when the parts of the building were made firm and stable by authority." *Jer. Taylor, Works,* vol. 10, pp. 151, 152.

Another specimen of doctrine, which no one will attempt to prove from Scripture, is the following:[62] —

"Eastwardly between two walls, was a vast place of purgatory, fixed, and beyond it a pond to rinse souls in that had waded through purgatory, the water being salt and cold beyond comparison. Over this purgatory, St. Nicholas was the owner.

"There was a mighty bridge, all beset with nails and spikes, and leading to the mount of joy; on which mount was a stately church, seemingly capable to contain all the inhabitants of the world, and into which the souls were no sooner entered but that they forgot all their former torments.

"Returning to the first church, there they found St. Michael the Archangel and the Apostles Peter and Paul, St Michael caused all the white souls to pass through the flames, unharmed to the mount of joy; and those that had black and white spots, St. Peter led into purgatory to be purified.

"In one part sat St. Paul, and the devil opposite to him with his guards, with a pair of scales between them, weighing all such souls as were all over black; when upon turning a soul, the scale turned towards St. Paul, he sent it to purgatory, there to expiate its sins; when towards the devil, his crew, with great triumph, plunged it into the flaming pit ...

"The rustic likewise saw near the entrance of the town hall, as it were, four streets; the first was full of innumerable furnaces and cauldrons filled with flaming pitch and other liquids, and boiling of souls whose heads were like those of black fishes in the seething liquor. The second had its cauldrons stored with snow and ice, to torment souls with horrid cold. The third had thereof boiling sulphur and other materials, affording the worst of stinks, for the vexing of souls that had wallowed in the filth of lust. The fourth had cauldrons of a most horrid salt and black water. Now sinners of all sorts were alternatively tormented in these cauldrons." *Purgatory proved by Miracle by S. Johnson,* pp. 8–10.[63]

[Let it be considered, then, whether, on the whole, the "Romish doctrine of Purgatory," which the Article condemns, and which was generally believed in the Roman Church three centuries since, as well as now, viewed in its essence, be not the doctrine, that the punishment of unrighteous Christians is temporary, not eternal, and that the purification of the righteous is a portion of the same punishment, together with the superstitions, and impostures for the sake of gain, consequent thereupon.]

2. Pardons, or Indulgences.[64]

The history of the rise of the Reformation will interrupt "the Romish doctrine concerning pardons," without going further. Burnet thus speaks on the subject.

"In the primitive church there were very severe rules made, obliging all that had sinned publicly (and they were afterwards applied to such as had sinned secretly) to continue for many years in a state of separation from the Sacrament, and of Penance and discipline. But because all such general rules admit of a great variety of circumstances, taken from men's sins, their persons, and their repentance, there was a power given to all Bishops, by the Council of Nicea[65] to shorten the time, and to relax the severity of those Canons, and such favour as they saw cause to grant, was called *indulgence.* This was just and necessary, and was a provision without which no constitution or society can be well governed. But after the tenth century, as the Popes came to take this power in the whole extent of it into their own hands, so they found it too feeble to carry on the great designs that they grafted upon it.

"They gave it high names, and called it a plenary remission, and the pardon of all sins; which the world was taught to look on as a thing of a much higher nature, than the bare excusing of men from discipline and penance. Purgatory was then got to be firmly believed, and all men were strangely possessed with the terror of it: so a deliverance from purgatory, and by consequence an immediate admission into heaven, was believed to be the certain effect of it. Multitudes were by these means, engaged to go to the Holy Land, to recover it out of the hands of the Saracens; afterwards they armed vast numbers against the heretics, to extirpate them: they fought also all those quarrels which their ambitious pretensions engaged them in, with emperors and other princes, by the same pay; and at last *they set it to sale* with the same impudence, and almost with the same methods, that mountebanks use in venting[66] of their secrets.

"This was so gross, even in an ignorant age and among the ruder sort, that it gave the first rise to the Reformation: and as the progress of it was a very signal work of GOD, so it was in a great measure owing to the scandals that *this shameless practice* had given to the world." *Burnet on Article 14*, p. 190.[67]

Again:

"The virtue of indulgences is the applying the treasure of the Church upon *such terms* as Popes shall think fit to prescribe, in order to the redeeming souls from purgatory, and from all other temporal punishments, and that for such a number of years as shall be specified in the bulls; some of which have gone to thousands of years; one I have seen to then hundred thousand: and as these indulgences are sometimes granted by special tickets, like tallies struck on that treasure; so sometimes they are affixed to particular churches and altars, to particular times, or days, chiefly to the year of jubilee; they are also affixed to such things as may be carried about, to Agnus Deis,[68] to medals, to rosaries, and scapularies;[69] they are also affixed to some prayers, the devout saying of them being a mean to procure great indulgences. The granting of these is left to the Pope's discretion, who ought to distribute them as he thinks may tend most to the honour of GOD and the good of the Church; and he ought not to be too profuse, much less to be too scanty in dispensing them.

"This has been the received doctrine and practice of the Church of Rome since the twelfth century: and the Council of Trent in a hurry, in its last session, did *in very general words* approve of the practice of the Church in this matter, and decreed that indulgences should be continues; only *they restrained some abuses*, in particular that of *selling them*."[70] *Burnet on Article 22*, p. 305.

Burnet goes on to maintain that the act of the Council was incomplete and evaded. If it be necessary to say more on the subject, let us attend to the following passage from Jeremy Taylor:

"I might have instances in worst matters, made by the Popes of Rome to be pious works, the condition of obtaining indulgence. Such as was the bull of Pope Julius II,[71] giving indulgence to him that meeting a Frenchman should kill him, and another for the killing of a Venetian ... I desire this only instance may be added to it, that Pope Paul the Third, he that convened the Council of Trent, and Julius the Third,[72] for fear, as I suppose, the Council should forbid any more such follies, for a farewell to this game, gave an indulgence to the fraternity of the Sacrament of the Altar, or of the Blessed Body of our LORD JESUS CHRIST, of such a vastness and unreasonable folly, that it puts us beyond the question of religion, to an inquiry, whether it were not done either in perfect distraction, or with a worse design, to make religion to be ridiculous, and to expose it to a contempt and scorn. The conditions of the indulgence are, either to visit the Church of St. Hilary of Chartres, to say a 'Pater Noster' and an 'Ave Mary' every Friday, or, at most, to be present at processions and other divine service upon 'Corpus Christi day.'[73] The gift is – as many privileges, indults, exemptions, liberties, immunities, plenary pardons of sins and other spiritual graces, as were given to the fraternity of the Image of our SAVIOUR 'ad Sancta Sanctorum;' the fraternity of the charity and great hospital of St. James in Augusta, of St. John Baptist, of St. Cosmas and Damianus; of the Florentine nations; of the hospital of the HOLY GHOST in Saxia; of the order of St. Austin and St Champ; of the fraternities of the said city; of the churches of our Lady 'de populo et verbo;'[74] and all those that were ever given to them that visited these churches, or those which should ever be given hereafter; a pretty large gift! in which there were so many pardons, quarter-pardons, half-pardons, plenary pardons, quarantines,[75] and years of quarantines; that it is a harder thing to number them than to purchase them. I shall remark in these some particulars to be considered.

"1. That a most scandalous and unchristian dissolution and death of all ecclesiastical discipline, is consequent to the making all sin so cheap and trivial a thing; that the horrible demerits and exemplary punishment and remotion of scandal and satisfactions to the Church, are indeed reduced to trifling and mock penances. He that shall send a servant with a candle to attend the Holy Sacrament when it shall be carried to sick people, or shall go himself; or, if he shall have a hundred years of true pardon. This is fair and easy. But then,

"2. It would be considered what is meant by so many years of pardon, and so many years of true pardon. I know but of one natural interpretation of it; and that it can mean nothing but that some of the pardons are but fantastical, and not true; and in this I find no fault, save only that it ought to have been said, that all of them are fantastical.

"3. It were fit we learned how to compute four thousand and eight hundred years of quarantines, and a remission of a third part of all their sins; for so much is given to every brother and sister of this fraternity, upon Easter day, and eight days after. Now if a brother needs not thus many, it would be considered whether it did not encourage a brother or a frail sister to use all their medicine and sin more freely, lest so great a gift become useless.

"4. And this is so much the more considerable, because the gift is vast beyond all imagination. The first four days in Lent they may purchase thirty-three thousand years of pardon, besides a plenary remission of all their sins, and two third parts besides, and the delivery of one soul out of purgatory. The fourth week in Lent, three score thousand years of pardon, besides a remission of two thirds of all their sins, and one plenary remission, and one soul delivered. The fifth week, seventy-nine thousand years of pardon, and the deliverance of two souls: only the two thousand seven hundred years are given for the Sunday, may be had twice that day, if they will visit the altar twice, and as many quarantines. The sixth week, two hundred and five thousand years, besides quarantine, and four plenary pardons. Only on Palm Sunday, whose portion is twenty-five thousand years, it may be had twice that day. And all this is the price of him that shall, upon these days, visit the altar in the church of St. Hilary. And this runs on to the Fridays, and many festivals and other solemn days in the others part of the year." *Jer. Taylor,* vol. 11, pp. 53–56.

[The doctrine then of pardons, spoken of in the Article, is the doctrine maintained and acted on in the Roman Church, that remission of the penalties of sin in the next life may be obtained by the power of the Pope, with such abuses as money payments consequent thereupon.][7]

3. Veneration and worshipping of Images and Relics.

That the Homilies do not altogether discard reverence towards relics, has already been shown. Now let us see what they do discard.

"What meaneth it that Christian men, after the use of the Gentiles idolaters, *cap and kneel* before images?[76] which, if they had any sense and gratitude, would kneel before men, carpenters, masons, plasterers, founders and goldsmiths, their makers and framers, by whose means they have attained this honour, which else should have been evil-favoured, and rude lumps of clay or plaster, pieces of timber, stone, or metal, without shape or fashion, and so without all estimation and honour, as that idol in the Pagan poet confesseth, saying, 'I was once a vile block, but now I am become a god,' &c. What a fond thing is it for man, who hath life and reason, to bow himself to a dead and insensible image, the work of his own hand! Is not this stooping and kneeling before them, which is forbidden so earnestly by GOD's word? Let such as so fall down before images of saints, know and confess that they exhibit that honour to dead stocks and stones, which the saints themselves, Peter, Paul and Barnabas, would not to be given to them, being alive;[77] which the angel of GOD forbiddeth to be given to him. And if they say they exhibit such honour not to the image, but to the saint whom it represent, they are convicted of folly, to believe that they please saints with that honour, which they abhor as a spoil of GOD's honour." – *Homily on Peril of Idolatry*, p. 191.

Again:[78]

"Thus far Lactantius, and much more, too long here to write, of *candle lighting* in temples *before images and idols* for religion; whereby

---

[7] The pardons, then, spoken of in the Article, are large and reckless indulgences from the penalties of sin obtained on money payments. 1st. ed.

appeareth both the foolishness thereof, and also that in opinion and act we do agree altogether in our candle religion with the Gentiles idolaters. What meaneth it that they, after the example of the Gentiles idolaters, *burn incense, offer up gold* to images, *hang up crutches*, chains, and ships, legs, arms and whole men and women of wax, before images, as though by them, or saints (as they say) they were delivered from lameness, sickness, captivity, or shipwreck? Is this not 'colere imagines,' to worship images, so earnestly forbidden by GOD's word? If they deny it, let them read the eleventh chapter of Daniel the Prophet, who saith of Antichrist, 'He shall worship GOD, whom his fathers knew not with gold, silver, and with precious stones, and other things of pleasure:'[79] in which place the Latin word is *colet* ... To increase this madness, wicked men, which have the keeping of such images, for their great lucre and advantage, after the example of the Gentiles idolaters, have reported and spread abroad, as well by *lying tales* as written fables, diver miracles of images: as that such an image miraculously was sent from heaven, even like the Palladium, or Magna Diana Ephesiorum.[80] Such another was as miraculously found in the earth, as the man's head was in the Capitol, or the horse's head in Capua.[81] Such an image was brought by angels.[82] Such an one came itself far from the East to the West and Dame Fortune fled to Rome. Such an image of our Lady was painted by St. Luke, whom of a physician they have made a painter for that purpose.[83] Such An one an hundred yokes of oxen could not move, like Bona Dea, whom the ship could not carry;[84] or Jupiter Olympius, which laughed the artificers to scorn, that went about to remove him to Rome. Some images, though they were hard and stony, yet, for tender heart and pity, wept. Some, like Castor and Polux, helping their friends in battle, sweat, as marble pillars do in dankish weather.[85] Some spake more monstrously than ever did Balaam's ass, who had life and breath in him.[86] Such a cripple came and saluted this saint of oak, and by and by he was made whole; and lo! here hangeth his crutch. Such an one in a tempest vowed to St. Christopher, and 'scaped; and behold, her is a ship of wax. Such an one, by St. Leonard's help,[87] brake out of prison; and see where his fetters hang .... The Relics we must kiss and *offer unto,* especially on Relic Sunday.[88] And while we offer, (that we should not be weary, or repent us of our cost,) the *music and minstrelsy* goeth merrily and the offertory time, with praising and calling upon those saints whose relics be then in presence. Yea, and the water wherein those relics have been dipped, must with great reverence be reserved, as very holy and effectuous ... Because relics were so gainful, few places were there but they had Relics provided for them. And for more *plenty* of Relics, some one saint had many heads, one in one place and another in another place. Some had six arms, and twenty-six fingers. And where our LORD bare His cross alone, if all the pieces of the relics thereof were gathered together, the greatest ship in England would scarcely bare them; and yet the greatest part of it, they say, doth yet remain in the hands of the Infidels; for the which they pray in their beads-bidding,[89] that they may get it also into their hands, for such godly use and purpose. And not only the bones of the saints, but everything appertaining to them, was a holy relic. In some places they offer a sword, in some the scabbard, in some a shoe, in some a saddle that had been set upon some holy horse, in some the coals wherewith St. Lawrence was roasted,[90] in some place the tail of the ass which our LORD JESUS CHRIST sat on, to be *kissed and offered unto* for a relic. For rather than they would lack a relic, they would offer you a *horse bone instead of a virgin's arm* or the tail of the ass to be kissed and offered unto for relics. O wicked, impudent, and most shameless men, the devisers of these things! O silly, foolish, and dastardly daws,[91] and more beastly than the ass whose tail they kissed, that believe such things! ... Of these things already rehearsed, it is evident that our image maintainers have not only made images, which the Gentiles idolaters had of their false gods; and have not only *worshipped* their images with the same rites, ceremonies, super-stition, and all circumstances, as did the Gentiles idolaters their idols, but in many points have also far exceeded them in all wicked-ness, foolishness, and madness." *Homily on the Peril of Idolatry,* pp. 193–197.[92]

It will be observed that in this extract, as elsewhere in the Homilies, it is implied that the Bishop of the Church of Rome is Antichrist; but this is a statement bearing on prophetical interpretation, not on doctrine; and one besides which cannot be reasonably brought to illustrate or explain any of the positions of the Articles; and therefore it may be suitably passed over.

In another place the Homilies speak as follows:

"Our churches stand full of such great puppets, *wondrously decked and adorned;* garlands and coronets be set on their heads, precious pearls hanging about their necks; their fingers shine with ring, set with precious stones; their dead and stiff bodies are clothed with garments still with gold. You would believe that the images of our men saints were some princes of Persia land with their proud apparel; and the idols of our women saints were *nice and well-trimmed harlots, tempting their paramours to wantonness;* whereby the saints of GOD are not honoured, but most dishonoured, and their godliness, soberness, chastity, contempt of riches, and of the vanity of the world, defaced and brought into doubt by such *monstrous decking,* most differing from their sober and godly lives. And because the whole pageant must thoroughly be played, it is not enough thus to deck idols, but at last come in the priests themselves, likewise decked in gold and pearl, that they may be meet servants for such lords and ladies, and fit worshippers of such gods and goddesses. And with a solemn pace they pass forth before these *golden puppets,* and *fall down* to the ground on their marrow bones before these honourable idols; and then rising up again, *offer up odours and incense* unto them, to give the people an example of double idolatry, by worshipping not only the idol, but the gold also, and riches, wherewith it is garnished. Which thing, the most part of our old Martyrs, rather than they would do, or once *kneel* or *offer* up one crumb of *incense* before an image, suffered most cruel and terrible deaths, as the histories of them at large do declare … O books and scriptures, in the which the devilish schoolmaster, Satan, hath penned the lewd lessons of wicked idolatry, for his dastardly disciples and scholars to behold, read, and learn, to GOD's most high dishonor, and their most horrible damnation![93] Have we not been much bound, think you, to those which should have taught us the truth out of GOD's Book and his Holy Scripture, that they have shut up that Book and Scripture from us, and none of us so bold as once to open it, or read in it? And instead thereof, to spread abroad these goodly carved and gilded books and painted scriptures, to teach us such good and godly lessons? Have not they done well, after they ceased to stand in the pulpits themselves, and to teach the people committed to their instruction, keeping silence of GOD's word, and become dumb dogs, (as the prophet calls them,)[94] to set up in their stead, on every pillar and corner of the church, such goodly doctors, as dumb, but more wicked than themselves be? We need not to complain of the lack of one dumb parson, having so many dumb devilish vicars (I mean these idols and painted puppets) to teach in their stead. Now in the mean season, whilst the dumb and dead idols stand thus *decked and clothed*, contrary to GOD's law and commandment, the poor Christian people, the lively images of GOD, commended to us so tenderly by our SAVIOUR CHRIST, as most dear to Him, stand naked, shivering for cold, and their teeth chattering in their heads, and no man covereth them, are pined with hunger and thirst, and no man giveth them a penny to refresh them; whereas pounds be ready at all time (contrary to GOD's word and will) to *deck and trim* dead stocks and stones, which neither feel cold, hunger, nor thirst." *Homily on Peril of Idolatry,* pp. 219–222.

Again, with a covert allusion to the abuses of the day, the Homilist says elsewhere, of Scripture,[95]

"There shall you read of Baal, Moloch, Chamos, Melchom, Baalpeor, Astaroth, Bel the Dragon, Priapus, the brazen Serpent,[96] the twelve signs, and many others, unto whose images the people, with great devotion, invented *pilgrimages, precious decking* and *censing* them, *kneeling down* and *offering* to them, thinking that an high merit before GOD, and to be esteemed above the precepts and commandments of GOD." *Homily on Good Works,* p. 42.

Again, soon after:

"What man, having any judgment or learning, joined with a true zeal unto GOD, doth not see and lament to have entered into CHRIST's religion, such false doctrine, superstition, idolatry, hypocrisy, and other enormities and abuses, so as by little and little, through the sour leaven thereof, the sweet bread of GOD's holy word hath been much hindered and laid apart? Never had the Jews, in their most blindness, so many *pilgrimages* unto images, nor used so much *kneeling, kissing* and *censing of* them, as hath been used in our time. Sects and feigned religions were neither the fortieth part so many among the Jews, nor more superstitiously and ungodly abused, than of late years they have been among us: which sects and religions had so many hypocritical and feigned works in their state of religion, as they arrogantly named it, that their lamps, as they said, ran always over, able to satisfy not only for their own sins, but also for all other their benefactors, brothers, and sisters of religion, as most ungodly and craftily they had persuaded the multitude of ignorant people; keeping in divers places, as it were, marts or markets of merits, being full of their holy relics, images, shrines, and works of overflowing abundance, ready to be sold; and all things which they had were called holy – holy cowls, holy girdles, holy pardons, holy beads, holy shoes, holy rules, and all full of holiness. And what thing can be more foolish, more superstitious, or ungodly, than that men, women, and children should wear a friar's coat to deliver them from agues or pestilence; or when they die, or they be buried, cause it be cast upon them, *in hope thereby to be saved*?[97] Which superstition, although (thanks be to GOD) it hath been little used in this realm, yet in divers other realms it hath been, and yet is, used among many, both learned and unlearned." – *Homily on Good Works,* pp. 45, 46.

[Once more: —

"True religion then, and pleasing of GOD, standeth not in making, setting up, painting, gilding, clothing, and decking of dumb and dead images (which be but great puppets and babies for old fools in dotage, and wicked idolatry, to dally and play with,) nor in kissing of them, capping, kneeling, offering to them, incensing of them, setting up of candles, hanging up of legs, arms, or whole bodies of wax before them, or praying or asking of them, or of saints, thing belonging only to GOD to give. But all these things be vain and abominable, and most damnable before GOD." *Homily on Peril of Idolatry,* p. 223.]

Now the veneration and worship condemned in these and other passages are such as these: kneeling before images,

lighting candles to them, offering them incense, going on
pilgrimage to them, hanging up crutches, &c. before them,
lying tales about them, belief in miracles as if wrought by
them through illusion of the devil, decking them up immod-
estly, and providing incentives by them to bad passions; and,
in like manner, merry music and minstrelsy and licentious
practices in honour of relics, counterfeit relics, multiplication
of them, absurd pretences about them. This is what the
Article means by "the Romish doctrine," which, in
agreement to one of the above extracts, it calls "a fond
thing," *res futilis;* for who can ever hope, except the grossest
and most blinded minds, to be gaining the favour of the
blessed saints, while they come with unchaste thoughts and
eyes, that cannot cease from sin; and to be profited by
"pilgrimage-going," in which "Lady Venus and her son
Cupid were rather worshipped wantonly in the flesh, than
GOD the FATHER, and our SAVIOUR CHRIST HIS SON, truly
worshipped in the SPIRIT?"

Here again it is remarkable that, urged by the truth of the
allegation, the Council of Trent is obliged, both to confess
the above-mentioned enormities in the veneration of relics
and images, and to forbid them.

"Into these holy and salutary observances should any abuses creep
of these the Holy Council strongly [vehementer] desires the utter
extinction; so that no images of a false doctrine, and supplying to
the uninstructed opportunity of perilous error, should be set up ...
All superstition also in invocation of the saints, veneration of relics,
and sacred use of images, be put away; all *filthy lucre* be cast out of
doors; and *all wantonness* be avoided; *so that images be not painted or
adorned with an immodest beauty;* or the celebration of Saints and
attendance on Relics *be abused to revelries and drunkenness;* as though
festival days were kept in honour of saints by *luxury and lascivious-
ness.*" Session 25.

[On the whole, then, by the Romish doctrine of the veneration and worshipping of images and relics, the article means

all maintenance of those idolatrous honours which have been paid and are paid them so commonly throughout the church of Rome, with the superstitions, profanities, and impurities consequent thereupon.][98]

4. Invocation of Saints.

By "invocation" here is not meant the mere circumstance of addressing beings out of sight, because we use the Psalms in our daily service, which are frequent in invocations of Angels to praise and bless GOD. In the Benedicite too we address "the spirits and souls of the righteous."[99]

Nor is it a "fond" invocation to pray that unseen beings may bless us; for this [Bishop Ken does in his Evening Hymn: –

> O may my Guardian, while I sleep,
> Close to my bed his vigils keep,
> His love angelical *instill*,
> Stop all the avenues of ill, &c.][100]

On the other hand, judging from the example set us in the Homilies themselves, invocations are not censurable, and certainly not "fond," is we mean nothing definite by them, addressing them to beings which we *know* cannot hear, and using them as interjections. The Homilist seems to avail himself of this proviso in a passage, which will serve to begin our extracts in illustration of the *superstitious* use of invocations.

"We have left Him neither heaven, nor earth, nor water, nor country, or city, peace nor war to rule and govern, neither men, nor beasts, nor their diseases to cure; that a godly man might justly, for zealous indignation, cry out, *O heaven, O earth, and seas*,[8] what madness and wickedness against GOD are men fallen into ! What dishonor do the creatures to their CREATOR and MAKER! And if we remember GOD sometimes, yet, because we doubt of His ability or

---

[8] O coelum, o terra, o maria Neptuni. Terence, *Adelphi*, v. 3.

will to help, we join to Him another helper, as if He were a noun adjective, using these sayings: such as learn, GOD and St. Nicholas be my speed[101] such as these, GOD help and St. John: to the horse, GOD and St. Loy save thee.[102] Thus are we become like horses and mules, which have no understanding. For is there not one GOD only, who by His power and wisdom made all things, and by His providence governeth the same, and by His goodness maintaineth and saveth them? Be not all things of Him, by Him, and through Him? Why dost thou *turn from the* CREATOR *to the creatures*? This is the manner of the Gentiles idolaters: but thou art a Christian, and therefore by CHRIST alone hast access to GOD the FATHER, and help of Him only." *Homily on Peril of Idolatry*, p. 189.

Again, just before –

"Terentius Varro[103] sheweth, that there were three hundred Jupiters in his time: there were not fewer Veneres and Dianae: we had no fewer Christophers, Ladies and Mary Magdalens, and other saints. Oenomaus and Hesiodus[104] shew, that in their time there were thirty thousands gods. I think we had no fewer saints, to whom we gave the honour due to GOD. And they have not only spoiled the true living GOD of his due honour in temples, cities, countries, and lands, by such devices and inventions as the Gentile idolaters have done before them: but the sea and waters have as well special saints with them, as they had gods with the Gentiles, Neptune, Triton, Nereus, Castor and Pollux, Venus, and such other: in whose places be come St. Christopher, St. Clement,[105] and divers other, and specially our Lady, to whom shipmen sing, 'Ave, maris stella.'[106] Neither hath the fire escaped their idolatrous inventions. For instead of Vulcan and Vesta, the Gentiles' gods of the fire, our men have placed St. Agatha,[107] and make litters on her day for to quench fire with. Every artificer and profession hath his special saints, as a peculiar god. As for example, scholars have St. Nicholas and St. Gregory; painters, St. Luke; neither lack soldiers their Mars nor lovers their Venus, amongst Christians. All diseases have their special saints, as gods the curers of them ... the falling-evil St Cornelio,[108] the toothache St. Apollin,[109] &c. Neither do beast nor cattle lack their gods with us; for St. Loy is the horse-leech, and St. Anthony the swineherd."[110] *Ibid.*, p. 188.

The same subject is introduced in connexion with a lament over the falling off of attendance on religious worship consequent upon the Reformation:

"GOD's vengeance hath been and is daily provoked, because much wicked people pass nothing to resort to the Church, either for that they are so sore blinded, that they understand nothing of GOD and godliness, and care not with devilish example to offend their neighbours; or else for that they see the Church altogether scoured of such *gay gazing sights*, as their gross fantasy was greatly delighted with, because they see the false religion abandoned, and the true restored, which seemeth an unsavoury thing to their unsavoury taste; as may appear by this, that a woman said to her neighbor, 'Alas, gossip, what shall we now do at church, since all the saints are taken away, since all the *goodly sights* we were wont to have are gone, since we cannot hear the like *piping, singing, chanting,* and *playing upon the organs,* that we could before?' But, dearly beloved, we ought greatly to rejoice, and give GOD thanks, that our churches are delivered of all those things which displeased GOD so sore, and *filthily defiled* his house and his place of prayer, for the which He hath justly destroyed many nations, according to the saying of St. Paul: 'If any man defile the temple of GOD, GOD will him destroy.'[111] And this ought we greatly to praise GOD for, that *superstitious* and *idolatrous* manners as were utterly naught, and defaced GOD's glory, are utterly abolished, as they most justly deserved: and yet those things that either GOD was honoured with, or his people edified, are decently retained, and in our churches comely practiced." *On the Place and Time of Prayer,* pp. 293, 294.

Again:[112]

"There are certain conditions most requisite to be found in every such a one that must be called upon, which if they are not found in Him unto whom we pray, then doth prayer avail us nothing, but is altogether in vain.

"The first is this, that He, to whom we make our prayers, be able to help us. The second is, that He will help us. The third, is, that He be such a one as may hear our prayers. The fourth is, that He understand better than ourselves what we lack, saving only GOD, then may we lawfully call upon some other besides GOD. But what man is so gross, that he well understandeth that these things are only proper to Him, who is omnipotent, and knoweth all things, even the very secrets of the heart; that is to say, only and to GOD alone? Whereof it followeth that we must call neither upon angel, nor yet upon saint, but only and solely upon GOD, as St. Paul doth write: 'How shall men call upon Him, in whom they have not believed?'[113] So that *invocation* or *prayer* may not be made without faith in Him on whom they call but that we must first *believe* in Him before we can make our prayer unto Him, whereupon we must only and solely pray unto GOD. For to say that we should *believe* in either angel or saint, or in any other living creature, were *most horrible blasphemy* against GOD and his holy word; neither ought this fancy to enter into the heart of any Christian man, because we are expressly taught in the word of the LORD only to repose our faith in the blessed TRINITY, in whose name we are also baptized, according to the express commandment of our SAVIOUR JESUS CHRIST, in the last of St. Matthew.[114]

"But that the truth thereof may better appear, even to them that be most simple and unlearned, let us consider what prayer is. St. Augustine calleth it a lifting up of the mind to GOD;[115] that is to say, an humble and lowly pouring out of the heart to GOD. Isidorus[116] saith, that it is an affection of the heart, and not a labour of the lips. So that, by these plan, true prayer doth consist not so much in the outward sound and voice of words, as in the inward groaning and crying of the heart to GOD.

"Now, then, is there any angel, any virgin, any patriarch, or prophet, among the dead, that can understand or know the meaning of the heart? The Scripture saith, 'it is God that searcheth the heart and the reins, and that He only knoweth the hearts of the children of men.'[117] As for the saints, they have so little knowledge of the secrets of the heart, that many of the ancient fathers greatly doubt whether they know anything at all, that is commonly done on earth. And albeit some think they do, yet St. Augustine, a doctor of great authority, and also antiquity, hath this opinion of them; that they know no more what we do on earth, than we know what they do in heaven. For proof whereof, he allegeth the words of Isaiah the prophet, where it is said, 'Abraham is ignorant of us, and

Israel knoweth us not.' His mind therefore is this, not that we should put any religion in *worshipping* them, or *praying* unto them; but that we should honour them by following their virtuous and godly life. For, as he witnesseth in another place, the martyrs, and holy men in time past, were wont, after their death, to be *remembered*, and *named* of the priest at divine service; but never to be *invoked* or *called upon*. And why so? Because the priest, saith he is GOD's priest, and not theirs: whereby he is bound to call upon GOD, and not upon them ... O but I dare not (will some men say) trouble GOD at all times with my prayers; we see that in king's houses, and courts of princes, men cannot be admitted, unless they first use the help and means of some special nobleman, to come to the speech of the king, and to obtain the thing that they would have.

"CHRIST sitting in heaven, hath an everlasting priesthood, and always prayeth to His FATHER for them that be penitent, obtaining, by virtue of His wounds, which are evermore in the sight of GOD, not only perfect remission of our sins, but also all other necessaries that we lack in this world; so that this Holy Mediator is sufficient in heaven, and needeth no others to help Him.

"Invocation is a thing *proper unto* GOD, which if we attribute unto the saints, it soundeth unto their reproach, neither can they well bear it at our hands. When Paul healed a certain lame man, which was impotent in his feet, at Lystra, the people would have *done sacrifice* unto him and Barnabas; who, rending their clothes, refused it, and exhorted them to *worship* the true GOD. Likewise in Revelation, when St. John *fell before the angel's feet to worship him,* the angel would not permit him to do it, but commanded him that he should worship GOD.[118] Which examples declare unto us, that the saints and angels in heaven will not have us to do *any honour* unto them, *that is due and proper unto* GOD." – *Homily on Prayer*, pp. 272–277.

Whereas, then, it has already been shown that not *all* invocation is wrong, this last passage plainly tells us *what kind* of invocation is not allowable, or what is meant by invocation in the exceptional sense: viz. "a thing proper to GOD," as being part of the "honour that is due and proper unto GOD."

And two instances are specially given of such calling and invocating, viz., *sacrificing ,*and *falling down in worship*. Besides this, the Homilist adds, that it is wrong to pray to them for "necessaries in this world," and to accompany their services with "piping, singing, chanting, and playing" on the organ, and of invoking saints as patrons of particular elements, countries, arts, or remedies.

Here again, as before, the Article gains a witness and concurrence from the Council of Trent. "Though," say the divines there assembled, "the Church has been accustomed sometimes to celebrate a few masses to the honour and remembrance of saints, yet she *doth not teach that sacrifice is offered to them,* but to GOD alone, who crowned them;[119] wherefore neither is the priest wont to say, *I offer sacrifice to thee, O Peter, or O Paul,* but to God." (Session 22.) Or, to know what is meant by found invocations, we may refer to the following passage of Bishop Andrew's Answer to Cardinal Perron:[120]

"This one point is needed to be observed throughout all the Cardinal's answer, that he hath framed to himself five distinctions: – (1) Prayer *direct*, and prayer *oblique*, or indirect. (2) Prayer *absolute,* and Prayer *relative*. (3) Prayer *sovereign and Prayer subaltern*. (4) Prayer *final* and prayer *transitory*. (5) Prayer *sacrificial* and Prayer *out of, or from the sacrifice*. Prayer *direct, absolute, final, sovereign, sacrificial,* that must not be made to the saints, but to GOD only; but as for prayer *oblique, relative, transitory, subaltern, from, or out of the sacrifice, that* (saith he*)* we may make to the saints.

"For all the world like the question in Scotland, which was made some fifty years since, whether the *Pater noster* might not be said to *saints*? For then they in like sort devised the distinction of – (1) *Ultimate, et non ultimate*. (2) *Principaliter, et minus principaliter*. (3) *Primarie, et secundarie: Capiendo stricte, et capiendo large*.[121] And as for *ultimate, principaliter, primarie, et capiendo stricte,* they conclude it must go to GOD; but *not ultimate, minus principaliter, secundarie, et capiendo large,* it might be allowed *saints*.

"Yet it is sure, that in these distinctions is the whole substance of his answer.[122] And whensoever he is pressed, he flees straight to his *prayer relative* and *prayer transitory;*as if *prier pour prier,*[123] were all the Church of Rome did hold: and that they made no prayers to the saints, but only to pray for them. The Bishop well remembers, that Master Casaubon[124] more than once told him, that reasoning with the Cardinal, touching the invocation of saints, the Cardinal freely confessed to him *that he had never prayed to saint in all his life, save only when he happened to follow the procession;* and that then he sung *Ora pro nobis* with the clerks indeed, *but else not.*

"Which cometh much to this opinion he now seemeth to defend: but wherein *others* of the Church of Rome will surely give him over, so that it is to be feared that the Cardinal will be silent for this, and *some censure come out against him* by the Sorbonne. For the world cannot believe that *oblique relative* prayer is all that is sought; seeing it is most evident in their breviaries, hours, and rosaries, that they pray *directly, absolutely, and finally to saints,* and make no mention at all of *prier pour prier,* to pray to GOD to forgive them; but to the saints, to give it themselves. So that all he saith comes to nothing. They say to the blessed Virgin, 'Sancta Maria,' not only 'Ora pro nobis:' but 'Succurre miseris, juva pusillanimes, resolve flebiles, accipe quod offerimus, dona quod rogamus, excusa quod timemus,' &c. &c.[125]

"All which, and many more, show plainly that the *practice* of the Church of Rome, in this point of invocation of saints, is far otherwise than Cardinal Perron would bear the world in hand : and that *prier pour prier,* is not all, but that 'Tu dona caelum, Tu laxa, Tu solve crimina, Tu duc, conduc, induc, perduc ad gloriam; Tu serva, Tu fer opem, Tu aufer, Tu confer vitam,' are said to them (*totidem verbis*) : *more than which cannot be said to* GOD *Himself.* And again, 'Hic nos solvate a peccatis, His nostros tergat reatus, Hic arma conferat, Hic hostem fuget, Haec gubernet, Hic aptet tuo conspec-tui;'[126] which is they be not *direct* and *absolute,* it would be asked of them what is *absolute* or *direct?*" *Bishop Andrews' Answer to Chapter 20 of Cardinal Perron's Reply*, pp. 57–62.

Bellarmine's admissions quite bear out the principles laid
down by Bishop Andrews and the Homilist: —

"It is not lawful," he says, "to ask of the saints to grant to us, as if
they were the *authors* of divine benefits, glory or grace, or the other
means of blessedness ... This is proved, first, from Scripture, 'The
Lord will give grace and glory.' (Ps. 84) Secondly, from the usage
of the Church; for in the mass prayers, and the saints' offices, we
never ask anything else, but that at their prayers benefits may be
granted to us by GOD. Thirdly, from reason; for *what we need
surpasses the powers of the creature*, and therefore even of saints;
therefore we ought to ask nothing of saints beyond their impetrating from GOD what is profitable for us. Fourthly, from Augustine
and Theodoret, who expressly teach that saints are not to be
invoked *as gods*, but as able to gain from GOD what they wish.
However, if must be observed, when we say, that nothing should
be asked of saints but their prayers for us, the question is not about
the words but about the *sense* of the words. For, as far as words go,
it is lawful to say: 'St Peter, pity me, save me, open for me the gates
of heaven;' also 'give me health of body, patience, fortitude,' &c.,
provided that we mean 'save and pity me *by praying for me*;' 'grant
me this or that '*by thy prayers and merits*.' For so speaks Gregory
Nazianzen, and many others of the ancients, &c." De Sanct[a],
Beat[itudine] et Canonizatione Sanctorum, i.17.[127]

[By the doctrine of the invocation of Saints, then, the article
means all maintenance of addresses to them which intrench
upon the incommunicable honour due to GOD alone, such as
have been, and are in the church of Rome, and such as,
equally with the peculiar doctrine of purgatory, pardons, and
worshipping and adoration of images and relics, as actually
taught in that church, are unknown to the Catholic
Church.][128]

§7. *The Sacraments.*

Article 25. – "Those five, commonly called Sacraments, that
is to say, Confirmation, Penance, Orders, Matrimony, and

Extreme Unction, are not to be counted for Sacraments of the Gospel, being such as have grown, partly of the corrupt following (prava imitatione) of the Apostles, partly from states of life allowed in the Scriptures; but yet have not like nature of sacraments, (sacramentorum eandem rationem) with Baptism and the LORD's Supper, for that they have not any visible sign or ceremony ordained of GOD."

This Article does not deny the five rites in question to be sacraments, but to be sacraments in *the sense* in which Baptism and the LORD's Supper are sacraments; "sacraments of *the Gospel*," sacraments *with an outward sign ordained of* GOD.

They are not sacraments in *any* sense, *unless* the Church has the power of dispensing grace through rites of its own appointing, or is endued with the gift of blessing and hallowing the "rites and ceremonies," which, according to the twentieth article, it "hath power to decree." But we may well believe that the Church has this gift.

If, then, a sacrament be merely *an outward sign of an invisible grace given under it,* the five rites may be sacraments; but if it must be an outward sign *ordained by* GOD *or* CHRIST, then only Baptism and the LORD's Supper are sacraments.

Our Church acknowledges both definitions; in the article before us, *the stricter;* and again in the Catechism, where a sacrament is defined to be "an outward sign of an inward spiritual grace, given unto us, *ordained by* CHRIST *himself.*" And this, it should be remarked, is a characteristic of our formularies in various places, not to deny the *truth* or *obligation* of certain doctrines or ordinances, but simply to deny (what no Roman opponent now can successfully maintain), that CHRIST for certain directly ordained them. For instance, in regard to the visible Church, it is sufficient that the ministration of the sacraments should be "*according to* CHRIST'S *ordinance.*"

Article 19. – And it is added, "in all those things that *of necessity* are requisite to the same." The question entertained is, what is *the least* that God requires of us. Again, "the baptism of young children is to be retained, as most agreeable to *the institution of* CHRIST."

Article 27. – Again, "the sacrament of the LORD's Supper was not by CHRIST's *ordinance* reserved, carried about, lifted up, or worshipped."

Article 28. – Who will maintain the paradox that what the Apostles "set in order when they came"[129] had been already done by CHRIST? Again, "both parts of the LORD's sacrament, *by* CHRIST's *ordinance and commandment,* ought to be administered to all Christian men alike."

Article 30. – Again, "bishops, priests, and deacons, *are not commanded by* GOD's *law* either to vow the estate of a single life, or to abstain from marriage."

Article 32. – [In making this distinction, however, it is not here insinuated, though the question is not entered on in these particular articles, that every one of these points, of which it is only said that they are not ordained by CHRIST is justifiable on grounds short of His appointment.]

On the other hand, our Church takes the *wider* sense of the meaning of the word sacrament in the Homilies, observing –

"In the second Book against the adversary of the Law and the Prophets,[130] he [St Augustine] calleth the sacraments *holy signs.* And writing to Bonifacius of the baptism of infants, he saith, 'if sacraments had not a certain similitude of those things whereof they be sacraments, they should be no sacraments at all. And of this similitude they do for the most part receive the names of the selfsame things they signify.'[131] By these words of St. Augustine it appeareth, that he alloweth the common description of a sacrament, which is, that it is *a visible sign of an invisible grace;*[132] that is to say, that setteth out to the eyes and other outward senses the inward working of God's free mercy, and doth, as it were, seal in our hearts the promises of God." *Homily on Common Prayer and Sacraments*, pp. 296–297.

Accordingly, starting with this definition of St. Augustine's, the writer is necessarily carried on as follows: –

"You shall hear how many sacraments there be, that were instituted by our SAVIOUR CHRIST, and are to be continued, and received of every Christian, in due time and order, and for such purpose as our SAVIOUR CHRIST willed them to be received. And as for the number of them, if they should be considered according to the *exact* signification of a sacrament, namely, for visible signs expressly commanded in the New Testament, whereunto is annexed the promise of free forgiveness of our sins, and of our holiness and joining in CHRIST, there be but two; namely Baptism, and the Supper of the LORD. For although absolution hath the promise of forgiveness of sin; yet by the *express* word of the New Testament, it hath not this promise annexed and tied to the visible sign, which is the imposition of hands. For this visible sign (I mean laying on of hands) is not *expressly* commanded in the New Testament to be used in absolution as the visible signs in Baptism and the Communion are. And though the ordering of ministers hath this visible sign and promise; yet it lacks the promise of remission of sin, as all other sacraments besides the two above named do. Therefore neither it, nor any *other* sacrament else, be *such* sacraments as Baptism and Communion are. But in a general acception, the name of a sacrament may be attributed to anything, whereby an holy thing is signified. In which understanding of the word, the ancient writers have given this name, not only to the other five, commonly of late years taken and used for supplying the number of the seven sacraments; but also to divers and sundry other ceremonies, as to oil, washing of feet, and such like; not meaning thereby to repute them as sacraments, *in the same signification* that the two forenamed sacraments are. And therefore St. Augustine, weighing the true signification and exact meaning of the word, writing to Januarius,[133] and also in the third book of Christian Doctrine, affirmeth, that the sacraments of the Christians, as they are most excellent in signification, so are they most few in number, and in both places maketh mention expressly of two, the sacrament of Baptism, and the Supper of the LORD. And although there are retained by order of the Church of England, besides these two, certain other rites and ceremonies, about the institution of ministers in the Church, Matrimony, Confirmation of Children, by examining them of their knowledge in the Articles of the Faith, and joining thereto the prayers of the Church for them, and likewise for the Visitation of the Sick; yet no man ought to take these for sacraments, in *such* signification and meaning as the sacraments of Baptism and the LORD's Supper are; but either for godly states of life, necessary in Christ's Church, and therefore worthy to be set forth by public action and solemnity, by the ministry of the Church, or else judged to be such ordinances as may make for the instruction, comfort, and edification of CHRIST's Church." *Homily on Common Prayer and Sacraments,* pp. 298–300.

Another definition of the word sacrament, which equally succeeds in limiting it to the two principal rites of the Christian Church, is also contained in the Catechism, as well as alluded to in the above passage: – "Two only, as *generally necessary* to salvation, Baptism and the Supper of the LORD." On this subject the following remark has been made:

"The Roman Catholic considers that there are seven [sacraments]; we do not strictly determine the number. We define the word generally to be an 'outward sign of an inward grace,' without saying to how many ordinances this applies. However, what we do determine is, that CHRIST has ordained two special sacraments as *generally necessary to salvation*. This, then, is the characteristic mark of those two, separating them from all other whatever; and this is nothing else but saying in other words, that they are the only *justifying* rites, or instruments of communicating the Atonement, which is the one thing necessary to us. Ordination, for instance, gives *power,* yet without making the soul *acceptable to* GOD; Confirmation gives *light and strength*, yet is the mere *completion* of Baptism; and Absolution may be viewed as a negative ordinance removing the *barrier* which sin has raised between us and grace, which by inheritance is ours. But the two sacraments 'of the Gospel,' as they may be emphatically styled, are the instruments of inward *life*, according to our LORD's declaration, that Baptism is a new *birth*, and that in the Eucharist we eat the *living* bread."

§8. *Transubstantiation*.

Articles 28. "Transubstantiation, or the change of the substance of bread and wine in the supper of the LORD, cannot be proved by Holy Writ; but is repugnant to the plain words of Scripture, overthroweth the nature of a sacrament, and hath given occasion to many superstitions."

What is here opposed as "Transubstantiation," is the shocking doctrine that "the body of CHRIST," as the Article goes on to express it, is *not* "given, taken, and eaten, after an heavenly and spiritual manner, but is carnally pressed with the teeth;" that it is a body or substance of a certain extension and bulk in space, and a certain figure and due disposition of parts, whereas we hold that the only substance such, is the bread which we see.

This is plain from Article 29, which quotes St. Augustine as speaking of the wicked as "carnally and visibly pressing with their teeth the *sacrament* of the body and blood of CHRIST,"[134] not the real substance, a statement which even the Breviary introduces into the service for Corpus Christi day.[135]

This is plain also from the words of the Homily: "Saith Cyprian, 'When we do these things *we need not whet our teeth,* but with sincere faith we break and divide that holy bread. It is well known that the meat we seek in this supper is spiritual food, the nourishment of the soul, a heavenly refection, *and not earthly;* an invisible meat *and not bodily*: a ghostly substance, *and not carnal.*' "

Some extracts may be quoted to the same effect from Bishop Taylor. Speaking of what has been believed in the Church of Rome, he says:[136]

"Sometimes CHRIST hath appeared in His own shape, and blood and flesh hath been pulled out of the mouths of the communicants; and Plegilus, the priest, saw an angel, showing CHRIST to him in form of a child upon the altar, whom first he took in his arms and kissed, but did eat Him up presently in his other shaped, in the shape of a wafer.[137] 'Speciosa certe pax nebulonis, ut qui oris prae-buerat basium dentium inferret exitum,' said Berengarius: 'It was but a Judas' kiss to kiss with the lip, and bite with the teeth.'" [138] – *Bp. Taylor*, vol. 10, p. 12.

Again: –

"Yet if this and the other miracles pretended, had not been illusions of directly fabulous, it had made very much against the present doctrine of the Roman Church: for they represent the body in such measure, as by their explications it is not, and it cannot be: they represent it broken, a finger, or a piece of flesh, or bloody, or bleed-ing, or in the form of an infant; and then, when it is in the species of bread: for if, as they say CHRIST's body is present no longer than the form of bread remained, how can it be CHRIST's body in the miracle, when the species being gone, it is not longer a sacrament? But the full inventors of miracles in those ages considered nothing of this; the article itself was then gross and rude, and so were the instruments of probation. I noted this, not only to show at what door so incredible a persuasion entered, but that the zeal of prevail-ing in it hath blinded the refiners of it in this age, that they still urge those miracles for proof, when, if they do anything at all, they reprove the present doctrine." – *Bp. Taylor's Works*, vol. 9, p. 411.

Again: the change which is denied in the Article is accurately specified in another passage of the same author: —

"I will not insist upon the unworthy questions which this carnal doctrine introduces ... neither will I make scrutiny concerning CHRIST's bones, hair, and nails; nor suppose the Roman priests to be such *κάρχαροδουτες*,[139] and to have such 'saws in their mouths:' these are appendages of their persuasion, but to be abom-inated by all Christian and modest persons, who use to eat not the bodies but the flesh of beasts, and not to devour, but to worship the body of CHRIST in the exaltation, and now in union with His divinity." *On the Real Presence*, 11.

And again:

"They that *deny the spiritual sense,* and affirm the natural, are to remember that CHRIST reproved all senses of these words that were not *spiritual.* And by the way let me observe, that the expressions of some chief men among the Romanists are so crude and crass, *that it will be impossible to excuse them from the understanding the words in the sense of the men of Capernaum*: for as they understood CHRIST to mean His 'true flesh, natural and proper,' so do they: as they thought CHRIST intended they should *tear Him with their teeth and suck His blood,* for which they were offended;[140] so do these men not only think so, but say so, and are not offended. So said Alanus, 'Assertissime loquimur, corpus Christi vere a nobis contrectari, manducari, circumgestari,[141] *dentibus teri* [ground by the teeth], *sensibiliter sacrificari* [sensibly sacrificed], non minus quam ante consecrationem panis.' [not less than the bread before consecration] ... I thought that the Romanists had been glad to separate their own opinion from the carnal conceit of the men of Capernaum and the offended disciples ... but I find that Bellarmine owns it, even in them, in their rude circumstances, for he affirms that 'CHRIST corrected them *not for supposing so*, but reproved them *for not believing it to be so.*' And indeed himself says as much: 'The body of CHRIST is *truly and properly manducated or chewed* with the bread in the Eucharist;' and to take off the foulness of the expression, by avoiding a worse, he is pleased to speak nonsense: 'A thing may be manducated or chewed, thought it be not attrite[142] or broken.' But Bellarmine adds, that if you will not allow him to say so, then he grants it in plain terms, that CHRIST's body is chewed, *is attrite or broken with the teeth,* and that not tropically,[143] *but properly* ... How? under the species of bread, and invisibly." – *Ibid.,* 3.

Take again the statement of Ussher: —

"Paschasius Radbertus, who was one of the first setters forward of this doctrine in the West, spendeth a large chapter upon this point, wherein he telleth us, that CHRIST in the Sacrament did show

himself 'oftentimes in a visible shape, either in the form of a lamb,
or in the colour of flesh and blood; so that while the host was
breaking or an offering, a lamb in the priest's hands, and blood in
the chalice should be seen as it were flowing from the sacrifice, that
what lay hid in a mystery might to them that yet doubted be made
manifest in a miracle.'[144] ... The first [tale] was ... of a Roman
matron, who found a piece of the sacramental bread turned into the
fashion of a finger, all bloody; which afterwards, upon the prayers
of St. Gregory, was converted to its former shape again. The other
two were first coined by the Grecian liars ... The former of these is
not only related there, but also in the legend of Simeon
Metaphrastes[145] (which is another author among the Grecians as
Jacobus de Voragine was among the Latins)[146] in the life of
Arsenius, ... how that a little child was seen upon the altar, and an
angel cutting him into small pieces with a knife, and receiving his
blood into the chalice, as long as the priest was breaking the bread
into little parts. The latter is a of a certain Jew, receiving the
sacrament at St. Basil's hands, converted visibly into true flesh and
blood." *Ussher's Answer to a Jesuit,* pp. 62–64.

Or the following:

"When St. Odo[147] was celebrating the mass in the presence of
certain of the clergy of Canterbury, (who maintained that the bread
and wine, after consecration, do remain in their former substance,
and are not CHRIST's true body and blood, but a figure of it when
he was come to confraction,[148] presently the fragments of the body
of CHRIST which he held in his hands, began to pour forth blood
into the chalice. Whereupon he shed tears of joy; and beckoning to
them that wavered in their faith, to come near and see the
wonderful work of GOD: as soon as they beheld it they cried out,
'O holy Prelate! to whom the SON of GOD has been pleased to
reveal Himself visibly in the flesh, pray for us, that the blood we see
here present to our eyes, may again be changed, lest for our
unbelief the Divine vengeance fall upon us.' He prayed accordingly; after which, looking in the chalice, he saw the species of
bread and wine, where he had left blood ...

"St Wittekundus,[149] in the administration of the Eucharist, saw a child enter into everyone's mouth, playing and smiling when some received him, and with an abhorring countenance when he went into the mouths of others; CHRIST thus showing this saint in His countenance, who were worthy, and who unworthy receivers." – *Johnson's Miracles of Saints,* pp. 27, 28.

The same doctrine was imposed by Nicholas the Second[150] on Berengarius, as the confession of the latter shows, which runs thus:

"I, Berengarius ... anathematize every heresy, and more particularly that of which I have hitherto been accused. ... I agree with the Roman Church ... that the bread and wine which are placed on the altar are, after consecration, not only a sacrament, but even the true body and blood of our LORD JESUS CHRIST; and that these are *sensibly,* and not merely sacramentally, but in truth *handled and broken* by the hands of the priest, and *ground by the teeth of the faithful.*" *Bowden's Life of Gregory VII,* vol. 2, p. 243.[151]

Another illustration of the sort of doctrine offered in the Article, may be given from Bellarmine, whose controversial statements have already been introduced in the course of the above extracts. He thus opposes the doctrine of *introsusception,*[152] which the spiritual view of the Real Presence suggests:

He observes, that there are "two particular opinions, false and erroneous, excogitated in the schools: that of Durandus,[153] who thought it probably that the substance of the body of CHRIST in the Eucharist was *without magnitude;* and that of certain ancients, which Occam[154] seems afterwards to have followed, that though it has magnitude, (which they think not really separable from substance) yet every part is so penetrated by every other, that the body of CHRIST is *without figure,* without distinction and order of parts." With this he contrasts the doctrine which, he maintains, is that of the Church of Rome as well as the general doctrine of the schools, that "in the Eucharist whole

CHRIST exists with *magnitude* and *all accidents,* except that relation to a heavenly location which He has as He is in heaven, and those things which are concomitants on His existence in that location; and that the parts and members of CHRIST's body do *not* penetrate each other, but are so distinct and arranged one with another, as to have a *figure and order* suitable to a human body." *De Euch.* 3.5.

We see then, that by transubstantiation, our Article does not confine itself to any abstract theory, nor aim at any definition of the word substance, nor in rejecting it, rejects a word, nor in denying a "mutatio panis et vini"[155] is denying *every kind* of change, but opposed itself to a certain plain and unambiguous statement, not of this or that council, but one generally received or taught both in the schools and in the multitude, that the material elements are changed into an earthly, fleshly, and organized body, extended in size, distinct in its parts, which is there where the outward appearances of bread and wine are, and only does not meet the senses, nor even that always.

Objections against "substance," "nature," "change," "accidents," and the like, seem more or less questions of words, and inadequate expressions of the great offence which we find in the received Roman view of this sacred doctrine.

In this connexion it may be suitable to proceed to notice the Explanation appended to the Communion Service, of our kneeling at the LORD's Supper, which requires explanation itself, more perhaps than any part of our formularies. It runs as follows:

"Whereas it is ordained in this office for the Administration of the LORD's Supper, that the communicants should receive the same kneeling; (which order is well meant, for a signification of our humble and grateful acknowledgement of the benefits of CHRIST therein given to all worthy receivers, and for the avoiding of such profanation and disorder in the holy communion, as might otherwise ensue) yet, lest the same kneeling should by any persons, either out of ignorance and infirmity, or out of malice and obstinacy, be misconstrued and depraved, – It is hereby declared, that thereby no adoration is intended, or ought to be done, either unto the sacramental bread or wine there bodily received, or unto any corporal presence of CHRIST's natural flesh and blood. For the sacramental bread and wine remain still in their very natural substances, and therefore may not be adored; (for that were idolatry, to be abhorred of all faithful Christians) and the natural body and blood of our SAVIOUR CHRIST are in heaven, and not here; it being against the truth of CHRIST's natural body to be at one time in more places than one."

Now it may be admitted without difficulty, – 1. That "no adoration ought to be done unto the sacramental bread and wine there bodily received." 2. Nor "unto any *corporal* (*i.e.* carnal) presence of CHRIST's natural flesh and blood." 3. That "the sacramental bread remain still in their very natural substances." 4. That to adore them "were idolatry to be abhorred by all faithful Christians;" and 5. That "the natural body and blood of our SAVIOUR CHRIST are in heaven."

But "to heaven" is added "*and not here.*" Now, though it be allowed that there is no "*corporal* presence" [*i.e.* carnal] of "CHRIST's natural flesh and blood" here, it is a further point to allow that "CHRIST's natural body and blood" are "*not here.*" And the question is, how can there be any *presence* at all of His body and blood, yet a presence such, as not be *here*? How can there be any *presence*, yet not *local*?

Yet that is the meaning of the paragraph in question is plain, from what goes on to say in proof of its position: "It being against the truth of CHRIST's natural body to be at one time in more places than one." It is here asserted then, 1. Generally, "no natural body can be in more places than one;" therefore, 2. CHRIST's natural body cannot be in the bread and wine, or there where the bread and wine are seen. In other words, there is no local presence in the Sacrament. Yet, that there is *a* presence is asserted in the Homilies, as quoted above, and the question is, as just now stated, "How can there be a presence, yet not a local one?"

Now, first, let it be observed, that the question to be solved is the truth of a certain philosophical deduction, not of a certain doctrine of Scripture. That there is a real presence, Scripture asserts, and the Homilies, Catechism and Communion Service confess; but the explanation before us adds, that it is philosophically impossible that it should be a particular kind of presence, a presence of which one can say "it is here," or which is "local." It states then a philosophical deduction; but to such deduction none of us have subscribed. We have professed, in the words of the Canon, "That the Book of Prayer, &c. containeth in it *nothing contrary to the word of God.*" Now, a position like this may not be, and is not, "contrary to the word of God," and yet need not be true; *e.g.* we may accept St. Clement's Epistle to the Corinthians, as containing nothing contrary to Scripture, nay, as altogether most scriptural, and yet this would not hinder us from rejecting the account of the Phoenix – as contrary to GOD's word, but to matter of fact.[156] Even the infallibility of the Roman see is not considered to extend to matters of fact or points of philosophy. Nay, we commonly do not consider that we need take the words of Scripture itself literally about the sun's standing still or the earth being fixed, or the firmament being above. Those at least who distinguish between what is theological in Scripture and what is scientific, and yet admit that Scripture is true, have no ground for wondering at such persons as subscribe to a paragraph, of which at the same time they disallow the philosophy; especially considering they expressly subscribe it only as not "contrary to the word of GOD." This then is what must be said first of all.

Next, the philosophical position is itself capable of a very specious defence. The truth is, we do not at all know what is meant by distance or intervals absolutely, any more than we know what is meant by absolute time. Late discoveries in geology have tended to make it probably that time may under circumstances go indefinitely faster or slower than it does at present; or in other words, that indefinitely more may be accomplished in a given portion of it.[157] What Moses calls a day,[158] geologists wish to prove to be thousands of years, if we measure time by the operations at present effected by it. It is equally difficult to determine what we mean by distance, or why we should not be at this moment closer to the throne of GOD, though we seem far from it. Our measure of distance is our hand or our foot; but as an object a foot off is not called distant, though an interval if indefinitely divisible; neither need it be distant either, after it has been multiplied indefinitely. Why should any conventual measure of ours – why should the perceptions of our eyes or our ears, be the standard of presence or distance? CHRIST may really be close to us, though in heaven, and His presence in the Sacrament may but be a manifestation the worshipper of that nearness, not a change of place, which may be unnecessary. But on this subject some extracts may be suitably made from a pamphlet published several years since, and admitting of one or two verbal corrections, which, as in the case of other similar quotations above, shall here be made without scruple:[159]

"In the note at the end of the Communion Service, it is argued, that a body cannot be in two places at once; and that therefore the Body of CHRIST is not *locally* present, in the sense in which we speak of the bread as being locally present. On the other hand, in the Communion Service itself, Catechism, Articles, and Homilies, it is plainly declared, that the Body of CHRIST is in a mysterious way, if not *locally,* yet *really* present, so that we are able after some ineffable manner to receive it. Whereas, then, the objection stands, 'CHRIST is not really here, because He is not locally here,' our formularies answer, 'He is really here, yet not locally.'

"But it may be asked, What is the meaning of saying that CHRIST is really present, yet not locally? I will make a suggestion on the subject. What do we mean by being *present*? How do we define and measure it? To a blind and deaf man, that only is present which he touches: give him hearing, and the range of things present enlarges; everything is present to him which he hears. Give him at length sight, and the sun may be said to be present to him in the daytime, and myriads of stars by night. The *presence,* then of a thing is a relative word, depending, in the popular sense of it, upon the channels of communication between it and him to whom it is present; and thus it is a word of degree.

"Such is the meaning of *presence*, when used of material objects; – very different from this is the conception we form of the presence of spirit with spirit. The most intimate presence we can fancy is a spiritual presence in the soul; it is nearer to us than any material object can possibly be; for our body, which is the organ of conveying to us the presence of matter, sets bounds to its approach towards us. If, then, spiritual beings can be brought near to us, (and that they can, we know, from what is told us of the influences of Divine grace, and again of evil angels upon our souls) their presence is something *sui generis*, of a more perfect and simple character than any presence we commonly call local. And further, their presence has nothing to do with the degrees of nearness; they are either present or not present, or, in other words, their coming is not measured by space, nor their absence ascertained by distance. In the case of things material, a transit through space is the necessary condition of approach and presence; but in things spiritual, (whatever be the condition) such a transit seems not to be a condition. The condition is unknown. Once more: while beings simply spiritual seem not to exist in space, the Incarnate Son does;

according to our Church's statement already alluded to that 'the natural body and blood of our SAVIOUR CHRIST are in heaven and not here, it being against the *truth* of CHRIST's natural body to be at one time *in more places than one.*"

"Such seems to be the mystery attending our LORD and SAVIOUR; He has a *body*, and that *spiritual*. He is in place; and yet, as being a spirit, His mode of approach – the mode in which He makes Himself present here or there – may be, for what we know, as different from the mode in which material bodies approach and come, as a spiritual presence is more perfect. As material bodies approach by moving from place to place, so the approach and presence of a spiritual body may be in some other way, – probably is in some other way, since in some other way, (as it would appear) not gradual, progressive, approximating, that is, locomotive, but at once, spirits become present, – may be such as to be consistent with His remaining on GOD's right hand while He becomes present here, – that is may be real, yet not local, or, in a word, is *mysterious*. The Body and Blood of CHRIST may be really, literally present in the holy Eucharist, yet not having become present by local passage, may still literally and really be on GOD's right hand; so that, though they be present in deed and truth, it may be impossible, it may be untrue to say, that they are literally *in* the elements, or *about* them, or *in* the soul of the receiver. These may be useful modes of speech according to the occasion; but the true determination of all such questions may be this, that CHRIST's Body and Blood are *locally* at GOD's right hand, *yet* really *present* here, present here, but not here in place, – because they are spirit.

"To assist our conceptions on this subject, I would recur to what I said just now about the presence of material objects, by way of putting my meaning in a different point of view. The presence of a material object, in the popular sense of the word, is a matter of degree, and ascertained by the means of apprehending it which belong to him to whom it is present. It is in some sense a correlative of the senses. A fly may be as near an edifice as a man; yet we do not call it present to the fly, because it cannot see it; and we call it present to the man, because he can. This, however, is but a popular view of the matter: when we consider it carefully, it certainly is difficult to say what is meant by the presence of a material object relatively to us. It is in some respects truer to say that a thing is present, which is so circumstanced as to act upon us and influence us, whether we are sensible of it or not. Now this is what the Catholic Church seems to hold concerning our LORD's Presence in the Sacrament, that He then personally and bodily is with us in the way an object is which we call present: how He is so, we know not, but that He should be so,[160] though He be millions of miles away, is not more inconceivable than the influence of eyesight upon us is to be blind man. The stars are millions of miles off, yet they impress ideas upon our souls through our sight. We know but of five senses: we know not whether or not human nature be capable of more; we know not whether or not the soul possesses anything analogous to them. We know nothing to negative the notion that the soul may be capable of having CHRIST present to it by the stimulating of dormant, or the development of possible energies.

"As sight for certain purposes annihilates space, so other unknown capacities, bodily or spiritual, may annihilate it for other purposes. Such a practical annihilation was involved in the appearance of CHRIST to St. Paul on his conversion. Such a practical annihilation is involved in the doctrine of CHRIST's ascension; to speak according to the ideas of space and time commonly received, what must have been the rapidity of that motion by which, within ten days, He placed our human nature at the right hand of GOD? Is it more mysterious that He should 'open the heavens,' to use the Scriptural phrase,[161] in the sacramental rite; that He should then dispense with time and space, in the sense in which they are daily dispensed with, in the sun's warming us at the distance of 100,000,000 of miles, than that He should have dispensed with them on occasion of His ascending on high? He who showed what the passage of an incorruptible body was ere it reached GOD's throne,[162] thereby suggests to us what may be its coming back and presence with us now, when at length glorified and become a spirit.

"In answer, then, to the problem, *how* CHRIST comes to us while remaining on high, I answer just as much as this, – that He comes by the agency of the HOLY GHOST, *in* and *by the Sacrament.* Locomotion is the means of a material presence; the Sacrament is the means of His spiritual Presence. As faith is the means of our receiving It, so the HOLY GHOST is the Agent and the Sacrament the means of His imparting It; and therefore we call It a Sacramental Presence. We kneel before His heavenly throne, and the distance is as nothing: it is as if that Throne were the Altar close to us.

"Let it be carefully observed, that I am not proving or determining anything; I am only showing how it is that certain propositions which at first sight seem contradictions in terms, are not so, – I am but pointing out *one* way of reconciling them. If there is but one way assignable, the force of all antecedent objection against the possibility of any at all is removed, and then of course there may be other ways supposable though not assignable. It seems at first sight a mere idle use of words to say that CHRIST is really and literally, yet not locally, present in the Sacrament; that He is there given to us, not in figure but in truth, and yet is still only on the right hand of GOD. I have wished to remove this seeming impossibility.

"If it be asked, *why* attempt to remove it, I answer that I have no wish to do so, if persons will not urge it against the Catholic doctrine. Men maintain it as an impossibility, a contradiction in terms, and force a believer in it to say why it should not be so accounted. And then when he gives a reason, they turn round and accuse him of subtleties, and refinements, and scholastic trifling. Let them but believe and act on the truth that the consecrated bread is CHRIST's body, as He says, and no officious comment on His words will be attempted by any well judging mind. But when they say 'this *cannot* be literally true, *because* it is impossible;' then they force those who think it is literally true to explain how, according to their notions, it is not impossible. And those who ask hard questions must put up with hard answers."[163]

There is nothing, then, in the Explanatory Paragraph which has given rise to these remarks, to interfere with the doctrine, elsewhere taught in our formularies, of a real super-local presence in the Holy Sacrament.

§9. *Masses.*

Article 31. – "The sacrifice (sacrificia) of Masses, in the which it was commonly said, that the priest did offer CHRIST for the quick and the dead, to have remission of pain or guilt, were blasphemous fables and dangerous deceits (perniciosae imposturae)."[164]

Nothing can show more clearly than this passage that the Articles are not written against the creed of the Roman Church, but against actual existing errors in it, whether taken into its system or not. Here the sacrifice of the *Mass* is not spoken of, in which the special question of doctrine would be introduced; but "the sacrifice of *Masses*," certain observances, for the most part private and solitary, which the writers of the Articles knew to have been in force in time past and saw before their eyes, and which involved certain opinions and a certain teaching. Accordingly the passage proceeds, "in which it *was commonly said;*" which surely is a strictly historical mode of speaking.

If any testimony is necessary in aid of what is so plain from the wording of the Article itself, it is found in the drift of the following passage from Burnet:

"It were easy from all the rituals of the ancients to shew, that they had none of those ideas that are now in the Roman Church. They had but one altar in a Church, and probably but one in a city: they had but one communion in a day at that altar: so far were they from the many altars in every church, and *the many masses* at every altar, that are now in the Roman Church. They did not know what *solitary masses* were, without a communion. All the liturgies and all the writings of the ancients are as express in this matter as is possible. The whole constitution of their worship and discipline shews it. Their worship always concluded with the Eucharist: such as were not capable of it, as the catechumens, and those who were doing public penance for their sins, assisted at the more general parts of the worship; and so much of it was called their mass, because they were dismissed at the conclusion of it. When that was done, then the faithful stayed, and did partake of the Eucharist; and at the conclusion of it, they were likewise dismissed, from whence it came to be called the mass of the faithful." *Burnet on the 31ˢᵗ Article,* p. 482.

These sacrifices are said to be "blasphemous fables and pernicious impostures." Now the "blasphemous fable" is the teaching that there is a sacrifice for sin other than CHRIST's death, and that masses are that sacrifice. And the "pernicious imposture" is the turning this belief into a means of filthy lucre.

1. That the "blasphemous fable" is the teaching that masses are sacrifices for sin distinct from the sacrifice of CHRIST's death, is plain from the first sentence of the Article. "The offering of CHRIST *once made,* is that perfect redemption, propitiation, and satisfaction for *all* the sins of the *whole world, both original and actual*. And *there is none other satisfaction* for sin, but *that alone. Wherefore* the sacrifice of masses, &c." It is observable too that the heading of the Article runs, "Of the one oblation of CHRIST finished upon the Cross," which interprets the *drift* of the statement contained in it about masses.

Our Communion Service shows it also, in which the

prayer of consecration commences pointedly with a declaration, which has the force of a protest, that CHRIST made on the cross, "by His *one* oblation of Himself *once* offered, a *full, perfect,* and *sufficient* sacrifice, oblation, and *satisfaction* for the sins of the whole world."

And again in the offering of the sacrifice: "We entirely desire thy fatherly goodness mercifully to accept our sacrifice of praise and thanksgiving, most humbly beseeching Thee to grant that *by the merits and death of Thy* SON JESUS CHRIST, and through faith in His blood, we and all Thy whole Church may obtain *remission of our sins* and all *other benefits* of His passion.

[And in the notice of the celebration: "I purpose, through God's assistance, to administer to all such as shall be religiously and devoutly disposed, the most comfortable Sacrament of the Body and Blood of CHRIST; to be by them received in remembrance of His meritorious Cross and Passion; *whereby alone* we obtain remission of our sins, and are made partakers of the kingdom of heaven."]

But the popular charge still urged against the Roman system, as introducing in the Mass a second or rather continually recurring atonement, is a sufficient illustration, without further quotations, of this part of the Article.

2. That the "blasphemous and pernicious imposture" is the turning the Mass into a gain, is plain from such passages as the following:

"With what earnestness, with what vehement zeal, did our SAVIOUR CHRIST drive the buyers and sellers out of the temple of GOD, and hurled down the tables of the changers of money, and the seats of the dove-sellers, and could not abide that a man should carry a vessel through the temple. He told them, that they had made His FATHER's house a den of thieves, partly through their superstition, hypocrisy, false worship, false doctrine, and insatiable covetousness, and partly through contempt, abusing that place with walking and talking, with worldly matters, without all fear of GOD, and due reverence to that place. What dens of thieves the Churches of England have been made by the *blasphemous buying and selling the most precious body and blood of* CHRIST *in the Mass,* as the world was made to believe, at dirges, at months minds, at trentalls,[165] in abbeys and chantries, besides other horrible abuses, (GOD's holy name be blessed for ever,) which we now see and understand. All these abominations they that supply the room of CHRIST have cleansed and purged the Churches of England of, taking away all such fulsomeness and filthiness, as through blind devotion and ignorance hath crept into the Church these many hundred years." – *On repairing and keeping clean of Churches,* pp. 229, 230.[166]

Other passages are as follows:

"Have not the Christians of late days, and even in our days also, in like manner provoked the displeasure and indignation of ALMIGHTY GOD; partly because they have profaned and defiled their Churches with heathenish and Jewish abuses, with images and idols, with numbers of altars, too superstitiously and intolerably abused, with gross abusing and filthy corrupting of the LORD's holy Supper, the blessed sacrament of His body and blood, with an infinite number of toys and trifles of their own devices, to make a goodly outward shew, and to deface the homely, simple, and sincere religion of CHRIST JESUS; partly they resort to the Church like hypocrites, full of all iniquity and sinful life, having a vain and dangerous fancy and persuasion, that if they come to the Church, besprinkle them with holy water, *hear a mass, and be blessed with a chalice,* though they understand not one word of the whole service, nor feel one motion of repentance in their heart, all is well, all is sure ?" *On the Place and Time of Prayer,* p. 293.

Again:

"What hath been the cause of this gross idolatry, but the ignorance hereof? What hath been the cause of this *mummish massing,*[167] but the ignorance hereof? Yes, what hath been, and what is at this day the cause of this want of love and charity, but the ignorance hereof? Let us therefore so travel to understand the LORD's Supper, that we be no cause of the decay of GOD's worship, of no idolatry, of no *dumb massing,* of no hate and malice; so may we the bolder have access thither to our comfort." *Homily concerning the Sacrament,* pp. 377, 378.

To the same purpose is the following passage from Bishop Bull's Sermons:

"It were easy to shew, how the whole frame of religion and doctrine of the Church of Rome, as it is distinguished from that Christianity which we hold in common with them, is evidently designed and contrived *to serve the interest and profit* of them that rule the Church, by the disservices, yea, and ruin of those souls that are under their government ... What can the doctrine of men's playing an after game[168] for their salvation in purgatory be designed for, but to enhance *the price of the priest's masses* and dirges for the dead? Why must a *solitary* mass, *bought for a piece of money,* performed and participated by a priest alone, in a private corner of a church, be, not only against the sense of Scripture and the Primitive Church, but also against common sense and grammar, called a Communion, and be accounted useful to him that buys it, though he never himself receive the sacrament, or but once a year, but for this reason, that there is *great gain,* but no godliness at all, in this doctrine?" *Bp. Bull's*[169] *Sermons,* p. 10.

And Burnet says,

"Without going far in tragical expressions, we cannot hold saying what our SAVIOUR said upon another occasion, 'My house is a house of prayer, but ye have made it a den of thieves.'[170] A trade was set up on this foundation. The world was made believe, that by the virtue of so many *masses, which were to be purchased by great endowments,* souls were redeemed out of purgatory, and scenes of visions and apparitions, sometimes of the tormented, and sometimes of the delivered souls, were published in all places: which had so wonderful an effect, that in two or three centuries, *endowments* increased to so vast a degree, that if the scandals of he clergy on the one hand, and the statutes of mortmain[171] on the other, had not restrained the profuseness that the world was wrought up to on this account, it is not easy to imagine how far this might have gone; perhaps to an entire subjecting of the temporality to the spirituality. The practices by which this was managed, and the effects that followed on it, we can call by no other name than downright *impostures*; worse than the making or vending false coin: when the world was drawn in by such arts to plain bargain, to *redeem* their own souls, and the souls of their ancestors and posterity, *so many masses were to be said*, and forfeitures were to follow upon their not being said: thus the *masses were really the price* of the lands." *On Article 22*, pp. 303, 304.

The Truth of these representations cannot be better shewn than by extracting the following passage from the Session 22 of the Council of Trent:

"Whereas many things appear to have crept in heretofore, whether by fault of the times or by neglect and wickedness of men, foreign to the dignity of so great a sacrifice, in order that it may regain its due honour and observance, to the glory of GOD and the edification of His faithful people, the Holy Council decrees, that the bishops, ordinaries of each place, diligently take care and be bound, to forbid and put an end to all those things, which either *avarice,* which is idolatry, or *irreverence*, which is scarcely separable from impiety, or *superstition*, the pretence of true piety, has introduced. And to say much in a few words, first of all, as to avarice, let them altogether forbid agreements, and bargains of *payment* of whatever kind, and *whatever is given for celebrating new masses;* moreover importunate and mean extortion, rather than petition of alms, and such like practices, which border on simoniacal sin, certainly on *filthy lucre* ... And let them banish from the church those musical practices, *when with the organ or with the chant anything lascivious or impure is mingled;* also all secular practices, vain and therefore profane conversations, promenading, bustle, clamour; so that the house of GOD may truly seem and be called the house of prayer. Lastly, lest any opening be given to superstition, let them provide by edict and punishments appointed, that the priests celebrate it at no other than the due hours, nor use rites or ceremonies and prayers in the celebration of masses, other than those which have been approved by the Church, and received on frequent and laudable use. And let them altogether remove form the Church *a set number of certain masses and candles*, which has proceeded rather from *superstitious observance* than from true religion, and teach the people in what it consists, and from whom, above all, proceeds the so precious and heavenly fruit of this most holy sacrifice. And let them admonish the same people to come frequently to their parish Churches, at least on Sundays and the greater feasts," &c.[172]

On the whole, then, it is conceived that the Article before us neither speaks against the Mass in itself, nor against its being [an offering, though commemorative][9] for the quick and the dead for the remission of sin; [(especially since the decree of Trent says, that "the fruits of the Bloody Oblation are through this most abundantly obtained; so far is the latter from detracting in any way from the former;")] but against its being viewed, on the one hand, as independent of or distinct from the Sacrifice on the Cross, which is blasphemy; and, on the other, its being directed to the emolument of those to whom it pertains to celebrate it, which is imposture in addition.

§10. *Marriage of Clergy.*

Article 32. – "Bishops, Priests, and Deacons, are not commanded by God's law, either to vow the estate of single life, or to abstain from marriage."

There is literally no subject for controversy in these words, since even the most determined advocates of the celibacy of the clergy admit their truth. [as far as clerical celibacy is a duty, it] is grounded not on GOD's law, but on the Church's rule, or on vow. No one, for instance, can question the vehement zeal of St. Jerome in behalf of this observance, yet

---

[9] "An offering for the quick," [i.e. the living], 1st Edition.

he makes the following admission, in his attack upon Jovinian:

"Jovinian says, 'You speak in vain, since the Apostle appointed Bishops and Presbyters, and Deacons, the husbands of one wife, and having children.' But, as the Apostle says, that he has not a precept concerning virgins, yet gives a counsel, as having received mercy of the Lord, and urges throughout that discourse, a preference of virginity to marriage, and *advises what he does not command,*[173] lest he seem to cast a snare, and to impose a burden too great for man's nature; *so also,* in ecclesiastical order, seeing that an infant Church was then forming out of the Gentiles, he gives the lighter precepts to recent converts, lest they should fail under them through fear." *Adv. Jovinian* 1.34[174]

And the Council of Trent merely lays down:

"If any shall say that clerks in holy orders, or regulars, who have solemnly professed chastity, can contract matrimony, and that the contract is valid *in spite of ecclesiastical law or vow,* let him be anathema." – Sess. 24, Can. 9.

Here the observance is placed simply upon rule of the Church or upon vow, neither of which exists in the English Church; "*therefore,*" as the Article logically proceeds, "it *is* lawful for them, as for all other Christian men, to marry *at their own discretion,* as they shall judge the same to serve better to godliness." Our Church leaves the discretion with the clergy; and most persons will allow that, *under our circumstances,* she acts wisely in doing so. That she has *power,* did she so choose, to take from them this discretion, and to oblige them either to marriage [(as is said to be the case as regards the parish priests of the Greek Church)] or to celibacy, would seem to be involved in the doctrine of the following extract from the Homilies; though, whether an enforcement either of the one or the other rule would be expedient and pious, is another matter. Speaking of fasting, the Homily says:

"GOD's Church ought not, neither may it, be so tied to that or any other order now made, or hereafter to be made and devised by the authority of man, but that *it may lawfully, for just causes, alter, change, or mitigate* those ecclesiastical decrees and orders, yea, *recede wholly from them, and break them,* when they tend either to superstition or to impiety; when they draw the people from GOD rather than work any edification in them. This authority CHRIST Himself used, and *left it to His Church.* He used it, I say, for the order or decree made by the elders for washing ofttimes, which was diligently observed of the Jews; yet tending to superstition our SAVIOUR CHRIST altered and changed the same in His Church into a profitable sacrament, the sacrament of our regeneration, or new birth. This authority to mitigate laws and decrees ecclesiastical, the Apostles practiced, when they, writing from Jerusalem unto the congregation that was at Antioch, signified unto them, that they would not lay an further burden upon them, but these necessaries: that is, 'that they should abstain from things offered unto idols, from blood, from that which is strangled, and from fornication;'[175] notwithstanding that Moses's law required many other observances. This authority to change the orders, decrees, and constitutions of the Church, was, after the Apostles' time, used of the fathers about the manner of fasting, as it appeareth in the Tripartite History[176] ... Thus ye have heard, good people, first, that Christian subjects are bound even in conscience to obey princes' laws, which are not repugnant to the laws of God. Ye have also heard that CHRIST's Church is not so bound to observe any order, law or decree made by man, to prescribe a form of religion, but that the Church hath full power and authority from GOD to change and alter the same, when need shall require; which hath been shewed you by the example of our SAVIOUR CHRIST, by the practice of the Apostles, and of the fathers since that time." *Homily on Fasting,* pp. 242–244.

To the same effect the 34th Article declares that,

"It is necessary that traditions and ceremonies be in all places one, and utterly like; for at all times there have been divers, and *may be changed* according to diversities of countries, times, and men's manners, so that nothing be ordained against GOD's Word. Whosoever, *through his private judgment,* willingly and purposely doth openly *break* the traditions and ceremonies of the Church, which be not repugnant to the Word of GOD, and be ordained and approved by common authority, ought to be rebuked openly."

§11. *The Homilies.*

Article 35. – "The second Book of Homilies doth contain a godly and wholesome doctrine, and necessary for these times, as doth the former Book of Homilies."

This Article has been treated in No. 82 of these Tracts,[177] in the course of an answer given to an opponent, who accused its author of not fairly receiving the Homilies, because he dissented from their doctrine, that the Bishop of Rome is Antichrist, and that regeneration was vouchsafed under the law. The passage of the Tract shall here be inserted, with some abridgement.

"I say plainly, then, I have not *subscribed* the Homilies, nor was it ever intended that any member of the English Church should be subjected to what, if considered as an extended confession, would indeed be a yoke of bondage. Romanism surely is innocent, compared with that system which should impose upon the conscience a thick octavo volume, written flowingly and freely by fallible men, to be received exactly, sentence by sentence: I cannot conceive any grosser instance of a pharisaical tradition than this would be.[178] No: such a proceeding would render it impossible (I would say), for any one member, lay or clerical, of the church to remain in it, who was subjected to such an ordeal. For instance; I do not

suppose that any reader would be satisfied with the political
reasons for fasting, though indirectly introduced, yet fully
admitted and dwelt upon in the Homily on the subject. He
would not like to subscribe the declaration that eating fish
was a duty, not only as being a kind of fasting, but as making
provision cheap, and encouraging the fisheries. He would
not like the association of religion with earthly politics.[179]

"How, then, are we bound to the Homilies? By the
Thirty-fifth Article, which speaks as follows: – 'The second
Book of Homilies ... doth *contain* a godly and wholesome
doctrine, and necessary for these times as doth the former *Book
of Homilies.*' Now, observe, this Article does not speak of
every statement made in them, but of the '*doctrine.*' It speaks
of the *view or cast or body of doctrine* contained in them. In spite
of ten thousand incidental propositions, as in any large book,
there is, it is obvious, a certain line of doctrine, which may
be contemplated continuously in its shape and direction.[180]
For instance; if you say you disapprove the doctrine
contained in the Tracts for the Times, no one supposed you
to mean that every sentence and half sentence is a lie. I say
then, that in like manner, when the Article speaks of the
doctrine of the Homilies, it does not measure the letter of
them by the inch, it does not imply that they contain no
propositions which admit of two opinions; but it speaks of a
certain determinate line of doctrine, and moreover adds, it is
'*necessary for these times.*' Does not *this,* too, show the same
thing? If a man said, the Tracts for the Times are *seasonable* at
this moment, as their title signifies, would he not speak of
them as taking a certain line, and bearing in a certain way?
Would he not be speaking, not of phrases or sentences, but
of a 'doctrine' in them tending one way, viewed as a whole?
Would he be inconsistent, if after praising them as seasonable, he continued, 'yet I do not pledge myself to every view
or sentiment; there are some things in them hard of
digestion, or overstated, or doubtful, or subtle?'

"If anything could add to the irrelevancy of the charge in question, it is the particular point in which it is urged that I dissent from the Homilies, – a question concerning the fulfillment of prophecy; viz., whether Papal Rome is Antichrist! An iron yoke indeed you would forge for the conscience, when you oblige us to assent, not only to all matters of *doctrine* which the Homilies contain, but even to their opinion concerning the fulfillment of prophecy. Why, *we* do not ascribe authority in such matters even to the unanimous consent of the fathers.

"I will put what I have been saying in a second point of view. The Homilies are subsidiary to the Articles; therefore they are of authority so far as they *bring out* the sense of the Articles, and are not of authority where they do not. For instance, they say that David, though unbaptized, was regenerated, as you have quoted. This statement cannot be of authority, because it not only does not agree, but it even disagrees, with the ninth Article,[181] which translates the Latin word 'renatis' by the English 'baptized.' But, observe, if this mode of viewing the Homilies be taken, as it fairly may, *you* suffer from it, for the Apocrypha, *being the subject of an Article*, the comment furnished in the Homily is binding on you, whereas you reject it.

"A further remark will bring us to the same point. Another test of acquiescence in the doctrine of the Homilies is this: – Take their table of contents; examine the headings; these surely, taken together, will give the substance of their teaching. Now I hold fully and heartily to the doctrine of the Homilies, under every one of these headings: the only points to which I should not accede, nor think myself called on the accede, would be certain matters, subordinate to the doctrines to which the headings refer – matters not of doctrine, but of opinion, as that Rome is the Antichrist; or of historical fact, as that there was a Pope Joan. But now, on the other hand can *you* subscribe the doctrine of the Homilies under every one of its formal headings? I believe you *cannot*. The Homily against Disobedience and Wilful Rebellion is,[182] in many of its elementary principles, decidedly uncongenial with your sentiments."

This illustration of the subject may be thought enough; yet it may be allowable to add from the Homilies a number or propositions and statements of more or less importance, which are too much forgotten at this day, and are decidedly opposed to the views of certain schools of religion, which at the present moment are so eager in claiming the Homilies to themselves. This is not done, as the extract already will show, with the intention of maintaining that they are one and all binding on the conscience of those who subscribe the Thirty-fifty Article; but since the strong language of the Homilies against the Bishop of Rome is often quoted, as if it were thus proved to be the doctrine of our Church, it may be as well to show that, following the same rule, we shall be also introducing Catholic doctrines, which indeed it far more belongs to a Church to profess than a certain view of prophecy, but which do not approve themselves to those who hold it. For instance, we read as follows:

1. "The great clerk and godly preacher, St. John Chrysostom." 1st Book, 1.1. And, in like manner, mention is made elsewhere of St. Augustine, St. Ambrose, St. Hilary, St. Basil, St. Cyprian, St. Hierome, St. Martin, Origen, Prosper, Ecumenius, Photius, Bernardus, Anselm, Didymus, Theophylactus, Tertullian, Athanasius, Lactantius, Cyrillus, Epiphanius, Gregory, Irenaeus, Clemens, Rabanus, Isidorus, Eusebius, Justinus Martyr, Optatus, Eusebius Emissenus, and Bede.

2. "Infants, being baptized, and dying in their infancy, are by this Sacrifice washed from their sins ... and they, which in act or deed do sin after this baptism, when the turn to GOD unfeignedly, they are *likewise* washed by this Sacrifice," &c. 1st Book of Homilies, 3.1. *init.*

3. "Our office is, not to pass the time of this present life unfruitfully and idly after we are *baptized or justified*," &c. 1 B, 3.3.

4. "By holy promises we be made lively members of CHRIST, receiving the sacrament of Baptism. By like holy promises *the sacrament of Matrimony* knitteth man and wife in perpetual love." 1 B, 7.1.

5. "Let us learn also here [in the Book of Wisdom,] by *the infallible and undeceivable Word of* GOD, that, &c. 1 B, 10.1.

6. "The due receiving of His blessed Body and Blood, *under the form* of bread and wine." *Note at end of* B 1.

7. "In the Primitive Church, *which was most holy and godly* ... open offenders were not suffered once to enter into the house of the LORD ... until they had done open penance ... but this was practiced, not only upon mean persons, but also upon the *rich, noble, and mighty persons,* yea upon Theodosius, *that puissant and mighty Emperor,* whom ... St. Ambrose ... did ... excommunicate."[183]. 2nd Book, 1.2.

8. "Open offenders were not ... admitted to common prayer, and the use of the holy *sacraments*." *Ibid.*

9. Let us amend this our negligence and contempt in coming to the house of the LORD; and resorting diligently together, let us there ... celebrating also reverently the LORD's holy *sacraments,* serve the LORD in His holy house." – *Ibid.,* 5.

10. "Contrary to the ... most manifest doctrine of the Scriptures, and contrary to the usage of the Primitive Church, *which was most pure and uncorrupt,* and contrary to the sentences and judgments of the *most ancient, learned, and godly* doctors of the Church." 2 B, 2.1. *init.*

11. "This truth ... was believed and taught by the *old holy fathers,* and *most ancient learned doctors* of the old Primitive Church, *which was most uncorrupt and pure.*" 2 B, 2.2. *init.*

12. "Athanasius, a very ancient, holy and learned bishop and doctor." *Ibid.*

13. "Cyrillus, an old and holy doctor." *Ibid.*

14. "Epiphanius, Bishop of Salamine, in Cyprus, a very holy and learned man." *Ibid.*

15. "To whose (Epiphanius's) judgment you have ... all the learned and godly bishops and clerks, yea, and the whole Church of that age," [the Nicene] "and so upward to our SAVIOUR CHRIST's time, by the space of about four hundred years, consenting and agreeing." *Ibid.*

16. "Epiphanius, a bishop and doctor of such antiquity, holiness and authority." *Ibid.*

17. "St. Augustine, the best learned of all ancient doctors." *Ibid.*

18. "That ye may know why and when, and by whom images were first used privately, and afterwards not only received into Christian churches and temples, but, in seclusion, worshipped also; and how the same was gainsaid, resisted, and forbidden, as well by *godly bishops and learned doctors,* as also by sundry Christian princes, I will briefly collect," &c. [The bishops and doctors which follow are:] "St. Jerome, Serenus, Gregory, the Fathers of the Council of Eliberis."[184]

19. "Constantine, Bishop of Rome, assembled a Council of bishops of the West, and did condemn Philippicus, the *Emperor,* and John, Bishop of Constantinople, of the *heresy of the Monothelites,* not without a cause indeed, but *very justly.*" *Ibid.*[185]

20. "Those six Councils *which were allowed and received of all men.*" *Ibid.*[186]

21. "There were no images publicly by the space of almost *seven hundred years.* And there is *no doubt* but the Primitive Church, next the Apostles' times, was *most pure.*" *Ibid.*

22. "Let us beseech GOD that we, being *warned* by His holy Word ... and by *the writings of old godly doctors* and ecclesiastical histories," &c. *Ibid.*

23. "It shall be declared, both by GOD's Word, and the

sentences of the ancient doctors, and *judgment* of the Primitive Church," &c. 2 B, 2.3.

24. "Saints, whose souls *reign* in joy with GOD." *Ibid.*

25. "That the law of GOD is likewise to be *understood* against all our images ... appeareth further by the *judgment* of the doctors and the Primitive Church." *Ibid.*

26. "The Primitive Church, *which is specially to be followed, as most incorrupt and pure." *Ibid.*

27. "Thus it is declared by GOD's Word, the *sentences* of the doctors and the *judgment* of the Primitive Church." *Ibid.*

28. "The rude[187] people, who specially, as the *Scripture* teacheth, are in danger of superstition and idolatry; viz. Wisdom 13.14." *Ibid.*

29. "They [the 'learned and holy bishops and doctors of the Church' of the eight first centuries] were the preaching bishops ... And as they were most zealous and diligent, so were they of excellent learning and godliness of life, and by both of great authority and credit with the people." *Ibid.*

30. "The most virtuous and best learned, the most diligent also, and in number almost infinite, ancient fathers, bishops, and doctors ... could do nothing against images and idolatry." *Ibid.*

31. "As the *Word of* GOD testifieth, Wisdom 14." *Ibid.*

32. "The Saints, *now reigning in heaven with* GOD." *Ibid.*

33. The *fountain of our regeneration is there* [in GOD's house] presented unto us." 2 B, 3.

36. "Somewhat shall now be spoken of one particular *good work*, whose commendation is both in the Law and in the Gospel [fasting]." 2 B, 4.1.

37. "If any man shall say ... we are not now under the yoke of the Law, we are set at liberty by the freedom of the Gospel: therefore these rites and customs of the old law bind not us, except it can be showed by the Scriptures of the New Testament, or by examples of the same, that fasting, now under the Gospel, is a *restraint of meat, drink, and all bodily food*

and pleasures from the body, as before: first that we ought to fast, is a *truth more manifest, then it should here need to be proved* … Fasting, even by CHRIST's assent, is a withholding meat, drink, and all natural food from the body," &c. *Ibid.*

38. "That it [fasting] was used in the Primitive Church, appeareth most evidently by the Chalcedon council, one of the *first four general councils.* The fathers assembled there … decreed in that council, that every person, as well in his private as public fast, should continue all the day without meat and drink, till after the evening prayer … This Canon teacheth how fasting was used in the *Primitive* Church." *Ibid.* [The Council was AD 452.]

39. "Fasting, then, by the *decree* of those 630 fathers, *grounding* their determinations in this matter upon the sacred Scriptures … is a withholding of meat, drink, and all natural food from the body, for the determined time of fasting." *Ibid.*

40. "The order or decree made by the elders for washing ofttimes, tending to superstition, our SAVIOUR CHRIST altered and changed the same in His Church, into a profitable sacrament, the sacrament of our *regeneration* or *new birth.*" 2 B, 4.2.

41. "Fasting thus used with prayer is of *great efficacy,* and *weigheth much* with GOD, so the angel Raphael told Tobias."[188] *Ibid.*

42. "As he" [St. Augustine] "witnesseth in another place, the martyrs and holy men in times past, were wont after their death to be *remembered* and *named* of the priest at divine service; but never to be invocated or called upon." 2 B, 7.2.

43. "Thus you see the *authority both* of Scripture and *also* of Augustine, doth not admit that we should pray to them." *Ibid.*

44. "To temples have the *Christians* customably used to resort from time to time as to most meet places, where they might … receive His holy *sacraments* ministered unto them duly and purely." 2 B, 8.1.

45. "The which thing both Christ and His apostles, *with all the rest of the holy fathers* do sufficiently declare so." *Ibid.*

46. "Our godly *predecessors,* and the *ancient* fathers of the Primitive Church, spared not their goods to build churches." *Ibid.*

47. "If we show ourselves true Christians, if we will be followers of Christ our Master, and of those *godly fathers* that have lived before us, and now have received the reward of true and faithful Christians," &c. *Ibid.*

48. "We must ... come unto the material churches and temples to pray ... whereby we may reconcile ourselves to God, be partakers of His holy *sacraments,* and be devout hears of His holy Word," &c. *Ibid.*

49. "It [ordination] lacks the promise of remission of sin, as all *other* sacraments as Baptism and Communion are." 2 *Hom.* 9.

50. "Thus we are taught, both by the Scriptures and ancient doctors, that," &c. *Ibid.*

51. "The holy apostles and disciples of Christ ... the godly fathers also, that were both *before* and *since* Christ *endued without doubt with the* Holy Ghost, ... they both do most earnestly exhort us, &c ... that we should remember the poor ... St. Paul crieth unto us after this sort[189] ... Isaiah the Prophet teaches us on this wise[190] ... *And the holy father Tobit* giveth this counsel.[191] And *the learned and godly doctor Chrysostom* giveth this admonition[192] ... But what mean these often admonitions and earnest exhortations of the prophets, apostles, fathers, and holy doctors?" 2 B, 11.1.

52. "The holy fathers, Job and Tobit." *Ibid.*

53. "Christ, whose especial *favour* we may be assured by *this means* to *obtain,"* [viz. by almsgiving] 2 B 11.2.

54. "Now will I ... show unto you how *profitable* it is for us to exercise them [alms deeds] ... [Christ's saying] serveth to ... prick us forwards ... to learn ... *how* we may *recover* our health, if it be lost or impaired, and how it may be

defended and maintained if we have it. Yea, He teacheth us also therefore to esteem that as a *precious medicine* and an *inestimable jewel*, that hath such *a precious medicine* and an *inestimable jewel,* that hath such *strength and virtue* in it, that can either *procure* or preserve so incomparable a treasure." *Ibid.*

55. "Then He and His disciples were grievously accused of the Pharisees ... because they went to meat and washed not their hands before,[193] ... CHRIST, answering their *superstitious* complaint, teacheth them an especial *remedy* how to *keep clean* their souls ... Give alms," &c. *Ibid.*

56. "Merciful alms-dealing *is profitable to purge* the soul from the *infection and filthy spots of sin.*" *Ibid.*

57. "The same lesson *doth the* HOLY GHOST *teach* in sundry places of the *Scripture, saying,* 'Mercifulness and alms-giving,' &c. [Tobit 4] ... The wise preacher, the son of Sirach, confirmeth the same, when he says, that 'as water quencheth burning fire,' " &c.[194] *Ibid.*

58. "A great *confidence* may they have *before the high* GOD, that show mercy and compassion to them that are afflicted." *Ibid.*

59. "If ye have by any infirmity or weakness been touched or annoyed with them ... straightaway shall mercifulness *wipe and wash away, as salves and remedies* to heal their *sores and grievous diseases.*" *Ibid.*

60. "And therefore that *holy father* Cyprian[195] admonisheth to consider how *wholesome* and *profitable* it is to relieve the needy, &c. ... by *the which* we may *purge our sins* and *heal our wounded souls.*" *Ibid.*

61. "We therefore *washed* in our baptism from the *filthiness of sin,* that we should live afterwards in the pureness of life." 2 B, 13.1.

62. "By these means [by love, compassion, &c.] shall we *move* GOD *to be merciful to our sins.*" *Ibid.*

63. " 'He was dead,' saith St. Paul, 'for our sins, and rose

again for our *justification*' ... He died to destroy the rule of the devil in us, and He rose again to send down His HOLY SPIRIT *to rule in our hearts,* to [endow] us with *perfect righteousness.*" 2 B, 14.

64. "The *ancient Catholic fathers,*" [in marg.] Irenaeus, Ignatius, Dionysius, Origen, Optatus, Cyprian, Athanasius ... "were not afraid to call this supper, some of them, *the salve of immortality and sovereign preservative against death;* other, the sweet dainties of our SAVIOUR, the pledge of eternal health, the defence of faith, the hope of the resurrection; other, the *food of immortality,* the healthful grace, and the conservatory to everlasting life." 2 B, 15.1.

65. "The meat we seek in this supper is spiritual food, the nourishment of our soul. a heavenly refection, and not earthly; an *invisible meat,* and not bodily, a *ghostly substance*, and not carnal. *Ibid.*

66. "Take this lesson ... of Emissenus,[196] a godly father, that ... thou *look up* with faith upon the *holy body and blood of thy* GOD, thou marvel with reverence, thou *touch* it with thy mind, thou receive it with the hand of thy heart, and thou take it fully with thy inward man." *Ibid.*

67. "The saying of the holy martyr of GOD, St Cyprian." 2 B, 20.3.

Thus we see the authority of the fathers, of the first six councils, and of the judgments of the Church generally, the holiness of the Primitive Church, the inspiration of the Apocrypha, the sacramental character of Marriage, and other ordinances, the Real Presence in the Eucharist, the Church's power of excommunication kings, the profitableness of fasting, the propitiatory value of good works, the Eucharistic commemoration, and justification by a righteousness [within us],[10] are taught in the Homilies. Let it be said again, it is not here asserted that a subscription to all and every of these

[10] "By inherent righteousness," 1*st Edition.*

quotations is involved in the subscription of an Article which does but generally approve the Homilies: but they who insist so strongly on our Church's holding out that the Bishop of Rome is Antichrist because the Homilies declare it, should recollect that there are other doctrines contained in them beside it, which they [themselves] should be understood to hold, before their argument has the force of consistency.

§12. *The Bishop of Rome.*

Article 38. – "The Bishop of Rome hath no jurisdiction in this realm of England."

By "hath" is meant "ought to have," as the Article in the 36th Canon and the Oath of Supremacy[197] show, in which the same doctrine is drawn out more at length. "No foreign prince, person, *prelate,* state, or potentate, hath, *or ought to have,* any jurisdiction, power, superiority, preeminence, or authority, ecclesiastical or spiritual, within this realm."

This is the profession which everyone must in consistency make, who does not join the Roman Church. If the Bishop of Rome has jurisdiction and authority here, why do we not acknowledge it, and submit to him? To say then the above words, is nothing more or less to say, "I am not a Roman Catholic;" and whatever reasons there are against saying them, are do far reasons against remaining in the English Church. They are a mere enunciation of the principle of Anglicanism.

Anglicans maintain that the supremacy of the Pope is not directly from revelation, but an event in Providence. All things may be undone by the agents and causes by which they are done. What revelation gives, revelation takes away; what Providence give, Providence takes away. GOD ordained by miracle, He reversed by miracle, the Jewish election; He promoted in the way of Providence, and He cast down by the same way, the Roman empire. "The powers that be, are ordained of GOD,"[198] *while* they be, they cease to have a claim. They cease to be, when GOD removes them. He may be considered to remove them when He undoes what He had done. The Jewish election did not cease to be, when the Jews went into captivity: this was an event in Providence; and what miracle had ordained, it was miracle that annulled. But the Roman power ceased to be when the barbarians overthrew it; for it rose by the sword, and it therefore perished by the sword. The Gospel Ministry began in CHRIST and His Apostles; and what they began, they only can end. The Papacy began in the exertions and passions of man; and what man can make, man can destroy. Its jurisdiction, while it lasted, was "ordained of GOD;" when it ceased to be, it ceased to claim our obedience; and it ceased to be at the Reformation. The Reformers, who could not destroy a Ministry, which the Apostles began, could destroy a Dominion which the Popes founded.

Perhaps the following passage will throw additional light upon this point: –

"The Anglican view of the Church has ever been this: that its portions need not otherwise have been united together for their essential completeness, than as being descended from one original. They are like a number of colonies sent out from a mother country ... Each Church is independent of all the rest, and is to act on the principle of what may be called Episcopal independence, except, indeed, so far as the civil power unites any number of them together ... Each diocese is a perfect independent Church, sufficient for itself; and the communion of Christians one with another, and the unity of them altogether, lie, not in mutual understanding, intercourse, and combination, not in what they do in common but in what they are and have in common, in their possession of the Succession, their Episcopal form, their Apostolical faith, and the use of the Sacraments ... Mutual intercourse is but an *accident* of the Church, not of its essence ...

Intercommunion is a duty, as other duties, but is not the tenure or instrument of the communion between the unseen world and this; and much more the confederacy of sees and churches, the metropolitan, patriarchal and papal systems, are matters of expedience or of natural duty, from long custom, or of propriety from gratitude and reverence, or of necessity from voluntary oaths and engagements, or of ecclesiastical force from the canons of Councils, but not necessary in order to the conveyance of grace, or for fulfillment of the ceremonial law, as it may be called, of unity. Bishop is superior to bishop only in rank, not in real power; and the Bishop of Rome, the head of the Catholic world, is not the centre of unity, except as having a primacy of order. Accordingly, even granting for argument's sake, that the English Church violated a duty in the 16th century, in releasing itself from the Roman supremacy, still it did not thereby commit that special sin, which cuts off from it the fountains of grace, and is called schism. It was essentially complete without Rome, and naturally independent of it; it had, in the course of years, whether by usurpation or not, come under the supremacy of Rome; and now, whether by rebellion or not, it is free from it: and as it did not enter into the Church invisible by joining Rome, so it was not cast out of it by breaking from Rome. These were accidents in its history, involving, indeed, sin in individuals, but not affecting the Church as a Church.

"Accordingly, the Oath of Supremacy declares 'that no foreign prelate hath or ought to have any jurisdiction, power, preeminence, or authority within this realm.' In other words, there is nothing in the Apostolic system which gives an authority to the Pope over the Church, such as it does not give to a Bishop. It is altogether an ecclesiastical arrangement; not a point *de fide*, but of expedience, custom, or piety, which cannot be claimed as if the Pope *ought* to have it, any more than, on the other hand, the King could of Divine right claim the supremacy; the claim of both one and the other resting, not on duty or revelation, but on specific engagement. We find ourselves, as a Church, under the King now, and we obey him; we were under the Pope formerly, and we obeyed him. 'Ought' does not in any degree, come into the question."[199]

Conclusion

One remark may be made in conclusion. It may be objected that the tenor of the above explanation is anti-Protestant, whereas it is notorious that the Articles were drawn up by Protestants, and intended for the establishment of Protestantism; accordingly, that it is an evasion of their meaning to give them any other than a Protestant drift, possible as it may be to do so grammatically, or in each separate part.

But the answer is simple:

1. In the first place, it is a *duty* which we owe both to the Catholic Church and to our own, to take our reformed confessions in the most Catholic sense they will admit; we have no duties toward their framers. [Nor do we receive the Articles from their original framers, but from several successive convocations after their time; in the last instance, from that of 1662.[200]

2. In giving the Articles a Catholic interpretation, we bring them into harmony with the Book of Common Prayer, an object of the most serious moment in those who have given their assent to both formularies.

3. Whatever be the authority of the [Declaration] prefixed to the Articles,[201] so far as it has any weight at all, it sanctions the mode of interpreting them above given. For its injoining the "literal and grammatical sense," relieves us from the necessity of making the known opinions of their framers a comment upon their text; and its forbidding any person to "affix any *new sense* to any Article," was promulgated at a

time when the leading me of our Church were especially noted for those Catholic views which have been here advocated.

4. It may be remarked, moreover, that such an interpretation is in accordance with the well known general leading of Melanchthon,[202] from whose writings our Articles are principally drawn and whose Catholic tendencies gained for him that same reproach of popery, which has ever been so freely bestowed upon members of our own reformed Church.

"Melanchthon was of opinion," says Mosheim, "that, for the sake of peace and concord many things might be given up and tolerated in the Church of Rome, which Luther considered could by no means be endured ... In the class of matters indifferent, his great man and his associates placed many things which had appeared of the highest importance to Luther, and could not of consequence be considered indifferent to his true disciples. For he regarded as such, the doctrine of justification by faith alone; the necessity of good works to eternal salvation; the number of the sacraments; the jurisdiction claimed by the Pope and the Bishops; extreme unction; the observation of certain religious festivals, and several superstitious rites and ceremonies." *Cent.* 16. §3, part 2.27, 28.[203]

5. Further: the Articles are evidently framed on the principle of leaving open large questions, on which the controversy hinges. They state broadly extreme truths, and are silent about their adjustment. For instance, they say that all necessary faith must be proved from Scripture, but do not say *who* is to prove it. They say that the Church has authority in controversies, they do not say *what* authority. They say that it may enforce nothing beyond Scripture, but do not say *where* the remedy lies when it does. They say that works *before* grace *and* justification are acceptable, but they do not speak at all of works *with* GOD's aid, *before* justification. They say that men are lawfully called and sent to minister and preach, who are chosen and called by men who have public authority *given* them in the congregation to call and send; but they do

not add *by whom* the authority is to be given. They say that councils called *by princes* may err; they do not determine whether councils called *in the name of* CHRIST will err.

[6. The variety of doctrinal views contained in the Homilies, as above shown, views which cannot be brought under Protestantism itself, in its widest comprehension of opinions, is an additional proof, considering the connexion of the Articles with the Homilies, that the Articles are not framed on the principle of excluding those who prefer the theology of the early ages to that of the Reformation; or rather since both Homilies and Articles appeal to the Fathers and Catholic antiquity, let it be considered whether, in interpreting them by these, we are not going to the very authority to which they profess to submit themselves.]

7. Lastly, their framers constructed them in such a way as best to comprehend those who did not go so far in Protestantism as themselves. Anglo-Catholics then are but the successors and representatives of those moderate reformers; and their case has been directly anticipated in the wording of the Articles. It follows that they are not perverting, they are using them, for an express purpose for which among others their authors framed them. The interpretation they take was intended to be admissible; though not that which their authors took themselves. Had it not been provided for, possibly the Articles never would have been accepted by our Church at all. If, then, their framers have gained their side of the compact in effecting the reception of the Articles, let Catholics have theirs too in retaining their own Catholic interpretation of them.

An illustration of this occurs in the history of the 28th Article. In the beginning of Elizabeth's reign a paragraph formed part of it, much like that which is now appended to the Communion Service, but in which the Real Presence was *denied in words*. It was adopted by the clergy at the first convocation, but not published. Burnet observes on it thus:—

"When these Articles were first prepared by the convocation in Queen Elizabeth's reign, this paragraph was made a part of them; for the original subscription by both houses of Convocation, yet extant, shows this. But the *design of the government* was at that time much turned *to the drawing over the body of the nation to the Reformation,* in whom the old leaven had gone deep: and no part of it deeper than the belief of the corporal presence of CHRIST in the Sacrament; therefore it was *thought not expedient to offend* them by so particular a definition in this matter; in which the very word Real Presence was rejected. It might, perhaps, be also suggested, that here a definition was made that went too much upon the principles of natural philosophy; though it was a part of the Article that was subscribed, yet it was not published, but the paragraph that follows, The Body of CHRIST, &c. was put in its stead, and was received and published by the next convocation; which upon the matter was a full explanation of the way of CHRIST's presence in this Sacrament; that 'He is present in a heavenly and spiritual manner, and that faith is the mean by which He is received.' This seemed to be more theological; and it does indeed amount to the same thing. But howsoever we see what was the sense of the first convocation in Queen Elizabeth's reign, it differed in nothing from that in King Edward's time; and therefore though this paragraph is now no part of our Articles, yet we are certain that the clergy at that time did not at all doubt of the truth of it; we are sure it was their opinion; since they subscribed it, though *they did not think fit* to publish it at first; and though it was afterwards changed for another, that was the same in sense." *Burnet on Article 28,* p. 416.

What has lately taken place in the political world will afford an illustration in point. A French minister, desirous of war, nevertheless, as a matter of policy, draws up his state papers in such moderate language, that his successor, who is for peace, can act up to them, without compromising his own principles.[204] The world, observing this, has considered it a circumstance for congratulation; as if the former minister, who acted a double part, had been caught in his own snare. It is neither decorous, nor necessary, nor altogether fair, to urge the parallel rigidly; but it will explain what it is here meant to convey. The Protestant Confession was drawn up with the purpose of including Catholics; and Catholics now will not be excluded. What was an economy[205] in the reformers, is a protection to us. What would have been a perplexity to us then, is a perplexity to Protestants now. We could not then have found fault with their words; they cannot now repudiate our meaning.

OXFORD,
The Feast of the Conversion of St Paul, 1841.

EDITOR'S NOTES

Notes for Tract 1:
[1] Gen. 42:1.

[2] 2 Cor. 11:28.

[3] 2 Tim. 1:13; 1 Tim. 6:20.

[4] Isa. 30:10.

[5] John 1:13.

[6] The Form and Manner of Making of Deacons (BCP).

[7] The Ordering of Priests (BCP).

[8] 2 Tim. 1:6.

[9] Matt. 12:30.

Notes for Tract 2:
[1] John 18:36.

[2] Jas. 2:4.

[3] Ezek. 33:6: "a solemn duty of the Church under certain circumstances", see Tr. 41. Cf. Newman's letter to *The Record*, 11 November 1833, LD 4, pp. 94–96.

[4] John 18:36.

[5] The Irish Church Temporalities Bill proposed the extinction of 2 out of the 4 archbishoprics and 8 out of 8 bishoprics. It was carried in August 1833. An Act of 1836 proposed the suppression of Sodor and Man diocese. It was repealed by a Bill of 1838.

[6] Newman preached in July 1828 that Christ "left his Apostles ... to preach, to write, to make converts and form them into a well arranged society." MS Sermon 171, July 1828. Cf. also MS Sermon 323 preached in December 1831.

[7] John Pearson (1613–1686) became bishop of Chester in 1673. His *Exposition of the Creed* was published in 1659.

[8] Acts 4:12.

[9] 1 Tim. 6:14; 4:14.

[10] Reference perhaps to Chidiock Tichborne's (1558–1586) *Elegy*.

[11] The Root & Branch Bill & Petition was introduced in 1641 for the abolition of episcopacy by the Puritans with Cromwell's support.

Notes for Tract 3:
[1] "They would eviscerate the Prayer-Book, reduce the Articles to a deistic formulary ... These notions are widely spread." William Palmer, *A Narrative of Events ...,* (1843), p. 29. Cf. also Appendix to Tract 4 with reference to Canon 36. The *title* is mentioned in Matt. 5:18.

[2] The book of 1549 included the Prayer of Consecration and the Prayer of Oblation, based upon the Sarum Missal.

[3] Psalms which invoke God's vengeance: Pss. 58, 68, 69, 109, 137.

[4] This refers to Aesop's fable of the Miller, his son and the ass. The moral is that you cannot satisfy everyone.

[5] The priest rehearses all the Ten Commandments, the people responding, "Lord, have mercy upon us, and incline our hearts to keep this law." (BCP)

[6] "Dearly beloved in the Lord, ye that mind to come to the holy Communion of the Body and Blood of our Saviour Christ, must consider how Saint Paul exhorteth all persons diligently to try and examine themselves ..." (BCP)

[7] "... We acknowledge and bewail our manifold sins and wickedness, which we, from time to time, most grievously have committed, by thought, word and deed ..." (BCP)

[8] Newman later talks of *the unseen state*; but cf. Tract 79, *On Purgatory*.

[9] Newman deals with the question of "improving the mind" in *The Tamworth Reading Room* (DA, pp. 254ff.).

[10] The Athanasian Creed replaced the Apostles' Creed on thirteen holy-days.

[11] A reference to the Reform Bill of 1832. "The true principles of Churchmanship seem so radically decayed . . ." (Apo, p. 30).

[12] Matt. 10:29.

[13] Matt. 13:25.

[14] Newman was faced with the problem. He declined to marry an unbaptized Miss Jubber at St Mary's. LD 4, pp. 288–93. Both Miss Jubbers subsequently asked for baptism. LD 5, p. 126.

Notes for Tract 6:
[1] *Article 22*: On Purgatory (BCP).

[2] Exo. 23:14; Deut. 16:16.

[3] Jer. 34:13–14; Neh. 10:32; 2 Chr. 36:20–21; 2 Kg. 19:20–30.

[4] Luke 1:6.

[5] Cf. 2 Tim. 1:6.

[6] Rev. 2:5.

[7] Joseph Bingham, country rector (1668–1723), author of *Origines Ecclesiasticae* or *The Antiquities of the Christian Church* (10 vols, 1708–1722).

[8] Luke 12:47.

[9] Matt. 24:12.

Notes for Tract 7:
[1] Refers to Richard Hooker (1554–1600), *Treatise on the Laws of Ecclesiastical Polity* (1594ff.) which was a justification of episcopacy.

[2] Matt. 28:20.

Notes for Tract 8:
[1] Acts 2:42.

[2] 1 Cor. 11:24.

[3] Matt. 19:14–16.

[4] Gen. 2:2.

[5] Deut. 14:22; 1 Cor. 9:7.

[6] Matt. 21:30.

Notes for Tract 10:
[1] 28 October. In 1833 it was a Monday. Newman preached on the feast day in 1834 *On Christian Zeal*, PPS II, pp. 379–402.

[2] John 15:17–27 (BCP).

[3] John 15:24.

[4] John 15:18–21.

[5] Luke 10:16.

[6] Heb. 11:1.

[7] 1 Pet. 2:25.

[8] One who goes to meetings, i.e. a Dissenter (OED).

[9] 30 August 1833. LD 4, p. 33.

[10] A General Thanksgiving (BCP).

[11] Thirty-one bishops voted against the Reform Bill in October 1831. Archbishop Howley was called Judas and mobbed; the Bishops of Exeter and Winchester were burned in effigy outside their homes; Bishop Gray's Palace at Bristol was burned to the ground.

[12] Luke 21:19.

Notes for Tract 11:
[1] Newman preached sermon 184 in February 1829 : "Beware, on the other of supposing faith is a mere feeling."

[2] Evangelicals believe in 'renewal and sanctification by the Holy Spirit' as part of the process of conversion cf. Matt. 7:8.

[3] Compare Newman's remarks about Dr. Achilli in *Prepos,* LD 14, Appendix 3, p. 501–3.

[4] 1 John 3:7.

[5] Matt. 5:19.

[6] Newman summarizes the tenets of Evangelical belief.

[7] Cf. PPS 3.17, *The Visible Church, An Encouragement to Faith.*

[8] "Two only, as generally necessary to salvation, that is to say, Baptism, and the Supper of the Lord." (BCP).

[9] "I appeal to you, brethren, by the name of our Lord Jesus Christ, that all of you agree and that there be no dissensions [schisms] among you, but that you be united in the same mind and the same judgment." (1 Cor. 1:10). Cf. also Irenaeus, *Adversus Haereses* 4,33,7.

[10] ". . . received into Christ's holy Church, and be made a lively member of the same" (BCP).

[11] "The Christian Church is like a company or corporation", Newman, MS Sermon 157, p. 3.

[12] Matt. 18:20.

[13] "It is not lawful for any man to take upon himself the office of publick preaching, or ministering the Sacraments in the Congregation . . ." (*Article 23,* BCP).

[14] Matt. 5:19.

[15] The burden of proof.

Notes for Tract 15:
[1] Newman credited Revd William James for teaching him the doctrine, Apo, p. 10.

[2] John 20:22.

[3] Matt. 28:20.

[4] 2 Tim. 4:2: "... be unfailing in patience and in teaching."

[5] In his first *Essay on Miracles*, Newman states, "There was no Age of Miracles, after which miracles ceased; that there have been at all times true miracles and false miracles, true accounts and false accounts." *Mir,* p. 100.

[6] 2 Tim. 4:3: "For the time is coming when people will not endure sound teaching, but having itching ears they will accumulate for themselves teachers to suit their own likings, and will turn away from listening to the truth and wander into myths."

[7] Convocation prorogued 1717. "Not a real and existing power", Newman to Keble, LD 8, p. 411.

[8] The Act of Parliament (25 Hen VIII, c.19) incorporated The Submission of Clergy of 1532, whereby they promised not to make new canons without royal licence.

[9] "Rome was the natural mediator between Alexandria and Antioch, and at that time possessed extensive influence among the Churches of the West." *Ari,* p. 285.

[10] DEC I, pp. 68–9.

[11] Ibid., pp. 8–9. Pentapolis, the five cities, part of the Roman province of Cyrenaica in modern Libya. Council of Milevis, 416. Pope Zosimus (417); Pope Celestine I (422–433). The relations with North Africa were fraught. Celestine reconciled the priest Apiarius who had been previously reconciled by Zosimus and had recanted. This gave the African bishops the chance to insist on their legitimate autonomy.

[12] Council of Milevis (Milev) in 402, presided over by Aurelius, Bishop of Carthage.

[13] 1 Cor. 7:20.

[14] The Creed of Pope Pius IV, in which every Roman Priest professes and promises to maintain all the errors of Popery, was only imposed *after* the Council of Trent. Cf. Apo, p. 79. [Newman's note in a different edition.]

[15] Hence Newman's opposition to the project of a Jerusalem Bishopric in which England and Prussia were to nominate in turn with the bishop ordaining German ministers who subscribed to the Confession of Augsburg. The Act became law in October 1841.

[16] Newman in his *Retractation of Anti-Catholic Statements* says of this Tract, "The words are often mine, though I cannot claim it as a whole." VM 2, p. 429. (The Tract was written by William Palmer but revised and completed by Newman.)

Notes for Tract 19:

[1] Joseph Butler (1692–1752) Bishop of Durham and author of *Analogy of Religion* (1736). Newman in his *Apologia* writes, "Butler teaches us that probability is the guide of life." Apo, p. 19, and cf. GA, p. 496ff.

[2] 1 Cor. 1:18,20,25.

[3] Matt. 25:25.

[4] Heb. 12:16.

[5] Ps. 78:9.

[6] Matt. 23:23.

Notes for Tract 20:

[1] 2 Cor. 6:14. "Our subtle Enemy has so contrived, that by affixing to this blessed truth the stigma of Popery, numbers among us are effectually deterred from profiting by a gracious provision." Cf. Appendix 1, 2.

[2] In 1834 Newman preached, "Thus a man is at once thrown out of himself, by the very voice which speaks within him … He looks out of himself for that Living Word to which he may attribute what has echoed in his heart." PPS 2, p. 18.

[3] Bishop Hobart of New York met Newman and Rose in 1824 (LD 1, p. 173). 1834 saw the consecration of James Otey who would order the words 'First Bishop of the Catholic Church in Tennessee' to be inscribed on his tombstone.

[4] Newman preached in 1828, "Such is their calm worship, the foretaste of heaven, who for a season shut themselves out from the world, and seek Him in invisible Presence, whom they shall hereafter see face to face." PPS 7, p. 159.

[5] The 1830s saw the beginning of the Irvingites, Adventists, Mormons and Plymouth Brethren.

[6] *Since you are such, would that you would be with us.* Newman refers to these "often-quoted words" in his essay on William Palmer's *View of Faith and Unity.* Ess 1, p. 217.

[7] Gen. 19:22. Zoar was Lot's place of refuge after leaving Sodom.

[8] Luke 16:8.

Notes for Tract 21:
[1] Heb. 11:37, 38.

[2] The Day of Atonement (Lev 23:27.29). Josaphat and Ezra proclaimed fasts (2 Chr. 20:3; Ezra 8:21) and 'ceremonial' fasts appear in Jer. 36:9; 1 Kings 21:9–12; Joel 1:14; Jonah 3:5.

[3] Both Nazirites and Rechabites abstained from wine.

[4] Num. 11:5.

[5] Deut. 18:15.

[6] Newman omits Matt. 9:15.

Notes for Tract 31:
[1] George Herbert (1593–1633). The poem was published posthumously in *The Temple.* Herbert was a poet and rector of Fugglestone with Bemerton near Salisbury.

[2] The Church of Ephesus is blamed because "thou hast left thy first love." Rev 2:4.

[3] Sanballat and Geshem opposed Nehemiah (Neh. 6:2ff)

[4] 2 Cor. 3:3.

[5] The child of the wife of Phineas, 1 Sam. 4:21.

[6] "He did not say this of his own accord, but being high priest that year he prophesied ..." (John 11:51).

[7] Palestine was governed in the 3rd century BC by the Greek dynasty of the Ptolemies whose capital was Alexandria.

[8] The name of the dynasty founded by Seleucus I, Nicator c.312 BC. Antiochus Epiphanes succeeded his brother, Seleucus IV, in 187 BC. This is the background to the Books of Maccabees.

[9] The Commonwealth under Oliver Cromwell.

[10] Benjamin Hoadly (1676–1761) became Bishop of Bangor in 1716. He preached a sermon in 1717 before George I on 'The Nature of the Kingdom of Christ' which argued that the Gospels did not provide any argument for a visible Church authority. He held that the Lord's Supper was purely a memorial.

[11] John Keble, *The Christian Year.*

[12] Luke 1:11.

Notes for Tract 33:
[1] A bishop of a country district in full Episcopal orders who could only ordain to minor orders.

[2] The Emperor Valens decided to divide Cappadocia in AD 371, making Podandus (at the food of Mount Taurus) the chief city. Basil intervened and Tyana was substituted but the province was divided.

[3] Newman wrote a pamphlet in 1835, *The Restoration of Suffragan Bishops,* cf. VM 2, pp. 51–92.

[4] Joseph Bingham (1668–1723) author of *Origines Ecclesiasticae; The Antiquities of the Christian Church* (1708–1722).

[5] Naples has at present 12 suffragan sees.

[6] Archdeacons since 1662 must be in priest's orders. They examine candidates for ordination.

[7] Thomas Cranmer (1489–1556) succeeded Warham as Archbishop of Canterbury in 1532.

[8] Gilbert Burnet (1643–1715) Bishop of Salisbury author of *History of the Reformation* (1679–).

[9] Thomas Cromwell (1485–1540), Vicar General in 1535. He arranged for the dissolution of the monasteries between 1536 and 1539 and ordered a bible should be kept in every Church.

[10] He proposed a plan for synodical government in 1647.

[11] Council of Nicea (325).

[12] *Antiquities of the Christian Church* (10 vols, 1708–1722).

[13] Gregory Nazianzen (329–389), Suffragan to his father, about St Basil of Caesarea (330–379).

[14] Robert Henry Henley, *A Plan for Church Reform* (1833).

Notes for Tract 34:
[1] 1 Cor. 11:16.

[2] 1 Cor. 11:1.

[3] 1 Cor. 11:22.

[4] 1 Cor. 14:16.

[5] From the twelfth century the chalice was withdrawn from the laity.

[6] "Hear us, O merciful Father, we most humbly beseech thee; and grant that we receiving these thy creatures of bread and wine according to thy Son our Saviour Jesus Christ's holy institution, in remembrance of his death and passion, may be partakers of his most blessed Body and Blood ..."

[7] "By nature, the children of wrath ..." (Eph. 2:3).

[8] "... Out of his heart will flow rivers of living water.' Now this he said about the Spirit, which those who believed in him were to receive." (John 7:38–39).

[9] Quintus Septimius Florens Tertullian (160–c. 225) wrote De Corona (The Crown) in 211. It concerns the problems of a Christian in military service.

[10] The *Disciplina Arcani* or practice of concealing certain truths from catechumens and pagans. This would be treated fully in Tract 80 *On*

Reserve in Communicating Religious Knowledge. It would cause the Evangelicals to distance themselves from the Tracts. Cf. Robin Selby, *The Principle of Reserve in the Writings of J H Newman*. Oxford, 1975, pp. 67–75.

[11] St Basil (330–379), Bishop of Caesarea wrote his treatise on the Holy Spirit in 375.

[12] Christians of the Orient, claiming the authority of St. Philip and St. John celebrated Easter on 17th Nisan, no matter on what day of the week it fell.

Notes for Tract 38:

[1] Published in a revised version, 1877 in VM 2, pp. 21–34.

[2] *Laicus/Clericus* = Layman/Clergyman.

[3] "But to *us*, probability is the very guide of life." Joseph Butler, *Analogy of Religion* (Intro.).

[4] More extreme Protestants who advocated Presbyterian policies and were among the 'seditious sectaries' of Archbishop Whitgift's Act of 1583.

[5] In 1560, the Reformed Church of Scotland was established on Presbyterian lines.

[6] Nine Bishops and 400 Clergy refused to take the Oath of Allegiance and Supremacy in 1688.

[7] Hoadley (or Hoadly) became Bishop of Bangor in 1716. Socinianism (from Lelio Sozini and Fausto Sozzini in the 16th century) resembles Arianism and declared that the Bible could be interpreted by human reason alone.

[8] "All priests and Deacons are to say daily the Morning and Evening Prayer either privately or openly". *Concerning the Service of the Church.* (BCP).

[9] "And in Cathedral and Collegiate Churches, and Colleges where there are many Priests and Deacons, they shall all receive the Communion with the Priest every Sunday at the least" (BCP).

[10] Saints' days to be observed. *Tables & Rules* (BCP).

[11] Vigils, Fasts and Days of Abstinence. Ibid.

[12] "And I by his authority committed to me, I absolve thee from all thy sins, in the Name of the Father, and of the Son, and of the Holy Ghost" (BCP).

[13] "Receive the Holy Ghost for the Office and Work of a Priest in the Church of God, now committed unto thee by the Imposition of our hands. Whose sins thou dost forgive, they are forgiven; and whose sins thou dost retain, they are retained." (BCP).

[14] To be said on major Holy Days and certain feast days at Morning Prayer.

[15] On Ash Wednesday (Denouncing of God's anger and judgments against sinners).

[16] In the Holy Communion "to accept our alms and *oblations*." (BCP).

[17] Newman wrote in 1825, "I think, I am not certain, I must give up the doctrine of imputed righteousness and that of regeneration as apart from baptism." Early Journal 2, AW, p. 203.

[18] 1 & 2 Esdras, Tobit, Judith, Rest of Esther, Wisdom, Ecclesiasticus, Baruch, Parts of Daniel, Prayer of Manasses, 1 & 2 Maccabees.

[19] The consecratory prayer, the oblatory words, the Invocation of the Holy Spirit. Cf. Ess 1, p. 339.

[20] Martin Bucer (1491–1551), the successor to Zwingli in 1531. He came to England at Cranmer's invitation and was made Regius Professor of Divinity at Cambridge in 1548.

[21] Term already used by George Herbert and Bishop Simon Patrick.

[22] The Lutheran Confession of Faith was presented to the Diet in 1530.

[23] At the Synod of Chanforans, in 1532, which accepted Predestination.

[24] John Calvin (1509–1564).

[25] The Wesleyan Methodists are the original and continuing foundation of John Wesley.

[26] The quotation on the Lord's Supper is from *The Institutes of Christian Religion*.

[27] Article VI.

[28] The Decrees of 1564, known as the Creed of Pius IV.

[29] Acts 20:27.

[30] Thomas Cartwright (1535–1603). A learned Puritan and one-time Lady Margaret Professor of Divinity at Cambridge. He championed the cause of Presbyterianism for the Puritan cause.

[31] William Pitt the Elder, Earl of Chatham, on 19 May 1772, in the House of Lords.

[32] This section is omitted from VM 2. Newman later added, "How mistaken we may ourselves be on many points that are only gradually opening to us." VM 2, p. 431.

[33] Bishop Joseph Hall (1574–1656). His book was published posthumously with the sub-heading: "The true state of the difference betwixt the Reformed and Roman Church, and the blame for this schism is cast upon the True Authors."

[34] The Council of Trent declared in its Canon 28 on Justification, "If anyone says that the justified man sins when he performs good works with a view to an eternal reward, *anathema sit*."

[35] Article 31.

[36] Article 22.

Notes for Tract 41:
[1] Newman reprinted it, with some word changes and additional notes, in VM 2, pp. 35–48.

[2] Article 33.

[3] A proposal to admit Dissenters to parliament in 1834.

[4] Baptism and the Eucharist.

[5] Naaman's reply to Elisha in 2 Kings 5:12.

[6] Believers' Baptism or Credobaptists.

[7] The Society of Friends consider both as 'shadows'.

[8] Article 6 *Of the Sufficiency of the holy Scriptures for salvation.*

[9] Erastianism (after Thomas Erastus, 1524–83) proposed the supreme importance of the State even in Church matters. Latitudinarianism or broad Churchmanship was the forerunner of liberalism.

[10] George III attended concerts in Gloucester Cathedral in 1743 and Worcester Cathedral in 1788.

[11] Meeting of parishioners, often in the vestry, to conduct parochial business.

[12] In his *Principles of Church Reform* (1833), Dr. Thomas Arnold put forward this suggestion.

[13] Newman would preach in February 1843, "Creeds and dogmas live in the one idea which they are designed to express, and which alone is substantive; and are necessary only because the human mind cannot reflect upon that idea, except piecemeal." US, p. 331.

[14] Convocation was prorogued by Royal writ in 1717 to prevent the condemnation of Bishop Hoadley's views expressed in a sermon on 'The Nature of the Kingdom or Church of Christ'.

[15] The arts used by ambitious or worldly priests to further their own interests. (OED).

[16] Devotion to the Sacred Heart of Jesus, a Roman Catholic devotion dating from 1674.

[17] Heb. 11:1.

[18] Cf. The instructions to the Seventy, "Remain in the same house . . ." Luke 10:7.

[19] The Commination Service was for use on Ash Wednesday. The quotation is from Is. 53:5.

[20] Matt. 11:30.

[21] Gal. 3:10.

[22] *Justification by faith* is the article on which the *Church stands or falls*. Cf. Luther, *Lecture on Galatians, Introduction* (1535).

[23] Psalms which call on God to avenge: Pss 58; 68:21–23; 69:23–29; 109: 5–19; 137:7–9).

[24] "He that hath clean hands and a pure heart," Ps. 24:4. "For thy lovingkindness is before mine eyes; and I have walked in thy truth," Ps. 26:3. "They also do no iniquity, they walk in his ways," Ps. 119:3.

[25] "Truly God is good to Israel, even to such as are of a clean heart," Ps. 73:1.

[26] Richard Hooker (1554–1600), Anglican divine. In his *Treatise on the Laws of Ecclesiastical Polity* (1594ff.). Puritan objections to the Book of Common Prayer formed part of the *Millenary Petition* presented in April 1603 to King James on his journey to London from Scotland, asking to be relieved from their "common burden of human rites and ceremonies."

Notes for Tract 45:
[1] The 1830 second French revolution led to the formation of radical parties in all Cantons, and eventually the formation of the Swiss Confederation.

[2] Elijah on Mount Horeb (1 Kings 19:12).

[3] The parable of the rich man and Lazarus (Luke 16:21).

[4] Acts 16:14, 34; 1 Cor. 1:16.

[5] Matt. 19:14.

[6] Mark 8:12.

[7] Cf. Tracts 1, 4, 7, 10, 11, 15, 17, 19, 24, 33.

[8] James 3:5.

Notes for Tract 47:
[1] George Canning (1770–1827) said to the House of Commons in 1801, "Away with the cant of 'Measures not men'! — the idle supposition that it is the harness and not the horses that draw the chariot along."

[2] After Jacobus Arminius (1560–1609), a Dutch divine who adopted a

more liberal approach to Calvinism, having doubted the teaching on Predestination.

[3] Presbyterian.

[4] Bramhall in *A Just Vindication* . . . (1654) (OED).

[5] Matt. 11:21.

[6] Cf. "For unto whomsoever much is given, of him shall be much required."(Luke 12:48).

[7] Mark 12:42.

[8] 1 Kings 19:18.

[9] John 4:22.

[10] Luke 19:20.

[11] Luke 4:26, 27.

[12] Rom. 11:20.

[13] "Many of you are weak and sickly" (1 Cor. 11:30).

[14] Is. 55:8.

[15] Rom. 3:4.

Notes for Tract 71:
[1] An amended version with notes is reprinted in VM 2, pp. 93–143.

[2] *Macbeth,* Act 3. Scene 4.

[3] It is estimated that, by 1839, there were about 700,000 Roman Catholics; of these, fewer than 200,000 were English (Rosemary Hill, *God's Architect,* London, 2008, p. 206).

[4] She [Rome] is considered too absurd to be inquired into, and too corrupt to be defended, and too dangerous to be treated with equity and fair dealing." *Prepos,* p. 11.

[5] G. M. Trevelyan notes, after 1829, "The Roman Catholic community went on increasing in numbers and influence" (*English Social History*, London, 1948, p. 521). Newman would mention "the solemn captivating services of Rome" in his Advertisement, cf. Appendix 1, 2 (2nd volume).

[6] 1 Cor. 7:20.

[7] The Society of Friends and Baptists believe in a spiritual baptism or baptism of conscious believers. The Puritans and, later, the Congregationalists maintained that their churches should be independent of the State.

[8] Henry Hammond (1605–1660) Anglican divine, defended episcopacy at the Conference of Uxbridge, in 1645 but was deprived under the Commonwealth; Richard Hooker (1554–1600), see earlier note.

[9] Thomas Ken (1637–1711), Bishop of Bath and Wells, one of the nine Bishops who refused the oath to William and was deposed from his see.

[10] "Bind us by *bands* of love," Hos. 11:4. Newman's own preferred variation.

[11] Onesimus (in the Letter to Philemon, v. 10).

[12] "As thou didst send me into the world, so I have sent them into the world. And for their sake I consecrate myself, that they also may be consecrated in truth." (John 17:19; cf. also 16:12).

[13] Exo. 32:7ff.

[14] Acts 17:28.

[15] Article 6: "Holy Scripture containeth all things necessary to salvation: so that whatsoever is not read thereby, is not required of any man, that it should be believed as an Article of the Faith."

[16] Newman will later cite *A Lecture on Popery delivered by the Rev. Dr Cooke*: "And now I charge the Romish system as being Anti-Christ because the Pope takes the very name of God." *Prepos,* ([Millennium Edition, Gracewing], Leominster, 2000), p. 448n.

[17] Act of Supremacy, 1558. Cf. also Article 37, *Of the Civil Magistrates.*

[18] The labourers in the vineyard (Matt. 20:12).

[19] Heb. 12:28.

[20] Edward Stillingfleet (1639–1699), advocated a union between Episcopalians and Presbyterians. He was the author of *The Doctrine of the Trinity and Transubstantiation compared as to Scripture and Tradition,* in 1687. The term transubstantiation, he argued, 'contradicts sense.'

[21] Article 30, *Of both kinds.*

[22] John 6:53.

[23] Baptists practice baptism by immersion.

[24] The Council of Trent decreed 'That ministers need the intention of *at least doing what the Church does,'* Canon 11 on Baptism. An unbeliever can consecrate validly.

[25] The Council of Trent states the obligation of confessing in Session 14 c. 5 and also that 'all mortal sins of which penitents after a diligent self-examination are conscious must be recounted by them in confession.'

[26] 1 Cor. 11:29.

[27] An over dramatic presentation, which does not take into account the element of obstinacy needed to justify such a harsh judgment. Canon 751: "Heresy is the *obstinate* denial or obstinate doubt after the reception of baptism of some truth which is to be believed by divine and Catholic faith." The Roman Church's power to grant indulgences is in Trent: Decree 1 in Session 25.

[28] The *Catechism of the Catholic Church* quotes St John Chrysostom: "If Job's sons were purified by their father's sacrifice, why would we doubt that our offerings for the dead bring them some consolation? Let us not hesitate to help those who have died and to offer our prayers for them." (*Hom. In 1 Cor. 41,5*). Newman adds that those who die in invincible ignorance are not lost but are either in purgatory or in heaven. *Via Media II,* p. 110 n. 6.

[29] Austin (or Augustine) states, "It is certain that these, being purified before the day of judgment ... are not to be given over to eternal fire," *City of God,* Book 21, ch. 24. Cf. Tract 79, On Purgatory: "These Fathers do not teach Purgatory, they do not teach any one view at all."

[30] Rev. 14:13: "... and their works do follow them."

[31] 1 Tim. 2:5.

[32] John Bunyan, *Works*, Vol. I, p. 130, *The Work of Jesus Christ as Advocate.*

[33] Rev. 19:10; 22:8.9.

[34] "Let no one disqualify you, insisting on self-abasement and worship of angels." (Col. 2:18).

[35] The papal *Absolution* of Gregory XVI [Bartolomeo Cappellari] (1830–1846).

[36] "That due honour and reverence is owed to them, not because some divinity or power is believe to reside in them ... but because the honour showed to them is referred to the original which they represent: thus ... we give adoration to Christ and veneration to the saints, whose likeness they bear." Session 25 (December 1563).

[37] John 11:51.

[38] Benjamin Hoadley [or Hoadly] (1676–1761), Bishop of Bangor in 1716, Hereford in 1721, Salisbury in 1723, and Winchester in 1734. His views were broad Church.

[39] Session 25 of the Council of Trent, *Decree on Purgatory* (during the pontificate of Pius IV, 1559–1565).

[40] *Of one substance with the Father,* as distinct from the Arian *homoiousion* (of *like* substance).

[41] Council of Ariminum (Rimini) in 359 dominated by the Semi-Arians. The orthodox bishops were persuaded to subscribe to *homoiousion.* Cf. Ari, pp. 344ff.

[42] Cf. Matt. 22:13.

[43] Profession of Faith of Pius IV (1564).

[44] Matt. 18:7; Rom. 14:13.

[45] William Wake (1657–1737), Archbishop of Canterbury. He negotiated with representatives of Gallicanism between 1717–1720.

[46] Jacques Bénigne Bossuet (1627–1704), Bishop of Meaux, drew up the Four Gallican Articles.

[47] Jean Crasset, SJ (1618–1692), author of *La Grande Vie de Notre Seigneur Jésus* (1686).

[48] 'without formal notice being taken'.

[49] Albertus Magnus [Albert the Great] (1200–1280), Dominican philosopher and theologian. However a Decree of Inquisition, 28 February 1875 "warned and reprehended (those who by such language) have not conformed to the right Catholic sense (but) ascribe power to her (the Blessed Virgin) as issuing from her divine maternity, beyond its due limits ... although she has the greatest influence with her Son, still it cannot be piously affirmed that she exercises command over Him."VM 2, p. 129 n. 1.

[50] The brown scapular of the Carmelites consists of two strips of cloth joined across the shoulders. The promises given for wearers of the scapular derive from a private vision to St. Simon Stock, the superior general of the Order in 1251 and another to Pope John XXII (1316–1334).

[51] Those enrolled in the Third Order of Carmelites or Tertiaries.

[52] Matt. 18:7–10.

[53] Francois Véron (1575–1649) was a Jesuit controversialist. His *Regle de la Foi Catholique* (1647) was translated into English and was praised by Leibnitz.

[54] *Exposition de la Doctrine Catholique* (1672).

[55] Henri de la Tour d'Auverge, Vicomte de Turenne (1611–1675) was made Marshal-general in 1661 and defeated Conde. He became a Catholic in 1668.

[56] Innocent XI (1676–1689) saw the Holy Office issue decrees against moral errors, and condemn the views of Molinos. The Holy Office would condemn Jansenism in the following pontificate.

[57] Gallicanism tended to limit the authority of the Pope in relation to the Bishops and to subordinate the rights of the Church to the power of the State.

[58] Newman maybe has in mind J. N Darby (1800–1882). His brother, Francis, joined the Plymouth brethren in 1830 as a missionary to Persia. Also Edward Irving (1792–1834) whose followers founded the Catholic

Apostolic Church and gave him a subordinate role. Cf. Private Judgement Ess. 2, p. 340.

[59] Roberto Francesco Romolo Bellarmino (1542–1621), his *Disputatio de Controversiis* (1586–93).

[60] Newman adds: "Bellarmine says that the Eight General Council (869–70) and Pope Hadrian II say that *latria* is *not* to be paid to the Cross but only reverence, because blest.VM 2, pp. 126–7.

[61] "If anyone says that the sacrifice of the Mass is merely an offering of praise and thanksgiving, or that it is a simple commemoration of the sacrifice accomplished on the cross, but not a propitiatory sacrifice ... anathema sit." 22nd Session, Canon 3, On the Eucharist.

[62] Bishop James Warren Doyle (1786–1834) of Kildare and Leighlin. He gave evidence in 1825, 1830 and 1832. He was the leader of the non-violent wing of resistance in the Tithe War.

[63] John Gother, (d. 1704) priest, author of *A Papist Misrepresented and Represented*.

[64] Richard Challoner (1691–1781), Vicar Apostolic of London district in 1758 and author of *Garden of the Soul* (1740).

[65] John Jewel (1522–1571) Bishop of Salisbury carried on a long dispute with Thomas Harding (1516–1572) who defended the papacy.

[66] St Bernard (1090–1153), Abbot of Clairvaux. Dante's "faithful servant ..."

[67] Peter Damiani or Damian (1007–1072), Benedictine reformer and Cardinal Bishop of Ostia. He makes the comparison between the Blessed Virgin Mary and Queen Esther.

[68] This section (until the paragraph which begins 'Enough perhaps . . .' is omitted in VM 2.

[69] Trent teaches attrition is Session 14, ch. 4, *On Penance*. It also states that it does "prepare for grace" (Canon 5) and joined to the Sacrament of Penance, forgiveness is obtained.

[70] Pietro Sforza Pallavicino (1607–1667), Jesuit Cardinal who answered Sarpi's work by *Istoria del Concilio di Trento* (1656–7).

[71] The Catechism was issued three years after the close of the Council, in 1566.

[72] Literally '*of faith*'. A classification deriving from the fact that it has been solemnly defined or taught by the ordinary teaching authority as binding on conscience.

[73] Article 26, *Of the Unworthiness of the Ministers, which hinders not the effect of the Sacrament.*

[74] Article 19, *Of the Church.*

[75] 'proves the rule'.

[76] The Western Church holds the doctrine that the Holy Ghost proceeds from the Father and the Son – the double procession; while Eastern theologians, arguing for a single fount of Godhead, maintain that the Holy Ghost proceeds from the Father through the Son.

[77] Acts 20:27.

[78] Used by St Cyprian (d.258), *De Unitate Ecclesiae* of the Church, 'hoc unitatis sacramentum', the sacrament or sign of unity.

[79] Thomas Ken (1637–1711), Bishop of Bath and Wells and one of the nine nonjuring bishops who refused to decline to take the oath to William III.

[80] The Ten Articles adopted by Convocation in 1536.

[81] Gilbert Burnett (1643–1715), Bishop of Salisbury and author of *The History of the Reformation in England* (1679–1714).

[82] Martin Bucer (1491–1551), Successor to Zwingli, came to England in 1548 and was made Regius Professor at Cambridge and advisor to Thomas Cranmer.

[83] Fausto of Riez (408–490), *De Spiritu Sancto* I, 2, ML 62,71.

[84] Lancelot Andrewes (1555–1629), Bishop of Winchester, author of *Preces Privatae.*

[85] Anabaptist views on Scripture, ordination and infant baptism. The Swiss reformers view the Sacraments as signs of grace independently received.

[86] Nicholas Ridley (1500–1555), Bishop of London, assisted in compiling the Book of Common Prayer in 1549. He gradually came to reject the Real Presence but was initially very circumspect.

[87] Bucer (qv). His views influenced the Ordinal of 1550.

[88] "We are accounted righteous before God, only for the merit of our Lord and Saviour Jesus Christ by Faith, and not for our own works or deservings: Wherefore, that we are justified by Faith only is a most wholesome Doctrine, and very full of comfort, as more largely is expressed in the Homily of Justification."

[89] The view that Christians are freed by grace from the obligations of any moral law.

[90] A service to commemorate the frustration of the Gunpowder Plot of 5 November 1605 was added to the Book of Common Prayer in 1605. It was amended when William III landed at Torbay on 5 November 1688 and was finally revoked in 1859.

[91] John Tillotson (1630–1694), Archbishop of Canterbury, had latitudinarian views, wishing to exclude the Athanasian Creed and held Zwinglian views on the Eucharist. His life by T. Birch was written in 3 volumes in 1752.

[92] Forces hostile to the veneration of icons, from c. 725 to 842, and the Council called by Charlemagne in 794. It condemned the worship of icons which the Second Council of Nicea had approved in 787.

[93] Henry Hammond (1605–1660), Anglican divine.

[94] Jeremy Taylor (1613–1667), Bishop of Down and Connor, author of *The Rule and Exercise of Holy Living* (1650).

Notes for Tract 73:
[1] Reprinted in Ess 1, pp. 30–101, with amendments and notes.

[2] Thomas Erskine (1788–1870) Scots Episcopalian, author of *Remarks on the Internal Evidence for the Truth of Revealed Religion* (1820) and *Essay on Faith* (1822).

[3] Jacob Abbott (1803–1879), American Congregational minister and author of *The Corner-Stone, A Familiar Illustration of the Principles of Christian Truth*. Boston (1835).

[4] Newman recasts this in Ess. 1. The text continues with "When the rich Lord ..."

[5] 2 Kings 7:2.

[6] 2 Kings 5:12.

[7] John 3:4, "How can a man be born when he is old?"

[8] John 6:52.

[9] John 20:24; Gen. 3:6.

[10] Josh. 10:12–14, "for the sun stood still and the moon stayed ..."

[11] Matt. 22:29, in answer to the question, "To which of the seven will she be wife ...?"

[12] Newman recasts this section down to "... of things or realities."

[13] David Hume (1711–1776), Scottish philosopher and economist has been called the first true phenomenalist, dissolving material objects into sense data. His works include *A Treatise of Human Nature* (1739). Newman records his reactions to Hume's works in Apo, p. 3.

[14] Heb. 10:13–14.

[15] 1 Pet. 10–13.

[16] *The Edinburgh Review*, No. CXXIII (1835). The article is a book review of Biela's *Comet* by Sir J. F. W. Herschel.

[17] Ps.19:1.

[18] Rev. 1:19. The Royal Astronomical Society was founded in 1820.

[19] Newman puts at the end '(abridged)'. See *The Tamworth Reading Room* on a study of astronomy where "the god we attain is our own mind", p. 301.

[20] Descartes argued that space was filled with matter in various forms whirling around the sun.

[21] This section was recast. Newman preaches in May 1836 on *The*

Mysteriousness of our Present Being, "Mysteries in religion are measured by the proud according to their own comprehension, by the humble according to the power of God." PPS 4, p. 283.

[22] In June 1829, Newman preached on *The Christian Mysteries,* "We detect in Revelation this remarkable principle, which is not openly propounded, *that religious light is intellectual darkness.* As if our gracious Lord had said to us, 'Scripture does not *aim* at making mysteries, but they are as shadows brought out by the Sun of Truth.' " PPS 1, p. 211.

[23] George Campbell (1719–1796), Scottish Professor of Divinity. He published *The Four Gospels* in 1789.

[24] Matt. 13:11.

[25] Luke 8:17.

[26] Rom. 16:25.

[27] "Many prophets and righteous men have longed to see what you see . . ." Matt. 13:17.

[28] "Now when they heard of the resurrection of the dead, some mocked; but others said, 'We will hear you again about this.' " Acts 17:32.

[29] Eph. 5:32.

[30] Eph 3:6, "That the Gentiles should be fellow-heirs, and of the same body. . ." Cf. infra.

[31] 1 Cor. 1:23, "We preach Christ crucified, a stumbling block to Jews and folly to Gentiles."

[32] Eph. 3:6.

[33] Jeremy Taylor (1613–1667), Bishop of Down and Connor, and devotional writer.

[34] Newman preached in August 1836 on *Elisha, a Type of Christ,* "Never then, my brethren, come to Church, or to Holy Communion, never be present at a baptism, marriage, or burial, or at any other rite, without feeling that there is a great deal more there than you see . . . *Angels are among us, and are powerful to do any thing. And they do wonders for the believing* . . ." SD, p. 179.

[35] Heb. 12:23.

[36] 2 Cor. 12:2.

[37] "And he slew some of the men of Bethshemesh, because they looked into the ark of the Lord." 1 Sam. 6:19.

[38] Cf. Newman's 'Elucidations of Dr Hampden's Theological Statement, 1836'. Henceforth Elu. "It means nothing but the simple history of Christ's mercy," p. 23.

[39] There were changes made between these two texts and Ess. 1.

[40] Ezek. 10:11ff.

[41] The end of all ends (*The Nicomachean Ethics,* 1.7).

[42] John 11:52.

[43] Dan. 9:24.

[44] Joseph Butler 1692–1752), Bishop of Durham, author of *Analogy of Religion* (1736). (This passage is taken from Part 2 ch. 4.)

[45] Newman omits the next passages until, "The author says . . .".

[46] "I will turn aside and see this great sight why this bush is not burnt . . ." Exo. 3:3.

[47] Newman recasts the following paragraphs to "That I am not unfair."

[48] Equivalent to Unitarianism: "All doctrine is a matter of opinion, whether a man believes in the Divinity of Christ or not." Elu., p. 11.

[49] The heresy named after Sabellius of Pentapolis, also called Monarchism, taught that God was one person only: The Word *is God, manifested in Creation* (flourished from 3rd to 5th century.)

[50] John 14:26, "But the Comforter, which is the Holy Ghost, whom the Father will send . . ."

[51] 2 Tim. 1:13.

[52] Jude 3, "That ye should earnestly contend for the faith which was once delivered to the saints."

[53] "If there come any unto you and bring not this doctrine, receive him not into your home." 2 John 10.

[54] 1 Cor. 1:23.

[55] John 1:5.

[56] Dan.7:8, describing the fourth beast. Cf. "A truth of Scripture cannot be stated otherwise than in the form of a *conclusion* from Scripture." Elu., p. 10.

[57] I.e., *apocatastasis,* which believes that all will be saved, because hell is temporary.

[58] Newman ends the quotation at this point in Ess. 1.

[59] Newman recasts this paragraph down to the quotation of Mr. Scott.

[60] Summarised by Jeremy Bentham (1748–1832), "The greatest happiness of the greatest number is the foundation of morals and legislation."

[61] Thomas Scott (1745–1821) succeeded John Newton at Olney before moving to Aston Sandford. His *Commentary on the Bible* was published between 1788 and 1792. For Newman's regard for Scott, see Apo, p. 5.

[62] Polybius, History Book 11.

[63] Arrested by the Etruscan army, attempting to kill Porsenna and threatened with torture, he showed his courage by putting his left hand in the fire. Pindar, *Olympian Odes* 10. 17–18.

[64] The Patriarchal, the Mosaic and the Christian.

[65] The full title of Butler's work is *The Analogy of Religion Natural and Revealed to the Constitution and the Course of Nature.*

[66] Newman recasts this paragraph in Ess 1.

[67] George Bull (1634–1710), Bishop of St Davids. His *Defensio Fidei Nicaenae* was published in 1685). Daniel Waterland (1683–1740), Anglican theologian, wrote *A Vindication of Christ's Divinity* (1719) and took a middle course between Socinianism and that of the Nonjurors.

[68] *Observations on Heresy and Orthodoxy* (1835) by Joseph Blanco White

(1775–1841), a former colleague of Newman at Oriel. He became a Socinian and then a Unitarian.

[69] Cf. Newman's letter to Bowden, LD 5, p. 114, "[Blanco White] says he has been for some time a Sabellian — but he perceives now that Sabellianism is but Unitarianism in disguise."

[70] World soul. Originating with Plato, "We may consequently say that this world is indeed a living being endowed with a soul and intelligence." (*Timaeus* n. 29), cf. also Friedrich Schelling (1775–1854), *Von der Weltseeele* (1798).

[71] Rom. 6:23.

[72] Rom. 3:25.

[73] "In Christian theology, man's reconciliation with God through the sacrificial death of Christ." Cross, p. 104.

[74] Newman omits this expression in Ess. 1.

[75] The Calvinist distinction between the converted (real) and the unconverted (nominal) Christian.

[76] "Not by conversion of the Godhead into flesh; but by taking of the Manhood into God."

[77] The seat of the soul or controlling part (Stoic philosophy).

[78] Matt. 4:11; Luke 22:43.

[79] On 10 May 1796 Napoleon led his armies victoriously against the Austrians. He wrote later, "It was on the evening of Lodi that I believed myself a superior man." Marcus Regulus, the consul, was taken prisoner BC 255, by the Carthaginians and chose to remain their slave.

[80] Matt. 6:28.

[81] Dan. 8:10 (in Newman's version of AV).

[82] Asiatic Cholera (thought to be an air-borne disease) occurred in epidemic proportions in 1832. Harriet Newman said in 1836, "I was attacked by a sort of Cholerina." LD 5, p. 311.

[83] 1 Cor. 3:15.

[84] Jacob Abbott became famous as a writer of children's books, including the Rollo and Lucy and Franconia series. Gillian Avery says, "His writing has a rare humanity, tolerance and gentleness which make it stand out among children's books of any age." *Behold the Child: American Children and Their Books 1621–1922,* London, 1994. Newman records that Mr Abbott called on him in 1843 to confess that these comments 'had the greatest effect on his mind, and he would write very differently now.' Ess. 1, pp. 100–101.

[85] The Young Christian (published in 1832).

[86] Dr John Pye Smith (1775–1851), leading Congregationalist theologian.

[87] Pelagius (fourth-century British theologian) who emphasized innate freedom to choose good; Socinus, Lelio Sozini (1525–1562) and Fausto Sozzini (1539–1604) considered the forerunners of Unitarianism. Episcopius (Simon Bischop, 1583–1643), Professor of Theology at Leyden, condemned for Arminian teaching by the Synod of Dort; Samuel Clarke (1675–1729), Rector of St James, Piccadilly, his *Scripture-Doctrine of the Trinity* had Unitarian overtones. The Lower House of Convocation sought to condemn his view. William Law (1686–1761), was a Nonjuring spiritual writer; Richard Watson (1737–1816), Bishop of Llandaff, Fellow of the Royal Society and Regius Professor of Divinity; Nathaniel Lardner (1684–1768), Nonconformist who wrote *The Credibility of the Gospel History* (1727–1757); Joseph Priestley (1733–1804), Presbyterian minister who embraced Socinianism and published the *Theological Repository* and became one of the founders of the Unitarian Society; William Ellery Channing (1780–1842), American Unitarian pastor of the Congregational Church in Federal Street, Boston, who adopted Unitarian views from 1820.

[88] Luke 23:53.

[89] Pope Victor excommunicated Theodotus the cobbler, founder of this 'God-denying apostasy'. Eusebius, *Ecclesiastical History,* 5.28.6.

[90] Friedrich Daniel Ernst Schliermacher (1768–1834), emphasized feeling as the basis for religion. It was partly an over-reaction to German rationalism.

[91] The term used for Canada in the 1830s.

[92] Translation and review done not by Newman but by Moses Stuart (1780–1852), American Congregationalist biblical scholar.

[93] In himself.

Notes for Tract 75:
[1] On 22 May, Francis Kilvert had urged the publication of a Manual of Prayers for the seven hours of the day, in which prayer was wont to be made in the early Church. LD 5, p. 305n.

[2] Breviarum sive ordo officium per totam anni discursionem.

[3] Gregory VII (1073–1085), Hildebrand, elected by popular acclaim and canonized in 1606.

[4] The pre-metric size was 5¼ x 8⅛. Recent research has discovered that there was no reform of the breviary but codification of rubrics. The breviary was given its form under Innocent III and revised by Honorius III (A. G. Martimort, *The Church at Prayer,* vol. 4, London, 1986, p. 252).

[5] Matins and Lauds, Prime, Terce, Sext, None, Vespers and Compline.

[6]. Dan. 6:10.

[7] Acts 2:15.

[8] Acts 10:9.

[9] Acts 3:1.

[10] Acts 1:14.

[11] Acts 16:25.

[12] Ps. 119:164.

[13] "... Who does thy sevenfold gifts impart," from the hymn for the Ordering of Priests (BCP)

[14] Matt. 12:45, "... and the last state of that man becomes worse than the first."

[15] Prov. 24:16.

[16] On Sundays and feast days there were three Nocturns, on simple feasts and ferias, one only.

[17] Eccl. 11:2.

[18] A short passage of Scripture (the *capitulum*) and a Responsory.

[19] Edersheim states, "According to general agreement, the morning sacrifice was brought at the 'third hour', corresponding to our nine o'clock. ... The evening sacrifice was fixed by the Law as 'between the evenings,' that is, between the darkness of the gloaming and that of the night." *The Temple,* (London, 1959 ed.), pp. 143–144.

[20] Ps 55:17.

[21] To offer light.

[22] Lord, have mercy; Christ, have mercy; Lord, have mercy; Our Father. In the name of our Lord Jesus Christ, light with peace. R. Amen. This is light offered. R. Thanks be to God.

[23] Ps. 50.

[24] Also known as Terce, Sext and None.

[25] The Eastern Church service is known as αποδειπνον (after Supper).

[26] The monks of Spain had 12 daylight hours and 12 night-time hours. *Martimort,* iam cit., p. 179. The medieval abridgement did reduce the readings to a few verses.

[27] The faithful steward: Luke 12:42.

[28] The Investiture controversy, Albigensianism, Illuminism and the Waldenses.

[29] Coptic, Chaldean, Syriac, Byzantine, Armenian and Maronite Offices had different versions.

[30] Gregory I (590–604); Leo I (440–461); Gelasius I (492–496).

[31] Pepin le Bref (741–768), King of the Franks, father of Charlemagne (742–814).

[32] St. Ambrose (339–397), Governor of Aemilia-Liguria and chosen to succeed Auxentius as Bishop of Milan. The Ambrosian Rite of Milan and the Mozarabic Rite of Toledo still survive.

[33] Charles II (837–877), Emperor and King of the Western Franks, son of Louis the Pious.

[34] Septuagesima, the third Sunday before the start of Lent. Sexagesima, the second Sunday.

[35] See earlier remark on Gregory's reform.

[36] "According to the custom of the Roman curia."

[37] Haymo of Faversham (d. 1244), General of the Franciscans, 1240. His revisions date from 1243.

[38] Nicholas III (1277–1280), Giovanni Gaetano, previously Protector (Patron) of the Franciscans.

[39] The Cistercians popularized the *Salve Regina* at the end of Compline; the breviary of the Roman curia added the *Ave Regina Caelorum*. The Little Office of the Blessed Virgin was introduced by religious orders.

[40] Most of the additions, such as the legendary hagiographies, the Little Office of the Blessed Virgin, &c. have been eliminated in the liturgical changes of 1971. The final antiphon at Compline has been retained.

[41] *Prayers and Thanksgivings upon Several Occasions*. In particular *A Prayer for the High Court of Parliament, to be read during their Session*. (BCP).

[42] 1 Tim. 5:21.

[43] After the Martyrology: 'Holy Mary and all the Saints intercede for us to the Lord ...' Bartolomeo Gavanti (1569–1638) was involved in the reform of the breviary, writing a commentary in 1628 on the origin and significance of the Western liturgy.

[44] '... invocation of Saints, is a fond thing vainly invented, and grounded upon no warranty of Scripture, but rather repugnant to the Word of God.' *Article* 22.

[45] Cardinal Cesare Baronius (1538–1607) author of *Annales Ecclesiastici*, a history of the Church.

[46] Jean Grancolas (1660–1732) was a Doctor of the Sorbonne and liturgist. Palmer cites Gavani, *Thesaurus a Gavanti Merari,* t. 2, pp. 103–4. Merari collaborated with Gavanti, cf. supra.

[47] Otho (fl. 1200), Bishop of Päris, near Basle.

[48] Cf. Gibbon, *Decline & Fall of the Roman Empire,* Vol. 4, c. 69.

[49] A Council was held in Oxford in 1250.

[50] Pope Pius V (1566–1572). Trent ended in 1563. Perhaps the date should be 1568, as stated infra?

[51] Hermann of Reichenau (1013–1054), poet and chronicler.

[52] Martimort suggests the authorship of Adhemar (d. 1098), bishop of Puy in Velay.

[53] Peter Damian (1007–1072), Benedictine monk and Cardinal Bishop of Ostia.

[54] John Damascene (675–749), Greek theologian, author of *De Fide Orthodoxa.*

[55] Authorised by Urban II at the Council of Clermont in 1096.

[56] Issued by Archbishop de Vintimille on his own authority.

[57] Cardinal Francisco Quinonez (d. 1540). His breviary was published in 1535. The Psalms were distributed in an arbitrary manner with no regard for traditional usage. Patristic readings were only introduced in the second edition. The hagiographical readings were however purified of many legends.

[58] Published in 1568 with the collaboration of Cardinal Guglielmo Sirleto and his commission.

[59] "confused arrangement."

[60] The 1970 reform of the breviary gives emphasis to 'historical truth' in hagiographic readings, all the books of the Bible are arranged to be read during the year and feast days do not take precedence over the major seasons of the year.

[61] The laws governing the life and activity of the Pontiffs.

[62] Paul III (1534–1549), Alessandro Farnese.

[63] The readings at Matins used to end 'et reliqua . . .'

[64] Medieval book for finding the Church service for any particular day. — from The Preface (BCP).

[65] Newman notes in his diary "Thursday 9 November (1837) began [Breviary] Services regularly" LD 6, p. 161.

Notes for Tract 79:
[1] This subject was touched on in Tract 71 §5.

[2] Archbishop James Ussher (1581–1656) Professor of Divinity at Dublin (1607), Archbishop of Armagh (1625), his mother was a Catholic and his uncle, Richard Stanihurst, a Jesuit.

[3] The distinction between Christ being of the *same* substance and the Arian contention that he was of *like* substance (homoiousion) to the Father.

[4] The Via Media approach but especially followed by Laud and the Caroline divines.

[5] 'These truths lead to real evils.' Horace, *Ars Poetica,* v. 451.

[6] Indulgences grant remission by the Church of temporal punishment due to sin.

[7] Article 22 says Purgatory is "a fond thing vainly invented, and grounded upon no warranty of Scripture, but rather repugnant to the Word of God."

[8] Most were founded in Rome as Confraternities, including *The Relief of Needy Souls* (1687) and the Archconfraternity of *The Mother of Sorrows* (1818).

[9] From stipends for the saying of Mass. This was largely the raison d'être of the *Chantries.*

[10] Pius V laid particular emphasis on the *Catechism,* telling the Cistercians that they should always have the Bible and the *Catechism* to hand. (*Apostolic Constitution 8 March 1570).*

[11] Part I, chapter 6, Q. 3 (De Symb. 5).

[12] *De Controversiis Christianae Fidei Adversus hujus temporis haereticos* published 1584–1593. R. F. Christie gave Newman a 1608 edition in July 1836. (LD 5, p. 317n.)

[13] 'prison' (in 2.4.): "The tormented pious souls atone for a certain time in purgatorial fire."

[14] 1 Cor. 11:31.

[15] *De Amiss. Grat.* i.2 (in section *De Purgatorio* of Bellarmine's *Disputationes de Controversiis*).

[16] 1 Cor. 3:15.

[17] The vision of God in heaven.

[18] Ibid., 2, 4.

[19] Because 'souls *descend.'DS 570.* Suarez considers it in the heart of the earth, but St Thomas says it is could be in various places . . .

[20] Limbus (fringe or outskirts) cf. Lazarus in Abraham's bosom, Luke 16:23.

[21] Pain/penalty of loss (because temporality deprived of the beatific vision) and pain of the senses: 'the *fire*'.

[22] The text can be found in *Mansi* 31.485–488.

[23] "The pains of Purgatory are most dreadful and the Fathers constantly teach that they cannot be compared with any in this life." St Augustine comments similarly in *Enarrationes in Pss.* 37.3.

[24] Tertullian refers to the treasure of merits in *De Puditia*, ML 2, 1027.

[25] Ibid., I.11: "Many more similar accounts can be read . . . but those mentioned have more authenticity."

[26] 2 Macc. 12:42–45.

[27] Council of Carthage AD 419 which passed the collection of Canons known as *Codex Canonum Ecclesiae Africanae.*

[28] Council of Braga AD 363.

[29] Council of Chalons AD 814

[30] Synod of Worms AD 868.

[31] Pope Symmachus (498–514). The Sixth Roman Council took place in 504.

[32] The Liturgy of St Basil prays, 'Remember also all who have fallen asleep in the hope of the Resurrection to eternal life and grant them rest, our God where the light of your countenance shines.' The Liturgy of St James, or Syrian, prays, 'for our fathers and brothers who have fallen asleep aforetime.'

[33] Cf. Council of Worms (supra).

[34] As part of the prayer for the Church Militant in the Communion Service: 'And we also bless thy holy Name for all thy servants departed this life in thy faith and fear, beseeching thee to give us grace so to follow their good examples, that with them we may be partakers of thy heavenly kingdom.' (BCP)

[35] Joseph Butler (1692–1752) Bishop of Durham, in his book *Analogy of Religion Natural and Revealed, to the Constitution and Course of Nature* (1736).

[36] Their morally unanimous consent is needed to establish a decisive authority in matters of faith.

[37] Quintus Septimius Florens Tertullianus (AD 155–244) in his *The Crown*, "We offer sacrifices for the dead on their birthday anniversaries."(AD 211).

[38] *On Monogamy* (post AD 213).

[39] Caecilius Cyprianus Thascius (d. 258) Bishop of Carthage.

[40] Eusebius Pamphilius (260–340) Bishop of Caesarea author of *A Life of Constantine.*

[41] As an illustration in the martyrdom of Polycarp, 'the Adversary contrived that his [Polycarp's] poor body might not be obtained by us, though many much desired to secure it, and communicate over his holy remains.' *Records of the Church No. 12.*

[42] Cyril (315–386) Bishop of Jerusalem. His catechetical lectures were delivered c. 350.

[43] Gregory Nazianzen (329–389) author of *Forty-Five Theological Orations.*

[44] Letter to Faustinus, Bishop of Bologna on the death of his sister (387) and *On the death of Theodosius Flavius* (395) preached 40 days after the Emperor's death.

[45] Eusebius Hieronymus (347–419) to Pammachius (c.340–410), who was a Christian Roman senator. He entered a monastic community after his wife's death.

[46] John Chrysostom (344/354–407) Bishop of Constantinople.

[47] Paulinus (353/4–431) Bishop of Nola.

[48] Aurelius Augustinus (354–430) Bishop of Hippo *The Care that should be taken of the Dead* (AD 421).

[49] Theodoret (393–466) Bishop of Cyr. His *History of the Church* was written AD 439. Theodosius II succeeded Arcadius in 408. Cf. *The Intermediate State*, PPS 3, pp. 371–2.

[50] Isidore (560–636) Archbishop of Seville. *On Ecclesiastical Duties.*

[51] Gregory I (540–604) His *Dialogues* date from 593/4.

[52] Origen (185–254) His *Homilies on Exodus* are post 244.

[53] His *The Soul* dates between 208 and 212.

[54] *On the Holy Lights* (AD 381).

[55] *Commentaries on Twelve of David's Psalms.*

[56] Basil (330–379) Bishop of Caesarea, composed his work on Isaiah in sixteen chapters ca. 365.

[57] Gregory Nyssen (c.330–395), Bishop of Nyssa 371, younger brother of St. Basil.

[58] Eusebius Emissenus (d. 360) Bishop of Edessa.

[59] Hilary (316–367) Bishop of Poitiers. His *Commentary on the Psalms* was written c. 365.

[60] Lucius Caelius Firmianus Lactantius (250–317) became private tutor to the son of Constantine after his conversion in 303. His *Divine Institutions* were written 304–311, "But also when God will judge the just, it is likewise in fire that He will try them."

[61] Jerome wrote his *Commentaries on Isaiah* 408–410. His *Dialogue against the Pelagians* in 415.

[62] Augustine's *City of God* was written 413–426. Gregory in his *Dialogues* says "There is, for the sake of lesser faults, a purgatorial fire before the judgment." (4.40)

[63] Newman would point out later, "Those who die in invincible ignorance are not in the place of lost souls; those who are not lost, are either in purgatory or in heaven." VM 2, p. 110n.

[64] See supra where Newman says that "all must be in favour" and note.

[65] "These opinions, taken as written, contain a manifest error ... In addition, it cannot be clearly understood what the said Fathers say (Origen excepted).

[66] Certainly the opinion [which teaches that all pass through fire, though not all are wounded by it], I would not dare to confirm as true nor reject as erroneous."

[67] censures or condemns.

[68] Rev. 21:19ff.; Ezek. 1:15ff.

[69] 1 Cor. 3:13; Matt. 3:11.

[70] A transitory state providing a second chance to respond fully to God's saving will.

[71] "For he is like a refiner's fire and like fuller's soap; he will sit as a refiner and purifier of silver, and he will purify the sons of Levi and refine them like gold and silver ..." (Mal. 3:2–3).

[72] Matt. 5:26.

[73] Rev. 5:3.

[74] 'For if we sin willfully after that we have received the knowledge of the truth, there remaineth no more sacrifice for sins, but a certain fearful looking for of judgment and fiery indignation.' Heb 10:26–27

[75] The paralysed man: John 5:14.

[76] Dan. 3:27.

[77] Rev. 20:15.

[78] A word that occurs only once.

[79] Deut. 4:20.

[80] Ps. 68:18.

[81] John 21:22.

[82] Ps. 66:12.

[83] Luke 17:7.

[84] Cant. 8:7.

[85] Isa. 49:23.

[86] Simeon in Luke 2:35.

[87] Job 1:20.

[88] Job 42:6.

[89] Mount Tabor, cf. 2 Pet. 1:16ff.

[90] *The Divine Institutions.*

[91] Paulinus, Bishop of Nola, to Sulpicius Severus, the rhetorician, ca. 395.

[92] 'to prove the rule.'

[93] "... Or that man's worldly desires (being venial) shall pass the purging

fire of tribulation only in this world, and not in the other; if any hold thus, I contradict him not; perhaps he may hold the truth." *City of God,* Book 21, ch. 26.

[94] Letter to Antonianus, Bishop in Numidia ca. 251/252.

[95] Nicholas Rigaltius (1577–1654) French classical scholar; George Stanley Faber (1773–1854) Evangelical divine and controversialist.

[96] 'sent to prison' 'to be purified for a long time by fire.'

[97] Montanism started about AD 156, claiming a new mandate from the Holy Spirit, with an invitation to severe penance and even martyrdom. Tertullian became a Montanist in the 190s.

[98] Clement of Alexandria, Origen and Gregory of Nyssa equate the fiery trial with the day of judgment.

[99] 1 Cor. 3:1.

[100] *The City of God* (AD 413–426); *Genesis defended against the Manicheans* (AD 389).

[101] Sir. 27:6.

[102] 1 Cor. 6:9.

[103] *Enchiridion of Faith, Hope and Love* (AD 421); Letter 204 to the Tribune Dulcitius (AD 418); Faith and Works (AD 413).

[104] Benedictine Congregation of St. Maur (founded 1618) translated the works of St Augustine.

[105] Jeremy Taylor (1613–1667), *Dissuasive from Popery* (1664), vol. 2, p. 75; Bellarmine, vol. 2. 1.

[106] Rev. 20:14; 21:8.

[107] *De Mortalitate* (AD 252/3).

[108] Rev. 7:9; 19:14.

[109] Matt. 8:11.

[110] Luke 14:19.

[111] *Death as a Blessing* (AD 388/390).

[112] The parable of the rich man and Lazarus, Luke 16:19–31.

[113] Macarius the Great (300–c. 390). Some dispute his authorship of the homilies.

[114] Vid. Athanasius (295–373) Bishop of Alexandria. *Life of St. Antony* §65; St Basil the Great, *in Psalm* 7§2.

[115] Italy was being devastated by an exceptional drought for much of 591, followed by plague in 592/3 in which a third of the population died. These were seen as signs of the last days.

[116] Gregory the Great's *Dialogues* were written AD 593/4. The Lombard invasion coincided with a serious attack of fever for Gregory.

[117] Matt. 24:29.

[118] *Speculum Exemplorum* (published in Cologne, c. 1483) contains a collection of medieval predictions and visions.

[119] Newman repeats this in Tract 90.

[120] Bishop Theobald (d. 1161) was the Archbishop of Canterbury who crowned King Stephen in 1141.

[121] Conrad, Bishop of Constance (d. 975) and Ulric/Udelric, Bishop of Augsburg (d. 975) saw a pool from which two birds emerged and saw it as a vision of two souls in purgatory.

[122] The *Dream of Scipio* is the sixth book of *De Re Publica*. The general Scipio Aemilianus, while in Carthage, muses on the nature of the soul from the Stoic point of view. Plato's *Gorgias* ends with the judgment of naked souls. His *Phaedo* discusses the immortality of the soul.

[123] "They should not allow uncertain speculation or what borders on falsehood to be publicly treated. And they should prohibit all that panders to curiosity and superstition..." *Decree on Purgatory,* Session 25 (1563).

[124] St Odilio (967–1048) was the fifth abbot of Cluny. He introduced the commemoration of All Souls' Day into the liturgy.

[125] St Damianus, Bishop of Pavia in the seventh century.

[126] Published 1664 and described by Cross as 'a violent invective against Popery.'

[127] Synod summoned by Charlemagne in AD 809.

[128] '*Of the vanity of the* age' and '*Of Correctness in Catholic Association.*'

[129] Otto (1114–1158). Cistercian Abbot and later Bishop of Freising, his principal work is 'Chronicon seu historia de duabus civitatibus' (1143–1146).

[130] Johann Franz de Trevern, Bishop of Strasbourg (1827–1841) engaged in debate with Faber.

[131] St John Fisher (1469–1535) Bishop of Rochester and Chancellor of Cambridge.

[132] Alphonsus a Castro or de Castro (1495–1558), Spanish Franciscan friar and theologian.

[133] Polydore Virgil (1470–1555), Italian historian, author of a History of England.

[134] Understood as 'station – meaning assembly – *church*'. The custom originated with Gregory I.

[135] *Assertionis Lutheranae Confutatio,* Antwerp, 1523.

[136] Gal.1:8.

[137] Pope Gregory XI (1371–1378) returned from Avignon to Rome in 1377.

[138] The Greeks objected to the material fire and the distinction between punishment and guilt.

[139] Eugenius IV (Gabriele Condulmaro) 1431–1447.

[140] Guiliano Cesarini (1398–1444) created Cardinal by Martin V in 1426.

[141] Emperor John VIII (1423–1448). His successor, Constantine XI would be the last.

[142] By this time the Ottoman frontier was two day's ride from the walls of the city.

[143] Sylvester Syropulus, a Church dignitary and chronicler, in *Vera Historia Unionis* (trans. R. Creyghten, Hague, 1660).

[144] Markus Eugenikos.

[145] Amurath (b. 1326) was Sultan from 1359–1389. He expanded his lands from 90,000 km to 500,000 by the time of his death in battle.

[146] John Bessarion (1403–1472), consecrated Archbishop of Nicea in 1437, he made his home in Italy and was made Cardinal in 1439.

[147] Isidore of Kiev (1385–1463). After his imprisonment, he escaped to Rome. He was received by Pope Nicholas V and made a Cardinal. He became Dean of the College in 1461.

Notes for Tract 82:
[1] Reprinted and re-cast with additional notes in VM 2, pp. 143–194.

[2] Samuel Charles Wilks, Editor of the Christian Observer (1816–1847). Cf. LD 6, p. 9n.

[3] Tract 69. *Scriptural Views on Holy Baptism (Part 3)*.

[4] Probably, Henry Churton (1811–1891) of Brasenose. Hulmeian Divinity Lecturer 1837, evangelical curate of St. Ebb's, Oxford and enthusiast for a Martyrs' Memorial. (LD 6, p. 332)

[5] Gilbert Burnet (1643–1715), Bishop of Salisbury. His *Exposition of the 39 Articles* was published in 1699.

[6] 'By the act done' in contrast to *opus operantis* 'by the act of the doer.'

[7] Samuel Horsley (1733–1806), Bishop of St Asaph.

[8] Article 19, *Of the Church*.

[9] John 4:24.

[10] Rev. 21:27.

[11] predisposed.

[12] *The Catechism:* 'What is the inward and spiritual grace?' *Answer:* 'A death unto sin and a new birth unto righteousness ...' (BCP).

[13] Richard Mant (1776–1848), Bishop of Down and Connor. His Tract on Infant Baptism (1815) was an extract of his Bampton Lecture of 1812.

[14] Eph. 2:3.

[15] Renn Dickson Hampden (1793–1868) became Regius Professor of Divinity in 1836 despite liberal views, but was suspended from the Board appointing select preachers in 1837.

[16] "... feed on him in thy heart by faith with thanksgiving," Holy Communion (BCP).

[17] The story (from the *Fioretti of St Francis*) is that at Rimini preaching to many heretics, without much response, he went and addressed the fishes.

[18] Those who assumed legal responsibility. In this case, godparents.

[19] Advertisement to the 2nd Volume of *The Tracts of the Times* in 1835. See Appendix 1.

[20] Edward Bouverie Pusey (1800–1882), appointed Regius Professor of Hebrew in 1828. He authored Tracts 18, 67, 68 and 69.

[21] Maynooth College in Co. Kildare, was established for the training of Catholic clergy by the Irish Parliament in 1795. The annual grant was raised to £9000 in 1813.

[22] A martyrs' memorial would be erected in 1839 in Oxford.

[23] *The Christian Observer*, a monthly founded in 1802 and connected with the 'Clapham Sect.'

[24] The form of government of a Church; the reference being to Hooker's *Laws of Ecclesiastical Polity* (1594–1597).

[25] The editor of the *Christian Observer* wrote in 1833, "We see a society formed at Oxford, the members of which, professing themselves to be the most orthodox upholders of the Church, have begun to scatter throughout the land publications which, for bigotry, Popery and intolerance surpass the writings even of Laud and Sacheverell."

[26] Henry Sacheverell (1674–1724), High Church pamphleteer who challenged the Whig government and, although impeached, received a derisory sentence. The Non-jurors would not take the oath to William III.

[27] Daniel's reply to Nebuchadnezzar, Dan. 2:36.

[28] Mr Abbott subsequently thanked Newman for the 'fairness of the review.' Ess 1, p. 101.

[29] Dr. Pusey's *Earnest Remonstrance to the Author of the Pope's Letter* (1836) in Tracts, vol. 3.

[30] 'into the same old song'. A Proverb, and in Terence, *Phormio* l. 495.

[31] 'Where one is removed there is no shortage of another.' Virgil, *Aeneid,* Book 6. L.

[32] Herbert Marsh (1757–1839), Bishop of Peterborough, who devised 87 questions for ordinands to filter out followers of Charles Simeon (1759–1836), a leader of the Evangelical revival.

[33] Zuingli. Ulrich Zwingly (1484–1531), Swiss Reformer and People's Preacher in Zurich. He upheld a purely symbolical presence of Christ in the Eucharist.

[34] Luther posted his 95 theses in Wittenberg on October 31, 1517.

[35] John 7:39.

[36] 1 Pet. 1:10–11.

[37] "For the law of the Spirit of life in Christ Jesus has set me free from the law of sin and death ... If the Spirit of him who raised Jesus from the dead dwells in you, he who raised Christ Jesus from the dead will give life to your mortal bodies also through his Spirit who dwells in you." (Rom. 8:2, 11).

[38] Job 2:1.

[39] "Jesus answered them, 'Did I not chose you, the twelve, and one of you is a devil?' " (John 6:70).

[40] Newman did not write a third part, but later published *Lectures on the Doctrine of Justification* in book form in 1838 and later made reference to the subject in Tract 90.

[41] "There are two sacraments ordained of Christ our Lord in the Gospel, that is to say, Baptism, and the Supper of the Lord." Article 25.

[42] "Hence we have almost embraced the doctrine, that GOD conveys grace only through faith, prayer, active contemplation, or (what is called) communion with GOD." Cf. Appendix 1, 2.

[43] See Appendix 1, 2.

[44] The tradition of following Jewish practice, believed to derive from St John, centred on Asia Minor (Quartodecimam). The Alexandrians put Easter after the vernal equinox.

[45] The PAS was founded in 1836 to help the home mission of the Church of England. Newman expressed reservations about the Church Missionary Society in 1830, VM 2, pp. 1–19.

[46] Gilbert Burnet, Bishop of Salisbury (1643–1715) put forward a scheme to incorporate dissenters into the Church of England.

[47] The Church of St Katharine Cree in London was consecrated by Laud in 1631. The form of service and his vestments were used as evidence of heresy at his trial in 1645.

[48] Vincent of Lerins (d. ca. 450), *Commonitorium,* "Quod ubique, quod semper, quod ab omnibus creditum est."

[49] "... The Body of Christ is given, taken and eaten in the Supper, only after an heavenly and spiritual manner." Article 28.

[50] John Keble (1792–1866), Tr. 57 *Sermons on Saints' Days. No 3. St. Mark's Day,* pp. 14–15.

[51] "Hold fast the form of sound words, which thou hast heard of me ..." 2 Tim 1:13.

[52] Dionysius Petavius/Dennis Pétau (1583–1652) introduced a discussion on *appropriation*. Newman writes in Jfc.: "At least English divines teach that our holiness and works done in the Spirit are something towards salvation, but not enough ... According to them, we are saved in Christ's righteousness, yet not without our own; or considering Christ's righteousness as a formal cause, we are saved by two contemporaneous formal causes, by a righteousness, meritorious on Christ's part, inchoate on ours." p. 367.

[53] The Homilies in Article 35 (BCP) are those of the Second Book of Homilies. The majority composed by John Jewel (1522–1571) Bishop of Salisbury, 'to be read in Churches by the ministers, diligently and distinctly, that they may be understood of the people.'

[54] No. 21 was added because of the rebellion of 1569 in which Durham cathedral was sacked.

[55] The reward or recompense.

[56] The 2nd Part of Homily 5, 'Of Good Works': First of Fasting advocates, "the maintaining of fisher towns bordering upon the seas, and for the increase of fisher men, to the furnishing of the navy of the Realm." And adds that the purchase of fish would be beneficial, increasing the spending of "victual upon the land ... sooner reducing to a more moderate price to the better sustenance of the poor." In 1560, Queen Elizabeth also decreed a fine on butchers who slaughtered meat in Lent.

[57] The First Book of 12 Homilies was composed by Thomas Cranmer in 1547.

[58] A syllogistic fallacy when the middle term is not distributed.

[59] The legend, which was probably an old Roman folk tale, says that after 900 a woman in male disguise became Pope and gave birth during a procession to St John Lateran and died.

[60] The *Christian Observer* held that subjects might rebel against authority [Newman's 1877 note].

[61] Achar, the troubler of Israel (1 Chr. 2:7).

[62] The accusation against Paul made before Felix, Acts 24:5.

[63] Oxford declaration against the admission of Dissenters, April 24, 1834.

[64] Tract 43 (21 September 1834) *Richard Nelson, No 4: Length of The Public Service* (by Thomas Keble).

[65] From the Holy Communion, BCP.

[66] 'a nose of wax' i.e. something which can be twisted to suit any meaning.

[67] "... the essence of Sectarian Doctrine ... to consider faith and not the sacraments, as the instrument of justification and other Gospel gifts." See Appendix 1, 2.

[68] Peter Heylyn (1600–1662) "Some take the Articles in the literal and grammatical sense, which is the fairest and most approved way of interpretation...Others there are (of which his late Majesty complained) who draw the Articles aside and put their own sense or comment to be the meaning of the Articles of the Church to speak for them, exclusive wholly of the other, but with a notable difference in the application." *Historia Quinquarticularis* (1681).

[69] 'That all agree on the true, usual, literal meaning of the said Articles ... Not to suffer unnecessary Disputations, Altercations or Questions to be raised, which may nourish Faction within the Church and Commonwealth.' (1628 – drawn up by Archbishop Laud.)

[70] "Of faith in the Holy Trinity; Of Christ the Son of God; Of his going down into Hell; Of his Resurrection; Of the Holy Ghost."

[71] The Convocation of 1571 restored Article 29 and the Articles in their final form gained synodical approval through Convocation.

[72] 'abusus non tollit usum', 'the abuse does not take away the use.'

[73] *The Apology of the Church of England* (1562) by Bishop John Jewel.

[74] Ignatius, Bishop of Antioch (35–107); Cyprian, Bishop of Carthage (d. 258); Gregory I (540–604).

[75] Edward VI (1537–1553). His reign saw the Book of Homilies, the Book of Common Prayer and the Forty-two Articles of Religion.

[76] Walter Farquhar Hook (1798–1875) Vicar of Holy Trinity, Coventry (1828–1837) and Vicar of Leeds (1837–1859). His five sermons before the University of Oxford was published 1837. He had contacts with the Tractarians, was a High Anglican and became Dean of Chichester in 1859.

[77] *On the controversy with the Romanists.* Newman was the author.

[78] Antinomianism or freedom by grace from moral constraints.

[79] Pusey was the first to sign his name to a Tract (No. 18) as E. B. P.

[80] Thomas Comber (1645–1699) Dean of Durham advocated admission of Dissenters.

[81] 'To the man' i.e. appealing to one's prejudice.

[82] A series.

[83] The agreement between the Fathers.

[84] William Palmer (1803–1885). His book *Origines Liturgicae* on the history of the English liturgy was published in 1832.

[85] Archbishop Ussher tried to impose a Calvinistic set of Articles upon the Irish Church in 1615.

Notes for Tract 90:
[1] Printed in VM 2 with additional notes, pp. 259–356.

[2] *Subscription* to the 39 Articles was required of all clergy until 1865.

[3] Cf. Tract 41, "Corruptions are pouring in, which, sooner or later, will need a SECOND REFORMATION."

[4] "No city divided against itself will stand." Matt. 12:25

[5] "Let the Church sit still; let her be content to be in bondage," &c. The author meant them in the sense of the lines in the *Lyra Apostolica* "Bide thou thy time! Watch with meek eyes the race of pride and crime; Sit in the gate and be the heathen's jest, Smiling and self-possest."

[6] "With stammering lips." 1st edition

[7] From the Greek 'hidden'. In the Old Testament: 1 & 2 Esdras, Tobit, Judith, the Rest of Esther, the Wisdom of Solomon, Sirach (Ecclesiasticus), Baruch, the Song of the Three Children, Susanna, Bel and the Dragon, the Prayer of Manasses and 1 & 2 Maccabees.

[8] St Jerome [Eusebius Hieronymus] (342–420).

[9] Preface to the Three Solomonic Books (AD 398), ML 28, 1242.

[10] The Council of Trent (4th Session, 1546) declared the Vulgate the only authentic Latin text.

[11] i.e. means.

[12] *Dr Wiseman's Lectures on the Catholic Church,* British Critic XIX, October, 1836, pp. 386–388.

[13] King William III, ruling with Mary II. (1688–1702).

[14] Article 3. *Of his going down into Hell.*

[15] *Answer to a Jesuit and other Tracts on Popery* (Dublin, 1624).

[16] *Dissuasive from Popery* (1664).

[17] Nicea (325), 1st Constantinople (381), Ephesus (431), Chalcedon (451).

[18] William Laud (1573–1645) Archbishop of Canterbury. His *Conference with Fisher,* (1639).

[19] John Bramhall (1594–1663) Archbishop of Armagh (1661). His *Works,* 5 vols, (Dublin, 1676).

[20] Edward Stillingfleet (1635–1699) Bishop of Worcester. His *Rational Account of the Grounds of the Protestant Religion* was a response to Fr Fisher's book.

[21] Herbert Thorndike (1598–1672) Theologian, published his *De Ratione ac Jure finiendi controversias Ecclesiae disputatio* in 1670.

[22] Thomas Jackson (1579–1640) Theologian and Dean of Peterborough.

[23] Richard Field (1561–1616) Dean of Gloucester. His treatise *Of the Church,* published 1606–1610, was an apology for the Church of England against Rome.

[24] Justification is the application of Christ's *merits* to the individual, that application is the imparting of an inward gift." Jfc, p. 144.

[25] James 2:18, The Authorised King James Version of the Bible.

[26] Jfc., pp. x, xii, 226, 276. The Arian heresy said that the Father was eternal and the Son was not.

[27] 'Supplicating or entreating by prayer'.

[28] And it came to pass, when Moses held up his hand, that Israel prevailed. (Exo. 17:11).

[29] Justification is a perfect act, anticipating at once in the sight of God what sanctification does but tend towards. Jfc, p. 73.

[30] Congruous merit appeals to the generosity of the giver, 'justified *freely* by his grace' (Rom. 3:24).

[31] John 8:11; 15:5.

[32] The fourth-century heresy that humanity can attain salvation by its own efforts, apart from Divine Grace, condemned at the Council of Carthage in AD 418.

[33] Habitual grace resides in the soul as a permanent quality; actual grace aids the soul to acts of supernatural virtue.

[34] Luke 19:17; Luke 12:48.

[35] Acts 10:17ff.

[36] Simon Magus offered money to be able to bestow the Holy Spirit (Acts 8;9ff); Felix was the Roman Procurator of Judea appointed by Claudius (Acts 23:24ff).

[37] Jean de Launoy (1603–1678) French historian. He wrote a treatise, *Explicata Ecclesiae Traditio circa Canonem* (1672).

[38] Newman omits the next passage in VM 2.

[39] John 14:16; Matt. 28:20. A brunt is a violent blow.

[40] John 17:20.

[41] Rom. 8:9, 15.

[42] That is, since the Eastern schism of 1054.

[43] i.e. Presbyterian or Methodist.

[44] Matt. 13:47–51.

[45] Matt. 18:20.

[46] In the sense of 'determined by a superior authority' (Webster's Dictionary).

[47] In the sense of 'diversity.'

[48] St Gregory Nazianzen (329–389) Newman quotes this in Ari, p. 388.

[49] This section was specifically attacked by the Four College Tutors in their letter of March 1841.VM 2, p. 359.

[50] Flavius Cassiodorus (485–580), Roman monk whose *Historia Ecclesiastica Tripartita* is a compilation of Socrates, Sozomen and Theodoret.

[51] Epiphanius (315–403) Bishop of Salamis, zealous defender of the faith of Nicea.

[52] Article 22 was drafted in 1553 and the Decree on Purgatory on 3/4 December, 1563. The 'Romish doctrine' was added to the original Article in 1563.

[53] The poena damni is the pain of loss because their sins for a time exclude them from the sight of God. The poena sensus means that they undergo suffering in the soul. Cf. Tr. 79.

[54] "animas poenis purgatoriis post mortem purgari" their souls are cleansed after death by cleansing pains." 6 July 1439.

[55] Parts of the next passage – down to "Now it [would seem] ..." – were omitted by Newman in VM 2.

[56] 'helped'.

[57] Eccli. 11:3.

[58] John 3:36.

[59] Cf, Augustine, *in Ps. 104 Sermon 3; City of God 16:24;* Cyprian, *De Mortalitate* 9; Chrysostom, *Homily 24 on Ephesians.* And cf. References in §3 of Tr. 79.

[60] Richard Hooker (1554–1600); his *A Learned Sermon on the Nature of Pride* was published posthumously in 1612.

[61] See Tr. 79 *On Purgatory*.

[62] Newman omits the next two paragraphs in VM 2.

[63] Rev. Samuel Johnson (1649–1703), 'The Whig,' Pamphleteer. *Purgatory proved by miracles collected out of Roman Catholic Authors* (1668).

[64] Newman omits the subsequent passages until "The virtue of indulgences. . ." in VM 2.

[65] Council of Nicea (325), Canon 11.

[66] Venting, i.e. quacks *selling* their secrets.

[67] Gilbert Burnet (1643–1715) in *Exposition of the Thirty-nine Articles* (1699).

[68] Wax medallion with the figure of a lamb which is blessed by the Pope on the Thursday after Easter in the first and seventh years of his pontificate.

[69] Scapularies/scapulars, ordinarily two pieces of cloth worn over the shoulders, connected by cords signifying the wearer is a member of a religious confraternity.

[70] ". . . that all base gain for securing indulgences, which has been the source of abundant abuses among the Christian people, should be totally abolished." Decree on 2nd Day of Session 25. The regulations concerning indulgences were revised in *Indulgentiarum Doctrina* (1967) restricting plenary indulgences to one a day and making all other indulgences partial.

[71] Julius II (Giuliano della Rovere) 1503–1513; and Paul III (Alessandro Farnese) 1534–1549.

[72] Julius III (Giovanni Maria de' Ciocchi del Monte) 1550–1555.

[73] The feast of the Body and Blood of Christ (Thursday or following Sunday after Trinity).

[74] The image of our Saviour 'ad Sancta Sanctorum' is a mosaic in St. John Lateran; the hospital of San Giacomo inAugusta, is in the Via Corso; the Church of St John the Baptist is St. John Lateran; of Sts Cosmas and Damian is in the Forum of Vespasian; of San Giovanni dei Fiorentini is in the Ponte Rione district and the hospital of Santo Spiritu in Sassia, one of Europe's oldest, is in the Via dei Penitenzieri near the Vatican. The Church of S. Agostino is near the Porta del Popolo.

[75] Quarantines are indulgences of forty days.

[76] Take off one's cap and kneel as a sign of reverence.

[77] Acts 14:15.

[78] Newman omits the passage up to "Because relics were so gainful ..." in VM 2.

[79] Dan. 11:43.

[80] The Palladium was the image on whom civic safety was said to depend. Diana of the Ephesian was the statue reverenced by the citizens of Ephesus, cf. Acts 19:28ff.

[81] Augustus decorated his villa at Capua; the head of a man was excavated on Capitol hill, which Etruscan augurs said, meant Rome would become the head of Italy.

[82] The image of Pallas at Troy.

[83] The icon of the Hodegetria.

[84] The Good Goddess, the Goddess of fertility.

[85] The Dioscuri came to the aid of the Argonauts and rescued Helen.

[86] Num. 22:28ff.

[87] St Leonard of Noblac (6th century) is the patron of prisoners of war.

[88] Relic Sunday was celebrated in mid July.

[89] 'beads-bidding' – Bidding Prayers occurring after the Gospel.

[90] St Lawrence (d. 258), Archdeacon to St Sixtus, roasted to death on a gridiron.

[91] 'daws', sluggards, lazy people.(OED)

[92] Newman omits this paragraph in VM 2 and cf. VM 2, p. 429 n. 3.

[93] Newman omits the rest of this paragraph in VM 2.

[94] Isa. 56:10.

[95] Newman substitutes the following paragraph with *Homily on Good Works*, pp.45–46, and omits up to "Now the veneration ..." in VM 2.

[96] Baal/Bel and Ashtaroth, Phoenician gods, Chemosh (Chamos) and Moloch and Baalpeor from Moab, Priapus, God of fertility, the brazen serpent worshipped in Canaan; the zodiac had particular significance for Sabean (ancient Chaldean) astrolaters.

[97] The wearers of the brown scapular (of the Carmelites) were promised that "no one dying will suffer eternal burning." But doubts remain about the Bull of Benedict XIV granting this.

[98] Newman omits this paragraph in VM 2.

[99] Dan. 3.

[100] Bishop Ken's *Glory to Thee my God this* night (of which this is the tenth verse). A passage here occurred in the 1st. edition upon Rev. 1:4, in which the author still thinks that "the seven spirits" are seven created angels.

[101] St Nicholas was the patron saint of steam threshing machines during the Kentish 'Captain Swing' uproar in 1830.

[102] St Eloi or Egidius (588–660), patron saint of smiths and metal workers.

[103] Marcus Terentius Varro (116 BC – 23 AD) in his *Antiquitates Rerum Humanorum et divinorum*.

[104] Oenomaus or Oinomaos, in mythology, was King of Pisa and father of Hippodamia; and Hesiodus was an eighth-century Greek poet, author of a *Theogony* or genealogy of the gods.

[105] St Clement (d.100) is the patron saint of sailors and lighthousemen.

[106] Ave, Maris Stella – ninth-century anonymous hymn to Mary, Star of the Sea.

[107] St Agatha, early Christian martyr, died in Catania (Sicily) and invoked against the eruptions of Etna and against fire.

[108] Cornelius (d.253) Pope and martyr.

[109] Apollinaris (dates unknown), Bishop of Ravenna and martyr.

[110] Antony of Egypt (251–356), Abbot, Patriarch of monks.

[111] 1 Cor. 3:17.

[112] Newman omits the following up to "Christ, sitting in heaven . . ." in VM 2.

[113] Rom. 10:14.

[114] Matt. 28:19.

[115] Generally attributed to St Augustine, but more probably to St John Damascene (*De Fide Orthodoxa*, 3, 24).

[116] St Isidore of Seville (560–636), author of *Sententiarum Libri Tres*, a manual of Christian doctrine and practice which draws on the teaching of St Augustine and St Gregory the Great.

[117] Ps. 7:9.

[118] Acts 14:8ff; Rev. 19:10.

[119] 'You are glorified in your saints, for their glory is the crowning of your gifts', Preface of Holy Men and Women from *Roman Missal*, 1973.

[120] Lancelot Andrewes (1555–1626), Bishop of Winchester in his first answer (published in 1618, p. 213), to Cardinal Jacques Davy du Perron (1556–1626), Bishop of Evreux, who supported King James I's use of the title 'Catholic.'

[121] 'taken strictly, taken broadly.'

[122] Newman omits what follows until "*Bellarmine's admissions quite bear out . . .*"

[123] 'to pray for prayer's sake.'

[124] Isaac Casaubon (1559–1614), Classical scholar and translator for Bishop Andrewes.

[125] 'Aid the miserable, help the fainthearted, comfort the tearful, accept what we offer' [from a prayer of Fulbert of Chartres (960–1028)]. "... grant what we ask, spare us what we fear." [Prayer, *O Beata Virgo*]. But cf. 'Excesses in Devotion to the Blessed Virgin' in *Diff.* 2, pp. 63, 105.

[126] (*in so many words*) 'You grant heaven, you release, you restore to health, you free the criminal; lead us, unite us, represent us, guide us to glory; protect, bring aid, take away what is harmful, give us life ... Here you free us from our sins, you cleanse our guilt, you give us weapons to fight, here may you vanquish the enemy, here make us worthy to be in your presence.' From prayers to St Erasmus, St Godard, St Bridget, St Martin, St Christopher, St Nicholas and All Saints. (*Answer to the 20th Chapter of the 5th Book,* London).

[127] De. Beatitudine Sanctorum, Cap. 7. Exposition of the Last Psalm.

[128] Newman omits this paragraph in VM 2.

[129] 1 Cor. 11:34.

[130] A work written in AD 420 against someone who attributed the Old Testament to a demon.

[131] Letter to Bishop Boniface, AD 408 (Letters 98, 2).

[132] *The City of God*, 10, 5.

[133] Letter to Januarius, AD 400 (Letters 54,1). In the Third Book of Christian Doctrine (AD 426) treats of the method of dealing with unknown signs.

[134] "Some understood this foolishly, and thought of it carnally, and supposed the Lord was going to cut off some parts of His body to give them." *Explanations of the Psalms* 98, 9.

[135] Corpus Christi, the feast of the Body and Blood of Christ is celebrated on the Thursday following Trinity Sunday (or the following Sunday)."Jesus *in form* of bread and wine/His loving sacrifice displays." (Hymn Verbum supernum prodiens at Lauds.)

[136] Newman omits the next three paragraphs and resumes with "They that deny ..." in VM 2.

[137] Paschasius Rhadbertus (790–865) the Benedictine theologian relates this story in *De Corpore et Sanguine Domini* (831).

[138] Berengarius of Tours (1010–1088), Canon of Chartres, criticized the theology of the Eucharist and was condemned in 1050.

[139] 'with sharp jagged teeth'. Scylla has 3 rows of such teeth in Ovid *Metamorphoses,* 13.732ff.

[140] "How can this man give us his flesh to eat? ... Many of his disciples, when they heard it, said, 'This is a hard saying; who can listen to it?' " (John 6:52, 60).

[141] Alan de Lille (d.1203), theologian and preacher: "We speak most certainly that the body of Christ is truly handled, eaten, carried around ..."

[142] 'worn down.'

[143] 'figuratively.'

[144] Newman omits the following passages in VM 2, until: 'The same doctrine was imposed ...'

[145] Simeon Metaphrastes (fl. c. 960), Hagiographer.

[146] Jacob of Voragine (1230–1298), Archbishop of Genoa, author of *The Golden Legend*.

[147] Odo (d.959), Archbishop of Canterbury, known as Odo the Good.

[148] 'the breaking of the Bread'.

[149] Widukind was a Saxon warrior, baptized in 785, whom legend subsequently made a saint.

[150] Nicholas II (Pope, 1059–1061), debated Berengar's views at the legatine synod in 1059.

[151] Gregory VII (Pope 1073–1079), in the Roman Council of 1079. John William Bowden published his *The Life and Pontificate of Gregory VII* in 1840.

[152] Rather, *Intussusception*: The Real Presence of Christ *in* the Eucharist (impanation).

[153] Durandus of Saint-Pourcain (1275–1334), 'Doctor Resolutissimus' philosopher.

[154] William of Occam (1285–1347), 'Venerabilis Inceptor', Franciscan theologian.

[155] The change of the bread and wine (into the body and blood of Christ).

[156] "There is a bird known as a Phoenix, which is the only specimen of its kind and has a life of five hundred years. When the hour of its dissolution and death approaches, it makes a nest for itself out of frankincense and myrrh and other fragrant spices, and in the fullness of time it enters into this and expires." Letter to the Corinthians, n. 25 (AD 96).

[157] In 1819, Newman had attended the lectures on Geology of William Buckland (1784–1856) who was Reader in mineralogy. He published his *Reliquiae Diluvianae* in 1823. AW, p. 44.

[158] Gen. 1:1—2:4. "Time and space have no portion in the spiritual Kingdom which He has founded; and the rites of His Church are mysterious spells by which He annuls them both." PPS 3, p. 277.

[159] Newman omits the remainder of this Tract in VM 2.

[160] "We call His presence in this Holy Sacrament a spiritual presence, not as if 'spiritual' were but a name or mode of speech, and He were really absent, but by way of expressing that He who is present there can neither be seen nor heard; that He cannot be approached or ascertained by any of the senses; that He is not present in space, that He is not present carnally, though He is really present. And how this is, of course is a mystery." Newman preaching in May 1838, PPS 6, p. 137.

[161] "You shall see heaven opened, and the angels of God ascending and descending on the Son of man." (John 1:51).

[162] In the Transfiguration or in his appearances after the Resurrection.

[163] Cf. Letter to Geoffrey Fausett, in VM 2, pp. 235ff.

[164] The substance of this Article dates from 1553 with only slight alterations later. The Creed of Pius IV of 1564 states, "I also profess that in the Mass there is offered a true sacrifice, properly speaking, which is propitiatory for the living and the dead."

[165] Month's Mind is a Mass said a month after the death; chantries were endowed chapels where daily Mass was offered for the souls of those

specified; trentalls were a collection of thirty Masses offered on behalf of the donor.

[166] Newman omits the next three paragraphs but gives references to them in VM 2.

[167] Mummish massing: making a folk performance, like the mummers.

[168] After game: a second game played in order to improve the issues of the first (OED).

[169] George Bull (1634–1710), Bishop of St. David's.

[170] Matt. 21:13.

[171] Lands held inalienably by an ecclesiastical corporation.

[172] *Decree on things to be observed and avoided in celebrating Mass* (17 September, 1562).

[173] 1 Cor. 7:8ff.

[174] Jovinian was a renegade Roman monk. The treatise is ca. AD 393.

[175] Acts 15:28–30.

[176] Senator Flavius Cassiodorus (485–580), *Historia Ecclesiastica Tripartita*.

[177] *Letter to a Magazine on the Subject of Dr. Pusey's Tract on Baptism.*

[178] Newman omits the rest of this paragraph in VM 2.

[179] See reference in Tr. 82.

[180] Newman omits the following passages until "This illustration of the subject . . ." in VM 2.

[181] *Of Original or Birth-Sin.*

[182] Homily 21 in the Second Book of Homilies.

[183] Theodosius I (346–395) was excommunicated for the massacre in Thessalonica in 390.

[184] Council of Elvira (AD 305).

[185] Constantine (Pope: 708–715) condemned Philippicus Bardanes for his heresy (which held that in Jesus there is only one divine will) in 711.

[186] First Nicea, First Constantinople, Ephesus, Chalcedon, Second Constantinople, Third Constantinople.

[187] 'simple'.

[188] Tob. 12:8.

[189] Gal. 2:10.

[190] Isa. 25:4.

[191] Tob. 2:2; 12:9.

[192] "Six Homilies on Lazarus and the Rich Man" (preached AD 389).

[193] Matt. 15:2ff.

[194] "Water extinguishes a blazing fire: so almsgiving atones for sin." Sir. 3:30.

[195] "Whatever stains we subsequently contract, we may wash away by almsgiving." *On Works and Almsgiving,* 1. (AD 253).

[196] Eusebius (300–360), Bishop of Emesa in Syria. He was a biblical exegete and homilist.

[197] The Act of Supremacy by which the sovereign is declared the only supreme head in earth of the Church of England, called *Anglicana Ecclesia* passed in November 1534.

[198] Rom. 13:1.

[199] '*Catholicity of the English Church*', British Critic (January 1840), pp. 54–58. Newman became Editor in January 1838.

[200] The Ten Articles of 1536; The Thirty-Eight Articles of 1563; The Thirty-Nine Articles of 1571, and 1662 with the revision of the Book of Common Prayer.

[201] Edward VI's Declaration of 1562, prefacing the Articles (BCP)

[202] Philipp Melanchthon (1497–1560), mainly responsible for the Augsburg Confession and organizing the Church in Saxony.

[203] Johann Lorenz von Mosheim (1694–1755), historian and divine. His *Institutiones Historiae Ecclesiasticae (1726)* was translated into English in 1841. Cf. LD 5, p. 122.

[204] Louis Adolphe Thiers published his *Histoire du Consulat et de l'Empire"* in 1845, his rival and successor was Francois Pierre Guillaume Guizot who had been Ambassador to Britain.

[205] An arrangement or adaptation of means to ends. (OED)

APPENDIX 1

ADVERTISEMENTS TO THE FIRST AND SECOND EDITIONS OF THE TRACTS

1st Volume[1]

The following Tracts were published with the object of contributing something towards the practical revival of doctrines, which, although held by the great divines of our Church, at present have become obsolete with the majority of her members, and are withdrawn from public view even by the more learned and orthodox few who still adhere to them. The Apostolic Succession, the Holy Catholic Church, were principles of action in the minds of our predecessors of the 17th century; but, in proportion as the maintenance of the Church has been secured by law, her ministers have been under the temptation of leaning on an arm of flesh instead of her own divinely-provided discipline, a temptation increased by political events and arrangements which need not here be alluded to. A lamentable increase of sectarianism has followed; being occasioned (in addition to other more obvious causes,) first, by the cold aspect which the new Church doctrines have presented to the religious sensibilities of the mind, next to their meagerness in suggesting motives to

restrain it from seeking out a more influential discipline. Doubtless obedience to the law of the land,
and the careful maintenance of "decency and order,"
(the topics in usage among us,) are plain duties of
the Gospel, and a reasonable ground for keeping in
communion with the Established Church; yet, if
Providence has graciously provided for our weakness
more interesting and constraining motives, it is a sin
thanklessly to neglect them; just as it would be a
mistake to rest the duties of temperance or justice
on the mere law of natural religion, when they are
mercifully sanctioned in the Gospel by the more
winning authority of our Saviour Christ. Experience
has shown the inefficacy of the mere injunctions of
Church order, however scripturally enforced, in
restraining from schism the awakened and anxious
sinner, who goes to a dissenting preacher "because
(as he expresses it) he gets good from him:" and
though he does not stand excused in God's sight for
yielding to the temptation, surely the Ministers of
the Church are not blameless if, by keeping back
the more gracious and consoling truths provided for
the little ones of Christ, they indirectly lead him
into it. Had he been taught as a child, that the
Sacraments, not preaching, are the sources of Divine
Grace; that the Apostolical ministry had a virtue in
it which went out over the whole Church, when
sought by the prayer of faith; that fellowship with
it was a gift and privilege, as well as a duty, we
could not have had so many wanderers from our
fold, nor so many cold hearts within it.

This instance may suggest many others of the
superior *influence* of an apostolical over a mere secular

method of teaching. The awakened mind knows its wants, but cannot provide for them; and in its hunger will feed upon ashes, if it cannot obtain the pure milk of the word. Methodism and Popery are in different ways the refuge of those whom the Church stints of the gifts of grace; they are the foster-mothers of abandoned children. The neglect of the daily service, the desecration of festivals, the Eucharist scantily administered, insubordination permitted in all ranks of the Church, orders and offices imperfectly developed, the want of Societies for particular religious objects, and the like deficiencies, lead the feverish mind, desirous of a vent to its feelings, and a stricter rule of life, to the smaller religious communities, to prayer and bible meetings, and ill-advised institutions and societies, on the one hand, – on the other, to the solemn and captivating services by which Popery gains its proselytes. Moreover, the multitude of men cannot teach or guide themselves; and an injunction given them to depend on their private judgment, cruel in itself, is doubly hurtful, as throwing them on such teachers as speak daringly and promise largely, and not only aid but supersede individual exertion.

These remarks may serve as a clue, for those who care to pursue it, to the views which have led to the publication of the following Tracts. The Church of Christ was intended to cope with human nature in all its forms, and surely the gifts vouchsafed it are adequate for that gracious purpose. There are zealous sons and servants of her English branch, who see with sorrow that she is defrauded of her full usefulness by particular theories and principles of the present age, which interfere with the execution of one portion of her commission; and while they consider that the revival of this portion of the truth is especially adapted to break up existing parties in the Church, and to form instead a bond of union among those who love the Lord Jesus Christ in sincerity, they believe that nothing but these neglected doctrines, faithfully preached, will repress that extension of Popery, for which the ever multiplying divisions of the religious world are too clearly preparing the way.

2nd Volume[2]

The present Volume will be found to persevere in the change of plan adopted in the latter part of the Second, the substitution of Tracts of considerable extent of subject for the short and incomplete papers with which the publication commenced. The reason for this change is to be found in the altered circumstances under which they now make their appearance. When the series began, the prospects of Catholic Truth were especially gloomy, from the circumstance that irreligious principles and false doctrines, which had hitherto been avowed only in the closet or on paper, had just been admitted into public measures on a large scale, with the probability of that admission becoming a precedent for future. A great proportion of the Irish Sees had been suppressed by the State against the Church's wish, all parties who were concerned to resist the measure, acquiescing either in utter apathy or in despair. Scarcely a protesting voice was heard, and the attempt to remonstrate was treated on all hands with coldness and disapprobation. A sense of the dreariness of such a state of things naturally led to those earnest appeals and abrupt sketches of doctrine with which the Tracts opened. They were written with the hope of rousing members of our Church to comprehend her alarming position, of helping them to realize the fact of the gradual growth, allowance, and establishment of unsound principles in the management of her internal concerns; and, having this object, they spontaneously used the language of alarm and complaint. They were written, as a man might give notice of a fire or inundation, to startle all who heard him, with only so much of doctrine and argument as might be necessary to account for their publication, or might answer more obvious objections to the views therein advocated.

This peculiarity in their composition has occasioned them to be censured as intemperate and violent. If this be true in such sense that they discover any personal feeling, bitterness, wrath, want of candour, unkindness, or reviling, of course nothing can be said in their defence. Or if they contain an extravagant doctrine, crudely imagined, confusedly or hastily expressed, and unsanctioned by our standard Divines, then, too, they are entitled to very little respect. But if the charge of intemperance simply means that they contain strong expressions of high and delicate matters, suddenly introduced, unexplained, and therefore harsh, though not intrinsically erroneous, then by intemperance is meant nothing else than want of judgment. Want of judgment, however, is commonly imputed to proceedings which tend to defeat their object, though allowable in themselves, and based upon true principles; and if so, the style of the Tracts in question is *not* injudicious, for their object has *not* been defeated. Naked statements, which offend the accurate and

cautious, are necessary upon occasions to infuse seri-
ousness into the indifferent.

These are the reasons, whether satisfactory or not in
the judgment of others, for the style and manner of the
earlier Tracts. When, however, from the circumstances of the times or from other causes, more interest
seemed to be excited among Churchmen concerning
these doctrines which it was their object to enforce,
discussion became more seasonable than the simple
statements of doctrine with which the series began;
and their character accordingly changed.

It would be unbecoming to go into this detail in this
place, were not a prejudice entertained against these
Tracts by many who know them only by a few
detached sentences, complete indeed in themselves,
and on the whole not unfairly selected, but which, so
detached, will not be understood in their true sense
and bearings by readers unacquainted with the
language of our old divinity. Dr. Pusey's valuable
pamphlet in answer to one objector, is, with the kind
consent of the Author, appended to this
Advertisement.[3]

Notes

1. The first volume which includes Tracts 1–46 was published on
   November 1, 1834.
2. The 2nd volume includes Tracts 71–76. It was published on
   November 1, 1836.
3   "*An Earnest Remonstrance to the Author of the Pope's Letter*". The
    pamphlet professed to be a 'Pastoral Epistle from the Pope to
    some Members of the University of Oxford faithfully trans-
    lated from the original Latin.' The author was Dr. Dickinson,
    chaplain to Archbishop Whately and afterwards, Bishop of
    Meath, LD 5, p. 270n.

APPENDIX 2

EDITIONS OF THE TRACTS

Published by Turrill with King the Printer in 1833 and by J. G. & F. Rivington & J. H. Parker, Oxford, 1834–1841.

Volume I (1833–1834) Tracts 1–46.

Volume II, Part I (1834–1835) Tracts 47–66.

Volume II, Part II (1834–1835) Tracts 67–70 and 4th Edition (1842).

Volume III (1835–1836) Tracts 71–76 and Tract 77 (contained in 'Note to Advertisement') 1836, 1837 (2nd Edition), 1840 (new Edition).

Volume IV (1836–1837) Tracts 78–82.

Volume V (1838–1840) Tracts 83–88.

Volume VI (1841–1842) Tracts 89–90.

With kind acknowledgements to the late Vincent Blehl, SJ and the Bibliographical Society of the University of Virginia.

APPENDIX 3

LIST OF TRACTS FOR THE TIMES

1 9 September 1833 'Thoughts on the Ministerial Commission' [NEWMAN]

2 9 September 'The Catholic Church' [NEWMAN]

3 9 September 'Thoughts respectfully addressed to the Clergy on Alterations in the Liturgy; 'The Burial Service'; The Principle of Unity' (Episcopal Authority) [NEWMAN]

4 21 September 'Adherence to the Apostolic Succession the Safest Course'; 'On Alterations in the Prayer Book' [J. KEBLE]

5 18 October 'A Short Address to his Brethren on the Nature and Constitution of the Church of Christ, and of the Branch of it established in England. By a Layman' [J. W. BOWDEN]

6 29 October 'The Present Obligation of Primitive Practice';'A Sin of the Church (infrequent celebration of the Eucharist) [NEWMAN]

7 29 October 'The Episcopal Church Apostolical' [NEWMAN]

8 31 October 'The Gospel a Law of Liberty'; 'Church Reform' (need for 'godly discipline') [NEWMAN or R. H. FROUDE]

9 31 October 'On Shortening the Church Service'; 'Sunday Lessons' [R. H. FROUDE]

10 4 November 'Heads of a Week-Day Lecture, delivered to a Country Congregation'

(Bishops the successors of the Apostles)
[NEWMAN]

11	11 November	'The Visible Church' Letters I and II [NEWMAN]
12	4 December	'Richard Nelson, No. 1, Bishops, Priests and Deacons' [T. KEBLE]
13	5 December	'Sunday Lessons. The Principle of Selection' [J. KEBLE]
14	12 December	'The Ember Days' [A. MENZIES]
15	13 December	'On the Apostolical Succession in the English Church' [W. PALMER, *revised and completed by* NEWMAN]
16	17 December	'Advent' [B. HARRISON]
17	20 December	'The Ministerial Commission: A Trust from Christ for the Benefit of His People' [B. HARRISON]
18	21 December	'Thoughts on the Benefits of the System of Fasting enjoined by our Church' [E. B. PUSEY]
19	23 December	'On arguing concerning the Apostolical Succession. On Reluctance to confess the Apostolical Succession. [NEWMAN]
20	24 December	'The Visible Church', Letter III [NEWMAN]
21	1 January 1834	'Mortification of the Flesh a Scripture Duty' [NEWMAN]
22	6 January	'Richard Nelson, No. 2, The Athanasian Creed' [T. KEBLE]
23	6 January	'The Faith and Obedience of Churchmen the strength of the Church' [A. P. PERCEVAL]
24	25 January	'The Scripture View of the Apostolic Commission' [B. HARRISON]
25	25 January	'The Great Necessity and Advantage of Public Prayer' [reprinted from Bishop Beveridge]

26	2 February	'The Necessity and Advantage of Frequent Communion' [reprinted from Bishop Beveridge]
27	24 February	'The History of Popish Transubstantiation' [reprinted from Bishop Cosin]
28	25 March	The same, concluded
29	25 March	'Christian Liberty; or, Why should we belong to the Church of England? By a Layman. [J. W. BOWDEN]
30	25 March	the same, concluded [J. W. BOWDEN]
31	25 April	'The Reformed Church' [NEWMAN]
32	25 April	'The Standing Ordinances of Religion' [C. P. EDEN]
33	1 May	'Primitive Episcopacy' [NEWMAN]
34	1 May	'Rites and Customs of the Church' [NEWMAN]
35	8 May	'The People's Interest in their Minister's Commission' [A. P. PERCEVAL]
36	11 June	'Account of Religious Sects at present existing in England' [A. P. PERCEVAL]
37	24 June	'Bishop Wilson's Form of Excommunication' (reprinted from Bishop Wilson: 1663–1755)
38	25 July	'Via Media' No. I [NEWMAN]
39	25 July	'Bishop Wilson's Form of Receiving Penitents' (reprinted from Bishop Wilson)
40	25 July	'Richard Nelson, No. 3, On Baptism' [T. KEBLE]
41	24 August	'Via Media' No. II [NEWMAN]
42	24 August	'Bishop Wilson's Meditations on his Sacred Office', No. 1, Sunday. (reprinted from Bishop Wilson)
43	21 September	'Richard Nelson, No. 4, Length of the Public Service' [T. KEBLE]

44	29 September	'Bishop Wilson's Meditations on his Sacred Office', No. 2, Monday. (A reprint)
45	18 October	'The Grounds of our Faith' [NEWMAN]
46	28 October	'Bishop Wilson's Meditations on his Sacred Office', No. 3, Tuesday. (A reprint)
47	1 November	'The Visible Church, Letter 4' [NEWMAN]
48	30 November	'Bishop Wilson's Meditations on his Sacred Office', No. 4, Wednesday' (A reprint) [NEWMAN]
49	25 December	'The Kingdom of Heaven' [B. HARRISON]
50	26 December	'Bishop Wilson's Meditations on his Sacred Office' No. 4, Wednesday, continued. (reprint)
51	6 January 1835	'On Dissent without reason in conscience' [R. F. WILSON]
52	undated	'Sermons for Saints' Days and Holidays, No. 1, St. Matthias' [J. KEBLE]
53	24 February	'Bishop Wilson's Meditations on his Sacred Office, No. 5' (A reprint)
54	2 February	'Sermons for Saints' Days and Holidays, No. 2, The Annunciation' [J. KEBLE]
55	25 March	'Bishop Wilson's Meditations on his Sacred Office, No. 5, continued (A reprint)
56	25 March	'Holy Days observed in the English Church' [J. W. BOWDEN]
57	25 March	'Sermons for Saints' Days and Holidays, No. 3, St. Mark's Day [J. KEBLE]
58	19 April	'On the Church as Viewed by Faith and by the World' [J. W. BOWDEN]
59	25 April	The Position of the Church of Christ in England, Relatively to the State and the

Nation' [R. H. FROUDE]

60 25 April Sermons for Saints' Days and Holidays, No. 4, St Philip and St James' [J. KEBLE]

61 1 May 'The Catholic Church a Witness against illiberality' [A. BULLER]

62 1 May 'Bishop Wilson's Meditations on his Sacred Office', No. 5, continued (A reprint)

63 1 May 'The Antiquity of the Existing Liturgies' [R. H. FROUDE]

64 11 June 'Bishop Bull on the Ancient Liturgies' (A reprint)

65 29 June 'Bishop Wilson's Meditations on his Sacred Office, No. 6' (A reprint)

66 25 July 'On the Benefits of the System of Fasting prescribed by our Church, supplement to Tract 18' [E. B. PUSEY]

67 24 August 'Scriptural Views of Holy Baptism' [E. B. PUSEY]

68 29 September 'Scriptural Views of Holy Baptism' [E. B. PUSEY]

69 18 October 'Scriptural Views of Holy Baptism' [E. B. PUSEY]

70 28 October 'Bishop Wilson's Meditations on His Sacred Office, No. 7' (A reprint)

71 1 January 1836 'On the Controversy with the Romanists' [NEWMAN]

72 6 January 'Archbishop Usher on Prayers for the Dead' (A reprint)

73 2 February 'On the Introduction of Rationalistic Principles into Religion' [NEWMAN]

74 25 April 'Catena Patrum, No. 1, on the Apostolic Succession' [NEWMAN]

75 24 June 'On the Roman Breviary as embodying the substance of the devotional services

		of the Church Catholic' [NEWMAN]
76	29 September	'Catena Patrum, No. 2, on Baptism Regeneration' [NEWMAN]
77	1 November	'An Earnest Remonstrance to the Author of the Pope's Letter' [E. B. PUSEY]
78	2 February 1837	'Catena Patrum, No. 3, Testimony of Writers of the Later English Church to the Duty of maintaining *Quod Semper, quod ubique, quod ab omnibus traditum est*' [H. E. MANNING, C. MARRIOTT & NEWMAN]
79	25 March	'On Purgatory (Against Romanism, No. 3)' [NEWMAN]
80	undated	'On Reserve in Communicating Religious Knowledge, Parts 1–3' [I. WILLIAMS]
81	1 November	'Catena Patrum, No. 4. Testimony of Writers of the Later English Church to the Doctrine of the Eucharistic Sacrifice, with an Historical Account of the Changes made in the Liturgy as to the Expression of that Doctrine' [E. B. PUSEY with assistance of B. HARRISON]
82	1 November	'Letter to a Magazine on the Subject of Dr. Pusey's Tract on Baptism' [NEWMAN]
83	29 June 1838	'Advent Sermons on Antichrist' [NEWMAN]
84	24 August	'Whether a Clergyman of the Church of England be now bound to have Morning and Evening Prayers daily in his Parish Church' [T. KEBLE and G. PREVOST]
85	21 September	'Lectures on the Scriptural Proof of the Doctrines of the Church, Part I' [NEWMAN]

86	25 March	1839 'Indications of a Superintending Providence in the Preservation of the Prayer Book and the Changes it has undergone' [I. WILLIAMS]
87	2 February 1840	'On Reserve in Communicating Religious Knowledge, Parts 4–6' [I. WILLIAMS]
88	25 March	'The Greek Devotions of Bishop Andrews, Translated and Arranged' [NEWMAN]
89	undated	'On the Mysticism attributed to the Early Fathers of the Church, (First Part) [J. KEBLE]
90	25 January 1841	(published 27 Feb.) 'Remarks on Certain Passages in the Thirty-Nine Articles' [NEWMAN]